JUSTICE STATISTICS

AN EXTENDED LOOK AT CRIME IN THE UNITED STATES

JUSTICE STATISTICS

AN EXTENDED LOOK AT CRIME IN THE UNITED STATES

SECOND EDITION
2016

Edited by
Shana Hertz Hattis

Lanham, MD

 **Bernan** Press

Published in the United States of America
by Bernan Press, a wholly owned subsidiary of
The Rowman & Littlefield Publishing Group, Inc.
4501 Forbes Boulevard, Suite 200
Lanham, Maryland 20706

Bernan Press
800-462-6420
www.rowman.com

ISBN-13: 978-1-59888-861-4
eISBN-13: 978-1-59888-862-1

∞™ The paper used in this publication meets the minimum requirements of
American National Standard for Information Sciences—Permanence of
Paper for Printed Library Materials, ANSI/NISO Z39.48-1992.

Manufactured in the United States of America.

Contents

129   Part 4. Capital Punishment, 2013

217 Part 7. Law Enforcement Officers Killed and Assaulted, 2014

INTRODUCTION

Bernan Press is pleased to present the second edition of its comprehensive collection of justice statistics in the United States. This volume provides valuable information compiled by the Department of Justice, including its subsidiaries, the Bureau of Justice Statistics and the Federal Bureau of Investigation.

This volume brings together nine key reports that fall under this category. Topics covered include capital punishment, criminal victimization, correctional populations, crime in the United States, hate crimes, probation, parole, and law enforcement officers killed and assaulted. Tables in this volume provide a comprehensive account of each of these subjects; for more information, including full-scope methodologies and information about standard errors for each table, please see the full reports at the URLs listed below.

Each section contains statistical tables and figures highlighting the data, as well as a brief summary of the report's methodology and at-a-glance highlights of the most compelling information.

This publication includes information from the following reports:

Criminal Victimization, 2014, takes a close look at the victims of violent and property crime in the United States. The full report is accessible at http://www.bjs.gov/index.cfm?ty=pbdetail&iid=5366

Correctional Populations in the United States, 2014, discusses the trends and changes in the incarcerated populations of the country's prisons. The full report is http://www.bjs.gov/index.cfm?ty=pbdetail&iid=5519

Crime in the United States, 2014, provides an introduction to overall crime trends. This report is more fully presented in Bernan Press's *Crime in the United States*; however, given the importance of the report in the understanding of justice and crime trends in the United States, its most relevant tables have been included in this volume. Once again appearing in this book, and not contained in the complementary *Crime* volume, are the expanded offense tables. The full report can be accessed at https://www.fbi.gov/about-us/cjis/ucr/crime-in-the-u.s/2014/crime-in-the-u.s.-2014

Capital Punishment, 2013, details statistics about inmates condemned to death. The full report can be accessed at http://www.bjs.gov/content/pub/pdf/cp13st.pdf

Hate Crime Statistics, 2014, details the hate crimes committed in the United States throughout 2014. It can be accessed at https://www.fbi.gov/about-us/cjis/ucr/hate-crime/2014

Jail Inmates at Midyear, 2014, presents estimates of the inmate populations of jails based on various demographic characteristics. The full report can be accesses at http://www.bjs.gov/content/pub/pdf/jim14.pdf

Law Enforcement Officers Killed and Assaulted, 2014, is the primary resource for data about harm done to law enforcement officers. This volume provides a comprehensive sample of the report; further information can be obtained at https://www.fbi.gov/about-us/cjis/ucr/leoka/2014

Probation and Parole in the United States, 2014, details data about post-release inmates still in the legal system. The report can be accessed at http://www.bjs.gov/index.cfm?ty=pbdetail&iid=5415

Human Trafficking, 2014, is the second iteration of FBI Uniform Crime Report (UCR) Program's data collection on trafficking in the United States. The full report is available at https://www.fbi.gov/about-us/cjis/ucr/crime-in-the-u.s/2014/crime-in-the-u.s.-2014/additional-reports/human-trafficking-report/human-trafficking.pdf

ABOUT THE EDITOR

Shana Hertz Hattis is an editor with over a decade of experience in statistical and government research publications. Past titles include *State Profiles: The Population and Economy of Each U.S. State, Crime in the United States,* and *The United States Government Internet Directory.* She earned her bachelor of science in journalism and master of science in education degrees from Northwestern University.

PART 1

Criminal Victimization, 2014

HIGHLIGHTS

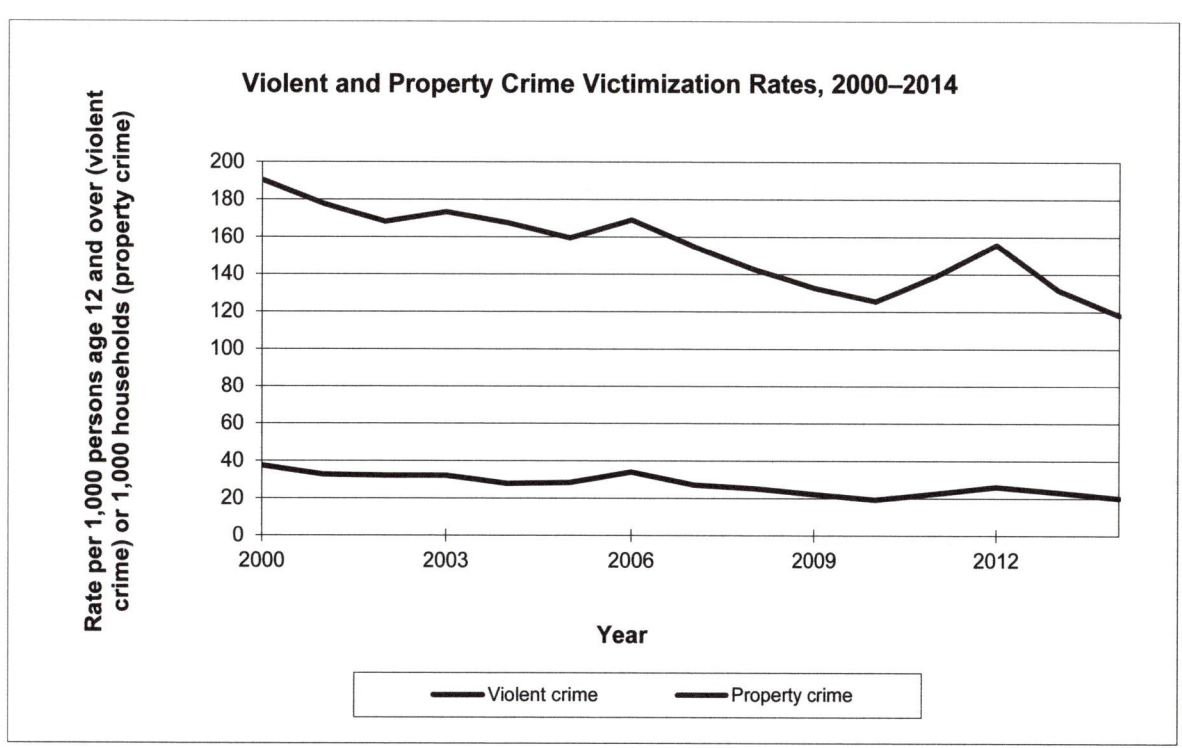

Violent and Property Crime Victimization Rates, 2000–2014

- In 2014, U.S. residents age 12 years or older experienced approximately 5.4 million violent victimizations and 15.3 million property victimizations.

- No significant change was noted in the violent crime victimization rate from 2013 to 2014 (23.2 to 20.1 incidents per 1,000 inhabitants age 12 years or over, respectively).

- The rate of property crime (per 1,000 households) decreased from 131.4 victimizations per 1,000 households in 2013 to 118.1 per 1,000 in 2014.

- Approximately 1.1 percent of all persons age years 12 or older (3 million persons) experienced at least one violent victimization, while approximately 8 percent of all households (10.4 million households) experienced one or more property victimizations.

- Victim service agencies assisted an estimated 12 percent of those who suffered serious violent crimes and 28 percent of intimate partner violence victims.

Table 1. Violent Victimization, by Type of Violent Crime, 2005, 2013, and 2014

(Number; rate per 1,000 persons age 12 years or older.)

	Number						Rate per 1,000 persons age 12 years or older					
Type of crime	2005	2005 confidence notes	2013	2013 confidence notes	2014[1]	2014 confidence notes	2005	2005 confidence notes	2013	2013 confidence notes	2014[1]	2014 confidence notes
Violent Crime[2]	6,947,800	Ü	6,126,420		5,359,570		28.4	Ü	23.2		20.1	
Rape/sexual assault	207,760		300,170		284,350		0.8		1.1		1.1	
Robbery	769,150		645,650		664,210		3.1		2.4		2.5	
Assault	5,970,890	Ü	5,180,610		4,411,010		24.4	Ü	19.6	á	16.5	
Aggravated assault	1,281,490		994,220		1,092,090		5.2	á	3.8		4.1	
Simple assault	4,689,400	Ü	4,186,390	Ü	3,318,920		19.2	Ü	15.8	Ü	12.4	
Domestic violence[3]	1,242,290		1,116,090		1,109,880		5.1	Ü	4.2		4.2	
Intimate partner violence[4]	816,010		748,800		634,610		3.3	á	2.8		2.4	
Stranger violence	2,829,600	Ü	2,098,170		2,166,130		11.6	Ü	7.9		8.1	
Violent crime involving injury	1,759,210	á	1,603,960		1,375,950		7.2	Ü	6.1		5.2	
Serious Violent Crime[5]	2,258,400		1,940,030		2,040,650		9.2		7.3		7.7	
Serious domestic violence[3]	425,270		464,730		400,030		1.7		1.8		1.5	
Serious intimate partner violence[4]	311,480		360,820		265,890		1.3		1.4		1.0	
Serious stranger violence	1,096,480		737,940		930,690		4.5		2.8		3.5	
Serious violent crime involving weapons	1,659,030		1,174,370		1,306,900		6.8	Ü	4.4		4.9	
Serious violent crime involving injury	824,800		739,210		692,470		3.4		2.8		2.6	

Note: Detail may not sum to total due to rounding. Total population age 12 or older was 244,505,300 in 2005; 264,411,700 in 2013; and 266,665,160 in 2014.
Ü = Significant difference from comparison year at the 95% confidence level.
á = Significant difference from comparison year at the 90% confidence level.
[1] Comparison year.
[2] Excludes homicide because the NCVS is based on interviews with victims and therefore cannot measure murder.
[3] Includes victimization committed by intimate partners and family members.
[4] Includes victimization committed by current or former spouses, boyfriends, or girlfriends.
[5] In the NCVS, serious violent crime includes rape or sexual assault, robbery, and aggravated assault.

Table 2. Firearm Victimizations, 2005–2014

(Number; rate per 1,000 persons age 12 years or older; percent.)

Characteristic	2005	2005 confidence notes	2006	2006 confidence notes	2007	2007 confidence notes	2008	2008 confidence notes	2009	2009 confidence notes
Firearm incidents	446,370		552,040		448,410		331,620		383,390	
Firearm victimizations	503,530		614,410		554,780		371,290		410,110	
Rate of firearm victimizations[2]	2.1		2.5	á	2.0		1.5		2.0	
Percent of firearms victimizations reported to police	72.3		71.0		52.9	Ü	70.8		61.5	Ü

Characteristic	2010	2010 confidence notes	2011	2011 confidence notes	2012	2012 confidence notes	2013	2013 confidence notes	2014[1]	2014 confidence notes
Firearm incidents	378,800		415,160		427,700		290,620		414,700	
Firearm victimizations	415,000		467,930		460,720		332,950		466,110	
Rate of firearm victimizations[2]	1.6		2.0		1.8		1.3		1.7	
Percent of firearms victimizations reported to police	50.9	Ü	1.0		66.4	Ü	75.3		81.9	

Note: Includes violent incidents and victimizations in which the offender had, showed, or used a firearm.
Ü = Significant difference from comparison year at the 95% confidence level.
á = Significant difference from comparison year at the 90% confidence level.
[1] Comparison year.
[2] Per 1,000 persons age 12 or older.

Table 3. Property Victimization, by Type of Property Crime, 2005, 2013, and 2014

(Number; rate per 1,000 households.)

Type of crime	Number						Rate per 1,000 households					
	2005	2005 confidence notes	2013	2013 confidence notes	2014[1]	2014 confidence notes	2005	2005 confidence notes	2013	2013 confidence notes	2014[1]	2014 confidence notes
Total	18,673,360	Ü	16,774,090	Ü	15,288,470		159.5	Ü	131.4	Ü	118.1	
Burglary	3,584,850	Ü	3,286,210		2,993,480		30.6	Ü	25.7	á	23.1	
Motor vehicle theft	1,003,150	Ü	661,250		534,370		8.6	Ü	5.2	Ü	4.1	
Theft...........................	14,085,360	Ü	12,826,620	Ü	11,760,620		120.3	Ü	100.5	Ü	90.8	

Note: Detail may not sum to total due to rounding. Total number of households was 117,099,820 in 2005; 127,622,320 in 2013; and 129,492,740 in 2014.
Ü = Significant difference from comparison year at the 95% confidence level.
á = Significant difference from comparison year at the 90% confidence level.
[1] Comparison year.

Table 4. Number of Victims and Prevalence Rate, by Type of Crime, 2005, 2013, and 2014

(Number; rate per 1,000 persons age 12 years or older.)

Type of crime	Number of persons victimized[1]						Prevalence rate[2]					
	2005	2005 confidence notes	2013	2013 confidence notes	2014[3]	2014 confidence notes	2005	2005 confidence notes	2013	2013 confidence notes	2014[3]	2014 confidence notes
Violent Crime[4]	3,350,630	Ü	3,041,170		2,948,540		1.4	Ü	1.2		1.1	
Rape/sexual assault	118,700		173,610		150,420		0.5		0.1		0.1	
Robbery..	414,740		369,070		435,830		0.2		0.1		0.2	
Assault...	2,868,470	Ü	2,600,920		2,449,820		1.2	Ü	1.0		0.9	
Aggravated assault...	721,750		633,090		681,280		0.3		0.2		0.3	
Simple assault	2,211,580	Ü	2,046,600		1,842,100		0.9	Ü	0.8	á	0.7	
Domestic violence[5]...	526,470		589,140		596,270		0.2		0.2		0.2	
Intimate partner violence[6]...........................	323,060		369,310		319,950		0.1		0.1		0.1	
Stranger violence	1,601,500	Ü	1,244,560		1,274,100		0.7	Ü	0.5		0.5	
Violent crime involving injury	975,790		849,240		856,760		0.4	Ü	0.3		0.3	
Serious Violent Crime[7]	1,238,410		1,145,350		1,235,290		0.5		0.4		0.5	
Serious domestic violence[5]	172,600	á	231,170		239,330		0.1		0.1		0.1	
Serious intimate partner violence[6]..............	98,360		163,480		128,090		0.0		0.1		0.1	
Serious stranger violence.................................	651,400		497,920	á	600,650		0.3		0.2	á	0.2	
Serious violent crime involving weapons........	905,930		738,540		815,380		0.4	Ü	0.3		0.3	
Serious violent crime involving injury	433,370		420,890		440,690		0.2		0.2		0.2	
Property Crime	11,781,400	Ü	11,531,420	Ü	10,352,520		10.1	Ü	9.0	Ü	8.0	
Burglary..	2,457,040	Ü	2,458,360	Ü	2,166,890		2.1	Ü	1.9	Ü	1.7	
Motor vehicle theft	730,970	Ü	555,660	Ü	429,840		0.6	Ü	0.4	Ü	0.3	
Theft...	9,259,190	Ü	9,070,680	Ü	8,297,290		7.9	Ü	7.1	Ü	6.4	

Note: Detail may not sum to total because a person or household may experience multiple types of crime.
Ü = Significant difference from comparison year at the 95% confidence level.
á = Significant difference from comparison year at the 90% confidence level.
[1] Number of persons age 12 or older who experienced at least one victimization during the year for violent crime, and number of households that experienced at least one victimization during the year for property crime.
[2] Percent of persons age 12 or older who experienced at least one victimization during the year for violent crime, and percent of households that experienced at least one victimization during the year for property crime.
[3] Comparison year.
[4] Excludes homicide because the NCVS is based on interviews with victims and therefore cannot measure murder.
[5] Includes victimization committed by intimate partners and family members.
[6] Includes victimization committed by current or former spouses, boyfriends, or girlfriends.
[7] In the NCVS, serious violent crime includes rape or sexual assault, robbery, and aggravated assault.

Table 5. Prevalence of Violent Crime, by Victim Demographic Characteristics, 2005, 2013, and 2014

(Number; rate per 1,000 persons age 12 years or older.)

Characteristic	Number of persons victimized[1]						Prevalence rate[2]					
	2005	2005 confidence notes	2013	2013 confidence notes	2014[3]	2014 confidence notes	2005	2005 confidence notes	2013	2013 confidence notes	2014[3]	2014 confidence notes
Total	3,350,630	Ü	3,041,170		2,948,540		1.4	Ü	1.2		1.1	
Sex....................................												
Male	1,972,270	Ü	1,567,070		1,497,430		1.7	Ü	1.2		1.2	
Female.................................	1,378,360		1,474,090		1,451,110		1.1		1.1		1.1	
Race/Hispanic Origin.......												
White[4]	2,192,670	Ü	1,860,870		1,848,860		1.3	Ü	1.1		1.1	
Black/African American[4].....	474,420		430,380		453,650		1.7		1.3		1.4	
Hispanic/Latino	489,410		540,130		457,320		1.5	Ü	1.3	á	1.1	
Other[4,5]	194,130		209,800		188,710		1.4	á	1.1		1.0	
Age.....................................												
12–17 years......................	691,670	Ü	545,370	á	422,460		2.7	Ü	2.2	Ü	1.7	
18–24 years......................	751,860	Ü	527,410		478,740		2.6	Ü	1.7		1.6	
25–34 years......................	621,640		604,500		650,560		1.6		1.4		1.5	
35–49 years......................	793,800		684,150		703,980		1.2		1.1		1.2	
50–64 years......................	421,600	Ü	566,990		579,770		0.8		0.9		0.9	
65 years and over	70,080	Ü	112,760		113,030		0.2		0.3		0.3	
Marital Status.................												
Never married...................	1,850,330	Ü	1,626,980		1,482,570		2.3	Ü	1.8		1.6	
Married..............................	851,590		738,410		806,200		0.7		0.6		0.6	
Widowed............................	60,270		74,880		77,420		0.4		0.5		0.5	
Divorced............................	435,660		405,420		410,540		2.0	Ü	1.6		1.6	
Separated	134,660		171,630		151,630		3.1		3.3		3.0	

Note: Detail may not sum to total due to rounding.
Ü = Significant difference from comparison year at the 95% confidence level.
á = Significant difference from comparison year at the 90% confidence level.
[1] Number of persons age 12 or older who experienced at least one victimization during the year for violent crime, and number of households that experienced at least one victimization during the year for property crime.
[2] Percent of persons age 12 or older who experienced at least one victimization during the year for violent crime, and percent of households that experienced at least one victimization during the year for property crime.
[3] Comparison year.
[4] Excludes persons of Hispanic or Latino origin.
[5] Includes American Indians and Alaska Natives; Asians, Native Hawaiians, and other Pacific Islanders; and persons of two or more races.

Table 6. Percent of Victimizations Reported to Police, by Type of Crime, 2005, 2013, and 2014

(Percent.)

Type of crime	2005	2005 confidence notes	2013	2013 confidence notes	2014[1]	2014 confidence notes
Violent Crime[2]	45.8		45.6		46.0	
Rape/sexual assault	35.0		35.0		34.0	
Robbery	55.4		68.0		60.9	
Assault	45.0		43.0		45.0	
Aggravated assault	65.0		64.0		58.0	
Simple assault	39.0		39.0		40.0	
Domestic violence[3]	53.0		57.0		56.0	
Intimate partner violence[4]	57.0		57.0		58.0	
Stranger violence	48.0		50.0		49.0	
Violent crime involving injury	60.0		56.0		55.0	
Serious Violent Crime[5]	59.0		61.0		56.0	
Serious domestic violence[3]	61.0		65.0		60.0	
Serious intimate partner violence[4]	57.0		60.0		57.0	
Serious stranger violence	53.0	á	62.0		65.0	
Serious violent crime involving weapons	64.0		66.0		58.0	
Serious violent crime involving injury	65.0		66.0		61.0	
Property Crime	38.7		36.0		37.0	
Burglary	55.3	á	57.3		60.0	
Motor vehicle theft	82.0		76.0	á	83.0	
Theft	32.0	á	29.0		29.0	

á = Significant difference from comparison year at the 90% confidence level.
[1] Comparison year.
[2] Excludes homicide because the NCVS is based on interviews with victims and therefore cannot measure murder.
[3] Includes victimization committed by intimate partners and family members.
[4] Includes victimization committed by current or former spouses, boyfriends, or girlfriends.
[5] In the NCVS, serious violent crime includes rape or sexual assault, robbery, and aggravated assault.

Table 7. Rates of Victimization Reported and Not Reported to the Police, by Type of Crime, 2005, 2013, and 2014

(Rates per 1,000 persons age 12 or older for violent crime and per 1,000 households for property crime.)

Type of crime	Reported to police						Not reported to police					
	2005	2005 confidence notes	2013	2013 confidence notes	2014[1]	2014 confidence notes	2005	2005 confidence notes	2013	2013 confidence notes	2014[1]	2014 confidence notes
Violent Crime[2]	13.0	Ü	11.0		9.0		15.0	Ü	12.2		10.5	
Rape/sexual assault	0.3	Ü	0.4		0.0		0.6		0.7		0.7	
Robbery	1.7	Ü	2.0		2.0		1.4		0.8		1.0	
Assault	11.0	Ü	9.0		7.0		13.1	Ü	10.7		8.9	
Aggravated assault	3.0	á	2.0		2.0		1.8	Ü	1.3		1.7	
Simple assault	8.0	Ü	6.0		5.0		11.3	Ü	9.5	á	7.2	
Domestic violence[3]	6.0		2.0		2.0		2.4		1.7		1.7	
Intimate partner violence[4]	2.0		2.0		1.0		1.4	á	1.2		0.9	
Stranger violence	5.6	Ü	4.0		4.0		5.7		3.8		4.1	
Violent crime involving injury	4.3	Ü	3.4		2.8		2.8		2.6		2.3	
Serious Violent Crime[5]	5.4	Ü	5.0		4.0		3.7		2.8		3.3	
Serious domestic violence[3]	1.0		1.0		1.0		0.7		0.6		0.6	
Serious intimate partner violence[4]	1.0		1.0		1.0		0.5		0.5		0.4	
Serious stranger violence	2.4		2.0		2.0		2.1	Ü	1.0		1.2	
Serious violent crime involving weapons	4.3	Ü	3.0		3.0		2.4		1.5		2.0	
Serious violent crime involving injury	2.2		2.0		2.0		1.2		0.9		1.0	
Property Crime	61.8	Ü	47.4	Ü	43.7		95.9	Ü	83.1	Ü	72.8	
Burglary	16.9	Ü	15.0		14.0		13.4	Ü	10.9	Ü	8.8	
Motor vehicle theft	7.0	Ü	4.0		3.0		1.5	Ü	1.2	Ü	0.7	
Theft	38.0	Ü	29.0	á	26.0		81.0	Ü	71.0	Ü	63.3	

Ü = Significant difference from comparison year at the 95% confidence level.
á = Significant difference from comparison year at the 90% confidence level.
[1] Comparison year.
[2] Excludes homicide because the NCVS is based on interviews with victims and therefore cannot measure murder.
[3] Includes victimization committed by intimate partners and family members.
[4] Includes victimization committed by current or former spouses, boyfriends, or girlfriends.
[5] In the NCVS, serious violent crime includes rape or sexual assault, robbery, and aggravated assault.

Table 8. Violent Crime Victims Who Received Assistance from a Victim Service Agency, by Type of Crime, 2005, 2013, and 2014

(Percent.)

Type of crime	2005	2005 confidence notes	2013	2013 confidence notes	2014[1]	2014 confidence notes
Violent Crime[2]	9.7		9.5		10.5	
Serious violent crime[3]	13.3		13.7		12.0	
Simple assault	8.0		7.6		9.5	
Intimate partner violence	24.4		31.0		28.0	
Violent crime involving injury	15.7		17.0		15.0	
Violent crime involving weapon	13.0	Ü	7.0		7.0	

Ü = Significant difference from comparison year at the 95% confidence level.
[1] Comparison year.
[2] Includes rape or sexual assault, robbery, aggravated assault, and simple assault. Excludes homicide because the NCVS is based on interviews with victims and therefore cannot measure murder.
[3] In the NCVS, serious violent crime includes rape or sexual assault, robbery, and aggravated assault.

Table 9. Rate of Violent Victimization, by Victim Demographic Characteristics, 2005, 2013, and 2014

(Rate per 1,000 persons age 12 years or older.)

Characteristic	Violent crime[1]						Serious violent crime[2]					
	2005	2005 confidence notes	2013	2013 confidence notes	2014[3]	2014 confidence notes	2005	2005 confidence notes	2013	2013 confidence notes	2014[3]	2014 confidence notes
Total	28.4	Ü	23.2		20.0		9.0		7.3		7.7	
Sex...............................												
Male..............................	34.0	Ü	23.7		21.0		11.4	á	7.7		8.3	
Female...........................	23.1		23.0		19.0		7.2		7.0		7.0	
Race/Hispanic Origin.............												
White[4]...........................	27.7	Ü	22.0		20.0		7.6		6.8		7.0	
Black/African American[4].........	32.7	Ü	25.0		23.0		15.4	á	9.5		10.1	
Hispanic/Latino	25.9	Ü	24.8	Ü	16.2		11.9		7.5		8.3	
Other[4,5].........................	34.3	á	25.0		23.0		10.7		8.8		7.7	
Age..............................												
12–17 years.....................	59.8	Ü	52.1	Ü	30.0		15.0	Ü	10.8		8.8	
18–24 years.....................	61.0	Ü	34.0		27.0		23.5	Ü	10.7		13.6	
25–34 years.....................	29.7		30.0		29.0		11.5		10.2		8.6	
35–49 years.....................	24.9		20.0		22.0		7.1		7.1		8.9	
50–64 years.....................	15.0		19.0		18.0		4.4	á	6.9		7.0	
65 years and over	3.6		3.1		3.0		2.0		1.1		1.3	
Marital Status..................												
Never married...................	47.3		36.0	Ü	28.0		15.2	Ü	9.6		10.7	
Married..........................	15.1		11.0		12.0		5.1		3.2		4.0	
Widowed.........................	8.9		9.0		9.0		5.3		5.2		2.9	
Divorced	40.0		34.0		30.0		12.7		16.0		14.2	
Separated	68.0		73.0		53.0		16.5		33.3		27.7	

Ü = Significant difference from comparison year at the 95% confidence level.
á = Significant difference from comparison year at the 90% confidence level.
[1] Includes rape or sexual assault, robbery, aggravated assault, and simple assault. Excludes homicide because the NCVS is based on interviews with victims and therefore cannot measure murder.
[2] In the NCVS, serious violent crime includes rape or sexual assault, robbery, and aggravated assault.
[3] Comparison year.
[4] Excludes persons of Hispanic or Latino origin.
[5] Includes American Indians and Alaska Natives; Asians, Native Hawaiians, and other Pacific Islanders; and persons of two or more races.

Table 10. Violent and Property Victimization, by Household Location, 2005, 2013, and 2014

(Rate per 1,000 persons age 12 years or older for violent crime; rate per 1,000 households for property crime.)

Characteristic	Violent crime[1]						Serious violent crime[2]						Property crime[3]					
	2005	2005 confidence notes	2013	2013 confidence notes	2014[4]	2014 confidence notes	2005	2005 confidence notes	2013	2013 confidence notes	2014[4]	2014 confidence notes	2005	2005 confidence notes	2013	2013 confidence notes	2014[4]	2014 confidence notes
Total	28.4	Ü	23.2		20.1		9.2		7.3		7.7		159.5	Ü	131.4	Ü	118.1	
Region.......................																		
Northeast....................	25.9	á	27.5	Ü	18.9		7.8		7.8		6.2		113.3	Ü	92.1		85.8	
Midwest	34.6	Ü	23.7		20.6		12.3	Ü	7.5		7.5		165.9	Ü	122.3	Ü	111.8	
South........................	23.4		18.0		20.2		7.8		5.5		7.6		148.8	Ü	125.8	Ü	116.2	
West.........................	32.0	Ü	27.3	á	20.3		9.4		9.6		8.9		209.3	Ü	182.1	Ü	153.0	
Location of Residence..																		
Urban	37.2	Ü	25.9		22.2		15.3	Ü	8.8		9.3		202.5	Ü	165.3	Ü	148.8	
Suburban....................	25.6	Ü	23.3		19.3		6.9		6.8		6.9		146.8	Ü	115.3	Ü	101.7	
Rural........................	22.4		16.9		18.3		6.4		6.1		6.5		126.2	Ü	109.4		103.2	

Ü = Significant difference from comparison year at the 95% confidence level.
á = Significant difference from comparison year at the 90% confidence level.
[1] Includes rape or sexual assault, robbery, aggravated assault, and simple assault. Excludes homicide because the NCVS is based on interviews with victims and therefore cannot measure murder.
[2] Includes rape or sexual assault, robbery, and aggravated assault.
[3] Includes household burglary, motor vehicle theft, and theft.
[4] Comparison year.

Table 11. Percent Change in the Number of Crimes Reported in the UCR and the NCVS, 2013–2014

(Percent.)

Type of crime	UCR[1]	NCVS	
		Total	Reported to police
Violent Crime[2]	NA	−12.5	−11.8
Serious violent crime[3]	−4.6	5.2	−3.9
Murder	−6.0	NA	NA
Rape[4]	−10.1	−5.3	−8.7
Robbery	−10.3	2.9	−7.9
Aggravated assault	−1.6	9.8	−0.3
Property Crime			
Burglary	−14.0	−8.9	−4.6
Motor vehicle theft	−5.7	−19.2	−10.8

NA = Not available.
[1] Includes commercial crimes.
[2] NCVS estimates exclude murder, and include simple assault.
[3] NCVS measures include rape or sexual assault, robbery, and aggravated assault.
[4] NCVS estimates include sexual assault. UCR estimate is based on the revised definition of rape but does not include agencies that used the legacy definition in 2013 and the revised definition in 2014.

Table 12. Distribution of Types of Rape and Sexual Assault Victimizations, 2005–2014

(Percent.)

Type of rape/sexual assault	Percent
Total	100
Completed rape	30
Attempted rape	23
Sexual assault	24
Unwanted sexual contact without force	6
Verbal threats of rape and sexual assault	18

METHODOLOGY

The National Crime Victimization Survey (NCVS) is an annual data collection conducted by the U.S. Census Bureau for the Bureau of Justice Statistics (BJS). The NCVS is a self-report survey in which interviewed persons are asked about the number and characteristics of victimizations experienced during the prior 6 months. The NCVS collects information on nonfatal personal crimes (rape or sexual assault, robbery, aggravated and simple assault, and personal larceny) and household property crimes (burglary, motor vehicle theft, and other theft) both reported and not reported to police. In addition to providing annual level and change estimates on criminal victimization, the NCVS is the primary source of information on the nature of criminal victimization incidents.

Survey respondents provide information about themselves (e.g., age, sex, race and Hispanic origin, marital status, education level, and income) and whether they experienced a victimization. The NCVS collects information for each victimization incident about the offender (e.g., age, race and Hispanic origin, sex, and victim—offender relationship), characteristics of the crime (including time and place of occurrence, use of weapons, nature of injury, and economic consequences), whether the crime was reported to police, reasons the crime was or was not reported, and victim experiences with the criminal justice system.

The NCVS is administered to persons age 12 or older from a nationally representative sample of households in the United States. The NCVS defines a household as a group of persons who all reside at a sampled address. Persons are considered household members when the sampled address is their usual place of residence at the time of the interview and when they have no usual place of residence elsewhere. Once selected, households remain in the sample for 3 years, and eligible persons in these households are interviewed every 6 months either in person or over the phone for a total of 7 interviews.

All first interviews are conducted in person with subsequent interviews conducted either in person or by phone. New households rotate into the sample on an ongoing basis to replace outgoing households that have been in the sample for the 3-year period. The sample includes persons living in group quarters, such as dormitories, rooming houses, and religious group dwellings, and excludes persons living in military barracks and institutional settings such as correctional or hospital facilities, and persons who are homeless.

Nonresponse and Weighting Adjustments

In 2014, 90,380 households and 158,090 persons age 12 or older were interviewed for the NCVS. Each household was interviewed twice during the year. The response rate was 84 percent for households and 87 percent for eligible persons.

Victimizations that occurred outside of the United States were excluded from this report. In 2014, less than 1 percent of the unweighted victimizations occurred outside of the United States and were excluded from the analyses.

Estimates in this report use data from the 1993 to 2014 NCVS data files, weighted to produce annual estimates of victimization for persons age 12 or older living in U.S.households. Because the NCVS relies on a sample rather than a census of the entire U.S. population, weights are designed to inflate sample point estimates to known population totals and to compensate for survey nonresponse and other aspects of the sample design.

The NCVS data files include both person and household weights. Person weights provide an estimate of the population represented by each person in the sample. Household weights provide an estimate of the U.S. household population represented by each household in the sample. After proper adjustment, both household and person weights are also typically used to form the denominator in calculations of crime rates.

Victimization weights used in this analysis account for the number of persons present during an incident and for high frequency repeat victimizations (i.e., series victimizations). Series victimizations are similar in type but occur with such frequency that a victim is unable to recall each individual event or describe each event in detail. Survey procedures allow NCVS interviewers to identify and classify these similar victimizations as series victimizations and to collect detailed information on only the most recent incident in the series.

The weight counts series incidents as the actual number of incidents reported by the victim, up to a maximum of 10 incidents. Including series victimizations in national rates results in large increases in the level of violent victimization; however, trends in violent crime are generally similar, regardless of whether series victimizations are included.

In 2014, series incidents accounted for about 1 percent of all victimizations and 4 percent of all violent victimizations.

Weighting series incidents as the number of incidents up to a maximum of 10 incidents produces more reliable estimates of crime levels, while the cap at 10 minimizes the effect of extreme outliers on rates. Additional information on the series enumeration is detailed in the report *Methods for Counting High-Frequency Repeat Victimizations in the National Crime Victimization Survey* (NCJ 237308, BJS web, April 2012).

Standard Error Computations

When national estimates are derived from a sample, as with the NCVS, caution must be used when comparing one estimate to another estimate or when comparing estimates over time.

Although one estimate may be larger than another, estimates based on a sample have some degree of sampling error. The sampling error of an estimate depends on several factors, including the amount of variation in the responses and the size of the sample. When the sampling error around an estimate is taken into account, the estimates that appear different may not be statistically different.

One measure of the sampling error associated with an estimate is the standard error. The standard error can vary from one estimate to the next. Generally, an estimate with a small standard error provides a more reliable approximation of the true value than an estimate with a large standard error. Estimates with relatively large standard errors are associated with less precision and reliability and should be interpreted with caution.

To generate standard errors around numbers and estimates from the NCVS, the Census Bureau produced generalized variance function (GVF) parameters for BJS. The GVFs take into account aspects of the NCVS complex sample design and represent the curve fitted to a selection of individual standard errors based on the Jackknife Repeated Replication technique. The GVF parameters were used to generate standard errors for each point estimate (e.g., counts, percentages, and rates).

BJS conducted tests to determine whether differences in estimated numbers, percentages, and rates in this report were statistically significant once sampling error was taken into account. Using statistical programs developed specifically for the NCVS, all comparisons in the text were tested for significance. The primary test procedure was the Student's t-statistic, which tests the difference between two sample estimates. Differences described as higher, lower, or different passed a test at the 0.05 level of statistical significance (95 percent confidence level). Differences described as somewhat, slightly, or marginally different, or with some indication of difference, passed a test at the 0.10 level of statistical significance (90 percent confidence level). Caution is required when comparing estimates not explicitly discussed in this report.

Data users can use the estimates and the standard errors of the estimates provided in this report to generate a confidence interval around the estimate as a measure of the margin of error.

In this report, BJS also calculated a coefficient of variation (CV) for all estimates, representing the ratio of the standard error to the estimate. CVs provide a measure of reliability and a means for comparing the precision of estimates across measures with differing levels or metrics.

NCVS Measurement of Rape and Sexual Assault

Definition of rape and sexual assault

The measurement of rape and sexual assault presents many challenges. Victims may not be willing to reveal or share their experiences with an interviewer. The level and type of sexual violence reported by victims is sensitive a variety of factors related to the interview process, including how items are worded, definitions are used, and the data collection mode. In addition, the legal definitions of rape and sexual assault vary across jurisdictions.

For the NCVS, survey respondents are asked to respond to a series of questions about the nature and characteristics of their victimization. The NCVS classifies victimizations as rape or sexual assault even if other crimes, such as robbery or assault, occurred at the same time. Then, the NCVS uses the following rape and sexual assault definitions:

Rape is the unlawful penetration of a person against the will of the victim, with use or threatened use of force, or attempting such an act. Rape includes psychological coercion and physical force, and forced sexual intercourse means vaginal, anal, or oral penetration by the offender. Rape also includes incidents where penetration is from a foreign object (e.g., a bottle), victimizations against male and female victims, and both heterosexual and homosexual rape. Attempted rape includes verbal threats of rape.

Sexual assault is defined across a wide range of victimizations, separate from rape or attempted rape. These crimes include attacks or attempted attacks generally involving unwanted sexual contact between a victim and offender. Sexual assault may or may not involve force and includes grabbing or fondling.

From 2005 to 2014, 30 percent of NCVS rape and sexual assault victimizations were classified as completed rape. Attempted rape or other sexual assault accounted for nearly 50 percent of rape or sexual assault victimizations. About 1 in 5 (18 percent) were verbal threats of rape or sexual assault.

Comparison of NCVS Estimates to Other Survey Estimates

Over the past several decades, a number of other surveys have also been used to study rape and sexual assault in the general population. BJS estimates of rape and sexual assault from the NCVS have typically been lower than estimates derived from other federal and private surveys. However, the NCVS methodology and definitions of rape and sexual assault differ from many of these surveys in important ways that contribute to the variation in estimates of the prevalence and incidence of these victimization. Additional information about differences in self-report estimates of rape and sexual assault is available on the BJS website. BJS continues an active research program on the collection of rape and sexual assault data in an effort to improve the quality and accuracy of these estimates.

Despite the current differences in methods and estimates that exist between the NCVS and other surveys, a strength of the NCVS is its capacity to be used to make comparisons over time, as year-to-year comparisons are not affected by the NCVS methodology.

PART 2

Correctional Populations in the United States, 2014

HIGHLIGHTS

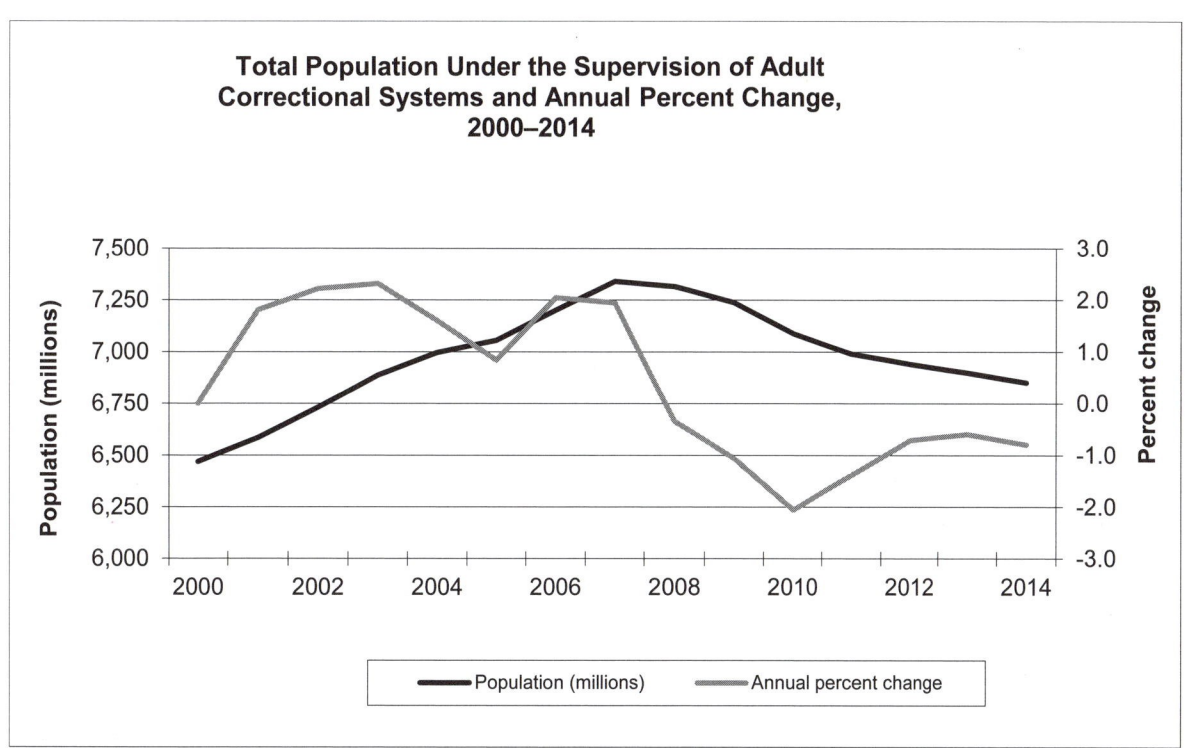

Total Population Under the Supervision of Adult Correctional Systems and Annual Percent Change, 2000–2014

- An estimated 6,851,000 persons were supervised by the correctional system at yearend 2014, about 52,200 less than at yearend 2013.

- About 1 in 36 adults (or 2.8 percent of adults in the United States) had some form of correctional supervision at yearend 2014, the lowest rate since 1996; the correctional population has declined by an average of 1 percent every year since 2007.

- In 2014, the reduction in the community supervision population (1 percent) accounted for the whole decrease in the correctional population.

- The incarcerated population slightly increased during 2014, rising by 1,900 people.

- Approximately 88 percent of the decrease in the correctional population (totaling 488,600 offenders) was attributable to the decline in the probation population.

- Seven jurisdictions—Texas, California, Georgia, Florida, Pennsylvania, Ohio, and the federal jurisdiction—accounted for 48 percent of the nation's correctional population at yearend 2014.

Table 1. Estimated Number of Persons Supervised by U.S. Adult Correctional Systems, by Correctional Status, Selected Years, 2000, 2005–2010, and 2013–2014

(Number; percent.)

Year	Total correctional population[1]	Community supervision			Incarcerated[1]		
		Total[2,3]	Probation	Parole	Total[1]	Local jail	Prison
2000	6,467,800	4,564,900	3,839,400	725,500	1,945,400	621,100	1,394,200
2005	7,055,600	4,946,600	4,162,300	784,400	2,200,400	747,500	1,525,900
2006	7,199,700	5,035,000	4,236,800	798,200	2,256,600	765,800	1,568,700
2007	7,339,600	5,119,000	4,293,000	826,100	2,296,400	780,200	1,596,800
2008	7,313,600	5,094,400	4,270,100	828,200	2,310,300	785,500	1,608,300
2009	7,235,200	5,015,900	4,196,200	824,100	2,297,700	767,400	1,615,500
2010	7,086,500	4,886,000	4,053,600	840,700	2,279,100	748,700	1,613,800
2013	6,903,200	4,753,400	3,910,600	855,200	2,222,500	731,200	1,577,000
2014	6,851,000	4,708,100	3,864,100	856,900	2,224,400	744,600	1,561,500
Average annual percent change, 2007–2014	-1.0	-1.2	-1.5	0.5	-0.5	-0.7	-0.3
Percent change, 2013–2014	-0.8	-1.0	-1.2	0.2	0.1	1.8	-1.0

Note: Estimates were rounded to the nearest 100 and may not be comparable to previously published BJS reports due to updated information or rounding. Counts include estimates for nonresponding jurisdictions. All probation, parole, and prison counts are for December 31; jail counts are for the last weekday in June. Detail may not sum to total due to rounding and adjustments made to account for offenders with multiple correctional statuses.
[1] Includes inmates held in local jails or under the jurisdiction of state or federal prisons.
[2] Total was adjusted to account for offenders with multiple correctional statuses.
[3] Includes some offenders held in a prison or jail but who remained under the jurisdiction of a probation or parole agency.

Table 2. Estimated Rate of Persons Supervised by U.S. Adult Correctional Systems, by Correctional Status, Selected Years, 2000 and 2005–2014

(Number; rate per 100,000 U.S. residents.)

Year	Total correctional population[1]			Community supervision population		Incarcerated population[2]	
	Number supervised per 100,000 U.S. residents age 18 or older[3]	U.S. adult residents under correctional supervision[3]	Number supervised per 100,000 U.S. residents of all ages[4]	Number on probation or parole per 100,000 U.S. residents age 18 or older[3]	Number on probation or parole per 100,000 U.S. residents of all ages[4]	Number in prison or local jail per 100,000 U.S. residents age 18 or older[3]	Number in prison or local jail per 100,000 U.S. residents of all ages[4]
2000	3,060	1 in 33	2,280	2,160	1,610	920	690
2005	3,160	1 in 32	2,370	2,210	1,660	990	740
2006	3,190	1 in 31	2,400	2,230	1,680	1,000	750
2007	3,210	1 in 31	2,420	2,240	1,690	1,000	760
2008	3,160	1 in 32	2,390	2,200	1,670	1,000	760
2009	3,100	1 in 32	2,350	2,150	1,630	980	750
2010	3,000	1 in 33	2,280	2,070	1,570	960	730
2011	2,930	1 in 34	2,230	2,010	1,540	940	720
2012	2,880	1 in 35	2,200	1,980	1,520	920	710
2013	2,830	1 in 35	2,170	1,950	1,500	910	700
2014	2,780	1 in 36	2,140	1,910	1,470	900	690

Note: Rates were estimated to the nearest 10. Estimates may not be comparable to previously published BJS reports due to updated information or rounding.
[1] Includes offenders in the community under the jurisdiction of probation or parole agencies, under the jurisdiction of state or federal prisons, or held in local jails.
[2] Includes inmates under the jurisdiction of state or federal prisons or held in local jails.
[3] Rates were computed using estimates of the U.S. resident population for persons age 18 or older.
[4] Rates were computed using estimates of the U.S. resident population for persons of all ages.

Table 3. Estimated Number of Persons Supervised by U.S. Adult Correctional Systems, by Correctional Status, 2007 and 2014

(Number; percent.)

Correctional populations	2007		2014	
	Population	Percent of total population	Population	Percent of total population
Total[1]	7,339,600	100.0	6,851,000	100.0
Probation[2]	4,293,000	58.5	3,864,100	56.4
Prison[2]	1,596,800	21.8	1,561,500	22.8
Parole[2]	826,100	11.3	856,900	12.5
Local jail[3]	780,200	10.6	744,600	10.9
Offenders with multiple correctional statuses[4]	156,400	:	176,100	:

Note: Counts were rounded to the nearest 100 and include estimates for nonresponding jurisdictions. Detail may not sum to total due to rounding and because offenders with multiple correctional statuses were excluded from the total correctional population.
: = Not calculated.
[1] Adjusted to exclude offenders with multiple correctional statuses to avoid double counting.
[2] Population as of December 31.
[3] Population as of the last weekday in June.
[4] Some probationers and parolees on December 31 were held in a prison or jail but still remained under the jurisdiction of a probation or parole agency, and some parolees were also on probation. In addition, some prisoners were held in jail. They were excluded from the total correctional population to avoid double counting. See Table 6.

Table 4. Change in the Estimated Number of Persons Supervised by U.S. Adult Correctional Systems, 2000–2007 and 2007–2014

(Number; percent.)

Characteristic	2000–2007		2007–2014	
	Change in population[1]	Percent of total change[1]	Change in population[1]	Percent of total change[1]
Total Change[2]	871,900	100.0	-488,600	100.0
Probation...	453,600	52.0	-428,800	87.8
Prison	202,600	23.2	-35,300	7.2
Local jail...	159,000	18.2	-35,600	7.3
Parole	100,600	11.5	30,800	-6.3
Offenders with mulitple correction statuses[3]	43,900	:	19,700	:

Note: Estimates were rounded to the nearest 100 and include estimates for nonresponding jurisdictions. Detail may not sum to total due to rounding.
: = Not calculated.
[1] Detail may not sum to total due to adjustments to exclude offenders with multiple correctional statuses from the total to avoid double counting. See Table 6.
[2] Includes the change in the number of offenders with multiple correctional statuses. See Table 6.
[3] Some probationers and parolees on December 31 were held in a prison or local jail but still remained under the jurisdiction of a probation or parole agency, and some parolees were also on probation. Some prisoners were held in a local jail on December 31. These offenders were excluded from the total correctional population prior to calculating change to avoid double counting. See Table 6.

Table 5. Estimated Number and Rate of Persons Supervised by U.S. Adult Correctional Systems, by Jurisdiction and Correctional Status, 2013 and 2014

(Number; rate per 100,000 U.S. residents of all ages.)

Jurisdiction	Total correctional population, 12/31/13					Total correctional population, 12/31/14				
	Number			Rate[1]		Number			Rate[1]	
	Total[2]	Male	Female	Male	Female	Total[2]	Male	Female	Male	Female
U.S. Total[3]	6,903,600	5,647,300	1,256,300	3,610	780	6,814,600	5,563,100	1,251,600	3,530	770
Federal[4]	347,000	308,600	38,400	200	20	338,000	300,600	37,400	190	20
State	6,556,600	5,338,700	1,217,900	3,410	750	6,476,600	5,262,500	1,214,100	3,340	750
Alabama[4]	115,500	98,500	17,100	4,200	690	104,900	87,400	17,500	3,710	700
Alaska	14,600	12,200	2,500	3,150	710	14,600	12,100	2,400	3,130	690
Arizona	132,300	111,100	21,200	3,350	630	133,600	111,900	21,700	3,330	640
Arkansas	70,100	56,400	13,700	3,870	910	69,100	55,500	13,500	3,800	890
California	601,800	506,800	95,000	2,640	490	589,600	495,500	94,100	2,560	480
Colorado	120,500	95,000	25,500	3,560	960	119,800	94,000	25,800	3,470	960
Connecticut	62,900	52,700	10,200	3,000	550	62,300	51,500	10,700	2,930	580
Delaware	23,700	19,100	4,600	4,240	960	23,300	18,800	4,500	4,130	930
District of Columbia[5]	13,700	11,700	2,000	3,770	580	11,900	10,200	1,800	3,230	520
Florida	389,200	314,400	74,800	3,260	740	382,600	308,800	73,700	3,150	720
Georgia[6]	623,500	496,600	126,800	10,120	2,470	579,600	463,800	115,800	9,370	2,230
Hawaii	28,900	22,800	6,200	3,190	890	28,300	22,300	6,000	3,100	850
Idaho[7]	46,200	35,900	10,300	4,410	1,270	48,600	37,700	10,900	4,580	1,330
Illinois	222,700	183,500	39,200	2,900	600	219,000	181,000	38,000	2,860	580
Indiana	179,100	142,200	36,900	4,380	1,100	175,200	139,300	35,900	4,280	1,070
Iowa	45,900	36,300	9,600	2,360	610	46,500	36,600	9,900	2,360	630
Kansas	37,100	30,900	6,200	2,140	430	37,400	31,200	6,200	2,150	420
Kentucky[4]	97,500	73,500	24,000	3,390	1,070	103,600	77,900	25,700	3,580	1,150
Louisiana	115,300	97,700	17,700	4,300	750	113,600	96,300	17,400	4,220	730
Maine	10,500	8,900	1,700	1,370	250	10,100	8,400	1,700	1,290	250
Maryland[4]	74,900	67,200	7,700	2,330	250	109,700	92,100	17,700	3,170	570
Massachusetts	90,700	76,100	14,600	2,330	420	90,300	75,900	14,400	2,310	410
Michigan[4]	253,500	203,300	50,200	4,180	1,000	256,700	203,200	53,400	4,170	1,060
Minnesota	123,500	97,400	26,100	3,600	950	120,500	95,500	25,000	3,510	910
Mississippi	67,600	52,400	15,200	3,600	990	69,700	58,200	11,500	4,000	750
Missouri	113,400	93,000	20,400	3,130	660	109,500	89,400	20,100	3,000	650
Montana	14,800	12,100	2,700	2,360	530	14,500	11,700	2,800	2,270	550
Nebraska	23,200	18,500	4,600	1,980	490	22,500	17,800	4,700	1,890	500
Nevada	37,200	31,000	6,300	2,190	450	37,500	31,400	6,100	2,190	430
New Hampshire	11,100	9,300	1,800	1,420	270	11,200	9,300	1,900	1,420	280
New Jersey	164,100	137,900	26,300	3,170	580	164,500	137,300	27,200	3,140	590
New Mexico	34,500	27,700	6,900	2,680	650	32,500	26,000	6,500	2,520	620
New York	227,200	197,500	29,700	2,060	290	222,100	192,300	29,800	2,000	290
North Carolina	156,100	126,500	29,600	2,620	580	153,600	124,100	29,500	2,550	580
North Dakota	8,300	6,500	1,800	1,730	500	9,300	7,300	2,000	1,900	550
Ohio	335,600	255,800	79,900	4,510	1,350	326,300	251,000	75,300	4,410	1,270
Oklahoma[7]	67,600	55,900	11,700	2,920	600	69,600	57,700	11,900	2,990	610
Oregon	82,300	68,200	14,100	3,490	710	82,700	68,200	14,500	3,460	720
Pennsylvania	357,400	286,700	70,700	4,590	1,080	360,800	284,700	76,100	4,540	1,160
Rhode Island	24,600	20,900	3,700	4,090	680	25,100	21,300	3,800	4,160	700
South Carolina	73,500	62,700	10,800	2,680	440	71,900	61,000	10,800	2,580	430
South Dakota	14,800	11,900	2,900	2,790	690	14,500	11,600	2,800	2,690	660
Tennessee	121,700	97,600	24,200	3,070	720	119,900	95,900	24,000	2,990	710
Texas	712,000	574,200	137,800	4,330	1,020	699,300	564,200	135,100	4,180	990
Utah	25,300	20,500	4,800	1,390	330	25,700	20,600	5,100	1,380	350
Vermont	8,600	6,900	1,800	2,230	570	8,400	6,700	1,700	2,170	540
Virginia	114,500	95,900	18,600	2,350	440	115,300	95,900	19,400	2,330	460
Washington[4]	139,400	112,600	26,900	3,210	770	133,000	106,600	26,500	3,000	750
West Virginia[4]	20,500	16,000	4,500	1,750	480	19,600	15,500	4,100	1,700	440
Wisconsin	97,900	83,000	14,900	2,910	510	97,300	82,300	15,000	2,870	520
Wyoming	9,700	7,700	2,000	2,590	700	9,700	7,700	2,000	2,580	700

Note: Counts were rounded to the nearest 100, and rates were rounded to the nearest 10. Detail may not sum to total due to rounding and because offenders with multiple correctional statuses were excluded from totals. Counts include estimates for nonresponding jurisdictions.
[1] Rates were computed using estimates of the resident population of persons of all ages within jurisdiction, by sex. U.S. resident population estimates of persons age 18 or older were not available by sex. For this reason, jurisdiction-level rates in other tables of this report may not be comparable to the rates in this table.
[2] Excludes, by jurisdiction, an estimated 154,100 males and 16,700 females in 2013 and 157,900 males and 18,200 females with multiple correctional statuses.
[3] Total correctional population includes local jail counts that are based on December 31 in order to produce jurisdiction-level estimates. For this reason, the estimates in this table differ from other datasets from this source.
[4] Estimates may not be comparable between years due to updated information or changes in reporting.
[5] After 2001, responsibility for sentenced prisoners was transferred to the Federal Bureau of Prisons. Therefore, the 2005 and 2013 incarcerated populations represent inmates held in local jails.
[6] Estimates include misdemeanant probation cases, not individuals, supervised by private companies and may overstate the number of offenders under supervision.
[7] Includes estimates of probationers supervised for a misdemeanor based on admissions and may overstate the number of offenders under supervision.

Table 6. Estimated Number of Offenders with Multiple Correctional Statuses at Yearend, by Correctional Status, 2000–2014

(Number; percent.)

Year	Total	Prisoners held in local jail	Probationers		Parolees		On probation
			Local jail	State or federal prison	Local jail	State or federal prison	
2000..	112,500	70,000	20,400	22,100	:	:	:
2001..	116,100	72,500	23,400	20,200	:	:	:
2002..	122,800	72,600	29,300	20,900	:	:	:
2003..	120,400	73,400	25,500	21,500	:	:	:
2004..	130,400	74,400	34,400	21,600	:	:	:
2005..	164,500	73,100	32,600	22,100	18,300	18,400	:
2006..	169,900	77,900	33,900	21,700	20,700	15,700	:
2007..	156,400	80,600	19,300	23,100	18,800	14,600	:
2008..	178,500	83,500	23,800	32,400	19,300	15,600	3,900
2009..	168,100	85,200	21,400	23,100	19,100	14,300	5,000
2010..	170,300	83,400	21,300	21,500	21,400	14,400	8,300
2011..	169,300	82,100	21,100	22,300	18,000	14,900	11,000
2012..	168,200	83,500	21,200	21,600	18,500	10,700	12,700
2013..	170,800	85,600	22,400	16,700	21,800	11,800	12,500
2014..	176,100	81,700	23,500	24,600	21,800	11,600	12,900

Note: Estimates were rounded to the nearest 100 and may not be comparable to previously published BJS reports due to updated information. Detail may not sum to total due to rounding.
: = Not collected or excluded from total correctional population.

Table 7. Estimated Number and Rate of Persons Supervised by U.S. Adult Correctional Systems, by Jurisdiction and Correctional Status, 2014

(Number as of 12/31/14; rate per 100,000 adults.)

Jurisdiction	Total correctional population[1]		Community supervision		Incarcerated	
	Number on probation or parole[2]	Correctional supervision rate[3]	Number on probation or parole[2]	Community supervision rate[3]	Number in prison or local jail[4]	Incarceration rate[3]
U.S. Total[5]...	6,814,600	2,760	4,708,100	1,910	2,188,000	890
Federal[6]..	338,000	140	128,400	50	209,600	90
State..	6,476,600	2,630	4,579,700	1,860	1,978,300	800
Alabama..	104,900	2,790	61,400	1,640	45,800	1,220
Alaska...	14,600	2,650	9,300	1,690	5,300	960
Arizona..	133,600	2,590	80,700	1,570	54,800	1,060
Arkansas..	69,100	3,050	49,300	2,170	23,100	1,020
California...	589,600	1,980	382,600	1,280	207,100	690
Colorado	119,800	2,890	89,100	2,150	31,500	760
Connecticut	62,300	2,200	45,600	1,610	16,600	590
Delaware	23,300	3,170	16,300	2,220	7,000	950
District of Columbia[7]................................	11,900	2,180	11,400	2,070	1,600	300
Florida...	382,600	2,390	231,600	1,450	153,600	960
Georgia[8]	579,600	7,580	491,800	6,430	91,000	1,190
Hawaii...	28,300	2,540	22,500	2,010	5,900	530
Idaho[9]...	48,600	4,010	37,700	3,110	11,000	910
Illinois...	219,000	2,210	151,800	1,530	67,200	680
Indiana..	175,200	3,480	128,100	2,540	47,100	940
Iowa..	46,500	1,940	35,500	1,490	12,700	530
Kansas...	37,400	1,710	20,400	930	17,000	780
Kentucky	103,600	3,040	70,800	2,080	33,500	980
Louisiana	113,600	3,200	70,600	1,990	49,100	1,380
Maine..	10,100	940	6,600	610	4,100	380
Maryland...	109,700	2,360	91,100	1,960	31,100	670
Massachusetts	90,300	1,680	70,200	1,310	20,300	380
Michigan..	256,700	3,330	199,000	2,580	59,400	770
Minnesota..	120,500	2,870	104,300	2,490	16,200	390
Mississippi...	69,700	3,070	44,300	1,950	25,400	1,120
Missouri...	109,500	2,340	65,800	1,400	43,700	930
Montana..	14,500	1,810	9,700	1,210	5,500	680
Nebraska	22,500	1,580	14,000	990	8,500	600
Nevada	37,500	1,710	18,000	820	19,600	890
New Hampshire	11,200	1,050	6,300	590	4,900	460
New Jersey..	164,500	2,370	130,800	1,880	35,200	510
New Mexico..	32,500	2,050	18,100	1,140	14,400	910
New York..	222,100	1,430	149,100	960	77,500	500
North Carolina	153,600	2,000	99,300	1,290	54,300	710
North Dakota..	9,300	1,610	6,200	1,070	3,200	550
Ohio..	326,300	3,630	256,200	2,850	71,200	790
Oklahoma[7]..	69,600	2,370	31,100	1,060	38,400	1,310
Oregon..	82,700	2,640	61,900	1,980	20,900	670
Pennsylvania...	360,800	3,570	281,400	2,780	85,200	840
Rhode Island...	25,100	2,970	24,100	2,850	3,400	400
South Carolina..	71,900	1,910	40,000	1,060	31,900	850
South Dakota..	14,500	2,240	9,400	1,460	5,100	800
Tennessee	119,900	2,360	76,400	1,500	46,900	920
Texas...	699,300	3,490	496,900	2,480	219,100	1,090
Utah..	25,700	1,250	15,300	740	12,600	620
Vermont	8,400	1,670	6,800	1,340	2,000	390
Virginia..	115,300	1,780	56,700	880	58,600	900
Washington..	133,000	2,420	104,000	1,890	30,900	560
West Virginia	19,600	1,330	9,900	680	9,900	670
Wisconsin	97,300	2,180	64,500	1,440	34,600	770
Wyoming..	9,700	2,180	5,900	1,330	3,800	850

Note: Counts were rounded to the nearest 100, and rates were rounded to the nearest 10. Detail may not sum to total due to rounding and because offenders with multiple correctional statuses were excluded from totals. Counts include estimates for nonresponding jurisdictions.
[1] Excludes an estimated 81,700 prisoners held in local jails; 23,500 probationers in prisons; 24,600 probationers in local jails; 21,800 parolees in local jails; 11,600 parolees in prisons; and 12,900 parolees on probation. See Table 6.
[2] Excludes an estimated 12,900 parolees on probation. See Table 6.
[3] Rates were computed using estimates of the U.S. resident population of persons age 18 or older within jurisdiction.
[4] Excludes an estimated 81,700 prisoners held in local jails. See Table 6.
[5] Total correctional population and total number in prison or local jail include local jail counts that are based on December 31, 2014, in order to produce jurisdiction-level estimates. For this reason, the totals in this table differ from the national estimates presented in most other data in this report.
[6] Excludes about 11,900 inmates who were not held in locally operated jails but in facilities that were operated by the Federal Bureau of Prisons and functioned as jails.
[7] After 2001, responsibility for sentenced prisoners was transferred to the Federal Bureau of Prisons. Therefore, the 2005 and 2013 incarcerated populations represent inmates held in local jails.
[8] Total correctional population and community supervision population estimates include misdemeanant probation cases, not individuals, supervised by private companies and may overstate the number of offenders under supervision.
[9] Total correctional population and community supervision population include estimates of probationers supervised for a misdemeanor based on admissions and may overstate the number of offenders under supervision.

Table 8. Inmates Held in Custody in State or Federal Prisons or in Local Jails, 2000 and 2013–2014

(Number; percent.)

Characteristic	Number of inmates			Average annual change, 2000–2013	Percent change, 2013–2014
	2000	2013	2014		
Inmates in Custody	1,938,500	2,217,000	2,222,900	1.0	0.3
Federal prisoners[1]	140,100	215,000	209,600	3.3	-2.5
Prisons	133,900	205,700	200,000	3.3	-2.8
Federal facilities	124,500	173,800	169,500	2.6	-2.5
Privately operated facilities	9,400	31,900	30,500	9.4	-4.4
Community corrections centers[2]	6,100	9,300	9,500	3.2	2.2
State prisoners	1,177,200	1,270,300	1,268,700	0.6	-0.2
State facilities[3]	1,101,200	1,177,900	1,177,500	0.5	0.0
Privately operated facilities	76,100	92,200	91,200	1.5	-1.0
Local jails	621,100	731,200	744,600	1.3	1.8
Incarceration rate[4]	690	700	690	0.1	-1.4
Adult incarceration rate[4]	920	910	900	-0.1	-1.1

Note: Estimates may not be comparable to previously published BJS reports due to updated information. Counts were rounded to the nearest 100 and include estimates for nonresponding jurisdictions. Rates were rounded to the nearest 10. Detail may not to sum to total due to rounding. Prison counts are for December 31; jail counts are for the last weekday in June. Total includes all inmates held in local jails, state or federal prisons, or privately operated facilities. It does not include inmates held in U.S. territories, military facilities, U.S. Immigration and Customs Enforcement facilities, in jails in Indian country, or juvenile facilities.
[1] After 2001, responsibility for sentenced prisoners from the District of Columbia was transferred to the Federal Bureau of Prisons.
[2] Nonsecure, privately operated community corrections centers.
[3] The total number in the custody of local jails, state or federal prisons, or privately operated facilities per 100,000 U.S. residents of all ages.
[4] The total number in custody per 100,000 U.S. residents age 18 or older.

Table 9. Estimated Number of Inmates Incarcerated by Other Adult Correctional Systems, 2000, 2005, and 2013–2014

(Number; percent.)

Characteristic	Number of inmates				Average annual change, 2000–2013	Percent change, 2013–2014
	2000	2005	2013	2014		
Other Adult Correctional Systems	20,400	19,800	17,600	16,800	-1.1	1.1
Territorial prisons[1]	16,200	15,800	13,900	14,000	-1.1	0.9
Military facilties[2]	2,400	2,300	1,400	1,400	-4.1	-0.8
Jails in Indian country[3]	1,800	1,700	2,300	2,400	1.9	4.1

Note: Estimates were rounded to the nearest 100. Total excludes inmates held in local jails, under the jurisdiction of state or federal prisons, in U.S. Immigration and Customs Enforcement facilities, or in juvenile facilities.
[1] Population counts are for December 31. The 2013–2014 totals include population counts that were estimated for some territories due to nonresponse. See Prisoners in 2014 (NCJ 248955, BJS web, September 2015).
[2] Population counts are for December 31. See Prisoners in 2014 (NCJ 248955, BJS web, September 2015).
[3] Population counts are for the last weekday in June. The 2005 population was estimated as the 2004 population because the Survey of Jails in Indian Country was not conducted in 2005 or 2006. See Jails in Indian Country, 2014 (NCJ 248974, BJS web, October 2015).

Table 10. Incarceration Rate of Inmates Under the Jurisdiction of State or Federal Prisons or Held in Local Jails and Imprisonment Rate of Sentenced Prisoners Under the Jurisdiction of State or Federal Prisons, 2004–2014

(Rate.)

Year	Rate per 100,000 U.S. residents age 18 years or older[1]		Rate per 100,000 U.S. residents of all ages[2]	
	Incarceration rate[3]	Imprisonment rate[4]	Incarceration rate[3]	Imprisonment rate[4]
2004........................	970	650	730	490
2005........................	990	660	740	490
2006........................	1,000	670	750	500
2007........................	1,000	670	760	510
2008........................	1,000	670	760	510
2009........................	980	660	750	500
2010........................	960	660	730	500
2011........................	940	640	720	490
2012........................	920	630	710	480
2013........................	910	620	700	480
2014........................	900	610	690	470

Note: Rates were rounded to the nearest 10 and include estimates for nonresponding jurisdictions.
[1] Rates were computed using estimates of the U.S. resident population for persons age 18 or older.
[2] Rates were computed using estimates of the U.S. resident population for persons of all ages.
[3] Includes inmates under the jurisdiction or legal authority of state or federal prisons or held in local jails.
[4] Includes prisoners sentenced to more than 1 year who were under the jurisdiction or legal authority of state or federal prisons. The imprisonment rate excludes unsentenced prisoners, prisoners with sentences of less than 1 year, and all inmates held in local jails.

METHODOLOGY

About the Data

The statistics presented in this chapter include data from *Correctional Populations in the United States, 2014*, which itself relies on various Bureau of Justice Statistics (BJS) data collections, each relying on the voluntary participation of federal, state, and local respondents. This report presents statistics on offenders supervised by adult correctional systems in the United States at yearend 2014, including offenders supervised in the community on probation or parole and those incarcerated in prison or local jail. The report provides the size and change in the total correctional population during 2014. It details the slowing rate of decline in the population since 2010 and the downward trend in the correctional supervision rate since 2007. It also examines the impact of changes in the community supervision and incarcerated populations on the total correctional population in recent years. Findings cover the size of the male and female correctional populations and compare the rates of change in the populations by correctional status since 2000. Other information comprises correctional populations, including prisoners under military jurisdiction, inmates held by correctional authorities in the U.S. territories and commonwealths, and jail inmates held in Indian country facilities, and estimates of the total correctional population by jurisdiction and correctional status.

For more information about any of the following data collections, or to see the full report, please see http://www.bjs.gov/content/pub/pdf/cpus14.pdf.

Annual Probation Survey and Annual Parole Survey

Collect administrative data from probation and parole agencies in the U.S. Data collected include the total number of adults on state and federal probation and parole on January 1 and December 31 of each year, the number of adults entering and exiting probation and parole supervision each year, and the characteristics of adults under the supervision of probation and parole agencies. Published data include both national and state-level data. The surveys cover all 50 states, the federal system, and the District of Columbia. They began in 1980 and are conducted annually. Probation data are also available dating back to 1977. Through BJS's National Probation Reports, probation data were collected from 1977 to 1979. Parole data are available dating back to 1975. The parole data from 1975 to 1979 were collected through BJS's Uniform Parole Reports.

Annual Survey of Jails

Collects data from a nationally representative sample of local jails on jail inmate populations, jail capacity, and related information. The collection began in 1982 and has been conducted annually, except for years 1983, 1988, 1993, 1999, and 2005, during which a complete census of U.S. local jails was conducted.

Census of Jails

The 2006 Census of Jail Facilities is part of a series of data collections that study the nation's local jails. To reduce respondent burden and improve data quality and timeliness, the original jail census was split into two parts in 2005: the Census of Jail Inmates (2005) and the Census of Jail Facilities (2006). In 2013, BJS expanded the 2013 Deaths in Custody Reporting Program—Annual Summary on Inmates under Jail Jurisdiction to act as the 2013 Census of Jails. The Census of Jail Facilities collects information on each facility, including admissions and releases, court orders, programs that offer alternatives to incarceration, counts of inmates on hold for other jurisdictions, use of space and crowding, staffing, inmate work assignments, and education and counseling programs. The census provides the sampling frame for the nationwide Survey of Inmates in Local Jails (SILJ) and the Annual Survey of Jails (ASJ).

Deaths in Custody Reporting Program (DCRP)

Collects inmate death records from each of the nation's 50 state prison systems and approximately 2,800 local jail jurisdictions. In addition, this program collects records of all deaths occurring during the process of arrest. Data are collected directly from state and local law enforcement agencies. To reduce respondent burden for the 2013 iteration, BJS combined the 2013 DCRP collection with the 2013 Census of Jails.

Death records include information on decedent personal characteristics (age, race or Hispanic origin, and sex), decedent criminal background (legal status, offense type, and time served), and the death itself (date, time, location, and cause of death, as well as information on the autopsy and medical treatment provided for any illness or disease).

Data collections covering these populations were developed in annual phases: Annual collection of individual death records from local jail facilities began in 2000, followed by a separate collection for state prison facilities in 2001. Collection of state juvenile correctional agencies began in 2002 but was discontinued in 2006, and collection of arrest-related death records began in 2003. Datasets are produced in an annual format.

National Prisoner Statistics (NPS) Program

Produces annual national and state-level data on the number of prisoners in state and federal prison facilities. Aggregate data are collected on race and sex of prison inmates, inmates held in private facilities and local jails, system capacity, noncitizens, and persons under age 18. Findings are released in the Prisoners series. Data are from the 50 state department of corrections, the Federal Bureau of Prisons, and until 2001, from the District of Columbia (after 2001, felons sentenced under the District of Columbia criminal code were housed in federal facilities).

Survey of Jails in Indian Country

Collects detailed information on confinement facilities, detention centers, jails, and other facilities operated by tribal authorities or the Bureau of Indian Affairs (BIA). Information is gathered on inmate counts, movements, facility operations, and staff. In selected years (1998, 2004, 2007, and 2011), additional information is collected on facility programs and services, such as medical assessments and mental health screening procedures, inmate work assignments, counseling, and educational programs.

Additional Information

Counts Adjusted for Offenders with Multiple Correctional Statuses

Offenders under correctional supervision may have multiple correctional statuses for several reasons. For example, probation and parole agencies may not always be notified immediately of new arrests, jail admissions, or prison admissions; absconders included in a probation or parole agency's population in one jurisdiction may actually be incarcerated in another jurisdiction; persons may be admitted to jail or prison before formal revocation hearings and potential discharge by a probation or parole agency; and persons may be serving separate probation and parole sentences concurrently. In addition, state and federal prisons may hold inmates in county facilities or local jails to reduce crowding in their prisons.

In 1998, through the ASPP, BJS began collecting data on the number of probationers and parolees with multiple correctional statuses and has since expanded on the information collected. In 1999, through the NPS, BJS began collecting data on the number of prisoners under the jurisdiction of state or federal prisons that were held in county facilities or local jails. Table 6 includes adjustments that were made to the total correctional population, total community supervision population, and total incarcerated population estimates presented in this report to exclude offenders with multiple correctional statuses to avoid double counting offenders. The estimates from the ASPP are based on data reported by the probation and parole agencies that were able to provide the information within the specific reporting year. Because some probation and parole agencies did not provide these data each year, the numbers may underestimate the total number of offenders who had multiple correctional statuses between 2000 and 2013. Due to these adjustments, the sum of correctional statuses in Tables 1, 2, 3, 4, 5 and appendix table 1 will not equal the total correctional population. In addition, the sum of the probation and parole populations for 2008 through 2013 will not yield the total community supervision population because the total was adjusted for parolees who were also on probation. In addition, the sum of the prison and local jail populations for 2000 through 2013 will not equal the total incarcerated population because prisoners held in local jails were excluded from the total.

Adjustments for Nonresponse

Probation, parole, jail, and prison population counts were adjusted to account for nonresponse across the data collections. The methods varied and depended on the type of collection, type of respondent, and availability of information. The local jail population counts that were collected through the 2013 Census of Jails to produce the jurisdiction-level estimates that are reported in appendix table 1 were adjusted for unit and item nonresponse. Nonresponse in the 2013 jail census was minimal as the unit response rate was 92.4 percent and the item response rate for the December 31, 2013, population total was 99.7 percent. For jails that did not participate in the census or were unable to provide the 2013 yearend count, a sequential hot deck imputation procedure was used to impute values.

Estimates of Males and Females under Correctional Supervision

The number of males and the number of females on probation or parole were adjusted to account for nonresponse using a ratio adjustment method. For jurisdictions that did not provide data on sex for a portion of their population, the sex distribution of the known portion of the population was used to impute for the unknown portion because it was assumed that the distributions were the same. For states that were unable to provide any data on sex, the state national average was used to impute the number of males and females supervised in those states. Adjusted jurisdiction totals were then aggregated to produce national estimates of the number of males and females on probation and parole. The number of prisoners by sex represents the reported number of males and females under the jurisdiction of state or federal prisons within the reference year. The number of local jail inmates by sex represents the adjusted number of males and females in the custody of local jails within the reference year.

PART 3

Crime in the United States, 2014

HIGHLIGHTS

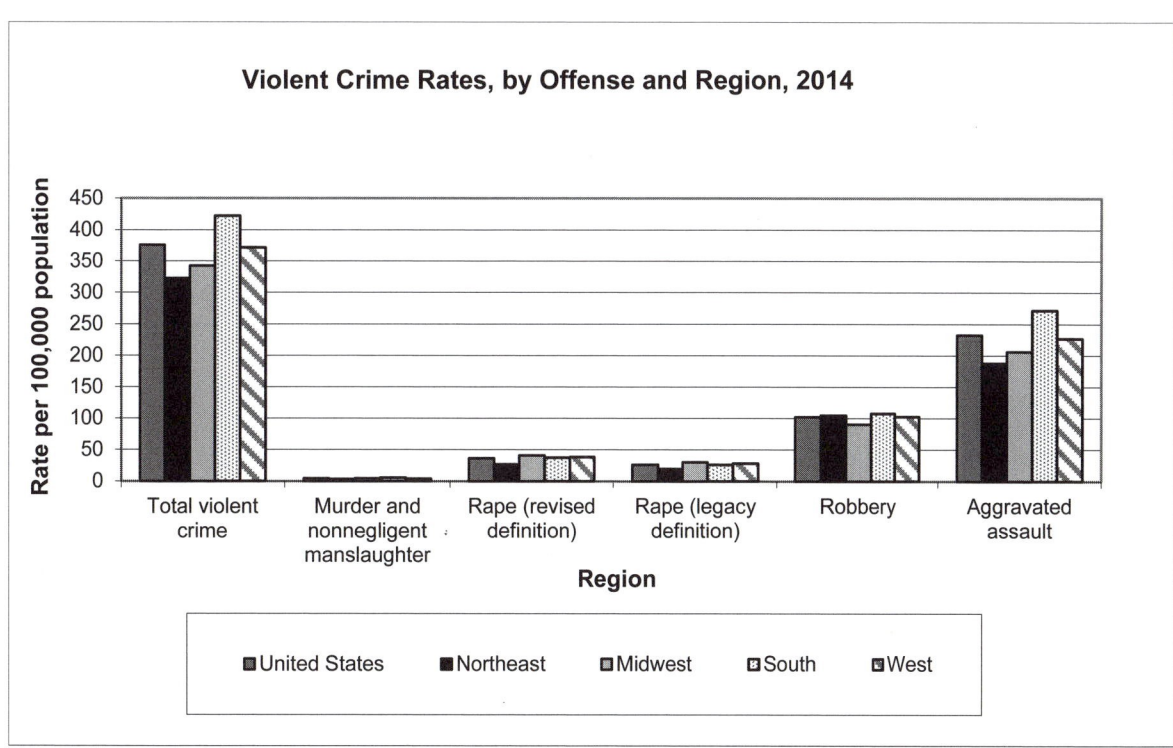

Violent Crime Rates, by Offense and Region, 2014

- In 2014, an estimated 1,165,383 violent crimes occurred nationwide, a decrease of 0.2 percent from the 2013 estimate. Aggravated assaults accounted for 63.6 percent of violent crimes reported to law enforcement in 2014.

- There were an estimated 8,277,829 property crime offenses in the nation in 2014. Of all property crimes in 2014, larceny-theft accounted for 70.8 percent.

- Approximately 47.4 percent of violent crimes and 20.2 percent of property crimes were cleared by arrest or exceptional means.

- Nationwide, law enforcement made an estimated 11,205.833 arrests in 2014. Of these arrests, 498,666 were for violent crimes, and 1,553,980 were for property crimes. The highest number of arrests were for drug abuse violations (estimated at 1,561,231 arrests).

- A total of 12,656 law enforcement agencies provided data on the number of full-time law enforcement employees

(sworn officers and civilian personnel) on staff in 2014; nationwide, the rate of sworn officers was 2.3 per 1,000 inhabitants.

- White males accounted for 31.2 percent of all reported murders in 2014, while White females comprised 13.9 percent of the total. Black males and females accounted for 43.5 percent and 7.4 percent of murders, respectively.

- Males of other and unknown racial origins accounted for 2.5 percent of murders, while their female counterparts accounted for 1.1 percent of murders.

- Approximately 41 percent of robberies took place on the street or highway, representing the largest number of robberies in a location category.

- Cities with 250,000 to 499,999 inhabitants had the highest arson rate in 2014 (29.6 incidents per 100,000 inhabitants), while nonmetropolitan counties had the lowest rate (10.0 incidents per 100,000 inhabitants).

Table 1. Crime in the United States, by Volume and Rate Per 100,000 Inhabitants, 1995–2014

(Number, rate per 100,000 population.)

Year	Population[1]	Violent crime[2]		Murder and nonnegligent manslaughter		Rape (revised definition)[3]		Rape (legacy definition)[4]		Robbery	
		Number	Rate	Number	Rate	Number	Rate	Number	Rate	Number	Rate
1995....................	262,803,276	1,798,792	684.5	21,606	8.2	X	X	97,470	37.1	580,509	220.9
1996....................	265,228,572	1,688,540	636.6	19,645	7.4	X	X	96,252	36.3	535,594	201.9
1997....................	267,783,607	1,636,096	611.0	18,208	6.8	X	X	96,153	35.9	498,534	186.2
1998....................	270,248,003	1,533,887	567.6	16,974	6.3	X	X	93,144	34.5	447,186	165.5
1999....................	272,690,813	1,426,044	523.0	15,522	5.7	X	X	89,411	32.8	409,371	150.1
2000....................	281,421,906	1,425,486	506.5	15,586	5.5	X	X	90,178	32.0	408,016	145.0
2001[5]	285,317,559	1,439,480	504.5	16,037	5.6	X	X	90,863	31.8	423,557	148.5
2002....................	287,973,924	1,423,677	494.4	16,229	5.6	X	X	95,235	33.1	420,806	146.1
2003....................	290,788,976	1,383,676	475.8	16,528	5.7	X	X	93,883	32.3	414,235	142.5
2004....................	293,656,842	1,360,088	463.2	16,148	5.5	X	X	95,089	32.4	401,470	136.7
2005....................	296,507,061	1,390,745	469.0	16,740	5.6	X	X	94,347	31.8	417,438	140.8
2006....................	299,398,484	1,435,123	479.3	17,309	5.8	X	X	94,472	31.6	449,246	150.0
2007....................	301,621,157	1,422,970	471.8	17,128	5.7	X	X	92,160	30.6	447,324	148.3
2008....................	304,059,724	1,394,461	458.6	16,465	5.4	X	X	90,750	29.8	443,563	145.9
2009....................	307,006,550	1,325,896	431.9	15,399	5.0	X	X	89,241	29.1	408,742	133.1
2010....................	309,330,219	1,251,248	404.5	14,722	4.8	X	X	85,593	27.7	369,089	119.3
2011....................	311,587,816	1,206,005	387.1	14,661	4.7	X	X	84,175	27.0	354,746	113.9
2012....................	313,914,040	1,214,462	386.9	14,827	4.7	X	X	84,376	26.9	354,520	112.9
2013[6]	316,128,839	1,168,146	367.9	14,196	4.5	113,695	35.9	79,770	25.2	345,031	109.1
2014....................	318,857,056.0	1,165,383	365.5	14,249	4.5	116,645	36.6	84,041	26.4	325,802	102.2

Table 1. Crime in the United States, by Volume and Rate Per 100,000 Inhabitants, 1995–2014—*Continued*

(Number, rate per 100,000 population.)

Year	Aggravated assault		Property crime		Burglary		Larceny-theft		Motor vehicle theft	
	Number	Rate	Number	Rate	Number	Rate	Number	Rate	Number	Rate
1995	1,099,207	418.3	12,063,935	4,590.5	2,593,784	987.0	7,997,710	3,043.2	1,472,441	560.3
1996	1,037,049	391.0	11,805,323	4,451.0	2,506,400	945.0	7,904,685	2,980.3	1,394,238	525.7
1997	1,023,201	382.1	11,558,475	4,316.3	2,460,526	918.8	7,743,760	2,891.8	1,354,189	505.7
1998	976,583	361.4	10,951,827	4,052.5	2,332,735	863.2	7,376,311	2,729.5	1,242,781	459.9
1999	911,740	334.3	10,208,334	3,743.6	2,100,739	770.4	6,955,520	2,550.7	1,152,075	422.5
2000	911,706	324.0	10,182,584	3,618.3	2,050,992	728.8	6,971,590	2,477.3	1,160,002	412.2
2001[5]	909,023	318.6	10,437,189	3,658.1	2,116,531	741.8	7,092,267	2,485.7	1,228,391	430.5
2002	891,407	309.5	10,455,277	3,630.6	2,151,252	747.0	7,057,379	2,450.7	1,246,646	432.9
2003	859,030	295.4	10,442,862	3,591.2	2,154,834	741.0	7,026,802	2,416.5	1,261,226	433.7
2004	847,381	288.6	10,319,386	3,514.1	2,144,446	730.3	6,937,089	2,362.3	1,237,851	421.5
2005	862,220	290.8	10,174,754	3,431.5	2,155,448	726.9	6,783,447	2,287.8	1,235,859	416.8
2006	874,096	292.0	10,019,601	3,346.6	2,194,993	733.1	6,626,363	2,213.2	1,198,245	400.2
2007	866,358	287.2	9,882,212	3,276.4	2,190,198	726.1	6,591,542	2,185.4	1,100,472	364.9
2008	843,683	277.5	9,774,152	3,214.6	2,228,887	733.0	6,586,206	2,166.1	959,059	315.4
2009	812,514	264.7	9,337,060	3,041.3	2,203,313	717.7	6,338,095	2,064.5	795,652	259.2
2010	781,844	252.8	9,112,625	2,945.9	2,168,459	701.0	6,204,601	2,005.8	739,565	239.1
2011	752,423	241.5	9,052,743	2,905.4	2,185,140	701.3	6,151,095	1,974.10	716,508	230.0
2012	760,739	242.3	8,975,438	2,859.2	2,103,787	670.2	6,150,598	1,959.30	721,053	229.7
2013[6]	724,149	229.1	8,632,512	2,730.7	1,928,465	610.0	6,004,598	1,899.40	699,594	221.3
2014	741,921	232.5	8,277,829	2,596.1	1,729,806	542.5	5,858,496	1,837.30	689,527	216.2

Note: Although arson data are included in the trend and clearance tables, sufficient data are not available to estimate totals for this offense. Therefore, no arson data are published in this table.
X = Not applicable.
[1] Populations are U.S. Census Bureau provisional estimates as of July 1 for each year except 2000 and 2010, which are decennial census counts.
[2] The violent crime figures include the offenses of murder, rape (legacy definition), robbery, and aggravated assault.
[3] The figures shown in this column for the offense of rape were estimated using the revised UCR definition of rape.
[4] The figures shown in this column for the offense of rape were estimated using the legacy UCR definition of rape.
[5] The murder and nonnegligent homicides that occurred as a result of the events of September 11, 2001, are not included in this table.
[6] The crime figures have been adjusted.

Table 1A. Crime in the United States, Percent Change in Volume and Rate Per 100,000 Inhabitants for 2 Years, 5 Years, and 10 Years, 2005–2014

(Percent change.)

Year	Violent crime		Murder and nonnegligent manslaughter		Rape (revised definition)[2]		Rape (legacy definition)[3]		Robbery		Aggravated assault		Property crime		Burglary		Larceny-theft		Motor vehicle theft	
	Number	Rate	Number	Rate	Number	Rate	Number	Rate	Number	Rate	Number	Rate	Number	Rate	Number	Rate	Number	Rate	Number	Rate
2005–2014	-16.2	-22.1	-14.9	-20.8	X	X	-10.9	-17.2	-22.0	-27.4	-14.0	-20.1	-18.6	-24.3	-19.7	-25.4	-13.6	-19.7	-44.2	-48.1
2009–2014	-6.9	-9.6	-3.2	-6.1	X	X	-1.8	-4.7	-11.7	-14.4	-5.2	-8.0	-9.2	-11.9	-20.2	-22.6	-5.6	-8.4	-6.8	-9.6
2013–2014	-0.2	-1.0	-0.5	-1.2	+2.6	+1.8	+2.4	+1.6	-5.6	-6.3	+2.0	+1.2	-4.3	-5.0	-10.5	-11.1	-2.7	-3.4	-1.5	-2.3

X = Not applicable.
[1] The violent crime figures include the offenses of murder, rape (legacy definition), robbery, and aggravated assault.
[2] The figures shown in this column for the offense of rape were estimated using the revised UCR definition of rape.
[3] The figures shown in this column for the offense of rape were estimated using the legacy UCR definition of rape.

Table 2. Crime in the United States, by Community Type, 2014

(Number, percent, rate per 100,000 population)

Area	Population[1]	Violent crime[2]	Murder and nonnegligent manslaughter	Rape (revised definition)[3]	Rape (legacy definition)[4]	Robbery	Aggravated assault	Property crime	Burglary	Larceny-theft	Motor vehicle theft
United States.................................	318,857,056	1,197,987	14,249	116,645	84,041	325,802	741,291	8,277,829	1,729,806	5,858,496	689,527
Rate per 100,000 inhabitants....................		375.7	4.5	36.6	26.4	102.2	232.5	2,596.1	542.5	1,837.3	216.2
Metropolitan Statistical Areas	271,962,556										
Area actually reporting (percent)[5]	98.6	1,068,409	12,600	96,897	70,270	311,586	647,326	7,202,237	1,465,579	5,102,543	634,115
Estimated total (percent)...........................	100.0	1,076,239	12,676	98,014	71,109	313,281	652,268	7,284,542	1,481,541	5,164,276	638,725
Rate per 100,000 inhabitants....................	X	395.7	4.7	36.0	26.1	115.2	239.8	2,678.5	544.8	1,898.9	234.9
Cities Outside Metropolitan Areas	19,117,450										
Area actually reporting (percent)[5]	91.6	65,600	650	8,984	6,551	8,375	47,591	569,554	115,458	430,023	24,073
Estimated total (percent)...........................	100.0	71,887	738	9,862	7,236	9,443	51,844	627,863	128,227	473,331	26,305
Rate per 100,000 inhabitants....................	X	376.0	3.9	51.6	37.9	49.4	271.2	3,284.2	670.7	2,475.9	137.6
Nonmetropolitan Counties......................	27,777,050										
Area actually reporting (percent)[5]	92.6	46,895	774	8,184	5,332	2,885	35,052	343,387	112,279	207,859	23,249
Estimated total (percent)...........................	100.0	49,861	835	8,769	5,696	3,078	37,179	365,424	120,038	220,889	24,497
Rate per 100,000 inhabitants....................	X	179.5	3.0	31.6	20.5	11.1	133.8	1,315.6	432.1	795.2	88.2

Note: Although arson data are included in the trend and clearance tables, sufficient data are not available to estimate totals for this offense. Therefore, no arson data are published in this table.
X = Not applicable.
[1] Population figures are U.S. Census Bureau provisional estimates as of July 1, 2014.
[2] The violent crime figures include the offenses of murder, rape (revised definition), robbery, and aggravated assault.
[3] The figures shown in this column for the offense of rape were estimated using the revised Uniform Crime Reporting (UCR) definition of rape. See chapter notes for more detail.
[4] The figures shown in this column for the offense of rape were estimated using the legacy Uniform Crime Reporting (UCR) definition of rape. See chapter notes for more detail.
[5] The percentage reported under "Area actually reporting" is based upon the population covered by agencies providing 3 months or more of crime reports to the FBI.

Table 3. Crime in the United States, Population and Offense Distribution, by Region, 2014

(Percent distribution.)

Region	Population	Violent crime	Murder and nonnegligent manslaughter	Rape (revised definition)[1]	Rape (legacy definition)[2]	Robbery	Aggravated assault	Property crime	Burglary	Larceny-theft	Motor vehicle theft
United States[3]....................................	100.0	100.0	100.0	100.0	100.0	100.0	100.0	100.0	100.0	100.0	100.0
Northeast..	17.6	15.1	13.1	12.9	13.1	18.0	14.2	12.3	10.5	13.3	8.5
Midwest	21.2	19.4	20.5	24.0	24.3	18.8	18.9	19.5	19.1	19.8	17.9
South...	37.6	42.2	46.0	38.3	37.5	39.5	43.9	43.5	46.3	43.6	36.5
West..	23.6	23.3	20.5	24.8	25.1	23.7	23.0	24.6	24.1	23.3	37.1

Note: Although arson data are included in the trend and clearance tables, sufficient data are not available to estimate totals for this offense. Therefore, no arson data are published in this table.
[1] The figures shown in this column for the offense of rape were estimated using the revised Uniform Crime Reporting (UCR) definition of rape. See chapter notes for more detail.
[2] The figures shown in this column for the offense of rape were estimated using the legacy Uniform Crime Reporting (UCR) definition of rape. See chapter notes for more detail.
[3] Because of rounding, the percentages may not add to 100.0.

Table 4. Crime,[1] by Region, Geographic Division, and State, 2013–2014

(Number, rate per 100,000 population, percent.)

Area	Population[2]	Violent crime[3]		Murder and nonnegligent manslaughter		Rape (revised definition)[4]		Rape (legacy definition)[5]	
		Number	Rate	Number	Rate	Number	Rate	Number	Rate
United States[6,7,8,9]									
2013	316,497,531	1,199,684	379.1	14,319	4.5	113,695	35.9	82,109	25.9
2014	318,857,056	1,197,987	375.7	14,249	4.5	116,645	36.6	84,041	26.4
Percent change	X	-0.1	-0.9	-0.5	-1.2	+2.6	+1.8	+2.4	+1.6
Northeast[6,7]									
2013	56,028,220	191,037	341.0	1,974	3.5	13,584	24.2	9,867	17.6
2014	56,152,333	181,066	322.5	1,866	3.3	15,046	26.8	11,028	19.6
Percent change	X	-5.2	-5.4	-5.5	-5.7	+10.8	+10.5	+11.8	+11.5
New England[6,7]									
2013	14,639,742	44,901	306.7	315	2.2	5,052	34.5	3,703	25.3
2014	14,680,722	42,158	287.2	286	1.9	4,512	30.7	3,370	23.0
Percent change	X	-6.1	-6.4	-9.2	-9.5	-10.7	-10.9	-9.0	-9.2
Connecticut[6]									
2013	3,599,341	9,439	262.2	91	2.5	891	24.8	647	18.0
2014	3,596,677	8,522	236.9	86	2.4	782	21.7	571	15.9
Percent change	X	-9.7	-9.6	-5.5	-5.4	-12.2	-12.2	-11.7	-11.7
Maine[7]									
2013	1,328,702	1,761	132.5	24	1.8	495	37.3	366	27.5
2014	1,330,089	1,700	127.8	21	1.6	485	36.5	360	27.1
Percent change	X	-3.5	-3.6	-12.5	-12.6	-2.0	-2.1	-1.6	-1.7
Massachusetts[7]									
2013	6,708,874	27,264	406.4	138	2.1	2,303	34.3	1,722	25.7
2014	6,745,408	26,399	391.4	132	2.0	2,180	32.3	1,629	24.1
Percent change	X	-3.2	-3.7	-4.3	-4.9	-5.3	-5.9	-5.4	-5.9
New Hampshire[6]									
2013	1,322,616	2,952	223.2	21	1.6	778	58.8	522	39.5
2014	1,326,813	2,602	196.1	12	0.9	594	44.8	458	34.5
Percent change	X	-11.9	-12.1	-42.9	-43.0	-23.7	-23.9	-12.3	-12.5
Rhode Island[7]									
2013	1,053,354	2,710	257.3	31	2.9	449	42.6	333	31.6
2014	1,055,173	2,313	219.2	25	2.4	361	34.2	253	24.0
Percent change	X	-14.6	-14.8	-19.4	-19.5	-19.6	-19.7	-24.0	-24.2
Vermont[6]									
2013	626,855	775	123.6	10	1.6	136	21.7	113	18.0
2014	626,562	622	99.3	10	1.6	110	17.6	99	15.8
Percent change	X	-19.7	-19.7	0.0	*	-19.1	-19.1	-12.4	-12.3
Middle Atlantic[6,7]									
2013	41,388,478	146,136	353.1	1,659	4.0	8,532	20.6	6,164	14.9
2014	41,471,611	138,908	334.9	1,580	3.8	10,534	25.4	7,658	18.5
Percent change	X	-4.9	-5.1	-4.8	-5.0	+23.5	+23.2	+24.2	+24.0
New Jersey									
2013	8,911,502	25,748	288.9	404	4.5	1,189	13.3	861	9.7
2014	8,938,175	23,346	261.2	349	3.9	1,274	14.3	953	10.7
Percent change	X	-9.3	-9.6	-13.6	-13.9	+7.1	+6.8	+10.7	+10.4
New York[7]									
2013	19,695,680	77,563	393.8	644	3.3	3,548	18.0	2,575	13.1
2014	19,746,227	75,398	381.8	617	3.1	5,433	27.5	3,918	19.8
Percent change		-2.8	-3.0	-4.2	-4.4	+53.1	+52.7	+52.2	+51.8
Pennsylvania[6]									
2013	12,781,296	42,825	335.1	611	4.8	3,795	29.7	2,728	21.3
2014	12,787,209	40,164	314.1	614	4.8	3,827	29.9	2,787	21.8
Percent change	X	-6.2	-6.3	+0.5	+0.4	+0.8	+0.8	+2.2	+2.1
Midwest[6,7]									
2013	67,567,871	237,138	351.0	3,076	4.6	29,049	43.0	21,297	31.5
2014	67,745,108	231,856	342.2	2,917	4.3	27,943	41.2	20,380	30.1
Percent change	X	-2.2	-2.5	-5.2	-5.4	-3.8	-4.1	-4.3	-4.6
East North Central[6,7]									
2013	46,674,416	170,180	364.6	2,345	5.0	20,593	44.1	14,926	32.0
2014	46,739,039	163,854	350.6	2,179	4.7	19,334	41.4	14,010	30.0
Percent change	X	-3.7	-3.9	-7.1	-7.2	-6.1	-6.2	-6.1	-6.3
Illinois[6]									
2013	12,890,552	51,956	403.1	722	5.6	5,340	41.4	3,895	30.2
2014	12,880,580	47,663	370.0	685	5.3	4,159	32.3	3,081	23.9
Percent change	X	-8.3	-8.2	-5.1	-5.1	-22.1	-22.1	-20.9	-20.8
Indiana[7]									
2013	6,570,713	23,627	359.6	357	5.4	2,241	34.1	1,623	24.7

Table 4. Crime,[1] by Region, Geographic Division, and State, 2013–2014—*Continued*

(Number, rate per 100,000 population, percent.)

Area	Robbery		Aggravated assault		Property crime		Burglary		Larceny-theft		Motor vehicle theft	
	Number	Rate	Number	Rate	Number	Rate	Number	Rate	Number	Rate	Number	Rate
United States[6,7,8,9]												
2013..	345,095	109.0	726,575	229.6	8,650,761	2,733.3	1,931,835	610.4	6,018,632	1,901.6	700,294	221.3
2014..	325,802	102.2	741,291	232.5	8,277,829	2,596.1	1,729,806	542.5	5,858,496	1,837.3	689,527	216.2
Percent change	-5.6	-6.3	+2.0	+1.3	-4.3	-5.0	-10.5	-11.1	-2.7	-3.4	-1.5	-2.3
Northeast[6,7]												
2013..	66,060	117.9	109,419	195.3	1,097,316	1,958.5	208,409	372.0	826,119	1,474.5	62,788	112.1
2014..	58,712	104.6	105,442	187.8	1,020,576	1,817.5	181,179	322.7	780,813	1,390.5	58,584	104.3
Percent change	-11.1	-11.3	-3.6	-3.8	-7.0	-7.2	-13.1	-13.3	-5.5	-5.7	-6.7	-6.9
New England[6,7]												
2013..	11,996	81.9	27,538	188.1	307,903	2,103.2	64,082	437.7	224,028	1,530.3	19,793	135.2
2014..	10,635	72.4	26,725	182.0	279,285	1,902.4	52,968	360.8	208,214	1,418.3	18,103	123.3
Percent change	-11.3	-11.6	-3.0	-3.2	-9.3	-9.5	-17.3	-17.6	-7.1	-7.3	-8.5	-8.8
Connecticut[6]												
2013..	3,551	98.7	4,906	136.3	71,274	1,980.2	12,934	359.3	52,099	1,447.5	6,241	173.4
2014	3,159	87.8	4,495	125.0	69,070	1,920.4	11,955	332.4	51,005	1,418.1	6,110	169.9
Percent change	-11.0	-11.0	-8.4	-8.3	-3.1	-3.0	-7.6	-7.5	-2.1	-2.0	-2.1	-2.0
Maine[7]												
2013..	335	25.2	907	68.3	30,454	2,292.0	6,480	487.7	23,063	1,735.8	911	68.6
2014	304	22.9	890	66.9	26,421	1,986.4	5,030	378.2	20,592	1,548.2	799	60.1
Percent change	-9.3	-9.3	-1.9	-2.0	-13.2	-13.3	-22.4	-22.5	-10.7	-10.8	-12.3	-12.4
Massachusetts[7]												
2013..	6,705	99.9	18,118	270.1	137,274	2,046.2	30,716	457.8	97,437	1,452.4	9,121	136.0
2014	6,036	89.5	18,051	267.6	125,267	1,857.1	24,964	370.1	92,043	1,364.5	8,260	122.5
Percent change	-10.0	-10.5	-0.4	-0.9	-8.7	-9.2	-18.7	-19.2	-5.5	-6.0	-9.4	-9.9
New Hampshire[6]												
2013..	647	48.9	1,506	113.9	29,278	2,213.6	4,979	376.5	23,355	1,765.8	944	71.4
2014	537	40.5	1,459	110.0	26,041	1,962.7	4,162	313.7	21,022	1,584.4	857	64.6
Percent change	-17.0	-17.3	-3.1	-3.4	-11.1	-11.3	-16.4	-16.7	-10.0	-10.3	-9.2	-9.5
Rhode Island[7]												
2013..	683	64.8	1,547	146.9	25,741	2,443.7	5,621	533.6	17,881	1,697.5	2,239	212.6
2014	529	50.1	1,398	132.5	22,935	2,173.6	4,823	457.1	16,279	1,542.8	1,833	173.7
Percent change	-22.5	-22.7	-9.6	-9.8	-10.9	-11.1	-14.2	-14.3	-9.0	-9.1	-18.1	-18.3
Vermont[6]												
2013	75	12.0	554	88.4	13,882	2,214.5	3,352	534.7	10,193	1,626.1	337	53.8
2014	70	11.2	432	68.9	9,551	1,524.4	2,034	324.6	7,273	1,160.8	244	38.9
Percent change	-6.7	-6.6	-22.0	-22.0	-31.2	-31.2	-39.3	-39.3	-28.6	-28.6	-27.6	-27.6
Middle Atlantic[6,7]												
2013..	54,064	130.6	81,881	197.8	789,413	1,907.3	144,327	348.7	602,091	1,454.7	42,995	103.9
2014..	48,077	115.9	78,717	189.8	741,291	1,787.5	128,211	309.2	572,599	1,380.7	40,481	97.6
Percent change	-11.1	-11.3	-3.9	-4.1	-6.1	-6.3	-11.2	-11.3	-4.9	-5.1	-5.8	-6.0
New Jersey												
2013..	12,084	135.6	12,071	135.5	167,634	1,881.1	35,883	402.7	118,005	1,324.2	13,746	154.3
2014	10,498	117.5	11,225	125.6	154,993	1,734.1	31,710	354.8	111,578	1,248.3	11,705	131.0
Percent change	-13.1	-13.4	-7.0	-7.3	-7.5	-7.8	-11.6	-11.9	-5.4	-5.7	-14.8	-15.1
New York[7]												
2013..	27,241	138.3	46,130	234.2	358,603	1,820.7	56,444	286.6	286,676	1,455.5	15,483	78.6
2014	24,045	121.8	45,303	229.4	339,282	1,718.2	50,781	257.2	272,765	1,381.4	15,736	79.7
Percent change	-11.7	-12.0	-1.8	-2.0	-5.4	-5.6	-10.0	-10.3	-4.9	-5.1	+1.6	+1.4
Pennsylvania[6]												
2013..	14,739	115.3	23,680	185.3	263,176	2,059.1	52,000	406.8	197,410	1,544.5	13,766	107.7
2014	13,534	105.8	22,189	173.5	247,016	1,931.7	45,720	357.5	188,256	1,472.2	13,040	102.0
Percent change	-8.2	-8.2	-6.3	-6.3	-6.1	-6.2	-12.1	-12.1	-4.6	-4.7	-5.3	-5.3
Midwest[6,7]												
2013..	67,045	99.2	137,968	204.2	1,733,118	2,565.0	383,762	568.0	1,221,208	1,807.4	128,148	189.7
2014..	61,138	90.2	139,858	206.4	1,614,561	2,383.3	330,908	488.5	1,160,493	1,713.0	123,160	181.8
Percent change	-8.8	-9.0	+1.4	+1.1	-6.8	-7.1	-13.8	-14.0	-5.0	-5.2	-3.9	-4.1
East North Central[6,7]												
2013..	54,257	116.2	92,985	199.2	1,177,763	2,523.4	273,551	586.1	818,132	1,752.8	86,080	184.4
2014..	48,036	102.8	94,305	201.8	1,089,474	2,331.0	231,146	494.5	777,925	1,664.4	80,403	172.0
Percent change	-11.5	-11.6	+1.4	+1.3	-7.5	-7.6	-15.5	-15.6	-4.9	-5.0	-6.6	-6.7
Illinois[6]												
2013..	17,733	137.6	28,161	218.5	296,048	2,296.6	59,093	458.4	216,059	1,676.1	20,896	162.1
2014	15,299	118.8	27,520	213.7	267,385	2,075.9	50,008	388.2	199,926	1,552.2	17,451	135.5
Percent change	-13.7	-13.7	-2.3	-2.2	-9.7	-9.6	-15.4	-15.3	-7.5	-7.4	-16.5	-16.4
Indiana[7]												
2013..	7,114	108.3	13,915	211.8	187,472	2,853.1	42,754	650.7	130,534	1,986.6	14,184	215.9

Table 4. Crime,[1] by Region, Geographic Division, and State, 2013–2014—*Continued*

(Number, rate per 100,000 population, percent.)

Area	Population[2]	Violent crime[3]		Murder and nonnegligent manslaughter		Rape (revised definition)[4]		Rape (legacy definition)[5]	
		Number	Rate	Number	Rate	Number	Rate	Number	Rate
2014	6,596,855	24,099	365.3	330	5.0	2,186	33.1	1,615	24.5
Percent change	X	+2.0	+1.6	-7.6	-7.9	-2.5	-2.8	-0.5	-0.9
Michigan[6]									
2013	9,898,193	44,757	452.2	625	6.3	6,785	68.5	4,506	45.5
2014	9,909,877	42,348	427.3	535	5.4	6,273	63.3	4,049	40.9
Percent change	X	-5.4	-5.5	-14.4	-14.5	-7.5	-7.7	-10.1	-10.2
Ohio[7]									
2013	11,572,005	33,722	291.4	478	4.1	4,391	37.9	3,594	31.1
2014	11,594,163	33,030	284.9	464	4.0	5,042	43.5	4,097	35.3
Percent change	X	-2.1	-2.2	-2.9	-3.1	+14.8	+14.6	+14.0	+13.8
Wisconsin[7]									
2013	5,742,953	16,118	280.7	163	2.8	1,836	32.0	1,308	22.8
2014	5,757,564	16,714	290.3	165	2.9	1,674	29.1	1,168	20.3
Percent change	X	+3.7	+3.4	+1.2	+1.0	-8.8	-9.1	-10.7	-10.9
West North Central[6,7]									
2013	20,893,455	66,958	320.5	731	3.5	8,456	40.5	6,371	30.5
2014	21,006,069	68,002	323.7	738	3.5	8,609	41.0	6,370	30.3
Percent change	X	+1.6	+1.0	+1.0	+0.4	+1.8	+1.3	+0.0	-0.6
Iowa[6]									
2013	3,092,341	8,443	273.0	41	1.3	1,133	36.6	873	28.2
2014	3,107,126	8,497	273.5	60	1.9	1,128	36.3	828	26.6
Percent change	X	+0.6	+0.2	+46.3	+45.6	-0.4	-0.9	-5.2	-5.6
Kansas[6]									
2013	2,895,801	9,928	342.8	117	4.0	1,295	44.7	1,003	34.6
2014	2,904,021	10,123	348.6	91	3.1	1,411	48.6	1,075	37.0
Percent change	X	+2.0	+1.7	-22.2	-22.4	+9.0	+8.6	+7.2	+6.9
Minnesota[6]									
2013	5,422,060	12,710	234.4	114	2.1	2,014	37.1	1,453	26.8
2014	5,457,173	12,505	229.1	88	1.6	2,001	36.7	1,452	26.6
Percent change	X	-1.6	-2.2	-22.8	-23.3	-0.6	-1.3	-0.1	-0.7
Missouri[6]									
2013	6,044,917	26,216	433.7	369	6.1	2,305	38.1	1,679	27.8
2014	6,063,589	26,856	442.9	403	6.6	2,379	39.2	1,706	28.1
Percent change	X	+2.4	+2.1	+9.2	+8.9	+3.2	+2.9	+1.6	+1.3
Nebraska[7]									
2013	1,868,969	4,949	264.8	56	3.0	847	45.3	621	33.2
2014	1,881,503	5,275	280.4	54	2.9	862	45.8	620	33.0
Percent change	X	+6.6	+5.9	-3.6	-4.2	+1.8	+1.1	-0.2	-0.8
North Dakota[6]									
2013	723,857	1,979	273.4	16	2.2	355	49.0	288	39.8
2014	739,482	1,960	265.1	22	3.0	358	48.4	276	37.3
Percent change	X	-1.0	-3.1	+37.5	+34.6	+0.8	-1.3	-4.2	-6.2
South Dakota[6]									
2013	845,510	2,733	323.2	18	2.1	507	60.0	454	53.7
2014	853,175	2,786	326.5	20	2.3	470	55.1	413	48.4
Percent change	X	+1.9	+1.0	+11.1	+10.1	-7.3	-8.1	-9.0	-9.8
South[6,7,8,9]									
2013	118,522,802	490,913	414.2	6,273	5.3	43,186	36.4	30,651	25.9
2014	119,771,934	505,389	422.0	6,552	5.5	44,733	37.3	31,523	26.3
Percent change	X	+2.9	+1.9	+4.4	+3.4	+3.6	+2.5	+2.8	+1.8
South Atlantic[6,8,9]									
2013	61,852,944	250,657	405.2	3,213	5.2	19,938	32.2	13,913	22.5
2014	62,514,615	263,801	422.0	3,486	5.6	21,391	34.2	14,892	23.8
Percent change	X	+5.2	+4.1	+8.5	+7.3	+7.3	+6.2	+7.0	+5.9
Delaware[6]									
2013	925,240	4,633	500.7	41	4.4	399	43.1	278	30.0
2014	935,614	4,576	489.1	54	5.8	386	41.3	249	26.6
Percent change	X	-1.2	-2.3	+31.7	+30.2	-3.3	-4.3	-10.4	-11.4
District of Columbia[6,8]									
2013	649,111	8,415	1,296.4	103	15.9	395	60.9	297	45.8
2014	658,893	8,199	1,244.4	105	15.9	472	71.6	352	53.4
Percent change	X	-2.6	-4.0	+1.9	+0.4	+19.5	+17.7	+18.5	+16.8
Florida[6]									
2013	19,600,311	91,993	469.3	972	5.0	6,767	34.5	4,765	24.3
2014	19,893,297	107,521	540.5	1,149	5.8	8,563	43.0	6,051	30.4
Percent change	X	+16.9	+15.2	+18.2	+16.5	+26.5	+24.7	+27.0	+25.1
Georgia[9]									
2013	9,994,759	37,519	375.4	563	5.6	2,891	28.9	2,022	20.2
2014	10,097,343	38,097	377.3	580	5.7	3,048	30.2	2,159	21.4

Table 4. Crime,[1] by Region, Geographic Division, and State, 2013–2014—*Continued*

(Number, rate per 100,000 population, percent.)

Area	Robbery Number	Robbery Rate	Aggravated assault Number	Aggravated assault Rate	Property crime Number	Property crime Rate	Burglary Number	Burglary Rate	Larceny-theft Number	Larceny-theft Rate	Motor vehicle theft Number	Motor vehicle theft Rate
2014	6,897	104.5	14,686	222.6	174,776	2,649.4	36,893	559.3	124,022	1,880.0	13,861	210.1
Percent change	-3.1	-3.4	+5.5	+5.1	-6.8	-7.1	-13.7	-14.1	-5.0	-5.4	-2.3	-2.7
Michigan[6]												
2013	10,093	102.0	27,254	275.3	230,135	2,325.0	56,256	568.3	149,794	1,513.3	24,085	243.3
2014	8,021	80.9	27,519	277.7	202,547	2,043.9	44,184	445.9	137,206	1,384.5	21,157	213.5
Percent change	-20.5	-20.6	+1.0	+0.9	-12.0	-12.1	-21.5	-21.6	-8.4	-8.5	-12.2	-12.3
Ohio[7]												
2013	14,483	125.2	14,370	124.2	338,414	2,924.4	91,090	787.2	227,799	1,968.5	19,525	168.7
2014	12,753	110.0	14,771	127.4	324,528	2,799.1	78,845	680.0	227,668	1,963.6	18,015	155.4
Percent change	-11.9	-12.1	+2.8	+2.6	-4.1	-4.3	-13.4	-13.6	-0.1	-0.2	-7.7	-7.9
Wisconsin[7]												
2013	4,834	84.2	9,285	161.7	125,694	2,188.7	24,358	424.1	93,946	1,635.8	7,390	128.7
2014	5,066	88.0	9,809	170.4	120,238	2,088.3	21,216	368.5	89,103	1,547.6	9,919	172.3
Percent change	+4.8	+4.5	+5.6	+5.4	-4.3	-4.6	-12.9	-13.1	-5.2	-5.4	+34.2	+33.9
West North Central[6,7]												
2013	12,788	61.2	44,983	215.3	555,355	2,658.0	110,211	527.5	403,076	1,929.2	42,068	201.3
2014	13,102	62.4	45,553	216.9	525,087	2,499.7	99,762	474.9	382,568	1,821.2	42,757	203.5
Percent change	+2.5	+1.9	+1.3	+0.7	-5.5	-6.0	-9.5	-10.0	-5.1	-5.6	+1.6	+1.1
Iowa[6]												
2013	937	30.3	6,332	204.8	67,976	2,198.2	15,918	514.8	47,803	1,545.9	4,255	137.6
2014	1,045	33.6	6,264	201.6	65,056	2,093.8	14,428	464.4	46,477	1,495.8	4,151	133.6
Percent change	+11.5	+11.0	-1.1	-1.5	-4.3	-4.8	-9.4	-9.8	-2.8	-3.2	-2.4	-2.9
Kansas[6]												
2013	1,339	46.2	7,177	247.8	85,704	2,959.6	17,476	603.5	61,557	2,125.7	6,671	230.4
2014	1,362	46.9	7,259	250.0	79,431	2,735.2	15,828	545.0	56,697	1,952.4	6,906	237.8
Percent change	+1.7	+1.4	+1.1	+0.9	-7.3	-7.6	-9.4	-9.7	-7.9	-8.2	+3.5	+3.2
Minnesota[6]												
2013	3,674	67.8	6,908	127.4	131,193	2,419.6	22,713	418.9	100,514	1,853.8	7,966	146.9
2014	3,687	67.6	6,729	123.3	125,377	2,297.5	20,773	380.7	96,237	1,763.5	8,367	153.3
Percent change	+0.4	-0.3	-2.6	-3.2	-4.4	-5.0	-8.5	-9.1	-4.3	-4.9	+5.0	+4.4
Missouri[6]												
2013	5,486	90.8	18,056	298.7	189,655	3,137.4	38,797	641.8	134,514	2,225.2	16,344	270.4
2014	5,592	92.2	18,482	304.8	176,237	2,906.5	35,258	581.5	124,622	2,055.3	16,357	269.8
Percent change	+1.9	+1.6	+2.4	+2.0	-7.1	-7.4	-9.1	-9.4	-7.4	-7.6	+0.1	-0.2
Nebraska[7]												
2013	1,035	55.4	3,011	161.1	49,197	2,632.3	8,945	478.6	35,791	1,915.0	4,461	238.7
2014	1,043	55.4	3,316	176.2	47,479	2,523.5	7,950	422.5	35,074	1,864.1	4,455	236.8
Percent change	+0.8	+0.1	+10.1	+9.4	-3.5	-4.1	-11.1	-11.7	-2.0	-2.7	-0.1	-0.8
North Dakota[6]												
2013	161	22.2	1,447	199.9	15,356	2,121.4	2,979	411.5	10,942	1,511.6	1,435	198.2
2014	173	23.4	1,407	190.3	15,605	2,110.3	2,707	366.1	11,384	1,539.5	1,514	204.7
Percent change	+7.5	+5.2	-2.8	-4.8	+1.6	-0.5	-9.1	-11.1	+4.0	+1.8	+5.5	+3.3
South Dakota[6]												
2013	156	18.5	2,052	242.7	16,274	1,924.8	3,383	400.1	11,955	1,413.9	936	110.7
2014	200	23.4	2,096	245.7	15,902	1,863.9	2,818	330.3	12,077	1,415.5	1,007	118.0
Percent change	+28.2	+27.1	+2.1	+1.2	-2.3	-3.2	-16.7	-17.4	+1.0	+0.1	+7.6	+6.6
South[6,7,8,9]												
2013	130,005	109.7	311,449	262.8	3,671,750	3,097.9	872,877	736.5	2,556,361	2,156.9	242,512	204.6
2014	128,703	107.5	325,401	271.7	3,604,877	3,009.8	800,905	668.7	2,552,096	2,130.8	251,876	210.3
Percent change	-1.0	-2.0	+4.5	+3.4	-1.8	-2.8	-8.2	-9.2	-0.2	-1.2	+3.9	+2.8
South Atlantic[6,8,9]												
2013	69,734	112.7	157,772	255.1	1,855,373	2,999.7	431,676	697.9	1,306,022	2,111.5	117,675	190.2
2014	68,997	110.4	169,927	271.8	1,873,950	2,997.6	405,083	648.0	1,345,189	2,151.8	123,678	197.8
Percent change	-1.1	-2.1	+7.7	+6.6	+1.0	-0.1	-6.2	-7.2	+3.0	+1.9	+5.1	+4.0
Delaware[6]												
2013	1,233	133.3	2,960	319.9	29,001	3,134.4	6,299	680.8	21,347	2,307.2	1,355	146.4
2014	1,269	135.6	2,867	306.4	27,900	2,982.0	5,768	616.5	20,865	2,230.1	1,267	135.4
Percent change	+2.9	+1.8	-3.1	-4.2	-3.8	-4.9	-8.4	-9.4	-2.3	-3.3	-6.5	-7.5
District of Columbia[6,8]												
2013	4,082	628.9	3,835	590.8	31,097	4,790.7	3,316	510.9	24,547	3,781.6	3,234	498.2
2014	3,497	530.7	4,125	626.1	34,147	5,182.5	3,466	526.0	26,898	4,082.3	3,783	574.1
Percent change	-14.3	-15.6	+7.6	+6.0	+9.8	+8.2	+4.5	+3.0	+9.6	+8.0	+17.0	+15.2
Florida[6]												
2013	23,200	118.4	61,054	311.5	607,170	3,097.8	138,915	708.7	433,344	2,210.9	34,911	178.1
2014	24,914	125.2	72,895	366.4	679,446	3,415.5	143,220	719.9	493,647	2,481.5	42,579	214.0
Percent change	+7.4	+5.8	+19.4	+17.6	+11.9	+10.3	+3.1	+1.6	+13.9	+12.2	+22.0	+20.2
Georgia[9]												
2013	12,704	127.1	21,361	213.7	339,808	3,399.9	83,459	835.0	229,190	2,293.1	27,159	271.7
2014	12,417	123.0	22,052	218.4	331,316	3,281.2	76,428	756.9	228,034	2,258.4	26,854	266.0

Table 4. Crime,[1] by Region, Geographic Division, and State, 2013–2014—*Continued*

(Number, rate per 100,000 population, percent.)

Area	Population[2]	Violent crime[3]		Murder and nonnegligent manslaughter		Rape (revised definition)[4]		Rape (legacy definition)[5]	
		Number	Rate	Number	Rate	Number	Rate	Number	Rate
Percent change	X	+1.5	+0.5	+3.0	+2.0	+5.4	+4.4	+6.8	+5.7
Maryland..................									
2013	5,938,737	28,235	475.4	384	6.5	1,679	28.3	1,179	19.9
2014	X	26,661	446.1	365	6.1	1,619	27.1	1,144	19.1
Percent change		-5.6	-6.2	-4.9	-5.5	-3.6	-4.2	-3.0	-3.6
North Carolina									
2013	9,848,917	33,587	341.0	463	4.7	2,524	25.6	1,790	18.2
2014	9,943,964	32,767	329.5	510	5.1	2,420	24.3	1,740	17.5
Percent change	X	-2.4	-3.4	+10.2	+9.1	-4.1	-5.0	-2.8	-3.7
South Carolina[6]									
2013	4,771,929	24,263	508.5	305	6.4	2,233	46.8	1,739	36.4
2014	4,832,482	24,052	497.7	311	6.4	2,068	42.8	1,480	30.6
Percent change	X	-0.9	-2.1	+2.0	+0.7	-7.4	-8.5	-14.9	-16.0
Virginia[6]									
2013	8,270,345	16,355	197.8	320	3.9	2,350	28.4	1,476	17.8
2014	8,326,289	16,340	196.2	338	4.1	2,310	27.7	1,432	17.2
Percent change	X	-0.1	-0.8	+5.6	+4.9	-1.7	-2.4	-3.0	-3.6
West Virginia[6]									
2013	1,853,595	5,657	305.2	62	3.3	700	37.8	367	19.8
2014	1,850,326	5,588	302.0	74	4.0	505	27.3	285	15.4
Percent change	X	-1.2	-1.0	+19.4	+19.6	-27.9	-27.7	-22.3	-22.2
East South Central[6,7]									
2013........................	18,723,054	76,480	408.5	1,070	5.7	7,225	38.6	5,030	26.9
2014........................	18,806,265	78,253	416.1	1,065	5.7	7,034	37.4	4,944	26.3
Percent change	X	+2.3	+1.9	-0.5	-0.9	-2.6	-3.1	-1.7	-2.1
Alabama[6]									
2013	4,833,996	20,834	431.0	346	7.2	2,055	42.5	1,449	30.0
2014	4,849,377	20,727	427.4	276	5.7	2,005	41.3	1,436	29.6
Percent change	X	-0.5	-0.8	-20.2	-20.5	-2.4	-2.7	-0.9	-1.2
Kentucky[6]									
2013	4,399,583	9,280	210.9	172	3.9	1,646	37.4	951	21.6
2014	4,413,457	9,340	211.6	160	3.6	1,440	32.6	883	20.0
Percent change	X	+0.6	+0.3	-7.0	-7.3	-12.5	-12.8	-7.2	-7.4
Mississippi[7]									
2013	2,992,206	8,303	277.5	217	7.3	1,024	34.2	726	24.3
2014	2,994,079	8,338	278.5	258	8.6	1,058	35.3	764	25.5
Percent change	X	+0.4	+0.4	+18.9	+18.8	+3.3	+3.3	+5.2	+5.2
Tennessee[7]									
2013	6,497,269	38,063	585.8	335	5.2	2,500	38.5	1,904	29.3
2014	6,549,352	39,848	608.4	371	5.7	2,531	38.6	1,861	28.4
Percent change	X	+4.7	+3.9	+10.7	+9.9	+1.2	+0.4	-2.3	-3.0
West South Central[6]									
2013........................	37,946,804	163,776	431.6	1,990	5.2	16,023	42.2	11,708	30.9
2014........................	38,451,054	163,335	424.8	2,001	5.2	16,308	42.4	11,687	30.4
Percent change	X	-0.3	-1.6	+0.6	-0.8	+1.8	+0.4	-0.2	-1.5
Arkansas[6]									
2013	2,958,765	13,705	463.2	158	5.3	1,490	50.4	1,135	38.4
2014	2,966,369	14,243	480.1	165	5.6	1,763	59.4	1,182	39.8
Percent change	X	+3.9	+3.7	+4.4	+4.2	+18.3	+18.0	+4.1	+3.9
Louisiana[6]									
2013	4,629,284	24,127	521.2	494	10.7	1,763	38.1	1,248	27.0
2014	4,649,676	23,934	514.7	477	10.3	1,375	29.6	992	21.3
Percent change	X	-0.8	-1.2	-3.4	-3.9	-22.0	-22.3	-20.5	-20.9
Oklahoma[6]									
2013	3,853,118	17,187	446.1	198	5.1	2,314	60.1	1,715	44.5
2014	X	15,744	406.0	175	4.5	1,777	45.8	1,277	32.9
Percent change		-8.4	-9.0	-11.6	-12.2	-23.2	-23.7	-25.5	-26.0
Texas[6]									
2013	26,505,637	108,757	410.3	1,140	4.3	10,456	39.4	7,610	28.7
2014	26,956,958	109,414	405.9	1,184	4.4	11,393	42.3	8,236	30.6
Percent change	X	+0.6	-1.1	+3.9	+2.1	+9.0	+7.1	+8.2	+6.4
West[6,7]									
2013........................	74,378,638	280,596	377.3	2,996	4.0	27,876	37.5	20,294	27.3
2014........................	75,187,681	279,676	372.0	2,914	3.9	28,923	38.5	21,110	28.1
Percent change	X	-0.3	-1.4	-2.7	-3.8	+3.8	+2.6	+4.0	+2.9
Mountain[6,7]									
2013........................	22,899,189	87,804	383.4	935	4.1	12,051	52.6	8,735	38.1
2014........................	23,197,119	88,243	380.4	893	3.8	12,027	51.8	8,620	37.2

Table 4. Crime,[1] by Region, Geographic Division, and State, 2013–2014—*Continued*

(Number, rate per 100,000 population, percent.)

Area	Robbery		Aggravated assault		Property crime		Burglary		Larceny-theft		Motor vehicle theft	
	Number	Rate	Number	Rate	Number	Rate	Number	Rate	Number	Rate	Number	Rate
Percent change	-2.3	-3.3	+3.2	+2.2	-2.5	-3.5	-8.4	-9.4	-0.5	-1.5	-1.1	-2.1
Maryland												
2013	10,048	169.2	16,124	271.5	157,918	2,659.1	31,950	538.0	112,551	1,895.2	13,417	225.9
2014	9,544	159.7	15,133	253.2	149,859	2,507.5	28,012	468.7	108,745	1,819.6	13,102	219.2
Percent change	-5.0	-5.6	-6.1	-6.7	-5.1	-5.7	-12.3	-12.9	-3.4	-4.0	-2.3	-3.0
North Carolina												
2013	9,275	94.2	21,325	216.5	305,631	3,103.2	90,182	915.7	201,043	2,041.3	14,406	146.3
2014	8,416	84.6	21,421	215.4	285,697	2,873.1	79,373	798.2	192,694	1,937.8	13,630	137.1
Percent change	-9.3	-10.1	+0.5	-0.5	-6.5	-7.4	-12.0	-12.8	-4.2	-5.1	-5.4	-6.3
South Carolina[6]												
2013	3,965	83.1	17,760	372.2	173,261	3,630.8	40,930	857.7	119,730	2,509.0	12,601	264.1
2014	3,997	82.7	17,676	365.8	167,217	3,460.3	36,721	759.9	117,594	2,433.4	12,902	267.0
Percent change	+0.8	-0.5	-0.5	-1.7	-3.5	-4.7	-10.3	-11.4	-1.8	-3.0	+2.4	+1.1
Virginia[6]												
2013	4,574	55.3	9,111	110.2	171,558	2,074.4	26,717	323.0	136,215	1,647.0	8,626	104.3
2014	4,292	51.5	9,400	112.9	160,720	1,930.3	23,122	277.7	129,933	1,560.5	7,665	92.1
Percent change	-6.2	-6.8	+3.2	+2.5	-6.3	-6.9	-13.5	-14.0	-4.6	-5.3	-11.1	-11.7
West Virginia[6]												
2013	653	35.2	4,242	228.9	39,929	2,154.1	9,908	534.5	28,055	1,513.5	1,966	106.1
2014	651	35.2	4,358	235.5	37,648	2,034.7	8,973	484.9	26,779	1,447.3	1,896	102.5
Percent change	-0.3	-0.1	+2.7	+2.9	-5.7	-5.5	-9.4	-9.3	-4.5	-4.4	-3.6	-3.4
East South Central[6,7]												
2013	17,638	94.2	50,547	270.0	555,514	2,967.0	145,044	774.7	377,545	2,016.5	32,925	175.9
2014	17,732	94.3	52,422	278.7	541,169	2,877.6	133,953	712.3	373,639	1,986.8	33,577	178.5
Percent change	+0.5	+0.1	+3.7	+3.3	-2.6	-3.0	-7.6	-8.1	-1.0	-1.5	+2.0	+1.5
Alabama[6]												
2013	4,645	96.1	13,788	285.2	161,835	3,347.9	42,410	877.3	108,862	2,252.0	10,563	218.5
2014	4,701	96.9	13,745	283.4	154,094	3,177.6	39,715	819.0	104,238	2,149.5	10,141	209.1
Percent change	+1.2	+0.9	-0.3	-0.6	-4.8	-5.1	-6.4	-6.7	-4.2	-4.6	-4.0	-4.3
Kentucky[6]												
2013	3,247	73.8	4,215	95.8	104,448	2,374.0	26,331	598.5	72,048	1,637.6	6,069	137.9
2014	3,336	75.6	4,404	99.8	99,166	2,246.9	23,244	526.7	69,604	1,577.1	6,318	143.2
Percent change	+2.7	+2.4	+4.5	+4.2	-5.1	-5.4	-11.7	-12.0	-3.4	-3.7	+4.1	+3.8
Mississippi[7]												
2013	2,413	80.6	4,649	155.4	81,548	2,725.3	24,969	834.5	52,192	1,744.3	4,387	146.6
2014	2,430	81.2	4,592	153.4	87,462	2,921.2	24,352	813.3	58,591	1,956.9	4,519	150.9
Percent change	+0.7	+0.6	-1.2	-1.3	+7.3	+7.2	-2.5	-2.5	+12.3	+12.2	+3.0	+2.9
Tennessee[7]												
2013	7,333	112.9	27,895	429.3	207,683	3,196.5	51,334	790.1	144,443	2,223.1	11,906	183.2
2014	7,265	110.9	29,681	453.2	200,447	3,060.6	46,642	712.2	141,206	2,156.0	12,599	192.4
Percent change	-0.9	-1.7	+6.4	+5.6	-3.5	-4.3	-9.1	-9.9	-2.2	-3.0	+5.8	+5.0
West South Central[6]												
2013	42,633	112.3	103,130	271.8	1,260,863	3,322.7	296,157	780.5	872,794	2,300.0	91,912	242.2
2014	41,974	109.2	103,052	268.0	1,189,758	3,094.2	261,869	681.0	833,268	2,167.1	94,621	246.1
Percent change	-1.5	-2.8	-0.1	-1.4	-5.6	-6.9	-11.6	-12.7	-4.5	-5.8	+2.9	+1.6
Arkansas[6]												
2013	2,261	76.4	9,796	331.1	106,477	3,598.7	30,369	1,026.4	70,430	2,380.4	5,678	191.9
2014	2,050	69.1	10,265	346.0	99,018	3,338.0	24,790	835.7	68,627	2,313.5	5,601	188.8
Percent change	-9.3	-9.6	+4.8	+4.5	-7.0	-7.2	-18.4	-18.6	-2.6	-2.8	-1.4	-1.6
Louisiana[6]												
2013	5,539	119.7	16,331	352.8	165,679	3,578.9	41,214	890.3	115,300	2,490.7	9,165	198.0
2014	5,695	122.5	16,387	352.4	160,824	3,458.8	38,337	824.5	112,596	2,421.6	9,891	212.7
Percent change	+2.8	+2.4	+0.3	-0.1	-2.9	-3.4	-7.0	-7.4	-2.3	-2.8	+7.9	+7.4
Oklahoma[6]												
2013	3,023	78.5	11,652	302.4	126,418	3,280.9	33,512	869.7	81,624	2,118.4	11,282	292.8
2014	3,048	78.6	10,744	277.0	115,982	2,990.7	29,508	760.9	75,891	1,956.9	10,583	272.9
Percent change	+0.8	+0.2	-7.8	-8.4	-8.3	-8.8	-11.9	-12.5	-7.0	-7.6	-6.2	-6.8
Texas[6]												
2013	31,810	120.0	65,351	246.6	862,289	3,253.2	191,062	720.8	605,440	2,284.2	65,787	248.2
2014	31,181	115.7	65,656	243.6	813,934	3,019.4	169,234	627.8	576,154	2,137.3	68,546	254.3
Percent change	-2.0	-3.6	+0.5	-1.2	-5.6	-7.2	-11.4	-12.9	-4.8	-6.4	+4.2	+2.4
West[6,7]												
2013	81,985	110.2	167,739	225.5	2,148,577	2,888.7	466,787	627.6	1,414,944	1,902.4	266,846	358.8
2014	77,249	102.7	170,590	226.9	2,037,815	2,710.3	416,814	554.4	1,365,094	1,815.6	255,907	340.4
Percent change	-5.8	-6.8	+1.7	+0.6	-5.2	-6.2	-10.7	-11.7	-3.5	-4.6	-4.1	-5.1
Mountain[6,7]												
2013	18,565	81.1	56,253	245.7	678,971	2,965.0	144,740	632.1	477,270	2,084.2	56,961	248.7
2014	19,100	82.3	56,223	242.4	650,981	2,806.3	130,696	563.4	462,044	1,991.8	58,241	251.1

Table 4. Crime,[1] by Region, Geographic Division, and State, 2013–2014—*Continued*

(Number, rate per 100,000 population, percent.)

Area	Population[2]	Violent crime[3]		Murder and nonnegligent manslaughter		Rape (revised definition)[4]		Rape (legacy definition)[5]	
		Number	Rate	Number	Rate	Number	Rate	Number	Rate
Percent change	X	+0.5	-0.8	-4.5	-5.7	-0.2	-1.5	-1.3	-2.6
Arizona[6]									
2013	6,634,997	27,576	415.6	355	5.4	3,174	47.8	2,344	35.3
2014	6,731,484	26,916	399.9	319	4.7	3,378	50.2	2,464	36.6
Percent change	X	-2.4	-3.8	-10.1	-11.4	+6.4	+4.9	+5.1	+3.6
Colorado[6]									
2013	5,272,086	16,099	305.4	174	3.3	2,963	56.2	2,198	41.7
2014	5,355,866	16,554	309.1	151	2.8	3,039	56.7	2,121	39.6
Percent change	X	+2.8	+1.2	-13.2	-14.6	+2.6	+1.0	-3.5	-5.0
Idaho[6]									
2013	1,612,843	3,471	215.2	29	1.8	674	41.8	516	32.0
2014	1,634,464	3,468	212.2	32	2.0	609	37.3	468	28.6
Percent change	X	-0.1	-1.4	+10.3	+8.9	-9.6	-10.8	-9.3	-10.5
Montana[6]									
2013	1,014,864	2,924	288.1	23	2.3	467	46.0	382	37.6
2014	1,023,579	3,313	323.7	37	3.6	541	52.9	430	42.0
Percent change	X	+13.3	+12.3	+60.9	+59.5	+15.8	+14.9	+12.6	+11.6
Nevada[6]									
2013	2,791,494	16,888	605.0	163	5.8	1,482	53.1	1,090	39.0
2014	2,839,099	18,045	635.6	170	6.0	1,357	47.8	995	35.0
Percent change	X	+6.9	+5.1	+4.3	+2.5	-8.4	-10.0	-8.7	-10.2
New Mexico									
2013	2,086,895	12,990	622.5	123	5.9	1,565	75.0	1,135	54.4
2014	2,085,572	12,459	597.4	101	4.8	1,475	70.7	1,071	51.4
Percent change	X	-4.1	-4.0	-17.9	-17.8	-5.8	-5.7	-5.6	-5.6
Utah[7]									
2013	2,902,787	6,644	228.9	51	1.8	1,522	52.4	926	31.9
2014	2,942,902	6,346	215.6	67	2.3	1,454	49.4	945	32.1
Percent change	X	-4.5	-5.8	+31.4	+29.6	-4.5	-5.8	+2.1	+0.7
Wyoming[6]									
2013	583,223	1,212	207.8	17	2.9	204	35.0	144	24.7
2014	584,153	1,142	195.5	16	2.7	174	29.8	126	21.6
Percent change	X	-5.8	-5.9	-5.9	-6.0	-14.7	-14.8	-12.5	-12.6
Pacific[6,7]									
2013	51,479,449	192,792	374.5	2,061	4.0	15,825	30.7	11,559	22.5
2014	51,990,562	191,433	368.2	2,021	3.9	16,896	32.5	12,490	24.0
Percent change	X	-0.7	-1.7	-1.9	-2.9	+6.8	+5.7	+8.1	+7.0
Alaska[6]									
2013	737,259	4,709	638.7	34	4.6	925	125.5	657	89.1
2014	736,732	4,684	635.8	41	5.6	771	104.7	555	75.3
Percent change	X	-0.5	-0.5	+20.6	+20.7	-16.6	-16.6	-15.5	-15.5
California[7]									
2013	38,431,393	154,739	402.6	1,746	4.5	10,324	26.9	7,464	19.4
2014	38,802,500	153,709	396.1	1,699	4.4	11,527	29.7	8,398	21.6
Percent change	X	-0.7	-1.6	-2.7	-3.6	+11.7	+10.6	+12.5	+11.4
Hawaii[6]									
2013	1,408,987	3,585	254.4	32	2.3	508	36.1	366	26.0
2014	1,419,561	3,680	259.2	26	1.8	445	31.3	314	22.1
Percent change	X	+2.6	+1.9	-18.8	-19.4	-12.4	-13.1	-14.2	-14.8
Oregon[7]									
2013	3,928,068	9,536	242.8	82	2.1	1,464	37.3	1,000	25.5
2014	3,970,239	9,224	232.3	81	2.0	1,458	36.7	1,052	26.5
Percent change	X	-3.3	-4.3	-1.2	-2.3	-0.4	-1.5	+5.2	+4.1
Washington[7]									
2013	6,973,742	20,223	290.0	167	2.4	2,604	37.3	2,072	29.7
2014	7,061,530	20,136	285.2	174	2.5	2,695	38.2	2,171	30.7
Percent change	X	-0.4	-1.7	+4.2	+2.9	+3.5	+2.2	+4.8	+3.5
Puerto Rico									
2013	3,595,839	9,328	259.4	883	24.6	34	0.9	26	0.7
2014	3,548,397	8,383	236.2	681	19.2	56	1.6	41	1.2
Percent change	X	-10.1	-8.9	-22.9	-21.8	+64.7	+66.9	+57.7	+59.8

(Number, rate per 100,000 population, percent.)

Area	Robbery Number	Robbery Rate	Aggravated assault Number	Aggravated assault Rate	Property crime Number	Property crime Rate	Burglary Number	Burglary Rate	Larceny-theft Number	Larceny-theft Rate	Motor vehicle theft Number	Motor vehicle theft Rate
Percent change	+2.9	+1.6	-0.1	-1.3	-4.1	-5.4	-9.7	-10.9	-3.2	-4.4	+2.2	+0.9
Arizona[6]												
2013	6,656	100.3	17,391	262.1	223,294	3,365.4	48,292	727.8	158,036	2,381.9	16,966	255.7
2014	6,249	92.8	16,970	252.1	215,240	3,197.5	43,562	647.1	154,091	2,289.1	17,587	261.3
Percent change	-6.1	-7.5	-2.4	-3.8	-3.6	-5.0	-9.8	-11.1	-2.5	-3.9	+3.7	+2.2
Colorado[6]												
2013	3,136	59.5	9,826	186.4	139,974	2,655.0	25,075	475.6	102,375	1,941.8	12,524	237.6
2014	3,039	56.7	10,325	192.8	135,510	2,530.1	23,472	438.2	99,464	1,857.1	12,574	234.8
Percent change	-3.1	-4.6	+5.1	+3.4	-3.2	-4.7	-6.4	-7.9	-2.8	-4.4	+0.4	-1.2
Idaho[6]												
2013	220	13.6	2,548	158.0	30,230	1,874.3	6,693	415.0	21,999	1,364.0	1,538	95.4
2014	204	12.5	2,623	160.5	30,316	1,854.8	6,428	393.3	22,227	1,359.9	1,661	101.6
Percent change	-7.3	-8.5	+2.9	+1.6	+0.3	-1.0	-4.0	-5.2	+1.0	-0.3	+8.0	+6.6
Montana[6]												
2013	217	21.4	2,217	218.5	26,195	2,581.1	4,122	406.2	20,192	1,989.6	1,881	185.3
2014	203	19.8	2,532	247.4	25,312	2,472.9	3,595	351.2	19,674	1,922.1	2,043	199.6
Percent change	-6.5	-7.2	+14.2	+13.2	-3.4	-4.2	-12.8	-13.5	-2.6	-3.4	+8.6	+7.7
Nevada[6]												
2013	5,183	185.7	10,060	360.4	79,177	2,836.4	23,047	825.6	46,132	1,652.6	9,998	358.2
2014	5,954	209.7	10,564	372.1	74,538	2,625.4	21,927	772.3	42,426	1,494.3	10,185	358.7
Percent change	+14.9	+12.9	+5.0	+3.2	-5.9	-7.4	-4.9	-6.5	-8.0	-9.6	+1.9	+0.2
New Mexico												
2013	1,832	87.8	9,470	453.8	78,958	3,783.5	21,828	1,046.0	51,146	2,450.8	5,984	286.7
2014	2,086	100.0	8,797	421.8	73,877	3,542.3	18,505	887.3	49,082	2,353.4	6,290	301.6
Percent change	+13.9	+13.9	` -7.1	-7.0	-6.4	-6.4	-15.2	-15.2	-4.0	-4.0	+5.1	+5.2
Utah[7]												
2013	1,247	43.0	3,824	131.7	88,334	3,043.1	13,727	472.9	67,115	2,312.1	7,492	258.1
2014	1,312	44.6	3,513	119.4	84,711	2,878.5	11,518	391.4	65,895	2,239.1	7,298	248.0
Percent change	+5.2	+3.8	-8.1	-9.4	-4.1	-5.4	-16.1	-17.2	-1.8	-3.2	-2.6	-3.9
Wyoming[6]												
2013	74	12.7	917	157.2	12,809	2,196.2	1,956	335.4	10,275	1,761.8	578	99.1
2014	53	9.1	899	153.9	11,477	1,964.7	1,689	289.1	9,185	1,572.4	603	103.2
Percent change	-28.4	-28.5	-2.0	-2.1	-10.4	-10.5	-13.7	-13.8	-10.6	-10.8	+4.3	+4.2
Pacific[6,7]												
2013	63,420	123.2	111,486	216.6	1,469,606	2,854.7	322,047	625.6	937,674	1,821.5	209,885	407.7
2014	58,149	111.8	114,367	220.0	1,386,834	2,667.5	286,118	550.3	903,050	1,736.9	197,666	380.2
Percent change	-8.3	-9.2	+2.6	+1.6	-5.6	-6.6	-11.2	-12.0	-3.7	-4.6	-5.8	-6.7
Alaska[6]												
2013	623	84.5	3,127	424.1	21,211	2,877.0	2,917	395.7	16,599	2,251.4	1,695	229.9
2014	629	85.4	3,243	440.2	20,334	2,760.0	3,150	427.6	15,445	2,096.4	1,739	236.0
Percent change	+1.0	+1.0	+3.7	+3.8	-4.1	-4.1	+8.0	+8.1	-7.0	-6.9	+2.6	+2.7
California[7]												
2013	53,640	139.6	89,029	231.7	1,018,907	2,651.2	232,058	603.8	621,557	1,617.3	165,292	430.1
2014	48,680	125.5	91,803	236.6	947,192	2,441.1	202,670	522.3	592,670	1,527.4	151,852	391.3
Percent change	-9.2	-10.1	+3.1	+2.1	-7.0	-7.9	-12.7	-13.5	-4.6	-5.6	-8.1	-9.0
Hawaii[6]												
2013	934	66.3	2,111	149.8	45,266	3,212.7	7,777	552.0	32,928	2,337.0	4,561	323.7
2014	1,107	78.0	2,102	148.1	43,297	3,050.0	7,778	547.9	31,640	2,228.9	3,879	273.3
Percent change	+18.5	+17.6	-0.4	-1.2	-4.3	-5.1	*	-0.7	-3.9	-4.6	-15.0	-15.6
Oregon[7]												
2013	2,394	60.9	5,596	142.5	125,083	3,184.3	20,808	529.7	94,363	2,402.3	9,912	252.3
2014	2,093	52.7	5,592	140.8	114,305	2,879.0	17,230	434.0	87,526	2,204.6	9,549	240.5
Percent change	-12.6	-13.5	-0.1	-1.1	-8.6	-9.6	-17.2	-18.1	-7.2	-8.2	-3.7	-4.7
Washington[7]												
2013	5,829	83.6	11,623	166.7	259,139	3,715.9	58,487	838.7	172,227	2,469.6	28,425	407.6
2014	5,640	79.9	11,627	164.7	261,706	3,706.1	55,290	783.0	175,769	2,489.1	30,647	434.0
Percent change	-3.2	-4.4	*	-1.2	+1.0	-0.3	-5.5	-6.6	+2.1	+0.8	+7.8	+6.5
Puerto Rico												
2013	6,016	167.3	2,395	66.6	48,851	1,358.5	13,961	388.3	29,360	816.5	5,530	153.8
2014	5,171	145.7	2,475	69.7	45,622	1,285.7	12,035	339.2	28,948	815.8	4,639	130.7
Percent change	-14.0	-12.9	+3.3	+4.7	-6.6	-5.4	-13.8	-12.6	-1.4	-0.1	-16.1	-15.0

Note: Although arson data are included in the trend and clearance tables, sufficient data are not available to estimate totals for this offense. Therefore, no arson data are published in this table.
X = Not applicable.
* = Less than one-tenth of 1 percent.
[1] The previous year's crime figures have been adjusted.
[2] Population figures are U.S. Census Bureau provisional estimates as of July 1, 2014.
[3] The violent crime figures include the offenses of murder, rape (revised definition), robbery, and aggravated assault.
[4] The figures shown in this column for the offense of rape were estimated using the revised Uniform Crime Reporting (UCR) definition of rape. See chapter notes for more detail.
[5] The figures shown in this column for the offense of rape were estimated using the legacy Uniform Crime Reporting (UCR) definition of rape. See chapter notes for more detail.
[6] This state's agencies submitted rape data according to the revised UCR definition of rape.
[7] Agencies within this state submitted rape data according to both the revised UCR definition of rape and the legacy UCR definition of rape.
[8] Includes offenses reported by the Metro Transit Police and the District of Columbia Fire and Emergency Services Fire Investigation Unit.
[9] Because of changes in the state/local agency's reporting practices, figures are not comparable to previous years' data.

Table 5. Crime, by State and Area, 2014

(Number, percent, rate per 100,000 population.)

Area	Population	Violent crime[1]	Murder and nonnegligent manslaughter	Rape (revised definition)[2]	Rape (legacy definition)[3]	Robbery	Aggravated assault	Property crime	Burglary	Larceny-theft	Motor vehicle theft
Alabama[4]											
Metropolitan statistical area	3,692,100										
Area actually reporting	95.5%	16,204	232	1,435	1,033	4,131	10,406	118,226	29,903	80,430	7,893
Estimated total	100.0%	16,702	236	1,494	1,076	4,228	10,744	122,299	31,007	83,126	8,166
Cities outside metropolitan areas	529,129										
Area actually reporting	93.3%	2,605	17	294	214	363	1,931	21,747	5,005	15,516	1,226
Estimated total	100.0%	2,769	18	310	226	386	2,055	23,058	5,330	16,420	1,308
Nonmetropolitan counties	628,148										
Area actually reporting	99.4%	1,247	22	199	133	86	940	8,683	3,357	4,663	663
Estimated total	100.0%	1,256	22	201	134	87	946	8,737	3,378	4,692	667
State total	4,849,377	20,727	276	2,005	1,436	4,701	13,745	154,094	39,715	104,238	10,141
Rate per 100,000 inhabitants		427.4	5.7	41.3	29.6	96.9	283.4	3,177.6	819.0	2,149.5	209.1
Alaska[4]											
Metropolitan statistical area	351,408										
Area actually reporting	100.0%	2,899	17	442	329	557	1,883	13,905	1,626	11,148	1,131
Cities outside metropolitan areas	128,681										
Area actually reporting	96.6%	722	3	128	93	45	546	3,362	413	2,702	247
Estimated total	100.0%	748	3	133	98	47	565	3,480	427	2,797	256
Nonmetropolitan counties	256,643										
Area actually reporting	100.0%	1,037	21	196	128	25	795	2,949	1,097	1,500	352
State total	736,732	4,684	41	771	555	629	3,243	20,334	3,150	15,445	1,739
Rate per 100,000 inhabitants		635.8	5.6	104.7	75.3	85.4	440.2	2,760.0	427.6	2,096.4	236.0
Arizona[4]											
Metropolitan statistical area	6,382,968										
Area actually reporting	98.1%	24,006	288	2,762	2,024	6,117	14,839	201,780	39,504	146,202	16,074
Estimated total	100.0%	24,291	293	2,791	2,045	6,155	15,052	204,214	40,034	147,926	16,254
Cities outside metropolitan areas	123,617										
Area actually reporting	78.4%	1,721	20	452	323	55	1,194	7,020	2,111	3,996	913
Estimated total	100.0%	2,192	25	574	409	70	1,523	8,952	2,692	5,096	1,164
Nonmetropolitan counties	224,899										
Area actually reporting	100.0%	433	1	13	10	24	395	2,074	836	1,069	169
State total	6,731,484	26,916	319	3,378	2,464	6,249	16,970	215,240	43,562	154,091	17,587
Rate per 100,000 inhabitants		399.9	4.7	50.2	36.6	92.8	252.1	3,197.5	647.1	2,289.1	261.3
Arkansas[4]											
Metropolitan statistical area	1,818,380										
Area actually reporting	98.5%	9,939	109	958	699	1,671	7,201	65,236	15,309	46,042	3,885
Estimated total	100.0%	10,058	109	976	712	1,683	7,290	66,163	15,532	46,704	3,927
Cities outside metropolitan areas	507,788										
Area actually reporting	88.9%	2,349	27	383	227	284	1,655	18,688	5,059	12,892	737
Estimated total	100.0%	2,648	30	438	268	319	1,861	21,015	5,689	14,497	829
Nonmetropolitan counties	640,201										
Area actually reporting	87.9%	1,340	23	296	170	42	979	10,407	3,137	6,527	743
Estimated total	100.0%	1,537	26	349	202	48	1,114	11,840	3,569	7,426	845
State total	2,966,369	14,243	165	1,763	1,182	2,050	10,265	99,018	24,790	68,627	5,601
Rate per 100,000 inhabitants		480.1	5.6	59.4	39.8	69.1	346.0	3,338.0	835.7	2,313.5	188.8
California[5]											
Metropolitan statistical area	37,970,617										
Area actually reporting	99.9%	150,171	1,652	11,088	8,096	48,278	89,153	928,421	197,039	581,578	149,804
Estimated total	100.0%	150,192	1,652	11,089	8,097	48,285	89,166	928,584	197,074	581,682	149,828
Cities outside metropolitan areas	268,396										
Area actually reporting	100.0%	1,524	16	168	126	257	1,083	10,256	2,635	6,832	789
Nonmetropolitan counties	563,487										
Area actually reporting	100.0%	1,993	31	270	175	138	1,554	8,352	2,961	4,156	1,235
State total	38,802,500	153,709	1,699	11,527	8,398	48,680	91,803	947,192	202,670	592,670	151,852
Rate per 100,000 inhabitants		396.1	4.4	29.7	21.6	125.5	236.6	2,441.1	522.3	1,527.4	391.3
Colorado[4]											
Metropolitan statistical area	4,664,010										
Area actually reporting	98.5%	15,229	126	2,700	1,943	2,952	9,451	122,570	21,212	89,448	11,910
Estimated total	100.0%	15,365	127	2,728	1,961	2,963	9,547	123,592	21,419	90,164	12,009
Cities outside metropolitan areas	334,211										
Area actually reporting	93.2%	735	15	191	96	60	469	8,603	1,257	7,018	328
Estimated total	100.0%	790	16	207	109	64	503	9,233	1,349	7,532	352
Nonmetropolitan counties	357,645										
Area actually reporting	99.6%	398	8	104	51	12	274	2,674	701	1,761	212

Table 5. Crime, by State and Area, 2014—*Continued*

(Number, percent, rate per 100,000 population.)

Area	Population	Violent crime[1]	Murder and nonnegligent manslaughter	Rape (revised definition)[2]	Rape (legacy definition)[3]	Robbery	Aggravated assault	Property crime	Burglary	Larceny-theft	Motor vehicle theft
Estimated total	100.0%	399	8	104	51	12	275	2,685	704	1,768	213
State total....................	5,355,866	16,554	151	3,039	2,121	3,039	10,325	135,510	23,472	99,464	12,574
Rate per 100,000 inhabitants		309.1	2.8	56.7	39.6	56.7	192.8	2,530.1	438.2	1,857.1	234.8
Connecticut[4]											
Metropolitan statistical area...................	2,948,198										
Area actually reporting	100.0%	8,068	82	686	513	3,106	4,194	63,397	10,737	46,890	5,770
Cities outside metropolitan areas...........	115,968										
Area actually reporting	100.0%	108	2	11	8	22	73	1,850	274	1,499	77
Nonmetropolitan counties	532,511										
Area actually reporting	100.0%	346	2	85	50	31	228	3,823	944	2,616	263
State total....................	3,596,677	8,522	86	782	571	3,159	4,495	69,070	11,955	51,005	6,110
Rate per 100,000 inhabitants		236.9	2.4	21.7	15.9	87.8	125.0	1,920.4	332.4	1,418.1	169.9
Delaware[4]											
Metropolitan statistical area...................	935,614										
Area actually reporting	100.0%	4,575	54	385	249	1,269	2,867	27,899	5,768	20,864	1,267
Cities outside metropolitan areas...........	None										
Area actually reporting	None										
State total....................	100.0%	1	0	1	0	0	0	1	0	1	0
Rate per 100,000 inhabitants	935,614	4,576	54	386	249	1,269	2,867	27,900	5,768	20,865	1,267
		489.1	5.8	41.3	26.6	135.6	306.4	2,982.0	616.5	2,230.1	135.4
District of Columbia[4,6]											
Metropolitan statistical area...................	658,893										
Area actually reporting	100.0%	8,199	105	472	352	3,497	4,125	34,147	3,466	26,898	3,783
Cities outside metropolitan areas...........	None										
Nonmetropolitan counties	None										
District total....................	658,893	8,199	105	472	352	3,497	4,125	34,147	3,466	26,898	3,783
Rate per 100,000 inhabitants		1,244.4	15.9	71.6	53.4	530.7	626.1	5,182.5	526.0	4,082.3	574.1
Florida[4]											
Metropolitan statistical area...................	19,186,005										
Area actually reporting	99.9%	104,161	1,133	8,298	5,872	24,552	70,178	661,692	138,134	481,755	41,803
Estimated total	100.0%	104,272	1,133	8,308	5,880	24,582	70,249	662,580	138,301	482,424	41,855
Cities outside metropolitan areas...........	148,283										
Area actually reporting	97.0%	921	4	53	38	163	701	5,937	1,324	4,355	258
Estimated total	100.0%	949	4	54	39	168	723	6,121	1,365	4,490	266
Nonmetropolitan counties	559,009										
Area actually reporting	94.1%	2,159	11	184	121	154	1,810	10,115	3,346	6,338	431
State total....................	100.0%	2,300	12	201	132	164	1,923	10,745	3,554	6,733	458
Rate per 100,000 inhabitants	19,893,297	107,521	1,149	8,563	6,051	24,914	72,895	679,446	143,220	493,647	42,579
		540.5	5.8	43.0	30.4	125.2	366.4	3,415.5	719.9	2,481.5	214.0
Georgia[7]											
Metropolitan statistical area...................	8,320,348										
Area actually reporting	99.4%	32,097	508	2,487	1,769	11,368	17,734	276,099	63,221	188,100	24,778
Estimated total	100.0%	32,360	508	2,539	1,809	11,447	17,866	278,295	63,621	189,741	24,933
Cities outside metropolitan areas...........	662,709										
Area actually reporting	90.3%	3,041	30	255	188	704	2,052	29,412	6,160	22,485	767
Estimated total	100.0%	3,352	33	269	202	779	2,271	32,554	6,818	24,887	849
Nonmetropolitan counties	1,114,286										
Area actually reporting	91.5%	2,179	36	215	134	175	1,753	18,737	5,483	12,273	981
Estimated total	100.0%	2,385	39	240	148	191	1,915	20,467	5,989	13,406	1,072
State total....................	10,097,343	38,097	580	3,048	2,159	12,417	22,052	331,316	76,428	228,034	26,854
Rate per 100,000 inhabitants		377.3	5.7	30.2	21.4	123.0	218.4	3,281.2	756.9	2,258.4	266.0
Hawaii[4]											
Metropolitan statistical area...................	1,156,263										
Area actually reporting	100.0%	2,901	15	310	225	994	1,582	35,245	5,759	26,162	3,324
Cities outside metropolitan areas...........	None										
Nonmetropolitan counties	263,298										
Area actually reporting	100.0%	779	11	135	89	113	520	8,052	2,019	5,478	555
State total....................	1,419,561	3,680	26	445	314	1,107	2,102	43,297	7,778	31,640	3,879
Rate per 100,000 inhabitants		259.2	1.8	31.3	22.1	78.0	148.1	3,050.0	547.9	2,228.9	273.3
Idaho[4]											
Metropolitan statistical area...................	1,086,169										
Area actually reporting	99.9%	2,431	18	433	318	157	1,823	21,605	4,103	16,290	1,212
Estimated total	100.0%	2,432	18	433	318	157	1,824	21,616	4,105	16,298	1,213
Cities outside metropolitan areas...........	250,458										

Table 5. Crime, by State and Area, 2014—*Continued*

(Number, percent, rate per 100,000 population.)

Area	Population	Violent crime[1]	Murder and nonnegligent manslaughter	Rape (revised definition)[2]	Rape (legacy definition)[3]	Robbery	Aggravated assault	Property crime	Burglary	Larceny-theft	Motor vehicle theft
Area actually reporting	100.0%	628	4	111	93	36	477	5,510	1,283	3,999	228
Nonmetropolitan counties	297,837										
Area actually reporting	100.0%	408	10	65	57	11	322	3,190	1,040	1,930	220
State total	1,634,464	3,468	32	609	468	204	2,623	30,316	6,428	22,227	1,661
Rate per 100,000 inhabitants		212.2	2.0	37.3	28.6	12.5	160.5	1,854.8	393.3	1,359.9	101.6
Illinois[4]											
Metropolitan statistical area	11,380,871										
Area actually reporting	96.3%	43,827	656	3,577	2,647	14,844	24,750	237,056	43,542	177,082	16,432
Estimated total	100.0%	44,639	665	3,690	2,735	15,060	25,224	244,145	44,777	182,621	16,747
Cities outside metropolitan areas	832,015										
Area actually reporting	86.1%	2,049	15	296	221	184	1,554	15,693	3,139	12,141	413
Estimated total	100.0%	2,377	17	341	260	214	1,805	18,227	3,646	14,101	480
Nonmetropolitan counties	667,694										
Area actually reporting	93.6%	599	3	114	78	23	459	4,691	1,483	2,998	210
Estimated total	100.0%	647	3	128	86	25	491	5,013	1,585	3,204	224
State total	12,880,580	47,663	685	4,159	3,081	15,299	27,520	267,385	50,008	199,926	17,451
Rate per 100,000 inhabitants		370.0	5.3	32.3	23.9	118.8	213.7	2,075.9	388.2	1,552.2	135.5
Indiana[5]											
Metropolitan statistical area	5,123,600										
Area actually reporting	89.1%	20,655	289	1,742	1,283	6,514	12,110	139,542	30,229	97,466	11,847
Estimated total	100.0%	21,655	300	1,851	1,364	6,697	12,807	149,875	31,963	105,352	12,560
Cities outside metropolitan areas	520,959										
Area actually reporting	68.2%	923	2	136	103	102	683	10,928	1,530	8,854	544
Estimated total	100.0%	1,352	3	199	153	149	1,001	16,013	2,242	12,974	797
Nonmetropolitan counties	952,296										
Area actually reporting	70.5%	764	19	90	70	36	619	6,266	1,895	4,016	355
Estimated total	100.0%	1,092	27	136	98	51	878	8,888	2,688	5,696	504
State total	6,596,855	24,099	330	2,186	1,615	6,897	14,686	174,776	36,893	124,022	13,861
Rate per 100,000 inhabitants		365.3	5.0	33.1	24.5	104.5	222.6	2,649.4	559.3	1,880.0	210.1
Iowa[4]											
Metropolitan statistical area	1,816,911										
Area actually reporting	97.6%	5,597	37	761	576	916	3,883	45,159	9,323	32,729	3,107
Estimated total	100.0%	5,673	38	777	587	919	3,939	45,646	9,453	33,049	3,144
Cities outside metropolitan areas	601,521										
Area actually reporting	91.6%	1,811	15	220	151	106	1,470	13,720	2,995	10,125	600
Estimated total	100.0%	1,980	16	243	168	116	1,605	14,984	3,271	11,058	655
Nonmetropolitan counties	688,694										
Area actually reporting	86.4%	726	5	90	62	9	622	3,824	1,472	2,048	304
Estimated total	100.0%	844	6	108	73	10	720	4,426	1,704	2,370	352
State total	3,107,126	8,497	60	1,128	828	1,045	6,264	65,056	14,428	46,477	4,151
Rate per 100,000 inhabitants		273.5	1.9	36.3	26.6	33.6	201.6	2,093.8	464.4	1,495.8	133.6
Kansas[4]											
Metropolitan statistical area	1,950,218										
Area actually reporting	98.4%	7,209	75	985	756	1,202	4,947	55,694	10,119	39,991	5,584
Estimated total	100.0%	7,262	75	991	760	1,208	4,988	56,297	10,220	40,448	5,629
Cities outside metropolitan areas	612,758										
Area actually reporting	95.3%	2,062	11	325	251	132	1,594	17,440	3,655	12,934	851
Estimated total	100.0%	2,161	12	337	261	139	1,673	18,303	3,836	13,574	893
Nonmetropolitan counties	341,045										
Area actually reporting	96.4%	673	4	79	51	14	576	4,656	1,708	2,578	370
Estimated total	100.0%	700	4	83	54	15	598	4,831	1,772	2,675	384
State total	2,904,021	10,123	91	1,411	1,075	1,362	7,259	79,431	15,828	56,697	6,906
Rate per 100,000 inhabitants		348.6	3.1	48.6	37.0	46.9	250.0	2,735.2	545.0	1,952.4	237.8
Kentucky[4]											
Metropolitan statistical area	2,574,779										
Area actually reporting	99.8%	7,057	100	727	420	2,827	3,403	72,864	15,478	52,618	4,768
Estimated total	100.0%	7,065	100	727	420	2,831	3,407	72,991	15,502	52,715	4,774
Cities outside metropolitan areas	538,647										
Area actually reporting	97.7%	869	11	173	135	315	370	14,649	2,799	11,298	552
Estimated total	100.0%	887	11	175	137	322	379	14,995	2,865	11,565	565
Nonmetropolitan counties	1,300,031										
Area actually reporting	99.2%	1,378	49	534	323	182	613	11,093	4,839	5,283	971
Estimated total	100.0%	1,388	49	538	326	183	618	11,180	4,877	5,324	979
State total	4,413,457	9,340	160	1,440	883	3,336	4,404	99,166	23,244	69,604	6,318
Rate per 100,000 inhabitants		211.6	3.6	32.6	20.0	75.6	99.8	2,246.9	526.7	1,577.1	143.2

Table 5. Crime, by State and Area, 2014—*Continued*

(Number, percent, rate per 100,000 population.)

Area	Population	Violent crime[1]	Murder and nonnegligent manslaughter	Rape (revised definition)[2]	Rape (legacy definition)[3]	Robbery	Aggravated assault	Property crime	Burglary	Larceny-theft	Motor vehicle theft
Louisiana[4]											
Metropolitan statistical area	3,882,923										
Area actually reporting	98.8%	20,348	413	1,148	833	5,252	13,535	136,338	32,197	95,266	8,875
Estimated total	100.0%	20,567	414	1,161	844	5,286	13,706	138,370	32,569	96,799	9,002
Cities outside metropolitan areas	274,036										
Area actually reporting	79.6%	1,702	30	85	62	253	1,334	11,295	2,718	8,275	302
Estimated total	100.0%	2,142	38	109	82	318	1,677	14,197	3,416	10,401	380
Nonmetropolitan counties	492,717										
Area actually reporting	100.0%	1,225	25	105	66	91	1,004	8,257	2,352	5,396	509
State total	4,649,676	23,934	477	1,375	992	5,695	16,387	160,824	38,337	112,596	9,891
Rate per 100,000 inhabitants		514.7	10.3	29.6	21.3	122.5	352.4	3,458.8	824.5	2,421.6	212.7
Maine[5]											
Metropolitan statistical area	783,169										
Area actually reporting	100.0%	984	13	247	187	215	509	16,216	3,083	12,662	471
Cities outside metropolitan areas	266,485										
Area actually reporting	100.0%	476	4	158	121	71	243	7,036	1,013	5,836	187
Nonmetropolitan counties	280,435										
Area actually reporting	100.0%	240	4	80	52	18	138	3,169	934	2,094	141
State total	1,330,089	1,700	21	485	360	304	890	26,421	5,030	20,592	799
Rate per 100,000 inhabitants		127.8	1.6	36.5	27.1	22.9	66.9	1,986.4	378.2	1,548.2	60.1
Maryland											
Metropolitan statistical area	5,823,196										
Area actually reporting	100.0%	26,186	360	1,583	1,118	9,488	14,755	146,392	27,175	106,222	12,995
Cities outside metropolitan areas	53,207										
Area actually reporting	100.0%	310	2	23	18	43	242	2,015	347	1,624	44
Nonmetropolitan counties	100,004										
Area actually reporting	100.0%	165	3	13	8	13	136	1,452	490	899	63
State total	5,976,407	26,661	365	1,619	1,144	9,544	15,133	149,859	28,012	108,745	13,102
Rate per 100,000 inhabitants		446.1	6.1	27.1	19.1	159.7	253.2	2,507.5	468.7	1,819.6	219.2
Massachusetts[5]											
Metropolitan statistical area	6,646,017										
Area actually reporting	98.2%	25,694	131	2,093	1,576	5,940	17,530	121,137	23,956	89,098	8,083
Estimated total	100.0%	26,077	132	2,130	1,604	6,010	17,805	123,126	24,348	90,571	8,207
Cities outside metropolitan areas	91,692										
Area actually reporting	76.8%	237	0	30	12	20	187	1,645	473	1,131	41
Estimated total	100.0%	310	0	41	19	26	243	2,141	616	1,472	53
Nonmetropolitan counties	7,699										
Area actually reporting	100.0%	12	0	9	6	0	3	0	0	0	0
State total	6,745,408	26,399	132	2,180	1,629	6,036	18,051	125,267	24,964	92,043	8,260
Rate per 100,000 inhabitants		391.4	2.0	32.3	24.1	89.5	267.6	1,857.1	370.1	1,364.5	122.5
Michigan[4]											
Metropolitan statistical area	8,107,118										
Area actually reporting	99.1%	37,965	504	4,630	2,989	7,858	24,973	174,589	38,467	115,908	20,214
Estimated total	100.0%	38,176	505	4,674	3,021	7,896	25,101	176,132	38,736	117,069	20,327
Cities outside metropolitan areas	603,680										
Area actually reporting	89.6%	1,324	8	496	309	71	749	11,588	1,441	9,848	299
Estimated total	100.0%	1,491	9	567	363	79	836	12,929	1,608	10,987	334
Nonmetropolitan counties	1,199,079										
Area actually reporting	96.0%	2,554	20	971	625	44	1,519	12,950	3,687	8,787	476
Estimated total	100.0%	2,681	21	1,032	665	46	1,582	13,486	3,840	9,150	496
State total	9,909,877	42,348	535	6,273	4,049	8,021	27,519	202,547	44,184	137,206	21,157
Rate per 100,000 inhabitants		427.3	5.4	63.3	40.9	80.9	277.7	2,043.9	445.9	1,384.5	213.5
Minnesota[4]											
Metropolitan statistical area	4,216,484										
Area actually reporting	99.9%	10,578	77	1,494	1,095	3,530	5,477	103,320	16,621	79,633	7,066
Estimated total	100.0%	10,579	77	1,494	1,095	3,530	5,478	103,337	16,623	79,647	7,067
Cities outside metropolitan areas	490,823										
Area actually reporting	100.0%	1,110	7	269	199	127	707	13,223	1,796	10,765	662
Nonmetropolitan counties	749,866										
Area actually reporting	100.0%	816	4	238	158	30	544	8,817	2,354	5,825	638
State total	5,457,173	12,505	88	2,001	1,452	3,687	6,729	125,377	20,773	96,237	8,367
Rate per 100,000 inhabitants		229.1	1.6	36.7	26.6	67.6	123.3	2,297.5	380.7	1,763.5	153.3
Mississippi[5]											
Metropolitan statistical area	1,365,250										
Area actually reporting	72.7%	3,137	104	400	299	1,214	1,419	32,956	8,088	22,660	2,208

Table 5. Crime, by State and Area, 2014—*Continued*

(Number, percent, rate per 100,000 population.)

Area	Population	Violent crime[1]	Murder and nonnegligent manslaughter	Rape (revised definition)[2]	Rape (legacy definition)[3]	Robbery	Aggravated assault	Property crime	Burglary	Larceny-theft	Motor vehicle theft
Estimated total	100.0%	3,739	122	463	346	1,344	1,810	40,942	9,959	28,361	2,622
Cities outside metropolitan areas	588,934										
Area actually reporting	48.5%	1,404	40	150	111	444	770	15,536	4,055	10,933	548
Estimated total	100.0%	2,898	82	311	238	916	1,589	32,064	8,369	22,564	1,131
Nonmetropolitan counties	1,039,895										
Area actually reporting	42.4%	716	23	115	73	72	506	6,134	2,556	3,253	325
Estimated total	100.0%	1,701	54	284	180	170	1,193	14,456	6,024	7,666	766
State total	2,994,079	8,338	258	1,058	764	2,430	4,592	87,462	24,352	58,591	4,519
Rate per 100,000 inhabitants		278.5	8.6	35.3	25.5	81.2	153.4	2,921.2	813.3	1,956.9	150.9
Missouri[4]											
Metropolitan statistical area	4,507,971										
Area actually reporting	99.9%	22,257	348	2,002	1,441	5,295	14,612	140,143	27,421	98,371	14,351
Cities outside metropolitan areas	100.0%	22,258	348	2,002	1,441	5,295	14,613	140,163	27,424	98,387	14,352
	665,780										
Area actually reporting	99.6%	2,649	22	217	160	255	2,155	24,487	4,085	19,441	961
Estimated total	100.0%	2,658	22	217	160	256	2,163	24,581	4,101	19,515	965
Nonmetropolitan counties	889,838										
Estimated total	100.0%	1,940	33	160	105	41	1,706	11,493	3,733	6,720	1,040
State total	6,063,589	26,856	403	2,379	1,706	5,592	18,482	176,237	35,258	124,622	16,357
Rate per 100,000 inhabitants		442.9	6.6	39.2	28.1	92.2	304.8	2,906.5	581.5	2,055.3	269.8
Montana[4]											
Metropolitan statistical area	362,656										
Area actually reporting	100.0%	1,049	14	191	145	133	711	11,788	1,538	9,329	921
Cities outside metropolitan areas	215,364										
Area actually reporting	98.0%	1,169	14	196	160	42	917	7,073	976	5,514	583
Estimated total	100.0%	1,194	14	201	164	43	936	7,219	996	5,628	595
Nonmetropolitan counties	445,559										
Area actually reporting	94.0%	1,003	8	138	114	25	832	5,930	998	4,436	496
Estimated total	100.0%	1,070	9	149	121	27	885	6,305	1,061	4,717	527
State total	1,023,579	3,313	37	541	430	203	2,532	25,312	3,595	19,674	2,043
Rate per 100,000 inhabitants		323.7	3.6	52.9	42.0	19.8	247.4	2,472.9	351.2	1,922.1	199.6
Nebraska[5]											
Metropolitan statistical area	1,210,548										
Area actually reporting	99.2%	4,086	42	588	427	987	2,469	36,129	5,735	26,472	3,922
Estimated total	100.0%	4,097	42	591	430	989	2,475	36,288	5,759	26,599	3,930
Cities outside metropolitan areas	338,087										
Area actually reporting	91.0%	817	4	191	139	45	577	7,954	1,360	6,279	315
Estimated total	100.0%	900	4	213	157	49	634	8,736	1,494	6,896	346
Nonmetropolitan counties	332,868										
Area actually reporting	78.7%	214	6	41	24	4	163	1,933	549	1,243	141
Estimated total	100.0%	278	8	58	33	5	207	2,455	697	1,579	179
State total	1,881,503	5,275	54	862	620	1,043	3,316	47,479	7,950	35,074	4,455
Rate per 100,000 inhabitants		280.4	2.9	45.8	33.0	55.4	176.2	2,523.5	422.5	1,864.1	236.8
Nevada[4]											
Metropolitan statistical area	2,565,531										
Area actually reporting	100.0%	17,199	157	1,233	909	5,903	9,906	69,217	20,344	39,084	9,789
Cities outside metropolitan areas	48,964										
Area actually reporting	100.0%	348	4	45	34	17	282	1,931	555	1,235	141
Nonmetropolitan counties	224,604										
Area actually reporting	97.9%	486	9	76	50	33	368	3,321	1,007	2,064	250
Estimated total	100.0%	498	9	79	52	34	376	3,390	1,028	2,107	255
State total	2,839,099	18,045	170	1,357	995	5,954	10,564	74,538	21,927	42,426	10,185
Rate per 100,000 inhabitants		635.6	6.0	47.8	35.0	209.7	372.1	2,625.4	772.3	1,494.3	358.7
New Hampshire[4]											
Metropolitan statistical area	830,790										
Area actually reporting	96.4%	1,702	11	323	250	421	947	15,633	2,403	12,679	551
Estimated total	100.0%	1,745	11	336	261	428	970	16,125	2,474	13,085	566
Cities outside metropolitan areas	442,983										
Area actually reporting	86.7%	684	1	206	158	93	384	8,304	1,379	6,686	239
Estimated total	100.0%	795	1	244	188	107	443	9,575	1,590	7,709	276
Nonmetropolitan counties	53,040										
Area actually reporting	100.0%	62	0	14	9	2	46	341	98	228	15
State total	1,326,813	2,602	12	594	458	537	1,459	26,041	4,162	21,022	857
Rate per 100,000 inhabitants		196.1	0.9	44.8	34.5	40.5	110.0	1,962.7	313.7	1,584.4	64.6

Table 5. Crime, by State and Area, 2014—*Continued*

(Number, percent, rate per 100,000 population.)

Area	Population	Violent crime[1]	Murder and nonnegligent manslaughter	Rape (revised definition)[2]	Rape (legacy definition)[3]	Robbery	Aggravated assault	Property crime	Burglary	Larceny-theft	Motor vehicle theft
New Jersey	8,938,175										
Metropolitan statistical area	100.0%	23,346	349	1,274	953	10,498	11,225	154,993	31,710	111,578	11,705
Area actually reporting	None										
Cities outside metropolitan areas	None										
Nonmetropolitan counties	8,938,175	23,346	349	1,274	953	10,498	11,225	154,993	31,710	111,578	11,705
State total		261.2	3.9	14.3	10.7	117.5	125.6	1,734.1	354.8	1,248.3	131.0
Rate per 100,000 inhabitants											
New Mexico	1,390,853										
Metropolitan statistical area	99.9%	8,653	63	1,031	751	1,771	5,788	51,763	12,135	34,681	4,947
Area actually reporting	100.0%	8,656	63	1,031	751	1,771	5,791	51,785	12,140	34,697	4,948
Estimated total	397,993										
Cities outside metropolitan areas	97.9%	2,847	28	338	252	259	2,222	17,471	4,290	12,284	897
Area actually reporting	100.0%	2,908	29	345	257	265	2,269	17,844	4,382	12,546	916
Estimated total	296,726										
Nonmetropolitan counties	92.7%	828	8	91	58	46	683	3,937	1,838	1,704	395
Area actually reporting	100.0%	895	9	99	63	50	737	4,248	1,983	1,839	426
Estimated total	2,085,572	12,459	101	1,475	1,071	2,086	8,797	73,877	18,505	49,082	6,290
State total		597.4	4.8	70.7	51.4	100.0	421.8	3,542.3	887.3	2,353.4	301.6
Rate per 100,000 inhabitants											
New York[5]	18,339,380										
Metropolitan statistical area	99.9%	72,890	588	4,591	3,349	23,787	43,924	314,802	45,880	253,815	15,107
Area actually reporting	100.0%	72,930	588	4,592	3,350	23,802	43,948	315,220	45,937	254,164	15,119
Estimated total	518,307										
Cities outside metropolitan areas	97.7%	1,187	10	229	168	190	758	13,033	2,274	10,503	256
Area actually reporting	100.0%	1,217	10	236	174	195	776	13,344	2,328	10,754	262
Estimated total	888,540										
Nonmetropolitan counties	97.0%	1,204	18	577	376	47	562	10,395	2,440	7,611	344
Area actually reporting	100.0%	1,251	19	605	394	48	579	10,718	2,516	7,847	355
Estimated total	19,746,227	75,398	617	5,433	3,918	24,045	45,303	339,282	50,781	272,765	15,736
State total		381.8	3.1	27.5	19.8	121.8	229.4	1,718.2	257.2	1,381.4	79.7
Rate per 100,000 inhabitants											
North Carolina	7,727,957										
Metropolitan statistical area	99.1%	25,907	358	1,946	1,410	7,112	16,491	220,587	57,805	151,974	10,808
Area actually reporting	100.0%	26,053	359	1,952	1,416	7,148	16,594	222,495	58,252	153,363	10,880
Estimated total	648,863										
Cities outside metropolitan areas	92.1%	3,655	71	192	145	835	2,557	31,335	7,687	22,533	1,115
Area actually reporting	100.0%	3,958	77	198	151	907	2,776	34,021	8,346	24,464	1,211
Estimated total	1,567,144										
Nonmetropolitan counties	97.0%	2,673	72	261	168	350	1,990	28,309	12,393	14,423	1,493
Area actually reporting	100.0%	2,756	74	270	173	361	2,051	29,181	12,775	14,867	1,539
Estimated total	9,943,964	32,767	510	2,420	1,740	8,416	21,421	285,697	79,373	192,694	13,630
State total		329.5	5.1	24.3	17.5	84.6	215.4	2,873.1	798.2	1,937.8	137.1
Rate per 100,000 inhabitants											
North Dakota[4]	363,187										
Metropolitan statistical area	100.0%	1,055	8	190	156	116	741	8,298	1,369	6,359	570
Area actually reporting	180,439										
Cities outside metropolitan areas	100.0%	683	12	130	95	47	494	5,385	897	3,852	636
Area actually reporting	195,856										
Nonmetropolitan counties	99.3%	221	2	38	25	10	171	1,909	438	1,165	306
Area actually reporting	100.0%	222	2	38	25	10	172	1,922	441	1,173	308
Estimated total	739,482	1,960	22	358	276	173	1,407	15,605	2,707	11,384	1,514
State total		265.1	3.0	48.4	37.3	23.4	190.3	2,110.3	366.1	1,539.5	204.7
Rate per 100,000 inhabitants											
Ohio[5]	9,218,545										
Metropolitan statistical area	91.2%	28,580	406	3,963	3,274	11,782	12,429	255,451	64,006	175,491	15,954
Area actually reporting	100.0%	29,798	417	4,233	3,479	12,195	12,953	274,917	67,601	190,658	16,658
Estimated total	1,049,077										
Cities outside metropolitan areas	81.8%	1,525	19	371	314	364	771	26,877	5,139	21,197	541
Area actually reporting	100.0%	1,861	23	451	369	445	942	32,841	6,279	25,901	661
Estimated total	1,326,541										
Nonmetropolitan counties	90.4%	1,234	22	318	223	102	792	15,161	4,489	10,043	629
Area actually reporting	100.0%	1,371	24	358	249	113	876	16,770	4,965	11,109	696
Estimated total	11,594,163	33,030	464	5,042	4,097	12,753	14,771	324,528	78,845	227,668	18,015
State total		284.9	4.0	43.5	35.3	110.0	127.4	2,799.1	680.0	1,963.6	155.4
Rate per 100,000 inhabitants											

Table 5. Crime, by State and Area, 2014—*Continued*

(Number, percent, rate per 100,000 population.)

Area	Population	Violent crime[1]	Murder and nonnegligent manslaughter	Rape (revised definition)[2]	Rape (legacy definition)[3]	Robbery	Aggravated assault	Property crime	Burglary	Larceny-theft	Motor vehicle theft
Oklahoma[4]	2,526,767										
Metropolitan statistical area											
Area actually reporting	100.0%	11,796	141	1,321	960	2,680	7,654	81,680	20,708	52,585	8,387
Cities outside metropolitan areas	728,921										
Area actually reporting	100.0%	3,189	24	372	264	337	2,456	26,975	6,244	19,215	1,516
Nonmetropolitan counties	622,363										
Area actually reporting	100.0%	759	10	84	53	31	634	7,327	2,556	4,091	680
State total	3,878,051	15,744	175	1,777	1,277	3,048	10,744	115,982	29,508	75,891	10,583
Rate per 100,000 inhabitants		406.0	4.5	45.8	32.9	78.6	277.0	2,990.7	760.9	1,956.9	272.9
Oregon[5]	3,317,292										
Metropolitan statistical area											
Area actually reporting	90.0%	7,436	55	1,114	817	1,840	4,427	92,252	12,754	71,579	7,919
Estimated total	100.0%	7,928	58	1,232	900	1,903	4,735	97,757	13,901	75,432	8,424
Cities outside metropolitan areas	306,040										
Area actually reporting	94.1%	805	9	148	100	148	500	10,629	1,780	8,250	599
Estimated total	100.0%	854	10	155	106	157	532	11,299	1,892	8,770	637
Nonmetropolitan counties	346,907										
Area actually reporting	98.4%	434	13	69	45	32	320	5,165	1,414	3,271	480
Estimated total	100.0%	442	13	71	46	33	325	5,249	1,437	3,324	488
State total	3,970,239	9,224	81	1,458	1,052	2,093	5,592	114,305	17,230	87,526	9,549
Rate per 100,000 inhabitants		232.3	2.0	36.7	26.5	52.7	140.8	2,879.0	434.0	2,204.6	240.5
Pennsylvania[4]	11,296,254										
Metropolitan statistical area											
Area actually reporting	99.5%	37,560	587	3,358	2,465	13,252	20,363	224,980	40,869	171,772	12,339
Estimated total	100.0%	37,654	588	3,362	2,468	13,278	20,426	225,908	41,009	172,530	12,369
Cities outside metropolitan areas	688,032										
Area actually reporting	97.9%	1,470	6	136	102	150	1,178	10,840	1,812	8,754	274
Estimated total	100.0%	1,499	6	137	103	153	1,203	11,068	1,850	8,938	280
Nonmetropolitan counties	802,923										
Area actually reporting	100.0%	1,011	20	328	216	103	560	10,040	2,861	6,788	391
State total	12,787,209	40,164	614	3,827	2,787	13,534	22,189	247,016	45,720	188,256	13,040
Rate per 100,000 inhabitants		314.1	4.8	29.9	21.8	105.8	173.5	1,931.7	357.5	1,472.2	102.0
Puerto Rico											
Metropolitan statistical area	3,394,621										
Area actually reporting	100.0%	8,134	657	55	41	5,062	2,360	44,180	11,558	28,051	4,571
Cities outside metropolitan areas	153,776										
Area actually reporting	100.0%	249	24	1	0	109	115	1,442	477	897	68
Total	3,548,397	8,383	681	56	41	5,171	2,475	45,622	12,035	28,948	4,639
Rate per 100,000 inhabitants		236.2	19.2	1.6	1.2	145.7	69.7	1,285.7	339.2	815.8	130.7
Rhode Island[5]											
Metropolitan statistical area	1,055,173										
Area actually reporting	100.0%	2,287	25	341	247	528	1,393	22,874	4,823	16,253	1,798
Cities outside metropolitan areas	None										
Nonmetropolitan counties	None										
Area actually reporting	100.0%	26	0	20	6	1	5	61	0	26	35
State total	1,055,173	2,313	25	361	253	529	1,398	22,935	4,823	16,279	1,833
Rate per 100,000 inhabitants		219.2	2.4	34.2	24.0	50.1	132.5	2,173.6	457.1	1,542.8	173.7
South Carolina[4]	4,078,154										
Metropolitan statistical area											
Area actually reporting	98.4%	19,644	252	1,716	1,225	3,423	14,253	138,237	29,121	98,137	10,979
Estimated total	100.0%	19,942	255	1,740	1,242	3,467	14,480	140,229	29,590	99,497	11,142
Cities outside metropolitan areas	208,220										
Area actually reporting	95.7%	1,677	19	104	81	307	1,247	11,294	2,433	8,363	498
Estimated total	100.0%	1,751	20	107	84	321	1,303	11,797	2,541	8,736	520
Nonmetropolitan counties	546,108										
Area actually reporting	100.0%	2,359	36	221	154	209	1,893	15,191	4,590	9,361	1,240
State total	4,832,482	24,052	311	2,068	1,480	3,997	17,676	167,217	36,721	117,594	12,902
Rate per 100,000 inhabitants		497.7	6.4	42.8	30.6	82.7	365.8	3,460.3	759.9	2,433.4	267.0
South Dakota[4]	405,686										
Metropolitan statistical area											
Area actually reporting	99.5%	1,374	9	259	238	150	956	9,265	1,663	6,981	621
Estimated total	100.0%	1,376	9	259	238	150	958	9,285	1,667	6,996	622
Cities outside metropolitan areas	218,451										
Area actually reporting	95.8%	1,168	6	163	139	43	956	5,171	832	4,032	307
Estimated total	100.0%	1,220	6	171	146	45	998	5,396	868	4,208	320

Table 5. Crime, by State and Area, 2014—*Continued*

(Number, percent, rate per 100,000 population.)

Area	Population	Violent crime[1]	Murder and nonnegligent manslaughter	Rape (revised definition)[2]	Rape (legacy definition)[3]	Robbery	Aggravated assault	Property crime	Burglary	Larceny-theft	Motor vehicle theft
Nonmetropolitan counties	229,038										
Area actually reporting	78.0%	144	4	27	22	4	109	953	221	681	51
Estimated total	100.0%	190	5	40	29	5	140	1,221	283	873	65
State total	853,175	2,786	20	470	413	200	2,096	15,902	2,818	12,077	1,007
Rate per 100,000 inhabitants		326.5	2.3	55.1	48.4	23.4	245.7	1,863.9	330.3	1,415.5	118.0
Tennessee[4]											
Metropolitan statistical area	5,053,537										
Area actually reporting	99.4%	33,938	319	2,154	1,575	6,823	24,642	162,661	36,810	115,487	10,364
Estimated total	100.0%	34,046	320	2,164	1,582	6,837	24,725	163,447	36,930	116,117	10,400
Cities outside metropolitan areas	516,197										
Area actually reporting	100.0%	3,203	21	183	144	312	2,687	21,421	4,146	16,367	908
Nonmetropolitan counties	979,618										
Area actually reporting	100.0%	2,599	30	184	135	116	2,269	15,579	5,566	8,722	1,291
State total	6,549,352	39,848	371	2,531	1,861	7,265	29,681	200,447	46,642	141,206	12,599
Rate per 100,000 inhabitants		608.4	5.7	38.6	28.4	110.9	453.2	3,060.6	712.2	2,156.0	192.4
Texas[4]											
Metropolitan statistical area	23,907,066										
Area actually reporting	99.7%	100,224	1,079	10,227	7,407	30,369	58,549	745,490	149,988	530,355	65,147
Estimated total	100.0%	100,400	1,080	10,252	7,428	30,409	58,659	746,997	150,305	531,426	65,266
Cities outside metropolitan areas	1,421,341										
Area actually reporting	97.3%	5,676	50	603	438	609	4,414	43,056	10,053	31,360	1,643
Estimated total	100.0%	5,832	51	623	456	624	4,534	44,192	10,320	32,187	1,685
Nonmetropolitan counties	1,628,551										
Area actually reporting	98.2%	3,117	52	502	342	145	2,418	22,326	8,450	12,310	1,566
Estimated total	100.0%	3,182	53	518	352	148	2,463	22,745	8,609	12,541	1,595
State total	26,956,958	109,414	1,184	11,393	8,236	31,181	65,656	813,934	169,234	576,154	68,546
Rate per 100,000 inhabitants		405.9	4.4	42.3	30.6	115.7	243.6	3,019.4	627.8	2,137.3	254.3
Utah[5]											
Metropolitan statistical area	2,627,376										
Area actually reporting	99.8%	5,739	54	1,290	839	1,287	3,108	78,386	10,465	61,010	6,911
Estimated total	100.0%	5,749	54	1,292	841	1,289	3,114	78,558	10,488	61,145	6,925
Cities outside metropolitan areas	140,374										
Area actually reporting	95.9%	287	1	100	63	13	173	3,526	559	2,808	159
Estimated total	100.0%	300	1	105	67	14	180	3,678	583	2,929	166
Nonmetropolitan counties	175,152										
Area actually reporting	97.5%	290	12	55	36	9	214	2,414	436	1,776	202
Estimated total	100.0%	297	12	57	37	9	219	2,475	447	1,821	207
State total	2,942,902	6,346	67	1,454	945	1,312	3,513	84,711	11,518	65,895	7,298
Rate per 100,000 inhabitants		215.6	2.3	49.4	32.1	44.6	119.4	2,878.5	391.4	2,239.1	248.0
Vermont[4]											
Metropolitan statistical area	215,526										
Area actually reporting	100.0%	214	2	22	20	24	166	4,265	725	3,427	113
Cities outside metropolitan areas	207,162										
Area actually reporting	99.9%	260	1	47	41	38	174	3,536	626	2,852	58
Nonmetropolitan counties	100.0%	260	1	47	41	38	174	3,541	627	2,856	58
Area actually reporting	203,874										
Estimated total	100.0%	148	7	41	38	8	92	1,745	682	990	73
State total	626,562	622	10	110	99	70	432	9,551	2,034	7,273	244
Rate per 100,000 inhabitants		99.3	1.6	17.6	15.8	11.2	68.9	1,524.4	324.6	1,160.8	38.9
Virginia[4]											
Metropolitan statistical area	7,266,550										
Area actually reporting	99.9%	14,412	284	1,880	1,206	4,039	8,209	143,762	19,725	117,178	6,859
Estimated total	100.0%	14,413	284	1,880	1,206	4,039	8,210	143,779	19,727	117,192	6,860
Cities outside metropolitan areas	264,412										
Area actually reporting	98.7%	694	15	113	65	144	422	7,385	1,130	6,060	195
Estimated total	100.0%	702	15	113	65	146	428	7,484	1,145	6,141	198
Nonmetropolitan counties	795,327										
Area actually reporting	100.0%	1,225	39	317	161	107	762	9,457	2,250	6,600	607
State total	8,326,289	16,340	338	2,310	1,432	4,292	9,400	160,720	23,122	129,933	7,665
Rate per 100,000 inhabitants		196.2	4.1	27.7	17.2	51.5	112.9	1,930.3	277.7	1,560.5	92.1
Washington[5]											
Metropolitan statistical area	6,347,580										
Area actually reporting	99.9%	18,604	159	2,438	1,954	5,439	10,568	241,803	49,672	163,026	29,105
Estimated total	100.0%	18,611	159	2,439	1,955	5,441	10,572	241,934	49,694	163,120	29,120
Cities outside metropolitan areas	294,301										

Table 5. Crime, by State and Area, 2014—*Continued*

(Number, percent, rate per 100,000 population.)

Area	Population	Violent crime[1]	Murder and nonnegligent manslaughter	Rape (revised definition)[2]	Rape (legacy definition)[3]	Robbery	Aggravated assault	Property crime	Burglary	Larceny-theft	Motor vehicle theft
Area actually reporting	97.7%	944	7	170	144	148	619	12,503	2,897	8,665	941
Estimated total	100.0%	966	7	173	147	152	634	12,803	2,966	8,873	964
Nonmetropolitan counties	419,649										
Area actually reporting	100.0%	559	8	83	69	47	421	6,969	2,630	3,776	563
State total	7,061,530	20,136	174	2,695	2,171	5,640	11,627	261,706	55,290	175,769	30,647
Rate per 100,000 inhabitants		285.2	2.5	38.2	30.7	79.9	164.7	3,706.1	783.0	2,489.1	434.0
West Virginia[4]	1,138,730										
Metropolitan statistical area	1,138,730										
Area actually reporting	92.8%	3,310	44	333	175	530	2,403	26,935	6,481	19,081	1,373
Estimated total	100.0%	3,526	46	348	187	560	2,572	29,155	6,857	20,830	1,468
Cities outside metropolitan areas	190,438										
Area actually reporting	58.2%	425	6	29	22	29	361	2,211	385	1,764	62
Estimated total	100.0%	721	10	41	33	50	620	3,801	662	3,032	107
Nonmetropolitan counties	521,158										
Area actually reporting	89.6%	1,197	16	99	54	37	1,045	4,205	1,303	2,614	288
Estimated total	100.0%	1,341	18	116	65	41	1,166	4,692	1,454	2,917	321
State total	1,850,326	5,588	74	505	285	651	4,358	37,648	8,973	26,779	1,896
Rate per 100,000 inhabitants		302.0	4.0	27.3	15.4	35.2	235.5	2,034.7	484.9	1,447.3	102.5
Wisconsin[5]	4,251,567										
Metropolitan statistical area	4,251,567										
Area actually reporting	96.7%	14,725	142	1,232	851	4,918	8,433	95,066	16,637	69,341	9,088
Estimated total	100.0%	14,890	143	1,259	872	4,961	8,527	97,688	16,979	71,524	9,185
Cities outside metropolitan areas	637,105										
Area actually reporting	95.2%	1,019	11	214	163	73	721	14,099	1,715	12,054	330
Estimated total	100.0%	1,072	12	226	172	77	757	14,813	1,802	12,664	347
Nonmetropolitan counties	868,892										
Area actually reporting	100.0%	752	10	189	124	28	525	7,737	2,435	4,915	387
State total	5,757,564	16,714	165	1,674	1,168	5,066	9,809	120,238	21,216	89,103	9,919
Rate per 100,000 inhabitants		290.3	2.9	29.1	20.3	88.0	170.4	2,088.3	368.5	1,547.6	172.3
Wyoming[4]	178,196										
Metropolitan statistical area	178,196										
Area actually reporting	100.0%	305	6	37	25	30	232	4,292	733	3,356	203
Cities outside metropolitan areas	246,602										
Area actually reporting	97.4%	580	6	80	61	18	476	5,806	707	4,816	283
Estimated total	100.0%	594	6	81	62	18	489	5,962	726	4,945	291
Nonmetropolitan counties	159,355										
Area actually reporting	91.8%	222	4	50	35	5	163	1,123	211	812	100
Estimated total	100.0%	243	4	56	39	5	178	1,223	230	884	109
State total	584,153	1,142	16	174	126	53	899	11,477	1,689	9,185	603
Rate per 100,000 inhabitants		195.5	2.7	29.8	21.6	9.1	153.9	1,964.7	289.1	1,572.4	103.2

Note: Although arson data are included in the trend and clearance tables, sufficient data are not available to estimate totals for this offense. Therefore, no arson data are published in this table.
[1] The violent crime figures include the offenses of murder, rape (revised definition), robbery, and aggravated assault.
[2] The figures shown in this column for the offense of rape were estimated using the revised Uniform Crime Reporting (UCR) definition of rape. See chapter notes for more detail.
[3] The figures shown in this column for the offense of rape were estimated using the legacy Uniform Crime Reporting (UCR) definition of rape. See chapter notes for more detail.
[4] This state's agencies submitted rape data according to the revised UCR definition of rape.
[5] Agencies within this state submitted rape data according to both the revised UCR definition of rape and the legacy UCR definition of rape.
[6] Includes offenses reported by the Zoological Police and the Metro Transit Police.
[7] Because of changes in the state/local agency's reporting practices, figures are not comparable to previous years' data.

Table 6. Crime, by Selected Metropolitan Statistical Area, 2014

(Number, percent, rate per 100,000 population.)

Area	Population	Violent crime	Murder and nonnegligent manslaughter	Rape[1]	Robbery	Aggravated assault	Property crime	Burglary	Larceny-theft	Motor vehicle theft
Abilene, TX MSA	169,202									
Includes Callahan, Jones, and Taylor Counties										
City of Abilene.............	120,686	571	7	93	128	343	5,344	1,095	3,887	362
Total area actually reporting	100.0%	677	10	113	140	414	6,207	1,428	4,372	407
Rate per 100,000 inhabitants..............		400.1	5.9	66.8	82.7	244.7	3,668.4	844.0	2,583.9	240.5
Akron, OH MSA[2,3]	706,737									
Includes Portage and Summit Counties										
City of Akron.............	197,891	1,358	26	171	435	726	9,061	2,871	5,611	579
Total area actually reporting	92.3%	1,864	33	297	533	1,001		4,437		835
Estimated total..............	100.0%	1,944	34	313	561	1,036		4,678		882
Rate per 100,000 inhabitants..............		275.1	4.8	44.3	79.4	146.6		661.9		124.8
Albany, GA MSA[3]	155,769									
Includes Baker, Dougherty, Lee, Terrell, and Worth Counties[3]........										
City of Albany[3]..............	75,858	775	9	26	156	584	4,196	1,172	2,849	175
Total area actually reporting	97.7%	939	9	38	175	717	6,081	1,652	4,154	275
Estimated total..............	100.0%	954	9	39	180	726	6,236	1,679	4,271	286
Rate per 100,000 inhabitants..............		612.4	5.8	25.0	115.6	466.1	4,003.4	1,077.9	2,741.9	183.6
Albany, OR MSA	119,734									
Includes Linn County...............										
City of Albany..............	51,889	42	2	10	26	4	1,675	201	1,358	116
Total area actually reporting	100.0%	117	3	18	38	58	3,818	626	2,918	274
Rate per 100,000 inhabitants..............		97.7	2.5	15.0	31.7	48.4	3,188.7	522.8	2,437.1	228.8
Albany-Schenectady-Troy, NY MSA	881,039									
Includes Albany, Rensselaer, Saratoga, Schenectady, and Schoharie Counties................										
City of Albany..............	98,595	802	8	54	237	503	3,888	683	3,083	122
City of Schenectady..............	65,834	575	5	57	158	355	2,518	642	1,752	124
City of Troy..............	49,950	350	7	0	110	233	2,182	540	1,512	130
Total area actually reporting	100.0%	2,360	32	251	645	1,432	19,577	3,353	15,545	679
Rate per 100,000 inhabitants..............		267.9	3.6	28.5	73.2	162.5	2,222.0	380.6	1,764.4	77.1
Albuquerque, NM MSA	903,982									
Includes Bernalillo, Sandoval, Torrance, and Valencia Counties										
City of Albuquerque..............	558,874	4,934	30	402	1,381	3,121	30,437	6,123	20,756	3,558
Total area actually reporting	99.9%	6,689	43	489	1,547	4,610	38,583	8,441	25,895	4,247
Estimated total..............	100.0%	6,692	43	489	1,547	4,613	38,605	8,446	25,911	4,248
Rate per 100,000 inhabitants..............		740.3	4.8	54.1	171.1	510.3	4,270.5	934.3	2,866.3	469.9
Alexandria, LA MSA	155,023									
Includes Grant and Rapides Parishes...............										
City of Alexandria	48,618	858	9	9	170	670	3,761	1,073	2,484	204
Total area actually reporting	97.1%	1,239	10	47	193	989	6,712	1,887	4,366	459
Estimated total..............	100.0%	1,259	10	48	196	1,005	6,899	1,921	4,507	471
Rate per 100,000 inhabitants..............		812.1	6.5	31.0	126.4	648.3	4,450.3	1,239.2	2,907.3	303.8
Allentown-Bethlehem-Easton, PA-NJ MSA	828,360									
Includes Warren County, NJ and Carbon, Lehigh, and Northampton Counties, PA										
City of Allentown, PA..............	118,710	611	9	66	312	224	3,821	940	2,608	273
City of Bethlehem, PA..............	75,024	211	1	28	83	99	1,823	298	1,429	96
Total area actually reporting	99.5%	1,507	18	179	551	759	16,070	2,855	12,446	769
Estimated total..............	100.0%	1,514	18	180	553	763	16,135	2,865	12,499	771
Rate per 100,000 inhabitants..............		182.8	2.2	21.7	66.8	92.1	1,947.8	345.9	1,508.9	93.1
Altoona, PA MSA	126,112									
Includes Blair County										
City of Altoona	45,676	159	1	38	32	88	890	208	658	24
Total area actually reporting	100.0%	294	1	50	40	203	2,072	349	1,678	45
Rate per 100,000 inhabitants..............		233.1	0.8	39.6	31.7	161.0	1,643.0	276.7	1,330.6	35.7
Amarillo, TX MSA	261,505									
Includes Armstrong, Carson, Oldham, Potter, and Randall Counties...............										
City of Amarillo..............	197,724	1,344	7	228	283	826	9,343	1,834	6,659	850
Total area actually reporting	100.0%	1,464	10	255	289	910	10,039	1,998	7,137	904
Rate per 100,000 inhabitants..............		559.8	3.8	97.5	110.5	348.0	3,838.9	764.0	2,729.2	345.7

Table 6. Crime, by Selected Metropolitan Statistical Area, 2014—*Continued*

(Number, percent, rate per 100,000 population.)

Area	Population	Violent crime	Murder and nonnegligent manslaughter	Rape[1]	Robbery	Aggravated assault	Property crime	Burglary	Larceny-theft	Motor vehicle theft
Ames, IA MSA...	93,310									
Includes Story County										
City of Ames...	62,514	75	0	23	15	37	1,117	191	901	25
Total area actually reporting	92.7%	110	0	36	15	59	1,531	294	1,194	43
Estimated total..	100.0%	123	0	38	16	69	1,645	314	1,283	48
Rate per 100,000 inhabitants............................		131.8	0.0	40.7	17.1	73.9	1,762.9	336.5	1,375.0	51.4
Anchorage, AK MSA	316,696									
Includes Anchorage Municipality and										
Matanuska-Susitna Borough										
City of Anchorage...	301,306	2,605	12	392	496	1,705	11,531	1,375	9,217	939
Total area actually reporting	100.0%	2,672	13	402	502	1,755	12,514	1,447	10,066	1,001
Rate per 100,000 inhabitants............................		843.7	4.1	126.9	158.5	554.2	3,951.4	456.9	3,178.4	316.1
Ann Arbor, MI MSA	356,841									
Includes Washtenaw County										
City of Ann Arbor	117,768	194	0	56	24	114	2,200	320	1,779	101
Total area actually reporting	100.0%	1,017	5	217	141	654	6,577	1,123	5,066	388
Rate per 100,000 inhabitants............................		285.0	1.4	60.8	39.5	183.3	1,843.1	314.7	1,419.7	108.7
Anniston-Oxford-Jacksonville, AL MSA	116,381									
Includes Calhoun County										
City of Anniston..	22,567	536	4	42	77	413	1,711	650	969	92
City of Oxford..	17,059	59	2	2	8	47	837	108	706	23
City of Jacksonville..	12,462	67	1	6	17	43	460	143	304	13
Total area actually reporting	100.0%	719	7	66	104	542	3,896	1,223	2,515	158
Rate per 100,000 inhabitants............................		617.8	6.0	56.7	89.4	465.7	3,347.6	1,050.9	2,161.0	135.8
Appleton, WI MSA	231,052									
Includes Calumet and Outagamie Counties................										
City of Appleton...	73,841	197	0	23	21	153	1,381	168	1,190	23
Total area actually reporting	100.0%	317	0	36	26	255	3,396	495	2,837	64
Rate per 100,000 inhabitants............................		137.2	0.0	15.6	11.3	110.4	1,469.8	214.2	1,227.9	27.7
Asheville, NC MSA	441,690									
Includes Buncombe, Haywood, Henderson, and Madison										
Counties..										
City of Asheville...	88,184	501	4	43	194	260	4,277	841	3,164	272
Total area actually reporting	99.2%	900	13	83	258	546	10,090	2,730	6,704	656
Estimated total..	100.0%	908	13	84	260	551	10,198	2,752	6,786	660
Rate per 100,000 inhabitants............................		205.6	2.9	19.0	58.9	124.7	2,308.9	623.1	1,536.4	149.4
Athens-Clarke County, GA MSA[3].........................	199,695									
Includes Clarke, Madison, Oconee, and Oglethorpe Counties[3]										
City of Athens-Clarke County[3]	121,511	372	4	38	125	205	3,792	760	2,845	187
Total area actually reporting	99.4%	595	4	115	136	340	5,709	1,204	4,230	275
Estimated total..	100.0%	600	4	115	138	343	5,758	1,213	4,267	278
Rate per 100,000 inhabitants............................		300.5	2.0	57.6	69.1	171.8	2,883.4	607.4	2,136.8	139.2
Atlanta-Sandy Springs-Roswell, GA MSA[3]	5,597,635									
Includes Barrow, Bartow, Butts, Carroll, Cherokee, Clayton, Cobb,										
Coweta, Dawson, DeKalb, Douglas, Fayette, Forsyth, Fulton,										
Gwinnett, Haralson, Heard, Henry, Jasper, Lamar, Meriwether,										
Morgan, Newton, Paulding, Pickens, Pike, Rockdale, Spalding,										
and Walton Counties[3]										
City of Atlanta[3]..	454,363	5,577	93	151	2,329	3,004	26,114	5,470	16,498	4,146
City of Sandy Springs[3].....................................	101,184	159	6	21	92	40	2,745	639	1,930	176
City of Roswell[3]..	95,387	110	3	10	53	44	1,789	372	1,328	89
City of Alpharetta[3]...	63,478	38	0	3	21	14	1,254	150	1,070	34
City of Marietta[3]...	59,663	303	5	8	139	151	2,654	366	2,080	208
Total area actually reporting	99.9%	22,263	342	1,138	8,607	12,176	180,516	40,572	121,220	18,724
Estimated total..	100.0%	22,300	342	1,140	8,620	12,198	180,878	40,636	121,493	18,749
Rate per 100,000 inhabitants............................		398.4	6.1	20.4	154.0	217.9	3,231.3	725.9	2,170.4	334.9
Atlantic City-Hammonton, NJ MSA	276,587									
Includes Atlantic County										
City of Atlantic City...	39,544	523	6	15	302	200	2,450	282	2,104	64
City of Hammonton..	14,800	17	0	0	3	14	155	29	123	3
Total area actually reporting	100.0%	1,062	17	55	489	501	8,125	1,649	6,270	206
Rate per 100,000 inhabitants............................		384.0	6.1	19.9	176.8	181.1	2,937.6	596.2	2,266.9	74.5

Table 6. Crime, by Selected Metropolitan Statistical Area, 2014—*Continued*

(Number, percent, rate per 100,000 population.)

Area	Population	Violent crime	Murder and nonnegligent manslaughter	Rape[1]	Robbery	Aggravated assault	Property crime	Burglary	Larceny-theft	Motor vehicle theft
Auburn-Opelika, AL M.S.A	153,664									
Includes Lee County										
City of Auburn	59,854	126	1	19	19	87	1,654	257	1,326	71
City of Opelika	29,201	188	1	11	34	142	1,622	289	1,245	88
Total area actually reporting	100.0%	388	3	44	66	275	3,936	775	2,939	222
Rate per 100,000 inhabitants		252.5	2.0	28.6	43.0	179.0	2,561.4	504.3	1,912.6	144.5
Augusta-Richmond County, GA-SC MSA[3]	585,946									
Includes Burke, Columbia, Lincoln, McDuffie, and Richmond Counties, GA[3] and Aiken and Edgefield Counties, SC										
Total area actually reporting	98.8%	1,650	39	197	520	894	19,060	4,626	13,042	1,392
Estimated total	100.0%	1,681	39	199	531	912	19,363	4,679	13,271	1,413
Rate per 100,000 inhabitants		286.9	6.7	34.0	90.6	155.6	3,304.6	798.5	2,264.9	241.1
Austin-Round Rock, TX MSA	1,938,280									
Includes Bastrop, Caldwell, Hays, Travis, and Williamson Counties.										
City of Austin	903,924	3,581	32	571	873	2,105	37,444	5,733	29,423	2,288
City of Round Rock	112,199	140	0	29	39	72	2,189	247	1,891	51
Total area actually reporting	99.8%	5,631	46	948	1,115	3,522	55,709	9,501	43,095	3,113
Estimated total	100.0%	5,639	46	949	1,117	3,527	55,800	9,517	43,164	3,119
Rate per 100,000 inhabitants		290.9	2.4	49.0	57.6	182.0	2,878.8	491.0	2,226.9	160.9
Bakersfield, CA MSA	874,650									
Includes Kern County										
City of Bakersfield	367,406	1,678	17	21	660	980	14,595	4,065	8,247	2,283
Total area actually reporting	100.0%	4,465	59	181	1,106	3,119	28,283	8,546	14,992	4,745
Rate per 100,000 inhabitants		510.5	6.7	20.7	126.5	356.6	3,233.6	977.1	1,714.1	542.5
Baltimore-Columbia-Towson, MD MSA[3]	2,790,201									
Includes Anne Arundel, Baltimore, Carroll, Harford, Howard, and Queen Anne's Counties and Baltimore City										
City of Baltimore	623,513	8,346	211	245	3,677	4,213	29,420	6,926	18,008	4,486
Total area actually reporting	100.0%	16,420	268	569	6,208	9,375	77,944	14,738	56,106	7,100
Rate per 100,000 inhabitants		588.5	9.6	20.4	222.5	336.0	2,793.5	528.2	2,010.8	254.5
Bangor, ME MSA	153,425									
Includes Penobscot County										
City of Bangor	32,586	55	1	4	22	28	1,678	182	1,474	22
Total area actually reporting	100.0%	118	4	18	35	61	3,467	533	2,850	84
Rate per 100,000 inhabitants		76.9	2.6	11.7	22.8	39.8	2,259.7	347.4	1,857.6	54.7
Barnstable Town, MA MSA	215,384									
Includes Barnstable County										
City of Barnstable	44,642	279	0	19	28	232	1,080	223	793	64
Total area actually reporting	100.0%	917	3	87	69	758	4,308	1,334	2,792	182
Rate per 100,000 inhabitants		425.8	1.4	40.4	32.0	351.9	2,000.1	619.4	1,296.3	84.5
Baton Rouge, LA MSA[2]	824,758									
Includes Ascension, East Baton Rouge, East Feliciana, Iberville, Livingston,[2] Pointe Coupee, St. Helena, West Baton Rouge, and West Feliciana Parishes										
City of Baton Rouge	229,387	2,120	53	73	852	1,142	10,270	2,772	6,986	512
Total area actually reporting	99.7%		88	217	1,172		28,016	6,682	20,307	1,027
Estimated total	100.0%		88	218	1,174		28,126	6,702	20,390	1,034
Rate per 100,000 inhabitants			10.7	26.4	142.3		3,410.2	812.6	2,472.2	125.4
Battle Creek, MI M.S.A.	134,882									
Includes Calhoun County										
City of Battle Creek	61,225	480	3	54	66	357	2,350	770	1,477	103
Total area actually reporting	100.0%	725	4	121	87	513	3,653	1,028	2,493	132
Rate per 100,000 inhabitants		537.5	3.0	89.7	64.5	380.3	2,708.3	762.1	1,848.3	97.9
Bay City, MI MSA	106,711									
Includes Bay County										
City of Bay City	34,307	182	1	55	19	107	1,003	272	695	36
Total area actually reporting	100.0%	296	2	101	29	164	2,124	473	1,585	66
Rate per 100,000 inhabitants		277.4	1.9	94.6	27.2	153.7	1,990.4	443.3	1,485.3	61.8
Beaumont-Port Arthur, TX MSA	408,113									
Includes Hardin, Jefferson, Newton, and Orange Counties										
City of Beaumont	117,898	1,050	16	91	293	650	5,530	1,456	3,861	213

Table 6. Crime, by Selected Metropolitan Statistical Area, 2014—*Continued*

(Number, percent, rate per 100,000 population.)

Area	Population	Violent crime	Murder and nonnegligent manslaughter	Rape[1]	Robbery	Aggravated assault	Property crime	Burglary	Larceny-theft	Motor vehicle theft
City of Port Arthur	54,178	341	8	29	114	190	2,131	528	1,471	132
Total area actually reporting	99.9%	2,015	33	185	501	1,296	12,116	3,054	8,344	718
Estimated total	100.0%	2,016	33	185	501	1,297	12,130	3,056	8,355	719
Rate per 100,000 inhabitants		494.0	8.1	45.3	122.8	317.8	2,972.2	748.8	2,047.2	176.2
Beckley, WV M.S.A	124,037									
Includes Fayette and Raleigh Counties										
City of Beckley	17,595	186	0	19	37	130	2,267	280	947	41
Total area actually reporting	93.4%	441	7	45	83	306	3,467	1,053	2,230	184
Estimated total	100.0%	466	7	47	87	325	3,735	1,090	2,451	194
Rate per 100,000 inhabitants		375.7	5.6	37.9	70.1	262.0	3,011.2	878.8	1,976.0	156.4
Bellingham, WA M.S.A.	208,491									
Includes Whatcom County										
City of Bellingham	83,048	220	1	55	64	100	4,699	726	3,808	165
Total area actually reporting	100.0%	423	2	97	87	237	7,142	1,405	5,470	267
Rate per 100,000 inhabitants		202.9	1.0	46.5	41.7	113.7	3,425.6	673.9	2,623.6	128.1
Bend-Redmond, OR MSA	168,749									
Includes Deschutes County										
City of Bend	82,418	114	0	16	23	75	2,140	255	1,799	86
City of Redmond	27,733	88	0	15	24	49	965	106	812	47
Total area actually reporting	100.0%	284	0	50	50	184	3,981	560	3,241	180
Rate per 100,000 inhabitants		168.3	0.0	29.6	29.6	109.0	2,359.1	331.9	1,920.6	106.7
Billings, MT MSA	167,246									
Includes Carbon, Golden Valley, and Yellowstone Counties										
City of Billings	110,245	417	10	72	54	281	4,935	631	3,746	558
Total area actually reporting	100.0%	541	12	85	64	380	5,800	802	4,358	640
Rate per 100,000 inhabitants		323.5	7.2	50.8	38.3	227.2	3,467.9	479.5	2,605.7	382.7
Binghamton, NY MSA	247,250									
Includes Broome and Tioga Counties										
City of Binghamton	46,229	305	1	49	82	173	2,048	343	1,653	52
Total area actually reporting	100.0%	621	4	150	132	335	6,247	984	5,115	148
Rate per 100,000 inhabitants		251.2	1.6	60.7	53.4	135.5	2,526.6	398.0	2,068.8	59.9
Birmingham-Hoover, AL MSA[4]	1,143,854									
Includes Bibb, Blount, Chilton, Jefferson, St. Clair, Shelby, and Walker Counties										
City of Birmingham	212,115	3,369	52	182	1,051	2,084	13,929	3,750	8,743	1,436
City of Hoover	84,843	98	1	15	50	32	2,257	270	1,908	79
Total area actually reporting	88.3%	6,206	85	451	1,769	3,901		9,676		2,711
Estimated total	100.0%	6,594	89	497	1,843	4,165		10,558		2,924
Rate per 100,000 inhabitants		576.5	7.8	43.4	161.1	364.1		923.0		255.6
Bismarck, ND MSA	126,444									
Includes Burleigh, Morton, Oliver, and Sioux Counties										
City of Bismarck	68,492	185	1	23	14	147	1,705	211	1,382	112
Total area actually reporting	100.0%	428	3	72	21	332	2,687	365	2,129	193
Rate per 100,000 inhabitants		338.5	2.4	56.9	16.6	262.6	2,125.1	288.7	1,683.7	152.6
Blacksburg-Christiansburg-Radford, VA MSA	180,931									
Includes Floyd, Giles, Montgomery, and Pulaski Counties and Radford City										
City of Blacksburg	43,842	33	2	15	3	13	393	67	311	15
City of Christiansburg	21,663	21	0	8	3	10	458	42	407	9
City of Radford	17,383	103	0	22	7	74	373	74	291	8
Total area actually reporting	100.0%	343	8	108	24	203	3,073	555	2,440	78
Rate per 100,000 inhabitants		189.6	4.4	59.7	13.3	112.2	1,698.4	306.7	1,348.6	43.1
Bloomington, IL MSA	192,070									
Includes DeWitt and McLean Counties										
City of Bloomington	79,451	327	3	56	30	238	1,668	298	1,311	59
Total area actually reporting	97.9%	517	3	101	62	351	3,347	649	2,606	92
Estimated total	100.0%	525	3	102	64	356	3,420	661	2,664	95
Rate per 100,000 inhabitants		273.3	1.6	53.1	33.3	185.3	1,780.6	344.1	1,387.0	49.5
Bloomington, IN MSA[3]	163,976									
Includes Monroe and Owen Counties										
City of Bloomington	83,075	294	1	61	81	151	2,466	487	1,854	125
Total area actually reporting	87.1%	411	1	78	104	228	3,786	730	2,859	197

Table 6. Crime, by Selected Metropolitan Statistical Area, 2014—*Continued*

(Number, percent, rate per 100,000 population.)

Area	Population	Violent crime	Murder and nonnegligent manslaughter	Rape[1]	Robbery	Aggravated assault	Property crime	Burglary	Larceny-theft	Motor vehicle theft
Estimated total..........................	100.0%	433	1	81	107	244	4,012	785	3,012	215
Rate per 100,000 inhabitants................		264.1	0.6	49.4	65.3	148.8	2,446.7	478.7	1,836.9	131.1
Boise City, ID MSA........................	663,371									
Includes Ada, Boise, Canyon, Gem, and Owyhee Counties...........										
City of Boise	216,260	641	4	123	57	457	4,511	693	3,626	192
Total area actually reporting	99.9%	1,513	11	296	92	1,114	11,745	2,252	8,891	602
Estimated total.............................	100.0%	1,514	11	296	92	1,115	11,756	2,254	8,899	603
Rate per 100,000 inhabitants................		228.2	1.7	44.6	13.9	168.1	1,772.2	339.8	1,341.5	90.9
Boulder, CO MSA[4]........................	315,369									
Includes Boulder County										
City of Boulder.............................	104,284	242	1	41	28	172	2,777	481	2,146	150
Total area actually reporting	79.7%	611	5	181	72	353		930		354
Estimated total.............................	100.0%	731	6	205	81	439		1,111		438
Rate per 100,000 inhabitants................		231.8	1.9	65.0	25.7	139.2		352.3		138.9
Bowling Green, KY MSA....................	164,892									
Includes Allen, Butler, Edmonson, and Warren Counties...............										
City of Bowling Green.......................	62,117	201	1	49	64	87	2,938	440	2,384	114
Total area actually reporting	100.0%	259	1	63	73	122	3,825	706	2,953	166
Rate per 100,000 inhabitants................		157.1	0.6	38.2	44.3	74.0	2,319.7	428.2	1,790.9	100.7
Bremerton-Silverdale, WA MSA.............	255,676									
Includes Kitsap County......................										
City of Bremerton...........................	39,359	209	0	39	39	131	1,810	345	1,311	154
Total area actually reporting	100.0%	697	7	143	84	463	7,382	1,661	5,170	551
Rate per 100,000 inhabitants................		272.6	2.7	55.9	32.9	181.1	2,887.2	649.7	2,022.1	215.5
Bridgeport-Stamford-Norwalk, CT MSA.......	927,225									
Includes Fairfield County										
City of Bridgeport	147,822	1,338	11	92	546	689	4,285	1,129	2,402	754
City of Stamford	127,385	306	2	21	146	137	2,033	275	1,554	204
City of Norwalk.............................	88,232	258	3	9	64	182	1,597	219	1,285	93
City of Danbury.............................	84,281	150	1	31	64	54	1,352	230	1,007	115
City of Stratford	52,279	64	0	7	45	12	1,310	224	961	125
Total area actually reporting	100.0%	2,268	18	185	927	1,138	14,893	2,819	10,628	1,446
Rate per 100,000 inhabitants................		244.6	1.9	20.0	100.0	122.7	1,606.2	304.0	1,146.2	155.9
Brownsville-Harlingen, TX MSA.............	422,772									
Includes Cameron County										
City of Brownsville	183,433	558	5	103	138	312	7,505	1,068	6,258	179
City of Harlingen...........................	65,808	146	0	11	34	101	2,059	412	1,589	58
Total area actually reporting	100.0%	1,095	5	188	219	683	14,022	2,552	11,113	357
Rate per 100,000 inhabitants................		259.0	1.2	44.5	51.8	161.6	3,316.7	603.6	2,628.6	84.4
Brunswick, GA MSA[3]......................	114,492									
Includes Brantley, Glynn, and McIntosh Counties[3]										
City of Brunswick[3]........................	15,912	225	2	6	58	159	1,202	325	836	41
Total area actually reporting	98.4%	472	6	26	110	330	4,678	1,120	3,393	165
Estimated total.............................	100.0%	481	6	27	113	335	4,758	1,134	3,454	170
Rate per 100,000 inhabitants................		420.1	5.2	23.6	98.7	292.6	4,155.7	990.5	3,016.8	148.5
Buffalo-Cheektowaga-Niagara Falls, NY MSA........	1,135,581									
Includes Erie and Niagara Counties										
City of Buffalo.............................	258,419	3,174	60	174	1,277	1,663	12,449	3,119	8,362	968
City of Cheektowaga Town....................	78,209	202	1	25	66	110	2,699	300	2,324	75
City of Niagara Falls.......................	49,300	581	3	26	161	391	2,641	650	1,858	133
Total area actually reporting	100.0%	4,945	72	351	1,768	2,754	30,539	5,987	22,970	1,582
Rate per 100,000 inhabitants................		435.5	6.3	30.9	155.7	242.5	2,689.3	527.2	2,022.8	139.3
Burlington, NC MSA.......................	155,421									
Includes Alamance County....................										
City of Burlington	51,627	352	3	20	88	241	2,064	460	1,506	98
Total area actually reporting	100.0%	578	3	29	130	416	4,302	1,276	2,852	174
Rate per 100,000 inhabitants................		371.9	1.9	18.7	83.6	267.7	2,768.0	821.0	1,835.0	112.0
California-Lexington Park, MD M.S.A........	110,842									
Includes St. Mary's County..................										
Total area actually reporting	100.0%	263	0	22	58	183	2,211	513	1,625	73
Rate per 100,000 inhabitants................		237.3	0.0	19.8	52.3	165.1	1,994.7	462.8	1,466.1	65.9

Table 6. Crime, by Selected Metropolitan Statistical Area, 2014—*Continued*

(Number, percent, rate per 100,000 population.)

Area	Population	Violent crime	Murder and nonnegligent manslaughter	Rape[1]	Robbery	Aggravated assault	Property crime	Burglary	Larceny-theft	Motor vehicle theft
Canton-Massillon, OH M.S.A................................	404,136									
Includes Carroll and Stark Counties.....................										
City of Canton..........................	72,391	730	8	91	228	403	3,929	1,021	2,657	251
City of Massillon........................	32,196	85	1	13	28	43	1,094	281	777	36
Total area actually reporting.............	90.8%	1,106	12	161	335	598	9,972	2,365	7,115	492
Estimated total...........................	100.0%	1,160	12	172	354	622	10,881	2,530	7,826	525
Rate per 100,000 inhabitants...............		287.0	3.0	42.6	87.6	153.9	2,692.4	626.0	1,936.5	129.9
Cape Coral-Fort Myers, FL M.S.A.	677,068									
Includes Lee County.......................										
City of Cape Coral.......................	168,712	242	4	11	41	186	3,271	679	2,440	152
City of Fort Myers.......................	69,718	769	11	43	173	542	2,176	368	1,680	128
Total area actually reporting.............	100.0%	2,975	45	218	738	1,974	17,509	4,134	12,212	1,163
Rate per 100,000 inhabitants...............		439.4	6.6	32.2	109.0	291.6	2,586.0	610.6	1,803.7	171.8
Cape Girardeau, MO-IL M.S.A.	97,805									
Includes Alexander County, IL and Bollinger and Cape Girardeau Counties, MO										
City of Cape Girardeau, MO	39,012	226	4	11	66	145	1,793	336	1,389	68
Total area actually reporting.............	100.0%	391	8	22	78	283	2,665	595	1,941	129
Rate per 100,000 inhabitants...............		399.8	8.2	22.5	79.8	289.4	2,724.8	608.4	1,984.6	131.9
Carson City, NV M.S.A.	54,298									
Includes Carson City......................										
Total area actually reporting.............	100.0%	160	1	0	15	144	875	198	623	54
Rate per 100,000 inhabitants...............		294.7	1.8	0.0	27.6	265.2	1,611.5	364.7	1,147.4	99.5
Casper, WY M.S.A.	81,960									
Includes Natrona County...................										
City of Casper..........................	60,771	84	2	4	11	67	1,632	238	1,329	65
Total area actually reporting.............	100.0%	151	3	19	13	116	1,951	306	1,559	86
Rate per 100,000 inhabitants...............		184.2	3.7	23.2	15.9	141.5	2,380.4	373.4	1,902.1	104.9
Cedar Rapids, IA M.S.A.	263,979									
Includes Benton, Jones, and Linn Counties.....										
City of Cedar Rapids....................	128,901	385	8	41	128	208	4,953	933	3,740	280
Total area actually reporting.............	88.0%	502	9	64	142	287	6,187	1,278	4,563	346
Estimated total...........................	100.0%	552	10	73	144	325	6,469	1,372	4,723	374
Rate per 100,000 inhabitants...............		209.1	3.8	27.7	54.5	123.1	2,450.6	519.7	1,789.2	141.7
Chambersburg-Waynesboro, PA M.S.A.	152,602									
Includes Franklin County..................										
City of Chambersburg....................	20,561	79	2	10	19	48	754	123	596	35
City of Waynesboro......................	10,748	32	0	9	5	18	300	71	221	8
Total area actually reporting.............	100.0%	227	5	41	61	120	3,092	593	2,372	127
Rate per 100,000 inhabitants...............		148.8	3.3	26.9	40.0	78.6	2,026.2	388.6	1,554.4	83.2
Champaign-Urbana, IL M.S.A.	235,685									
Includes Champaign, Ford, and Piatt Counties										
City of Champaign......................	83,995	624	5	42	133	444	2,255	531	1,669	55
City of Urbana.........................	41,805	130	0	18	63	49	1,467	327	1,113	27
Total area actually reporting.............	98.2%	1,083	11	99	226	747	5,356	1,323	3,916	117
Estimated total...........................	100.0%	1,091	11	100	228	752	5,433	1,336	3,977	120
Rate per 100,000 inhabitants...............		462.9	4.7	42.4	96.7	319.1	2,305.2	566.9	1,687.4	50.9
Charleston, WV M.S.A.	223,677									
Includes Boone, Clay, and Kanawha Counties										
City of Charleston......................	50,693	622	9	48	119	446	3,326	688	2,497	141
Total area actually reporting.............	90.6%	1,062	18	97	167	780	7,526	1,696	5,438	392
Estimated total...........................	100.0%	1,117	19	102	174	822	8,067	1,792	5,859	416
Rate per 100,000 inhabitants...............		499.4	8.5	45.6	77.8	367.5	3,606.5	801.2	2,619.4	186.0
Charleston-North Charleston, SC M.S.A.	727,099									
Includes Berkeley, Charleston, and Dorchester Counties										
City of Charleston......................	129,867	270	8	25	70	167	2,971	350	2,442	179
City of North Charleston................	105,594	772	23	80	241	428	5,742	797	4,441	504
Total area actually reporting.............	99.5%	2,841	58	232	573	1,978	20,907	3,692	15,524	1,691
Estimated total...........................	100.0%	2,857	58	233	576	1,990	21,050	3,713	15,639	1,698
Rate per 100,000 inhabitants...............		392.9	8.0	32.0	79.2	273.7	2,895.1	510.7	2,150.9	233.5

Table 6. Crime, by Selected Metropolitan Statistical Area, 2014—*Continued*

(Number, percent, rate per 100,000 population.)

Area	Population	Violent crime	Murder and nonnegligent manslaughter	Rape[1]	Robbery	Aggravated assault	Property crime	Burglary	Larceny-theft	Motor vehicle theft
Charlotte-Concord-Gastonia, NC-SC M.S.A.	2,370,253									
Includes Cabarrus, Gaston, Iredell, Lincoln, Mecklenburg, Rowan, and Union Counties, NC and Chester, Lancaster, and York Counties, SC										
City of Charlotte-Mecklenburg, NC..............................	856,916	5,054	47	210	1,586	3,211	30,565	6,031	22,827	1,707
City of Concord, NC	84,558	96	2	11	41	42	2,408	347	1,957	104
City of Gastonia, NC.................................	73,576	484	1	23	113	347	3,688	636	2,852	200
City of Rock Hill, SC.................................	69,754	357	5	32	64	256	2,371	370	1,932	69
Total area actually reporting	99.3%	9,256	106	526	2,345	6,279	66,370	14,145	48,919	3,306
Estimated total....................	100.0%	9,297	107	529	2,356	6,305	66,891	14,250	49,317	3,324
Rate per 100,000 inhabitants....................		392.2	4.5	22.3	99.4	266.0	2,822.1	601.2	2,080.7	140.2
Charlottesville, VA M.S.A.	225,461									
Includes Albemarle, Buckingham, Fluvanna, Greene, and Nelson Counties and Charlottesville City....................										
City of Charlottesville....................	44,574	191	5	16	39	131	1,356	173	1,100	83
Total area actually reporting	100.0%	365	9	60	58	238	4,016	559	3,275	182
Rate per 100,000 inhabitants....................		161.9	4.0	26.6	25.7	105.6	1,781.2	247.9	1,452.6	80.7
Chattanooga, TN-GA M.S.A.[3]	546,512									
Includes Catoosa, Dade, and Walker Counties, GA[3] and Hamilton, Marion, and Sequatchie Counties, TN										
City of Chattanooga, TN....................	174,449	1,699	27	106	348	1,218	10,968	2,089	7,862	1,017
Total area actually reporting	100.0%	2,912	40	194	472	2,206	20,449	4,129	14,656	1,664
Rate per 100,000 inhabitants....................		532.8	7.3	35.5	86.4	403.7	3,741.7	755.5	2,681.7	304.5
Cheyenne, WY M.S.A.	96,236									
Includes Laramie County										
City of Cheyenne	63,155	89	2	6	13	68	1,795	246	1,465	84
Total area actually reporting	100.0%	154	3	18	17	116	2,341	427	1,797	117
Rate per 100,000 inhabitants....................		160.0	3.1	18.7	17.7	120.5	2,432.6	443.7	1,867.3	121.6
Chicago-Naperville-Elgin, IL-IN-WI M.S.A.[3]....................	9,546,349									
Includes the Metropolitan Divisions of Chicago-Naperville-Arlington Heights, IL; Elgin, IL; Gary, IN; and Lake County-Kenosha County, IL-WI....................										
City of Chicago, IL....................	2,724,121	24,089	411	1,343	9,804	12,531	85,161	14,537	60,601	10,023
City of Naperville, IL....................	145,510	113	1	8	20	84	1,634	176	1,421	37
City of Elgin, IL....................	110,595	221	3	46	65	107	1,997	299	1,614	84
City of Gary, IN....................	78,013	712	37	44	278	353	4,052	1,312	2,268	472
City of Arlington Heights, IL....................	76,200	43	0	4	12	27	743	134	588	21
City of Evanston, IL....................	75,817	151	1	3	54	93	1,900	334	1,500	66
City of Schaumburg, IL....................	75,060	73	0	20	21	32	1,870	146	1,648	76
City of Skokie, IL....................	65,263	170	2	11	46	111	1,353	259	1,046	48
City of Des Plaines, IL....................	59,041	53	0	8	11	34	718	129	571	18
City of Hoffman Estates, IL....................	52,512	50	0	9	13	28	558	78	458	22
Total area actually reporting	97.8%	35,866	601	2,650	13,570	19,045	199,903	33,898	150,185	15,820
Estimated total....................	100.0%	36,281	605	2,692	13,678	19,306	203,854	34,528	153,301	16,025
Rate per 100,000 inhabitants....................		380.1	6.3	28.2	143.3	202.2	2,135.4	361.7	1,605.9	167.9
Chicago-Naperville-Arlington Heights, IL M.D.....................	7,341,262									
Includes Cook, DuPage, Grundy, Kendall, McHenry, and Will Counties....................										
Total area actually reporting	98.5%	31,125	505	2,167	12,266	16,187	159,062	26,487	118,941	13,634
Estimated total....................	100.0%	31,344	508	2,192	12,329	16,315	161,027	26,809	120,498	13,720
Rate per 100,000 inhabitants....................		427.0	6.9	29.9	167.9	222.2	2,193.5	365.2	1,641.4	186.9
Elgin, IL M.D.	629,627									
Includes DeKalb and Kane Counties....................										
Total area actually reporting	97.8%	1,073	11	163	194	705	8,696	1,284	7,185	227
Estimated total....................	100.0%	1,100	11	166	202	721	8,944	1,325	7,381	238
Rate per 100,000 inhabitants....................		174.7	1.7	26.4	32.1	114.5	1,420.5	210.4	1,172.3	37.8
Gary, IN M.D.[3]	705,329									
Includes Jasper, Lake, Newton, and Porter Counties										
Total area actually reporting	90.8%	2,257	66	130	698	1,363	17,806	3,338	12,940	1,528
Estimated total....................	100.0%	2,392	67	140	725	1,460	19,240	3,555	14,062	1,623
Rate per 100,000 inhabitants....................		339.1	9.5	19.8	102.8	207.0	2,727.8	504.0	1,993.7	230.1

Table 6. Crime, by Selected Metropolitan Statistical Area, 2014—*Continued*

(Number, percent, rate per 100,000 population.)

Area	Population	Violent crime	Murder and nonnegligent manslaughter	Rape[1]	Robbery	Aggravated assault	Property crime	Burglary	Larceny-theft	Motor vehicle theft
Lake County-Kenosha County, IL-WI M.D.	870,131									
Includes Lake County, IL and Kenosha County, WI										
Total area actually reporting	98.0%	1,411	19	190	412	790	14,339	2,789	11,119	431
Estimated total	100.0%	1,445	19	194	422	810	14,643	2,839	11,360	444
Rate per 100,000 inhabitants		166.1	2.2	22.3	48.5	93.1	1,682.9	326.3	1,305.6	51.0
Chico, CA M.S.A.	223,878									
Includes Butte County										
City of Chico	88,562	340	1	53	100	186	3,213	483	2,385	345
Total area actually reporting	100.0%	678	11	76	149	442	6,631	1,667	4,204	760
Rate per 100,000 inhabitants		302.8	4.9	33.9	66.6	197.4	2,961.9	744.6	1,877.8	339.5
Cincinnati, OH-KY-IN M.S.A.[3]	2,145,462									
Includes Dearborn, Ohio, and Union Counties, IN; Boone, Bracken, Campbell, Gallatin, Grant, Kenton, and Pendleton Counties, KY; and Brown, Butler, Clermont, Hamilton, and Warren Counties, OH										
City of Cincinnati, OH	297,671	2,695	60	228	1,356	1,051	16,557	4,820	10,639	1,098
Total area actually reporting	92.8%	5,535	95	752	2,363	2,325	60,595	13,083	44,802	2,710
Estimated total	100.0%	5,734	98	787	2,416	2,433	63,461	13,680	46,936	2,845
Rate per 100,000 inhabitants		267.3	4.6	36.7	112.6	113.4	2,957.9	637.6	2,187.7	132.6
Clarksville, TN-KY M.S.A.	276,035									
Includes Christian and Trigg Counties, KY and Montgomery County, TN										
City of Clarksville, TN	144,639	967	10	65	100	792	4,272	973	3,114	185
Total area actually reporting	99.7%	1,268	17	104	160	987	6,900	1,670	4,924	306
Estimated total	100.0%	1,270	17	104	161	988	6,922	1,674	4,941	307
Rate per 100,000 inhabitants		460.1	6.2	37.7	58.3	357.9	2,507.7	606.4	1,790.0	111.2
Cleveland, TN M.S.A.	119,510									
Includes Bradley and Polk Counties										
City of Cleveland	43,135	370	1	20	28	321	2,583	481	1,955	147
Total area actually reporting	100.0%	591	2	32	34	523	4,086	947	2,864	275
Rate per 100,000 inhabitants		494.5	1.7	26.8	28.4	437.6	3,419.0	792.4	2,396.5	230.1
Coeur d'Alene, ID M.S.A.	146,681									
Includes Kootenai County										
City of Coeur d'Alene	46,952	239	2	40	22	175	1,822	334	1,347	141
Total area actually reporting	100.0%	405	4	56	36	309	3,870	790	2,813	267
Rate per 100,000 inhabitants		276.1	2.7	38.2	24.5	210.7	2,638.4	538.6	1,917.8	182.0
College Station-Bryan, TX M.S.A.	240,441									
Includes Brazos, Burleson, and Robertson Counties										
City of College Station	101,483	191	0	45	31	115	2,343	517	1,748	78
City of Bryan	79,267	338	5	68	58	207	2,521	549	1,865	107
Total area actually reporting	100.0%	703	5	126	95	477	6,026	1,388	4,419	219
Rate per 100,000 inhabitants		292.4	2.1	52.4	39.5	198.4	2,506.2	577.3	1,837.9	91.1
Colorado Springs, CO M.S.A.	689,470									
Includes El Paso and Teller Counties										
City of Colorado Springs	444,949	2,039	20	412	404	1,203	16,319	2,759	11,914	1,646
Total area actually reporting	100.0%	2,660	23	516	442	1,679	19,879	3,573	14,403	1,903
Rate per 100,000 inhabitants		385.8	3.3	74.8	64.1	243.5	2,883.2	518.2	2,089.0	276.0
Columbia, MO M.S.A.	172,934									
Includes Boone County										
City of Columbia	116,847	410	5	63	116	226	3,988	750	3,069	169
Total area actually reporting	100.0%	592	6	80	131	375	5,143	910	4,007	226
Rate per 100,000 inhabitants		342.3	3.5	46.3	75.8	216.8	2,974.0	526.2	2,317.1	130.7
Columbia, SC M.S.A.	803,559									
Includes Calhoun, Fairfield, Kershaw, Lexington, Richland, and Saluda Counties										
City of Columbia	134,124	1,004	8	71	320	605	7,191	1,102	5,416	673
Total area actually reporting	92.9%	4,446	49	341	802	3,254	25,798	4,531	18,871	2,396
Estimated total	100.0%	4,705	52	364	838	3,451	27,417	4,945	19,931	2,541
Rate per 100,000 inhabitants		585.5	6.5	45.3	104.3	429.5	3,411.9	615.4	2,480.3	316.2
Columbus, GA-AL M.S.A.[3]	322,951									
Includes Russell County, AL and Chattahoochee, Harris, Marion, and Muscogee Counties, GA[3]										

Table 6. Crime, by Selected Metropolitan Statistical Area, 2014—*Continued*

(Number, percent, rate per 100,000 population.)

Area	Population	Violent crime	Murder and nonnegligent manslaughter	Rape[1]	Robbery	Aggravated assault	Property crime	Burglary	Larceny-theft	Motor vehicle theft
City of Columbus, GA[3]	206,714	1,101	22	47	511	521	13,378	3,711	8,495	1,172
Total area actually reporting	96.8%	1,386	29	84	564	709	16,259	4,513	10,258	1,488
Estimated total	100.0%	1,420	29	86	576	729	16,592	4,587	10,490	1,515
Rate per 100,000 inhabitants		439.7	9.0	26.6	178.4	225.7	5,137.6	1,420.3	3,248.2	469.1
Columbus, IN M.S.A.[3]	80,345									
Includes Bartholomew County										
City of Columbus	46,196	45	0	12	20	13	2,001	204	1,630	167
Total area actually reporting	100.0%	88	0	14	24	50	2,573	332	2,032	209
Rate per 100,000 inhabitants		109.5	0.0	17.4	29.9	62.2	3,202.4	413.2	2,529.1	260.1
Columbus, OH M.S.A.	1,985,491									
Includes Delaware, Fairfield, Franklin, Hocking, Licking, Madison, Morrow, Perry, Pickaway, and Union Counties										
City of Columbus	830,811	4,563	83	738	2,098	1,644	35,334	9,066	23,328	2,940
Total area actually reporting	94.0%	5,677	93	1,035	2,465	2,084	58,583	13,723	41,181	3,679
Estimated total	100.0%	5,855	95	1,070	2,528	2,162	61,508	14,255	43,469	3,784
Rate per 100,000 inhabitants		294.9	4.8	53.9	127.3	108.9	3,097.9	718.0	2,189.3	190.6
Corpus Christi, TX M.S.A.	449,583									
Includes Aransas, Nueces, and San Patricio Counties										
City of Corpus Christi	319,211	2,094	27	280	377	1,410	14,110	2,316	11,233	561
Total area actually reporting	100.0%	2,650	30	342	424	1,854	18,365	3,471	14,136	758
Rate per 100,000 inhabitants		589.4	6.7	76.1	94.3	412.4	4,084.9	772.0	3,144.2	168.6
Corvallis, OR M.S.A.	87,222									
Includes Benton County										
City of Corvallis	55,541	72	0	16	12	44	1,737	225	1,476	36
Total area actually reporting	100.0%	105	0	22	16	67	2,219	321	1,835	63
Rate per 100,000 inhabitants		120.4	0.0	25.2	18.3	76.8	2,544.1	368.0	2,103.8	72.2
Crestview-Fort Walton Beach-Destin, FL M.S.A.	260,307									
Includes Okaloosa and Walton Counties										
City of Crestview	23,251	128	1	28	28	71	740	158	549	33
City of Fort Walton Beach	20,881	71	0	8	19	44	693	96	560	37
Total area actually reporting	99.7%	1,295	4	144	153	994	7,622	1,628	5,683	311
Estimated total	100.0%	1,298	4	144	154	996	7,649	1,633	5,703	313
Rate per 100,000 inhabitants		498.6	1.5	55.3	59.2	382.6	2,938.5	627.3	2,190.9	120.2
Cumberland, MD-WV M.S.A.	100,807									
Includes Allegany County, MD and Mineral County, WV										
City of Cumberland, MD	20,364	149	0	11	23	115	1,306	292	997	17
Total area actually reporting	98.5%	257	3	20	34	200	2,769	656	2,050	63
Estimated total	100.0%	261	3	20	35	203	2,818	663	2,090	65
Rate per 100,000 inhabitants		258.9	3.0	19.8	34.7	201.4	2,795.4	657.7	2,073.3	64.5
Dalton, GA M.S.A.[3]	142,646									
Includes Murray and Whitfield Counties[3]										
City of Dalton[3]	33,464	90	3	14	15	58	1,242	203	979	60
Total area actually reporting	98.3%	305	4	36	23	242	3,806	839	2,732	235
Estimated total	100.0%	316	4	37	27	248	3,912	858	2,812	242
Rate per 100,000 inhabitants		221.5	2.8	25.9	18.9	173.9	2,742.5	601.5	1,971.3	169.7
Danville, IL M.S.A.	79,939									
Includes Vermilion County										
City of Danville	32,404	348	0	43	77	228	1,878	630	1,191	57
Total area actually reporting	98.4%	470	1	73	85	311	2,770	912	1,767	91
Estimated total	100.0%	473	1	73	86	313	2,793	916	1,785	92
Rate per 100,000 inhabitants		591.7	1.3	91.3	107.6	391.5	3,493.9	1,145.9	2,233.0	115.1
Daphne-Fairhope-Foley, AL M.S.A.	198,874									
Includes Baldwin County										
City of Daphne	24,111	41	0	7	5	29	477	64	401	12
City of Fairhope	17,914	54	0	3	7	44	564	111	443	10
City of Foley	16,101	51	1	1	13	36	783	98	664	21
Total area actually reporting	96.2%	365	4	32	61	268	3,990	755	3,116	119
Estimated total	100.0%	396	4	35	68	289	4,265	811	3,318	136
Rate per 100,000 inhabitants		199.1	2.0	17.6	34.2	145.3	2,144.6	407.8	1,668.4	68.4
Davenport-Moline-Rock Island, IA-IL M.S.A.	384,694									
Includes Henry, Mercer, and Rock Island Counties, IL and Scott County, IA										

Table 6. Crime, by Selected Metropolitan Statistical Area, 2014—*Continued*

(Number, percent, rate per 100,000 population.)

Area	Population	Violent crime	Murder and nonnegligent manslaughter	Rape[1]	Robbery	Aggravated assault	Property crime	Burglary	Larceny-theft	Motor vehicle theft
City of Davenport, IA	102,715	636	2	100	166	368	4,190	932	3,008	250
City of Moline, IL	43,017	156	0	11	16	129	1,447	232	1,196	19
City of Rock Island, IL	38,844	157	1	14	22	120	875	157	676	42
Total area actually reporting	94.5%	1,335	4	175	227	929	9,059	1,777	6,900	382
Estimated total	100.0%	1,367	4	180	232	951	9,340	1,840	7,105	395
Rate per 100,000 inhabitants		355.3	1.0	46.8	60.3	247.2	2,427.9	478.3	1,846.9	102.7
Dayton, OH M.S.A.[4]	803,779									
Includes Greene, Miami, and Montgomery Counties										
City of Dayton	143,217	1,225	27	135	535	528	7,963	2,976	4,397	590
Total area actually reporting	97.8%	2,150	34	380	877	859		6,577		1,290
Estimated total	100.0%	2,176	34	385	886	871		6,656		1,306
Rate per 100,000 inhabitants		270.7	4.2	47.9	110.2	108.4		828.1		162.5
Decatur, AL M.S.A.	153,346									
Includes Lawrence and Morgan Counties										
City of Decatur	55,836	112	0	7	25	80	2,451	434	1,883	134
Total area actually reporting	98.4%	246	2	36	40	168	3,660	791	2,631	238
Estimated total	100.0%	256	2	37	42	175	3,750	809	2,697	244
Rate per 100,000 inhabitants		166.9	1.3	24.1	27.4	114.1	2,445.5	527.6	1,758.8	159.1
Decatur, IL M.S.A.	108,808									
Includes Macon County										
City of Decatur	74,373	355	1	10	93	251	2,225	644	1,519	62
Total area actually reporting	100.0%	397	2	12	101	282	2,647	739	1,843	65
Rate per 100,000 inhabitants		364.9	1.8	11.0	92.8	259.2	2,432.7	679.2	1,693.8	59.7
Deltona-Daytona Beach-Ormond Beach, FL M.S.A.	608,127									
Includes Flagler and Volusia Counties										
City of Daytona Beach	62,629	804	4	69	153	578	3,974	628	2,992	354
City of Ormond Beach	38,782	166	0	0	15	151	1,555	259	1,226	70
Total area actually reporting	99.7%	2,796	12	251	421	2,112	19,614	3,945	14,441	1,228
Estimated total	100.0%	2,804	12	252	423	2,117	19,672	3,956	14,485	1,231
Rate per 100,000 inhabitants		461.1	2.0	41.4	69.6	348.1	3,234.9	650.5	2,381.9	202.4
Denver-Aurora-Lakewood, CO M.S.A.[4]	2,750,394									
Includes Adams, Arapahoe, Broomfield, Clear Creek, Denver, Douglas, Elbert, Gilpin, Jefferson, and Park Counties										
City of Denver	665,353	3,983	31	448	1,091	2,413	22,352	4,555	14,363	3,434
City of Aurora	350,948	1,448	11	274	417	746	9,962	1,816	7,082	1,064
City of Lakewood	148,236	712	5	116	137	454	6,844	898	5,293	653
City of Broomfield	60,693	31	0	15	5	11	1,036	114	886	36
Total area actually reporting	99.9%	9,108	76	1,509	2,064	5,459			52,008	8,042
Estimated total	100.0%	9,109	76	1,509	2,064	5,460			52,026	8,044
Rate per 100,000 inhabitants		331.2	2.8	54.9	75.0	198.5			1,891.6	292.5
Des Moines-West Des Moines, IA M.S.A.	608,260									
Includes Dallas, Guthrie, Madison, Polk, and Warren Counties										
City of Des Moines	208,250	1,250	9	87	267	887	8,841	1,888	6,083	870
City of West Des Moines	62,359	116	0	17	15	84	1,562	136	1,363	63
Total area actually reporting	100.0%	1,927	11	196	299	1,421	15,198	2,910	11,023	1,265
Rate per 100,000 inhabitants		316.8	1.8	32.2	49.2	233.6	2,498.6	478.4	1,812.2	208.0
Detroit-Warren-Dearborn, MI M.S.A.	4,299,979									
Includes the Metropolitan Divisions of Detroit-Dearborn-Livonia and Warren-Troy-Farmington Hills										
City of Detroit	684,694	13,616	298	557	3,570	9,191	32,983	9,177	13,723	10,083
City of Warren	135,080	641	4	99	160	378	3,427	742	2,144	541
City of Dearborn	95,396	339	2	34	97	206	3,135	338	2,386	411
City of Livonia	94,833	120	1	16	20	83	1,772	207	1,417	148
City of Troy	83,279	50	1	8	10	31	1,359	156	1,133	70
City of Farmington Hills	81,682	95	0	17	19	59	977	190	707	80
City of Southfield	73,321	230	3	33	85	109	2,150	321	1,471	358
City of Taylor	61,527	343	2	52	70	219	1,797	435	1,160	202
City of Novi	58,654	47	1	13	7	26	853	53	760	40
Total area actually reporting	99.5%	22,712	374	1,920	5,388	15,030	94,351	20,016	57,874	16,461
Estimated total	100.0%	22,765	374	1,929	5,398	15,064	94,758	20,087	58,180	16,491
Rate per 100,000 inhabitants		529.4	8.7	44.9	125.5	350.3	2,203.7	467.1	1,353.0	383.5
Detroit-Dearborn-Livonia, MI M.D.	1,766,912									
Includes Wayne County										

Table 6. Crime, by Selected Metropolitan Statistical Area, 2014—*Continued*

(Number, percent, rate per 100,000 population.)

Area	Population	Violent crime	Murder and nonnegligent manslaughter	Rape[1]	Robbery	Aggravated assault	Property crime	Burglary	Larceny-theft	Motor vehicle theft
Total area actually reporting	98.9%	17,299	336	993	4,388	11,582	57,075	13,674	30,240	13,161
Estimated total	100.0%	17,352	336	1,002	4,398	11,616	57,482	13,745	30,546	13,191
Rate per 100,000 inhabitants		982.1	19.0	56.7	248.9	657.4	3,253.2	777.9	1,728.8	746.6
Warren-Troy-Farmington Hills, MI M.D.	2,533,067									
Includes Lapeer, Livingston, Macomb, Oakland, and St. Clair Counties										
Total area actually reporting	100.0%	5,413	38	927	1,000	3,448	37,276	6,342	27,634	3,300
Rate per 100,000 inhabitants		213.7	1.5	36.6	39.5	136.1	1,471.6	250.4	1,090.9	130.3
Dover, DE M.S.A.	171,672									
Includes Kent County										
City of Dover	37,671	242	2	14	64	162	1,874	74	1,736	64
Total area actually reporting	100.0%	726	5	101	121	499	4,699	711	3,810	178
Rate per 100,000 inhabitants		422.9	2.9	58.8	70.5	290.7	2,737.2	414.2	2,219.3	103.7
Dubuque, IA M.S.A.	96,347									
Includes Dubuque County										
City of Dubuque	58,421	145	0	27	20	98	1,513	383	1,071	59
Total area actually reporting	100.0%	171	0	35	22	114	1,728	448	1,203	77
Rate per 100,000 inhabitants		177.5	0.0	36.3	22.8	118.3	1,793.5	465.0	1,248.6	79.9
Duluth, MN-WI M.S.A.	280,297									
Includes Carlton and St. Louis Counties, MN and Douglas County, WI										
City of Duluth, MN	86,106	309	3	42	73	191	3,650	503	3,002	145
Total area actually reporting	100.0%	629	7	103	122	397	8,833	1,438	6,927	468
Rate per 100,000 inhabitants		224.4	2.5	36.7	43.5	141.6	3,151.3	513.0	2,471.3	167.0
Durham-Chapel Hill, NC M.S.A.	542,584									
Includes Chatham, Durham, Orange and Person Counties										
City of Durham	249,738	1,834	21	73	654	1,086	11,085	3,652	6,853	580
City of Chapel Hill	60,190	86	2	13	29	42	1,347	360	921	66
Total area actually reporting	100.0%	2,315	26	125	740	1,424	17,681	5,700	11,147	834
Rate per 100,000 inhabitants		426.7	4.8	23.0	136.4	262.4	3,258.7	1,050.5	2,054.4	153.7
East Stroudsburg, PA M.S.A.	166,423									
Includes Monroe County										
Total area actually reporting	99.6%	362	5	72	63	222	4,042	1,085	2,845	112
Estimated total	100.0%	363	5	72	63	223	4,054	1,087	2,855	112
Rate per 100,000 inhabitants		218.1	3.0	43.3	37.9	134.0	2,436.0	653.2	1,715.5	67.3
Eau Claire, WI M.S.A.[4]	165,411									
Includes Chippewa and Eau Claire Counties										
City of Eau Claire	67,937	110	1	21	16	72	1,727	287	1,368	72
Total area actually reporting	100.0%	217	1	45	19	152	2,874	522	2,227	125
Rate per 100,000 inhabitants		131.2	0.6	27.2	11.5	91.9	1,737.5	315.6	1,346.3	75.6
El Centro, CA M.S.A.	178,032									
Includes Imperial County										
City of El Centro	43,532	167	0	12	59	96	2,095	406	1,544	145
Total area actually reporting	96.1%	583	3	33	113	434	5,536	1,303	3,608	625
Estimated total	100.0%	604	3	34	120	447	5,699	1,338	3,712	649
Rate per 100,000 inhabitants		339.3	1.7	19.1	67.4	251.1	3,201.1	751.6	2,085.0	364.5
Elizabethtown-Fort Knox, KY M.S.A.	152,068									
Includes Hardin, Larue, and Meade Counties										
City of Elizabethtown	30,208	41	0	16	8	17	1,069	154	886	29
Total area actually reporting	100.0%	140	1	42	26	71	2,012	425	1,501	86
Rate per 100,000 inhabitants		92.1	0.7	27.6	17.1	46.7	1,323.1	279.5	987.1	56.6
Elkhart-Goshen, IN M.S.A.[3]	201,503									
Includes Elkhart County										
City of Elkhart	51,366	646	1	20	79	546	2,283	615	1,484	184
City of Goshen	32,337	36	0	13	15	8	1,240	240	934	66
Total area actually reporting	100.0%	720	4	49	106	561	4,331	1,048	2,948	335
Rate per 100,000 inhabitants		357.3	2.0	24.3	52.6	278.4	2,149.3	520.1	1,463.0	166.3
Elmira, NY M.S.A.	88,535									
Includes Chemung County										
City of Elmira	28,803	80	1	0	29	50	964	230	712	22

Table 6. Crime, by Selected Metropolitan Statistical Area, 2014—*Continued*

(Number, percent, rate per 100,000 population.)

Area	Population	Violent crime	Murder and nonnegligent manslaughter	Rape[1]	Robbery	Aggravated assault	Property crime	Burglary	Larceny-theft	Motor vehicle theft
Total area actually reporting	100.0%	159	1	19	33	106	1,981	344	1,593	44
Rate per 100,000 inhabitants		179.6	1.1	21.5	37.3	119.7	2,237.5	388.5	1,799.3	49.7
El Paso, TX M.S.A.	843,273									
Includes El Paso and Hudspeth Counties										
City of El Paso	680,273	2,671	21	335	415	1,900	14,570	1,579	12,170	821
Total area actually reporting	100.0%	3,109	27	388	440	2,254	17,116	2,044	14,110	962
Rate per 100,000 inhabitants		368.7	3.2	46.0	52.2	267.3	2,029.7	242.4	1,673.2	114.1
Erie, PA M.S.A.	280,129									
Includes Erie County										
City of Erie	100,403	406	10	52	96	248	2,640	772	1,794	74
Total area actually reporting	100.0%	635	13	103	139	380	5,948	1,329	4,484	135
Rate per 100,000 inhabitants		226.7	4.6	36.8	49.6	135.7	2,123.3	474.4	1,600.7	48.2
Evansville, IN-KY M.S.A.[3]	315,179									
Includes Posey, Vanderburgh, and Warrick Counties, IN and Henderson County, KY										
City of Evansville	120,372	623	9	69	223	322	6,883	1,087	5,250	546
Total area actually reporting	100.0%	919	10	101	248	560	10,282	1,888	7,704	690
Rate per 100,000 inhabitants		291.6	3.2	32.0	78.7	177.7	3,262.3	599.0	2,444.3	218.9
Fairbanks, AK M.S.A.	34,712									
Includes Fairbanks North Star Borough										
City of Fairbanks	32,477	214	4	39	52	119	1,247	155	969	123
Total area actually reporting	100.0%	225	4	38	55	128	1,391	179	1,082	130
Rate per 100,000 inhabitants		648.2	11.5	109.5	158.4	368.7	4,007.3	515.7	3,117.1	374.5
Fargo, ND-MN M.S.A.	227,885									
Includes Clay County, MN and Cass County, ND										
City of Fargo, ND	115,686	410	4	80	76	250	3,042	539	2,304	199
Total area actually reporting	100.0%	574	5	118	94	357	4,958	898	3,720	340
Rate per 100,000 inhabitants		251.9	2.2	51.8	41.2	156.7	2,175.7	394.1	1,632.4	149.2
Farmington, NM M.S.A.	125,309									
Includes San Juan County										
City of Farmington	45,289	301	2	56	52	191	1,521	307	1,116	98
Total area actually reporting	100.0%	670	5	101	57	507	2,485	570	1,750	165
Rate per 100,000 inhabitants		534.7	4.0	80.6	45.5	404.6	1,983.1	454.9	1,396.5	131.7
Fayetteville, NC M.S.A.	380,427									
Includes Cumberland and Hoke Counties										
City of Fayetteville	205,306	1,039	19	72	470	478	10,524	2,510	7,427	587
Total area actually reporting	100.0%	1,745	37	100	649	959	16,761	4,484	11,436	841
Rate per 100,000 inhabitants		458.7	9.7	26.3	170.6	252.1	4,405.8	1,178.7	3,006.1	221.1
Flagstaff, AZ M.S.A.	138,202									
Includes Coconino County										
City of Flagstaff	69,490	275	3	30	46	196	3,020	215	2,722	83
Total area actually reporting	100.0%	481	8	67	53	353	4,401	478	3,799	124
Rate per 100,000 inhabitants		348.0	5.8	48.5	38.3	255.4	3,184.5	345.9	2,748.9	89.7
Flint, MI M.S.A.	413,377									
Includes Genesee County										
City of Flint	99,166	1,694	28	115	277	1,274	3,891	1,677	1,944	270
Total area actually reporting	99.9%	2,695	32	289	484	1,890	11,293	3,637	7,096	560
Estimated total	100.0%	2,696	32	289	484	1,891	11,301	3,638	7,102	561
Rate per 100,000 inhabitants		652.2	7.7	69.9	117.1	457.5	2,733.8	880.1	1,718.0	135.7
Florence, SC M.S.A.	207,327									
Includes Darlington and Florence Counties										
City of Florence	37,951	332	2	18	60	252	2,800	481	2,196	123
Total area actually reporting	98.9%	1,071	11	60	190	810	9,086	2,206	6,393	487
Estimated total	100.0%	1,082	11	61	192	818	9,180	2,220	6,468	492
Rate per 100,000 inhabitants		521.9	5.3	29.4	92.6	394.5	4,427.8	1,070.8	3,119.7	237.3
Florence-Muscle Shoals, AL M.S.A.	147,427									
Includes Colbert and Lauderdale Counties										
City of Florence	40,236	202	1	25	44	132	1,476	250	1,137	89
City of Muscle Shoals	13,584	45	0	10	10	25	786	138	596	52
Total area actually reporting	99.8%	501	3	70	75	353	4,128	922	2,888	318

Table 6. Crime, by Selected Metropolitan Statistical Area, 2014—*Continued*

(Number, percent, rate per 100,000 population.)

Area	Population	Violent crime	Murder and nonnegligent manslaughter	Rape[1]	Robbery	Aggravated assault	Property crime	Burglary	Larceny-theft	Motor vehicle theft
Estimated total..............	100.0%	502	3	70	75	354	4,139	924	2,896	319
Rate per 100,000 inhabitants.............		340.5	2.0	47.5	50.9	240.1	2,807.5	626.8	1,964.4	216.4
Fond du Lac, WI M.S.A..............	101,856									
Includes Fond du Lac County.............										
City of Fond du Lac.............	42,953	141	1	30	12	98	1,203	100	1,075	28
Total area actually reporting.............	100.0%	203	2	42	15	144	1,597	188	1,362	47
Rate per 100,000 inhabitants.............		199.3	2.0	41.2	14.7	141.4	1,567.9	184.6	1,337.2	46.1
Fort Collins, CO M.S.A..............	321,817									
Includes Larimer County.............										
City of Fort Collins.............	154,015	329	1	41	36	251	3,782	489	3,142	151
Total area actually reporting.............	100.0%	617	4	114	53	446	6,927	942	5,668	317
Rate per 100,000 inhabitants.............		191.7	1.2	35.4	16.5	138.6	2,152.5	292.7	1,761.2	98.5
Fort Smith, AR-OK M.S.A..............	279,713									
Includes Crawford and Sebastian Counties, AR and Le Flore and Sequoyah Counties, OK										
City of Fort Smith, AR.............	87,989	663	4	74	106	479	4,672	866	3,625	181
Total area actually reporting.............	99.7%	1,186	6	146	131	903	8,656	1,950	6,303	403
Estimated total.............	100.0%	1,188	6	146	131	905	8,681	1,956	6,321	404
Rate per 100,000 inhabitants.............		424.7	2.1	52.2	46.8	323.5	·3,103.5	699.3	2,259.8	144.4
Fort Wayne, IN M.S.A.[3].............	426,293									
Includes Allen, Wells, and Whitley Counties.............										
City of Fort Wayne.............	257,172	816	12	104	347	353	8,352	1,765	6,223	364
Total area actually reporting.............	94.7%	956	13	121	394	428	10,186	2,069	7,652	465
Estimated total.............	100.0%	979	13	124	397	445	10,430	2,128	7,817	485
Rate per 100,000 inhabitants.............		229.7	3.0	29.1	93.1	104.4	2,446.7	499.2	1,833.7	113.8
Fresno, CA M.S.A..............	966,353									
Includes Fresno County.............										
City of Fresno.............	513,187	2,382	47	53	781	1,501	21,101	4,721	13,277	3,103
Total area actually reporting.............	100.0%	4,548	59	183	1,040	3,266	32,598	7,838	19,914	4,846
Rate per 100,000 inhabitants.............		470.6	6.1	18.9	107.6	338.0	3,373.3	811.1	2,060.7	501.5
Gadsden, AL M.S.A.[4].............	103,851									
Includes Etowah County.............										
City of Gadsden.............	36,455	358	3	31	89	235	2,806	733	1,879	194
Total area actually reporting.............	99.3%	512	3	71	95	343		1,161		281
Estimated total.............	100.0%	515	3	71	96	345		1,166		283
Rate per 100,000 inhabitants.............		495.9	2.9	68.4	92.4	332.2		1,122.8		272.5
Gainesville, FL M.S.A..............	274,003									
Includes Alachua and Gilchrist Counties.............										
City of Gainesville.............	128,185	817	2	102	150	563	4,580	594	3,688	298
Total area actually reporting.............	99.6%	1,808	11	193	279	1,325	8,800	1,677	6,649	474
Estimated total.............	100.0%	1,812	11	193	280	1,328	8,833	1,683	6,674	476
Rate per 100,000 inhabitants.............		661.3	4.0	70.4	102.2	484.7	3,223.7	614.2	2,435.7	173.7
Gainesville, GA M.S.A.[3].............	190,345									
Includes Hall County[3].............										
City of Gainesville[3].............	35,967	131	2	16	33	80	1,492	214	1,202	76
Total area actually reporting.............	100.0%	336	7	31	73	225	3,717	852	2,554	311
Rate per 100,000 inhabitants.............		176.5	3.7	16.3	38.4	118.2	1,952.8	447.6	1,341.8	163.4
Gettysburg, PA M.S.A..............	101,545									
Includes Adams County.............										
City of Gettysburg.............	7,667	29	0	6	2	21	130	17	112	1
Total area actually reporting.............	99.4%	103	0	20	10	73	1,118	221	864	33
Estimated total.............	100.0%	104	0	20	10	74	1,129	223	873	33
Rate per 100,000 inhabitants.............		102.4	0.0	19.7	9.8	72.9	1,111.8	219.6	859.7	32.5
Glens Falls, NY M.S.A..............	128,487									
Includes Warren and Washington Counties.............										
City of Glens Falls.............	14,518	25	0	8	4	13	338	39	293	6
Total area actually reporting.............	100.0%	143	0	60	10	73	1,787	273	1,481	33
Rate per 100,000 inhabitants.............		111.3	0.0	46.7	7.8	56.8	1,390.8	212.5	1,152.6	25.7
Goldsboro, NC M.S.A..............	125,267									
Includes Wayne County.............										

Table 6. Crime, by Selected Metropolitan Statistical Area, 2014—*Continued*

(Number, percent, rate per 100,000 population.)

Area	Population	Violent crime	Murder and nonnegligent manslaughter	Rape[1]	Robbery	Aggravated assault	Property crime	Burglary	Larceny-theft	Motor vehicle theft
City of Goldsboro	36,481	328	6	1	74	247	2,209	462	1,655	92
Total area actually reporting	97.7%	455	7	2	104	342	4,153	1,185	2,761	207
Estimated total	100.0%	462	7	2	106	347	4,243	1,203	2,830	210
Rate per 100,000 inhabitants		368.8	5.6	1.6	84.6	277.0	3,387.2	960.3	2,259.2	167.6
Grand Forks, ND-MN M.S.A.	101,602									
Includes Polk County, MN and Grand Forks County, ND										
City of Grand Forks, ND	55,438	127	1	24	15	87	1,545	246	1,208	91
Total area actually reporting	100.0%	210	1	52	15	142	2,222	392	1,694	136
Rate per 100,000 inhabitants		206.7	1.0	51.2	14.8	139.8	2,187.0	385.8	1,667.3	133.9
Grand Island, NE M.S.A.	84,623									
Includes Hall, Hamilton, Howard, and Merrick Counties										
City of Grand Island	50,999	131	0	34	8	89	2,223	403	1,719	101
Total area actually reporting	92.5%	164	0	37	8	119	2,604	540	1,937	127
Estimated total	100.0%	171	0	39	9	123	2,689	555	2,002	132
Rate per 100,000 inhabitants		202.1	0.0	46.1	10.6	145.4	3,177.6	655.9	2,365.8	156.0
Grand Junction, CO M.S.A.	148,670									
Includes Mesa County										
City of Grand Junction	59,972	286	1	64	42	179	2,530	265	2,164	101
Total area actually reporting	99.5%	518	3	110	57	348	3,874	541	3,118	215
Estimated total	100.0%	519	3	110	57	349	3,891	543	3,132	216
Rate per 100,000 inhabitants		349.1	2.0	74.0	38.3	234.7	2,617.2	365.2	2,106.7	145.3
Grand Rapids-Wyoming, MI M.S.A.[4]	1,024,499									
Includes Barry, Kent, Montcalm, and Ottawa Counties										
City of Grand Rapids[4]	193,385	1,381	7	86	426	862		1,126	3,755	
City of Wyoming	74,603	289	5	49	41	194	1,518	313	1,066	139
Total area actually reporting	99.2%	3,196	22	665	608	1,901		3,658	13,809	
Estimated total	100.0%	3,217	22	669	612	1,914		3,686	13,931	
Rate per 100,000 inhabitants		314.0	2.1	65.3	59.7	186.8		359.8	1,359.8	
Great Falls, MT M.S.A.	82,773									
Includes Cascade County										
City of Great Falls	59,501	162	0	28	21	113	2,561	314	2,130	117
Total area actually reporting	100.0%	205	0	37	23	145	2,722	353	2,249	120
Rate per 100,000 inhabitants		247.7	0.0	44.7	27.8	175.2	3,288.5	426.5	2,717.1	145.0
Greeley, CO M.S.A.	275,436									
Includes Weld County										
City of Greeley	97,406	485	1	74	61	349	3,292	499	2,593	200
Total area actually reporting	97.7%	778	5	114	75	584	5,413	936	4,126	351
Estimated total	100.0%	791	5	117	77	592	5,574	957	4,254	363
Rate per 100,000 inhabitants		287.2	1.8	42.5	28.0	214.9	2,023.7	347.4	1,544.5	131.8
Green Bay, WI M.S.A.[4]	313,920									
Includes Brown, Kewaunee, and Oconto Counties										
City of Green Bay	104,979	520	3	51	63	403	2,310	406	1,819	85
Total area actually reporting	84.1%	641	3	66	71	501		684		128
Estimated total	100.0%	687	3	72	81	531		796		155
Rate per 100,000 inhabitants		218.8	1.0	22.9	25.8	169.2		253.6		49.4
Greensboro-High Point, NC M.S.A.	746,709									
Includes Guilford, Randolph, and Rockingham Counties										
City of Greensboro	282,203	1,346	23	52	487	784	10,160	2,508	7,119	533
City of High Point	108,540	505	4	23	142	336	3,863	998	2,628	237
Total area actually reporting	99.8%	2,393	33	106	740	1,514	22,855	6,100	15,698	1,057
Estimated total	100.0%	2,396	33	106	741	1,516	22,895	6,108	15,729	1,058
Rate per 100,000 inhabitants		320.9	4.4	14.2	99.2	203.0	3,066.1	818.0	2,106.4	141.7
Greenville, NC M.S.A.	176,019									
Includes Pitt County										
City of Greenville	90,198	468	4	13	144	307	3,685	800	2,771	114
Total area actually reporting	98.3%	720	6	28	191	495	5,405	1,313	3,916	176
Estimated total	100.0%	728	6	29	193	500	5,498	1,332	3,987	179
Rate per 100,000 inhabitants		413.6	3.4	16.5	109.6	284.1	3,123.5	756.7	2,265.1	101.7
Hammond, LA M.S.A.	126,481									
Includes Tangipahoa Parish										
City of Hammond	20,416	240	1	7	54	178	2,152	782	1,368	2

Table 6. Crime, by Selected Metropolitan Statistical Area, 2014—*Continued*

(Number, percent, rate per 100,000 population.)

Area	Population	Violent crime	Murder and nonnegligent manslaughter	Rape[1]	Robbery	Aggravated assault	Property crime	Burglary	Larceny-theft	Motor vehicle theft
Total area actually reporting.......	98.4%	954	10	51	122	771	6,629	2,209	4,124	296
Estimated total.......	100.0%	963	10	52	123	778	6,711	2,224	4,186	301
Rate per 100,000 inhabitants.......		761.4	7.9	41.1	97.2	615.1	5,305.9	1,758.4	3,309.6	238.0
Hanford-Corcoran, CA M.S.A........	151,437									
Includes Kings County.......										
City of Hanford.......	54,824	305	1	27	31	246	1,857	259	1,442	156
City of Corcoran.......	23,057	86	0	5	5	76	292	105	168	19
Total area actually reporting.......	100.0%	696	7	65	72	552	3,475	702	2,362	411
Rate per 100,000 inhabitants.......		459.6	4.6	42.9	47.5	364.5	2,294.7	463.6	1,559.7	271.4
Harrisburg-Carlisle, PA M.S.A........	559,478									
Includes Cumberland, Dauphin, and Perry Counties.......										
City of Harrisburg.......	49,109	547	17	42	272	216	1,828	477	1,214	137
City of Carlisle.......	18,974	37	0	7	13	17	526	50	472	4
Total area actually reporting.......	99.7%	1,328	22	202	458	646	10,616	1,820	8,462	334
Estimated total.......	100.0%	1,331	22	202	459	648	10,648	1,825	8,488	335
Rate per 100,000 inhabitants.......		237.9	3.9	36.1	82.0	115.8	1,903.2	326.2	1,517.1	59.9
Harrisonburg, VA M.S.A........	130,160									
Includes Rockingham County and Harrisonburg City.......										
City of Harrisonburg.......	52,026	103	0	21	11	71	1,150	228	894	28
Total area actually reporting.......	100.0%	183	3	42	17	121	1,842	409	1,379	54
Rate per 100,000 inhabitants.......		140.6	2.3	32.3	13.1	93.0	1,415.2	314.2	1,059.5	41.5
Hartford-West Hartford-East Hartford, CT M.S.A........	1,024,517									
Includes Hartford, Middlesex, and Tolland Counties.......										
City of Hartford.......	124,943	1,380	19	45	502	814	5,280	888	3,642	750
City of West Hartford.......	63,360	49	1	1	37	10	1,395	200	1,129	66
City of East Hartford.......	51,185	131	2	24	55	50	1,220	283	800	137
City of Middletown.......	47,256	78	0	4	23	51	859	96	699	64
Total area actually reporting.......	100.0%	2,584	39	248	963	1,334	22,869	3,991	17,057	1,821
Rate per 100,000 inhabitants.......		252.2	3.8	24.2	94.0	130.2	2,232.2	389.5	1,664.9	177.7
Hickory-Lenoir-Morganton, NC M.S.A........	363,897									
Includes Alexander, Burke, Caldwell, and Catawba Counties.......										
City of Hickory.......	40,435	158	0	20	38	100	1,895	357	1,442	96
City of Lenoir.......	17,994	43	1	1	13	28	783	210	541	32
City of Morganton.......	16,786	43	3	3	11	26	645	147	479	19
Total area actually reporting.......	99.5%	701	17	60	142	482	9,935	3,028	6,453	454
Estimated total.......	100.0%	705	17	60	143	485	9,995	3,040	6,499	456
Rate per 100,000 inhabitants.......		193.7	4.7	16.5	39.3	133.3	2,746.7	835.4	1,785.9	125.3
Hilton Head Island-Bluffton-Beaufort, SC M.S.A........	202,116									
Includes Beaufort and Jasper Counties.......										
City of Bluffton.......	13,755	33	1	4	9	19	461	79	360	22
City of Beaufort.......	13,090	97	0	5	27	65	903	155	716	32
Total area actually reporting.......	99.9%	880	7	54	145	674	5,265	1,151	3,841	273
Estimated total.......	100.0%	880	7	54	145	674	5,270	1,152	3,845	273
Rate per 100,000 inhabitants.......		435.4	3.5	26.7	71.7	333.5	2,607.4	570.0	1,902.4	135.1
Hinesville, GA M.S.A.[3].......	81,944									
Includes Liberty and Long Counties[3].......										
City of Hinesville[3].......	34,525	162	1	6	35	120	1,426	347	1,040	39
Total area actually reporting.......	97.5%	275	5	11	52	207	2,123	618	1,415	90
Estimated total.......	100.0%	284	5	12	55	212	2,210	633	1,481	96
Rate per 100,000 inhabitants.......		346.6	6.1	14.6	67.1	258.7	2,697.0	772.5	1,807.3	117.2
Homosassa Springs, FL M.S.A........	139,880									
Includes Citrus County.......										
Total area actually reporting.......	97.8%	727	7	74	76	570	3,625	798	2,606	221
Estimated total.......	100.0%	739	7	75	79	578	3,726	817	2,682	227
Rate per 100,000 inhabitants.......		528.3	5.0	53.6	56.5	413.2	2,663.7	584.1	1,917.4	162.3
Houma-Thibodaux, LA M.S.A........	210,453									
Includes Lafourche and Terrebonne Parishes.......										
City of Houma.......	34,129	211	4	12	66	129	1,390	191	1,136	63
City of Thibodaux.......	14,565	79	1	4	9	65	612	65	540	7
Total area actually reporting.......	100.0%	510	9	24	122	355	6,051	1,084	4,766	201
Rate per 100,000 inhabitants.......		242.3	4.3	11.4	58.0	168.7	2,875.2	515.1	2,264.6	95.5

Table 6. Crime, by Selected Metropolitan Statistical Area, 2014—*Continued*

(Number, percent, rate per 100,000 population.)

Area	Population	Violent crime	Murder and nonnegligent manslaughter	Rape[1]	Robbery	Aggravated assault	Property crime	Burglary	Larceny-theft	Motor vehicle theft
Houston-The Woodlands-Sugar Land, TX M.S.A.	6,454,938									
Includes Austin, Brazoria, Chambers, Fort Bend, Galveston,										
Harris, Liberty, Montgomery, and Waller Counties										
City of Houston	2,219,933	22,008	242	812	10,186	10,768	104,197	21,629	68,125	14,443
City of Sugar Land	85,055	99	1	6	36	56	1,400	220	1,132	48
City of Baytown	76,253	241	5	32	84	120	3,157	638	2,091	428
City of Conroe	64,446	206	2	28	71	105	2,211	431	1,672	108
Total area actually reporting	99.9%	36,620	377	2,144	14,988	19,111	207,029	44,440	137,615	24,974
Estimated total	100.0%	36,625	377	2,145	14,989	19,114	207,083	44,449	137,656	24,978
Rate per 100,000 inhabitants		567.4	5.8	33.2	232.2	296.1	3,208.1	688.6	2,132.6	387.0
Huntsville, AL M.S.A.	440,192									
Includes Limestone and Madison Counties										
City of Huntsville	187,624	1,467	15	104	390	958	9,161	1,912	6,521	728
Total area actually reporting	100.0%	2,103	23	184	475	1,421	13,972	3,054	9,923	995
Rate per 100,000 inhabitants		477.7	5.2	41.8	107.9	322.8	3,174.1	693.8	2,254.2	226.0
Idaho Falls, ID M.S.A.	138,893									
Includes Bonneville, Butte, and Jefferson Counties										
City of Idaho Falls	58,606	126	0	36	7	83	1,502	239	1,164	99
Total area actually reporting	100.0%	215	0	48	9	158	2,450	432	1,862	156
Rate per 100,000 inhabitants		154.8	0.0	34.6	6.5	113.8	1,763.9	311.0	1,340.6	112.3
Indianapolis-Carmel-Anderson, IN M.S.A.[3]	1,971,378									
Includes Boone, Brown, Hamilton, Hancock, Hendricks, Johnson,										
Madison, Marion, Morgan, Putnam, and Shelby Counties										
City of Indianapolis[3]	858,238	10,768	136	573	3,808	6,251	41,394	12,125	24,090	5,179
City of Carmel	87,555	12	1	2	6	3	816	72	689	55
City of Anderson	55,545	190	1	59	73	57	2,490	553	1,739	198
Total area actually reporting	86.6%	12,229	148	723	4,029	7,329	58,483	14,591	37,520	6,372
Estimated total	100.0%	12,742	155	763	4,129	7,695	63,940	15,446	41,756	6,738
Rate per 100,000 inhabitants		646.3	7.9	38.7	209.4	390.3	3,243.4	783.5	2,118.1	341.8
Iowa City, IA M.S.A.	163,631									
Includes Johnson and Washington Counties										
City of Iowa City	72,522	213	1	31	51	130	1,756	269	1,411	76
Total area actually reporting	100.0%	425	1	69	70	285	2,965	463	2,375	127
Rate per 100,000 inhabitants		259.7	0.6	42.2	42.8	174.2	1,812.0	283.0	1,451.4	77.6
Jackson, MI M.S.A.	160,565									
Includes Jackson County										
City of Jackson	33,404	299	3	40	53	203	1,428	232	1,157	39
Total area actually reporting	98.7%	656	10	122	79	445	3,398	596	2,710	92
Estimated total	100.0%	662	10	123	80	449	3,443	604	2,744	95
Rate per 100,000 inhabitants		412.3	6.2	76.6	49.8	279.6	2,144.3	376.2	1,709.0	59.2
Jackson, MS M.S.A.	577,909									
Includes Copiah, Hinds, Madison, Rankin, Simpson, and Yazoo										
Counties										
City of Jackson	172,376	1,593	61	117	801	614	10,382	2,952	6,303	1,127
Total area actually reporting	77.3%	1,868	67	140	863	798	14,263	3,850	9,075	1,338
Estimated total	100.0%	2,103	74	157	918	954	17,330	4,522	11,331	1,477
Rate per 100,000 inhabitants		363.9	12.8	27.2	158.8	165.1	2,998.7	782.5	1,960.7	255.6
Jackson, TN M.S.A.	131,143									
Includes Chester, Crockett, and Madison Counties										
City of Jackson	67,869	734	10	34	131	559	3,063	646	2,244	173
Total area actually reporting	100.0%	991	12	44	148	787	4,114	975	2,878	261
Rate per 100,000 inhabitants		755.7	9.2	33.6	112.9	600.1	3,137.0	743.5	2,194.6	199.0
Jacksonville, FL M.S.A.	1,417,629									
Includes Baker, Clay, Duval, Nassau, and St. Johns Counties										
City of Jacksonville	856,021	5,853	96	479	1,419	3,859	33,732	6,806	24,945	1,981
Total area actually reporting	100.0%	7,955	108	656	1,723	5,468	48,665	9,575	36,524	2,566
Rate per 100,000 inhabitants		561.1	7.6	46.3	121.5	385.7	3,432.8	675.4	2,576.4	181.0
Janesville-Beloit, WI M.S.A.	160,897									
Includes Rock County										
City of Janesville	63,885	162	1	23	28	110	2,076	303	1,726	47
City of Beloit	36,872	148	8	15	53	72	1,239	229	967	43

Table 6. Crime, by Selected Metropolitan Statistical Area, 2014—*Continued*

(Number, percent, rate per 100,000 population.)

Area	Population	Violent crime	Murder and nonnegligent manslaughter	Rape[1]	Robbery	Aggravated assault	Property crime	Burglary	Larceny-theft	Motor vehicle theft
Total area actually reporting	100.0%	375	9	52	90	224	4,028	712	3,193	123
Rate per 100,000 inhabitants		233.1	5.6	32.3	55.9	139.2	2,503.5	442.5	1,984.5	76.4
Jefferson City, MO M.S.A.	150,805									
Includes Callaway, Cole, Moniteau, and Osage Counties										
City of Jefferson City	43,372	133	1	6	25	101	1,331	166	1,134	31
Total area actually reporting	100.0%	356	6	23	46	281	2,946	537	2,276	133
Rate per 100,000 inhabitants		236.1	4.0	15.3	30.5	186.3	1,953.5	356.1	1,509.2	88.2
Johnson City, TN M.S.A.	202,004									
Includes Carter, Unicoi, and Washington Counties										
City of Johnson City	65,541	242	4	15	38	185	2,367	383	1,886	98
Total area actually reporting	100.0%	583	6	34	53	490	4,980	1,044	3,717	219
Rate per 100,000 inhabitants		288.6	3.0	16.8	26.2	242.6	2,465.3	516.8	1,840.1	108.4
Johnstown, PA M.S.A.	139,742									
Includes Cambria County										
City of Johnstown	21,755	125	6	6	32	81	808	287	502	19
Total area actually reporting	98.9%	228	7	14	48	159	2,393	514	1,832	47
Estimated total	100.0%	231	7	14	49	161	2,418	518	1,852	48
Rate per 100,000 inhabitants		165.3	5.0	10.0	35.1	115.2	1,730.3	370.7	1,325.3	34.3
Jonesboro, AR M.S.A.	126,640									
Includes Craighead and Poinsett Counties										
City of Jonesboro	72,569	380	9	55	61	255	3,172	681	2,409	82
Total area actually reporting	98.0%	511	9	81	67	354	4,398	1,000	3,291	107
Estimated total	100.0%	522	9	83	68	362	4,485	1,021	3,353	111
Rate per 100,000 inhabitants		412.2	7.1	65.5	53.7	285.8	3,541.5	806.2	2,647.7	87.7
Joplin, MO M.S.A.	175,290									
Includes Jasper and Newton Counties										
City of Joplin	50,751	261	3	48	62	148	3,948	611	3,042	295
Total area actually reporting	100.0%	576	4	89	84	399	7,469	1,324	5,583	562
Rate per 100,000 inhabitants		328.6	2.3	50.8	47.9	227.6	4,260.9	755.3	3,185.0	320.6
Kahului-Wailuku-Lahaina, HI M.S.A.	162,229									
Includes Kalawao and Maui Counties										
Total area actually reporting	100.0%	508	4	88	80	336	5,800	1,046	4,184	570
Rate per 100,000 inhabitants		313.1	2.5	54.2	49.3	207.1	3,575.2	644.8	2,579.1	351.4
Kalamazoo-Portage, MI M.S.A.	333,814									
Includes Kalamazoo and Van Buren Counties										
City of Kalamazoo	75,857	884	6	111	157	610	2,901	677	2,035	189
City of Portage	47,819	77	0	17	18	42	1,497	187	1,268	42
Total area actually reporting	100.0%	1,523	8	294	224	997	8,404	1,804	6,180	420
Rate per 100,000 inhabitants		456.2	2.4	88.1	67.1	298.7	2,517.6	540.4	1,851.3	125.8
Kankakee, IL M.S.A.	111,679									
Includes Kankakee County										
City of Kankakee	27,026	221	6	28	93	94	1,232	292	906	34
Total area actually reporting	87.9%	323	11	43	112	157	2,678	521	2,078	79
Estimated total	100.0%	350	11	46	120	173	2,917	560	2,267	90
Rate per 100,000 inhabitants		313.4	9.8	41.2	107.5	154.9	2,612.0	501.4	2,029.9	80.6
Kansas City, MO-KS M.S.A.	2,066,584									
Includes Johnson, Leavenworth, Linn, Miami, and Wyandotte Counties, KS and Bates, Caldwell, Cass, Clay, Clinton, Jackson, Lafayette, Platte, and Ray Counties, MO										
City of Kansas City, MO	468,417	5,862	78	390	1,625	3,769	22,648	5,659	13,037	3,952
City of Overland Park, KS	183,108	327	6	127	29	165	3,033	384	2,130	519
City of Kansas City, KS	149,103	1,060	25	233	254	548	7,316	1,663	4,697	956
Total area actually reporting	98.9%	9,920	136	1,117	2,336	6,331	61,894	12,899	40,797	8,198
Estimated total	100.0%	9,962	136	1,124	2,340	6,362	62,354	12,976	41,146	8,232
Rate per 100,000 inhabitants		482.1	6.6	54.4	113.2	307.9	3,017.2	627.9	1,991.0	398.3
Kennewick-Richland, WA M.S.A.	276,409									
Includes Benton and Franklin Counties										
City of Kennewick	77,381	190	5	34	41	110	2,419	465	1,808	146
City of Richland	53,445	90	0	11	13	66	1,209	169	991	49
Total area actually reporting	100.0%	567	14	88	91	374	6,117	1,244	4,476	397
Rate per 100,000 inhabitants		205.1	5.1	31.8	32.9	135.3	2,213.0	450.1	1,619.3	143.6

Table 6. Crime, by Selected Metropolitan Statistical Area, 2014—*Continued*

(Number, percent, rate per 100,000 population.)

Area	Population	Violent crime	Murder and nonnegligent manslaughter	Rape[1]	Robbery	Aggravated assault	Property crime	Burglary	Larceny-theft	Motor vehicle theft
Killeen-Temple, TX M.S.A.	430,225									
Includes Bell, Coryell, and Lampasas Counties...........................										
City of Killeen	139,211	846	10	114	196	526	4,703	1,334	3,149	220
City of Temple..	71,049	175	5	21	62	87	2,421	494	1,804	123
Total area actually reporting	99.3%	1,460	20	209	324	907	11,811	2,815	8,498	498
Estimated total..	100.0%	1,468	20	210	326	912	11,897	2,830	8,563	504
Rate per 100,000 inhabitants........................		341.2	4.6	48.8	75.8	212.0	2,765.3	657.8	1,990.4	117.1
Kingsport-Bristol-Bristol, TN-VA M.S.A.	308,581									
Includes Hawkins and Sullivan Counties, TN and Scott and										
Washington Counties and Bristol City, VA										
City of Kingsport, TN	53,010	319	2	20	35	262	2,631	356	2,130	145
City of Bristol, TN.......................................	26,603	122	0	5	7	110	967	149	761	57
City of Bristol, VA.......................................	17,225	54	1	5	8	40	482	50	413	19
Total area actually reporting	100.0%	982	15	88	82	797	7,788	1,409	5,937	442
Rate per 100,000 inhabitants........................		318.2	4.9	28.5	26.6	258.3	2,523.8	456.6	1,924.0	143.2
Kingston, NY M.S.A.	180,937									
Includes Ulster County										
City of Kingston	23,702	67	2	5	25	35	672	87	578	7
Total area actually reporting	100.0%	303	5	60	49	189	2,935	523	2,368	44
Rate per 100,000 inhabitants........................		167.5	2.8	33.2	27.1	104.5	1,622.1	289.1	1,308.7	24.3
Knoxville, TN M.S.A.	858,559									
Includes Anderson, Blount, Campbell, Grainger, Knox, Loudon,										
Morgan, Roane, and Union Counties										
City of Knoxville	184,362	1,612	12	135	413	1,052	12,028	1,976	9,216	836
Total area actually reporting	96.6%	3,253	27	266	573	2,387	26,141	5,412	18,965	1,764
Estimated total..	100.0%	3,361	28	276	587	2,470	26,927	5,532	19,595	1,800
Rate per 100,000 inhabitants........................		391.5	3.3	32.1	68.4	287.7	3,136.3	644.3	2,282.3	209.7
Kokomo, IN M.S.A.[3]	82,820									
Includes Howard County										
City of Kokomo	56,904	162	3	22	42	95	2,074	501	1,515	58
Total area actually reporting	98.7%	185	3	25	44	113	2,278	602	1,608	68
Estimated total..	100.0%	188	3	25	45	115	2,311	606	1,635	70
Rate per 100,000 inhabitants........................		227.0	3.6	30.2	54.3	138.9	2,790.4	731.7	1,974.2	84.5
La Crosse-Onalaska, WI-MN M.S.A.	135,985									
Includes Houston County, MN and La Crosse County, WI										
City of La Crosse, WI	51,564	102	0	20	28	54	1,522	224	1,258	40
City of Onalaska, WI	18,437	6	0	0	3	3	402	16	381	5
Total area actually reporting	100.0%	154	0	31	34	89	2,469	357	2,057	55
Rate per 100,000 inhabitants........................		113.2	0.0	22.8	25.0	65.4	1,815.6	262.5	1,512.7	40.4
Lafayette, LA M.S.A.[2]	482,374									
Includes Acadia, Iberia, Lafayette, St. Martin, and Vermilion[2]										
Parishes										
City of Lafayette	125,122	814	7	10	248	549	6,800	1,186	5,208	406
Total area actually reporting	95.1%	2,024	35	62	459	1,468		3,322	9,990	
Estimated total..	100.0%	2,131	36	68	476	1,551		3,504	10,737	
Rate per 100,000 inhabitants........................		441.8	7.5	14.1	98.7	321.5		726.4	2,225.9	
Lafayette-West Lafayette, IN M.S.A.[3]	210,988									
Includes Benton, Carroll, and Tippecanoe Counties										
City of Lafayette	70,749	351	2	43	90	216	3,426	634	2,542	250
City of West Lafayette..................................	31,192	32	0	2	8	22	349	44	286	19
Total area actually reporting	86.7%	423	3	58	104	258	4,795	902	3,569	324
Estimated total..	100.0%	461	3	62	111	285	5,184	981	3,850	353
Rate per 100,000 inhabitants........................		218.5	1.4	29.4	52.6	135.1	2,457.0	465.0	1,824.7	167.3
Lake Havasu City-Kingman, AZ M.S.A.	205,249									
Includes Mohave County..										
City of Lake Havasu City	52,892	88	1	14	5	68	1,109	222	830	57
City of Kingman	28,526	73	1	6	9	57	1,471	248	1,151	72
Total area actually reporting	97.7%	409	7	68	49	285	6,339	1,670	4,265	404
Estimated total..	100.0%	421	7	69	52	293	6,483	1,695	4,375	413
Rate per 100,000 inhabitants........................		205.1	3.4	33.6	25.3	142.8	3,158.6	825.8	2,131.6	201.2
Lakeland-Winter Haven, FL M.S.A.	633,015									
Includes Polk County..										

Table 6. Crime, by Selected Metropolitan Statistical Area, 2014—*Continued*

(Number, percent, rate per 100,000 population.)

Area	Population	Violent crime	Murder and nonnegligent manslaughter	Rape[1]	Robbery	Aggravated assault	Property crime	Burglary	Larceny-theft	Motor vehicle theft
City of Lakeland	101,428	453	8	73	153	219	5,285	1,088	3,948	249
City of Winter Haven	35,935	224	2	14	49	159	1,351	284	1,025	42
Total area actually reporting	100.0%	2,867	19	208	497	2,143	20,842	5,761	13,807	1,274
Rate per 100,000 inhabitants		452.9	3.0	32.9	78.5	338.5	3,292.5	910.1	2,181.1	201.3
Lancaster, PA M.S.A.	531,837									
Includes Lancaster County										
City of Lancaster	59,325	403	6	68	165	164	2,291	347	1,874	70
Total area actually reporting	100.0%	878	13	200	270	395	8,386	1,447	6,698	241
Rate per 100,000 inhabitants		165.1	2.4	37.6	50.8	74.3	1,576.8	272.1	1,259.4	45.3
Lansing-East Lansing, MI M.S.A.	468,547									
Includes Clinton, Eaton, and Ingham Counties										
City of Lansing	113,901	1,272	10	117	250	895	3,576	955	2,252	369
City of East Lansing	48,555	135	2	27	27	79	698	147	489	62
Total area actually reporting	93.5%	1,905	14	317	323	1,251	8,708	1,982	6,156	570
Estimated total	100.0%	1,988	15	331	339	1,303	9,343	2,093	6,634	616
Rate per 100,000 inhabitants		424.3	3.2	70.6	72.4	278.1	1,994.0	446.7	1,415.9	131.5
Laredo, TX M.S.A.	267,304									
Includes Webb County										
City of Laredo	250,994	976	14	99	196	667	9,687	1,267	8,144	276
Total area actually reporting	100.0%	1,076	15	110	198	753	10,024	1,356	8,373	295
Rate per 100,000 inhabitants		402.5	5.6	41.2	74.1	281.7	3,750.0	507.3	3,132.4	110.4
Las Cruces, NM M.S.A.	213,753									
Includes Dona Ana County										
City of Las Cruces	102,113	295	7	55	60	173	4,614	828	3,563	223
Total area actually reporting	100.0%	611	11	130	76	394	6,521	1,403	4,746	372
Rate per 100,000 inhabitants		285.8	5.1	60.8	35.6	184.3	3,050.7	656.4	2,220.3	174.0
Las Vegas-Henderson-Paradise, NV M.S.A.	2,066,423									
Includes Clark County										
City of Las Vegas Metropolitan Police Department	1,530,899	12,876	122	780	4,885	7,089	44,754	14,150	23,432	7,172
City of Henderson	274,121	452	3	89	165	195	5,423	1,397	3,531	495
Total area actually reporting	100.0%	15,354	137	992	5,545	8,680	57,690	17,962	31,123	8,605
Rate per 100,000 inhabitants		743.0	6.6	48.0	268.3	420.0	2,791.8	869.2	1,506.1	416.4
Lawton, OK M.S.A.	131,086									
Includes Comanche and Cotton Counties										
City of Lawton	96,966	893	11	75	194	613	4,508	1,371	2,926	211
Total area actually reporting	100.0%	924	11	81	197	635	4,851	1,490	3,125	236
Rate per 100,000 inhabitants		704.9	8.4	61.8	150.3	484.4	3,700.6	1,136.7	2,383.9	180.0
Lebanon, PA M.S.A.	135,898									
Includes Lebanon County										
City of Lebanon	25,538	79	3	10	31	35	621	106	503	12
Total area actually reporting	100.0%	209	7	28	46	128	2,164	320	1,787	57
Rate per 100,000 inhabitants		153.8	5.2	20.6	33.8	94.2	1,592.4	235.5	1,315.0	41.9
Lewiston, ID-WA M.S.A.	62,666									
Includes Nez Perce County, ID and Asotin County, WA										
City of Lewiston, ID	32,521	59	1	10	9	39	1,133	212	847	74
Total area actually reporting	100.0%	118	3	16	14	85	1,875	364	1,400	111
Rate per 100,000 inhabitants		188.3	4.8	25.5	22.3	135.6	2,992.1	580.9	2,234.1	177.1
Lewiston-Auburn, ME M.S.A.	107,711									
Includes Androscoggin County										
City of Lewiston	36,402	84	2	21	31	30	894	220	637	37
City of Auburn	22,973	28	0	8	5	15	886	113	755	18
Total area actually reporting	100.0%	153	2	45	41	65	2,311	515	1,720	76
Rate per 100,000 inhabitants		142.0	1.9	41.8	38.1	60.3	2,145.6	478.1	1,596.9	70.6
Lexington-Fayette, KY M.S.A.[2]	494,197									
Includes Bourbon, Clark,[2] Fayette, Jessamine, Scott, and Woodford Counties										
City of Lexington	311,848	1,041	20	134	554	333	12,134	2,393	8,816	925
Total area actually reporting	100.0%	1,287	22	176	654	435			12,641	1,117
Rate per 100,000 inhabitants		260.4	4.5	35.6	132.3	88.0			2,557.9	226.0

Table 6. Crime, by Selected Metropolitan Statistical Area, 2014—*Continued*

(Number, percent, rate per 100,000 population.)

Area	Population	Violent crime	Murder and nonnegligent manslaughter	Rape[1]	Robbery	Aggravated assault	Property crime	Burglary	Larceny-theft	Motor vehicle theft
Lima, OH M.S.A.	105,180									
Includes Allen County										
City of Lima	38,265	353	3	40	71	239	1,868	592	1,201	75
Total area actually reporting	100.0%	406	5	49	88	264	3,467	925	2,431	111
Rate per 100,000 inhabitants		386.0	4.8	46.6	83.7	251.0	3,296.3	879.4	2,311.3	105.5
Lincoln, NE M.S.A.	317,498									
Includes Lancaster and Seward Counties										
City of Lincoln	271,208	918	7	152	205	554	9,082	1,305	7,452	325
Total area actually reporting	99.3%	954	7	161	209	577	9,637	1,398	7,888	351
Estimated total	100.0%	957	7	162	210	578	9,680	1,403	7,924	353
Rate per 100,000 inhabitants		301.4	2.2	51.0	66.1	182.0	3,048.8	441.9	2,495.8	111.2
Little Rock-North Little Rock-Conway, AR M.S.A.	729,360									
Includes Faulkner, Grant, Lonoke, Perry, Pulaski, and Saline Counties										
City of Little Rock	198,217	2,759	43	138	729	1,849	14,253	3,068	10,320	865
City of North Little Rock	67,031	426	8	14	86	318	2,846	517	2,126	203
City of Conway	64,895	257	1	27	62	167	3,008	501	2,347	160
Total area actually reporting	97.3%	4,990	61	348	1,012	3,569	31,294	6,698	22,498	2,098
Estimated total	100.0%	5,079	61	361	1,021	3,636	31,984	6,864	22,991	2,129
Rate per 100,000 inhabitants		696.4	8.4	49.5	140.0	498.5	4,385.2	941.1	3,152.2	291.9
Longview, TX M.S.A.	218,568									
Includes Gregg, Rusk, and Upshur Counties										
City of Longview	79,728	265	2	22	63	178	2,871	595	2,108	168
Total area actually reporting	98.4%	743	11	62	97	573	6,387	1,461	4,495	431
Estimated total	100.0%	752	11	63	99	579	6,482	1,477	4,568	437
Rate per 100,000 inhabitants		344.1	5.0	28.8	45.3	264.9	2,965.7	675.8	2,090.0	199.9
Longview, WA M.S.A.	102,175									
Includes Cowlitz County										
City of Longview	36,459	133	0	31	27	75	2,305	496	1,669	140
Total area actually reporting	100.0%	253	0	72	34	147	3,701	807	2,640	254
Rate per 100,000 inhabitants		247.6	0.0	70.5	33.3	143.9	3,622.2	789.8	2,583.8	248.6
Los Angeles-Long Beach-Anaheim, CA M.S.A.	13,277,942									
Includes the Metropolitan Divisions of Anaheim-Santa Ana-Irvine and Los Angeles-Long Beach-Glendale										
City of Los Angeles	3,906,772	19,171	260	1,126	7,949	9,836	83,139	15,070	54,281	13,788
City of Long Beach	471,123	2,304	23	110	889	1,282	12,438	3,482	6,875	2,081
City of Anaheim	346,956	1,101	14	79	418	590	8,196	1,301	5,620	1,275
City of Santa Ana	336,462	1,260	18	115	452	675	5,784	793	3,685	1,306
City of Irvine	242,971	120	0	28	36	56	3,045	575	2,344	126
City of Glendale	197,079	186	0	9	67	110	3,073	511	2,294	268
City of Torrance	147,971	155	2	18	73	62	2,623	582	1,784	257
City of Pasadena	140,373	394	10	23	126	235	3,469	826	2,413	230
City of Orange	140,767	142	0	10	53	79	2,241	366	1,631	244
City of Costa Mesa	112,709	318	0	45	120	153	3,462	573	2,583	306
City of Burbank	105,041	150	1	14	55	80	2,426	296	1,948	182
City of Carson	92,838	339	9	8	115	207	2,116	460	1,267	389
City of Santa Monica	93,151	338	0	30	120	188	3,026	535	2,314	177
City of Newport Beach	87,759	109	0	17	21	71	1,880	357	1,419	104
City of Tustin	79,046	132	0	16	39	77	1,356	193	1,047	116
City of Monterey Park	61,284	91	1	4	41	45	1,039	267	608	164
City of Gardena	60,233	276	1	10	164	101	1,389	335	785	269
City of Arcadia	57,950	60	1	7	24	28	1,159	276	839	44
City of Fountain Valley	57,024	86	0	0	21	65	1,023	196	759	68
Total area actually reporting	100.0%	48,982	587	2,874	18,140	27,381	272,247	53,479	175,884	42,884
Rate per 100,000 inhabitants		368.9	4.4	21.6	136.6	206.2	2,050.4	402.8	1,324.6	323.0
Anaheim-Santa Ana-Irvine, CA M.D.	3,156,440									
Includes Orange County										
Total area actually reporting	100.0%	6,257	61	650	1,949	3,597	54,754	9,255	39,201	6,298
Rate per 100,000 inhabitants		198.2	1.9	20.6	61.7	114.0	1,734.7	293.2	1,241.9	199.5
Los Angeles-Long Beach-Glendale, CA M.D.	10,121,502									
Includes Los Angeles County										
Total area actually reporting	100.0%	42,725	526	2,224	16,191	23,784	217,493	44,224	136,683	36,586
Rate per 100,000 inhabitants		422.1	5.2	22.0	160.0	235.0	2,148.8	436.9	1,350.4	361.5

Table 6. Crime, by Selected Metropolitan Statistical Area, 2014—*Continued*

(Number, percent, rate per 100,000 population.)

Area	Population	Violent crime	Murder and nonnegligent manslaughter	Rape[1]	Robbery	Aggravated assault	Property crime	Burglary	Larceny-theft	Motor vehicle theft
Louisville/Jefferson County, KY-IN M.S.A.[3]................	1,269,992									
Includes Clark, Floyd, Harrison, Scott, and Washington Counties, IN and Bullitt, Henry, Jefferson, Oldham, Shelby, Spencer, and Trimble Counties, KY..										
City of Louisville Metro, KY[3]..	677,710	4,005	56	184	1,531	2,234	28,364	6,417	19,669	2,278
Total area actually reporting	96.0%	4,937	68	267	1,835	2,767	40,925	8,656	29,166	3,103
Estimated total...	100.0%	5,016	69	275	1,850	2,822	41,775	8,811	29,802	3,162
Rate per 100,000 inhabitants...		395.0	5.4	21.7	145.7	222.2	3,289.4	693.8	2,346.6	249.0
Lubbock, TX M.S.A.	305,514									
Includes Crosby, Lubbock, and Lynn Counties........................										
City of Lubbock	241,826	2,084	12	128	333	1,611	10,617	2,288	7,563	766
Total area actually reporting	99.4%	2,249	14	157	345	1,733	12,023	2,586	8,586	851
Estimated total...	100.0%	2,254	14	158	346	1,736	12,077	2,595	8,627	855
Rate per 100,000 inhabitants...		737.8	4.6	51.7	113.3	568.2	3,953.0	849.4	2,823.8	279.9
Lynchburg, VA M.S.A.	257,560									
Includes Amherst, Appomattox, Bedford, and Campbell Counties and Bedford and Lynchburg Cities.................................										
City of Lynchburg..	78,639	367	5	30	56	276	1,992	403	1,483	106
Total area actually reporting	100.0%	590	14	88	79	409	4,242	845	3,188	209
Rate per 100,000 inhabitants...		229.1	5.4	34.2	30.7	158.8	1,647.0	328.1	1,237.8	81.1
Madera, CA M.S.A.	153,544									
Includes Madera County										
City of Madera..	63,495	415	6	15	72	322	1,686	472	1,007	207
Total area actually reporting	100.0%	888	9	38	99	742	3,380	1,116	1,819	445
Rate per 100,000 inhabitants...		578.3	5.9	24.7	64.5	483.2	2,201.3	726.8	1,184.7	289.8
Madison, WI M.S.A.	632,961									
Includes Columbia, Dane, Green, and Iowa Counties										
City of Madison	245,788	846	7	83	226	530	6,978	1,129	5,603	246
Total area actually reporting	96.5%	1,292	13	146	301	832	12,427	1,835	10,193	399
Estimated total...	100.0%	1,320	13	150	309	848	12,899	1,891	10,592	416
Rate per 100,000 inhabitants...		208.5	2.1	23.7	48.8	134.0	2,037.9	298.8	1,673.4	65.7
Manchester-Nashua, NH M.S.A.	405,230									
Includes Hillsborough County...										
City of Manchester	110,571	683	3	61	237	382	4,009	730	3,118	161
City of Nashua	87,279	202	3	57	52	90	1,855	271	1,508	76
Total area actually reporting	97.1%	1,066	7	155	313	591	8,217	1,362	6,533	322
Estimated total...	100.0%	1,082	7	159	316	600	8,409	1,390	6,691	328
Rate per 100,000 inhabitants...		267.0	1.7	39.2	78.0	148.1	2,075.1	343.0	1,651.2	80.9
Manhattan, KS M.S.A.	99,371									
Includes Pottawatomie and Riley Counties										
Total area actually reporting	100.0%	233	3	30	32	168	1,465	269	1,150	46
Rate per 100,000 inhabitants...		234.5	3.0	30.2	32.2	169.1	1,474.3	270.7	1,157.3	46.3
Mankato-North Mankato, MN M.S.A.	99,160									
Includes Blue Earth and Nicollet Counties.................................										
City of Mankato..	40,959	107	1	20	17	69	1,429	214	1,152	63
City of North Mankato..	13,448	26	0	7	3	16	255	44	196	15
Total area actually reporting	100.0%	178	2	42	23	111	2,166	401	1,663	102
Rate per 100,000 inhabitants...		179.5	2.0	42.4	23.2	111.9	2,184.3	404.4	1,677.1	102.9
Mansfield, OH M.S.A.	121,351									
Includes Richland County										
City of Mansfield	46,145	210	3	40	87	80	3,174	901	2,127	146
Total area actually reporting	95.3%	248	4	57	98	89	5,389	1,468	3,724	197
Estimated total...	100.0%	257	4	59	101	93	5,527	1,493	3,832	202
Rate per 100,000 inhabitants...		211.8	3.3	48.6	83.2	76.6	4,554.6	1,230.3	3,157.8	166.5
McAllen-Edinburg-Mission, TX M.S.A.	831,477									
Includes Hidalgo County										
City of McAllen...	138,122	181	6	18	68	89	4,947	411	4,364	172
City of Edinburg..	82,349	296	1	66	48	181	4,420	562	3,658	200
City of Mission	81,871	95	0	5	30	60	2,405	309	1,964	132
Total area actually reporting	100.0%	2,739	26	363	443	1,907	27,982	5,132	21,567	1,283
Rate per 100,000 inhabitants...		329.4	3.1	43.7	53.3	229.4	3,365.3	617.2	2,593.8	154.3

Table 6. Crime, by Selected Metropolitan Statistical Area, 2014—*Continued*

(Number, percent, rate per 100,000 population.)

Area	Population	Violent crime	Murder and nonnegligent manslaughter	Rape[1]	Robbery	Aggravated assault	Property crime	Burglary	Larceny-theft	Motor vehicle theft
Medford, OR M.S.A.	210,715									
Includes Jackson County										
City of Medford	78,356	393	0	45	93	255	5,127	536	4,358	233
Total area actually reporting	100.0%	664	3	75	121	465	8,292	1,018	6,853	421
Rate per 100,000 inhabitants		315.1	1.4	35.6	57.4	220.7	3,935.2	483.1	3,252.3	199.8
Memphis, TN-MS-AR M.S.A.	1,348,092									
Includes Crittenden County, AR; Benton, DeSoto, Marshall, Tate, and Tunica Counties, MS; and Fayette, Shelby, and Tipton Counties, TN										
City of Memphis, TN	654,922	11,399	140	501	3,285	7,473	39,217	11,451	24,791	2,975
Total area actually reporting	87.2%	13,685	165	663	3,593	9,264	52,269	14,382	34,212	3,675
Estimated total	100.0%	13,933	173	686	3,645	9,429	55,738	15,232	36,635	3,871
Rate per 100,000 inhabitants		1,033.5	12.8	50.9	270.4	699.4	4,134.6	1,129.9	2,717.5	287.1
Merced, CA M.S.A.	266,350									
Includes Merced County										
City of Merced	81,603	570	13	17	143	397	2,632	605	1,678	349
Total area actually reporting	100.0%	1,485	29	43	241	1,172	7,126	1,754	4,357	1,015
Rate per 100,000 inhabitants		557.5	10.9	16.1	90.5	440.0	2,675.4	658.5	1,635.8	381.1
Miami-Fort Lauderdale-West Palm Beach, FL M.S.A.	5,938,747									
Includes the Metropolitan Divisions of Fort Lauderdale-Pompano Beach-Deerfield Beach, Miami-Miami Beach-Kendall, and West Palm Beach-Boca Raton-Delray Beach										
City of Miami	421,996	4,473	81	110	1,790	2,492	20,394	3,659	14,514	2,221
City of Fort Lauderdale	174,056	1,345	18	78	618	631	8,933	1,942	6,317	674
City of West Palm Beach	103,028	849	15	45	326	463	4,788	929	3,567	292
City of Pompano Beach	105,523	869	6	62	259	542	4,568	1,004	3,250	314
City of Miami Beach	91,771	893	5	54	385	449	9,423	819	8,176	428
City of Boca Raton	90,496	167	0	16	52	99	2,066	346	1,628	92
City of Deerfield Beach	78,773	369	1	32	104	232	2,073	502	1,429	142
City of Delray Beach	64,917	432	5	30	122	275	2,733	434	2,136	163
City of Jupiter	59,039	126	1	7	40	78	1,049	167	836	46
Total area actually reporting	100.0%	35,348	419	2,214	11,176	21,539	230,954	42,567	171,138	17,249
Rate per 100,000 inhabitants		595.2	7.1	37.3	188.2	362.7	3,888.9	716.8	2,881.7	290.4
Fort Lauderdale-Pompano Beach-Deerfield Beach, FL M.D.	1,875,917									
Includes Broward County										
Total area actually reporting	100.0%	7,853	76	627	2,654	4,496	58,201	11,954	42,374	3,873
Rate per 100,000 inhabitants		418.6	4.1	33.4	141.5	239.7	3,102.5	637.2	2,258.8	206.5
Miami-Miami Beach-Kendall, FL M.D.	2,667,260									
Includes Miami-Dade County										
Total area actually reporting	100.0%	20,141	251	1,006	6,591	12,293	125,062	20,237	94,748	10,077
Rate per 100,000 inhabitants		755.1	9.4	37.7	247.1	460.9	4,688.8	758.7	3,552.3	377.8
West Palm Beach-Boca Raton-Delray Beach, FL M.D.	1,395,570									
Includes Palm Beach County										
Total area actually reporting	100.0%	7,354	92	581	1,931	4,750	47,691	10,376	34,016	3,299
Rate per 100,000 inhabitants		527.0	6.6	41.6	138.4	340.4	3,417.3	743.5	2,437.4	236.4
Michigan City-La Porte, IN M.S.A.[3]	111,335									
Includes La Porte County										
City of Michigan City	31,508	100	3	6	57	34	1,382	167	1,146	69
City of La Porte	22,002	34	2	1	14	17	747	121	600	26
Total area actually reporting	90.5%	156	6	7	75	68	2,583	462	2,001	120
Estimated total	100.0%	185	6	9	81	89	2,904	503	2,261	140
Rate per 100,000 inhabitants		166.2	5.4	8.1	72.8	79.9	2,608.3	451.8	2,030.8	125.7
Midland, MI M.S.A.	84,059									
Includes Midland County										
City of Midland	42,256	50	1	19	8	22	546	57	477	12
Total area actually reporting	100.0%	104	1	35	9	59	1,042	239	777	26
Rate per 100,000 inhabitants		123.7	1.2	41.6	10.7	70.2	1,239.6	284.3	924.4	30.9
Midland, TX M.S.A.	161,969									
Includes Martin and Midland Counties										
City of Midland	127,344	407	7	36	65	299	3,266	597	2,475	194
Total area actually reporting	100.0%	522	8	37	74	403	4,179	834	3,045	300
Rate per 100,000 inhabitants		322.3	4.9	22.8	45.7	248.8	2,580.1	514.9	1,880.0	185.2

(Number, percent, rate per 100,000 population.)

Area	Population	Violent crime	Murder and nonnegligent manslaughter	Rape[1]	Robbery	Aggravated assault	Property crime	Burglary	Larceny-theft	Motor vehicle theft
Milwaukee-Waukesha-West Allis, WI M.S.A.	1,573,272									
Includes Milwaukee, Ozaukee, Washington, and Waukesha Counties										
City of Milwaukee	600,374	8,864	90	395	3,520	4,859	27,499	5,929	14,917	6,653
City of Waukesha	71,093	90	1	17	15	57	1,204	208	957	39
City of West Allis	60,764	218	0	15	107	96	2,717	502	2,075	140
Total area actually reporting	96.2%	9,900	98	513	3,928	5,361	46,130	8,292	30,353	7,485
Estimated total	100.0%	9,974	99	523	3,950	5,402	47,383	8,440	31,413	7,530
Rate per 100,000 inhabitants		634.0	6.3	33.2	251.1	343.4	3,011.7	536.5	1,996.7	478.6
Minneapolis-St. Paul-Bloomington, MN-WI M.S.A.	3,491,062									
Includes Anoka, Carver, Chisago, Dakota, Hennepin, Isanti, Le Sueur, Mille Lacs, Ramsey, Scott, Sherburne, Sibley, Washington, and Wright Counties, MN and Pierce and St. Croix Counties, WI										
City of Minneapolis, MN	404,461	4,093	31	389	1,871	1,802	19,123	4,112	13,480	1,531
City of St. Paul, MN	297,984	1,974	11	181	654	1,128	10,383	2,330	6,045	2,008
City of Bloomington, MN	87,163	157	0	23	75	59	3,202	203	2,892	107
City of Plymouth, MN	74,833	54	1	13	12	28	1,059	177	846	36
City of Eagan, MN	65,754	24	0	1	12	11	1,177	152	995	30
City of Eden Prairie, MN	63,036	22	0	11	4	7	849	98	735	16
Total area actually reporting	99.8%	9,129	64	1,177	3,291	4,597	86,992	14,025	66,746	6,221
Estimated total	100.0%	9,138	64	1,178	3,293	4,603	87,153	14,044	66,882	6,227
Rate per 100,000 inhabitants		261.8	1.8	33.7	94.3	131.9	2,496.5	402.3	1,915.8	178.4
Missoula, MT M.S.A.	112,637									
Includes Missoula County										
City of Missoula	69,674	222	2	48	43	129	2,869	295	2,447	127
Total area actually reporting	100.0%	303	2	69	46	186	3,266	383	2,722	161
Rate per 100,000 inhabitants		269.0	1.8	61.3	40.8	165.1	2,899.6	340.0	2,416.6	142.9
Mobile, AL M.S.A.[5]	414,522									
Includes Mobile County										
City of Mobile[5]	250,655	1,488	31	136	428	893	11,603	2,847	8,225	531
Total area actually reporting	100.0%	2,120	39	196	559	1,326	16,605	4,395	11,209	1,001
Rate per 100,000 inhabitants		511.4	9.4	47.3	134.9	319.9	4,005.8	1,060.3	2,704.1	241.5
Modesto, CA M.S.A.	531,018									
Includes Stanislaus County										
City of Modesto	205,820	1,778	11	81	385	1,301	9,113	1,754	6,164	1,195
Total area actually reporting	100.0%	2,826	32	136	683	1,975	18,559	4,188	11,545	2,826
Rate per 100,000 inhabitants		532.2	6.0	25.6	128.6	371.9	3,495.0	788.7	2,174.1	532.2
Monroe, LA M.S.A.[2, 3]	179,150									
Includes Ouachita and Union Parishes										
City of Monroe[2]	49,900		10	49	243		5,098	1,299	3,660	139
Total area actually reporting	97.0%		13	67	307		9,332	2,570	6,450	312
Estimated total	100.0%		13	68	311		9,557	2,611	6,620	326
Rate per 100,000 inhabitants			7.3	38.0	173.6		5,334.6	1,457.4	3,695.2	182.0
Montgomery, AL M.S.A.	373,331									
Includes Autauga, Elmore, Lowndes, and Montgomery Counties										
City of Montgomery	200,194	1,046	35	35	450	526	9,025	2,548	5,817	660
Total area actually reporting	99.1%	1,456	40	101	541	774	13,357	3,727	8,671	959
Estimated total	100.0%	1,471	40	103	544	784	13,485	3,753	8,765	967
Rate per 100,000 inhabitants		394.0	10.7	27.6	145.7	210.0	3,612.1	1,005.3	2,347.8	259.0
Morgantown, WV M.S.A.	137,326									
Includes Monongalia and Preston Counties										
City of Morgantown	31,103	81	2	11	25	43	794	161	608	25
Total area actually reporting	93.4%	250	4	32	40	174	1,895	451	1,357	87
Estimated total	100.0%	277	4	34	44	195	2,189	491	1,600	98
Rate per 100,000 inhabitants		201.7	2.9	24.8	32.0	142.0	1,594.0	357.5	1,165.1	71.4
Morristown, TN M.S.A.	115,787									
Includes Hamblen and Jefferson Counties										
City of Morristown	29,401	191	0	10	23	158	1,467	167	1,237	63
Total area actually reporting	100.0%	444	0	34	35	375	3,121	584	2,390	147
Rate per 100,000 inhabitants		383.5	0.0	29.4	30.2	323.9	2,695.5	504.4	2,064.1	127.0
Mount Vernon-Anacortes, WA M.S.A.	119,835									
Includes Skagit County										

Table 6. Crime, by Selected Metropolitan Statistical Area, 2014—*Continued*

(Number, percent, rate per 100,000 population.)

Area	Population	Violent crime	Murder and nonnegligent manslaughter	Rape[1]	Robbery	Aggravated assault	Property crime	Burglary	Larceny-theft	Motor vehicle theft
City of Mount Vernon	32,805	85	1	16	21	47	1,505	223	1,178	104
City of Anacortes	16,119	23	0	7	1	15	413	64	333	16
Total area actually reporting	100.0%	247	3	62	37	145	4,394	980	3,157	257
Rate per 100,000 inhabitants		206.1	2.5	51.7	30.9	121.0	3,666.7	817.8	2,634.5	214.5
Muncie, IN M.S.A.[3]	117,526									
Includes Delaware County										
City of Muncie	70,347	277	2	37	101	137	2,899	490	2,232	177
Total area actually reporting	100.0%	330	2	50	105	173	3,488	627	2,650	211
Rate per 100,000 inhabitants		280.8	1.7	42.5	89.3	147.2	2,967.9	533.5	2,254.8	179.5
Muskegon, MI M.S.A.	170,933									
Includes Muskegon County										
City of Muskegon	36,964	305	2	24	69	210	1,764	443	1,218	103
Total area actually reporting	100.0%	761	11	120	140	490	6,077	1,196	4,624	257
Rate per 100,000 inhabitants		445.2	6.4	70.2	81.9	286.7	3,555.2	699.7	2,705.2	150.4
Napa, CA M.S.A.	142,015									
Includes Napa County										
City of Napa	79,572	249	2	34	39	174	1,315	290	900	125
Total area actually reporting	100.0%	534	5	45	59	425	2,385	566	1,606	213
Rate per 100,000 inhabitants		376.0	3.5	31.7	41.5	299.3	1,679.4	398.5	1,130.9	150.0
Naples-Immokalee-Marco Island, FL M.S.A.	346,776									
Includes Collier County										
City of Naples	20,779	16	0	1	8	7	541	86	440	15
City of Marco Island	17,343	5	1	0	1	3	118	20	92	6
Total area actually reporting	100.0%	1,374	8	130	243	993	7,349	1,312	5,623	414
Rate per 100,000 inhabitants		396.2	2.3	37.5	70.1	286.4	2,119.2	378.3	1,621.5	119.4
Nashville-Davidson–Murfreesboro–Franklin, TN M.S.A.	1,783,924									
Includes Cannon, Cheatham, Davidson, Dickson, Hickman, Macon, Maury, Robertson, Rutherford, Smith, Sumner, Trousdale, Williamson, and Wilson Counties										
City of Nashville	647,689	7,270	41	487	1,523	5,219	23,515	4,756	17,622	1,137
City of Murfreesboro	119,005	635	7	54	119	455	3,983	761	3,052	170
City of Franklin	70,485	99	0	19	5	75	990	103	868	19
Total area actually reporting	100.0%	10,898	70	834	1,946	8,048	45,794	9,100	34,488	2,206
Rate per 100,000 inhabitants		610.9	3.9	46.8	109.1	451.1	2,567.0	510.1	1,933.3	123.7
New Bern, NC M.S.A.	128,067									
Includes Craven, Jones, and Pamlico Counties										
City of New Bern	30,371	122	0	7	38	77	1,267	310	936	21
Total area actually reporting	92.4%	284	2	20	60	202	2,952	878	1,989	85
Estimated total	100.0%	299	2	21	62	214	3,125	941	2,090	94
Rate per 100,000 inhabitants		233.5	1.6	16.4	48.4	167.1	2,440.1	734.8	1,632.0	73.4
New Haven-Milford, CT M.S.A.	807,947									
Includes New Haven County										
City of New Haven	130,882	1,380	12	80	591	697	5,167	990	3,579	598
City of Milford	53,222	35	2	0	21	12	1,387	146	1,179	62
Total area actually reporting	100.0%	2,639	25	176	1,096	1,342	21,544	3,284	16,024	2,236
Rate per 100,000 inhabitants		326.6	3.1	21.8	135.7	166.1	2,666.5	406.5	1,983.3	276.8
New Orleans-Metairie, LA M.S.A.[3,4]	1,253,840									
Includes Jefferson, Orleans, Plaquemines, St. Bernard,[3] St. Charles, St. James, St. John the Baptist,[4] and St. Tammany Parishes										
City of New Orleans	387,113	3,770	150	244	1,470	1,906	16,382	3,458	10,309	2,615
Total area actually reporting	99.7%		211	408	2,178		40,391	7,583	28,840	3,968
Estimated total	100.0%		211	409	2,180		40,534	7,609	28,948	3,977
Rate per 100,000 inhabitants			16.8	32.6	173.9		3,232.8	606.9	2,308.7	317.2
New York-Newark-Jersey City, NY-NJ-PA M.S.A.[4]	20,070,688									
Includes the Metropolitan Divisions of Dutchess County-Putnam County, NY; Nassau County-Suffolk County, NY; Newark, NJ-PA; and New York-Jersey City-White Plains, NY-NJ										
City of New York, NY	8,473,938	50,564	333	2,190	16,581	31,460	135,747	15,916	112,107	7,724
City of Newark, NJ	279,110	3,008	93	49	1,922	944	7,958	1,736	3,810	2,412
City of Jersey City, NJ	260,005	1,381	24	35	620	702	4,240	887	2,804	549

Table 6. Crime, by Selected Metropolitan Statistical Area, 2014—*Continued*

(Number, percent, rate per 100,000 population.)

Area	Population	Violent crime	Murder and nonnegligent manslaughter	Rape[1]	Robbery	Aggravated assault	Property crime	Burglary	Larceny-theft	Motor vehicle theft
City of White Plains, NY	58,103	105	1	5	25	74	1,046	55	968	23
City of New Brunswick, NJ	56,193	418	4	18	222	174	1,582	523	979	80
City of Lakewood Township, NJ	93,749	167	2	3	65	97	1,118	223	849	46
Total area actually reporting	99.9%	74,512	632	3,325	27,152	43,403		44,277		20,225
Estimated total	100.0%	74,537	632	3,326	27,161	43,418		44,312		20,233
Rate per 100,000 inhabitants		371.4	3.1	16.6	135.3	216.3		220.8		100.8
Dutchess County-Putnam County, NY M.D.	396,951									
Includes Dutchess and Putnam Counties										
Total area actually reporting	99.1%	683	3	107	179	394	4,955	762	4,106	87
Estimated total	100.0%	688	3	107	181	397	5,013	770	4,154	89
Rate per 100,000 inhabitants		173.3	0.8	27.0	45.6	100.0	1,262.9	194.0	1,046.5	22.4
Nassau County-Suffolk County, NY M.D.	2,860,417									
Includes Nassau and Suffolk Counties										
Total area actually reporting	99.9%	3,842	47	185	1,541	2,069	39,611	5,265	32,249	2,097
Estimated total	100.0%	3,844	47	185	1,542	2,070	39,636	5,268	32,270	2,098
Rate per 100,000 inhabitants		134.4	1.6	6.5	53.9	72.4	1,385.7	184.2	1,128.2	73.3
Newark, NJ-PA M.D.	2,506,630									
Includes Essex, Hunterdon, Morris, Somerset, Sussex, and Union Counties, NJ and Pike County, PA										
Total area actually reporting	100.0%	7,922	145	273	4,398	3,106	39,972	8,276	25,877	5,819
Rate per 100,000 inhabitants		316.0	5.8	10.9	175.5	123.9	1,594.7	330.2	1,032.3	232.1
New York-Jersey City-White Plains, NY-NJ M.D.[4]	14,306,690									
Includes Bergen, Hudson, Middlesex, Monmouth, Ocean, and Passaic Counties, NJ and Bronx, Kings, New York, Orange, Queens, Richmond, Rockland, and Westchester Counties, NY										
Total area actually reporting	99.9%	62,065	437	2,760	21,034	37,834		29,974		12,222
Estimated total	100.0%	62,083	437	2,761	21,040	37,845		29,998		12,227
Rate per 100,000 inhabitants		433.9	3.1	19.3	147.1	264.5		209.7		85.5
Niles-Benton Harbor, MI M.S.A.	155,008									
Includes Berrien County										
City of Niles	11,389	64	0	14	13	37	332	57	258	17
City of Benton Harbor	10,014	253	1	33	80	139	539	175	341	23
Total area actually reporting	97.4%	651	2	139	124	386	3,605	717	2,748	140
Estimated total	100.0%	662	2	141	126	393	3,689	732	2,811	146
Rate per 100,000 inhabitants		427.1	1.3	91.0	81.3	253.5	2,379.9	472.2	1,813.5	94.2
North Port-Sarasota-Bradenton, FL M.S.A.	745,917									
Includes Manatee and Sarasota Counties										
City of North Port	59,668	103	1	30	12	60	892	179	688	25
City of Sarasota	53,620	357	2	23	108	224	2,537	479	1,947	111
City of Bradenton	52,350	338	3	24	71	240	2,009	416	1,515	78
City of Venice	21,378	40	0	4	5	31	396	74	311	11
Total area actually reporting	100.0%	4,049	28	413	709	2,899	24,973	5,395	18,558	1,020
Rate per 100,000 inhabitants		542.8	3.8	55.4	95.1	388.6	3,348.0	723.3	2,487.9	136.7
Norwich-New London, CT M.S.A.	146,061									
Includes New London County										
City of Norwich	40,296	153	0	16	23	114	848	210	588	50
City of New London	27,526	163	0	22	40	101	846	180	561	105
Total area actually reporting	100.0%	496	0	66	91	339	3,474	551	2,705	218
Rate per 100,000 inhabitants		339.6	0.0	45.2	62.3	232.1	2,378.5	377.2	1,852.0	149.3
Ocala, FL M.S.A.	341,542									
Includes Marion County										
City of Ocala	57,740	360	7	34	87	232	3,003	494	2,439	70
Total area actually reporting	100.0%	1,418	19	131	171	1,097	6,928	1,655	5,013	260
Rate per 100,000 inhabitants		415.2	5.6	38.4	50.1	321.2	2,028.4	484.6	1,467.8	76.1
Ocean City, NJ M.S.A.	95,711									
Includes Cape May County										
City of Ocean City	11,392	13	0	0	3	10	475	84	384	7
Total area actually reporting	100.0%	228	0	19	53	156	3,536	757	2,712	67
Rate per 100,000 inhabitants		238.2	0.0	19.9	55.4	163.0	3,694.5	790.9	2,833.5	70.0
Odessa, TX M.S.A.[4]	153,741									
Includes Ector County[4]										

Table 6. Crime, by Selected Metropolitan Statistical Area, 2014—*Continued*

(Number, percent, rate per 100,000 population.)

Area	Population	Violent crime	Murder and nonnegligent manslaughter	Rape[1]	Robbery	Aggravated assault	Property crime	Burglary	Larceny-theft	Motor vehicle theft
City of Odessa	113,619	1,068	11	65	148	844	4,217	735	3,004	478
Total area actually reporting	100.0%		17	75	165		5,974	1,118	4,128	728
Rate per 100,000 inhabitants			11.1	48.8	107.3		3,885.8	727.2	2,685.0	473.5
Ogden-Clearfield, UT M.S.A.	629,218									
Includes Box Elder, Davis, Morgan, and Weber Counties										
City of Ogden	84,557	444	4	83	113	244	3,645	531	2,844	270
City of Clearfield	30,535	39	1	16	8	14	645	97	520	28
Total area actually reporting	99.5%	970	11	313	157	489	13,030	1,876	10,299	855
Estimated total	100.0%	975	11	314	158	492	13,113	1,887	10,364	862
Rate per 100,000 inhabitants		155.0	1.7	49.9	25.1	78.2	2,084.0	299.9	1,647.1	137.0
Oklahoma City, OK M.S.A.	1,336,996									
Includes Canadian, Cleveland, Grady, Lincoln, Logan, McClain, and Oklahoma Counties										
City of Oklahoma City	617,975	4,782	45	434	1,126	3,177	27,258	6,638	17,111	3,509
Total area actually reporting	100.0%	6,199	69	667	1,409	4,054	44,800	10,560	29,432	4,808
Rate per 100,000 inhabitants		463.7	5.2	49.9	105.4	303.2	3,350.8	789.8	2,201.4	359.6
Olympia-Tumwater, WA M.S.A.	265,955									
Includes Thurston County										
City of Olympia	48,763	198	0	19	47	132	2,170	390	1,629	151
City of Tumwater	18,800	58	0	7	13	38	670	167	450	53
Total area actually reporting	100.0%	601	3	76	113	409	7,286	1,868	4,878	540
Rate per 100,000 inhabitants		226.0	1.1	28.6	42.5	153.8	2,739.6	702.4	1,834.1	203.0
Omaha-Council Bluffs, NE-IA M.S.A.	903,607									
Includes Harrison, Mills, and Pottawattamie Counties, IA and Cass, Douglas, Sarpy, Saunders, and Washington Counties, NE										
City of Omaha, NE	438,465	2,458	32	180	723	1,523	19,053	2,997	12,910	3,146
City of Council Bluffs, IA	61,864	338	1	47	72	218	4,108	744	2,906	458
Total area actually reporting	99.6%	3,291	37	323	846	2,085	28,209	4,745	19,484	3,980
Estimated total	100.0%	3,297	37	324	846	2,090	28,271	4,755	19,533	3,983
Rate per 100,000 inhabitants		364.9	4.1	35.9	93.6	231.3	3,128.7	526.2	2,161.7	440.8
Orlando-Kissimmee-Sanford, FL M.S.A.	2,319,802									
Includes Lake, Orange, Osceola, and Seminole Counties										
City of Orlando	259,675	2,340	15	167	620	1,538	16,515	3,342	12,182	991
City of Kissimmee	66,623	445	2	45	104	294	2,816	623	2,090	103
City of Sanford	56,601	455	2	29	108	316	2,982	641	2,163	178
Total area actually reporting	99.6%	15,861	157	1,447	3,570	10,687	92,753	22,580	64,455	5,718
Estimated total	100.0%	15,901	157	1,450	3,581	10,713	93,082	22,642	64,703	5,737
Rate per 100,000 inhabitants		685.4	6.8	62.5	154.4	461.8	4,012.5	976.0	2,789.2	247.3
Oshkosh-Neenah, WI M.S.A.	170,212									
Includes Winnebago County										
City of Oshkosh	66,962	154	0	10	23	121	1,432	263	1,137	32
City of Neenah	25,992	38	0	3	4	31	477	73	394	10
Total area actually reporting	100.0%	289	2	24	33	230	2,834	495	2,275	64
Rate per 100,000 inhabitants		169.8	1.2	14.1	19.4	135.1	1,665.0	290.8	1,336.6	37.6
Owensboro, KY M.S.A.	116,963									
Includes Daviess, Hancock, and McLean Counties										
City of Owensboro	58,659	122	0	28	41	53	2,252	385	1,763	104
Total area actually reporting	100.0%	150	0	34	42	74	2,792	542	2,119	131
Rate per 100,000 inhabitants		128.2	0.0	29.1	35.9	63.3	2,387.1	463.4	1,811.7	112.0
Oxnard-Thousand Oaks-Ventura, CA M.S.A.	847,935									
Includes Ventura County										
City of Oxnard	204,159	884	11	45	447	381	6,382	1,172	4,475	735
City of Thousand Oaks	129,175	128	1	25	22	80	1,599	357	1,148	94
City of Ventura	109,246	276	1	28	103	144	3,867	663	2,994	210
City of Camarillo	66,272	72	0	14	21	37	965	154	755	56
Total area actually reporting	100.0%	1,890	20	185	682	1,003	16,812	3,217	12,153	1,442
Rate per 100,000 inhabitants		222.9	2.4	21.8	80.4	118.3	1,982.7	379.4	1,433.2	170.1
Palm Bay-Melbourne-Titusville, FL M.S.A.	556,949									
Includes Brevard County										
City of Palm Bay	105,287	600	4	38	56	502	2,226	478	1,621	127
City of Melbourne	77,797	611	2	58	119	432	3,102	460	2,533	109
City of Titusville	44,310	267	0	15	53	199	1,447	384	930	133

Table 6. Crime, by Selected Metropolitan Statistical Area, 2014—*Continued*

(Number, percent, rate per 100,000 population.)

Area	Population	Violent crime	Murder and nonnegligent manslaughter	Rape[1]	Robbery	Aggravated assault	Property crime	Burglary	Larceny-theft	Motor vehicle theft
Total area actually reporting	100.0%	3,121	19	292	461	2,349	16,771	3,352	12,669	750
Rate per 100,000 inhabitants		560.4	3.4	52.4	82.8	421.8	3,011.2	601.9	2,274.7	134.7
Panama City, FL M.S.A.	193,811									
Includes Bay and Gulf Counties										
City of Panama City	37,204	343	8	7	65	263	2,581	451	1,952	178
Total area actually reporting	100.0%	969	18	83	141	727	7,432	1,357	5,663	412
Rate per 100,000 inhabitants		500.0	9.3	42.8	72.8	375.1	3,834.7	700.2	2,921.9	212.6
Parkersburg-Vienna, WV M.S.A.[4]	92,202									
Includes Wirt and Wood Counties										
City of Parkersburg[4]	31,139	88	1	14	6	67		259		53
City of Vienna	10,603	4	0	0	0	4		25		1
Total area actually reporting	100.0%	168	1	24	7	136		457		84
Rate per 100,000 inhabitants		182.2	1.1	26.0	7.6	147.5		495.7		91.1
Pensacola-Ferry Pass-Brent, FL M.S.A.	474,766									
Includes Escambia and Santa Rosa Counties										
City of Pensacola	52,873	373	3	28	82	260	2,390	451	1,836	103
Total area actually reporting	100.0%	3,194	33	269	539	2353	18,890	4451	13,411	1028
Rate per 100,000 inhabitants		672.8	7.0	56.7	113.5	495.6	3,978.8	937.5	2,824.8	216.5
Peoria, IL M.S.A.	382,542									
Includes Marshall, Peoria, Stark, Tazewell, and Woodford Counties										
City of Peoria	116,923	759	7	68	230	454	4,858	1,224	3,442	192
Total area actually reporting	94.3%	1,140	9	132	267	732	8,609	2,145	6,173	291
Estimated total	100.0%	1,183	10	137	279	757	8,998	2,209	6,481	308
Rate per 100,000 inhabitants		309.2	2.6	35.8	72.9	197.9	2,352.2	577.5	1,694.2	80.5
Philadelphia-Camden-Wilmington, PA-NJ-DE-MD M.S.A.	6,054,007									
Includes the Metropolitan Divisions of Camden, NJ; Montgomery County-Bucks County-Chester County, PA; Philadelphia, PA; and Wilmington, DE-MD-NJ.										
City of Philadelphia, PA	1,559,062	15,925	248	1,207	6,970	7,500	52,816	9,694	37,394	5,728
City of Wilmington, DE	71,713	1,174	27	23	397	727	3,765	900	2,530	335
Total area actually reporting	99.9%	27,821	424	2,076	10,875	14,446	141,113	26,148	105,437	9,528
Estimated total	100.0%	27,824	424	2,076	10,876	14,448	141,137	26,152	105,456	9,529
Rate per 100,000 inhabitants		459.6	7.0	34.3	179.6	238.7	2,331.3	432.0	1,741.9	157.4
Camden, NJ M.D.	1,256,578									
Includes Burlington, Camden, and Gloucester Counties										
Total area actually reporting	100.0%	3,466	56	214	1,294	1,902	26,142	6,075	19,027	1,040
Rate per 100,000 inhabitants		275.8	4.5	17.0	103.0	151.4	2,080.4	483.5	1,514.2	82.8
Montgomery County-Bucks County-Chester County, PA M.D.	1,954,080									
Includes Bucks, Chester, and Montgomery Counties										
Total area actually reporting	99.9%	2,460	26	236	794	1,404	29,654	4,255	24,241	1,158
Estimated total	100.0%	2,463	26	236	795	1,406	29,678	4,259	24,260	1,159
Rate per 100,000 inhabitants		126.0	1.3	12.1	40.7	72.0	1,518.8	218.0	1,241.5	59.3
Philadelphia, PA M.D.	2,121,653									
Includes Delaware and Philadelphia Counties										
Total area actually reporting	100.0%	18,276	295	1,413	7,668	8,900	64,229	11,520	46,406	6,303
Rate per 100,000 inhabitants		861.4	13.9	66.6	361.4	419.5	3,027.3	543.0	2,187.3	297.1
Wilmington, DE-MD-NJ M.D.	721,696									
Includes New Castle County, DE; Cecil County, MD; and Salem County, NJ										
Total area actually reporting	100.0%	3,619	47	213	1119	2,240	21,088	4,298	15,763	1,027
Rate per 100,000 inhabitants		501.5	6.5	29.5	155.1	310.4	2,922.0	595.5	2,184.2	142.3
Pine Bluff, AR M.S.A	94,694									
Includes Cleveland, Jefferson, and Lincoln Counties										
City of Pine Bluff	45,402	576	13	39	141	383	2,656	991	1,487	178
Total area actually reporting	100.0%	649	17	60	142	430	3,382	1,281	1,867	234
Rate per 100,000 inhabitants		685.4	18.0	63.4	150.0	454.1	3,571.5	1,352.8	1,971.6	247.1
Pittsburgh, PA M.S.A.	2,361,431									
Includes Allegheny, Armstrong, Beaver, Butler, Fayette, Washington, and Westmoreland Counties										

Table 6. Crime, by Selected Metropolitan Statistical Area, 2014—*Continued*

(Number, percent, rate per 100,000 population.)

Area	Population	Violent crime	Murder and nonnegligent manslaughter	Rape[1]	Robbery	Aggravated assault	Property crime	Burglary	Larceny-theft	Motor vehicle theft
City of Pittsburgh	307,613	2,455	69	91	986	1,309	9,883	2,129	7,157	597
Total area actually reporting	99.1%	6,745	128	361	1,976	4,280	42,597	8,137	32,769	1,691
Estimated total	100.0%	6,783	128	364	1,986	4,305	42,968	8,192	33,073	1,703
Rate per 100,000 inhabitants		287.2	5.4	15.4	84.1	182.3	1,819.6	346.9	1,400.5	72.1
Pittsfield, MA M.S.A.	129,547									
Includes Berkshire County										
City of Pittsfield	43,895	194	0	35	30	129	1,341	459	842	40
Total area actually reporting	91.9%	365	0	59	44	262	2,582	760	1,753	69
Estimated total	100.0%	398	0	62	50	286	2,756	794	1,882	80
Rate per 100,000 inhabitants		307.2	0.0	47.9	38.6	220.8	2,127.4	612.9	1,452.8	61.8
Portland-South Portland, ME M.S.A.[3]	522,033									
Includes Cumberland, Sagadahoc, and York Counties										
City of Portland	66,380	158	1	20	64	73	2,134	246	1,834	54
City of South Portland	25,327	39	0	5	8	26	797	107	676	14
Total area actually reporting	100.0%	666	7	137	139	383	10,438	2,035	8,092	311
Rate per 100,000 inhabitants		127.6	1.3	26.2	26.6	73.4	1,999.5	389.8	1,550.1	59.6
Portland-Vancouver-Hillsboro, OR-WA M.S.A.	2,345,482									
Includes Clackamas, Columbia, Multnomah, Washington, and										
Yamhill Counties, OR and Clark and Skamania Counties, WA										
City of Portland, OR	615,672	2,911	26	262	847	1,776	32,229	4,146	24,707	3,376
City of Vancouver, WA	168,688	577	6	89	151	331	5,259	821	3,617	821
City of Hillsboro, OR	98,635	186	2	40	58	86	2,205	246	1,825	134
City of Beaverton, OR	94,416	127	0	17	34	76	1,521	174	1,250	97
Total area actually reporting	90.7%	5,771	44	725	1,573	3,429	64,411	9,339	48,447	6,625
Estimated total	100.0%	6,068	46	779	1,613	3,630	67,979	10,090	50,935	6,954
Rate per 100,000 inhabitants		258.7	2.0	33.2	68.8	154.8	2,898.3	430.2	2,171.6	296.5
Port St. Lucie, FL M.S.A.	444,898									
Includes Martin and St. Lucie Counties										
City of Port St. Lucie	172,453	243	6	16	37	184	2,498	511	1,896	91
Total area actually reporting	100.0%	1,474	27	140	287	1,020	9,712	2,190	7,112	410
Rate per 100,000 inhabitants		331.3	6.1	31.5	64.5	229.3	2,183.0	492.2	1,598.6	92.2
Providence-Warwick, RI-MA M.S.A.	1,610,481									
Includes Bristol County, MA and Bristol, Kent, Newport,										
Providence, and Washington Counties RI										
City of Providence, RI	178,640	927	18	90	289	530	6,827	1,666	4,366	795
City of Warwick, RI	82,123	84	0	25	10	49	1,866	190	1,611	65
Total area actually reporting	100.0%	5,297	31	607	1,116	3,543	34,357	7,364	24,483	2,510
Rate per 100,000 inhabitants		328.9	1.9	37.7	69.3	220.0	2,133.3	457.3	1,520.2	155.9
Pueblo, CO M.S.A.	162,854									
Includes Pueblo County										
City of Pueblo	108,591	886	10	152	183	541	7,077	2,002	4,439	636
Total area actually reporting	100.0%	937	10	156	189	582	8,315	2,246	5,341	728
Rate per 100,000 inhabitants		575.4	6.1	95.8	116.1	357.4	5,105.8	1,379.1	3,279.6	447.0
Punta Gorda, FL M.S.A.	167,298									
Includes Charlotte County										
City of Punta Gorda	17,305	8	0	0	3	5	287	39	241	7
Total area actually reporting	100.0%	439	2	40	36	361	4,301	843	3,302	156
Rate per 100,000 inhabitants		262.4	1.2	23.9	21.5	215.8	2,570.9	503.9	1,973.7	93.2
Racine, WI M.S.A.	194,990									
Includes Racine County										
City of Racine	78,057	310	3	10	200	97	2,723	955	1,662	106
Total area actually reporting	100.0%	388	4	26	220	138	4,443	1,170	3,123	150
Rate per 100,000 inhabitants		199.0	2.1	13.3	112.8	70.8	2,278.6	600.0	1,601.6	76.9
Rapid City, SD M.S.A.	143,222									
Includes Custer, Meade, and Pennington Counties										
City of Rapid City	71,481	426	4	59	53	310	2,704	426	2,076	202
Total area actually reporting	100.0%	548	5	93	60	390	3,527	604	2678	245
Rate per 100,000 inhabitants		382.6	3.5	64.9	41.9	272.3	2,462.6	421.7	1,869.8	171.1
Reading, PA M.S.A.	413,879									
Includes Berks County										
City of Reading	87,848	760	9	55	288	408	2,551	852	1,494	205

Table 6. Crime, by Selected Metropolitan Statistical Area, 2014—*Continued*

(Number, percent, rate per 100,000 population.)

Area	Population	Violent crime	Murder and nonnegligent manslaughter	Rape[1]	Robbery	Aggravated assault	Property crime	Burglary	Larceny-theft	Motor vehicle theft
Total area actually reporting	100.0%	1,356	12	97	372	875	7,344	1,741	5,210	393
Rate per 100,000 inhabitants		327.6	2.9	23.4	89.9	211.4	1,774.4	420.7	1,258.8	95.0
Redding, CA M.S.A.	180,406									
Includes Shasta County										
City of Redding	91,426	610	4	52	142	412	3,924	802	2,636	486
Total area actually reporting	100.0%	1,275	8	111	171	985	5,705	1,331	3,511	863
Rate per 100,000 inhabitants		706.7	4.4	61.5	94.8	546.0	3,162.3	737.8	1,946.2	478.4
Reno, NV M.S.A.	444,810									
Includes Storey and Washoe Counties										
City of Reno	235,055	1,147	15	128	263	741	6,798	1,312	4,711	775
Total area actually reporting	100.0%	1,685	19	241	343	1,082	10,652	2,184	7,338	1,130
Rate per 100,000 inhabitants		378.8	4.3	54.2	77.1	243.2	2,394.7	491.0	1,649.7	254.0
Richmond, VA M.S.A.	1,255,599									
Includes Amelia, Caroline, Charles City, Chesterfield, Dinwiddie, Goochland, Hanover, Henrico, King William, New Kent, Powhatan, Prince George, and Sussex Counties and Colonial Heights, Hopewell, Petersburg, and Richmond Cities										
City of Richmond	216,747	1,254	41	39	569	605	8,388	1,685	5,969	734
Total area actually reporting	100.0%	2,916	78	253	1,059	1,526	29,204	5,122	22,578	1,504
Rate per 100,000 inhabitants		232.2	6.2	20.1	84.3	121.5	2,325.9	407.9	1,798.2	119.8
Riverside-San Bernardino-Ontario, CA M.S.A.	4,440,461									
Includes Riverside and San Bernardino Counties										
City of Riverside	319,453	1,384	12	143	441	788	9,864	1,531	6,794	1,539
City of San Bernardino	214,588	2,128	43	104	811	1,170	9,239	2,370	4,405	2,464
City of Ontario	168,278	431	6	20	163	242	4,654	780	2,987	887
City of Corona	161,128	171	0	25	68	78	3,440	541	2,389	510
City of Victorville	122,316	642	3	39	189	411	4,374	1,747	2,023	604
City of Temecula	108,308	100	2	7	54	37	2,535	656	1,668	211
City of Chino	81,600	186	0	8	42	136	1,816	418	1,121	277
City of Redlands	70,295	147	1	9	60	77	2,837	512	1,965	360
Total area actually reporting	100.0%	14,541	203	916	4,396	9,026	116,212	29,915	66,604	19,693
Rate per 100,000 inhabitants		327.5	4.6	20.6	99.0	203.3	2,617.1	673.7	1,499.9	443.5
Roanoke, VA M.S.A.	312,777									
Includes Botetourt, Craig, Franklin, and Roanoke Counties and Roanoke and Salem Cities										
City of Roanoke	98,941	340	2	35	89	214	4,127	557	3,386	184
Total area actually reporting	100.0%	634	7	88	118	421	7,043	958	5,797	288
Rate per 100,000 inhabitants		202.7	2.2	28.1	37.7	134.6	2,251.8	306.3	1,853.4	92.1
Rochester, MN M.S.A.	213,400									
Includes Dodge, Fillmore, Olmsted, and Wabasha Counties										
City of Rochester	111,712	205	2	46	52	105	2,223	338	1,775	110
Total area actually reporting	100.0%	301	3	61	55	182	2,947	487	2,303	157
Rate per 100,000 inhabitants		141.0	1.4	28.6	25.8	85.3	1,381.0	228.2	1,079.2	73.6
Rochester, NY M.S.A.	1,085,775									
Includes Livingston, Monroe, Ontario, Orleans, Wayne, and Yates Counties										
City of Rochester	210,347	1,765	27	190	698	850	8,856	2,125	6,058	673
Total area actually reporting	99.8%	2,809	32	451	919	1,407	24,368	4,559	18,716	1,093
Estimated total	100.0%	2,812	32	451	920	1,409	24,403	4,564	18,745	1,094
Rate per 100,000 inhabitants		259.0	2.9	41.5	84.7	129.8	2,247.5	420.3	1,726.4	100.8
Rockford, IL M.S.A.	343,135									
Includes Boone and Winnebago Counties										
City of Rockford	149,586	1,847	17	131	412	1,287	6,401	1,708	4,313	380
Total area actually reporting	83.8%	2,187	21	181	473	1,512	9,054	2,311	6,260	483
Estimated total	100.0%	2,281	23	195	493	1,570	9,844	2,477	6,847	520
Rate per 100,000 inhabitants		664.8	6.7	56.8	143.7	457.5	2,868.8	721.9	1,995.4	151.5
Rocky Mount, NC M.S.A.	150,531									
Includes Edgecombe and Nash Counties										
City of Rocky Mount	56,757	533	15	15	113	390	2,744	735	1,929	80
Total area actually reporting	97.7%	673	19	28	143	483	4,384	1,375	2,863	146
Estimated total	100.0%	682	19	29	145	489	4,495	1,397	2,948	150
Rate per 100,000 inhabitants		453.1	12.6	19.3	96.3	324.9	2,986.1	928.0	1,958.4	99.6

Table 6. Crime, by Selected Metropolitan Statistical Area, 2014—*Continued*

(Number, percent, rate per 100,000 population.)

Area	Population	Violent crime	Murder and nonnegligent manslaughter	Rape[1]	Robbery	Aggravated assault	Property crime	Burglary	Larceny-theft	Motor vehicle theft
Sacramento–Roseville–Arden-Arcade, CA M.S.A.	2,243,875									
Includes El Dorado, Placer, Sacramento, and Yolo Counties										
City of Sacramento	482,767	2,968	28	78	1,000	1,862	15,078	3,238	9,443	2,397
City of Roseville	128,997	193	1	17	50	125	3,070	470	2,367	233
City of Folsom	73,329	79	1	8	23	47	1,305	244	996	65
Total area actually reporting	100.0%	9,214	89	549	2,601	5,975	55,534	12,393	35,440	7,701
Rate per 100,000 inhabitants		410.6	4.0	24.5	115.9	266.3	2,474.9	552.3	1,579.4	343.2
Saginaw, MI M.S.A.	195,891									
Includes Saginaw County										
City of Saginaw	50,030	845	11	70	124	640	1,209	555	593	61
Total area actually reporting	100.0%	1,293	16	160	165	952	3,815	1,106	2,535	174
Rate per 100,000 inhabitants		660.1	8.2	81.7	84.2	486.0	1,947.5	564.6	1,294.1	88.8
Salem, OR M.S.A.	404,329									
Includes Marion and Polk Counties										
City of Salem	162,028	505	2	44	103	356	7,031	828	5,562	641
Total area actually reporting	100.0%	859	8	106	158	587	12,540	1,744	9,614	1,182
Rate per 100,000 inhabitants		212.5	2.0	26.2	39.1	145.2	3,101.4	431.3	2,377.8	292.3
Salinas, CA M.S.A.	434,416									
Includes Monterey County										
City of Salinas	156,908	997	15	32	449	501	5,227	1,281	2,330	1,616
Total area actually reporting	100.0%	1,833	34	125	587	1,087	10,577	2,594	5,595	2,388
Rate per 100,000 inhabitants		421.9	7.8	28.8	135.1	250.2	2,434.8	597.1	1,287.9	549.7
Salisbury, MD-DE M.S.A.	389,229									
Includes Sussex County, DE and Somerset, Wicomico, and Worcester Counties, MD										
City of Salisbury, MD	31,779	286	0	17	71	198	1,835	311	1,478	46
Total area actually reporting	100.0%	1,610	11	178	310	1,111	12,577	3,061	9,176	340
Rate per 100,000 inhabitants		413.6	2.8	45.7	79.6	285.4	3,231.3	786.4	2,357.5	87.4
Salt Lake City, UT M.S.A.	1,156,755									
Includes Salt Lake and Tooele Counties										
City of Salt Lake City	192,368	1,447	7	219	450	771	16,228	1,726	12,717	1,785
Total area actually reporting	99.9%	4,026	26	696	1,039	2,265	51,753	6,777	39,530	5,446
Estimated total	100.0%	4,026	26	696	1,039	2,265	51,763	6,778	39,538	5,447
Rate per 100,000 inhabitants		348.0	2.2	60.2	89.8	195.8	4,474.8	585.9	3,418.0	470.9
San Angelo, TX M.S.A.	118,519									
Includes Irion and Tom Green Counties										
City of San Angelo	98,477	325	3	46	38	238	3,786	808	2,738	240
Total area actually reporting	100.0%	348	5	55	38	250	4,222	955	2,996	271
Rate per 100,000 inhabitants		293.6	4.2	46.4	32.1	210.9	3,562.3	805.8	2,527.9	228.7
San Antonio-New Braunfels, TX M.S.A.	2,326,684									
Includes Atascosa, Bandera, Bexar, Comal, Guadalupe, Kendall, Medina, and Wilson Counties										
City of San Antonio	1,428,465	7,704	103	1,077	1,777	4,747	77,392	12,344	57,908	7,140
City of New Braunfels	64,622	182	1	9	21	151	2,101	313	1,614	174
Total area actually reporting	99.9%	9,337	133	1,374	2,006	5,824	97,124	16,823	71,928	8,373
Estimated total	100.0%	9,420	134	1,382	2,027	5,877	97,664	16,974	72,263	8,427
Rate per 100,000 inhabitants		404.9	5.8	59.4	87.1	252.6	4,197.6	729.5	3,105.8	362.2
San Diego-Carlsbad, CA M.S.A.	3,256,669									
Includes San Diego County										
City of San Diego	1,368,690	5,214	32	371	1,318	3,493	26,812	5,115	16,691	5,006
City of Carlsbad	112,297	204	1	14	44	145	1,731	331	1,272	128
Total area actually reporting	100.0%	10,590	74	763	2,706	7,047	59,059	10,962	38,633	9,464
Rate per 100,000 inhabitants		325.2	2.3	23.4	83.1	216.4	1,813.5	336.6	1,186.3	290.6
San Francisco-Oakland-Hayward, CA M.S.A.	4,585,742									
Includes the Metropolitan Divisions of Oakland-Hayward-Berkeley, San Francisco-Redwood City-South San Francisco, and San Rafael.										
City of San Francisco	850,294	6,761	45	355	3,224	3,137	45,093	5,237	33,730	6,126
City of Oakland	409,994	6,910	80	209	3,481	3,140	24,367	4,006	13,842	6,519
City of Hayward	153,319	605	9	53	329	214	4,873	985	2,444	1,444
City of Berkeley	117,753	431	3	35	263	130	5,102	932	3,615	555
City of San Leandro	88,690	369	1	18	226	124	3,757	599	2,236	922

Table 6. Crime, by Selected Metropolitan Statistical Area, 2014—*Continued*

(Number, percent, rate per 100,000 population.)

Area	Population	Violent crime	Murder and nonnegligent manslaughter	Rape[1]	Robbery	Aggravated assault	Property crime	Burglary	Larceny-theft	Motor vehicle theft
City of Redwood City....................	81,870	194	2	55	59	78	1,728	477	1,039	212
City of San Ramon.....................	75,049	23	0	3	11	9	748	209	463	76
City of Pleasanton.....................	75,060	61	0	8	14	39	1,244	169	919	156
City of Walnut Creek..................	67,555	74	0	4	24	46	2,439	434	1,788	217
City of South San Francisco............	66,793	156	1	27	49	79	1,274	287	836	151
City of San Rafael.....................	59,292	193	0	20	55	118	1,664	287	1,132	245
Total area actually reporting...........	100.0%	22,843	210	1,277	10,352	11,004	154,539	26,276	100,629	27,634
Rate per 100,000 inhabitants...........		498.1	4.6	27.8	225.7	240.0	3,370.0	573.0	2,194.4	602.6
Oakland-Hayward-Berkeley, CA M.D.	2,715,593									
Includes Alameda and Contra Costa Counties										
Total area actually reporting...........	100.0%	14,006	149	659	6,495	6,703	89,852	16,782	53,825	19,245
Rate per 100,000 inhabitants...........		515.8	5.5	24.3	239.2	246.8	3,308.7	618.0	1,982.1	708.7
San Francisco-Redwood City-South San Francisco, CA M.D. ..	1,608,949									
Includes San Francisco and San Mateo Counties.........										
Total area actually reporting...........	100.0%	8,383	56	578	3,746	4,003	60,122	8,422	43,852	7,848
Rate per 100,000 inhabitants...........		521.0	3.5	35.9	232.8	248.8	3,736.7	523.4	2,725.5	487.8
San Rafael, CA M.D.	261,200									
Includes Marin County										
Total area actually reporting	100.0%	454	5	40	111	298	4,565	1,072	2,952	541
Rate per 100,000 inhabitants...........		173.8	1.9	15.3	42.5	114.1	1,747.7	410.4	1,130.2	207.1
San Jose-Sunnyvale-Santa Clara, CA M.S.A.	1,950,374									
Includes San Benito and Santa Clara Counties............										
City of San Jose	1,009,679	3,242	32	306	1,072	1,832	24,577	5,167	11,850	7,560
City of Sunnyvale.....................	149,384	167	1	14	88	64	2,356	511	1,559	286
City of Santa Clara....................	121,114	162	0	26	89	47	3,268	577	2,287	404
City of Mountain View.................	78,759	156	1	14	29	112	1,608	263	1,237	108
City of Milpitas.......................	70,568	112	1	14	52	45	2,131	351	1,453	327
City of Palo Alto......................	67,169	59	0	3	29	27	1,299	257	976	66
City of Cupertino.....................	60,564	40	0	4	19	17	1,026	263	716	47
Total area actually reporting...........	100.0%	4,872	44	491	1,568	2,769	43,820	9,163	24,809	9,848
Rate per 100,000 inhabitants...........		249.8	2.3	25.2	80.4	142.0	2,246.7	469.8	1,272.0	504.9
San Luis Obispo-Paso Robles-Arroyo Grande, CA M.S.A.	279,628									
Includes San Luis Obispo County										
City of San Luis Obispo	46,672	240	0	47	25	168	1,439	206	1,162	71
City of Paso Robles	31,117	125	0	6	7	112	788	157	584	47
City of Arroyo Grande	17,829	52	0	1	7	44	356	82	243	31
Total area actually reporting...........	100.0%	1,177	3	97	71	1,006	5,683	1,395	3,893	395
Rate per 100,000 inhabitants...........		420.9	1.1	34.7	25.4	359.8	2,032.3	498.9	1,392.2	141.3
Santa Cruz-Watsonville, CA M.S.A.............	272,480									
Includes Santa Cruz County										
City of Santa Cruz....................	63,440	524	1	63	109	351	3,270	420	2,602	248
City of Watsonville....................	52,778	265	8	14	85	158	1,489	190	937	362
Total area actually reporting...........	100.0%	1,139	9	110	236	784	8,121	1,369	5,669	1,083
Rate per 100,000 inhabitants...........		418.0	3.3	40.4	86.6	287.7	2,980.4	502.4	2,080.5	397.5
Santa Fe, NM M.S.A.	147,809									
Includes Santa Fe County										
City of Santa Fe	70,438	244	3	23	73	145	3,017	1,157	1,747	113
Total area actually reporting	100.0%	403	4	31	91	277	4,174	1,721	2,290	163
Rate per 100,000 inhabitants...........		272.6	2.7	21.0	61.6	187.4	2,823.9	1,164.3	1,549.3	110.3
Santa Maria-Santa Barbara, CA M.S.A.	441,058									
Includes Santa Barbara County.........										
City of Santa Maria	102,885	439	3	44	149	243	3,045	666	1,496	883
City of Santa Barbara..................	90,889	302	1	39	56	206	2,389	454	1,843	92
Total area actually reporting...........	100.0%	1,294	16	167	263	848	9,088	2,020	5,864	1,204
Rate per 100,000 inhabitants...........		293.4	3.6	37.9	59.6	192.3	2,060.5	458.0	1,329.5	273.0
Santa Rosa, CA M.S.A.	500,416									
Includes Sonoma County										
City of Santa Rosa....................	172,991	636	2	70	130	434	3,850	598	2,873	379
Total area actually reporting	100.0%	1,821	7	172	239	1,403	8,583	1,643	6,100	840
Rate per 100,000 inhabitants...........		363.9	1.4	34.4	47.8	280.4	1,715.2	328.3	1,219.0	167.9

Table 6. Crime, by Selected Metropolitan Statistical Area, 2014—*Continued*

(Number, percent, rate per 100,000 population.)

Area	Population	Violent crime	Murder and nonnegligent manslaughter	Rape[1]	Robbery	Aggravated assault	Property crime	Burglary	Larceny-theft	Motor vehicle theft
Savannah, GA M.S.A.[3]	371,693									
Includes Bryan, Chatham, and Effingham Counties[3]										
City of Savannah-Chatham Metropolitan[3]	236,682	927	32	65	459	371	8,507	1,681	6,071	755
Total area actually reporting	97.4%	1,272	35	78	553	606	11,384	2,495	7,979	910
Estimated total	100.0%	1,316	35	81	568	632	11,806	2,569	8,298	939
Rate per 100,000 inhabitants		354.1	9.4	21.8	152.8	170.0	3,176.3	691.2	2,232.5	252.6
Scranton–Wilkes-Barre–Hazleton, PA M.S.A.	561,534									
Includes Lackawanna, Luzerne, and Wyoming Counties										
City of Scranton	75,749	216	4	21	79	112	2,102	449	1,522	131
City of Wilkes-Barre	41,017	179	2	22	92	63	1,449	348	1,037	64
City of Hazleton	25,023	119	3	7	67	42	575	162	367	46
Total area actually reporting	95.9%	1,231	16	97	343	775	11,110	2,157	8,481	472
Estimated total	100.0%	1,272	17	100	354	801	11,498	2,215	8,798	485
Rate per 100,000 inhabitants		226.5	3.0	17.8	63.0	142.6	2,047.6	394.5	1,566.8	86.4
Seattle-Tacoma-Bellevue, WA M.S.A.	3,667,968									
Includes the Metropolitan Divisions of Seattle-Bellevue-Everett and Tacoma-Lakewood										
City of Seattle	663,410	4,001	26	154	1,567	2,254	40,649	7,099	28,036	5,514
City of Tacoma	204,722	1,625	12	134	510	969	12,721	3,127	7,521	2,073
City of Bellevue	135,449	144	2	25	65	52	4,606	630	3,662	314
City of Everett	105,911	364	2	43	135	184	6,947	1,198	4,660	1,089
City of Kent	125,837	360	3	65	160	132	6,243	1,019	4,243	981
City of Renton	98,240	229	5	23	84	117	5,207	734	3,651	822
City of Auburn	76,020	299	1	38	105	155	4,578	846	3,116	616
City of Lakewood	59,313	380	1	42	88	249	2,465	644	1,604	217
City of Redmond	58,311	30	1	7	8	14	1,745	241	1,422	82
Total area actually reporting	99.9%	11,998	98	1,197	4,039	6,664	153,536	30,803	102,023	20,710
Estimated total	100.0%	12,005	98	1,198	4,041	6,668	153,667	30,825	102,117	20,725
Rate per 100,000 inhabitants		327.3	2.7	32.7	110.2	181.8	4,189.4	840.4	2,784.0	565.0
Seattle-Bellevue-Everett, WA M.D.	2,838,393									
Includes King and Snohomish Counties										
Total area actually reporting	99.9%	8,409	68	848	3,036	4,457	120,979	22,229	82,521	16,229
Estimated total	100.0%	8,416	68	849	3,038	4,461	121,110	22,251	82,615	16,244
Rate per 100,000 inhabitants		296.5	2.4	29.9	107.0	157.2	4,266.9	783.9	2,910.6	572.3
Tacoma-Lakewood, WA M.D.	829,575									
Includes Pierce County										
Total area actually reporting	100.0%	3,589	30	349	1,003	2,207	32,557	8,574	19,502	4,481
Rate per 100,000 inhabitants		432.6	3.6	42.1	120.9	266.0	3,924.5	1,033.5	2,350.8	540.2
Sebastian-Vero Beach, FL M.S.A.	144,091									
Includes Indian River County										
City of Sebastian	22,889	39	0	3	1	35	463	77	380	6
City of Vero Beach	15,876	70	3	7	18	42	606	142	440	24
Total area actually reporting	100.0%	406	7	24	47	328	3,173	735	2,341	97
Rate per 100,000 inhabitants		281.8	4.9	16.7	32.6	227.6	2,202.1	510.1	1,624.7	67.3
Sebring, FL M.S.A.	98,122									
Includes Highlands County										
City of Sebring	10,312	43	1	1	17	24	478	100	363	15
Total area actually reporting	91.0%	275	11	20	57	187	2,566	760	1,716	90
Estimated total	100.0%	311	11	23	67	210	2,858	815	1,936	107
Rate per 100,000 inhabitants		317.0	11.2	23.4	68.3	214.0	2,912.7	830.6	1,973.1	109.0
Sheboygan, WI M.S.A.	114,823									
Includes Sheboygan County										
City of Sheboygan	48,605	156	1	22	17	116	1,267	160	1,083	24
Total area actually reporting	100.0%	187	1	28	21	137	1,975	254	1,672	49
Rate per 100,000 inhabitants		162.9	0.9	24.4	18.3	119.3	1,720.0	221.2	1,456.2	42.7
Sherman-Denison, TX M.S.A.	123,565									
Includes Grayson County										
City of Sherman	39,522	142	0	25	22	95	1,150	282	818	50
City of Denison	22,838	88	0	17	16	55	714	169	486	59
Total area actually reporting	99.2%	333	3	47	44	239	2,628	654	1,809	165
Estimated total	100.0%	336	3	47	45	241	2,657	659	1,831	167
Rate per 100,000 inhabitants		271.9	2.4	38.0	36.4	195.0	2,150.3	533.3	1,481.8	135.2

Table 6. Crime, by Selected Metropolitan Statistical Area, 2014—*Continued*

(Number, percent, rate per 100,000 population.)

Area	Population	Violent crime	Murder and nonnegligent manslaughter	Rape[1]	Robbery	Aggravated assault	Property crime	Burglary	Larceny-theft	Motor vehicle theft
Shreveport-Bossier City, LA M.S.A.[4]	448,163									
Includes Bossier, Caddo, De Soto,[4] and Webster Parishes										
City of Shreveport	200,184	1,444	20	121	400	903	9,204	2,087	6,623	494
City of Bossier City	67,469	433	5	31	73	324	3,204	457	2,597	150
Total area actually reporting	98.4%		29	174	499		15,326	3,287	11,206	833
Estimated total	100.0%		29	176	504		15,620	3,341	11,428	851
Rate per 100,000 inhabitants			6.5	39.3	112.5		3,485.3	745.5	2,550.0	189.9
Sioux City, IA-NE-SD M.S.A.	169,008									
Includes Plymouth and Woodbury Counties, IA; Dakota and Dixon Counties, NE; and Union County, SD										
City of Sioux City, IA	82,372	289	1	45	41	202	3,166	533	2,427	206
Total area actually reporting	98.4%	404	5	67	47	285	4,420	813	3,337	270
Estimated total	100.0%	406	5	67	47	287	4,454	819	3,364	271
Rate per 100,000 inhabitants		240.2	3.0	39.6	27.8	169.8	2,635.4	484.6	1,990.4	160.3
Sioux Falls, SD M.S.A.	247,531									
Includes Lincoln, McCook, Minnehaha, and Turner Counties										
City of Sioux Falls	167,339	740	4	149	88	499	4,938	846	3,777	315
Total area actually reporting	100.0%	811	4	165	89	553	5,641	1,045	4,228	368
Rate per 100,000 inhabitants		327.6	1.6	66.7	36.0	223.4	2,278.9	422.2	1,708.1	148.7
South Bend-Mishawaka, IN-MI M.S.A.[3]	318,782									
Includes St. Joseph County, IN and Cass County, MI										
City of South Bend, IN	100,853	691	17	98	341	235	4,744	1,222	3,190	332
City of Mishawaka, IN	47,933	106	0	23	37	46	2,352	244	1,983	125
Total area actually reporting	98.0%	1,014	19	186	397	412	8,873	1,985	6,337	551
Estimated total	100.0%	1,031	19	189	400	423	9,012	2,008	6,443	561
Rate per 100,000 inhabitants		323.4	6.0	59.3	125.5	132.7	2,827.0	629.9	2,021.1	176.0
Spartanburg, SC M.S.A.	321,808									
Includes Spartanburg and Union Counties										
City of Spartanburg	37,795	365	2	25	101	237	2,436	415	1,878	143
Total area actually reporting	99.6%	1,263	14	138	246	865	9,683	2,309	6,726	648
Estimated total	100.0%	1,269	14	139	247	869	9,738	2,317	6,770	651
Rate per 100,000 inhabitants		394.3	4.4	43.2	76.8	270.0	3,026.0	720.0	2,103.7	202.3
Spokane-Spokane Valley, WA M.S.A.	539,925									
Includes Pend Oreille, Spokane, and Stevens Counties										
City of Spokane	211,025	1,156	10	117	416	613	18,062	3,365	12,455	2,242
City of Spokane Valley	91,382	297	3	38	86	170	5,245	1,000	3,780	465
Total area actually reporting	100.0%	1,720	15	220	551	934	29,233	5,918	20,048	3,267
Rate per 100,000 inhabitants		318.6	2.8	40.7	102.1	173.0	5,414.3	1,096.1	3,713.1	605.1
Springfield, IL M.S.A.	211,855									
Includes Menard and Sangamon Counties										
City of Springfield	117,134	1,248	4	97	258	889	5,535	1,110	4,300	125
Total area actually reporting	92.9%	1,596	18	148	284	1,146	6,724	1,388	5,124	212
Estimated total	100.0%	1,625	18	151	293	1,163	6,991	1,432	5,335	224
Rate per 100,000 inhabitants		767.0	8.5	71.3	138.3	549.0	3,299.9	675.9	2,518.2	105.7
Springfield, MA M.S.A.	629,676									
Includes Hampden and Hampshire Counties										
City of Springfield	153,766	1,662	13	94	583	972	5,903	1,793	3,478	632
Total area actually reporting	97.8%	3,151	16	318	847	1,970	15,672	3,881	10,671	1,120
Estimated total	100.0%	3,195	16	322	855	2,002	15,901	3,926	10,841	1,134
Rate per 100,000 inhabitants		507.4	2.5	51.1	135.8	317.9	2,525.3	623.5	1,721.7	180.1
Springfield, MO M.S.A.	452,154									
Includes Christian, Dallas, Greene, Polk, and Webster Counties										
City of Springfield	165,280	1,961	16	265	390	1,290	12,638	1,814	9,509	1,315
Total area actually reporting	100.0%	2,423	22	333	423	1,645	17,710	3,004	13,043	1,663
Rate per 100,000 inhabitants		535.9	4.9	73.6	93.6	363.8	3,916.8	664.4	2,884.6	367.8
Springfield, OH M.S.A.	135,676									
Includes Clark County										
City of Springfield	58,891	442	7	50	223	162	4,238	1,310	2,715	213
Total area actually reporting	99.8%	498	7	56	240	195	5,633	1,681	3,684	268
Estimated total	100.0%	498	7	56	240	195	5,640	1,682	3,690	268
Rate per 100,000 inhabitants		367.1	5.2	41.3	176.9	143.7	4,157.0	1,239.7	2,719.7	197.5

Table 6. Crime, by Selected Metropolitan Statistical Area, 2014—*Continued*

(Number, percent, rate per 100,000 population.)

Area	Population	Violent crime	Murder and nonnegligent manslaughter	Rape[1]	Robbery	Aggravated assault	Property crime	Burglary	Larceny-theft	Motor vehicle theft
State College, PA M.S.A...	155,684									
Includes Centre County..										
City of State College..	56,551	26	0	5	5	16	632	62	564	6
Total area actually reporting..............................	100.0%	127	0	39	12	76	1,843	247	1,555	41
Rate per 100,000 inhabitants..............................		81.6	0.0	25.1	7.7	48.8	1,183.8	158.7	998.8	26.3
Staunton-Waynesboro, VA M.S.A...............................	119,879									
Includes Augusta County and Staunton and Waynesboro Cities										
City of Staunton..	24,499	31	1	6	14	10	586	68	504	14
City of Waynesboro..	21,321	33	1	12	4	16	655	84	545	26
Total area actually reporting..............................	100.0%	177	6	34	25	112	2,036	314	1,639	83
Rate per 100,000 inhabitants..............................		147.6	5.0	28.4	20.9	93.4	1,698.4	261.9	1,367.2	69.2
St. Cloud, MN M.S.A...	192,150									
Includes Benton and Stearns Counties.......................										
City of St. Cloud..	66,366	261	0	47	53	161	2,510	382	1,973	155
Total area actually reporting..............................	100.0%	343	2	80	56	205	4,455	602	3,613	240
Rate per 100,000 inhabitants..............................		178.5	1.0	41.6	29.1	106.7	2,318.5	313.3	1,880.3	124.9
St. George, UT M.S.A...	150,723									
Includes Washington County.....................................										
City of St. George..	77,838	112	0	28	19	65	1,506	310	1,086	110
Total area actually reporting..............................	98.0%	198	2	49	28	119	2,535	481	1,900	154
Estimated total...	100.0%	203	2	50	29	122	2,614	492	1,962	160
Rate per 100,000 inhabitants..............................		134.7	1.3	33.2	19.2	80.9	1,734.3	326.4	1,301.7	106.2
St. Joseph, MO-KS M.S.A...	128,038									
Includes Doniphan County, KS and Andrew, Buchanan, and DeKalb Counties, MO										
City of St. Joseph, MO..	77,269	351	2	56	89	204	4,294	680	3,295	319
Total area actually reporting..............................	100.0%	443	2	65	92	284	5,123	930	3,816	377
Rate per 100,000 inhabitants..............................		346.0	1.6	50.8	71.9	221.8	4,001.2	726.3	2,980.4	294.4
St. Louis, MO-IL M.S.A...	2,807,175									
Includes Bond, Calhoun, Clinton, Jersey, Macoupin, Madison, Monroe, and St. Clair Counties, IL and Franklin, Jefferson, Lincoln, St. Charles, St. Louis, and Warren Counties and St. Louis City, MO										
City of St. Louis, MO..	318,574	5,348	159	279	1,562	3,348	19,919	4,209	12,463	3,247
City of St. Charles, MO..	67,970	125	1	19	31	74	1,699	178	1,443	78
Total area actually reporting..............................	95.3%	11,813	245	974	2,833	7,761	66,508	12,817	47,789	5,902
Estimated total...	100.0%	12,064	248	1,004	2,902	7,910	68,754	13,204	49,548	6,002
Rate per 100,000 inhabitants..............................		429.8	8.8	35.8	103.4	281.8	2,449.2	470.4	1,765.0	213.8
Stockton-Lodi, CA M.S.A...	712,619									
Includes San Joaquin County.....................................										
City of Stockton..	299,519	3,988	49	134	1,098	2,707	13,148	3,124	8,082	1,942
City of Lodi..	63,601	290	3	7	97	183	2,095	474	1,170	451
Total area actually reporting..............................	100.0%	5,346	67	175	1,487	3,617	25,092	5,685	15,578	3,829
Rate per 100,000 inhabitants..............................		750.2	9.4	24.6	208.7	507.6	3,521.1	797.8	2,186.0	537.3
Sumter, SC M.S.A...	108,748									
Includes Sumter County..										
City of Sumter	41,341	326	1	11	67	247	1,933	550	1,277	106
Total area actually reporting..............................	99.3%	721	7	50	93	571	4,065	1,379	2,424	262
Estimated total...	100.0%	724	7	50	94	573	4,093	1,383	2,447	263
Rate per 100,000 inhabitants..............................		665.8	6.4	46.0	86.4	526.9	3,763.7	1,271.7	2,250.2	241.8
Syracuse, NY M.S.A...	662,707									
Includes Madison, Onondaga, and Oswego Counties..................										
City of Syracuse..	144,534	1,164	20	70	406	668	5,755	1,404	3,986	365
Total area actually reporting..............................	100.0%	1,851	23	256	529	1,043	15,142	3,036	11,531	575
Rate per 100,000 inhabitants..............................		279.3	3.5	38.6	79.8	157.4	2,284.9	458.1	1,740.0	86.8
Tallahassee, FL M.S.A...	377,234									
Includes Gadsden, Jefferson, Leon, and Wakulla Counties............										
City of Tallahassee..	187,573	1,758	14	198	307	1,239	9,080	2,316	6,099	665
Total area actually reporting..............................	99.8%	2,559	18	265	353	1,923	13,790	3,548	9,337	905
Estimated total...	100.0%	2,562	18	265	354	1,925	13,810	3,552	9,352	906
Rate per 100,000 inhabitants..............................		679.2	4.8	70.2	93.8	510.3	3,660.9	941.6	2,479.1	240.2

Table 6. Crime, by Selected Metropolitan Statistical Area, 2014—*Continued*

(Number, percent, rate per 100,000 population.)

Area	Population	Violent crime	Murder and nonnegligent manslaughter	Rape[1]	Robbery	Aggravated assault	Property crime	Burglary	Larceny-theft	Motor vehicle theft
Tampa-St. Petersburg-Clearwater, FL M.S.A.............................	2,914,610									
Includes Hernando, Hillsborough, Pasco, and Pinellas Counties										
City of Tampa	357,124	2,080	28	62	514	1,476	8,670	1,820	6,355	495
City of St. Petersburg	250,772	2,169	19	154	619	1,377	14,150	2,612	10,139	1,399
City of Clearwater	110,075	641	7	56	195	383	4,283	755	3,318	210
City of Largo	78,502	338	4	42	92	200	2,876	564	2,182	130
Total area actually reporting	100.0%	13,043	159	1,059	2,857	8,968	94,329	19,518	68,808	6,003
Rate per 100,000 inhabitants.....................		447.5	5.5	36.3	98.0	307.7	3,236.4	669.7	2,360.8	206.0
Texarkana, TX-AR M.S.A.	150,328									
Includes Little River and Miller Counties, AR and										
Bowie County, TX										
City of Texarkana, TX	37,687	325	1	41	64	219	2,393	512	1,699	182
Total area actually reporting	100.0%	801	5	72	120	604	6,132	1,486	4,204	442
Rate per 100,000 inhabitants.....................		532.8	3.3	47.9	79.8	401.8	4,079.1	988.5	2,796.6	294.0
The Villages, FL M.S.A.	111,413									
Includes Sumter County										
Total area actually reporting	99.2%	208	2	27	18	161	1,094	353	687	54
Estimated total.......................................	100.0%	211	2	27	19	163	1,122	358	708	56
Rate per 100,000 inhabitants.....................		189.4	1.8	24.2	17.1	146.3	1,007.1	321.3	635.5	50.3
Toledo, OH M.S.A.[3, 4, 6]	608,517									
Includes Fulton, Lucas, and Wood Counties										
City of Toledo[6]	281,150	3,068	24	231	944	1,869		4,691		949
Total area actually reporting	92.6%	3,336	27	291	1,014	2,004		5,769		1,147
Estimated total.......................................	100.0%	3,404	28	304	1,038	2,034		5,970		1,187
Rate per 100,000 inhabitants.....................		559.4	4.6	50.0	170.6	334.3		981.1		195.1
Topeka, KS M.S.A.	234,274									
Includes Jackson, Jefferson, Osage, Shawnee, and										
Wabaunsee Counties										
City of Topeka	127,673	651	6	66	198	381	6,260	1,007	4,672	581
Total area actually reporting	97.6%	853	9	77	206	561	7,940	1,480	5,752	708
Estimated total.......................................	100.0%	863	9	79	207	568	8,049	1,498	5,835	716
Rate per 100,000 inhabitants.....................		368.4	3.8	33.7	88.4	242.5	3,435.7	639.4	2,490.7	305.6
Trenton, NJ M.S.A.......................................	371,608									
Includes Mercer County										
City of Trenton	84,324	931	32	23	403	473	2,029	819	870	340
Total area actually reporting	100.0%	1,290	32	42	558	658	6,749	1,767	4,356	626
Rate per 100,000 inhabitants.....................		347.1	8.6	11.3	150.2	177.1	1,816.2	475.5	1,172.2	168.5
Tulsa, OK M.S.A.	968,064									
Includes Creek, Okmulgee, Osage, Pawnee, Rogers, Tulsa, and										
Wagoner Counties										
City of Tulsa	399,556	3,217	46	313	920	1,938	20,304	5,500	12,494	2,310
Total area actually reporting	100.0%	4,463	59	552	1,059	2,793	30,013	8,080	18,728	3,205
Rate per 100,000 inhabitants.....................		461.0	6.1	57.0	109.4	288.5	3,100.3	834.7	1,934.6	331.1
Tuscaloosa, AL M.S.A.	237,088									
Includes Hale, Pickens, and Tuscaloosa Counties......................										
City of Tuscaloosa	96,412	466	9	53	176	228	4,138	1,042	2,913	183
Total area actually reporting	93.7%	858	12	103	233	510	7,327	1,812	5,129	386
Estimated total.......................................	100.0%	896	12	108	240	536	7,626	1,907	5,312	407
Rate per 100,000 inhabitants.....................		377.9	5.1	45.6	101.2	226.1	3,216.5	804.3	2,240.5	171.7
Utica-Rome, NY M.S.A.	297,852									
Includes Herkimer and Oneida Counties................................										
City of Utica..	61,702	402	6	35	124	237	2,366	432	1,826	108
City of Rome..	32,615	28	2	1	7	18	625	156	450	19
Total area actually reporting	98.5%	764	9	149	161	445	6,160	1,215	4,755	190
Estimated total.......................................	100.0%	772	9	150	164	449	6,235	1,225	4,818	192
Rate per 100,000 inhabitants.....................		259.2	3.0	50.4	55.1	150.7	2,093.3	411.3	1,617.6	64.5
Valdosta, GA M.S.A.[3]......................................	144,114									
Includes Brooks, Echols, Lanier, and Lowndes Counties[3]										
City of Valdosta[3]	56,862	184	7	9	65	103	3,289	542	2,627	120
Total area actually reporting	99.5%	377	9	19	83	266	4,846	1,008	3,622	216
Estimated total.......................................	100.0%	380	9	19	84	268	4,875	1,013	3,644	218
Rate per 100,000 inhabitants.....................		263.7	6.2	13.2	58.3	186.0	3,382.7	702.9	2,528.6	151.3

Table 6. Crime, by Selected Metropolitan Statistical Area, 2014—*Continued*

(Number, percent, rate per 100,000 population.)

Area	Population	Violent crime	Murder and nonnegligent manslaughter	Rape[1]	Robbery	Aggravated assault	Property crime	Burglary	Larceny-theft	Motor vehicle theft
Vallejo-Fairfield, CA M.S.A.	429,882									
Includes Solano County...										
City of Vallejo	119,504	1,034	18	63	368	585	4,877	2,258	1,579	1,040
City of Fairfield	110,300	519	6	41	201	271	3,873	656	2,582	635
Total area actually reporting	100.0%	2,109	27	146	723	1213	13,453	3773	7,417	2263
Rate per 100,000 inhabitants......................................		490.6	6.3	34.0	168.2	282.2	3,129.5	877.7	1,725.4	526.4
Victoria, TX M.S.A.	99,086									
Includes Goliad and Victoria Counties										
City of Victoria...	65,726	338	2	67	38	231	2,281	437	1,774	70
Total area actually reporting	100.0%	426	4	79	43	300	2,861	615	2,145	101
Rate per 100,000 inhabitants......................................		429.9	4.0	79.7	43.4	302.8	2,887.4	620.7	2,164.8	101.9
Vineland-Bridgeton, NJ M.S.A........................................	157,616									
Includes Cumberland County										
City of Vineland	61,115	267	2	13	113	139	2,243	450	1,762	31
City of Bridgeton	25,243	258	7	8	122	121	978	396	563	19
Total area actually reporting	100.0%	806	17	45	333	411	6,125	1,548	4,479	98
Rate per 100,000 inhabitants......................................		511.4	10.8	28.6	211.3	260.8	3,886.0	982.1	2,841.7	62.2
Virginia Beach-Norfolk-Newport News, VA-NC M.S.A.	1,715,279									
Includes Currituck and Gates Counties, NC and Gloucester, Isle of Wight, James City, Mathews, and York Counties and Chesapeake, Hampton, Newport News, Norfolk, Poquoson, Portsmouth, Suffolk, Virginia Beach, and Williamsburg Cities, VA..										
City of Virginia Beach, VA	451,102	660	17	107	252	284	9,811	1,050	8,396	365
City of Norfolk, VA	247,078	1,280	31	122	392	735	9,679	1,312	7,864	503
City of Newport News, VA	182,374	783	25	72	232	454	5,533	918	4,290	325
City of Hampton, VA..	136,590	347	9	35	110	193	4,399	591	3,580	228
City of Portsmouth, VA	96,435	581	9	48	173	351	4,838	1,225	3,298	315
Total area actually reporting	99.3%	5,277	109	568	1,481	3,119	47,534	7,010	38,242	2,282
Estimated total..	100.0%	5,293	109	569	1,483	3,132	47,732	7,085	38,355	2,292
Rate per 100,000 inhabitants......................................		308.6	6.4	33.2	86.5	182.6	2,782.8	413.1	2,236.1	133.6
Visalia-Porterville, CA M.S.A.	459,432									
Includes Tulare County										
City of Visalia	128,488	484	10	30	138	306	3,796	783	2,456	557
City of Porterville	55,391	158	4	10	38	106	1,204	343	702	159
Total area actually reporting	100.0%	1,937	38	91	378	1,430	11,424	2,938	6,686	1,800
Rate per 100,000 inhabitants......................................		421.6	8.3	19.8	82.3	311.3	2,486.5	639.5	1,455.3	391.8
Waco, TX M.S.A.	262,172									
Includes Falls and McLennan Counties										
City of Waco...	129,944	576	6	101	138	331	5,009	1,373	3,434	202
Total area actually reporting	97.9%	994	10	157	173	654	7,915	1,926	5,645	344
Estimated total..	100.0%	1,008	10	159	176	663	8,066	1,952	5,760	354
Rate per 100,000 inhabitants......................................		384.5	3.8	60.6	67.1	252.9	3,076.6	744.5	2,197.0	135.0
Walla Walla, WA M.S.A...	63,981									
Includes Columbia and Walla Walla Counties										
City of Walla Walla	31,833	104	1	21	12	70	1,560	268	1,198	94
Total area actually reporting	100.0%	129	2	22	13	92	2,260	442	1,682	136
Rate per 100,000 inhabitants......................................		201.6	3.1	34.4	20.3	143.8	3,532.3	690.8	2,628.9	212.6
Warner Robins, GA M.S.A.[3]	188,330									
Includes Houston, Peach, and Pulaski Counties[3]										
City of Warner Robins[3]..	73,418	328	2	20	119	187	4,524	867	3,451	206
Total area actually reporting	97.1%	631	8	28	158	437	7,497	1,636	5,558	303
Estimated total..	100.0%	657	8	30	167	452	7,736	1,678	5,739	319
Rate per 100,000 inhabitants......................................		348.9	4.2	15.9	88.7	240.0	4,107.7	891.0	3,047.3	169.4
Washington-Arlington-Alexandria, DC-VA-MD-WV M.S.A.	6,031,640									
Includes the Metropolitan Divisions of Silver Spring-Frederick-Rockville, MD and Washington-Arlington-Alexandria, DC-VA-MD-WV..										
City of Washington, D.C.	658,893	7,810	105	470	3,231	4,004	33,027	3,463	25,881	3,683
City of Alexandria, VA..	151,065	276	4	22	142	108	2,960	259	2,438	263
City of Frederick, MD	67,257	289	1	19	82	187	1,556	205	1,312	39
Total area actually reporting	99.9%	19,068	224	1,422	7,429	9,993	127,078	15,643	100,285	11,150
Estimated total..	100.0%	19,094	224	1,424	7,433	10,013	127,366	15,682	100,523	11,161
Rate per 100,000 inhabitants......................................		316.6	3.7	23.6	123.2	166.0	2,111.6	260.0	1,666.6	185.0

Table 6. Crime, by Selected Metropolitan Statistical Area, 2014—*Continued*

(Number, percent, rate per 100,000 population.)

Area	Population	Violent crime	Murder and nonnegligent manslaughter	Rape[1]	Robbery	Aggravated assault	Property crime	Burglary	Larceny-theft	Motor vehicle theft
Silver Spring-Frederick-Rockville, MD M.D.	1,272,900									
Includes Frederick and Montgomery Counties										
Total area actually reporting	100.0%	2,343	20	166	774	1,383	20,470	3,067	16,567	836
Rate per 100,000 inhabitants..................................		184.1	1.6	13.0	60.8	108.6	1,608.1	240.9	1,301.5	65.7
Washington-Arlington-Alexandria, DC-VA-MD-WV M.D.	4,758,740									
Includes District of Columbia; Calvert, Charles, and Prince George's Counties, MD; Arlington, Clarke, Culpeper, Fairfax, Fauquier, Loudoun, Prince William, Rappahannock, Spotsylvania, Stafford, and Warren Counties and Alexandria, Fairfax, Falls Church, Fredericksburg, Manassas, and Manassas Park Cities, VA; and Jefferson County, WV...										
Total area actually reporting	99.8%	16,725	204	1,256	6,655	8,610	106,608	12,576	83,718	10,314
Estimated total..................................	100.0%	16,751	204	1,258	6,659	8,630	106,896	12,615	83,956	10,325
Rate per 100,000 inhabitants..................................		352.0	4.3	26.4	139.9	181.4	2,246.3	265.1	1,764.2	217.0
Waterloo-Cedar Falls, IA M.S.A.	170,225									
Includes Black Hawk, Bremer, and Grundy Counties										
City of Waterloo	68,358	653	6	84	65	498	2,673	795	1,755	123
City of Cedar Falls	40,883	50	1	12	7	30	786	115	646	25
Total area actually reporting	100.0%	817	7	107	75	628	4,058	1,122	2,760	176
Rate per 100,000 inhabitants..................................		480.0	4.1	62.9	44.1	368.9	2,383.9	659.1	1,621.4	103.4
Watertown-Fort Drum, NY M.S.A.	120,437									
Includes Jefferson County										
City of Watertown	28,009	153	0	47	17	89	1,296	193	1,097	6
Total area actually reporting	97.6%	214	1	68	21	124	2,341	338	1,964	39
Estimated total..................................	100.0%	219	1	68	23	127	2,389	345	2,004	40
Rate per 100,000 inhabitants..................................		181.8	0.8	56.5	19.1	105.4	1,983.6	286.5	1,663.9	33.2
Wausau, WI M.S.A...	135,783									
Includes Marathon County										
City of Wausau	39,359	85	2	13	10	60	764	125	609	30
Total area actually reporting	97.5%	118	2	17	11	88	1,777	289	1,436	52
Estimated total..................................	100.0%	122	2	18	12	90	1,850	298	1,497	55
Rate per 100,000 inhabitants..................................		89.8	1.5	13.3	8.8	66.3	1,362.5	219.5	1,102.5	40.5
Wenatchee, WA M.S.A...	114,491									
Includes Chelan and Douglas Counties...........................										
City of Wenatchee	32,820	63	0	12	15	36	1,156	184	914	58
Total area actually reporting	100.0%	134	0	25	22	87	2,363	514	1,697	152
Rate per 100,000 inhabitants..................................		117.0	0.0	21.8	19.2	76.0	2,063.9	448.9	1,482.2	132.8
Wheeling, WV-OH M.S.A.	145,171									
Includes Belmont County, OH and Marshall and Ohio Counties, WV...										
City of Wheeling, WV	27,890	217	0	12	16	189	705	165	501	39
Total area actually reporting	88.8%	381	0	38	35	308	2,058	451	1,496	111
Estimated total..................................	100.0%	411	0	43	43	325	2,489	523	1,839	127
Rate per 100,000 inhabitants..................................		283.1	0.0	29.6	29.6	223.9	1,714.5	360.3	1,266.8	87.5
Wichita Falls, TX M.S.A.	152,243									
Includes Archer, Clay, and Wichita Counties										
City of Wichita Falls	104,949	426	2	87	130	207	4,258	939	3,082	237
Total area actually reporting	95.9%	508	3	98	134	273	5,021	1,139	3,585	297
Estimated total..................................	100.0%	523	3	100	137	283	5,190	1,168	3,714	308
Rate per 100,000 inhabitants..................................		343.5	2.0	65.7	90.0	185.9	3,409.0	767.2	2,439.5	202.3
Williamsport, PA M.S.A.	116,875									
Includes Lycoming County...										
City of Williamsport	29,340	132	3	9	54	66	1,011	137	848	26
Total area actually reporting	100.0%	255	4	41	77	133	2,224	387	1,787	50
Rate per 100,000 inhabitants..................................		218.2	3.4	35.1	65.9	113.8	1,902.9	331.1	1,529.0	42.8
Wilmington, NC M.S.A.	272,484									
Includes New Hanover and Pender Counties										
City of Wilmington	113,418	766	18	36	237	475	5,172	1,343	3,475	354
Total area actually reporting	99.1%	1,101	34	81	292	694	9,186	2,303	6,365	518
Estimated total..................................	100.0%	1,107	34	81	294	698	9,266	2,319	6,426	521
Rate per 100,000 inhabitants..................................		406.3	12.5	29.7	107.9	256.2	3,400.6	851.1	2,358.3	191.2

Table 6. Crime, by Selected Metropolitan Statistical Area, 2014—*Continued*

(Number, percent, rate per 100,000 population.)

Area	Population	Violent crime	Murder and nonnegligent manslaughter	Rape[1]	Robbery	Aggravated assault	Property crime	Burglary	Larceny-theft	Motor vehicle theft
Winchester, VA-WV M.S.A.	132,823									
Includes Frederick County and Winchester City, VA and										
Hampshire County, WV........................										
City of Winchester, VA........................	27,481	85	0	33	16	36	1,083	113	937	33
Total area actually reporting........................	99.7%	233	2	76	36	119	2,798	457	2,222	119
Estimated total........................	100.0%	234	2	76	36	120	2,809	459	2,231	119
Rate per 100,000 inhabitants........................		176.2	1.5	57.2	27.1	90.3	2,114.8	345.6	1,679.7	89.6
Winston-Salem, NC M.S.A.	654,625									
Includes Davidson, Davie, Forsyth, Stokes, and Yadkin Counties										
City of Winston-Salem	238,082	1,696	13	77	428	1,178	12,896	3,724	8,467	705
Total area actually reporting........................	99.3%	2,626	22	136	574	1,894	23,016	7,229	14,622	1,165
Estimated total........................	100.0%	2,637	22	137	577	1,901	23,157	7,257	14,730	1,170
Rate per 100,000 inhabitants........................		402.8	3.4	20.9	88.1	290.4	3,537.4	1,108.6	2,250.1	178.7
Worcester, MA-CT M.S.A.	856,152									
Includes Windham County, CT and Worcester County, MA										
City of Worcester, MA........................	183,248	1,762	6	7	402	1,347	5,604	1,414	3,824	366
Total area actually reporting........................	99.0%	3,576	8	212	629	2,727	15,903	3,730	11,355	818
Estimated total........................	100.0%	3,604	8	215	634	2,747	16,046	3,758	11,461	827
Rate per 100,000 inhabitants........................		421.0	0.9	25.1	74.1	320.9	1,874.2	438.9	1,338.7	96.6
Yakima, WA M.S.A.	248,862									
Includes Yakima County........................										
City of Yakima........................	93,667	408	2	39	115	252	4,616	1,087	2,808	721
Total area actually reporting........................	100.0%	605	7	56	152	390	8,191	2,091	4,937	1,163
Rate per 100,000 inhabitants........................		243.1	2.8	22.5	61.1	156.7	3,291.4	840.2	1,983.8	467.3
York-Hanover, PA M.S.A.	439,739									
Includes York County........................										
City of York........................	43,951	388	8	24	167	189	1,444	389	938	117
City of Hanover........................	15,380	35	1	2	11	21	413	23	389	1
Total area actually reporting........................	100.0%	902	14	94	267	527	7,349	1,208	5,858	283
Rate per 100,000 inhabitants........................		205.1	3.2	21.4	60.7	119.8	1,671.2	274.7	1,332.2	64.4
Youngstown-Warren-Boardman, OH-PA M.S.A.[2]	553,703									
Includes Mahoning and Trumbull Counties, OH and Mercer										
County, PA........................										
City of Youngstown, OH........................	64,669	424	14	34	132	244	3,180	1,462	1,486	232
City of Warren, OH........................	40,592	181	2	29	87	63	1,646	551	1,003	92
City of Boardman, OH........................	40,047	65	1	15	35	14	1,825	262	1,520	43
Total area actually reporting........................	95.3%	1,308	24	185	398	701		4,080	9,403	
Estimated total........................	100.0%	1,347	24	193	412	718		4,195	9,897	
Rate per 100,000 inhabitants........................		243.3	4.3	34.9	74.4	129.7		757.6	1,787.4	
Yuba City, CA M.S.A.	170,005									
Includes Sutter and Yuba Counties........................										
City of Yuba City........................	65,525	223	0	21	53	149	1,699	410	1,109	180
Total area actually reporting........................	100.0%	612	2	46	116	448	4,499	1,206	2,706	587
Rate per 100,000 inhabitants........................		360.0	1.2	27.1	68.2	263.5	2,646.4	709.4	1,591.7	345.3
Yuma, AZ M.S.A.	203,851									
Includes Yuma County........................										
City of Yuma........................	92,075	520	3	35	70	412	3,334	855	2,166	313
Total area actually reporting........................	100.0%	759	8	51	88	612	5,215	1,566	3,167	482
Rate per 100,000 inhabitants........................		372.3	3.9	25.0	43.2	300.2	2,558.2	768.2	1,553.6	236.4
Aguadilla-Isabela, Puerto Rico M.S.A.	322,641									
Includes Aguada, Aguadilla, Anasco, Isabela, Lares, Moca,										
Rincon, San Sebastian, and Utuado Municipios										
Total area actually reporting........................	100.0%	265	19	8	103	135	2,962	1,120	1,751	91
Rate per 100,000 inhabitants........................		82.1	5.9	2.5	31.9	41.8	918.0	347.1	542.7	28.2
Arecibo, Puerto Rico M.S.A.	191,864									
Includes Arecibo, Camuy, Hatillo, and Quebradillas Municipios......										
Total area actually reporting........................	100.0%	294	17	4	148	125	2,722	868	1,682	172
Rate per 100,000 inhabitants........................		153.2	8.9	2.1	77.1	65.2	1,418.7	452.4	876.7	89.6
Guayama, Puerto Rico M.S.A.	80,581									
Includes Arroyo, Guayama, and Patillas Municipios										

Table 6. Crime, by Selected Metropolitan Statistical Area, 2014—*Continued*

(Number, percent, rate per 100,000 population.)

Area	Population	Violent crime	Murder and nonnegligent manslaughter	Rape[1]	Robbery	Aggravated assault	Property crime	Burglary	Larceny-theft	Motor vehicle theft
Total area actually reporting	100.0%	159	13	1	50	95	1,014	357	632	25
Rate per 100,000 inhabitants		197.3	16.1	1.2	62.0	117.9	1,258.4	443.0	784.3	31.0
Mayaguez, Puerto Rico M.S.A.	98,661									
Includes Hormigueros and Mayaguez Municipios										
Total area actually reporting	100.0%	176	8	2	111	55	1,628	492	1,069	67
Rate per 100,000 inhabitants		178.4	8.1	2.0	112.5	55.7	1,650.1	498.7	1,083.5	67.9
Ponce, Puerto Rico M.S.A.	325,929									
Includes Guanica, Guyanilla, Juana Diaz, Penuelas, Ponce, Villalba, and Yauco Municipios										
Total area actually reporting	100.0%	778	68	12	353	345	3,074	821	2,140	113
Rate per 100,000 inhabitants		238.7	20.9	3.7	108.3	105.9	943.2	251.9	656.6	34.7
San German, Puerto Rico M.S.A.	132,660									
Includes Cabo Rojo, Lajas, Sabana Grande, and San German Municipios										
Total area actually reporting	100.0%	92	6	1	32	53	819	346	445	28
Rate per 100,000 inhabitants		69.4	4.5	0.8	24.1	40.0	617.4	260.8	335.4	21.1
San Juan-Carolina-Caguas, Puerto Rico M.S.A.	2,242,285									
Includes Aguas Buenas, Aibonito, Barceloneta, Barranquitas, Bayamon, Caguas, Canovanas, Carolina, Catano, Cayey, Ceiba, Ciales, Cidra, Comerio, Corozal, Dorado, Fajardo, Florida, Guaynabo, Gurabo, Humacao, Juncos, Las Piedras, Loiza, Luquillo, Manati, Maunabo, Morovis, Naguabo, Naranjito, Orocovis, Rio Grande, San Juan, San Lorenzo, Toa Alta, Toa Baja, Trujillo Alto, Vega Alta, Vega Baja, and Yabucoa Municipios										
Total area actually reporting	100.0%	6,356	526	13	4,265	1,552	31,961	7,554	20,332	4,075
Rate per 100,000 inhabitants		283.5	23.5	0.6	190.2	69.2	1,425.4	336.9	906.8	181.7

[1] The rape figures in this table are an aggregate total of the data submitted using both the revised and legacy Uniform Crime Reporting (UCR) definitions.
[2] The FBI determined that the agency's data were overreported. Consequently, affected data are not included in this table.
[3] Because of changes in the state/local agency's reporting practices, figures are not comparable to previous years' data.
[4] The FBI determined that the agency's data were underreported. Consequently, those data are not included in this table.
[5] The population for the city of Mobile, Alabama, includes 55,819 inhabitants from the jurisdiction of the Mobile County Sheriff's Department.
[6] The FBI determined that the agency did not follow national UCR Program guidelines for reporting an offense. Consequently, this figure is not included in this table.

Table 7. Offense Analysis, United States, 2010–2014

(Number.)

Classification	2010	2011	2012	2013[1]	2014
Murder	14,722	14,661	14,856	14,319	14,249
Rape (revised definition)[2]	X	X	X	113,695	116,645
Rape (legacy definition)[3]	85,593	84,175	85,141	82,109	84,041
Robbery[4]	369,089	354,746	355,051	345,093	325,802
By location					
Street/highway	159,307	155,218	154,289	146,499	133,456
Commercial house	48,804	46,156	47,151	45,760	45,679
Gas or service station	8,549	8,539	8,660	8,354	8,144
Convenience store	19,282	18,108	18,180	17,103	17,536
Residence	63,779	60,138	59,979	57,372	54,605
Bank	8,034	7,038	6,666	6,512	5,992
Miscellaneous	61,333	59,549	60,126	63,495	60,390
Burglary[4]	2,168,459	2,185,140	2,109,932	1,932,139	1,729,806
By location					
Residence (dwelling)	1,602,056	1,628,656	1,571,635	1,428,448	1,266,104
Residence, night	445,480	442,390	429,662	395,604	352,838
Residence, day	825,163	859,299	832,944	756,617	675,870
Residence, unknown	331,414	326,967	309,028	276,227	237,396
	566,403	556,484	538,297	503,691	463,702
Nonresidence (store, office, etc.)	233,765	227,446	220,784	206,031	189,837
Nonresidence, night	192,985	196,461	192,963	183,380	169,379
Nonresidence, day	139,652	132,577	124,550	114,280	104,485
Nonresidence, unknown					
	6,204,601	6,151,095	6,168,874	6,019,465	5,858,496
Larceny-theft (except motor vehicle theft)[4]	24,231	26,518	29,550	32,426	31,478
By type					
Pocket-picking	28,137	27,082	26,407	25,867	23,679
Purse-snatching	1,064,608	1,077,791	1,147,679	1,199,157	1,257,814
Shoplifting	1,638,670	1,523,950	1,480,790	1,405,858	1,344,269
From motor vehicles (except accessories)	549,905	497,980	467,369	439,151	412,022
Motor vehicle accessories	206,677	216,987	223,786	212,889	211,547
Bicycles	699,599	728,050	745,238	740,092	718,133
From buildings	20,309	19,536	17,240	15,906	13,442
From coin-operated machines	1,972,464	2,033,200	2,030,815	1,948,120	1,846,111
All others					
By value					
Under $50	2,811,555	2,850,302	2,872,445	2,819,518	2,710,465
$50 to $200	1,421,342	1,399,484	1,398,870	1,342,473	1,317,469
Over $200	1,971,705	1,901,309	1,897,560	1,857,474	1,830,562
Motor vehicle theft	739,565	716,508	723,186	700,288	689,527

X = Not applicable.
[1] The crime figures have been adjusted.
[2] The figures shown in this column for the offense of rape were estimated using the revised Uniform Crime Reporting (UCR) definition of rape. See chapter notes for more detail.
[3] The figures shown in this column for the offense of rape were estimated using the legacy Uniform Crime Reporting (UCR) definition of rape. See chapter notes for more detail.
[4] Because of rounding, the number of offenses may not add to the total.

Table 8. Crime Trends, by Population Group, 2013–2014

(Number, percent change.)

Population group	Violent crime	Murder and nonnegligent manslaughter	Rape (revised definition)[1]	Rape (legacy definition)[2]	Robbery	Aggravated assault	Property crime	Burglary	Larceny-theft	Motor vehicle theft	Arson	Number of agencies	Estimated population, 2014
Total, All Agencies...........................													
2013....................................	1,112,265	13,741	55,598	15,461	334,513	692,952	8,183,021	1,820,797	5,690,372	671,852	44,713		
2014....................................	1,094,854	13,472	55,355	16,372	311,936	697,719	7,738,735	1,611,882	5,470,741	656,112	42,934	15,324	303,380,767
Percent change	-1.6	-2.0	-0.4	+5.9	-6.7	+0.7	-5.4	-11.5	-3.9	-2.3	-4.0		
Total, Cities													
2013....................................	889,721	10,517	39,154	11,484	293,496	535,070	6,439,938	1,329,585	4,571,822	538,531	33,757		
2014....................................	874,127	10,446	39,093	12,343	272,517	539,728	6,107,458	1,176,693	4,404,964	525,801	32,617	11,079	204,409,381
Percent change	-1.8	-0.7	-0.2	+7.5	-7.1	+0.9	-5.2	-11.5	-3.6	-2.4	-3.4		
Group I (250,000 and over)...............													
2013....................................	411,799	5,320	10,536	3,374	162,094	230,475	2,108,022	448,942	1,413,360	245,720	12,512		
2014....................................	406,528	5,339	10,643	3,534	150,004	237,008	1,993,393	398,502	1,353,125	241,766	11,863	78	57,577,457
Percent change	-1.3	+0.4	+1.0	+4.7	-7.5	+2.8	-5.4	-11.2	-4.3	-1.6	-5.2		
1,000,000 and over (Group I subset)................................													
2013....................................	172,827	1,970	1,279	586	72,584	96,408	787,221	156,776	535,540	94,905	4,176		
2014....................................	168,884	2,013	1,207	677	67,350	97,637	737,241	139,623	504,789	92,829	3,782	11	27,023,807
Percent change	-2.3	+2.2	-5.6	+15.5	-7.2	+1.3	-6.3	-10.9	-5.7	-2.2	-9.4		
500,000 to 999,999 (Group I subset)..................................													
2013....................................	127,964	1,701	4,801	1,533	46,136	73,793	700,267	150,979	473,309	75,979	4,169		
2014....................................	129,281	1,693	4,802	1,452	43,158	78,176	672,755	134,578	460,179	77,998	3,735	22	15,200,484
Percent change	+1.0	-0.5	0.0	-5.3	-6.5	+5.9	-3.9	-10.9	-2.8	+2.7	-10.4		
250,000 to 499,999 (Group I subset)..................................													
2013....................................	111,008	1,649	4,456	1,255	43,374	60,274	620,534	141,187	404,511	74,836	4,167		
2014....................................	108,363	1,633	4,634	1,405	39,496	61,195	583,397	124,301	388,157	70,939	4,346	45	15,353,166
Percent change	-2.4	-1.0	+4.0	+12.0	-8.9	+1.5	-6.0	-12.0	-4.0	-5.2	+4.3		
Group II (100,000 to 249,999)...........													
2013....................................	143,066	1,787	6,510	1,933	47,792	85,044	1,108,364	242,440	761,012	104,912	5,401		
2014....................................	141,912	1,804	6,700	2,218	44,959	86,231	1,062,425	217,070	743,103	102,252	5,312	215	31,966,637
Percent change	-0.8	+1.0	+2.9	+14.7	-5.9	+1.4	-4.1	-10.5	-2.4	-2.5	-1.6		
Group III (50,000 to 99,999)													
2013....................................	111,658	1,171	6,168	1,879	33,372	69,068	953,036	196,372	682,019	74,645	4,573		
2014....................................	108,010	1,098	6,034	2,018	30,816	68,044	902,740	170,344	660,987	71,409	4,333	478	33,076,321
Percent change	-3.3	-6.2	-2.2	+7.4	-7.7	-1.5	-5.3	-13.3	-3.1	-4.3	-5.2		
Group IV (25,000 to 49,999)..............													
2013....................................	82,834	892	5,483	1,539	23,015	51,905	806,998	159,644	601,441	45,913	3,691		
2014....................................	79,602	908	5,287	1,551	21,223	50,633	764,465	139,921	580,206	44,338	3,698	857	29,556,524
Percent change	-3.9	+1.8	-3.6	+0.8	-7.8	-2.5	-5.3	-12.4	-3.5	-3.4	+0.2		
Group V (10,000 to 24,999)													
2013....................................	75,933	739	5,556	1,438	17,173	51,027	784,210	154,768	591,103	38,339	3,252		
2014....................................	74,344	724	5,422	1,520	16,007	50,671	743,189	137,120	568,854	37,215	3,241	1,817	28,982,145
Percent change	-2.1	-2.0	-2.4	+5.7	-6.8	-0.7	-5.2	-11.4	-3.8	-2.9	-0.3		
Group VI (under 10,000)....................													
2013....................................	64,431	608	4,901	1,321	10,050	47,551	679,308	127,419	522,887	29,002	4,328		
2014....................................	63,731	573	5,007	1,502	9,508	47,141	641,246	113,736	498,689	28,821	4,170	7,634	23,250,297
Percent change	-1.1	-5.8	+2.2	+13.7	-5.4	-0.9	-5.6	-10.7	-4.6	-0.6	-3.7		
Metropolitan Counties													
2013....................................	180,609	2,385	11,392	3,180	38,333	125,319	1,392,396	372,334	909,083	110,979	8,288		
2014....................................	179,197	2,321	11,200	3,281	36,816	125,579	1,311,113	330,297	872,040	108,776	7,649	1,872	74,401,790
Percent change	-0.8	-2.7	-1.7	+3.2	-4.0	+0.2	-5.8	-11.3	-4.1	-2.0	-7.7		
Nonmetropolitan Counties[3]													
2013....................................	41,935	839	5,052	797	2,684	32,563	350,687	118,878	209,467	22,342	2,668		
2014....................................	41,530	705	5,062	748	2,603	32,412	320,164	104,892	193,737	21,535	2,668	2,373	24,569,596
Percent change	-1.0	-16.0	+0.2	-6.1	-3.0	-0.5	-8.7	-11.8	-7.5	-3.6	0.0		
Suburban Areas[4]													
2013....................................	319,153	3,716	22,555	6,281	73,272	213,329	2,868,918	644,626	2,033,261	191,031	14,791		
2014....................................	313,838	3,637	22,015	6,614	69,062	212,510	2,703,237	569,218	1,947,792	186,227	13,868	8,393	133,928,066
Percent change	-1.7	-2.1	-2.4	+5.3	-5.7	-0.4	-5.8	-11.7	-4.2	-2.5	-6.2		

[1] The figures shown in the rape (revised definition) column include only those reported by law enforcement agencies that used the revised Uniform Crime Reporting (UCR) definition of rape.
[2] The figures shown in the rape (legacy definition) column include only those reported by law enforcement agencies that used the legacy UCR definition of rape.
[3] Includes state police agencies that report aggregately for the entire state.
[4] Suburban areas include law enforcement agencies in cities with less than 50,000 inhabitants and county law enforcement agencies that are within a Metropolitan Statistical Area. Suburban areas exclude all metropolitan agencies associated with a principal city. The agencies associated with suburban areas also appear in other groups within this table.

Table 9. Rate: Number of Crimes Per 100,000 Population, by Population Group, 2014

(Number, rate.)

Population group	Violent crime		Murder and nonnegligent manslaughter		Rape (revised definition)[1]		Rape (legacy definition)[2]		Robbery		Aggravated assault	
	Number of offenses known	Rate	Number of offenses known	Rate	Number of offenses known	Rate	Number of offenses known	Rate	Number of offenses known	Rate	Number of offenses known	Rate
Total, All Agencies..	1,107,564	374.9	13,280	4.5	84,885	38.5	16,261	21.6	307,590	104.1	685,548	232.1
Total, Cities	887,727	443.7	10,322	5.2	63,071	42.4	12,296	24.1	270,022	135.0	532,016	265.9
Group I (250,000 and over)................................	416,525	730.1	5,305	9.3	23,497	51.5	3,534	31.7	149,079	261.3	235,110	412.1
1,000,000 and over (Group I subset)	177,999	658.7	2,013	7.4	10,322	41.9	677	28.5	67,350	249.2	97,637	361.3
500,000 to 999,999 (Group I subset)	128,303	874.4	1,659	11.3	6,681	61.6	1,452	38.0	42,233	287.8	76,278	519.8
250,000 to 499,999 (Group I subset)	110,223	717.9	1,633	10.6	6,494	64.2	1,405	28.3	39,496	257.2	61,195	398.6
Group II (100,000 to 249,999)	143,779	461.8	1,784	5.7	10,310	46.5	2,193	24.5	44,390	142.6	85,102	273.3
Group III (50,000 to 99,999)	109,777	335.1	1,093	3.3	8,284	36.6	2,044	20.2	30,697	93.7	67,659	206.5
Group IV (25,000 to 49,999).............................	80,443	280.0	892	3.1	7,317	35.4	1,538	18.9	20,955	72.9	49,741	173.1
Group V (10,000 to 24,999)	74,451	264.0	707	2.5	6,938	33.6	1,501	19.8	15,717	55.7	49,588	175.8
Group VI (under 10,000).....................................	62,752	282.5	541	2.4	6,725	39.3	1,486	29.1	9,184	41.3	44,816	201.7
Metropolitan Counties	176,354	248.0	2,236	3.1	15,203	29.0	3,233	16.8	35,001	49.2	120,681	169.7
Nonmetropolitan Counties[3]	43,483	179.5	722	3.0	6,611	34.2	732	14.6	2,567	10.6	32,851	135.6
Suburban Areas[4]	309,144	239.8	3,511	2.7	27,287	29.1	6,180	17.3	66,729	51.8	205,437	159.4

Table 10. Rate: Number of Crimes Per 100,000 Inhabitants, by Suburban and Nonsuburban Cities,[1] by Population Group, 2014

(Number, rate.)

Population group	Violent crime		Murder and nonnegligent manslaughter		Rape (revised definition)[2]		Rape (legacy definition)[3]		Robbery		Aggravated assault	
	Number of offenses known	Rate	Number of offenses known	Rate	Number of offenses known	Rate	Number of offenses known	Rate	Number of offenses known	Rate	Number of offenses known	Rate
Total, Suburban Cities....................................	132,790	229.8	1,275	2.2	12,084	29.2	2,947	17.9	31,728	54.9	84,756	146.7
Group IV (25,000 to 49,999)........................	50,175	225.4	558	2.5	4,446	28.5	990	14.7	13,838	62.2	30,343	136.3
Group V (10,000 to 24,999)	46,574	216.7	429	2.0	4,136	27.0	953	15.3	11,298	52.6	29,758	138.5
Group VI (under 10,000)...............................	36,041	256.9	288	2.1	3,502	33.2	1,004	28.7	6,592	47.0	24,655	175.7
Total, Nonsuburban Cities	84,856	397.2	865	4.0	8,896	52.3	1,578	36.0	14,128	66.1	59,389	278.0
Group IV (25,000 to 49,999)........................	30,268	468.0	334	5.2	2,871	56.8	548	38.8	7,117	110.0	19,398	299.9
Group V (10,000 to 24,999)	27,877	415.3	278	4.1	2,802	52.2	548	40.3	4,419	65.8	19,830	295.4
Group VI (under 10,000)...............................	26,711	326.3	253	3.1	3,223	49.0	482	30.0	2,592	31.7	20,161	246.3

Table 9. Rate: Number of Crimes Per 100,000 Population, by Population Group, 2014—*Continued*

(Number, rate.)

Population group	Property crime		Burglary		Larceny-theft		Motor vehicle theft		Number of agencies	Estimated population, 2014
	Number of offenses known	Rate	Number of offenses known	Rate	Number of offenses known	Rate	Number of offenses known	Rate		
Total, All Agencies.........................	7,578,653	2,565.3	1,579,038	534.5	5,353,190	1,812.0	646,425	218.8	14,621	295,429,333
Total, Cities...............................	6,000,713	2,999.0	1,156,175	577.8	4,325,678	2,161.9	518,860	259.3	10,531	200,090,212
Group I (250,000 and over)...............	1,971,331	3,455.4	394,582	691.6	1,336,638	2,342.9	240,111	420.9	77	57,050,129
1,000,000 and over (Group I subset)	737,241	2,728.1	139,623	516.7	504,789	1,867.9	92,829	343.5	11	27,023,807
500,000 to 999,999 (Group I subset)	643,452	4,385.2	130,658	890.5	436,451	2,974.5	76,343	520.3	21	14,673,156
250,000 to 499,999 (Group I subset)	590,638	3,847.0	124,301	809.6	395,398	2,575.4	70,939	462.0	45	15,353,166
Group II (100,000 to 249,999)	1,036,492	3,328.8	212,938	683.9	723,596	2,323.9	99,958	321.0	210	31,137,166
Group III (50,000 to 99,999)	896,856	2,737.9	168,729	515.1	657,042	2,005.8	71,085	217.0	474	32,757,062
Group IV (25,000 to 49,999)...............	749,728	2,609.7	137,274	477.8	568,717	1,979.6	43,737	152.2	833	28,728,176
Group V (10,000 to 24,999)	725,478	2,572.5	133,114	472.0	555,934	1,971.3	36,430	129.2	1,768	28,200,971
Group VI (under 10,000)...................	620,828	2,794.4	109,538	493.0	483,751	2,177.4	27,539	124.0	7,169	22,216,708
Metropolitan Counties	1,259,723	1,771.4	318,716	448.2	835,181	1,174.4	105,826	148.8	1,791	71,115,093
Nonmetropolitan Counties[3]	318,217	1,313.6	104,147	429.9	192,331	794.0	21,739	89.7	2,299	24,224,028
Suburban Areas[4]	2,621,529	2,033.8	551,918	428.2	1,887,979	1,464.7	181,632	140.9	8,042	128,895,308

[1] The figures shown in the rape (revised definition) column include only those reported by law enforcement agencies that used the revised Uniform Crime Reporting (UCR) definition of rape.
[2] The figures shown in the rape (legacy definition) column include only those reported by law enforcement agencies that used the legacy UCR definition of rape.
[3] Includes state police agencies that report aggregately for the entire state.
[4] Suburban areas include law enforcement agencies in cities with less than 50,000 inhabitants and county law enforcement agencies that are within a Metropolitan Statistical Area. Suburban areas exclude all metropolitan agencies associated with a principal city. The agencies associated with suburban areas also appear in other groups within this table.

Table 10. Rate: Number of Crimes Per 100,000 Inhabitants, by Suburban and Nonsuburban Cities,[1] by Population Group, 2014—*Continued*

(Number, rate.)

Population group	Property crime		Burglary		Larceny-theft		Motor vehicle theft		Number of agencies	Estimated population, 2014
	Number of offenses known	Rate	Number of offenses known	Rate	Number of offenses known	Rate	Number of offenses known	Rate		
Total, Suburban Cities...................	1,361,806	2,356.9	233,202	403.6	1,052,798	1,822.1	75,806	131.2	6,251	57,780,215
Group IV (25,000 to 49,999)...............	497,600	2,235.3	87,307	392.2	378,962	1,702.4	31,331	140.7	651	22,261,087
Group V (10,000 to 24,999)	474,114	2,206.3	83,598	389.0	363,646	1,692.2	26,870	125.0	1,335	21,489,083
Group VI (under 10,000)..................	390,092	2,780.4	62,297	444.0	310,190	2,210.9	17,605	125.5	4,265	14,030,045
Total, Nonsuburban Cities	734,228	3,436.5	146,724	686.7	555,604	2,600.5	31,900	149.3	3,519	21,365,640
Group IV (25,000 to 49,999)...............	252,128	3,898.6	49,967	772.6	189,755	2,934.2	12,406	191.8	182	6,467,089
Group V (10,000 to 24,999)	251,364	3,745.1	49,516	737.7	192,288	2,864.9	9,560	142.4	433	6,711,888
Group VI (under 10,000)..................	230,736	2,818.4	47,241	577.0	173,561	2,120.0	9,934	121.3	2,904	8,186,663

[1] Suburban cities include law enforcement agencies in cities with less than 50,000 inhabitants that are within a Metropolitan Statistical Area. Suburban cities exclude all metropolitan agencies associated with a principal city. Nonsuburban cities include law enforcement agencies in cities with less than 50,000 inhabitants that are not associated with a Metropolitan Statistical Area.
[2] The figures shown in the rape (revised definition) column include only those reported by law enforcement agencies that used the revised Uniform Crime Reporting (UCR) definition of rape.
[3] The figures shown in the rape (legacy definition) column include only those reported by law enforcement agencies that used the legacy UCR definition of rape.

Table 11. Offense Analysis, Number and Percent Change, 2013–2014

(Number, percent, dollars; 14,137 agencies; 2014 estimated population 284,261,606.)

Classification	Number of offenses, 2014	Percent change from 2013	Percent distribution[1]	Average value (dollars)
Murder	12,064	-1.1	NA	X
Rape[2]	81,948	NA	NA	X
Robbery	283,820	-5.9	100.0	$1,227
By location				
Street/highway	116,259	-8.4	41.0	871
Commercial house	39,793	+0.1	14.0	1,872
Gas or service station	7,095	+4.3	2.5	1,026
Convenience store	15,276	+3.0	5.4	699
Residence	47,569	-5.6	16.8	1,466
Bank	5,220	-7.4	1.8	3,816
Miscellaneous	52,608	-8.1	18.5	1,235
Burglary	1,532,127	-11.6	100.0	2,251
By location				
Residence (dwelling)	1,121,416	-12.7	73.2	2,229
Residence, night	312,516	-11.1	20.4	1,760
Residence, day	598,633	-13.5	39.1	2,311
Residence, unknown	210,267	-13.1	13.7	2,691
Nonresidence (store, office, etc.)	410,711	-8.5	26.8	2,312
Nonresidence, night	168,143	-8.1	11.0	2,020
Nonresidence, day	150,023	-8.5	9.8	2,144
Nonresidence, unknown	92,545	-9.2	6.0	3,114
Larceny-theft (except motor vehicle theft)	5,111,544	-3.9	100.0	941
By type				
Pocket-picking	27,465	-8.8	0.5	548
Purse-snatching	20,660	-10.5	0.4	508
Shoplifting	1,097,444	+3.3	21.5	204
From motor vehicles (except accessories)	1,172,876	-5.7	22.9	835
Motor vehicle accessories	359,490	-7.4	7.0	553
Bicycles	184,575	-1.2	3.6	418
From buildings	626,572	-5.1	12.3	1,333
From coin-operated machines	11,728	-15.1	0.2	480
All others	1,610,734	-5.7	31.5	1,530
By value				
Over $200	2,364,884	-5.4	46.3	1,972
$50 to $200	1,149,493	-2.8	22.5	104
Under $50	1,597,167	-2.3	31.2	16
Motor Vehicle Theft	611,610	-4.3	NA	6,537

NA = Not available.
X = Not applicable.
[1] Because of rounding, the percentages may not add to 100.0.
[2] The rape figure in this table is an aggregate total of the data submitted using both the revised and legacy Uniform Crime Reporting definitions.

Table 12. Property Stolen and Recovered, by Type and Value, 2014

(Dollars, percent; 13,563 agencies; 2014 estimated population 275,323,431.)

Type of property	Value of property (dollars)		Percent recovered
	Stolen	Recovered	
Total	$12,315,037,768	$2,792,353,707	22.7
Currency, notes, etc.	1,145,928,344	39,056,171	3.4
Jewelry and precious metals	1,539,752,196	61,325,890	4.0
Clothing and furs	324,714,255	40,020,528	12.3
Locally stolen motor vehicles	4,050,775,087	2,237,942,124	55.2
Office equipment	551,418,671	30,967,359	5.6
Televisions, radios, stereos, etc.	547,061,935	31,141,958	5.7
Firearms	139,127,645	13,533,991	9.7
Household goods	279,501,459	12,418,248	4.4
Consumable goods	121,485,931	16,236,504	13.4
Livestock	19,166,046	1,961,215	10.2
Miscellaneous	3,596,106,199	307,749,719	8.6

Table 13. Number and Percent of Offenses Cleared by Arrest or Exceptional Means, by Population Group, 2014

(Number, percent.)

Population group	Violent crime	Murder and nonnegligent manslaughter	Rape (revised definition)[1]	Rape (legacy definition)[2]	Robbery	Aggravated assault	Property crime	Burglary	Larceny-theft	Motor vehicle theft	Arson[3]	Number of agencies	Estimated population, 2014
Total, All Agencies...........................													
Offenses known	1,085,156	12,879	83,309	16,456	297,819	674,693	7,515,512	1,573,560	5,302,190	639,762	42,539	15,033	292,235,983
Percent cleared by arrest...............	47.4	64.5	38.5	39.3	29.6	56.3	20.2	13.6	23.0	12.8	21.7		
Total Cities													
Offenses known	858,342	9,838	61,346	12,303	258,178	516,677	5,887,929	1,139,300	4,238,836	509,793	32,162	10,807	194,592,052
Percent cleared by arrest..............	45.6	63.5	36.7	38.4	29.1	54.7	20.3	13.0	23.3	11.6	21.1		
Group I (250,000 and over)................													
Offenses known	395,660	4,928	22,521	3,534	140,200	224,477	1,908,232	383,965	1,292,524	231,743	12,000	77	54,853,336
Percent cleared by arrest..............	40.7	60.7	39.4	33.3	26.3	49.6	14.7	10.0	17.2	8.1	16.1		
1,000,000 and over (Group I subset).													
Offenses known	153,910	1,602	8,979	677	57,546	85,106	652,080	125,086	444,188	82,806	3,721	10	24,299,686
Percent cleared by arrest..............	46.2	69.6	43.1	26.9	30.2	57.0	14.8	9.8	17.6	7.6	14.3		
500,000 to 999,999 (Group I subset).													
Offenses known	131,527	1,693	7,048	1,452	43,158	78,176	672,755	134,578	460,179	77,998	3,748	22	15,200,484
Percent cleared by arrest..............	36.0	56.2	37.0	29.2	22.5	43.1	13.1	9.2	15.2	7.6	18.4		
250,000 to 499,999 (Group I subset).													
Offenses known	110,223	1,633	6,494	1,405	39,496	61,195	583,397	124,301	388,157	70,939	4,531	45	15,353,166
Percent cleared by arrest..............	38.7	56.6	36.8	40.6	24.6	47.5	16.3	11.0	19.2	9.3	15.7		
Group II (100,000 to 249,999)............													
Offenses known	142,540	1,773	10,410	2,193	44,170	83,994	1,043,021	213,182	728,204	101,635	5,277	209	31,128,218
Percent cleared by arrest..............	44.5	63.7	35.3	41.8	29.1	53.5	18.5	12.3	21.4	11.1	23.1		
Group III (50,000 to 99,999)													
Offenses known	106,121	1,026	8,118	1,970	29,391	65,616	873,450	165,083	639,022	69,345	4,264	457	31,671,604
Percent cleared by arrest..............	49.8	64.8	35.5	38.8	33.3	59.1	22.4	14.3	25.5	12.9	21.1		
Group IV (25,000 to 49,999)................													
Offenses known	77,329	840	6,874	1,543	20,150	47,922	731,851	134,299	554,492	43,060	3,425	797	27,585,966
Percent cleared by arrest..............	49.9	67.7	33.9	40.8	34.4	58.8	24.6	14.1	27.9	15.5	25.2		
Group V (10,000 to 24,999)													
Offenses known	72,344	699	6,617	1,508	15,034	48,486	706,052	130,589	539,917	35,546	3,082	1,691	26,885,036
Percent cleared by arrest..............	53.6	69.0	36.0	38.9	35.7	61.7	27.1	16.3	30.2	18.6	28.7		
Group VI (under 10,000).....................													
Offenses known	64,348	572	6,806	1,555	9,233	46,182	625,323	112,182	484,677	28,464	4,114	7,576	22,467,892
Percent cleared by arrest..............	56.3	71.0	34.9	41.8	38.0	63.4	25.2	18.1	27.0	23.6	24.2		
Metropolitan Counties													
Offenses known	183,207	2,314	15,388	3,389	37,007	125,109	1,309,418	329,625	871,639	108,154	7,661	1,903	73,390,390
Percent cleared by arrest..............	53.6	67.1	43.9	42.1	31.8	61.3	19.5	14.5	21.8	15.9	22.4		
Nonmetropolitan Counties..............													
Offenses known	43,607	727	6,575	764	2,634	32,907	318,165	104,635	191,715	21,815	2,716	2,323	24,253,541
Percent cleared by arrest..............	58.5	70.6	43.0	40.8	45.0	62.8	19.6	16.5	20.7	25.1	26.7		
Suburban Areas[4]													
Offenses known	310,977	3,538	26,796	6,355	67,218	207,070	2,632,592	558,504	1,891,448	182,640	13,460	8,170	128,834,045
Percent cleared by arrest..............	53.6	66.9	40.6	41.4	33.4	62.0	22.2	15.2	24.9	16.1	24.2		

[1] The figures shown in this column for the offense of rape were reported using the revised Uniform Crime Reporting (UCR) definition of rape. See chapter notes for more detail.
[2] The figures shown in this column for the offense of rape were reported using the legacy Uniform Crime Reporting (UCR) definition of rape. See chapter notes for more detail.
[3] Not all agencies submit reports for arson to the FBI. As a result, the number of reports the FBI uses to compute the percent of offenses cleared for arson is less than the number it uses to compute the percent of offenses cleared for all other offenses.
[4] Suburban area includes law enforcement agencies in cities with less than 50,000 inhabitants and county law enforcement agencies that are within a Metropolitan Statistical Area. Suburban area excludes all metropolitan agencies associated with a principal city. The agencies associated with suburban areas also appear in other groups within this table.

Table 14. Number of Offenses Cleared by Arrest or Exceptional Means and Percent Involving Persons Under 18 Years of Age, by Population Group, 2014

(Number, percent.)

Population group	Violent crime	Murder and nonnegligent manslaughter	Rape (revised definition)[1]	Rape (legacy definition)[2]	Robbery	Aggravated assault	Property crime	Burglary	Larceny-theft	Motor vehicle theft	Arson[3]	Number of agencies	Estimated population, 2014
Total, All Agencies................................													
Offenses known	467,479	7,649	28,444	6,464	80,776	344,146	1,386,842	192,973	1,119,151	74,718	8,848	14,462	272,419,125
Percent under 18 years	8.6	4.3	15.4	9.5	12.9	7.2	10.3	9.9	10.4	10.7	25.8		
Total Cities													
Offenses known	366,465	5,883	20,827	4,724	70,850	264,181	1,122,781	138,086	929,156	55,539	6,621	10,492	185,097,227
Percent under 18 years	8.7	4.5	14.2	9.2	13.3	7.2	10.6	10.5	10.6	11.2	26.9		
Group I (250,000 and over)....................													
Offenses known	154,003	2,872	8,277	1,176	35,562	106,116	264,768	36,023	210,886	17,859	1,893	72	52,707,748
Percent under 18 years	8.7	4.9	12.9	7.2	15.1	6.4	10.8	11.4	10.6	12.5	25.3		
1,000,000 and over (Group I subset).......													
Offenses known	71,081	1,115	3,872	182	17,397	48,515	96,578	12,300	77,964	6,314	532	10	24,299,686
Percent under 18 years	8.6	5.3	12.3	7.1	15.5	5.9	9.7	9.7	9.8	9.6	22.0		
500,000 to 999,999 (Group I subset)......													
Offenses known	44,914	890	2,332	424	9,326	31,942	82,789	11,508	65,715	5,566	681	21	14,344,463
Percent under 18 years	9.2	4.6	13.4	6.6	16.4	7.0	11.5	13.0	10.9	15.8	22.8		
250,000 to 499,999 (Group I subset) ..													
Offenses known	38,008	867	2,073	570	8,839	25,659	85,401	12,215	67,207	5,979	680	41	14,063,599
Percent under 18 years	8.4	4.8	13.2	7.7	13.0	6.5	11.4	11.7	11.2	12.5	30.3		
Group II (100,000 to 249,999)................													
Offenses known	58,699	1,042	3,336	917	11,969	41,435	178,750	24,241	143,877	10,632	1,184	193	28,851,498
Percent under 18 years	8.5	4.1	15.0	8.9	12.0	7.1	11.8	11.5	11.8	11.3	24.3		
Group III (50,000 to 99,999)													
Offenses known	47,371	605	2,557	765	8,695	34,749	177,497	21,217	148,027	8,253	859	424	29,480,448
Percent under 18 years	8.5	5.0	13.8	8.2	12.1	7.2	11.6	9.9	11.9	9.9	29.3		
Group IV (25,000 to 49,999)..................													
Offenses known	35,429	517	2,154	629	6,307	25,822	168,052	17,306	144,611	6,135	835	761	26,285,490
Percent under 18 years	9.1	6.2	17.0	9.7	11.4	7.9	10.5	9.8	10.5	10.9	30.4		
Group V (10,000 to 24,999)													
Offenses known	35,994	453	2,220	587	4,960	27,774	180,543	19,853	154,525	6,165	864	1,624	25,807,366
Percent under 18 years	9.1	1.5	15.6	15.8	9.2	8.5	9.8	9.4	9.8	10.7	29.9		
Group VI (under 10,000)........................													
Offenses known	34,969	394	2,283	650	3,357	28,285	153,171	19,446	127,230	6,495	986	7,418	21,964,677
Percent under 18 years	9.0	2.8	14.2	7.7	11.2	8.4	8.9	10.1	8.7	10.2	25.8		
Metropolitan Counties													
Offenses known	77,034	1,268	4,910	1,428	8,841	60,587	204,490	38,577	152,057	13,856	1,519	1,720	63,594,611
Percent under 18 years	8.7	3.4	19.2	10.3	11.2	7.6	9.7	8.9	9.9	9.5	25.6		
Nonmetropolitan Counties.................													
Offenses known	23,980	498	2,707	312	1,085	19,378	59,571	16,310	37,938	5,323	708	2,250	23,727,287
Percent under 18 years	6.8	4.0	17.3	11.2	4.3	5.5	7.3	7.5	7.1	8.7	15.4		
Suburban Areas[4]													
Offenses known	139,830	2,008	8,680	2,629	18,608	107,905	513,507	72,514	415,742	25,251	3,030	7,771	116,626,974
Percent under 18 years	9.2	3.2	18.0	10.9	11.4	8.2	9.7	9.4	9.7	9.7	28.9		

[1] The figures shown in this column for the offense of rape were reported using the revised Uniform Crime Reporting (UCR) definition of rape. See chapter notes for more detail.
[2] The figures shown in this column for the offense of rape were reported using the legacy Uniform Crime Reporting (UCR) definition of rape. See chapter notes for more detail.
[3] Not all agencies submit reports for arson to the FBI. As a result, the number of reports the FBI uses to compute the percent of offenses cleared for arson is less than the number it uses to compute the percent of offenses cleared for all other offenses.
[4] Suburban area includes law enforcement agencies in cities with less than 50,000 inhabitants and county law enforcement agencies that are within a Metropolitan Statistical Area. Suburban area excludes all metropolitan agencies associated with a principal city. The agencies associated with suburban areas also appear in other groups within this table.

Table 15. Estimated Number of Arrests, 2014

(Number.)

Offense	Arrests
Total[1]	11,205,833
Violent crime[2]	498,666
Murder and nonnegligent manslaughter	10,571
Rape[3]	21,007
Robbery	94,403
Aggravated assault	372,685
Property crime[2]	1,553,980
Burglary	237,974
Larceny-theft	1,238,190
Motor vehicle theft	68,422
Arson	9,394
Other assaults	1,093,258
Forgery and counterfeiting	56,783
Fraud	141,293
Embezzlement	16,227
Stolen property; buying, receiving, possessing	88,946
Vandalism	198,400
Weapons; carrying, possessing, etc.	140,713
Prostitution and commercialized vice	47,598
Sex offenses (except forcible rape and prostitution)	55,456
Drug abuse violations	1,561,231
Gambling	5,637
Offenses against the family and children	102,336
Driving under the influence	1,117,852
Liquor laws	321,125
Drunkenness	414,854
Disorderly conduct	436,014
Vagrancy	27,380
All other offenses	3,274,430
Suspicion	1,310
Curfew and loitering law violations	53,654

[1] Does not include suspicion.
[2] Violent crimes are offenses of murder and nonnegligent manslaughter, rape, robbery, and aggravated assault. Property crimes are offenses of burglary, larceny-theft, motor vehicle theft, and arson.
[3] The rape figures in this table are an aggregate total of the data submitted using both the revised and legacy Uniform Crime Reporting definitions.

Table 16. Number and Rate of Arrests, by Geographic Region, 2014

(Number, rate per 100,000 inhabitants.)

Offense charged	United States total (12,327 agencies; population 250,219,374)		Northeast (3,078 agencies; population 44,861,741)		Midwest (3,115 agencies; population 50,295,343)		South (4,322 agencies; population 85,236,433)		West (1,812 agencies; population 69,825,857)	
	Total	Rate	Total	Rate	Total	Rate	Total	Rate	Total	Rate
Total[1]	8,789,559	3,512.7	1,352,573	3,015.0	1,739,863	3,459.3	3,247,981	3,810.6	2,449,142	3,507.5
Violent crime[2]	392,177	156.7	60,532	134.9	62,199	123.7	119,934	140.7	149,512	214.1
Murder and nonnegligent manslaughter	8,267	3.3	1,036	2.3	1,649	3.3	3,357	3.9	2,225	3.2
Rape[3]	16,473	6.6	2,565	5.7	3,902	7.8	5,253	6.2	4,753	6.8
Robbery	74,432	29.7	15,479	34.5	12,412	24.7	23,921	28.1	22,620	32.4
Aggravated assault	293,005	117.1	41,452	92.4	44,236	88.0	87,403	102.5	119,914	171.7
Property crime[2]	1,226,608	490.2	195,444	435.7	244,478	486.1	465,780	546.5	320,906	459.6
Burglary	187,474	74.9	26,917	60.0	26,207	52.1	65,869	77.3	68,481	98.1
Larceny-theft	978,033	390.9	160,925	358.7	205,750	409.1	382,634	448.9	228,724	327.6
Motor vehicle theft	53,744	21.5	6,124	13.7	11,266	22.4	14,923	17.5	21,431	30.7
Arson	7,357	2.9	1,478	3.3	1,255	2.5	2,354	2.8	2,270	3.3
Other assaults	859,214	343.4	148,134	330.2	173,354	344.7	336,676	395.0	201,050	287.9
Forgery and counterfeiting	44,609	17.8	7,667	17.1	7,229	14.4	19,579	23.0	10,134	14.5
Fraud	110,355	44.1	21,746	48.5	19,463	38.7	52,096	61.1	17,050	24.4
Embezzlement	12,772	5.1	1,438	3.2	2,165	4.3	7,071	8.3	2,098	3.0
Stolen property; buying, receiving, possessing	70,170	28.0	11,734	26.2	12,818	25.5	19,657	23.1	25,961	37.2
Vandalism	155,893	62.3	33,352	74.3	32,198	64.0	40,962	48.1	49,381	70.7
Weapons; carrying, possessing, etc.	110,367	44.1	14,960	33.3	22,908	45.5	36,854	43.2	35,645	51.0
Prostitution and commercialized vice	37,222	14.9	5,329	11.9	5,370	10.7	11,101	13.0	15,422	22.1
Sex offenses (except forcible rape and prostitution)	43,422	17.4	6,599	14.7	8,399	16.7	12,708	14.9	15,716	22.5
Drug abuse violations	1,223,505	489.0	203,938	454.6	231,208	459.7	445,928	523.2	342,431	490.4
Gambling	4,373	1.7	509	1.1	1,715	3.4	1,735	2.0	414	0.6
Offenses against the family and children	79,556	31.8	15,545	34.7	17,148	34.1	34,905	41.0	11,958	17.1
Driving under the influence	872,184	348.6	128,054	285.4	187,748	373.3	271,101	318.1	285,281	408.6
Liquor laws	249,970	99.9	30,657	68.3	84,575	168.2	60,628	71.1	74,110	106.1
Drunkenness	328,466	131.3	33,338	74.3	21,011	41.8	176,546	207.1	97,571	139.7
Disorderly conduct	341,979	136.7	86,874	193.6	109,220	217.2	92,281	108.3	53,604	76.8
Vagrancy	21,810	8.7	1,706	3.8	3,313	6.6	5,676	6.7	11,115	15.9
All other offenses (except traffic)	2,563,166	1,024.4	327,772	730.6	486,240	966.8	1,028,770	1,207.0	720,384	1,031.7
Suspicion	1,068	0.4	66	0.1	237	0.5	719	0.8	46	0.1
Curfew and loitering law violations	41,741	16.7	17,245	38.4	7,104	14.1	7,993	9.4	9,399	13.5

[1] Does not include suspicion.
[2] Violent crimes are offenses of murder and nonnegligent manslaughter, rape, robbery, and aggravated assault. Property crimes are offenses of burglary, larceny-theft, motor vehicle theft, and arson.
[3] The rape figures in this table are an aggregate total of the data submitted using both the revised and legacy Uniform Crime Reporting definitions.

Table 17. Number and Rate of Arrests, by Population Group, 2014

(Number, rate per 100,000 inhabitants.)

Offense charged	Total (12,327 agencies; population 250,219,374)		Total cities (8,872 cities; population 170,174,044)		Group I (68 cities, 250,000 and over; population 45,887,356)		Group II (182 cities, 100,000 to 249,999; population 26,979,784)		Group III (414 cities, 50,000 to 99,999; population 28,758,398)		Group IV (721 cities, 25,000 to 49,999; population 24,938,920)	
	Total	Rate	Total	Rate	Total	Rate	Total	Rate	Total	Rate	Total	Rate
Total[2]	8,789,559	3,512.7	6,411,512	3,767.6	1,652,592	3,601.4	992,430	3,678.4	1,000,541	3,479.1	892,381	3,578.3
Violent crime[3]	392,177	156.7	303,317	178.2	113,075	246.4	54,252	201.1	46,493	161.7	33,123	132.8
Murder and nonnegligent manslaughter	8,267	3.3	5,967	3.5	2,830	6.2	1,076	4.0	712	2.5	583	2.3
Rape[4]..	16,473	6.6	11,945	7.0	3,959	8.6	1,877	7.0	1,755	6.1	1,475	5.9
Robbery	74,432	29.7	63,216	37.1	28,238	61.5	11,019	40.8	9,094	31.6	6,656	26.7
Aggravated assault	293,005	117.1	222,189	130.6	78,048	170.1	40,280	149.3	34,932	121.5	24,409	97.9
Property crime[3].................................	1,226,608	490.2	1,004,135	590.1	237,879	518.4	160,030	593.1	170,007	591.2	155,306	622.7
Burglary...	187,474	74.9	137,034	80.5	36,441	79.4	25,644	95.0	24,566	85.4	18,022	72.3
Larceny-theft	978,033	390.9	821,597	482.8	185,096	403.4	126,027	467.1	138,574	481.9	132,570	531.6
Motor vehicle theft	53,744	21.5	39,987	23.5	15,045	32.8	7,508	27.8	5,925	20.6	3,867	15.5
Arson...	7,357	2.9	5,517	3.2	1,297	2.8	851	3.2	942	3.3	847	3.4
Other assaults..	859,214	343.4	642,556	377.6	182,031	396.7	106,371	394.3	101,830	354.1	88,249	353.9
Forgery and counterfeiting............................	44,609	17.8	32,696	19.2	7,306	15.9	5,205	19.3	5,232	18.2	4,817	19.3
Fraud	110,355	44.1	74,553	43.8	14,058	30.6	9,776	36.2	11,410	39.7	11,730	47.0
Embezzlement	12,772	5.1	9,700	5.7	2,148	4.7	1,650	6.1	1,685	5.9	1,585	6.4
Stolen property; buying, receiving, possessing.............	70,170	28.0	52,113	30.6	13,091	28.5	8,888	32.9	9,629	33.5	8,254	33.1
Vandalism..	155,893	62.3	120,491	70.8	32,053	69.9	18,336	68.0	19,469	67.7	17,473	70.1
Weapons; carrying, possessing, etc.	110,367	44.1	86,046	50.6	32,766	71.4	14,024	52.0	12,410	43.2	9,146	36.7
Prostitution and commercialized vice........................	37,222	14.9	33,701	19.8	23,189	50.5	4,668	17.3	2,521	8.8	1,731	6.9
Sex offenses (except forcible rape and prostitution).....	43,422	17.4	30,946	18.2	10,390	22.6	4,503	16.7	4,564	15.9	4,036	16.2
Drug abuse violations.....................................	1,223,505	489.0	875,373	514.4	256,099	558.1	134,889	500.0	138,303	480.9	113,842	456.5
Gambling..	4,373	1.7	3,482	2.0	2,305	5.0	195	0.7	284	1.0	97	0.4
Offenses against the family and children	79,556	31.8	38,895	22.9	6,383	13.9	6,964	25.8	5,632	19.6	6,251	25.1
Driving under the influence............................	872,184	348.6	503,164	295.7	108,472	236.4	68,052	252.2	76,125	264.7	72,365	290.2
Liquor laws	249,970	99.9	197,930	116.3	40,128	87.4	21,328	79.1	25,159	87.5	25,952	104.1
Drunkenness...	328,466	131.3	280,592	164.9	49,712	108.3	52,406	194.2	51,564	179.3	40,976	164.3
Disorderly conduct...	341,979	136.7	286,239	168.2	59,874	130.5	36,525	135.4	41,342	143.8	42,107	168.8
Vagrancy..	21,810	8.7	19,517	11.5	6,706	14.6	3,489	12.9	4,632	16.1	2,021	8.1
All other offenses (except traffic)....................	2,563,166	1,024.4	1,777,739	1,044.7	432,495	942.5	278,200	1,031.1	268,593	934.0	250,284	1,003.6
Suspicion	1,068	0.4	837	0.5	2	*	28	0.1	321	1.1	75	0.3
Curfew and loitering law violations	41,741	16.7	38,327	22.5	22,432	48.9	2,679	9.9	3,657	12.7	3,036	12.2

Table 17. Number and Rate of Arrests, by Population Group, 2014—*Continued*

(Number, rate per 100,000 inhabitants.)

Offense charged	Group V (1,516 cities, 10,000 to 24,999; population 24,164,183)		Group VI (5,971 cities, under 10,000; population 19,445,403)		Metropolitan counties (1,458 agencies; population 58,220,680)		Nonmetropolitan counties (1,997 agencies; population 21,824,650)		Suburban areas[1] (6,799 agencies; population 112,259,903)	
	Total	Rate	Total	Rate	Total	Rate	Total	Rate	Total	Rate
Total[2]	923,428	3,821.5	950,140	4,886.2	1,688,931	2,900.9	689,116	3,157.5	3,670,867	3,270.0
Violent crime[3]	30,565	126.5	25,809	132.7	68,455	117.6	20,405	93.5	134,006	119.4
Murder and nonnegligent manslaughter	436	1.8	330	1.7	1,692	2.9	608	2.8	2,578	2.3
Rape[4]	1,455	6.0	1,424	7.3	3,122	5.4	1,406	6.4	6,064	5.4
Robbery	4,884	20.2	3,325	17.1	9,850	16.9	1,366	6.3	21,990	19.6
Aggravated assault	23,790	98.5	20,730	106.6	53,791	92.4	17,025	78.0	103,374	92.1
Property crime[3]	159,253	659.0	121,660	625.6	172,410	296.1	50,063	229.4	490,176	436.6
Burglary	17,352	71.8	15,009	77.2	36,014	61.9	14,426	66.1	72,821	64.9
Larceny-theft	137,248	568.0	102,082	525.0	124,936	214.6	31,500	144.3	395,852	352.6
Motor vehicle theft	3,849	15.9	3,793	19.5	10,203	17.5	3,554	16.3	18,580	16.6
Arson	804	3.3	776	4.0	1,257	2.2	583	2.7	2,923	2.6
Other assaults	86,265	357.0	77,810	400.1	160,277	275.3	56,381	258.3	337,515	300.7
Forgery and counterfeiting	5,577	23.1	4,559	23.4	9,079	15.6	2,834	13.0	19,758	17.6
Fraud	11,766	48.7	15,813	81.3	24,810	42.6	10,992	50.4	51,166	45.6
Embezzlement	1,457	6.0	1,175	6.0	2,433	4.2	639	2.9	5,394	4.8
Stolen property; buying, receiving, possessing	7,076	29.3	5,175	26.6	14,096	24.2	3,961	18.1	30,341	27.0
Vandalism	16,607	68.7	16,553	85.1	26,531	45.6	8,871	40.6	62,239	55.4
Weapons; carrying, possessing, etc.	8,276	34.2	9,424	48.5	18,035	31.0	6,286	28.8	38,179	34.0
Prostitution and commercialized vice	1,023	4.2	569	2.9	3,321	5.7	200	0.9	6,224	5.5
Sex offenses (except forcible rape and prostitution)	3,826	15.8	3,627	18.7	9,075	15.6	3,401	15.6	17,642	15.7
Drug abuse violations	111,758	462.5	120,482	619.6	251,045	431.2	97,087	444.9	511,765	455.9
Gambling	273	1.1	328	1.7	751	1.3	140	0.6	1,036	0.9
Offenses against the family and children	6,487	26.8	7,178	36.9	30,152	51.8	10,509	48.2	42,617	38.0
Driving under the influence	84,570	350.0	93,580	481.2	218,040	374.5	150,980	691.8	402,498	358.5
Liquor laws	31,922	132.1	53,441	274.8	34,383	59.1	17,657	80.9	109,480	97.5
Drunkenness	41,814	173.0	44,120	226.9	33,054	56.8	14,820	67.9	120,546	107.4
Disorderly conduct	48,942	202.5	57,449	295.4	38,415	66.0	17,325	79.4	141,023	125.6
Vagrancy	1,496	6.2	1,173	6.0	2,107	3.6	186	0.9	5,660	5.0
All other offenses (except traffic)	261,598	1,082.6	286,569	1,473.7	569,340	977.9	216,087	990.1	1,133,431	1,009.6
Suspicion	176	0.7	235	1.2	7	*	224	1.0	349	0.3
Curfew and loitering law violations	2,877	11.9	3,646	18.7	3,122	5.4	292	1.3	10,171	9.1

[1] Suburban areas include law enforcement agencies in cities with less than 50,000 inhabitants and county law enforcement agencies that are within a Metropolitan Statistical Area. Suburban areas exclude all metropolitan agencies associated with a principal city. The agencies associated with suburban areas also appear in other groups within this table.
[2] Does not include suspicion.
[3] Violent crimes are offenses of murder and nonnegligent manslaughter, forcible rape, robbery, and aggravated assault. Property crimes are offenses of burglary, larceny-theft, motor vehicle theft, and arson.
[4] The rape figures in this table are an aggregate total of the data submitted using both the revised and legacy Uniform Crime Reporting definitions.

Table 18. Ten-Year Arrest Trends, 2005 and 2014

(Number, percent change; 6,082 agencies; 2014 estimated population 149,523,915; 2005 estimated population 138,435,918.)

Offense charged	Number of persons arrested								
	Total, all ages			Under 18 years of age			18 years of age and over		
	2005	2014	Percent change	2005	2014	Percent change	2005	2014	Percent change
Total[1]	6,557,708	5,267,843	-19.7	987,682	482,050	-51.2	5,570,026	4,785,793	-14.1
Violent crime[2]	296,436	248,666	-16.1	45,319	25,890	-42.9	251,117	222,776	-11.3
Murder and nonnegligent manslaughter	6,487	4,929	-24.0	598	331	-44.6	5,889	4,598	-21.9
Rape[3]	11,887	9,757	NA	1,786	1,501	NA	10,101	8,256	NA
Robbery	54,522	46,756	-14.2	13,790	9,150	-33.6	40,732	37,606	-7.7
Aggravated assault	223,540	187,224	-16.2	29,145	14,908	-48.8	194,395	172,316	-11.4
Property crime[2]	783,834	752,061	-4.1	204,717	110,729	-45.9	579,117	641,332	+10.7
Burglary	151,795	126,903	-16.4	39,843	20,602	-48.3	111,952	106,301	-5.0
Larceny-theft	556,806	587,221	+5.5	144,688	83,438	-42.3	412,118	503,783	+22.2
Motor vehicle theft	67,148	33,253	-50.5	16,121	5,142	-68.1	51,027	28,111	-44.9
Arson	8,085	4,684	-42.1	4,065	1,547	-61.9	4,020	3,137	-22.0
Other assaults	573,559	489,005	-14.7	114,737	63,260	-44.9	458,822	425,745	-7.2
Forgery and counterfeiting	58,723	26,782	-54.4	2,081	564	-72.9	56,642	26,218	-53.7
Fraud	136,954	63,492	-53.6	3,799	1,934	-49.1	133,155	61,558	-53.8
Embezzlement	7,739	5,783	-25.3	497	166	-66.6	7,242	5,617	-22.4
Stolen property; buying, receiving, possessing	68,530	48,273	-29.6	11,541	5,394	-53.3	56,989	42,879	-24.8
Vandalism	136,890	96,717	-29.3	51,732	22,070	-57.3	85,158	74,647	-12.3
Weapons; carrying, possessing, etc.	95,704	68,733	-28.2	22,824	10,323	-54.8	72,880	58,410	-19.9
Prostitution and commercialized vice	30,238	19,658	-35.0	709	381	-46.3	29,529	19,277	-34.7
Sex offenses (except forcible rape and prostitution)	46,036	29,784	-35.3	8,828	4,910	-44.4	37,208	24,874	-33.1
Drug abuse violations	876,940	771,213	-12.1	89,506	54,433	-39.2	787,434	716,780	-9.0
Gambling	2,580	1,586	-38.5	297	99	-66.7	2,283	1,487	-34.9
Offenses against the family and children	69,539	46,195	-33.6	2,859	1,541	-46.1	66,680	44,654	-33.0
Driving under the influence	681,202	532,384	-21.8	8,784	3,007	-65.8	672,418	529,377	-21.3
Liquor laws	251,938	131,358	-47.9	59,366	24,463	-58.8	192,572	106,895	-44.5
Drunkenness	280,849	215,257	-23.4	8,537	3,533	-58.6	272,312	211,724	-22.2
Disorderly conduct	316,037	194,593	-38.4	102,373	37,316	-63.5	213,664	157,277	-26.4
Vagrancy	18,230	14,314	-21.5	3,316	640	-80.7	14,914	13,674	-8.3
All other offenses (except traffic)	1,755,631	1,483,098	-15.5	175,741	82,506	-53.1	1,579,890	1,400,592	-11.3
Suspicion	2,343	544	-76.8	343	136	-60.3	2,000	408	-79.6
Curfew and loitering law violations	70,119	28,891	-58.8	70,119	28,891	-58.8	NA	NA	NA

NA = Not available.
[1] Does not include suspicion.
[2] Violent crimes are offenses of murder and nonnegligent manslaughter, rape, robbery, and aggravated assault. Property crimes are offenses of burglary, larceny-theft, motor vehicle theft, and arson.
[3] The 2005 rape figures are based on the legacy definition, and the 2014 rape figures are aggregate totals based on both the legacy and revised Uniform Crime Reporting definitions. For this reason, a percent change is not provided.

Table 19. Current Year Over Previous Year Arrest Trends, 2013–2014

(Number, percent change; 11,284 agencies; 2014 estimated population 235,423,438; 2013 estimated population 233,336,432; 2013 estimated population 233,336,432.)

Offense charged	Total, all ages			Under 15 years of age			Under 18 years of age			18 years of age and over		
	2013	2014	Percent change	2013	2014	Percent change	2013	2014	Percent change	2013	2014	Percent change
Total[1]	8,601,467	8,266,163	-3.9	295,239	270,173	-8.9	822,234	752,515	-8.5	7,779,233	7,513,648	-3.4
Violent crime[2]	373,074	370,074	-0.8	11,284	10,778	-4.7	39,950	38,414	-3.8	333,124	331,660	-0.4
Murder and nonnegligent manslaughter	7,725	7,379	-4.5	71	41	-42.3	562	511	-9.1	7,163	6,868	-4.1
Rape[3]	14,355	15,477	+7.8	927	955	+3.0	2,306	2,432	+5.5	12,049	13,045	+8.3
Robbery	72,618	67,885	-6.5	2,787	2,602	-6.6	14,016	13,260	-5.4	58,602	54,625	-6.8
Aggravated assault	278,376	279,333	+0.3	7,570	7,221	-4.6	23,066	22,211	-3.7	255,310	257,122	+0.7
Property crime[2]	1,185,731	1,154,168	-2.7	52,678	48,654	-7.6	185,359	173,500	-6.4	1,000,372	980,668	-2.0
Burglary	193,274	176,697	-8.6	8,784	8,285	-5.7	32,383	29,528	-8.8	160,891	147,169	-8.5
Larceny-theft	937,154	921,848	-1.6	40,612	37,078	-8.7	142,363	133,236	-6.4	794,791	788,612	-0.8
Motor vehicle theft	47,964	48,699	+1.5	1,773	1,927	+8.7	8,006	8,399	+4.9	39,958	40,300	+0.9
Arson	7,339	6,924	-5.7	1,509	1,364	-9.6	2,607	2,337	-10.4	4,732	4,587	-3.1
Other assaults	838,441	805,653	-3.9	43,813	39,674	-9.4	111,284	102,188	-8.2	727,157	703,465	-3.3
Forgery and counterfeiting	46,651	42,245	-9.4	90	110	+22.2	810	872	+7.7	45,841	41,373	-9.7
Fraud	109,592	104,299	-4.8	687	614	-10.6	3,485	3,215	-7.7	106,107	101,084	-4.7
Embezzlement	12,464	12,469	*	36	22	-38.9	311	365	+17.4	12,153	12,104	-0.4
Stolen property; buying, receiving, possessing	71,806	66,875	-6.9	1,866	1,751	-6.2	8,028	7,798	-2.9	63,778	59,077	-7.4
Vandalism	153,623	148,083	-3.6	13,764	13,204	-4.1	35,869	33,832	-5.7	117,754	114,251	-3.0
Weapons; carrying, possessing, etc.	104,340	100,878	-3.3	5,244	4,993	-4.8	15,321	14,798	-3.4	89,019	86,080	-3.3
Prostitution and commercialized vice	39,190	34,674	-11.5	61	74	+21.3	633	566	-10.6	38,557	34,108	-11.5
Sex offenses (except forcible rape and prostitution)	43,927	41,082	-6.5	3,851	3,441	-10.6	7,824	7,137	-8.8	36,103	33,945	-6.0
Drug abuse violations	1,116,612	1,120,133	+0.3	14,897	13,471	-9.6	86,070	80,741	-6.2	1,030,542	1,039,392	+0.9
Gambling	2,915	2,709	-7.1	63	32	-49.2	237	205	-13.5	2,678	2,504	-6.5
Offenses against the family and children	75,820	74,432	-1.8	695	809	+16.4	2,088	2,323	+11.3	73,732	72,109	-2.2
Driving under the influence	885,226	838,725	-5.3	119	113	-5.0	5,765	5,234	-9.2	879,461	833,491	-5.2
Liquor laws	270,884	236,920	-12.5	4,468	3,722	-16.7	46,848	40,231	-14.1	224,036	196,689	-12.2
Drunkenness	344,799	318,713	-7.6	650	598	-8.0	5,671	4,918	-13.3	339,128	313,795	-7.5
Disorderly conduct	347,333	312,676	-10.0	27,571	22,313	-19.1	69,989	58,706	-16.1	277,344	253,970	-8.4
Vagrancy	20,495	21,439	+4.6	169	169	0.0	704	718	+2.0	19,791	20,721	+4.7
All other offenses (except traffic)	2,511,791	2,419,888	-3.7	35,419	33,484	-5.5	149,235	136,726	-8.4	2,362,556	2,283,162	-3.4
Suspicion	813	1,027	+26.3	80	99	+23.8	171	346	+102.3	642	681	+6.1
Curfew and loitering law violations	46,753	40,028	-14.4	13,781	12,674	-8.0	46,753	40,028	-14.4	NA	NA	NA

NA = Not available.
* = Less than one-tenth of 1 percent.
[1] Does not include suspicion.
[2] Violent crimes are offenses of murder and nonnegligent manslaughter, rape, robbery, and aggravated assault. Property crimes are offenses of burglary, larceny-theft, motor vehicle theft, and arson.
[3] The rape figures in this table are aggregate totals of the data submitted based on both the legacy and revised Uniform Crime Reporting definitions.

Table 20. Full-Time Law Enforcement Employees,[1] by Region and Geographic Division and Population Group, 2014

(Number, rate per 1,000 inhabitants)

Region/geographic division	Total (9,792 cities; population 183,432,062)	Group I (72 cities, 250,000 and over; population 55,946,176)	Group II (192 cities, 100,000 to 249,999; population 28,478,947)	Group III (405 cities, 50,000 to 99,999; population 28,000,451)	Group IV (729 cities, 25,000 to 49,999; population 25,123,097)	Group V (1,579 cities, 10,000 to 24,999; population 25,167,878)
Total						
Number of employees	519,535	191,314	62,974	57,298	53,585	56,825
Average number of employees per 1,000 inhabitants	2.8	3.4	2.2	2.0	2.1	2.3
Northeast						
Number of employees	144,740	63,744	8,601	15,030	17,504	18,445
Average number of employees per 1,000 inhabitants	3.3	5.4	3.0	2.3	2.2	2.1
New England						
Number of employees	34,371	2,710	4,507	6,222	7,041	7,202
Average number of employees per 1,000 inhabitants	2.6	4.1	3.0	2.3	2.2	2.2
Middle Atlantic						
Number of employees	110,369	61,034	4,094	8,808	10,463	11,243
Average number of employees per 1,000 inhabitants	3.5	5.5	3.0	2.3	2.2	2.0
Midwest						
Number of employees	93,026	31,028	7,549	11,698	11,028	13,083
Average number of employees per 1,000 inhabitants	2.5	3.5	2.0	1.8	1.9	2.0
East North Central						
Number of employees	60,083	23,124	4,330	7,418	8,025	7,755
Average number of employees per 1,000 inhabitants	2.6	3.7	2.1	1.9	1.9	2.0
West North Central						
Number of employees	32,943	7,904	3,219	4,280	3,003	5,328
Average number of employees per 1,000 inhabitants	2.4	3.1	1.9	1.7	1.9	2.1
South						
Number of employees	169,441	47,478	27,025	16,122	16,524	18,689
Average number of employees per 1,000 inhabitants	3.3	3.1	2.7	2.6	2.7	2.9
South Atlantic						
Number of employees	81,897	21,902	13,136	8,459	7,983	8,730
Average number of employees per 1,000 inhabitants	3.8	3.9	2.7	2.7	2.9	3.0
East South Central						
Number of employees	29,705	6,351	4,721	2,568	3,444	3,597
Average number of employees per 1,000 inhabitants	3.4	2.8	3.4	2.8	2.6	3.0
West South Central						
Number of employees	57,839	19,225	9,168	5,095	5,097	6,362
Average number of employees per 1,000 inhabitants	2.8	2.6	2.3	2.3	2.4	2.6
West						
Number of employees	112,328	49,064	19,799	14,448	8,529	6,608
Average number of employees per 1,000 inhabitants	2.2	2.4	1.7	1.6	1.7	2.0
Mountain						
Number of employees	40,273	16,675	6,839	3,913	3,360	2,556
Average number of employees per 1,000 inhabitants	2.5	2.5	2.0	1.9	1.9	2.3
Pacific						
Number of employees	72,055	32,389	12,960	10,535	5,169	4,052
Average number of employees per 1,000 inhabitants	2.1	2.4	1.6	1.6	1.7	1.9

Table 20. Full-Time Law Enforcement Employees,[1] by Region and Geographic Division and Population Group, 2014—*Continued*

(Number, rate per 1,000 inhabitants)

Region/geographic division	Group VI (6,815 cities, under 10,000; population 20,715,513)	Total city agencies	City population, 2014, estimated	County[2] (2,864 agencies; population 84,864,300)	Total city and county agencies	Total agency population, 2014, estimated	Suburban areas[3] (6,730 agencies; population 114,360,957)
Total							
Number of employees	97,539	9,792	183,432,062	379,677	12,656	268,296,362	427,326
Average number of employees per 1,000 inhabitants	4.7			4.5			3.7
Northeast							
Number of employees	21,416	2,517	44,303,475				
Average number of employees per 1,000 inhabitants	3.4						
New England							
Number of employees	6,689	791	13,015,911				
Average number of employees per 1,000 inhabitants	3.9						
Middle Atlantic							
Number of employees	14,727	1,726	31,287,564				
Average number of employees per 1,000 inhabitants	3.3						
Midwest							
Number of employees	18,640	2,527	36,995,395				
Average number of employees per 1,000 inhabitants	3.3						
East North Central							
Number of employees	9,431	1,322	23,462,944				
Average number of employees per 1,000 inhabitants	3.1						
West North Central							
Number of employees	9,209	1,205	13,532,451				
Average number of employees per 1,000 inhabitants	3.6						
South							
Number of employees	43,603	3,374	51,013,291				
Average number of employees per 1,000 inhabitants	6.6						
South Atlantic							
Number of employees	21,687	1,430	21,774,071				
Average number of employees per 1,000 inhabitants	8.1						
East South Central							
Number of employees	9,024	794	8,677,869				
Average number of employees per 1,000 inhabitants	5.8						
West South Central							
Number of employees	12,892	1,150	20,561,351				
Average number of employees per 1,000 inhabitants	5.4						
West							
Number of employees	13,880	1,374	51,119,901				
Average number of employees per 1,000 inhabitants	6.0						
Mountain							
Number of employees	6,930	608	16,150,237				
Average number of employees per 1,000 inhabitants	6.2						
Pacific							
Number of employees	6,950	766	34,969,664				
Average number of employees per 1,000 inhabitants	5.8						

[1] Full-time law enforcement employees include civilians.
[2] The designation county is a combination of both metropolitan and nonmetropolitan counties.
[3] Suburban areas include law enforcement agencies in cities with less than 50,000 inhabitants and county law enforcement agencies that are within a Metropolitan Statistical Area (see Data Declaration). Suburban areas exclude all metropolitan agencies associated with a principal city. The agencies associated with suburban areas also appear in other groups within this table.

Table 21. Full-Time Law Enforcement Officers, by Region and Geographic Division, and Population Group, 2014

(Number, rate per 1,000 inhabitants.)

Region/geographic division	Total (9,792 cities; population 183,432,062)	Group I (72 cities, 250,000 and over; population 55,946,176)	Group II (192 cities, 100,000 to 249,999; population 28,478,947)	Group III (405 cities, 50,000 to 99,999; population 28,000,451)	Group IV (729 cities, 25,000 to 49,999; population 25,123,097)	Group V (1,579 cities, 10,000 to 24,999; population 25,167,878)
Total						
Number of officers	403,984	146,606	47,991	44,551	42,884	46,181
Average number of officers per 1,000 inhabitants	2.2	2.6	1.7	1.6	1.7	1.8
Northeast						
Number of officers	114,676	46,596	7,220	12,444	14,848	15,673
Average number of officers per 1,000 inhabitants	2.6	4.0	2.5	1.9	1.8	1.8
New England						
Number of officers	28,501	2,151	3,870	5,316	5,905	5,837
Average number of officers per 1,000 inhabitants	2.2	3.3	2.6	2.0	1.8	1.8
Middle Atlantic						
Number of officers	86,175	44,445	3,350	7,128	8,943	9,836
Average number of officers per 1,000 inhabitants	2.8	4.0	2.4	1.9	1.8	1.7
Midwest						
Number of officers	77,418	26,576	6,190	9,472	8,920	10,739
Average number of officers per 1,000 inhabitants	2.1	3.0	1.7	1.5	1.5	1.7
East North Central						
Number of officers	51,144	20,620	3,611	6,042	6,527	6,415
Average number of officers per 1,000 inhabitants	2.2	3.3	1.8	1.5	1.5	1.6
West North Central						
Number of officers	26,274	5,956	2,579	3,430	2,393	4,324
Average number of officers per 1,000 inhabitants	1.9	2.3	1.5	1.4	1.5	1.7
South						
Number of officers	131,307	37,737	20,633	12,447	12,989	14,711
Average number of officers per 1,000 inhabitants	2.6	2.5	2.0	2.0	2.1	2.3
South Atlantic						
Number of officers	63,515	16,834	10,216	6,626	6,290	7,027
Average number of officers per 1,000 inhabitants	2.9	3.0	2.1	2.1	2.3	2.5
East South Central						
Number of officers	23,579	5,414	3,546	2,000	2,809	2,847
Average number of officers per 1,000 inhabitants	2.7	2.4	2.5	2.2	2.1	2.3
West South Central						
Number of officers	44,213	15,489	6,871	3,821	3,890	4,837
Average number of officers per 1,000 inhabitants	2.2	2.1	1.7	1.7	1.8	2.0
West						
Number of officers	80,583	35,697	13,948	10,188	6,127	5,058
Average number of officers per 1,000 inhabitants	1.6	1.8	1.2	1.2	1.3	1.5
Mountain						
Number of officers	28,148	11,299	4,911	2,723	2,466	1,977
Average number of officers per 1,000 inhabitants	1.7	1.7	1.4	1.3	1.4	1.8
Pacific						
Number of officers	52,435	24,398	9,037	7,465	3,661	3,081
Average number of officers per 1,000 inhabitants	1.5	1.8	1.1	1.1	1.2	1.4

Table 21. Full-Time Law Enforcement Officers, by Region and Geographic Division, and Population Group, 2014—*Continued*

(Number, rate per 1,000 inhabitants.)

Region/geographic division	Group VI (6,815 cities, under 10,000; population 20,715,513)	Total city agencies	City population, 2014, estimated	County[1] (2,864 agencies; population 84,864,300)	Total city and county agencies	Total agency population, 2014, estimated	Suburban areas[2] (6,730 agencies; population 114,360,957)
Total							
Number of officers	75,771	9,792	183,432,062	223,965	12,656	268,296,362	279,954
Average number of officers per 1,000 inhabitants	3.7			2.6			2.4
Northeast							
Number of officers	17,895	2,517	44,303,475				
Average number of officers per 1,000 inhabitants	2.9						
New England							
Number of officers	5,422	791	13,015,911				
Average number of officers per 1,000 inhabitants	3.1						
Middle Atlantic							
Number of officers	12,473	1,726	31,287,564				
Average number of officers per 1,000 inhabitants	2.8						
Midwest							
Number of officers	15,521	2,527	36,995,395				
Average number of officers per 1,000 inhabitants	2.8						
East North Central							
Number of officers	7,929	1,322	23,462,944				
Average number of officers per 1,000 inhabitants	2.6						
West North Central							
Number of officers	7,592	1,205	13,532,451				
Average number of officers per 1,000 inhabitants	3.0						
South							
Number of officers	32,790	3,374	51,013,291				
Average number of officers per 1,000 inhabitants	5.0						
South Atlantic							
Number of officers	16,522	1,430	21,774,071				
Average number of officers per 1,000 inhabitants	6.2						
East South Central							
Number of officers	6,963	794	8,677,869				
Average number of officers per 1,000 inhabitants	4.5						
West South Central							
Number of officers	9,305	1,150	20,561,351				
Average number of officers per 1,000 inhabitants	3.9						
West							
Number of officers	9,565	1,374	51,119,901				
Average number of officers per 1,000 inhabitants	4.1						
Mountain							
Number of officers	4,772	608	16,150,237				
Average number of officers per 1,000 inhabitants	4.3						
Pacific							
Number of officers	4,793	766	34,969,664				
Average number of officers per 1,000 inhabitants	4.0						

[1] The designation county is a combination of both metropolitan and nonmetropolitan counties.
[2] Suburban areas include law enforcement agencies in cities with less than 50,000 inhabitants and county law enforcement agencies that are within a Metropolitan Statistical Area. Suburban areas exclude all metropolitan agencies associated with a principal city. The agencies associated with suburban areas also appear in other groups within this table.

Table 22. Full-Time State Law Enforcement Employees, by Selected State, 2014

(Number.)

State/agency	Law enforcement employees	Officers		Civilians	
		Male	Female	Male	Female
Alabama[1]					
Other state agencies	141	89	11	15	26
Alaska					
State Troopers..	633	378	17	100	138
Arizona					
Department of Public Safety................................	1,911	1,061	46	328	476
Arkansas[1]					
Other state agencies	31	29	0	0	2
California					
Highway Patrol	10,551	6,775	500	1,399	1,877
Other state agencies[2]	1,256	938	193	33	92
Colorado[3]					
Other state agencies	177	33	5	30	109
Connecticut..					
State Police	1,661	1,044	84	240	293
Other state agencies	44	32	1	8	3
Delaware					
State Police	948	622	84	100	142
Other state agencies	684	205	23	169	287
Florida[1]					
Other state agencies	3,332	1,415	219	597	1,101
Georgia[1]					
Other state agencies	1,090	317	92	214	467
Idaho					
State Police	463	246	14	50	153
Illinois...					
State Police	2,933	1,603	178	464	688
Indiana					
State Police	1,744	1,218	61	167	298
Other state agencies	88	72	15	0	1
Iowa					
Department of Public Safety................................	874	543	34	145	152
Kansas...					
Highway Patrol	742	449	19	108	166
Other state agencies	553	299	26	83	145
Kentucky...					
State Police	1,704	922	18	376	388
Other state agencies	281	214	10	19	38
Maine					
State Police	424	285	22	53	64
Other state agencies[2]	54	23	2	22	7
Maryland					
State Police	2,189	1,369	105	367	348
Other state agencies	1,690	858	132	365	335
Massachusetts					
State Police	2,727	2,050	137	222	318
Other state agencies	269	227	28	7	7
Michigan					
State Police	2,646	1,610	181	374	481

(Number.)

State/agency	Law enforcement employees	Officers		Civilians	
		Male	Female	Male	Female
Minnesota..					
State Patrol...	598	449	46	55	48
Other state agencies	68	16	4	41	7
Mississippi[1]					
Other state agencies	116	94	4	3	15
Missouri...					
State Highway Patrol..	2,274	1,122	62	495	595
Other state agencies	480	411	31	4	34
Montana					
Highway Patrol	294	223	14	20	37
Nebraska					
State Patrol...	688	420	27	86	155
Nevada					
Highway Patrol	531	404	41	40	46
New Hampshire...					
State Police...	504	305	24	60	115
Other state agencies	32	14	7	3	8
New Jersey					
State Police...	3,811	2,468	117	583	643
Other state agencies	318	239	22	29	28
Port Authority of New York and New Jersey[4]............	1,426	1,198	155	13	60
New Mexico..					
State Police...	658	486	31	33	108
Other state agencies	212	115	11	54	32
New York					
State Police...	5,650	4,414	415	307	514
Other state agencies	50	43	7	0	0
North Carolina..					
Highway Patrol	2,178	1,626	44	298	210
Other state agencies	1,081	680	122	118	161
North Dakota...					
Highway Patrol	190	140	8	14	28
Ohio					
Highway Patrol	2,402	1,457	141	399	405
Other state agencies	104	74	21	1	8
Oklahoma[1]					
Other state agencies	97	30	6	47	14
Oregon..					
State Police...	1,186	614	55	182	335
Other state agencies	57	37	10	0	10
Pennsylvania					
State Police...	6,195	3,954	220	1,005	1,016
Other state agencies	389	285	28	52	24
Rhode Island...					
State Police...	303	222	25	29	27
Other state agencies	80	60	4	10	6
South Carolina[1]..					
Other state agencies[2]..	1,079	631	88	119	241
South Dakota					
Highway Patrol	252	167	5	46	34
Other state agencies	168	44	4	44	76

Table 22. Full-Time State Law Enforcement Employees, by Selected State, 2014—*Continued*

(Number.)

State/agency	Law enforcement employees	Officers		Civilians	
		Male	Female	Male	Female
Tennessee					
Department of Safety...................................	1,701	784	37	276	604
Other state agencies	1,210	660	84	182	284
Utah[1]					
Other state agencies	131	123	5	1	2
Vermont..					
State Police..	352	283	28	10	31
Other state agencies	126	93	6	10	17
Virginia					
State Police..	2,697	1,866	108	247	476
Other state agencies	770	496	58	79	137
Washington					
State Patrol	2,190	974	94	566	556
Other state agencies	129	55	19	15	40
Wisconsin..					
State Patrol	622	431	50	62	79
Other state agencies	448	345	60	13	30

Note: Caution should be used when comparing data from one state to another. The responsibilities of the various state police, highway patrol, and department of public safety agencies range from full law enforcement duties to traffic patrol only, which can affect the data for the level of employment for agencies as well as the ratio of sworn officers to civilians employed. Any valid comparison must take these factors and the other identified variables affecting crime into consideration.
[1] Police Employee data were not received from the State Police/Highway Patrol/Department of Public Safety for the state.
[2] The total employee count includes employees from agencies that are not represented in other law enforcement employee tables.
[3] The FBI determined that the Colorado State Police's data were not comparable to previous year's data. Consequently, those data are not included in this table.
[4] Data reported are the number of law enforcement employees for the state of New Jersey.

Table 23. Murder Victims, by Race and Sex, 2014

(Number.)

Race	Total	Sex		
		Male	Female	Unknown
Total	11,961	9,246	2,681	34
White	5,937	3,733	1,664	0
Black..	6,095	5,209	881	5
Other race	309	208	100	1
Unknown race	160	96	36	28
Hispanic or Latino[1]	1,871	1,510	361	0
Not Hispanic or Latino[1]	6,764	5,145	1,616	3
Unknown[1]	1,913	1,475	420	18

[1] The ethnicity totals are representative of those agencies that provided ethnicity breakdowns. Not all agencies provide ethnicity data, therefore the race and ethnicity totals will not equal.

Table 24. Murder Victims, by Age, Sex, Race, and Ethnicity, 2014

(Number; percent; single victim/single offender.)

Age	Total	Sex			Race				Ethnicity		
		Male	Female	Unknown	White	Black or African American	Other[1]	Unknown	Hispanic/ Latino	Not Hispanic/ Latino	Unknown
Total	11,961	9,246	2,681	34	5,397	6,095	309	160	1,871	6,764	1,913
Percent distribution[2]	100.0	77.3	22.4	0.3	45.1	51.0	2.6	1.3	17.7	64.1	18.1
Under 18[3]	1,085	692	388	5	492	545	25	23	203	586	150
Under 22[3]	2,595	1,996	593	6	982	1,527	52	34	475	1,357	393
18 and over[3]	10,773	8,493	2,268	12	4,866	5,517	281	109	1,658	6,148	1,711
Infant (under 1).............................	177	92	80	5	90	68	6	13	29	101	28
1 to 4	283	147	136	0	142	134	4	3	52	163	40
5 to 8	83	43	40	0	48	28	6	1	16	49	13
9 to 12	63	35	28	0	41	19	3	0	13	39	3
13 to 16	273	206	67	0	102	163	5	3	54	123	43
17 to 19	861	733	127	1	294	549	12	6	167	444	125
20 to 24	2,181	1,879	301	1	712	1,414	39	16	374	1,151	351
25 to 29	1,760	1,470	290	0	637	1,068	36	19	280	1,012	276
30 to 34	1,389	1,111	276	2	586	753	39	11	238	756	208
35 to 39	1,072	856	215	1	492	531	32	17	195	597	146
40 to 44	836	616	220	0	439	367	21	9	147	469	131
45 to 49	747	546	197	4	402	299	32	14	87	474	109
50 to 54	669	485	183	1	390	251	22	6	88	405	111
55 to 59	514	362	152	0	315	173	23	3	55	331	88
60 to 64	304	229	75	0	191	100	9	4	27	197	54
65 to 69	227	159	67	1	149	69	7	2	20	135	55
70 to 74	148	83	65	0	112	29	5	2	9	97	33
75 and over	271	133	137	1	216	47	5	3	10	191	47
Unknown.......................................	103	61	25	17	39	33	3	28	10	30	52

[1] Includes American Indian or Alaska Native; Asian; Native Hawaiian or Other Pacific Islander.
[2] Because of rounding, the percentages may not add to 100.0.
[3] Does not include unknown ages.

Table 25. Murder Offenders, by Age, Sex, Race, and Ethnicity, 2014

(Number; percent; single victim/single offender.)

Age	Total	Sex			Race				Ethnicity[1]		
		Male	Female	Unknown	White	Black or African American	Other[2]	Unknown	Hispanic/ Latino	Not Hispanic/ Latino	Unknown
Total	13,897	8,770	1,169	3,958	4,367	5,173	225	4,132	1,264	3,782	3,554
Percent distribution[3]	100.0	63.1	8.4	28.5	31.4	37.2	1.6	29.7	14.7	44.0	41.3
Under 18[4]	653	594	50	9	255	372	10	16	111	204	67
Under 22[4]	2,580	2,333	231	16	893	1,608	38	41	378	896	270
18 and over[4]	8,758	7,640	1,091	27	4,038	4,387	212	121	1,116	3,414	918
Infant (under 1)..........................	0	0	0	0	0	0	0	0	0	0	0
1 to 4	0	0	0	0	0	0	0	0	0	0	0
5 to 8	0	0	0	0	0	0	0	0	0	0	0
9 to 12	8	8	0	0	5	3	0	0	1	1	1
13 to 16	323	291	29	3	139	172	7	5	65	109	29
17 to 19	1,234	1,128	98	8	436	758	19	21	192	409	125
20 to 24	2,300	2,038	256	6	802	1,425	39	34	299	830	236
25 to 29	1,615	1,405	208	2	690	872	38	15	226	612	175
30 to 34	1,112	951	158	3	551	516	30	15	165	430	112
35 to 39	779	670	108	1	406	340	19	14	110	317	73
40 to 44	550	467	82	1	304	217	22	7	69	224	68
45 to 49	453	393	58	2	263	167	18	5	37	200	33
50 to 54	405	344	57	4	237	144	12	12	26	173	60
55 to 59	277	231	42	4	181	86	5	5	16	128	33
60 to 64	142	120	22	0	102	33	5	2	12	71	14
65 to 69	91	76	15	0	77	12	2	0	2	46	10
70 to 74	42	38	3	1	34	5	3	0	1	25	6
75 and over	80	74	5	1	66	9	3	2	6	43	10
Unknown......................................	4,486	536	28	3,922	74	414	3	3,995	37	164	2,569

[1] The ethnicity totals are representative of those agencies that provided ethnicity breakdowns. Not all agencies provide ethnicity data, therefore the race and ethnicity totals will not equal.
[2] Includes American Indian or Alaska Native; Asian; Native Hawaiian or Other Pacific Islander.
[3] Because of rounding, the percentages may not add to 100.0.
[4] Does not include unknown ages.

Table 26. Murder, by Victim/Offender Situations, 2014

(Number; percent; single victim/single offender.)

Situation	Total	Percent distribution (may not add to 100.0 due to rounding)
Total	11,961	100.0
Single victim/single offender	5,703	47.7
Single victim/unknown offender or offenders...	3,648	30.5
Single victim/multiple offenders..	1,481	12.4
Multiple victims/single offender..	559	4.7
Multiple victims/unknown offender or offenders...	227	1.9
Multiple victims/multiple offenders...	343	2.9

Table 27. Murder Age of Victim, by Age of Offender, 2014

(Number; single victim/single offender.)

Age of victim	Total	Age of offender		
		Under 18 years	18 years and over	Unknown
Total	5,703	239	5,245	219
Under 18	547	80	457	10
18 and over	5,117	158	4,755	204
Unknown..	39	1	33	5

Note: This table is based on incidents where some information about the offender is known by law enforcement; therefore, when the offender age, sex, and race are all reported as unknown, these data are excluded from the table.

Table 28. Murder, Race, Ethnicity, and Sex of Victim by Race, Ethnicity, and Sex of Offender, 2014

(Number; single victim/single offender.)

Victim characteristic	Total	Sex			Race				Ethnicity		
		Male	Female	Unknown	White	Black or African American	Other[1]	Unknown	Hispanic/ Latino	Not Hispanic/ Latino	Unknown
Race..											
White	3,021	2,663	306	52	2,488	446	35	52	595	1,061	1,365
Black or African American.......................	2,451	2,160	247	44	187	2,205	15	44	81	1,040	1,330
Other race[1]	168	148	17	3	47	25	93	3	10	90	68
Unknown...	63	41	13	9	34	17	3	9	6	10	47
Sex..											
Male	3,949	3,448	421	80	1,708	2,070	91	80	511	1,517	1,921
Female...	1,691	1,523	149	19	1,014	606	52	19	175	674	842
Unknown...	63	41	13	9	34	17	3	9	5	11	47
Ethnicity...											
Hispanic or Latino	720	654	51	15	578	119	8	15	519	162	39
Not Hispanic or Latino...........................	2,213	1,977	211	25	956	1,148	84	25	151	1,996	66
Unknown...	2,770	2,381	321	68	1,222	1,426	54	68	21	44	2,705

Note: This table is based on incidents where some information about the offender is known by law enforcement; therefore, when the offender age, sex, and race are all reported as unknown, these data are excluded from the table.
[1] Includes American Indian or Alaska Native; Asian; Native Hawaiian or Other Pacific Islander.

Table 29. Murder, Types of Weapons Used, Percent Distribution by Region, 2014[1]

(Percent.)

Region	Total, all weapons[2]	Firearms	Knives or cutting instruments	Unknown or other dangerous weapons	Personal weapons (hands, fists, feet, etc.)[3]
Total	100.0	67.3	13.1	13.5	5.5
Northeast..................................	100.0	65.3	16.8	13.6	4.3
Midwest	100.0	70.8	9.7	14.5	5.0
South...	100.0	69.6	12.0	12.4	6.0
West...	100.0	64.2	15.6	14.3	5.9

[1] Guam and Virgin Islands totals are not included in this table.
[2] Because of rounding, the percentages may not add to 100.0.
[3] Pushed is included in personal weapons.

Table 30. Murder Victims, by Weapons, 2010–2014

(Number.)

Weapons	2010	2011	2012	2013	2014
Total	13,164	12,795	12,888	12,253	11,961
Total firearms	8,874	8,653	8,897	8,454	8,124
Handguns	6,115	6,251	6,404	5,782	5,562
Rifles	367	332	298	285	248
Shotguns	366	362	310	308	262
Other guns	93	97	116	123	93
Firearms, type not stated	1,933	1,611	1,769	1,956	1,959
Knives or cutting instruments	1,732	1,716	1,604	1,490	1,567
Blunt objects (clubs, hammers, etc.)	549	502	522	428	435
Personal weapons (hands, fists, feet, etc.)[1]	769	751	707	687	660
Poison	11	5	13	11	7
Explosives	4	6	8	2	6
Fire	78	76	87	94	71
Narcotics	45	33	38	53	62
Drowning	10	15	14	4	14
Strangulation	122	88	90	85	89
Asphyxiation	98	92	106	95	96
Other weapons or weapons not stated	872	858	802	850	830

[1] Pushed is included in personal weapons.

Table 31. Murder Victims by Age, by Weapon, 2014

(Number.)

Age	Total murder victims	Weapons										
		Firearms	Knives or cutting instruments	Blunt objects (clubs, hammers, etc.)	Personal weapons (hands, fists, feet, etc.)[1]	Poison	Explosives	Fire	Narcotics	Strangulation	Asphyxiation	Other weapon or weapon not stated[2]
Total	11,961	8,124	1,567	435	660	7	6	71	62	89	96	844
Percent distribution[3]	100.0	67.9	13.1	3.6	5.5	0.1	0.1	0.6	0.5	0.7	0.8	7.1
Under 18[4]	1,085	519	80	45	217	2	0	11	13	11	33	154
Under 22[4]	2,595	1,793	209	56	240	2	1	15	19	13	39	208
18 and over[4]	10,773	7,560	1,477	388	429	4	6	58	48	78	61	664
Infant (under 1)........................	177	10	5	17	88	0	0	0	3	0	9	45
1 to 4	283	44	12	20	109	1	0	6	7	4	12	68
5 to 8	83	34	11	3	9	1	0	1	1	3	7	13
9 to 12	63	36	9	2	2	0	0	1	0	2	2	9
13 to 16	273	220	22	2	6	0	0	3	1	2	3	14
17 to 19	861	728	80	2	14	0	0	3	1	1	3	29
20 to 24	2,181	1,821	188	22	40	0	1	5	8	8	5	83
25 to 29	1,760	1,378	206	27	43	0	0	5	9	9	2	81
30 to 34	1,389	1,037	169	38	35	0	0	5	7	16	2	80
35 to 39	1,072	772	148	30	31	1	1	10	9	6	4	60
40 to 44	836	561	127	33	48	0	0	5	5	3	5	49
45 to 49	747	453	135	25	37	1	0	4	3	10	10	69
50 to 54	669	366	143	50	46	0	1	7	3	3	4	46
55 to 59	514	247	102	48	41	0	0	8	0	4	4	60
60 to 64	304	131	58	36	31	0	1	3	0	8	5	31
65 to 69	227	85	55	32	24	0	0	1	2	3	4	21
70 to 74	148	60	29	18	16	1	2	0	0	1	4	17
75 and over	271	96	58	28	26	1	0	2	2	6	9	43
Unknown.............................	103	45	10	2	14	1	0	2	1	0	2	26

[1] Pushed is included in personal weapons.
[2] Includes drowning.
[3] Because of rounding, the percentages may not add to 100.0.
[4] Does not include unknown ages.

Table 32. Murder Circumstances, by Relationship, 2014[1]

(Number.)

Circumstances	Total murder victims	Husband	Wife	Mother	Father	Son	Daughter	Brother	Sister
Total	11,961	99	539	133	142	204	198	94	21
Felony type total	1,789	9	35	22	7	23	13	11	3
Rape	23	2	0	0	0	0	0	0	0
Robbery	565	0	0	2	0	0	0	1	0
Burglary	77	0	2	0	0	0	0	1	1
Larceny-theft	21	0	0	1	1	0	0	0	0
Motor vehicle theft	25	0	1	0	1	0	0	0	0
Arson	22	1	0	0	0	1	2	0	0
Prostitution and commercialized vice	19	0	0	0	0	0	0	0	0
Other sex offenses	3	1	0	0	0	0	1	0	0
Narcotic drug laws	371	1	1	0	0	0	0	0	0
Gambling	10	0	0	0	0	0	0	0	0
Other-not specified	653	4	31	19	5	22	10	9	2
Suspected felony type	83	0	5	0	1	0	3	0	0
Other than felony type total:	5,583	77	374	70	101	141	152	69	4
Romantic triangle	85	2	8	0	0	0	0	0	0
Child killed by babysitter	37	0	0	0	0	8	7	0	0
Brawl due to influence of alcohol	71	0	1	1	2	3	2	1	0
Brawl due to influence of narcotics	61	1	1	0	1	2	0	1	0
Argument over money or property	144	0	3	5	4	1	0	3	0
Other arguments	2,786	63	250	34	72	30	23	54	3
Gangland killings	145	0	0	0	0	0	0	0	0
Juvenile gang killings	570	0	0	0	0	0	0	0	0
Institutional killings	18	0	0	0	0	0	0	0	0
Sniper attack	3	0	0	0	0	0	0	0	0
Other-not specified	1,663	11	111	30	22	97	120	10	1
Unknown	4,506	13	125	41	33	40	30	14	14

Table 32. Murder Circumstances, by Relationship, 2014[1]—*Continued*

(Number.)

Circumstances	Other family	Acquaintance	Friend	Boyfriend	Girlfriend	Neighbor	Employee	Employer	Stranger	Unknown
Total	281	2,416	331	151	414	105	6	6	1,381	5,440
Felony type total	33	421	58	12	27	16	1	1	375	722
Rape	0	10	1	0	1	0	0	0	5	4
Robbery	9	119	10	3	2	5	1	1	195	217
Burglary	1	14	0	1	0	4	0	0	29	24
Larceny-theft	1	5	0	0	0	0	0	0	4	9
Motor vehicle theft	0	3	1	0	2	1	0	0	8	8
	0	2	1	0	0	0	0	0	7	8
Arson										
Prostitution and commercialized vice	0	7	0	0	0	0	0	0	6	6
Other sex offenses...	0	1	0	0	0	0	0	0	0	0
Narcotic drug laws	2	127	28	2	0	2	0	0	37	171
Gambling	0	8	0	0	0	0	0	0	1	1
Other-not specified..	20	125	17	6	22	4	0	0	83	274
Suspected felony type	1	6	0	1	4	0	0	0	7	55
Other than felony type total:	195	1,499	216	122	295	75	4	4	590	1,595
Romantic triangle	1	44	5	3	12	0	0	0	6	4
Child killed by babysitter	3	18	1	0	0	0	0	0	0	0
Brawl due to influence of alcohol	5	17	9	0	4	4	0	0	11	11
Brawl due to influence of narcotics.........................	1	28	4	1	2	1	0	0	5	13
Argument over money or property	4	80	11	4	4	6	0	0	9	10
Other arguments..	125	826	121	92	231	43	3	2	279	535
Gangland killings..	0	38	5	0	0	0	0	0	24	78
Juvenile gang killings...	0	80	1	0	0	0	0	0	90	399
Institutional killings...	0	11	0	0	0	0	0	0	2	5
Sniper attack	0	0	0	0	0	0	0	0	2	1
Other-not specified..	56	357	59	22	42	21	1	2	162	539
Unknown..	52	490	57	16	88	14	1	1	409	3,068

Note: The relationship categories of husband and wife include both common-law and ex-spouses. The categories of mother, father, sister, brother, son, and daughter include stepparents, stepchildren, and stepsiblings. The category of acquaintance includes homosexual relationships and the composite category of other known to victim.
[1] Relationship is that of victim to offender.

Table 33. Murder Circumstances, by Weapon, 2014

(Number.)

Circumstances	Total murder victims	Total firearms	Handguns	Rifles	Shotguns	Other guns or type not stated	Knives or cutting instruments	Blunt objects (clubs, hammers, etc.)	Personal weapons (hands, fists, feet, etc.)
Total	11,961	8,124	5,562	248	262	2,052	1,567	435	658
Felony type total	1,789	1,262	902	36	34	290	187	61	76
Rape	23	4	1	0	1	2	3	1	7
Robbery	565	451	345	10	10	86	39	25	22
Burglary	77	50	27	0	1	22	18	5	2
Larceny-theft	21	12	6	0	0	6	4	3	1
Motor vehicle theft	25	10	8	0	0	2	8	2	1
Arson	22	0	0	0	0	0	0	0	0
Prostitution and commercialized vice	19	6	5	0	0	1	2	1	6
Other sex offenses..	3	2	2	0	0	0	1	0	0
Narcotic drug laws	371	298	245	5	3	45	31	5	2
Gambling	10	10	8	1	0	1	0	0	0
Other-not specified......................................	653	419	255	20	19	125	81	19	35
Suspected felony type	83	68	47	2	0	19	6	2	1
Other than felony type total:	5,583	3,527	2,607	137	148	635	914	232	434
Romantic triangle..	85	60	47	0	3	10	15	2	2
Child killed by babysitter	37	2	0	0	0	2	0	7	16
Brawl due to influence of alcohol	71	40	26	5	3	6	15	1	10
Brawl due to influence of narcotics	61	35	24	3	2	6	5	3	4
Argument over money or property	144	85	61	1	12	11	36	10	7
Other arguments..	2,786	1,674	1,249	61	81	283	620	135	185
Gangland killings..	145	128	89	2	1	36	15	0	0
Juvenile gang killings....................................	570	539	426	16	5	92	24	1	2
Institutional killings......................................	18	1	1	0	0	0	1	1	7
Sniper attack	3	3	1	2	0	0	0	0	0
Other-not specified......................................	1,663	960	683	47	41	189	183	72	201
Unknown...	4,506	3,267	2,006	73	80	1,108	460	140	147

Table 33. Murder Circumstances, by Weapon, 2014—*Continued*

(Number.)

Circumstances	Poison	Pushed or thrown out window	Explosives	Fire	Narcotics	Drowning	Strangulation	Asphyxiation	Other
Total	7	2	6	71	62	14	89	96	830
Felony type total	2	1	3	31	30	2	12	13	109
Rape	0	0	0	0	1	0	0	4	3
Robbery	0	0	0	1	0	0	5	4	18
Burglary	0	0	0	1	0	0	1	0	0
Larceny-theft	0	0	0	0	0	0	0	0	1
Motor vehicle theft.........................	0	0	0	0	0	0	0	0	4
Arson...	0	0	0	19	0	0	0	0	3
Prostitution and commercialized vice	0	0	0	0	2	0	1	0	1
Other sex offenses...........................	0	0	0	0	0	0	0	0	0
Narcotic drug laws	2	0	0	1	22	0	0	0	10
Gambling	0	0	0	0	0	0	0	0	0
Other-not specified.........................	0	1	3	9	5	2	5	5	69
Suspected felony type	0	0	0	0	0	0	1	1	4
Other than felony type total:	5	0	0	15	22	9	49	55	321
Romantic triangle	0	0	0	0	0	0	2	1	3
Child killed by babysitter	0	0	0	0	1	0	0	2	9
Brawl due to influence of alcohol	0	0	0	0	0	0	0	0	5
Brawl due to influence of narcotics....	0	0	0	0	5	0	1	1	7
Argument over money or property	0	0	0	0	0	0	0	2	4
Other arguments.............................	0	0	0	8	2	2	29	17	114
Gangland killings............................	0	0	0	0	0	0	0	0	2
Juvenile gang killings......................	0	0	0	0	0	0	0	0	4
Institutional killings........................	0	0	0	0	1	0	2	1	4
Sniper attack	0	0	0	0	0	0	0	0	0
Other-not specified.........................	5	0	0	7	13	7	15	31	169
Unknown..	0	1	3	25	10	3	27	27	396

Table 34. Murder Circumstances, 2010–2014

(Number.)

Circumstances	2010	2011	2012	2013[1]	2014[1]
Total	13,164	12,795	12,888	12,253	11,961
Felony type total	1,974	1,842	1,842	1,909	1,789
Rape	41	16	16	20	23
Robbery	803	750	656	686	565
Burglary	85	95	91	94	77
Larceny-theft	21	12	15	16	21
Motor vehicle theft	35	23	22	27	25
Arson	35	38	32	37	22
Prostitution and commercialized vice	5	3	6	13	19
Other sex offenses	14	10	13	9	3
Narcotic drug laws	474	397	375	386	371
Gambling	7	8	7	7	10
Other-not specified	454	490	609	614	653
Suspected felony type	68	62	137	122	83
Other than felony type total:	6,485	6,056	6,320	5,782	5,583
Romantic triangle	90	88	98	69	85
Child killed by babysitter	36	38	26	30	37
Brawl due to influence of alcohol	122	113	84	93	71
Brawl due to influence of narcotics	60	121	65	59	61
Argument over money or property	187	156	152	133	144
Other arguments	3,280	3,163	3,147	2,889	2,786
Gangland killings	181	149	152	138	145
Juvenile gang killings	675	526	722	584	570
Institutional killings	17	22	13	15	18
Sniper attack	3	1	1	6	3
Other-not specified	1,834	1,679	1,860	1,766	1,663
Unknown	4,637	4,835	4,589	4,440	4,506

[1] The rape figures in this table are an aggregate total of the data submitted using both the revised and legacy Uniform Crime Reporting definitions.

Table 35. Murder Circumstances, by Sex of Victim, 2014

(Number.)

Circumstances	Total murder victims	Male	Female	Unknown
Total	11,961	9,246	2,681	34
Felony type total	1,789	1,434	349	6
Rape	23	3	20	0
Robbery	565	502	63	0
Burglary	77	58	19	0
Larceny-theft	21	15	5	1
Motor vehicle theft	25	16	8	1
Arson	22	11	11	0
Prostitution and commercialized vice	19	10	9	0
Other sex offenses	3	2	1	0
Narcotic drug laws	371	341	29	1
Gambling	10	10	0	0
Other-not specified	653	466	184	3
Suspected felony type	83	58	25	0
Other than felony type total:	5,583	4,126	1,444	13
Romantic triangle	85	62	23	0
Child killed by babysitter	37	22	15	0
Brawl due to influence of alcohol	71	58	13	0
Brawl due to influence of narcotics	61	46	15	0
Argument over money or property	144	116	28	0
Other arguments	2,786	2,009	773	4
Gangland killings	145	138	7	0
Juvenile gang killings	570	534	35	1
Institutional killings	18	16	2	0
Sniper attack	3	2	1	0
Other-not specified	1,663	1,123	532	8
Unknown	4,506	3,628	863	15

Table 36. Justifiable Homicide by Weapon, Law Enforcement,[1] 2010–2014

(Number.)

Year	Total	Total firearms	Handguns	Rifles	Shotguns	Firearms, type not stated	Knives or cutting instruments	Other dangerous weapons	Personal weapons
2010	397	396	323	29	6	38	0	1	0
2011	404	401	305	36	11	49	2	0	1
2012	426	423	339	38	7	39	0	3	0
2013	471	467	334	46	9	78	0	3	1
2014	444	442	323	45	5	69	1	1	0

[1] The killing of a felon by a law enforcement officer in the line of duty.

Table 37. Justifiable Homicide by Weapon, Private Citizen,[1] 2010–2014

(Number.)

Year	Total	Total firearms	Handguns	Rifles	Shotguns	Firearms, type not stated	Knives or cutting instruments	Other dangerous weapons	Personal weapons
2010	285	236	170	8	30	28	33	11	5
2011	270	209	156	13	11	29	49	9	3
2012	315	263	198	20	15	30	35	6	11
2013	286	227	174	6	11	36	35	13	11
2014	277	229	178	10	10	31	26	2	10

[1] The killing of a felon, during the commission of a felony, by a private citizen.

Table 38. Robbery, Location, Percent Distribution Within Region, 2014

(Percent.)

Region	Total[1]	Street/ highway	Commercial house	Gas or service station	Convenience store	Residence	Bank	Miscellaneous
Total	100.0	41.0	14.0	2.5	5.4	16.8	1.8	18.5
Northeast	100.0	49.9	8.3	2.1	5.1	12.7	2.2	19.9
Midwest	100.0	45.8	12.4	3.5	3.8	16.2	2.0	16.4
South	100.0	35.5	14.1	2.7	6.0	22.5	1.5	17.7
West	100.0	40.3	18.9	2.1	5.5	11.3	2.0	20.0

[1] Because of rounding, the percentages may not add to 100.0.

Table 39. Robbery, Location, Percent Distribution Within Population Group, 2014

(Percent.)

Type	Group I (74 cities, 250,000 and over; population 53,744,776)	Group II (204 cities, 100,000 to 249,999; population 30,349,229)	Group III (456 cities, 50,000 to 99,999; population 31,521,356)	Group IV (802 cities, 25,000 to 49,999; population 27,753,171)	Group V (1,713 cities, 10,000 to 24,999; population 27,124,934)	Group VI (7,153 cities, under 10,000; population 22,357,510)	County agencies (3,828 agencies; population 97,084,166)
Total[1]	100.0	100.0	100.0	100.0	100.0	100.0	100.0
Street/highway	49.4	38.8	37.9	32.4	27.3	22.5	30.1
Commercial house	12.4	15.3	15.7	15.3	15.9	13.4	15.8
Gas or service station	1.9	2.4	2.8	3.2	3.5	3.6	3.5
Convenience store	3.8	6.1	6.2	7.3	7.9	8.4	6.8
Residence	15.5	15.2	13.6	16.4	18.5	19.3	24.0
Bank	1.2	1.9	2.3	2.9	3.1	3.2	2.2
Miscellaneous	15.8	20.2	21.5	22.4	23.8	29.7	17.6

[1] Because of rounding, the percentages may not add to 100.0.

Table 40. Robbery, Types of Weapons Used, Percent Distribution Within Region, 2014

(Percent.)

Region	Total all weapons[1]	Armed			Strong arm
		Firearms	Knives or cutting instruments	Other weapons	
Total	100.0	40.3	7.9	8.8	43.0
Northeast	100.0	31.1	9.8	7.8	51.2
Midwest	100.0	45.3	5.8	9.0	39.9
South	100.0	49.9	6.7	8.3	35.0
West	100.0	29.3	9.5	10.2	51.0

[1] Because of rounding, the percentages may not add to 100.0.

Table 41. Aggravated Assault, Types of Weapons Used, Percent Distribution by Region, 2014

(Percent.)

Region	Total all weapons[1]	Firearms	Knives or cutting instruments	Other weapons (clubs, blunt objects, etc.)	Personal weapons (hands, feet, fists, etc.)
Total	100.0	22.5	18.8	31.9	26.9
Northeast	100.0	14.6	22.8	30.8	31.8
Midwest	100.0	25.1	16.7	28.4	29.8
South	100.0	26.7	18.8	32.3	22.2
West	100.0	18.1	17.6	34.0	30.3

[1] Because of rounding, the percentages may not add to 100.0.

Table 42. Larceny-Theft, Percent Distribution Within Region, 2014

(Percent.)

Region	Total[1]	Pocket- picking	Purse snatching	Shoplifting	From motor vehicles (except accessories)	Motor vehicle accessories	Bicycles	From buildings	From coin-operated machines	All others
Total	100.0	0.5	0.4	21.5	22.9	7.0	3.6	12.3	0.2	31.5
Northeast.............................	100.0	0.9	0.5	22.4	19.2	5.4	4.3	18.7	0.2	28.5
Midwest	100.0	0.4	0.3	22.1	18.7	7.2	3.0	15.3	0.2	32.7
South..................................	100.0	0.5	0.4	21.2	22.5	7.2	2.7	9.7	0.2	35.5
West..................................	100.0	0.5	0.4	21.1	28.4	7.5	5.3	11.4	0.2	25.2

[1] Because of rounding, the percentages may not add to 100.0.

Table 43. Motor Vehicle Theft, Percent Distribution Within Region, 2014

(Percent.)

Region	Total[1]	Autos	Trucks and buses	Other vehicles
Total	100.0	74.5	14.9	10.6
Northeast...	100.0	85.2	4.5	10.4
Midwest	100.0	76.8	13.1	10.1
South...	100.0	66.6	19.5	13.8
West..	100.0	78.5	13.6	7.9

[1] Because of rounding, the percentages may not add to 100.0.

Table 44. Arson Rates, by Population Group, 2014

(14,629 agencies; 2014 estimated population 295,821,623; rate per 100,000 inhabitants.)

Population group	Rate per 100,000 inhabitants
Total, All Agencies..	14.2
Total Cities	16.0
Group I (250,000 and over)...	21.6
1,000,000 and over (Group I subset)	15.5
500,000 to 999,999 (Group I subset)	24.6
250,000 to 499,999 (Group I subset)	29.6
Group II (100,000 to 249,999)	17.3
Group III (50,000 to 99,999)	13.2
Group IV (25,000 to 49,999)..	12.0
Group V (10,000 to 24,999)	10.9
Group VI (under 10,000)..	15.9
Metropolitan counties...	10.4
Nonmetropolitan counties...	10.0
Suburban areas[1]..	10.2

[1] Suburban areas include law enforcement agencies in cities with less than 50,000 inhabitants and county law enforcement agencies that are within a Metropolitan Statistical Area. Suburban areas exclude all metropolitan agencies associated with a principal city. The agencies associated with suburban areas also appear in other groups within this table.

Table 45. Arson, by Type of Property, 2014

(Number; percent; dollars. 14,750 agencies; 2014 estimated population 262,342,126)

Property classification	Number of arson offenses	Percent distribution[1]	Percent not in use	Average damage (dollars)	Total clearances	Percent of arsons cleared[2]	Percent of clearances under 18
Total	39,174	100.0	X	16,055	8,555	21.8	25.5
Total structure	17,854	45.6	14.6	29,779	4,577	25.6	25.6
Single occupancy residential	8,630	22.0	14.9	27,742	2,109	24.4	18.2
Other residential	3,071	7.8	10.1	26,786	848	27.6	15.2
Storage	1,113	2.8	18.9	11,341	233	20.9	41.6
Industrial/manufacturing	141	0.4	29.8	167,545	35	24.8	14.3
Other commercial	1,594	4.1	16.7	56,592	370	23.2	23.2
Community/public	1,513	3.9	14.9	15,948	579	38.3	63.0
Other structure	1,792	4.6	14.6	33,161	403	22.5	27.0
Total mobile	9,154	23.4	X	7,716	1,051	11.5	10.4
Motor vehicles	8,608	22.0	X	7,416	937	10.9	9.4
Other mobile	546	1.4	X	12,458	114	20.9	18.4
Other	12,166	31.1	X	2,189	2,927	24.1	30.6

X = Not applicable.
[1] Because of rounding, the percentages may not add to 100.0.
[2] Includes arsons cleared by arrest or exceptional means.

METHODOLOGY

Submitting Uniform Crime Reporting (UCR) program data to the Federal Bureau of Investigation (FBI) is a collective effort on the part of city, county, state, tribal, and federal law enforcement agencies to present a nationwide view of crime. Law enforcement agencies in 46 states and the District of Columbia voluntarily contribute crime data to the UCR program through their respective state UCR programs. For those states that do not have a state program, local agencies submit crime statistics directly to the FBI. The state UCR programs function as liaisons between local agencies and the FBI. Many states have mandatory reporting requirements, and many state programs collect data beyond the scope of the UCR program to address crime problems specific to their particular jurisdictions. In most cases, state programs also provide direct and frequent service to participating law enforcement agencies, make information readily available for statewide use, and help streamline the national program's operations.

A Note Regarding Rape

In 2013, the FBI UCR Program initiated collection of rape data under a revised definition within the Summary Reporting System. Previously, offense data for forcible rape was collected under the legacy UCR definition: the carnal knowledge of a female forcibly and against her will. Beginning with the 2013 data year, the term "forcible" was removed from the offense title, and the definition was changed. The revised UCR definition of rape is: Penetration, no matter how slight, of the vagina or anus with any body part or object, or oral penetration by a sex organ of another person, without the consent of the victim. Attempts or assaults to commit rape are also included; however, statutory rape and incest are excluded. For more information, please see https://www.fbi.gov/about-us/cjis/ucr/crime-in-the-u.s/2013/crime-in-the-u.s.-2013/rape-addendum/rape_addendum_final.

Criteria for State UCR Programs

The criteria established for state programs ensure consistency and comparability in the data submitted to the national program, as well as regular and timely reporting. These criteria are:

1. A UCR Program must conform to the FBI UCR Program's submission standards, definitions, specifications, and required deadlines.
2. A UCR Program must establish data integrity procedures and have personnel assigned to assist contributing agencies in quality assurance practices and crime reporting procedures. Data integrity procedures should include crime trend assessments, offense classification verification, and technical specification validation.
3. A UCR Program's submissions must cover more than 50 percent of the law enforcement agencies within its established reporting domain and be willing to cover any and all UCR-contributing agencies that wish to use the UCR Program from within its domain. (An agency wishing to become a UCR Program must be willing to report for all of the agencies within the state.)
4. A UCR Program must furnish the FBI UCR Program with all of the UCR data collected by the law enforcement agencies within its domain.

These requirements do not prohibit the state from gathering other statistical data beyond the national collection.

Data Completeness and Quality

National program staff members contact the state UCR program in connection with crime-reporting matters and, when necessary and approved by the state, they contact individual contributors within the state. To fulfill its responsibilities in connection with the UCR program, the FBI reviews and edits individual agency reports for completeness and quality. Upon request, they conduct training programs within the state on law enforcement record-keeping and crime-reporting procedures. The FBI conducts an audit of each state's UCR data collection procedures once every three years, in accordance with audit standards established by the federal government. Should circumstances develop in which the state program does not comply with the aforementioned requirements, the national program may institute a direct collection of data from law enforcement agencies within the state.

Reporting Procedures

Offenses known and value of property—Law enforcement agencies tabulate the number of Part I offenses reported based on records of all reports of crime received from victims, officers who discover infractions, or other sources, and submit these reports each month to the FBI directly or through their state UCR programs. Part I offenses include murder and nonnegligent manslaughter, forcible rape, robbery, aggravated assault, burglary, larceny-theft, motor vehicle theft, and arson. Each month, law enforcement agencies also submit to the FBI the value of property stolen and recovered in connection with the offenses and detailed information pertaining to criminal homicide.

Unfounded offenses and clearances—When, through investigation, an agency determines that complaints of crimes are unfounded or false, the agency eliminates that offense from its crime tally through an entry on the monthly report. The report also provides the total number of actual Part I offenses, the number of offenses cleared, and the number of clearances that involve only offenders under the age of 18. (Law enforcement can clear crimes in one of two ways: by the arrest of at least one person who is charged and turned over to the court for prosecution or by exceptional means—when some element beyond law enforcement's control precludes the arrest of a known offender.)

Persons arrested—In addition to reporting Part I offenses each month, law enforcement agencies also provide data on the age, sex, and race of persons arrested for Part I and Part II offenses. Part II offenses encompass all crimes, except traffic violations, that are not classified as Part I offenses.

Officers killed or assaulted—Each month, law enforcement agencies also report information to the UCR program regarding law enforcement officers killed or assaulted, and each year they report the number of full-time sworn and civilian law enforcement personnel employed as of October 31.

Editing Procedures

The UCR program thoroughly examines each report it receives for arithmetical accuracy and for deviations in crime data from month to month and from present to past years that may indicate errors. UCR staff members compare an agency's monthly reports with its previous submissions and with reports from similar agencies to identify any unusual fluctuations in the agency's crime count. Considerable variations in crime levels may indicate modified records procedures, incomplete reporting, or changes in the jurisdiction's geopolitical structure.

Evaluation of trends—Data reliability is a high priority of the FBI, which brings any deviations or arithmetical adjustments to the attention of state UCR programs or the submitting agencies. Typically, FBI staff members study the monthly reports to evaluate periodic trends prepared for individual reporting units. Any significant increase or decrease becomes the subject of a special inquiry. Changes in crime reporting procedures or annexations that affect an agency's jurisdiction can influence the level of reported crime. When this occurs, the FBI excludes the figures for specific crime categories or totals, if necessary, from the trend tabulations.

Training for contributors—In addition to the evaluation of trends, the FBI provides training seminars and instructional materials on crime reporting procedures to assist contributors in complying with UCR standards. Throughout the country, representatives from the national program coordinate with representatives of state programs and law enforcement personnel and hold training sessions to explain the purpose of the program, the rules of uniform classification and scoring, and the methods of assembling the information for reporting. When an individual agency has specific problems with compiling its crime statistics and its remedial efforts are unsuccessful, personnel from the FBI's Criminal Justice Information Services Division may visit the contributor to aid in resolving the problems.

UCR Handbook—The national UCR program publishes the *Uniform Crime Reporting (UCR) Handbook* (revised 2004), which details procedures for classifying and scoring offenses and serves as the contributing agencies' basic resource for preparing reports. The national staff also produces letters to UCR contributors, state program bulletins, and UCR newsletters as needed. These publications provide policy updates and new information, as well as clarification of reporting issues.

The final responsibility for data submissions rests with the individual contributing law enforcement agency. Although the FBI makes every effort through its editing procedures, training practices, and correspondence to ensure the validity of the data it receives, the accuracy of the statistics depends primarily on the adherence of each contributor to the established standards of reporting. Deviations from these established standards that cannot be resolved by the national UCR program may be brought to the attention of the Criminal Justice Information Systems Committees of the International Association of Chiefs of Police and the National Sheriffs' Association.

NIBRS Conversion

Thirty-three state programs are certified to provide their UCR data in the expanded National Incident-Based Reporting System (NIBRS) format. For presentation in this book, the NIBRS data were converted to the historical Summary Reporting System data. The UCR program staff constructed the NIBRS database to allow for such conversion so that UCR's long-running time series could continue.

Crime Trends

By showing fluctuations from year to year, trend statistics offer the data user an added perspective from which to study crime. Percent change tabulations in this publication are computed only for reporting agencies that provided comparable data for the periods under consideration. The FBI excludes from the trend calculations all figures except those received for common months from common agencies. Also excluded are unusual fluctuations of data that the FBI determines are the result of such variables as improved records procedures, annexations, and so on.

Caution to Users

Data users should exercise care in making any direct comparison between data in this publication and those in prior issues of *Crime in the United States*. Because of differing levels of participation from year to year and reporting problems that require the FBI to estimate crime counts for certain contributors, some data may not be comparable. In addition, this publication may contain updates to data provided in prior years' publications.

For information about the FBI's caution against ranking, including warnings about variables affecting crime and characteristics of jurisdictions, please see http://www.fbi.gov/about-us/cjis/ucr/ucr-statistics-their-proper-use.

Offense Estimation

Some tables in this publication contain statistics for the entire United States. Because not all law enforcement agencies provide data for complete reporting periods, the FBI includes estimated crime numbers in these presentations. The FBI estimates data for three areas: Metropolitan Statistical Areas (MSAs), cities outside MSAs, and nonmetropolitan counties; and computes estimates for participating agencies that do not provide 12 months of complete data. For agencies supplying 3 to 11 months of data, the national UCR program estimates for the missing data by following a standard estimation procedure using the data provided by the agency. If an agency has supplied less than 3 months of data, the FBI computes estimates by using the known crime figures of similar areas within a state and assigning the same proportion of crime volumes to nonreporting agencies. The estimation process considers the following: population size covered by the agency; type of jurisdiction; for example, police department versus sheriff's office; and geographic location.

Estimation of State-Level Data

In response to various circumstances, the FBI calculates estimated offense totals for certain states. For example, some states do not provide forcible rape figures in accordance with UCR guidelines. In addition, problems at the state level have, at times, resulted in no useable data. Also, the conversion of the National Incident-Based Reporting System (NIBRS) data to summary data has contributed to the need for unique estimation procedures.

Expanded Offense Tables

Expanded offense data are the details of the various offenses that the Uniform Crime Reporting Program collects beyond the count of how many crimes law enforcement agencies report. These details may include the type of weapon used in a crime, the type or value of items stolen, and so forth. Expanded homicide data provide supplemental details about murders such as the age, sex, and race of both the victim and the offender, the weapon used in the homicide, the circumstances surrounding the offense, and the relationship of the victim to the offender. In addition, expanded data includes trends (for example, 2-year comparisons) and rates per 100,000 inhabitants.

Expanded offense data, including expanded homicide data, are information collected in addition to the reports of the number of crimes known. As a result, law enforcement agencies can report an offense without providing the supplemental data about that offense.

PART 4

Capital Punishment, 2013

HIGHLIGHTS

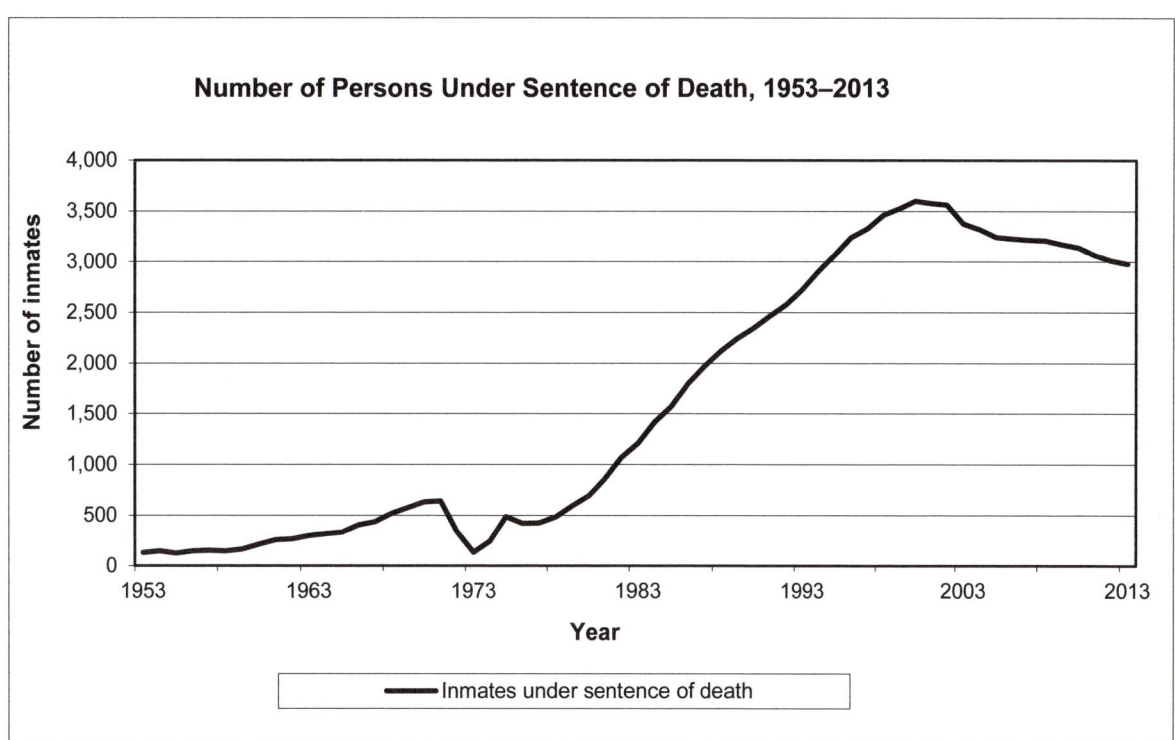

Number of Persons Under Sentence of Death, 1953–2013

- The 35 states and the Federal Bureau of Prisons held 2,979 inmates under sentence of death, which was 32 fewer than at yearend 2012.

- Five states (California, Florida, Texas, Pennsylvania, and Alabama) held 60% of all inmates on death row on December 31, 2013. The Federal Bureau of Prisons held 56 inmates under sentence of death.

- At yearend 2013, approximately 56 percent of death row inmates were White and 42 percent were Black; 98 percent were male and 2 percent were female.

- Nine states executed 39 inmates in 2013; 43 inmates were executed in 9 states in 2012.

- Among the 36 jurisdictions with prisoners under sentence of death on December 31, 2013, 6 jurisdictions had more inmates than a year earlier, 16 had fewer inmates, and 14 had the same number.

Table 1. Capital Offenses, by State, 2013

State	Offense
Alabama	Intentional murder (Ala. Stat. Ann. 13A-5-40(a)(1)-(18)) with 10 aggravating factors (Ala. Stat. Ann. 13A-5-49).
Arizona	First-degree murder, including premeditated murder and felony murder, accompanied by at least 1 of 14 aggravating factors (A.R.S. ß 13-703(F)).
Arkansas	Capital murder (Ark. Code Ann. ß 5-10-101) with a finding of at least 1 of 10 aggravating circumstances; treason (Ark. Code Ann. ß 5-51-201).
California	First-degree murder with special circumstances; sabotage; train wrecking causing death; treason; perjury in a capital case causing execution of an innocent person; fatal assault by a prisoner serving a life sentence.
Colorado	First-degree murder with at least 1 of 17 aggravating factors; first-degree kidnapping resulting in death; treason.
Connecticut[1]	Capital felony with 8 forms of aggravated homicide (C.G.S. ß 53a-54b).
Delaware	First-degree murder (11 Del. C. ß 636) with at least 1 statutory aggravating circumstance (11 Del. C. ß 4209).
Florida	First-degree murder; felony murder; capital drug trafficking; capital sexual battery.
Georgia	Murder with aggravating circumstances; rape, armed robbery, or kidnapping with bodily injury or ransom when the victim dies; aircraft hijacking; treason.
Idaho	First-degree murder with aggravating factors; first-degree kidnapping; perjury resulting in the execution of an innocent person.
Indiana	Murder with 16 aggravating circumstances (IC 35-50-2-9).
Kansas	Capital murder (K.S.A. 21-5401) with 8 aggravating circumstances (K.S.A. 21-6617 and K.S.A. 21-6624).
Kentucky	Capital murder with the presence of at least one statutory aggravating circumstance; capital kidnapping (KRS 532.025).
Louisiana	First-degree murder; treason (La. R.S. 14:30 and 14:113).
Mississippi	Capital murder (Miss. Code Ann. ß 97-3-19(2)); aircraft piracy (Miss. Code Ann. ß 97-25-55(1)).
Missouri	First-degree murder (565.020 RSMO 2000).
Montana	Capital murder with 1 of 9 aggravating circumstances (Mont. Code Ann. ß 46-18-303); aggravated kidnapping; felony murder; capital sexual intercourse without consent (Mont. Code Ann. ß 45-5-503).
Nebraska	First-degree murder with a finding of one or more statutory aggravating circumstances.
Nevada	First-degree murder with at least 1 of 15 aggravating circumstances (NRS 200.030, 200.033, and 200.035).
New Hampshire	Murder committed in the course of rape, kidnapping, drug crimes, or home invasion; killing of a police officer, judge, or prosecutor; murder for hire; murder by an inmate while serving a sentence of life without parole (RSA 630:1 and 630:5).
New Mexico[2]	First-degree murder with at least 1 of 7 aggravating factors (NMSA 1978 ß 31-20A-5).
New York[3]	First-degree murder with 1 of 13 aggravating factors (NY Penal Law ß125.27).
North Carolina	First-degree murder (N.C.G.S. ß14-17) with the finding of at least 1 of 11 statutory aggravating circumstances (N.C.G.S. ß 15A-2000).
Ohio	Aggravated murder with at least 1 of 10 aggravating circumstances (O.R.C. 2903.01, 2929.02, and 2929.04).
Oklahoma	First-degree murder in conjunction with a finding of at least 1 of 8 statutorily-defined aggravating circumstances.
Oregon	Aggravated murder (ORS 163.095).
Pennsylvania	First-degree murder with 18 aggravating circumstances.
South Carolina	Murder with at least 1 of 12 aggravating circumstances (ß 16-3-20(C)(a)).
South Dakota	First-degree murder with 1 of 10 aggravating circumstances.
Tennessee	First-degree murder (Tenn. Code Ann. ß 39-13-202) with 1 of 17 aggravating circumstances (Tenn. Code Ann. ß 39-13-204).
Texas	Criminal homicide with 1 of 9 aggravating circumstances (Tex. Penal Code ß 19.03).
Utah	Aggravated murder (Utah Code Ann. 76-5-202).
Virginia	First-degree murder with 1 of 15 aggravating circumstances (VA Code ß 18.2-31(1-15)).
Washington	Aggravated first-degree murder.
Wyoming	First-degree murder; murder during the commission of sexual assault, sexual abuse of a minor, arson, robbery, burglary, escape, resisting arrest, kidnapping, or abuse of a minor under 16 (W.S.A. ß 6-2-101(a)).

Note: Maryland repealed its capital statute effective October 1, 2013. Five men in Maryland remain under a previously imposed sentence of death.
[1] Connecticut enacted a prospective repeal of its capital statute as of April 25, 2012. Offenders who committed capital offenses prior to that date are eligible for the death penalty.
[2] New Mexico enacted a prospective repeal of its capital statute as of July 1, 2009. Offenders who committed capital offenses prior to that date are eligible for the death penalty.
[3] The New York Court of Appeals has held that a portion of New York's death penalty sentencing statute (CPL 400.27) was unconstitutional (People v. Taylor, 9 N.Y. 3d 129 (2007)). No legislative action has been taken to amend the statute. As a result, capital cases are no longer pursued in New York.

Table 1A. Prisoners Executed Under Civil Authority in the United States, by Year, Region, and Jurisdiction, 1977–2014

(Number.)

Region and jurisdiction	Total	1977	1978	1979	1980	1981	1982	1983	1984	1985	1986	1987	1988	1989	1990	1991	1992	1993	1994
U.S. Total	1,394	1	0	2	0	1	2	5	21	18	18	25	11	16	23	14	31	38	31
Federal	3	0	0	0	0	0	0	0	0	0	0	0	0	0	0	0	0	0	0
State	1,391	1	0	2	0	1	2	5	21	18	18	25	11	16	23	14	31	38	31
Northeast	4	0	0	0	0	0	0	0	0	0	0	0	0	0	0	0	0	0	0
Connecticut	1	0	0	0	0	0	0	0	0	0	0	0	0	0	0	0	0	0	0
Maine	0	0	0	0	0	0	0	0	0	0	0	0	0	0	0	0	0	0	0
Massachusetts	0	0	0	0	0	0	0	0	0	0	0	0	0	0	0	0	0	0	0
New Hampshire	0	0	0	0	0	0	0	0	0	0	0	0	0	0	0	0	0	0	0
New Jersey	0	0	0	0	0	0	0	0	0	0	0	0	0	0	0	0	0	0	0
New York	0	0	0	0	0	0	0	0	0	0	0	0	0	0	0	0	0	0	0
Pennsylvania	3	0	0	0	0	0	0	0	0	0	0	0	0	0	0	0	0	0	0
Rhode Island	0	0	0	0	0	0	0	0	0	0	0	0	0	0	0	0	0	0	0
Vermont	0	0	0	0	0	0	0	0	0	0	0	0	0	0	0	0	0	0	0
Midwest	171	0	0	0	0	1	0	0	0	1	0	0	0	1	5	1	1	4	3
Illinois	12	0	0	0	0	0	0	0	0	0	0	0	0	0	1	0	0	0	1
Indiana	20	0	0	0	0	1	0	0	0	1	0	0	0	0	0	0	0	0	1
Iowa	0	0	0	0	0	0	0	0	0	0	0	0	0	0	0	0	0	0	0
Kansas	0	0	0	0	0	0	0	0	0	0	0	0	0	0	0	0	0	0	0
Michigan	0	0	0	0	0	0	0	0	0	0	0	0	0	0	0	0	0	0	0
Minnesota	0	0	0	0	0	0	0	0	0	0	0	0	0	0	0	0	0	0	0
Missouri	80	0	0	0	0	0	0	0	0	0	0	0	0	1	4	1	1	4	0
Nebraska	3	0	0	0	0	0	0	0	0	0	0	0	0	0	0	0	0	0	1
North Dakota	0	0	0	0	0	0	0	0	0	0	0	0	0	0	0	0	0	0	0
Ohio	53	0	0	0	0	0	0	0	0	0	0	0	0	0	0	0	0	0	0
South Dakota	3	0	0	0	0	0	0	0	0	0	0	0	0	0	0	0	0	0	0
Wisconsin	0	0	0	0	0	0	0	0	0	0	0	0	0	0	0	0	0	0	0
South	1,131	0	0	1	0	0	2	5	21	16	18	24	10	13	17	13	26	30	26
Alabama	56	0	0	0	0	0	0	1	0	0	1	1	0	4	1	0	2	0	0
Arkansas	27	0	0	0	0	0	0	0	0	0	0	0	0	0	2	0	2	0	5
Delaware	16	0	0	0	0	0	0	0	0	0	0	0	0	0	0	0	1	2	1
District of Columbia	0	0	0	0	0	0	0	0	0	0	0	0	0	0	0	0	0	0	0
Florida	89	0	0	1	0	0	0	1	8	3	3	1	2	2	4	2	2	3	1
Georgia	55	0	0	0	0	0	0	1	2	3	1	5	1	1	0	1	0	2	1
Kentucky	3	0	0	0	0	0	0	0	0	0	0	0	0	0	0	0	0	0	0
Louisiana	28	0	0	0	0	0	0	1	5	1	0	8	3	0	1	1	0	1	0
Maryland	5	0	0	0	0	0	0	0	0	0	0	0	0	0	0	0	0	0	1
Mississippi	21	0	0	0	0	0	0	1	0	0	0	2	0	1	0	0	0	0	0
North Carolina	43	0	0	0	0	0	0	0	2	0	1	0	0	0	0	1	1	0	1
Oklahoma	111	0	0	0	0	0	0	0	0	0	0	0	0	0	1	0	2	0	0
South Carolina	43	0	0	0	0	0	0	0	0	1	1	0	0	0	1	1	0	0	0
Tennessee	6	0	0	0	0	0	0	0	0	0	0	0	0	0	0	0	0	0	0
Texas	518	0	0	0	0	0	1	0	3	6	10	6	3	4	4	5	12	17	14
Virginia	110	0	0	0	0	0	1	0	1	2	1	1	1	1	3	2	4	5	2
West Virginia	0	0	0	0	0	0	0	0	0	0	0	0	0	0	0	0	0	0	0
West	85	1	0	1	0	0	0	0	0	1	0	1	1	2	1	0	4	4	2
Alaska	0	0	0	0	0	0	0	0	0	0	0	0	0	0	0	0	0	0	0
Arizona	37	0	0	0	0	0	0	0	0	0	0	0	0	0	0	0	1	2	0
California	13	0	0	0	0	0	0	0	0	0	0	0	0	0	0	0	1	1	0
Colorado	1	0	0	0	0	0	0	0	0	0	0	0	0	0	0	0	0	0	0
Hawaii	0	0	0	0	0	0	0	0	0	0	0	0	0	0	0	0	0	0	0
Idaho	3	0	0	0	0	0	0	0	0	0	0	0	0	0	0	0	0	0	1
Montana	3	0	0	0	0	0	0	0	0	0	0	0	0	0	0	0	0	0	0
Nevada	12	0	0	1	0	0	0	0	0	1	0	0	0	2	1	0	0	0	0
New Mexico	1	0	0	0	0	0	0	0	0	0	0	0	0	0	0	0	0	0	0
Oregon	2	0	0	0	0	0	0	0	0	0	0	0	0	0	0	0	0	0	0
Utah	7	1	0	0	0	0	0	0	0	0	0	1	1	0	0	0	1	0	0
Washington	5	0	0	0	0	0	0	0	0	0	0	0	0	0	0	0	0	1	1
Wyoming	1	0	0	0	0	0	0	0	0	0	0	0	0	0	0	0	1	0	0

Table 1A. Prisoners Executed Under Civil Authority in the United States, by Year, Region, and Jurisdiction, 1977–2014—*Continued*

(Number.)

Region and jurisdiction	1995	1996	1997	1998	1999	2000	2001	2002	2003	2004	2005	2006	2007	2008	2009	2010	2011	2012	2013	2014
U.S. Total	56	45	74	68	98	85	66	71	65	59	60	53	42	37	52	46	43	43	39	35
Federal	0	0	0	0	0	0	2	0	1	0	0	0	0	0	0	0	0	0	0	0
State	56	45	74	68	98	85	64	71	64	59	60	53	42	37	52	46	43	43	39	35
Northeast	2	0	0	0	1	0	0	0	0	0	1	0	0	0	0	0	0	0	0	0
Connecticut	0	0	0	0	0	0	0	0	0	0	1	0	0	0	0	0	0	0	0	0
Maine	0	0	0	0	0	0	0	0	0	0	0	0	0	0	0	0	0	0	0	0
Massachusetts	0	0	0	0	0	0	0	0	0	0	0	0	0	0	0	0	0	0	0	0
New Hampshire	0	0	0	0	0	0	0	0	0	0	0	0	0	0	0	0	0	0	0	0
New Jersey	0	0	0	0	0	0	0	0	0	0	0	0	0	0	0	0	0	0	0	0
New York	0	0	0	0	0	0	0	0	0	0	0	0	0	0	0	0	0	0	0	0
Pennsylvania	2	0	0	0	1	0	0	0	0	0	0	0	0	0	0	0	0	0	0	0
Rhode Island	0	0	0	0	0	0	0	0	0	0	0	0	0	0	0	0	0	0	0	0
Vermont	0	0	0	0	0	0	0	0	0	0	0	0	0	0	0	0	0	0	0	0
Midwest	11	9	10	5	12	5	10	9	7	7	14	6	5	2	7	8	6	5	5	11
Illinois	5	1	2	1	1	0	0	0	0	0	0	0	0	0	0	0	0	0	0	0
Indiana	0	1	1	1	1	0	2	0	2	0	5	1	2	0	1	0	0	0	0	0
Iowa	0	0	0	0	0	0	0	0	0	0	0	0	0	0	0	0	0	0	0	0
Kansas	0	0	0	0	0	0	0	0	0	0	0	0	0	0	0	0	0	0	0	0
Michigan	0	0	0	0	0	0	0	0	0	0	0	0	0	0	0	0	0	0	0	0
Minnesota	0	0	0	0	0	0	0	0	0	0	0	0	0	0	0	0	0	0	0	0
Missouri	6	6	6	3	9	5	7	6	2	0	5	0	0	0	1	0	1	0	2	10
Nebraska	0	1	1	0	0	0	0	0	0	0	0	0	0	0	0	0	0	0	0	0
North Dakota	0	0	0	0	0	0	0	0	0	0	0	0	0	0	0	0	0	0	0	0
Ohio	0	0	0	0	1	0	1	3	3	7	4	5	2	2	5	8	5	3	3	1
South Dakota	0	0	0	0	0	0	0	0	0	0	0	0	1	0	0	0	0	2	0	0
Wisconsin	0	0	0	0	0	0	0	0	0	0	0	0	0	0	0	0	0	0	0	0
South	41	29	60	55	74	76	50	61	57	50	43	44	36	35	45	35	32	31	32	23
Alabama	2	1	3	1	2	4	0	2	3	2	4	1	3	0	6	5	6	0	1	0
Arkansas	2	1	4	1	4	2	1	0	1	1	1	0	0	0	0	0	0	0	0	0
Delaware	1	3	0	0	2	1	2	0	0	0	1	0	0	0	0	0	1	1	0	0
District of Columbia	0	0	0	0	0	0	0	0	0	0	0	0	0	0	0	0	0	0	0	0
Florida	3	2	1	4	1	6	1	3	3	2	1	4	0	2	2	1	2	3	7	8
Georgia	2	2	0	1	0	0	4	4	3	2	3	0	1	3	3	2	4	0	1	2
Kentucky	0	0	1	0	1	0	0	0	0	0	0	0	0	1	0	0	0	0	0	0
Louisiana	1	1	1	0	1	1	0	1	0	0	0	0	0	0	0	1	0	0	0	0
Maryland	0	0	1	1	0	0	0	0	0	1	1	0	0	0	0	0	0	0	0	0
Mississippi	0	0	0	0	0	0	0	2	0	0	1	1	0	2	0	3	2	6	0	0
North Carolina	2	0	0	3	4	1	5	2	7	4	5	4	0	0	0	0	0	0	0	0
Oklahoma	3	2	1	4	6	11	18	7	14	6	4	4	3	2	3	3	2	6	6	3
South Carolina	1	6	2	7	4	1	0	3	0	4	3	1	1	3	2	0	1	0	0	0
Tennessee	0	0	0	0	0	1	0	0	0	0	0	1	2	0	2	0	0	0	0	0
Texas	19	3	37	20	35	40	17	33	24	23	19	24	26	18	24	17	13	15	16	10
Virginia	5	8	9	13	14	8	2	4	2	5	0	4	0	4	3	3	1	0	1	0
West Virginia	0	0	0	0	0	0	0	0	0	0	0	0	0	0	0	0	0	0	0	0
West	2	7	4	8	11	4	4	1	0	2	2	3	1	0	0	3	5	7	2	1
Alaska	0	0	0	0	0	0	0	0	0	0	0	0	0	0	0	0	0	0	0	0
Arizona	1	2	2	4	7	3	0	0	0	0	0	0	1	0	0	1	4	6	2	1
California	0	2	0	1	2	1	1	1	0	0	2	1	0	0	0	0	0	0	0	0
Colorado	0	0	1	0	0	0	0	0	0	0	0	0	0	0	0	0	0	0	0	0
Hawaii	0	0	0	0	0	0	0	0	0	0	0	0	0	0	0	0	0	0	0	0
Idaho	0	0	0	0	0	0	0	0	0	0	0	0	0	0	0	0	1	1	0	0
Montana	1	0	0	1	0	0	0	0	0	0	0	1	0	0	0	0	0	0	0	0
Nevada	0	1	0	1	1	0	1	0	0	2	0	1	0	0	0	0	0	0	0	0
New Mexico	0	0	0	0	0	0	1	0	0	0	0	0	0	0	0	0	0	0	0	0
Oregon	0	1	1	0	0	0	0	0	0	0	0	0	0	0	0	0	0	0	0	0
Utah	0	1	0	0	1	0	0	0	0	0	0	0	0	0	0	1	0	0	0	0
Washington	0	0	0	1	0	0	1	0	0	0	0	0	0	0	0	1	0	0	0	0
Wyoming	0	0	0	0	0	0	0	0	0	0	0	0	0	0	0	0	0	0	0	0

Table 2. Method of Execution, by State, 2013

(Number.)

State	Lethal injection[1]	Electrocution	Lethal gas	Hanging	Firing squad
Total	35	8	3	3	2
Alabama...	x	x			
Arizona[2]..	x		x		
Arkansas[3]...	x	x			
California...	x				
Colorado	x				
Connecticut[4].....................................	x				
Delaware[5]	x			x	
Florida	x	x			
Georgia	x				
Idaho	x				
Indiana	x				
Kansas...	x				
Kentucky[6]	x	x			
Louisiana	x				
Mississippi..	x				
Missouri...	x		x		
Montana...	x				
Nebraska	x				
Nevada	x				
New Hampshire[7]	x			x	
New Mexico[8]	x				
New York..	x				
North Carolina	x				
Ohio	x				
Oklahoma[9]..	x	x			x
Oregon	x				
Pennsylvania	x				
South Carolina.....................................	x	x			
South Dakota.......................................	x				
Tennessee[10].......................................	x	x			
Texas...	x				
Utah[11]	x				x
Virginia..	x	x			
Washington	x			x	
Wyoming[12]	x		x		

Note: The method of execution of federal prisoners is lethal injection, pursuant to 28 CFR Part 26. For offenses prosecuted under the Violent Crime Control and Law Enforcement Act of 1994, the execution method is that of the state in which the conviction took place (18 U.S.C. 3596).

[1] Maryland repealed the death penalty effective October 1, 2013. The five men who remain under sentence of death are subject to execution by lethal injection.
[2] Authorizes lethal injection for persons sentenced after November 15, 1992; inmates sentenced before that date may select lethal injection or gas.
[3] Authorizes lethal injection for inmates whose capital offense occurred on or after July 4, 1983; inmates whose offense occurred before that data may select lethal injection or electrocution.
[4] Authorizes lethal injection for inmates whose capital offense occurred prior to April 25, 2012.
[5] Authorizes hanging if lethal injection is held to be unconstitutional by a court of competent jurisdiction.
[6] Authorizes lethal injection for persons sentenced on or after March 31, 1998; inmates sentenced before that data may select lethal injection or electrocution.
[7] Authorizes hanging only if lethal injection cannot be given.
[8] Authorizes lethal injection for inmates whose capital offense occurred prior to July 1, 2009.
[9] Authorizes electrocution if lethal injection is held to be unconstitutional, and firing squad if both lethal injection and electrocution are held to be unconstitutional.
[10] Authorizes lethal injection for inmates whose capital offense occurred after December 31, 1998; inmates whose offense occurred before that date may select electrocution by written waiver.
[11] Authorizes firing squad if lethal injection is held unconstitutional. Inmates who selected execution by firing squad prior to May 3, 2004, may still be entitled to execution by that method.
[12] Authorizes lethal gas if lethal injection is held to be unconstitutional.

Table 3. Federal Capital Offenses, 2013

Statute	Description
8 U.S.C. 1342	Murder related to the smuggling of aliens.
18 U.S.C. 32-34	Destruction of aircraft, motor vehicles, or related facilities resulting in death.
18 U.S.C. 36	Murder committed during a drug-related drive-by shooting.
18 U.S.C. 37	Murder committed at an airport serving international civil aviation.
18 U.S.C. 115(b)(3) [by cross-reference to 18 U.S.C. 1111]	Retaliatory murder of a member of the immediate family of law enforcement officials.
18 U.S.C. 241, 242, 245, 247	Civil rights offenses resulting in death.
18 U.S.C. 351 [by cross-reference to 18 U.S.C. 1111]	Murder of a member of Congress, an important executive official, or a Supreme Court Justice.
18 U.S.C. 794	Espionage.
18 U.S.C. 844(d), (f), (i)	Death resulting from offenses involving transportation of explosives, destruction of government property, or destruction of property related to foreign or interstate commerce.
18 U.S.C. 924(i)	Murder committed by the use of a firearm during a crime of violence or a drug-trafficking crime.
18 U.S.C. 930	Murder committed in a federal government facility.
18 U.S.C. 1091	Genocide.
18 U.S.C. 1111	First-degree murder.
18 U.S.C. 1114	Murder of a federal judge or law enforcement official.
18 U.S.C. 1116	Murder of a foreign official.
18 U.S.C. 1118	Murder by a federal prisoner.
18 U.S.C. 1119	Murder of a U.S. national in a foreign country.
18 U.S.C. 1120	Murder by an escaped federal prisoner already sentenced to life imprisonment.
18 U.S.C. 1121	Murder of a state or local law enforcement official or other person aiding in a federal investigation; murder of a state correctional officer.
18 U.S.C. 1201	Murder during a kidnapping.
18 U.S.C. 1203	Murder during a hostage taking.
18 U.S.C. 1503	Murder of a court officer or juror.
18 U.S.C. 1512	Murder with the intent of preventing testimony by a witness, victim, or informant.
18 U.S.C. 1513	Retaliatory murder of a witness, victim, or informant.
18 U.S.C. 1716	Mailing of injurious articles with intent to kill or resulting in death.
18 U.S.C. 1751 [by cross-reference to 18 U.S.C. 1111]	Assassination or kidnapping resulting in the death of the President or Vice President.
18 U.S.C. 1958	Murder for hire.
18 U.S.C. 1959	Murder involved in a racketeering offense.
18 U.S.C. 1992	Willful wrecking of a train resulting in death.
18 U.S.C. 2113	Bank robbery-related murder or kidnapping.
18 U.S.C. 2119	Murder related to a carjacking.
18 U.S.C. 2245	Murder related to rape or child molestation.
18 U.S.C. 2251	Murder related to sexual exploitation of children.
18 U.S.C. 2280	Murder committed during an offense against maritime navigation.
18 U.S.C. 2281	Murder committed during an offense against a maritime fixed platform.
18 U.S.C. 2332	Terrorist murder of a U.S. national in another country.
18 U.S.C. 2332a	Murder by the use of a weapon of mass destruction.
18 U.S.C. 2340	Murder involving torture.
18 U.S.C. 2381	Treason.
21 U.S.C. 848(e)	Murder related to a continuing criminal enterprise or related murder of a federal, state, or local law enforcement officer.
49 U.S.C. 1472-1473	Death resulting from aircraft hijacking.

Table 4. Prisoners Under Sentence of Death, by Region, Jurisdiction, and Race, 2012 and 2013

(Number.)

Region and jurisdiction	Under sentence of death, 12/31/12			Received under sentence of death, 2013			Removed from death row (excluding executions), 2013[3]			Executed, 2013			Under sentence of death, 12/31/13		
	All races[1]	White[2]	Black[2]	All races[1]	White[2]	Black[2]	All races[1]	White[2]	Black[2]	All races[1]	White[2]	Black[2]	All races[1]	White[2]	Black[2]
U.S. Total	3,011	1,684	1,258	83	49	33	76	44	30	39	26	13	2,979	1,663	1,248
Federal[4]	56	27	28	2	0	2	2	0	2	0	0	0	56	27	28
State	2,955	1,657	1,230	81	49	31	74	44	28	39	26	13	2,923	1,636	1,220
Northeast	204	87	114	4	2	2	7	2	5	0	0	0	201	87	111
Connecticut	10	4	6	0	0	0	0	0	0	0	0	0	10	4	6
New Hampshire	1	0	1	0	0	0	0	0	0	0	0	0	1	0	1
New York	0	0	0	0	0	0	0	0	0	0	0	0	0	0	0
Pennsylvania	193	83	107	4	2	2	7	2	5	0	0	0	190	83	104
Midwest	218	115	99	11	8	3	6	2	3	5	5	0	218	116	99
Indiana	12	9	3	3	2	1	1	0	1	0	0	0	14	11	3
Kansas	9	6	3	0	0	0	0	0	0	0	0	0	9	6	3
Missouri	45	26	19	3	3	0	1	0	1	2	2	0	45	27	18
Nebraska	11	7	2	0	0	0	0	0	0	0	0	0	11	7	2
Ohio	138	64	72	4	2	2	3	1	1	3	3	0	136	62	73
South Dakota	3	3	0	1	1	0	1	1	0	0	0	0	3	3	0
South	1,538	825	693	34	15	18	45	28	16	32	19	13	1,495	793	682
Alabama	191	98	92	5	1	4	5	3	2	1	1	0	190	95	94
Arkansas	38	15	23	0	0	0	1	0	1	0	0	0	37	15	22
Delaware	16	7	9	1	0	1	0	0	0	0	0	0	17	7	10
Florida	402	252	149	15	10	5	12	11	1	7	5	2	398	246	151
Georgia	89	46	43	0	0	0	6	2	4	1	1	0	82	43	39
Kentucky	34	29	5	0	0	0	1	0	1	0	0	0	33	29	4
Louisiana	85	28	56	0	0	0	1	0	1	0	0	0	84	28	55
Maryland	5	1	4	0	0	0	0	0	0	0	0	0	5	1	4
Mississippi	49	20	28	2	2	0	1	0	1	0	0	0	50	22	27
North Carolina	152	66	79	1	0	1	2	1	1	0	0	0	151	65	79
Oklahoma[5]	56	29	24	1	0	0	3	1	1	6	3	3	48	25	20
South Carolina[6]	49	20	29	0	0	0	4	2	2	0	0	0	45	18	27
Tennesseee	79	43	34	0	0	0	4	4	0	0	0	0	75	39	34
Texas	284	166	114	9	2	7	4	4	0	16	8	8	273	156	113
Virginia	9	5	4	0	0	0	1	0	1	1	1	0	7	4	3
West	995	630	324	32	24	8	16	12	4	2	2	0	1,009	640	328
Arizona	125	103	17	4	4	0	5	5	0	2	2	0	122	100	17
California[6]	718	423	263	25	17	8	8	6	2	0	0	0	735	434	269
Colorado	3	0	3	0	0	0	0	0	0	0	0	0	3	0	3
Idaho	12	12	0	0	0	0	0	0	0	0	0	0	12	12	0
Montana	2	2	0	0	0	0	0	0	0	0	0	0	2	2	0
Nevada	80	47	32	2	2	0	1	0	1	0	0	0	81	49	31
New Mexico	2	2	0	0	0	0	0	0	0	0	0	0	2	2	0
Oregon	36	30	4	0	0	0	2	1	1	0	0	0	34	29	3
Utah	8	6	1	0	0	0	0	0	0	0	0	0	8	6	1
Washington	8	4	4	1	1	0	0	0	0	0	0	0	9	5	4
Wyoming	1	1	0	0	0	0	0	0	0	0	0	0	1	1	0

Note: Counts for yearend 2012 have been revised from those reported in Capital Punishment, 2012 - Statistical Tables (NCJ 245789, BJS web, May 2014). Revised counts include 19 inmates who were either reported late to the National Prisoner Statistics program or were not in custody of state correctional authorities on December 31, 2012 (14 in California; 3 in Florida; and 1 each in Pennsylvania and Oregon) and exclude 42 inmates who were relieved of a death sentence before December 31, 2012 (9 each in Pennsylvania and California; 6 each in Georgia and Texas; 4 in Florida; 3 in Tennessee; 2 in Missouri; and 1 each in Ohio, Delaware, and Nevada). Data for December 31, 2012, also include 1 inmate in Pennsylvania who was erroneously reported as being removed from under sentence of death.
[1] Includes American Indians or Alaska Natives; Asians, Native Hawaiians, or other Pacific Islanders; and inmates of Hispanic or Latino origin for whom no other race was identified.
[2] Counts of white and black inmates include persons of Hispanic or Latino origin, which may differ from other tables in this report.
[3] Includes 25 deaths from natural causes (6 each in Florida and California; 2 each in Alabama and Tennessee; and 1 each in Pennsylvania, Missouri, Ohio, North Carolina, South Carolina, Texas, Arizona, Oregon, and the Federal Bureau of Prisons) and 6 deaths from suicide (2 in Arizona; and 1 each in Ohio, Florida, South Carolina, and California).
[4] Excludes persons held under Armed Forces jurisdiction with a military death sentence for murder.
[5] One inmate who was previously in the custody of Tennessee is now being reported in Oklahoma where he is under a separate sentence of death.
[6] One inmate who was previously in the custody of South Carolina is now being reported in California where he is under a separate sentence of death.

Table 5. Demographic Characteristics of Prisoners Under Sentence of Death, 2013

(Number; percent.)

Characteristic	Total year end	Admissions	Removals
Total Inmates	2,979	83	115
Sex			
Male	98.1	100.0	96.5
Female	1.9	0.0	3.5
Race[1]			
White	55.8	59.0	60.9
Black	41.9	39.8	37.4
All other races[2]	2.3	1.2	1.7
Hispanic/Latino origin[3]			
Hispanic/Latino	14.4	18.3	12.1
Non-Hispanic/Latino	85.6	81.7	87.9
Age			
18–19	X	X	X
20–24	0.7	6.0	0.9
25–29	3.4	12.0	3.5
30–34	9.2	20.5	4.3
35–39	13.2	18.1	10.4
40–44	18.3	16.9	17.4
45–49	16.1	7.2	17.4
50–54	16.3	8.4	15.7
55–59	10.6	6.0	10.4
60–64	6.4	2.4	8.7
65 or older	5.8	2.4	11.3
Average age			
Mean	47	39	49
Median	46	38	49
Education[4]			
8th grade or less	13.1	15.7	22.0
9th–11th grade	34.8	23.5	32.0
High school graduate/GED	42.8	47.1	40.0
Any college	9.4	13.7	6.0
Median education level	12th	12th	11th
Marital status[5]			
Married	21.5	22.4	26.5
Divorced/separated	20.0	20.9	27.5
Widowed	3.6	1.5	4.9
Never married	54.8	55.2	41.2

Note: Detail may not sum to total due to rounding.
X = Not applicable.
[1] Percentages for white and black inmates include persons of Hispanic or Latino origin, which may differ from other tables in this report.
[2] At yearend 2013, inmates in "all other races" consisted of 21 American Indian or Alaska Natives (AIAN); 42 Asian, Native Hawaiian, or other Pacific Islanders; and 5 self-identified Hispanics or Latinos. During 2013, 1 AIAN inmate was admitted and 2 AIAN inmates were removed.
[3] Calculations exclude count of inmates with unknown Hispanic or Latino origin: 278 at yearend, 1 admission, and 8 removals.
[4] Calculations exclude count of inmates with unknown education level: 544 at yearend, 32 admissions, and 15 removals.
[5] Calculations exclude count of inmates with unknown marital status: 335 at yearend, 16 admissions, and 13 removals.

Table 6. Female Prisoners Under Sentence of Death, by Region, Jurisdiction, and Race, 2012 and 2013

(Number.)

Region and jurisdiction	Under sentence of death, 12/31/12[1]			Received under sentence of death, 2013	Removed from death row (excluding executions), 2013[4]			Executed, 2013[4]	Under sentence of death, 12/31/13		
	All races[2]	White[3]	Black[3]		All races[2]	White[3]	Black[3]		All races[2]	White[3]	Black[3]
U.S. Total	60	41	15	0	3	3	0	1	56	38	14
Federal	1	1	0	0	0	0	0	0	1	1	0
State	59	40	15	0	3	3	0	1	55	37	14
Northeast	3	1	2	0	0	0	0	0	3	1	2
Pennsylvania	3	1	2	0	0	0	0	0	3	1	2
Midwest	2	1	1	0	1	1	0	0	1	0	1
Indiana	1	0	1	0	0	0	0	0	1	0	1
Ohio	1	1	0	0	1	1	0	0	0	0	0
South	29	19	10	0	1	1	0	1	27	18	9
Alabama	4	3	1	0	0	0	0	0	4	3	1
Florida	5	2	3	0	0	0	0	0	5	2	3
Georgia	1	1	0	0	0	0	0	0	1	1	0
Kentucky	1	1	0	0	0	0	0	0	1	1	0
Louisiana	2	1	1	0	0	0	0	0	2	1	1
Mississippi	2	2	0	0	0	0	0	0	2	2	0
North Carolina	3	2	1	0	1	1	0	0	2	1	1
Oklahoma	1	1	0	0	0	0	0	0	1	1	0
Tennesseee	1	1	0	0	0	0	0	0	1	1	0
Texas	9	5	4	0	0	0	0	1	8	5	3
West	25	19	2	0	1	1	0	0	24	18	2
Arizona	3	3	0	0	1	1	0	0	2	2	0
California	20	14	2	0	0	0	0	0	20	14	2
Idaho	1	1	0	0	0	0	0	0	1	1	0
Oregon	1	1	0	0	0	0	0	0	1	1	0

[1] Counts of female prisoners under sentence of death at yearend 2012 have been revised from those reported in Capital Punishment, 2012 - Statistical Tables (NCJ 245789 BJS web, May 2014). The revised figures exclude 1 female inmate in Texas whose removal from under sentence of death occurred prior to 2012 but was not reported until the 2013 data collection.
[2] Includes American Indians or Alaska Natives; Asians, Native Hawaiians, or other Pacific Islanders; and inmates of Hispanic or Latino origin for whom no other race was identified.
[3] Counts of white and black inmates include persons of Hispanic or Latino origin, which may differ from other tables in this report.
[4] One black female inmate was executed in Texas in 2013.

Table 7. Hispanic or Latino Prisoners Under Sentence of Death, by Region, Jurisdiction, and Race, 2012 and 2013

(Number.)

Region and jurisdiction	Under sentence of death, 12/31/12	Received under sentence of death, 2013	Removed from death row (excluding executions), 2013	Executed, 2013	Under sentence of death, 12/31/13
U.S. Total	387	15	10	3	389
Federal	8	0	1	0	7
State	379	15	9	3	382
Northeast	20	0	0	0	20
Pennsylvania	20	0	0	0	20
Midwest	9	0	0	0	9
Nebraska	5	0	0	0	5
Ohio	4	0	0	0	4
South	135	2	6	3	128
Alabama	2	0	0	0	2
Delaware	3	0	0	0	3
Florida	33	1	2	0	32
Georgia	3	0	1	0	2
Louisiana	2	0	0	0	2
North Carolina	4	0	0	0	4
Oklahoma	1	0	0	0	1
South Carolina	1	0	0	0	1
Tennesseee	1	0	0	0	1
Texas	85	1	3	3	80
West	215	13	3	0	225
Arizona	25	1	0	0	26
California	175	12	3	0	184
Idaho	1	0	0	0	1
Nevada	8	0	0	0	8
Oregon	3	0	0	0	3
Utah	3	0	0	0	3

Note: Counts of Hispanic or Latino inmates under sentence of death at yearend 2012 have been revised from those reported in Capital Punishment, 2012 - Statistical Tables (NCJ 245789, BJS web, May 2014). Revised counts exclude 1 inmate in New Mexico who was erroneously reported as Hispanic or Latino.

Table 8. Criminal History of Prisoners Under Sentence of Death, by Race and Hispanic Origin, 2013

(Percent.)

Characteristic	All races[1]	White[2]	Black[2]	Hispanic
U.S. Total	100.0	100.0	100.0	100.0
Prior felony convictions[3]				
Yes	67.3	63.9	72.6	64.8
No	32.7	36.1	27.4	35.2
Prior homicide convictions[4]				
Yes	9.0	9.0	9.6	6.6
No	91.0	91.0	90.4	93.4
Legal status at time of capital offense[5]				
Charges pending	8.7	9.6	8.7	6.2
Probation	11.4	9.9	12.0	13.8
Parole	16.5	14.1	18.5	18.3
On escape	1.3	1.8	0.8	1.1
Incarcerated	2.7	3.5	2.2	2.0
Other status	0.1	0.1	0.2	0.3
None	59.3	61.0	57.6	58.4

Note: Percentages are based on offenders for whom data were reported. Detail may not sum to total due to rounding.
[1] Includes American Indians or Alaska Natives and Asians, Native Hawaiians, or Other Pacific Islanders.
[2] Excludes persons of Hispanic or Latino origin.
[3] Data were not reported for 217 inmates.
[4] Data were not reported for 36 inmates.
[5] Data were not reported for 292 inmates.

Table 9. Inmates Removed from Under Sentence of Death, by Region, Jurisdiction, and Method of Removal, 2013

(Number.)

Region and jurisdiction	Total	Execution	Other death	Appeals or higher court overturned		
				Capital statute	Conviction	Sentence
U.S. Total	115	39	31	1	12	32
Federal	2	0	1	0	0	1
State	113	39	30	1	12	31
Northeast	7	0	1	0	0	6
Pennsylvania	7	0	1	0	0	6
Midwest	11	5	3	0	0	3
Indiana	1	0	0	0	0	1
Missouri	3	2	1	0	0	0
Ohio	6	3	2	0	0	1
South Dakota	1	0	0	0	0	1
South	77	32	15	0	11	19
Alabama	6	1	2	0	2	1
Arkansas	1	0	0	0	1	0
Florida	19	7	7	0	3	2
Georgia	7	1	0	0	0	6
Kentucky	1	0	0	0	1	0
Louisiana	1	0	0	0	0	1
Mississippi	1	0	0	0	0	1
North Carolina	2	0	1	0	0	1
Oklahoma	9	6	0	0	3	0
South Carolina	4	0	2	0	0	2
Tennesseee	4	0	2	0	0	2
Texas	20	16	1	0	1	2
Virginia	2	1	0	0	0	1
West	18	2	11	1	1	3
Arizona	7	2	3	1	1	0
California	8	0	7	0	0	1
Nevada	1	0	0	0	0	1
Oregon	2	0	1	0	0	1

Table 10. Average Time Between Sentencing and Execution, 1977–2013

(Number; time in months.)

Year[1]	Number executed	Average elapsed time from sentence to execution[2]
Total	1,359	137
1977....................................	1	:
1979....................................	2	:
1981....................................	1	:
1982....................................	2	:
1983....................................	5	:
1984....................................	21	74
1985....................................	18	71
1986....................................	18	87
1987....................................	25	86
1988....................................	11	80
1989....................................	16	95
1990....................................	23	95
1991....................................	14	116
1992....................................	31	114
1993....................................	38	113
1994....................................	31	122
1995....................................	56	134
1996....................................	45	125
1997....................................	74	133
1998....................................	68	130
1999....................................	98	143
2000....................................	85	137
2001....................................	66	142
2002....................................	71	127
2003....................................	65	131
2004....................................	59	132
2005....................................	60	147
2006....................................	53	145
2007....................................	42	153
2008....................................	37	139
2009....................................	52	169
2010....................................	46	178
2011....................................	43	198
2012....................................	43	190
2013....................................	39	186

Note: In 1972, the U.S. Supreme Court invalidated capital punishment statutes in several states (Furman v. Georgia, 408 U.S. 238 (1972)), effecting a moratorium on executions. Executions resumed in 1977 when the Supreme Court found that revisions to several state statutes had effectively addressed the issues previously held unconstitutional (Gregg v. Georgia, 428 U.S. 153 (1976) and its companion cases).
: = Not calculated. A reliable average could not be generated from fewer than 10 cases.
[1] No inmates were executed in 1978 or 1980.
[2] Average time was calculated from the most recent sentencing date.

Table 11. Number of Inmates Executed, by Race and Hispanic Origin, 1977–2013

(Ttime in months.)

Year[1]	All races	White[2]	Black[2]	Hispanic	All other races[2,3]
Total	1,359	770	464	111	14
1977..................................	1	1	0	0	0
1979..................................	2	2	0	0	0
1981..................................	1	1	0	0	0
1982..................................	2	1	1	0	0
1983..................................	5	4	1	0	0
1984..................................	21	13	8	0	0
1985..................................	18	9	7	2	0
1986..................................	18	9	7	2	0
1987..................................	25	11	11	3	0
1988..................................	11	6	5	0	0
1989..................................	16	6	8	2	0
1990..................................	23	16	7	0	0
1991..................................	14	6	7	1	0
1992..................................	31	17	11	2	1
1993..................................	38	19	14	4	1
1994..................................	31	19	11	1	0
1995..................................	56	31	22	2	1
1996..................................	45	29	14	2	0
1997..................................	74	41	26	5	2
1998..................................	68	40	18	8	2
1999..................................	98	53	33	9	3
2000..................................	85	43	35	6	1
2001..................................	66	45	17	3	1
2002..................................	71	47	18	6	0
2003..................................	65	41	20	3	1
2004..................................	59	36	19	3	1
2005..................................	60	38	19	3	0
2006..................................	53	25	20	8	0
2007..................................	42	22	14	6	0
2008..................................	37	17	17	3	0
2009..................................	52	24	21	7	0
2010..................................	46	28	13	5	0
2011..................................	43	22	16	5	0
2012..................................	43	25	11	7	0
2013..................................	39	23	13	3	0

Note: In 1972, the U.S. Supreme Court invalidated capital punishment statutes in several states (Furman v. Georgia, 408 U.S. 238 (1972)), effecting a moratorium on executions. Executions resumed in 1977 when the Supreme Court found that revisions to several state statutes had effectively addressed the issues previously held unconstitutional (Gregg v. Georgia, 428 U.S. 153 (1976) and its companion cases).
[1] No inmates were executed in 1978 or 1980.
[2] Excludes persons of Hispanic or Latino origin.
[3] Includes American Indians or Alaska Natives, and Asians, Native Hawaiians, or Other Pacific Islanders.

Table 12. Executions and Other Dispositions of Inmates Sentenced to Death, by Race and Hispanic Origin, 1977–2013

(Number; percent.)

Race/Hispanic origin	Number under sentence of death, 1977–2013[1]	Prisoners executed		Prisoners who received other dispensations[2]	
		Number	Percent of total	Number	Percent of total
Total	8,124	1,359	16.7	3,786	46.6
White[3]	3,907	770	19.7	1,843	47.2
Black[3]	3,334	464	13.9	1,635	49.0
Hispanic/Latino	755	111	14.7	255	33.8
All other races[3,4]...................................	128	14	10.9	53	41.4

Note: In 1972, the U.S. Supreme Court invalidated capital punishment statutes in several states (Furman v. Georgia, 408 U.S. 238 (1972)), effecting a moratorium on executions. Executions resumed in 1977 when the Supreme Court found that revisions to several state statutes had effectively addressed the issues previously held unconstitutional (Gregg v. Georgia, 428 U.S. 153 (1976) and its companion cases).

[1] Includes 4 persons sentenced to death prior to 1977 who were still under sentence of death on December 31, 2013; 375 persons sentenced to death prior to 1977 whose death sentence was removed between 1977 and December 31, 2013; and 7,745 persons sentenced to death between 1977 and 2013.

[2] Includes persons removed from under a sentence of death because of statutes struck down on appeal, sentences or convictions vacated, commutations, or death by other than execution.

[3] Excludes persons of Hispanic or Latino origin.

[4] Includes American Indians, Alaska Natives, Asians, Native Hawaiians, and Other Pacific Islanders.

Table 13. Executions, by Jurisdiction and Method, 1977–2013

(Number.)

Jurisdiction	All executions	Lethal injection	Electrocution	Lethal gas	Hanging	Firing squad
U.S. Total...................................	1,359	1,184	158	11	3	3
Federal..	3	3	0	0	0	0
Alabama..	56	32	24	0	0	0
Arizona...	36	34	0	2	0	0
Arkansas.......................................	27	26	1	0	0	0
California......................................	13	11	0	2	0	0
Colorado.......................................	1	1	0	0	0	0
Connecticut...................................	1	1	0	0	0	0
Delaware.......................................	16	15	0	0	1	0
Florida..	81	37	44	0	0	0
Georgia...	53	30	23	0	0	0
Idaho..	3	3	0	0	0	0
Illinois..	12	12	0	0	0	0
Indiana...	20	17	3	0	0	0
Kentucky.......................................	3	2	1	0	0	0
Louisiana......................................	28	8	20	0	0	0
Maryland.......................................	5	5	0	0	0	0
Mississippi....................................	21	17	0	4	0	0
Missouri..	70	70	0	0	0	0
Montana..	3	3	0	0	0	0
Nebraska.......................................	3	0	3	0	0	0
Nevada..	12	11	0	1	0	0
New Mexico....................................	1	1	0	0	0	0
North Carolina...............................	43	41	0	2	0	0
Ohio...	52	52	0	0	0	0
Oklahoma......................................	108	108	0	0	0	0
Oregon..	2	2	0	0	0	0
Pennsylvania..................................	3	3	0	0	0	0
South Carolina...............................	43	36	7	0	0	0
South Dakota.................................	3	3	0	0	0	0
Tennessee.....................................	6	5	1	0	0	0
Texas..	508	508	0	0	0	0
Utah...	7	4	0	0	0	3
Virginia...	110	79	31	0	0	0
Washington....................................	5	3	0	0	2	0
Wyoming.......................................	1	1	0	0	0	0

Note: In 1972, the U.S. Supreme Court invalidated capital punishment statutes in several states (Furman v. Georgia, 408 U.S. 238 (1972)), effecting a moratorium on executions. Executions resumed in 1977, when the Supreme Court found that revisions to several state statutes had effectively addressed the issues previously held unconstitutional (Gregg v. Georgia, 428 U.S. 153 (1976) and its companion cases).

Table 14. Executions, by Jurisdiction, 1930–2013

(Number.)

Jurisdiction	Since 1930	Since 1977
U.S. Total	5,218	1,359
Texas	805	508
Georgia	419	53
New York	329	0
North Carolina	306	43
California	305	13
Florida	251	81
Ohio	224	52
South Carolina	205	43
Virginia	202	110
Alabama	191	56
Mississippi	175	21
Oklahoma	168	108
Louisiana	161	28
Pennsylvania	155	3
Arkansas	145	27
Missouri	132	70
Kentucky	106	3
Illinois	102	12
Tennessee	99	6
Arizona	74	36
New Jersey	74	0
Maryland	73	5
Indiana	61	20
Washington	52	5
Colorado	48	1
Nevada	41	12
District of Columbia	40	0
West Virginia	40	0
Federal system	36	3
Delaware	28	16
Massachusetts	27	0
Connecticut	22	1
Oregon	21	2
Utah	20	7
Iowa	18	0
Kansas	15	0
Montana	9	3
New Mexico	9	1
Wyoming	8	1
Nebraska	7	3
Idaho	6	3
South Dakota	4	3
Vermont	4	0
New Hampshire	1	0

Note: Statistics on executions under civil authority have been collected by the federal government annually since 1930. Excludes 160 executions carried out by military authorities between 1930 and 1961.

Table 15. Prisoners Under Sentence of Death on December 31, 2013, by Jurisdiction and Year of Sentencing, 1974–2013

(Number.)

Jurisdiction	Year of sentence for prisoners under sentence of death, 12/31/13							
	1974–1979	1980–1982	1983–1985	1986–1988	1989–1991	1992–1994	1995–1997	1998–2000
Total	25	51	116	175	218	315	413	407
Florida	11	9	17	26	39	45	36	53
California..............................	5	24	37	56	70	88	106	100
Texas.....................................	4	3	5	12	11	21	26	42
Nevada	1	3	10	7	7	4	20	9
Arizona..................................	1	2	4	5	12	14	9	4
Georgia	1	2	0	7	5	9	16	15
Tennessee	1	1	10	9	9	3	13	8
Arkansas................................	1	0	0	0	1	8	9	5
Pennsylvania	0	2	5	18	19	29	24	23
Mississippi.............................	0	2	0	0	6	5	4	7
Kentucky	0	1	3	5	2	5	2	7
Alabama.................................	0	1	2	7	7	20	25	31
Idaho.....................................	0	1	0	1	2	1	2	0
Ohio.......................................	0	0	9	13	12	10	20	18
Maryland	0	0	3	0	0	0	1	1
Louisiana	0	0	2	5	2	6	19	19
Missouri.................................	0	0	2	1	3	2	7	5
Oklahoma...............................	0	0	2	1	0	2	3	9
South Carolina.......................	0	0	2	0	2	0	6	6
Utah.......................................	0	0	1	1	2	0	2	1
North Carolina.......................	0	0	1	0	3	33	45	28
Montana.................................	0	0	1	0	0	1	0	0
Nebraska................................	0	0	0	1	0	0	2	0
Connecticut............................	0	0	0	0	3	0	1	0
Washington	0	0	0	0	1	0	2	1
Oregon	0	0	0	0	0	5	5	7
Federal...................................	0	0	0	0	0	2	4	4
Indiana	0	0	0	0	0	1	1	3
South Dakota.........................	0	0	0	0	0	1	0	0
Colorado	0	0	0	0	0	0	1	0
Delaware	0	0	0	0	0	0	1	0
New Mexico............................	0	0	0	0	0	0	1	0
Virginia..................................	0	0	0	0	0	0	0	1
Kansas...................................	0	0	0	0	0	0	0	0
Wyoming................................	0	0	0	0	0	0	0	0
New Hampshire	0	0	0	0	0	0	0	0

Table 15. Prisoners Under Sentence of Death on December 31, 2013, by Jurisdiction and Year of Sentencing, 1974–2013—*Continued*

(Number.)

Jurisdiction	Year of sentence for prisoners under sentence of death, 12/31/13							Under sentence of death, 12/31/13	Average number of years under sentence of death, 12/31/13
	2001–2002	2003–2004	2005–2006	2007–2008	2009–2010	2011–2012	2013		
Total	188	194	217	204	211	162	83	2,979	14.6
Florida	15	15	25	30	26	36	15	398	15
California....................	38	29	37	37	59	24	25	735	16.1
Texas..........................	30	34	22	22	15	17	9	273	13
Nevada	0	3	3	4	6	2	2	81	17.7
Arizona.......................	1	11	11	11	22	11	4	122	12.4
Georgia	3	5	5	8	3	3	0	82	15.5
Tennessee	5	5	1	2	4	4	0	75	18.4
Arkansas.....................	3	1	2	4	2	1	0	37	14.7
Pennsylvania	12	8	12	13	8	13	4	190	15.4
Mississippi..................	7	2	4	2	6	3	2	50	13
Kentucky	2	1	3	0	1	1	0	33	18.3
Alabama.....................	12	13	24	15	14	14	5	190	12.4
Idaho	0	2	1	0	2	0	0	12	16.2
Ohio	10	10	7	7	8	8	4	136	15.2
Maryland	0	0	0	0	0	0	0	5	:
Louisiana	7	5	5	2	5	7	0	84	14
Missouri......................	4	4	5	7	1	1	3	45	12.4
Oklahoma...................	3	8	7	9	2	1	1	48	11.1
South Carolina.............	5	8	7	6	3	0	0	45	12
Utah	0	0	0	1	0	0	0	8	:
North Carolina	10	8	9	4	6	3	1	151	15.1
Montana......................	0	0	0	0	0	0	0	2	:
Nebraska	0	2	3	1	2	0	0	11	11.3
Connecticut.................	0	0	1	3	1	1	0	10	11.9
Washington	2	0	0	0	1	1	1	9	:
Oregon.......................	2	3	3	2	3	4	0	34	12
Federal.......................	7	10	11	8	7	1	2	56	9.1
Indiana	2	1	2	0	1	0	3	14	9.7
South Dakota..............	0	0	0	0	0	1	1	3	:
Colorado	0	0	0	1	1	0	0	3	:
Delaware	5	3	3	0	1	3	1	17	8.2
New Mexico.................	1	0	0	0	0	0	0	2	:
Virginia......................	0	0	3	2	0	1	0	7	:
Kansas........................	2	2	1	2	1	1	0	9	:
Wyoming....................	0	1	0	0	0	0	0	1	:
New Hampshire	0	0	0	1	0	0	0	1	:

Note: For persons sentenced to death more than once, the numbers are based on the most recent death sentence.
: = Not calculated. A reliable average could not be generated from fewer than 10 cases.

Table 16. Prisoners Sentenced to Death and the Outcome of the Sentence, by Year of Sentencing, 1973–2013

(Number.)

| Year of sentence | Number sentenced | Execution | Other death | Appeal or higher courts overturned | | | Sentence commuted | Other/ unknown removals | Remaining under sentence of death, 12/31/13 |
				Capital statute	Conviction	Sentence			
Total, 1973–2013...........	8,466	1,359	509	523	890	1,781	392	33	2,979
1973............................	42	2	0	14	9	8	9	0	0
1974............................	149	11	5	65	15	30	22	1	0
1975............................	298	6	5	171	24	67	21	2	2
1976............................	232	14	6	136	17	42	15	0	2
1977............................	137	19	5	40	26	34	7	0	6
1978............................	183	38	7	21	36	67	8	0	6
1979............................	150	28	16	2	28	60	6	1	9
1980............................	172	47	16	4	30	55	12	0	8
1981............................	223	58	16	0	43	82	12	1	11
1982............................	265	67	26	0	42	86	12	0	32
1983............................	252	69	28	1	31	72	15	2	34
1984............................	286	72	21	2	46	80	13	8	44
1985............................	258	53	14	1	44	89	15	4	38
1986............................	301	75	26	1	50	73	14	5	57
1987............................	288	59	29	7	45	83	10	7	48
1988............................	287	64	20	1	38	80	14	0	70
1989............................	255	48	23	0	33	73	13	1	64
1990............................	250	51	22	2	37	59	18	1	60
1991............................	267	45	15	2	38	62	11	0	94
1992............................	283	51	20	0	28	60	23	0	101
1993............................	290	67	21	3	23	49	15	0	112
1994............................	311	74	13	10	37	60	15	0	102
1995............................	310	67	20	6	22	50	14	0	131
1996............................	315	46	20	4	21	66	15	0	143
1997............................	266	35	15	3	21	42	11	0	139
1998............................	295	50	15	4	22	53	9	0	142
1999............................	279	36	16	8	23	39	10	0	147
2000............................	223	28	16	4	12	36	9	0	118
2001............................	153	16	12	3	7	26	2	0	87
2002............................	166	25	6	3	3	23	5	0	101
2003............................	151	19	10	1	8	14	1	0	98
2004............................	138	10	5	1	5	16	5	0	96
2005............................	140	1	6	0	3	14	1	0	115
2006............................	123	1	4	0	7	6	3	0	102
2007............................	126	2	3	2	7	5	2	0	105
2008............................	120	2	3	0	3	10	3	0	99
2009............................	118	1	1	1	0	7	1	0	107
2010............................	114	0	1	0	6	2	1	0	104
2011............................	85	2	1	0	0	1	0	0	81
2012............................	82	0	1	0	0	0	0	0	81
2013............................	83	0	0	0	0	0	0	0	83

Note: In 1972, the U.S. Supreme Court invalidated capital punishment statutes in several states (Furman v. Georgia, 408 U.S. 238 (1972)), effecting a moratorium on executions. Executions resumed in 1977 when the Supreme Court found that revisions to several state statutes had effectively addressed the issues previously held unconstitutional (Gregg v. Georgia, 428 U.S. 153 (1976) and its companion cases). Some inmates executed since 1977 or currently under sentence of death were sentenced prior to 1977. For persons sentenced to death more than once, the numbers are based on the most recent death sentence.

Table 17. Prisoners Sentenced to Death and the Outcome of the Sentence, by Jurisdiction, 1973–2013

(Number; percent.)

Jurisdiction	Total sentenced to death, 1973–2013	Number of prisoners removed from under sentence of death					Remaining under sentence of death, 12/31/13
		Execution	Other death	Sentence/ conviction overturned	Sentence commuted	Other/ unknown removals	
U.S. Total..	8,466	1,359	509	3,194	392	33	2,979
Federal..	71	3	1	10	1	0	56
Alabama..	439	56	36	155	2	0	190
Arizona...	307	36	21	120	7	1	122
Arkansas..	114	27	3	45	2	0	37
California..	1,013	13	92	158	15	0	735
Colorado	22	1	2	15	1	0	3
Connecticut...	15	1	0	4	0	0	10
Delaware	60	16	0	26	1	0	17
Florida	1,040	81	72	469	18	2	398
Georgia	325	53	19	160	10	1	82
Idaho...	42	3	3	21	3	0	12
Illinois	307	12	15	97	171	12	0
Indiana	103	20	4	57	6	2	14
Kansas	13	0	0	4	0	0	9
Kentucky	83	3	6	39	2	0	33
Louisiana	245	28	6	119	7	1	84
Maryland	53	5	3	36	4	0	5
Massachusetts	4	0	0	2	2	0	0
Mississippi...	197	21	6	117	0	3	50
Missouri..	186	70	11	57	3	0	45
Montana...	15	3	2	6	2	0	2
Nebraska	33	3	5	12	2	0	11
Nevada	156	12	15	44	4	0	81
New Hampshire	1	0	0	0	0	0	1
New Jersey...	52	0	3	33	8	8	0
New Mexico..	28	1	1	19	5	0	2
New York...	10	0	0	10	0	0	0
North Carolina......................................	536	43	25	309	8	0	151
Ohio..	419	52	26	183	22	0	136
Oklahoma..	353	108	17	176	4	0	48
Oregon...	63	2	3	24	0	0	34
Pennsylvania	417	3	30	188	6	0	190
Rhode Island	2	0	0	2	0	0	0
South Carolina......................................	204	43	8	105	3	0	45
South Dakota..	7	3	1	0	0	0	3
Tennessee	225	6	19	117	6	2	75
Texas...	1,075	508	45	194	55	0	273
Utah	27	7	1	10	1	0	8
Virginia...	152	110	6	17	11	1	7
Washington	40	5	1	25	0	0	9
Wyoming	12	1	1	9	0	0	1
Percent of inmates sentenced to death, 1973–2013........	100.0	16.1	6.0	37.7	4.6	0.4	35.2

Note: In 1972, the U.S. Supreme Court invalidated capital punishment statutes in several states (Furman v. Georgia, 408 U.S. 238 (1972)), effecting a moratorium on executions. Executions resumed in 1977 when the Supreme Court found that revisions to several state statutes had effectively addressed the issues previously held unconstitutional (Gregg v. Georgia, 428 U.S. 153 (1976) and its companion cases). Some inmates executed since 1977 or currently under sentence of death were sentenced prior to 1977. For persons sentenced to death more than once, the numbers are based on the most recent death sentence.

Table 18. Inmates Under Sentence of Death, by Demographic Characteristics, 2013

(Number.)

Characteristic	Total yearend	Admissions	Removals
Total inmates	2,979	83	115
Sex			
Male	2,923	83	111
Female	56	0	4
Race[1]			
White	1,663	49	70
Black	1,248	33	43
All other races[2]	68	1	2
Hispanic origin			
Hispanic	389	15	13
Non-Hispanic	2,312	67	94
Number unknown	278	1	8
Age			
18–19	0	0	0
20–24	21	5	1
25–29	101	10	4
30–34	273	17	5
35–39	392	15	12
40–44	545	14	20
45–49	479	6	20
50–54	487	7	18
55–59	315	5	12
60–64	192	2	10
65 or older	174	2	13
Education			
8th grade or less	318	8	22
9th–11th grade	847	12	32
High school graduate/GED	1,042	24	40
Any college	228	7	6
Unknown	544	32	15
Marital status			
Married	569	15	27
Divorced/separated	530	14	28
Widowed	95	1	5
Never married	1,450	37	42
Unknown	335	16	13

[1] Counts for white and black inmates include persons of Hispanic or Latino origin, which may differ from other tables in this report.
[2] At yearend 2013, inmates in "all other races" consisted of 21 American Indian or Alaska Natives (AIAN); 42 Asian, Native Hawaiian, and Other Pacific Islanders; and 5 self-identified Hispanics or Latinos. During 2013, 1 AIAN inmate was admitted and 2 AIAN inmates were removed.

METHODOLOGY

About the Data

Capital punishment information is collected annually as part of the National Prisoner Statistics program (NPS-8). This data series is collected in two parts: data on persons under sentence of death are obtained from the department of corrections in each jurisdiction currently authorizing capital punishment, and the status of death penalty statutes is obtained from the Office of the Attorney General in each of the 50 states, from the U.S. Attorney's Office in the District of Columbia, and from the Federal Bureau of Prisons for the federal government. Data collection forms are available on the BJS website at www.bjs.gov.

NPS-8 covers all persons under sentence of death at any time during the year who were held in a state or federal nonmilitary correctional facility. This includes capital offenders transferred from prison to mental hospitals and those who may have escaped from custody. It excludes persons whose death sentences have been overturned by the court, regardless of their current incarceration status.

The statistics included in this report may differ from data collected by other organizations for various reasons: (1) NPS-8 adds inmates to the population under sentence of death not at sentencing, but at the time they are admitted to a state or federal correctional facility; (2) if inmates entered prison under a death sentence or were reported as being relieved of a death sentence in one year but the court had acted in the previous year, the counts are adjusted to reflect the dates of court decisions (see note on Table 4 for the affected jurisdictions); and (3) NPS counts are always for the last day of the calendar year and will differ from counts for more recent periods. All data in this report have been reviewed for accuracy by the data providers in each jurisdiction prior to publication.

Changes to the Death Penalty

One state repealed its capital statute in 2013, and five states revised statutes relating to the death penalty.

As of December 31, 2013, 35 states and the federal government authorized the death penalty (Table 1 and Table 3). Although New Mexico repealed the death penalty in 2009 (2009 N.M. Laws, chapter 11 § 5) and Connecticut repealed the death penalty in 2012, the repeals were not retroactive, and offenders charged with a capital offense committed prior to the date of the repeal may be eligible for a death sentence. As of December 31, 2013, New Mexico held 2 men and Connecticut held 10 men under previously imposed death sentences.

In 2013, the Maryland legislature repealed the death penalty (2013 Maryland Laws, chapter 156), effective October 1, 2013. The repeal did not affect previously imposed death sentences, and as of December 31, 2013, Maryland held 5 men under sentence of death.

During 2013, the Arkansas legislature revised a portion of its capital statute pertaining to the selection and administration of drugs in lethal injections (the Method of Execution Act (MEA), Ark. Code Ann. § 5-4-617 (Repl. 2013)). The changes, which created specific steps to be followed by corrections officials when carrying out executions, were made following a decision by the Arkansas Supreme Court declaring the MEA unconstitutional (Hobbs v. Jones (2012 Ark. 293)) and became effective February 20, 2013.

Kansas amended an element of capital murder—intentional and premeditated murder of a child under age 14 during the commission of kidnapping with intent to commit a sex offense—to include "commercial sexual exploitation" in the definition of sex offenses (K.S.A. 2013 Supp. 21-5401, at subsection (b)), effective July 1, 2013. Mississippi added aggravating factors for which the death penalty can be imposed to include murder committed with the intent to influence government by intimidation, coercion, mass destruction or assassination, or to coerce civilians (Miss. Code Ann. § 99-19-101(4)(i)-(j)), effective July 1, 2013.

Texas amended its code of criminal procedure to require DNA analysis of all biological evidence in death penalty cases (Tex. C.C.P. Art. 38.43(i), (j), (k), (l), (m)), effective September 1, 2013. Utah amended its statute to codify that, for defendants younger than age 18 at the time of the offense, aggravated murder is a noncapital first-degree felony punishable as provided by Utah Code Ann. § 76-3-207.7 (Utah Code Ann. § 76-5-202(3)(e)), effective May 14, 2013.

Executions in 2014

Between January 1, 2014, and November 30, 2014, 7 states executed 33 inmates, which was 2 fewer than the number executed during the same period in 2013.

Three states accounted for 82% of the executions carried out during this period: Texas executed 10 inmates, Missouri executed 9 inmates, and Florida executed 8 inmates. Of the 33 executions carried out in the first 11 months of 2014, all were by lethal injection.

Two women were executed during this period in Texas.

For more information, please see the full report at http://www.bjs.gov/index.cfm?ty=pbdetail&iid=5156.

PART 5

Hate Crime Statistics, 2014

HIGHLIGHTS

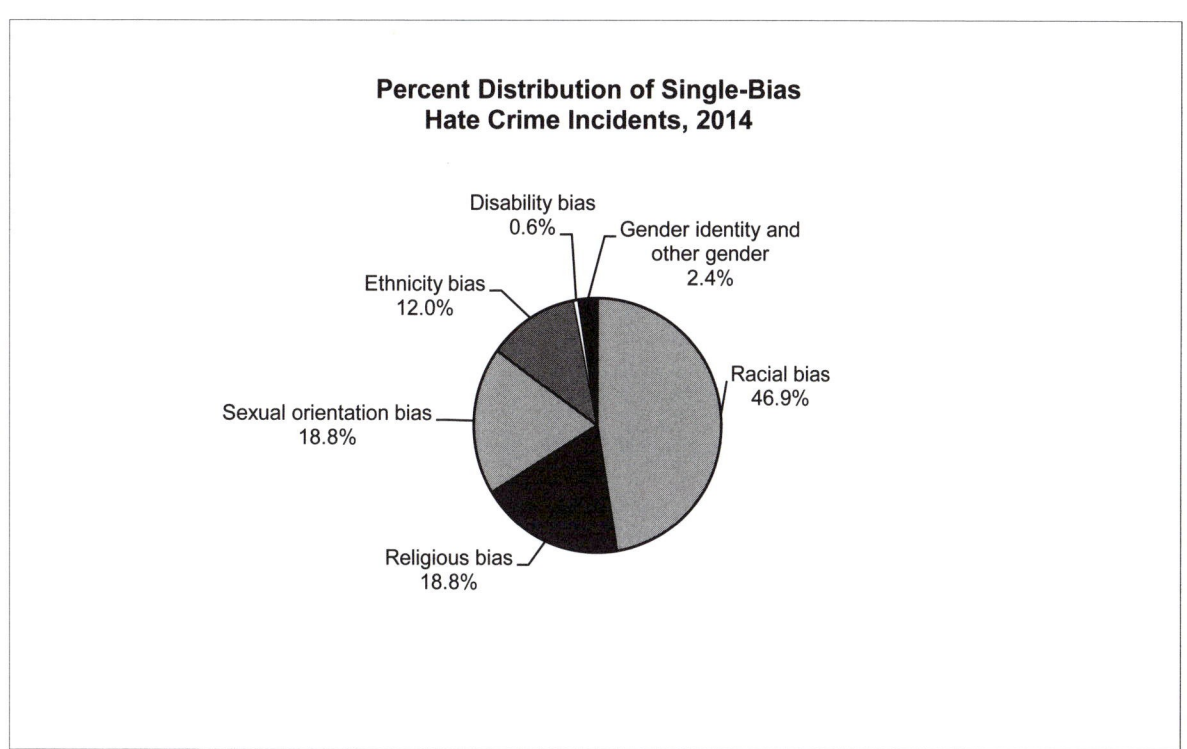

Percent Distribution of Single-Bias Hate Crime Incidents, 2014

- Disability bias 0.6%
- Gender identity and other gender 2.4%
- Ethnicity bias 12.0%
- Racial bias 46.9%
- Sexual orientation bias 18.8%
- Religious bias 18.8%

- In 2013, 1,666 law enforcement agencies reported 5,479 hate crime incidents involving 6,418 offenses.

- There were 5,462 single-bias incidents that involved 6,385 offenses, 6,681 victims, and 5,176 known offenders. Approximately 47.0 percent were racially motivated, 18.6 percent resulted from sexual-orientation bias, 18.6 percent were motivated by religious bias, 11.9 percent stemmed from ethnicity bias, 1.8 percent were motivated by gender-identity bias, 1.5 percent were prompted by disability bias, and 0.6 percent resulted from gender bias.

- The 17 multiple-bias incidents reported in 2014 involved 33 offenses, 46 victims, and 16 offenders.

- The majority of the 2,317 hate crime offenses that were crimes against property (73.1 percent) were acts of destruction/damage/vandalism; the remaining crimes against property consisted of robbery, burglary, larceny-theft, motor vehicle theft, arson, and other crime.

- There were 53 offenses defined as crimes against society (e.g., drug or narcotic offenses or prostitution).

Table 1. Incidents, Offenses, Victims, and Known Offenders, by Bias Motivation, 2014

(Number.)

Bias motivation	Incidents	Offenses	Victims[1]	Known offenders[2]
Total	5,479	6,418	6,727	5,192
Single-bias incidents	5,462	6,385	6,681	5,176
Race	2,568	3,081	3,227	2,431
Anti-White	593	701	734	635
Anti-Black or African American..	1,621	1,955	2,022	1,442
Anti-American Indian or Alaska Native...	130	142	148	108
Anti-Asian	140	168	201	187
Anti-Native Hawaiian or Other Pacific Islander	3	4	4	3
Anti-Multiple races, group...	81	111	118	56
Religion	1,014	1,092	1,140	687
Anti-Jewish	609	635	648	380
Anti-Catholic..	64	67	70	35
Anti-Protestant..	25	28	28	12
Anti-Islamic (Muslim)	154	178	184	148
Anti-other religion	107	120	125	70
Anti-multiple religions, group	44	51	71	29
Anti-atheism/agnosticism/etc.	11	13	14	13
Sexual orientation...	1,017	1,178	1,248	1,154
Anti-gay (male)..	599	683	703	732
Anti-lesbian..	129	168	174	126
Anti-lesbian, gay, bisexual, or transgender (mixed group).........	241	278	305	249
Anti-heterosexual..	18	18	19	10
Anti-bisexual	30	31	47	37
Ethnicity...	648	790	821	668
Anti-Hispanic or Latino...	299	376	389	325
Anti-Not Hispanic or Latino[3]	349	414	432	343
Disability..	84	95	96	74
Anti-physical	23	26	26	25
Anti-mental	61	69	70	49
Gender	33	40	40	25
Anti-male..	10	12	12	10
Anti-female...	23	28	28	15
Gender Identity..	98	109	109	137
Anti-transgender..	58	69	69	104
Anti-gender nonconforming...	40	40	40	33
Multiple-bias incidents[4]	17	33	46	16

[1] The term victim may refer to a person, business, institution, or society as a whole.
[2] The term known offender does not imply that the identity of the suspect is known, but only that an attribute of the suspect has been identified, which distinguishes him/her from an unknown offender.
[3] The term anti-not Hispanic or Latino does not imply the victim was targeted because he/she was not of Hispanic origin, but it refers to other or unspecified ethnic biases that are not Hispanic or Latino.
[4] A multiple-bias incident is an incident in which one or more offense types are motivated by two or more biases.

Table 2. Incidents, Offenses, Victims, and Known Offenders, by Offense Type, 2014

(Number.)

Offense type	Incidents[1]	Offenses	Victims[2]	Known offenders[3]
Total	5,479	6,418	6,727	5,192
Crimes against persons.........................	3,303	4,048	4,048	3,925
Murder and nonnegligent manslaughter	4	4	4	5
Rape (revised definition)[4]..............................	9	9	9	10
Rape (legacy definition)[5]..............................	0	0	0	0
Aggravated assault	599	770	770	899
Simple assault	1,307	1,514	1,514	1,664
Intimidation	1,378	1,745	1,745	1,336
Other[6]..	6	6	6	11
Crimes against property	2,317	2,317	2,624	1,455
Robbery	122	122	138	255
Burglary	162	162	208	185
Larceny-theft	239	239	256	152
Motor vehicle theft	22	22	22	15
Arson	26	26	39	20
Destruction/damage/vandalism	1,694	1,694	1,907	792
Other[6]..	52	52	54	36
Crimes against society[6]........................	53	53	55	61

[1] The actual number of incidents is 5,479. However, the column figures will not add to the total because incidents may include more than one offense type, and these are counted in each appropriate offense type category.
[2] The term victim may refer to a person, business, institution, or society as a whole.
[3] The term known offender does not imply that the identity of the suspect is known, but only that an attribute of the suspect has been identified, which distinguishes him/her from an unknown offender. The actual number of known offenders is 5,814. However, the column figures will not add to the total because some offenders are responsible for more than one offense type, and are, therefore, counted more than once in this table.
[4] The figures shown in this row for the offense of rape include only those reported by law enforcement agencies that used the revised Uniform Crime Reporting (UCR) definition of rape.
[5] The figures shown in this row for the offense of rape include only those reported by law enforcement agencies that used the legacy UCR definition of rape.
[6] Includes additional offenses collected in the National Incident-Based Reporting System.

Table 3. Offenses, Known Offender's Race and Ethnicity, by Offense Type, 2014

(Number.)

Bias motivation	Total offenses	Known offender's race							Known offender's ethnicity[1]				Unknown offender
		White	Black or African American	American Indian or Alaska Native	Asian	Native Hawaiian or Other Pacific Islander	Group of multiple races	Unknown race	Hispanic or Latino	Not Hispanic or Latino	Group of multiple ethnicities	Unknown ethnicity	
Total	6,418	2,694	1,006	53	42	2	189	758	48	477	9	400	1,674
Crimes against persons	4,048	2,239	851	42	37	2	162	312	44	408	5	317	403
Murder and nonnegligent manslaughter ...	4	1	2	0	0	0	0	0	0	2	0	0	1
Rape (revised definition)[2]	9	7	2	0	0	0	0	0	1	1	0	1	0
Rape (legacy definition)[3]	0	0	0	0	0	0	0	0	0	0	0	0	0
Aggravated assault..........................	770	468	175	11	9	0	35	33	12	88	3	71	39
Simple assault	1,514	771	384	20	12	2	96	161	19	160	1	115	68
Intimidation...............................	1,745	988	287	11	15	0	31	118	12	156	1	130	295
Other[4]	6	4	1	0	1	0	0	0	0	1	0	0	0
Crimes against property	2,317	419	146	11	5	0	26	446	4	65	4	82	1,264
Robbery	122	42	44	5	1	0	6	7	0	13	2	7	17
Burglary	162	31	22	0	0	0	10	25	0	3	0	2	74
Larceny-theft................................	239	80	21	1	0	0	1	30	2	10	1	7	106
Motor vehicle theft..........................	22	6	2	0	0	0	0	2	0	0	0	0	12
Arson..	26	8	4	0	0	0	0	3	0	0	0	0	11
Destruction/damage/ vandalism................	1,694	234	46	5	4	0	8	374	2	36	1	64	1,023
Other[4]....................................	52	18	7	0	0	0	1	5	0	3	0	2	21
Crimes against society[4]	53	36	9	0	0	0	1	0	0	4	0	1	7

[1] The sum of offenses by the known offender's ethnicity does not equal the sum of offenses by the known offender's race because not all law enforcement agencies that report offender race data also report offender ethnicity data.
[2] The figures shown in the rape (revised definition) row include only those reported by law enforcement agencies that used the revised Uniform Crime Reporting (UCR) definition of rape.
[3] The figures shown in the rape (legacy definition) row include only those reported by law enforcement agencies that used the legacy UCR definition of rape.
[4] Includes additional offenses collected in the National Incident-Based Reporting System.

Table 4. Offenses, Offense Type, by Bias Motivation, 2014

(Number.)

Bias motivation	Total offenses	Crimes against persons						
		Murder and nonnegligent manslaughter	Rape (revised definition)[1]	Rape (legacy definition)[2]	Aggravated assault	Simple assault	Intimidation	Other[3]
Total	6,418	4	9	0	770	1,514	1,745	6
Single-bias incidents	6,385	4	9	0	767	1,507	1,738	6
Race	3,081	4	3	0	404	684	971	2
Anti-White	701	3	0	0	96	185	168	1
Anti-Black or African American	1,955	1	2	0	265	421	701	1
Anti-American Indian or Alaska Native	142	0	1	0	10	23	25	0
Anti-Asian	168	0	0	0	17	38	42	0
Anti-Native Hawaiian or Other Pacific Islander	4	0	0	0	0	0	2	0
Anti-Multiple races, group	111	0	0	0	16	17	33	0
Religion	1,092	0	0	0	37	129	194	1
Anti-Jewish	635	0	0	0	4	65	93	0
Anti-Catholic	67	0	0	0	0	4	5	0
Anti-Protestant	28	0	0	0	1	2	4	0
Anti-Islamic (Muslim)	178	0	0	0	20	36	64	0
Anti-other religion	120	0	0	0	9	13	15	0
Anti-multiple religions, group	51	0	0	0	0	8	11	1
Anti-atheism/agnosticism/etc.	13	0	0	0	3	1	2	0
Sexual orientation	1,178	0	1	0	171	397	306	1
Anti-gay (male)	683	0	0	0	108	259	166	1
Anti-lesbian	168	0	0	0	23	40	66	0
Anti-lesbian, gay, bisexual, or transgender (mixed group)	278	0	1	0	36	88	66	0
Anti-heterosexual	18	0	0	0	0	4	5	0
Anti-bisexual	31	0	0	0	4	6	3	0
Ethnicity	790	0	3	0	122	238	215	2
Anti-Hispanic or Latino	376	0	2	0	56	99	124	0
Anti-Not Hispanic or Latino[4]	414	0	1	0	66	139	91	2
Disability	95	0	1	0	5	24	22	0
Anti-physical	26	0	0	0	2	6	8	0
Anti-mental	69	0	1	0	3	18	14	0
Gender	40	0	1	0	5	8	14	0
Anti-male	12	0	0	0	1	1	8	0
Anti-female	28	0	1	0	4	7	6	0
Gender Identity	109	0	0	0	23	27	16	0
Anti-transgender	69	0	0	0	18	21	16	0
Anti-gender nonconforming	40	0	0	0	5	6	0	0
Multiple-bias incidents[5]	33	0	0	0	3	7	7	0

Table 4. Offenses, Offense Type, by Bias Motivation, 2014—*Continued*

(Number.)

Bias motivation	Crimes against property							Crimes against society[3]
	Robbery	Burglary	Larceny- theft	Motor vehicle theft	Arson	Destruction/ damage/ vandalism	Other[3]	
Total	122	162	239	22	26	1,694	52	53
Single-bias incidents	121	160	237	22	25	1,684	52	53
Race	56	91	123	16	7	667	25	28
Anti-White	30	27	70	3	1	84	13	20
Anti-Black or African American..........................	17	24	17	2	4	491	5	4
Anti-American Indian or Alaska Native...................	5	13	28	8	0	21	6	2
Anti-Asian	3	27	5	2	2	31	1	0
Anti-Native Hawaiian or Other Pacific Islander	0	0	1	0	0	1	0	0
Anti-Multiple races, group...............................	1	0	2	1	0	39	0	2
Religion	4	25	30	1	12	637	10	12
Anti-Jewish	1	8	5	0	2	451	2	4
Anti-Catholic...	0	3	8	0	3	40	2	2
Anti-Protestant..	0	3	4	0	0	12	1	1
Anti-Islamic (Muslim).......................................	3	2	2	0	1	45	2	3
Anti-other religion..	0	6	6	1	6	60	3	1
Anti-multiple religions, group	0	2	3	0	0	25	0	1
Anti-atheism/agnosticism/etc.	0	1	2	0	0	4	0	0
Sexual orientation..	36	20	20	1	2	216	3	4
Anti-gay (male)..	24	14	4	1	2	102	1	1
Anti-lesbian..	5	2	4	0	0	27	0	1
Anti-lesbian, gay, bisexual, or transgender (mixed group)........	7	3	3	0	0	74	0	0
Anti-heterosexual..	0	0	4	0	0	5	0	0
Anti-bisexual	0	1	5	0	0	8	2	2
Ethnicity..	19	13	28	2	4	138	2	4
Anti-Hispanic or Latino	14	8	4	1	2	63	1	2
Anti-Not Hispanic or Latino[4]	5	5	24	1	2	75	1	2
Disability...	1	5	12	0	0	14	9	2
Anti-physical	0	0	3	0	0	1	6	0
Anti-mental..	1	5	9	0	0	13	3	2
Gender	1	2	2	0	0	3	1	3
Anti-male	0	2	0	0	0	0	0	0
Anti-female	1	0	2	0	0	3	1	3
Gender Identity..	4	4	22	2	0	9	2	0
Anti-transgender	3	1	5	1	0	4	0	0
Anti-gender nonconforming...............................	1	3	17	1	0	5	2	0
Multiple-bias incidents[5]	1	2	2	0	1	10	0	0

[1] The figures shown in this column for the offense of rape include only those reported by law enforcement agencies that used the revised Uniform Crime Reporting (UCR) definition of rape.
[2] The figures shown in this column for the offense of rape include only those reported by law enforcement agencies that used the legacy UCR definition of rape.
[3] Includes additional offenses collected in the National Incident-Based Reporting System.
[4] The term anti-not Hispanic or Latino does not imply the victim was targeted because he/she was not of Hispanic origin, but it refers to other or unspecified ethnic biases that are not Hispanic or Latino.
[5] A multiple-bias incident is an incident in which one or more offense types are motivated by two or more biases.

Table 5. Offenses, Known Offender's Race and Ethnicity, by Bias Motivation, 2014

(Number.)

Bias motivation	Total offenses	Known offender's race							Known offender's ethnicity[1]				Unknown offender
		White	Black or African American	American Indian or Alaska Native	Asian	Native Hawaiian or Other Pacific Islander	Group of multiple races	Unknown race	Hispanic or Latino	Not Hispanic or Latino	Group of multiple ethnicities	Unknown ethnicity	
Total	6,418	2,694	1,006	53	42	2	189	758	48	477	9	400	1,674
Single-bias incidents	6,385	2,675	1,004	53	42	2	189	756	48	473	9	398	1,664
Race	3,081	1,487	472	24	18	0	83	240	8	230	2	213	757
Anti-White	701	145	337	10	4	0	18	45	1	54	0	46	142
Anti-Black or African American	1,955	1,165	57	10	9	0	52	166	6	148	1	145	496
Anti-American Indian or Alaska Native	142	56	23	3	0	0	5	9	0	6	1	6	46
Anti-Asian	168	75	37	1	5	0	2	16	1	9	0	12	32
Anti-Native Hawaiian or Other Pacific Islander	4	4	0	0	0	0	0	0	0	1	0	0	0
Anti-Multiple races, group	111	42	18	0	0	0	6	4	0	12	0	4	41
Religion	1,092	242	47	7	10	1	19	302	6	42	2	33	464
Anti-Jewish	635	87	20	0	4	1	10	231	0	11	0	5	282
Anti-Catholic	67	10	3	0	0	0	0	18	0	2	0	1	36
Anti-Protestant	28	8	3	0	0	0	0	2	0	4	0	0	15
Anti-Islamic (Muslim)	178	82	9	6	1	0	7	23	1	19	2	21	50
Anti-other religion	120	41	5	1	4	0	1	16	2	3	0	2	52
Anti-multiple religions, group	51	13	5	0	1	0	1	6	0	2	0	4	25
Anti-atheism/agnosticism/etc.	13	1	2	0	0	0	0	6	3	1	0	0	4
Sexual orientation	1,178	447	301	12	12	0	59	111	19	72	3	75	236
Anti-gay (male)	683	252	194	5	10	0	46	72	18	47	3	48	104
Anti-lesbian	168	66	43	4	1	0	6	9	0	13	0	11	39
Anti-lesbian, gay, bisexual, or transgender (mixed group)	278	110	57	1	1	0	5	28	1	11	0	14	76
Anti-heterosexual	18	6	1	1	0	0	0	1	0	0	0	0	9
Anti-bisexual	31	13	6	1	0	0	2	1	0	1	0	2	8
Ethnicity	790	399	123	10	1	1	22	87	8	91	1	54	147
Anti-Hispanic or Latino	376	204	47	7	0	1	11	36	5	36	1	26	70
Anti-Not Hispanic or Latino[2]	414	195	76	3	1	0	11	51	3	55	0	28	77
Disability	95	41	19	0	0	0	2	8	1	11	0	10	25
Anti-physical	26	11	7	0	0	0	1	5	0	5	0	3	2
Anti-mental	69	30	12	0	0	0	1	3	1	6	0	7	23
Gender	40	22	6	0	1	0	0	2	1	9	0	0	9
Anti-male	12	8	2	0	0	0	0	1	0	3	0	0	1
Anti-female	28	14	4	0	1	0	0	1	1	6	0	0	8
Gender Identity	109	37	36	0	0	0	4	6	5	18	1	13	26
Anti-transgender	69	20	29	0	0	0	3	6	4	14	0	9	11
Anti-gender nonconforming	40	17	7	0	0	0	1	0	1	4	1	4	15
Multiple-bias incidents[3]	33	19	2	0	0	0	0	2	0	4	0	2	10

[1] The total number of offenses by the known offender's ethnicity do not equal the total number of offenses by the known offender's race because not all law enforcement agencies that report offender race data also report offender ethnicity data.

[2] The term anti-not Hispanic or Latino does not imply the victim was targeted because he/she was not of Hispanic origin, but it refers to other or unspecified ethnic biases that are not Hispanic or Latino.

[3] A multiple-bias incident is an incident in which one or more offense types are motivated by two or more biases.

Table 6. Offenses, Victim Type, by Offense Type, 2014

(Number.)

Offense type	Total offenses	Victim type					
		Individual	Business/ financial institution	Government	Religious organization	Society/ public[1]	Other/ unknown/ multiple
Total	6,418	5,287	307	146	153	53	472
Crimes against persons[2]	4,048	4,048	NA	NA	NA	NA	NA
Crimes against property	2,317	1,239	307	146	153	0	472
Robbery	122	114	3	0	0	0	5
Burglary	162	116	15	2	8	0	21
Larceny-theft...	239	157	63	3	5	0	11
Motor vehicle theft.......................................	22	22	0	0	0	0	0
Arson	26	11	3	0	11	0	1
Destruction/damage/vandalism......................	1,694	776	218	138	129	0	433
Other[2]	52	43	5	3	0	0	1
Crimes against society[2]	53	NA	NA	NA	NA	53	NA

NA = Not available.
[1] The victim type *society/public* is collected only in the National Incident-Based Reporting System (NIBRS).
[2] Includes additional offenses collected in the NIBRS.

Table 7. Victims, Offense Type, by Bias Motivation, 2014

(Number.)

Bias motivation	Total victims[1]	Total number of adult victims[2]	Total number of juvenile victims[2]	Crimes against persons				
				Murder and nonnegligent manslaughter	Rape (revised definition)[3]	Rape (legacy definition)[4]	Aggravated assault	Simple assault
Total	6,727	2,096	254	4	9	0	770	1,514
Single-bias incidents	6,681	2,083	254	4	9	0	767	1,507
Race	3,227	1,103	123	4	3	0	404	684
Anti-White	734	334	24	3	0	0	96	185
Anti-Black or African American	2,022	616	87	1	2	0	265	421
Anti-American Indian or Alaska Native	148	64	5	0	1	0	10	23
Anti-Asian	201	58	2	0	0	0	17	38
Anti-Native Hawaiian or Other Pacific Islander	4	1	0	0	0	0	0	0
Anti-Multiple races, group	118	30	5	0	0	0	16	17
Religion	1,140	207	14	0	0	0	37	129
Anti-Jewish	648	58	5	0	0	0	4	65
Anti-Catholic	70	8	1	0	0	0	0	4
Anti-Protestant	28	8	0	0	0	0	1	2
Anti-Islamic (Muslim)	184	71	5	0	0	0	20	36
Anti-other religion	125	23	2	0	0	0	9	13
Anti-multiple religions, group	71	31	1	0	0	0	0	8
Anti-atheism/agnosticism/etc.	14	8	0	0	0	0	3	1
Sexual orientation	1,248	380	54	0	1	0	171	397
Anti-gay (male)	703	209	34	0	0	0	108	259
Anti-lesbian	174	50	10	0	0	0	23	40
Anti-lesbian, gay, bisexual, or transgender (mixed group)	305	106	9	0	1	0	36	88
Anti-heterosexual	19	5	0	0	0	0	0	4
Anti-bisexual	47	10	1	0	0	0	4	6
Ethnicity	821	282	52	0	3	0	122	238
Anti-Hispanic or Latino	389	123	27	0	2	0	56	99
Anti-Not Hispanic or Latino[6]	432	159	25	0	1	0	66	139
Disability	96	46	7	0	1	0	5	24
Anti-physical	26	15	3	0	0	0	2	6
Anti-mental	70	31	4	0	1	0	3	18
Gender	40	19	2	0	1	0	5	8
Anti-male	12	4	0	0	0	0	1	1
Anti-female	28	15	2	0	1	0	4	7
Gender Identity	109	46	2	0	0	0	23	27
Anti-transgender	69	29	1	0	0	0	18	21
Anti-gender nonconforming	40	17	1	0	0	0	5	6
Multiple-bias incidents[7]	46	13	0	0	0	0	3	7

Table 7. Victims, Offense Type, by Bias Motivation, 2014—*Continued*

(Number.)

Bias motivation	Intimidation	Other[5]	Crimes against property							Crimes against society[5]
			Robbery	Burglary	Larceny-theft	Motor vehicle theft	Arson	Destruction/ damage/ vandalism	Other[5]	
Total	1,745	6	138	208	256	22	39	1,907	54	55
Single-bias incidents	1,738	6	137	204	252	22	33	1,893	54	55
Race	971	2	63	123	133	16	15	753	26	30
Anti-White	168	1	32	30	76	3	9	97	14	20
Anti-Black or African American...............	701	1	19	28	17	2	4	550	5	6
Anti-American Indian or Alaska Native........	25	0	6	16	30	8	0	21	6	2
Anti-Asian	42	0	5	49	7	2	2	38	1	0
Anti-Native Hawaiian or Other Pacific Islander	2	0	0	0	1	0	0	1	0	0
Anti-Multiple races, group	33	0	1	0	2	1	0	46	0	2
Religion	194	1	4	27	31	1	12	681	11	12
Anti-Jewish	93	0	1	9	5	0	2	463	2	4
Anti-Catholic...................................	5	0	0	3	8	0	3	42	3	2
Anti-Protestant.................................	4	0	0	3	4	0	0	12	1	1
Anti-Islamic (Muslim)..........................	64	0	3	2	2	0	1	51	2	3
Anti-other religion	15	0	0	6	7	1	6	64	3	1
Anti-multiple religions, group	11	1	0	3	3	0	0	44	0	1
Anti-atheism/agnosticism/etc.	2	0	0	1	2	0	0	5	0	0
Sexual orientation	306	1	37	23	23	1	2	279	3	4
Anti-gay (male).................................	166	1	24	15	4	1	2	121	1	1
Anti-lesbian	66	0	5	2	6	0	0	31	0	1
Anti-lesbian, gay, bisexual, or transgender (mixed group)....	66	0	8	5	4	0	0	97	0	0
Anti-heterosexual	5	0	0	0	4	0	0	6	0	0
Anti-bisexual	3	0	0	1	5	0	0	24	2	2
Ethnicity..	215	2	27	19	29	2	4	154	2	4
Anti-Hispanic or Latino	124	0	21	12	4	1	2	65	1	2
Anti-Not Hispanic or Latino[6]	91	2	6	7	25	1	2	89	1	2
Disability...	22	0	1	6	12	0	0	14	9	2
Anti-physical	8	0	0	0	3	0	0	1	6	0
Anti-mental	14	0	1	6	9	0	0	13	3	2
Gender	14	0	1	2	2	0	0	3	1	3
Anti-male	8	0	0	2	0	0	0	0	0	0
Anti-female	6		1		2			3	1	3
Gender Identity.....................................	16	0	4	4	22	2	0	9	2	0
Anti-transgender	16	0	3	1	5	1	0	4	0	0
Anti-gender nonconforming.....................	0	0	1	3	17	1	0	5	2	0
Multiple-bias incidents[7]	7	0	1	4	4	0	6	14	0	0

Note: The aggregate of adult and juvenile individual victims does not equal the total number of victims because total victims include individuals, businesses, institutions, and society as a whole. In addition, the aggregate of adult and juvenile individual victims does not equal the aggregate of victims of crimes against persons because not all law enforcement agencies report the ages of individual victims.
[1] A victim can be an individual, a business, an institution, or society as a whole.
[2] The figures shown in this column are individual victims only.
[3] The figures shown in this column for the offense of rape include only those reported by law enforcement agencies that used the revised Uniform Crime Reporting (UCR) definition of rape.
[4] The figures shown in this column for the offense of rape include only those reported by law enforcement agencies that used the legacy UCR definition of rape.
[5] Includes additional offenses collected in the National Incident-Based Reporting System.
[6] The term anti-not Hispanic or Latino does not imply the victim was targeted because he/she was not of Hispanic origin, but it refers to other or unspecified ethnic biases that are not Hispanic or Latino.
[7] A multiple-bias incident is an incident in which one or more offense types are motivated by two or more biases.

Table 8. Incidents, Victim Type, by Bias Motivation, 2014

(Number.)

Bias motivation	Total incidents	Victim type					
		Individual	Business/financial institution	Government	Religious organization	Society/public[1]	Other/unknown/ multiple
Total	5,479	4,364	299	144	144	41	487
Single-bias incidents..........................	5,462	4,351	297	143	144	41	486
Race...	2,568	2,184	127	80	10	23	144
Religion..	1,014	477	97	36	122	9	273
Sexual Orientation........................	1,017	923	28	17	5	3	41
Ethnicity.......................................	648	575	32	8	6	1	26
Disability......................................	84	71	6	2	1	2	2
Gender..	33	30	0	0	0	3	0
Gender Identity	98	91	7	0	0	0	0
Multiple-bias incidents[2]	17	13	2	1	0	0	1

[1] The victim type society/public is collected only in the National Incident-Based Reporting System.
[2] A multiple-bias incident is an incident in which one or more offense types are motivated by two or more biases.

Table 9. Known Offenders,[1] by Known Offender's Race, Ethnicity, and Age, 2014

(Number.)

Race/ethnicity/age	Total
Race..	5,192
White	2,699
Black or African American..	1,203
American Indian or Alaska Native...	58
Asian	39
Native Hawaiian or Other Pacific Islander	2
Group of multiple races[2]	359
Unknown race	832
Ethnicity[3]..	975
Hispanic or Latino	63
Not Hispanic or Latino..	464
Group of multiple ethnicities[4]...	17
Unknown ethnicity..	431
Age[3]...	1,875
Total known offenders 18 and over..	1,519
Total known offenders under 18	356

[1] The term known offender does not imply that the identity of the suspect is known, but only that an attribute of the suspect has been identified, which distinguishes him/her from an unknown offender.
[2] The term group of multiple races is used to describe a group of offenders of varying races.
[3] The total number of known offenders by age and the total number of known offenders by ethnicity do not equal the total number of known offenders by race because not all law enforcement agencies report the age and/or ethnicity of the known offenders.
[4] The term group of multiple ethnicities is used to describe a group of offenders of varying ethnicities.

Table 10. Incidents, Bias Motivation, by Location, 2014

(Number.)

Location	Total incidents	Bias motivation							Multiple-bias incidents[1]
		Race	Religion	Sexual orientation	Ethnicity	Disability	Gender	Gender Identity	
Total	5,479	2,568	1,014	1,017	648	84	33	98	17
Abandoned/condemned structure	3	2	1	0	0	0	0	0	0
Air/bus/train terminal	68	39	5	13	8	2	0	1	0
Amusement park	2	2	0	0	0	0	0	0	0
Arena/stadium/fairgrounds/coliseum	2	1	0	1	0	0	0	0	0
Auto dealership new/used..................................	1	1	0	0	0	0	0	0	0
Bank/savings and loan......................................	21	11	1	3	2	1	0	3	0
Bar/nightclub	90	48	5	23	13	0	1	0	0
Camp/campground	1	1	0	0	0	0	0	0	0
Church/synagogue/temple/mosque	195	21	158	9	6	1	0	0	0
Commercial office building	70	28	17	12	12	1	0	0	0
Community center	6	1	1	3	0	0	0	1	0
Construction site..	10	4	1	1	4	0	0	0	0
Convenience store	73	35	5	11	21	0	0	1	0
Daycare facility..	4	1	1	0	2	0	0	0	0
Department/discount store................................	58	36	2	8	6	1	2	3	0
Dock/wharf/freight/modal terminal	3	2	0	0	1	0	0	0	0
Drug store/doctor's office/hospital.....................	70	41	8	5	11	4	1	0	0
Farm facility	1	1	0	0	0	0	0	0	0
Field/woods	36	20	6	5	5	0	0	0	0
Government/public building................................	96	57	15	12	9	2	0	1	0
Grocery/supermarket	52	24	9	7	9	1	0	2	0
Highway/road/alley/street/sidewalk....................	974	493	96	231	107	11	6	26	4
Hotel/motel/etc...	35	19	1	7	6	0	1	1	0
Industrial site	6	6	0	0	0	0	0	0	0
Jail/prison/penitentiary/corrections facility..........	53	29	1	13	9	0	0	1	0
Lake/waterway/beach	10	4	1	3	2	0	0	0	0
Liquor store	8	4	2	1	1	0	0	0	0
Park/playground..	70	34	8	17	10	0	0	1	0
Parking/drop lot/garage	343	186	37	59	49	3	2	6	1
Rental storage facility.......................................	3	3	0	0	0	0	0	0	0
Residence/home...	1,732	828	249	318	239	36	14	41	7
Rest area..	6	1	1	2	2	0	0	0	0
Restaurant..	114	58	10	25	16	2	2	0	1
School/college[2]	165	78	46	27	11	1	2	0	0
School—college/university.................................	123	73	23	21	0	2	2	2	0
School—elementary/secondary	184	94	27	33	20	6	0	2	2
Service/gas station	62	35	5	9	10	1	0	1	1
Shelter—mission/homeless................................	5	4	0	1	0	0	0	0	0
Shopping mall...	15	5	6	2	1	1	0	0	0
Specialty store (TV, fur, etc.)	48	25	8	7	6	0	0	2	0
Other/unknown	654	210	258	126	48	8	0	3	1
Multiple locations	7	3	0	2	2	0	0	0	0

[1] A multiple-bias incident is an incident in which one or more offense types are motivated by two or more biases.
[2] The location designation School/college has been retained for agencies that have not updated their records management systems to include the new location designations of School—college/university and School—elementary/secondary, which allow for more specificity in reporting.

Table 11. Offenses, Offense Type, by Participating State, 2014

(Number.)

State	Total offenses	Crimes against persons							Crimes against property							Crimes against society[3]
		Murder and nonnegligent manslaughter	Rape (revised definition)[1]	Rape (legacy definition)[2]	Aggravated assault	Simple assault	Intimidation	Other[3]	Robbery	Burglary	Larceny-theft	Motor vehicle theft	Arson	Destruction/ damage/ vandalism	Other[3]	
Total	6,418	4	9	0	770	1,514	1,745	6	122	162	239	22	26	1,694	52	53
Alabama	10	0	0		0	2	5	0	0	1	0	0	0	2	0	0
Alaska....................	7	0	0		1	4	0	0	1	0	0	0	0	1	0	0
Arizona..................	304	0	0		45	70	104	1	3	1	3	0	0	76	0	1
Arkansas................	16	0	0		6	2	7	0	0	0	0	0	0	1	0	0
California................	943	1	0	0	187	202	237	0	28	10	7	0	5	266	0	0
Colorado	129	0	2		34	22	39	0	4	1	0	0	0	23	2	2
Connecticut............	144	0	0		3	20	66	0	3	1	10	2	0	38	0	1
Delaware	18	0	0		2	3	7	1	0	0	0	0	0	5	0	0
District of Columbia ..	87	0	1		18	31	19	0	2	0	0	0	0	16	0	0
Florida	72	1	0		15	23	6	0	1	2	2	0	0	22	0	0
Georgia..................	50	0		0	3	10	32	0	2	0	0	0	0	3	0	0
Idaho.....................	40	0	0		14	11	11	0	1	0	0	0	0	3	0	0
Illinois	136	0	0		30	31	40	0	2	1	4	0	0	28	0	0
Indiana	60	1	2	0	3	15	21	0	0	1	0	0	0	15	0	2
Iowa	12	0	0		0	5	1	0	1	1	0	0	0	4	0	0
Kansas	86	0	1		8	19	21	0	0	3	7	1	0	25	1	0
Kentucky	199	0	0		13	35	54	0	6	16	11	1	2	42	5	14
Louisiana	11	0	0		0	7	2	0	0	0	1	0	0	1	0	0
Maine.....................	34	0	0	0	4	7	16	0	0	0	1	0	0	6	0	0
Maryland	18	0		0	4	5	2	0	2	0	1	0	0	4	0	0
Massachusetts	418	0	0	0	45	80	106	1	7	11	32	2	1	116	11	6
Michigan	354	0	0		33	78	129	0	4	28	8	1	3	66	3	1
Minnesota	117	0	0		13	27	43	0	3	1	0	0	0	30	0	0
Mississippi..............	1	0	0	0	0	1	0	0	0	0	0	0	0	0	0	0
Missouri.................	106	0	0		27	18	30	0	1	2	0	0	0	27	0	1
Montana.................	43	0	0		11	9	3	0	0	1	8	1	0	8	2	0
Nebraska	61	0	0	0	3	15	21	0	1	1	0	0	0	19	1	0
Nevada	29	0	0		6	13	1	0	5	0	0	0	0	4	0	0
New Hampshire	22	0	0		0	5	10	0	0	1	0	0	0	5	1	0
New Jersey..............	347	0		0	5	11	190	0	2	3	1	0	0	135	0	0
New Mexico.............	13	0		0	4	2	3	0	0	1	0	0	1	2	0	0
New York................	558	0	0	0	33	221	1	0	0	20	10	0	4	269	0	0
North Carolina.........	186	0		0	21	42	65	0	2	2	2	1	0	51	0	0
North Dakota...........	51	0	0		5	19	17	0	0	0	2	1	0	7	0	0
Ohio	474	0	0		31	89	172	0	17	15	44	7	0	91	8	0
Oklahoma...............	37	0	0		3	8	15	0	0	0	1	0	2	8	0	0
Oregon...................	38	0	0	0	3	9	14	0	0	0	2	0	0	9	0	1
Pennsylvania	58	0	0		5	11	25	0	1	1	6	0	3	6	0	0
Rhode Island	5	0	0		0	1	0	0	0	2	0	0	0	2	0	0
South Carolina.........	60	0	0		12	16	7	2	1	2	2	0	0	10	0	8
South Dakota...........	18	0	0		2	9	2	0	0	0	0	0	0	5	0	0
Tennessee	220	1	1		35	79	33	1	4	2	9	1	2	50	1	1
Texas	165	0	0		24	60	34	0	6	1	2	0	0	38	0	0
Utah	58	0	1	0	0	7	1	0	0	5	8	1	0	20	4	11
Vermont	15	0	0		0	3	0	0	0	1	4	0	0	7	0	0
Virginia	131	0	0		8	43	26	0	3	2	5	0	0	44	0	0
Washington	367	0	1	0	44	89	90	0	8	19	36	3	1	66	10	0
West Virginia	28	0	0		1	7	1	0	0	1	7	0	1	8	1	1
Wisconsin	62	0	0	0	6	18	16	0	1	2	3	0	1	10	2	3
Wyoming.................	0	0	0		0	0	0	0	0	0	0	0	0	0	0	0

[1] The figures shown in this column for the offense of rape include only those reported by law enforcement agencies that used the revised Uniform Crime Reporting (UCR) definition of rape.
[2] The figures shown in this column for the offense of rape include only those reported by law enforcement agencies that used the legacy UCR definition of rape.
[3] Includes additional offenses collected in the National Incident-Based Reporting System.

Table 12. Agency Hate Crime Reporting, by Participating State and Territory, 2014

(Number.)

State	Number of participating agencies	Population covered	Agencies submitting incident reports	Total number of incidents reported
Total	15,494	297,926,030	1,666	5,479
Alabama..	39	794,907	4	9
Alaska..	33	732,371	1	6
Arizona..	99	6,433,584	22	265
Arkansas..	270	2,661,818	5	8
California..	743	38,802,500	208	759
Colorado	231	5,268,592	40	96
Connecticut..	95	3,375,662	54	123
Delaware	60	935,614	9	13
District of Columbia	2	658,893	2	70
Florida..	505	19,794,279	37	65
Georgia	479	8,204,655	4	41
Guam[1]...	1		0	0
Idaho...	112	1,634,011	10	25
Illinois	693	12,029,618	48	109
Indiana	348	6,093,574	15	50
Iowa..	221	2,974,604	10	11
Kansas	359	2,843,179	37	73
Kentucky	399	4,386,536	84	163
Louisiana	86	2,706,155	6	9
Maine	184	1,330,089	15	28
Maryland	154	5,976,407	9	16
Massachusetts	315	6,485,973	90	375
Michigan	607	9,732,430	119	311
Minnesota	292	5,287,138	27	98
Mississippi..	75	1,349,655	1	1
Missouri...	630	6,061,406	25	76
Montana...	98	992,702	12	30
Nebraska	216	1,763,318	7	47
Nevada	51	2,834,483	4	24
New Hampshire	158	1,238,190	11	14
New Jersey...	509	8,936,591	126	336
New Mexico..	7	717,010	3	13
New York..	572	19,652,379	59	545
North Carolina..	524	9,942,854	40	140
North Dakota..	111	738,176	16	40
Ohio	606	9,711,237	105	403
Oklahoma...	333	3,878,051	18	33
Oregon	92	1,526,458	15	26
Pennsylvania	1,457	12,587,318	22	50
Rhode Island...	48	1,054,130	4	4
South Carolina..	430	4,813,088	32	49
South Dakota..	121	776,484	12	18
Tennessee	465	6,519,911	53	194
Texas...	1,033	26,922,758	57	145
Utah	134	2,926,391	23	50
Vermont	91	626,306	10	15
Virginia	414	8,324,943	50	118
U.S. Virgin Islands[1]	1		0	0
Washington	262	7,051,748	67	308
West Virginia	269	1,648,198	16	26
Wisconsin	397	5,610,210	22	51
Wyoming..	63	579,446	0	0

[1] The 2014 population estimates were not available at the time of publication.

Table 13. Hate Crime Incidents Per Bias Motivation and Quarter, by Selected State and Agency, 2014

(Number.)

State/agency	Number of incidents per bias motivation							Number of incidents per quarter				Population[1]
	Race	Religion	Sexual orientation	Ethnicity	Disability	Gender	Gender identity	1st quarter	2nd quarter	3rd quarter	4th quarter	
ALABAMA............................												
Total	7	1	0	1	0	0	0					
Cities	7	1	0	1	0	0	0					
Fairfield..............................	1	0	0	0	0	0	0		1			10,913
Hoover................................	0	1	0	1	0	0	0	1	0	0	1	84,843
Prattville.............................	4	0	0	0	0	0	0		3	1		35,530
Sylacauga	2	0	0	0	0	0	0			1	1	12,722
ALASKA..............................												
Total	5	0	1	0	0	0	0					
Cities	5	0	1	0	0	0	0					
Anchorage..........................	5	0	1	0	0	0	0	0	0	4	2	301,306
ARIZONA............................												
Total	124	38	55	44	4	0	0					
Cities	117	35	47	44	3	0	0					
Apache Junction	0	0	0	1	0	0	0	0	0	0	1	37,274
Avondale	1	1	0	1	0	0	0	1	1	0	1	79,472
Chandler.............................	1	0	0	0	0	0	0	1	0	0	0	252,369
Cottonwood........................	1	0	0	0	0	0	0	1	0	0	0	11,490
El Mirage	1	0	0	0	0	0	0	0	1	0	0	33,307
Flagstaff.............................	0	0	1	0	0	0	0	0	0	0	1	69,490
Gilbert................................	2	0	0	0	0	0	0	1	0	1	0	235,430
Glendale.............................	4	2	2	1	0	0	0	2	3	3	1	236,780
Goodyear............................	1	0	0	0	0	0	0	1	0	0	0	74,826
Kingman.............................	0	1	1	0	0	0	0	0	1	1	0	28,526
Mesa..................................	4	1	3	2	0	0	0	0	3	1	6	462,092
Oro Valley	0	1	0	0	0	0	0	0	1	0	0	41,764
Phoenix..............................	91	19	35	35	3	0	0	37	41	47	58	1,529,852
Scottsdale...........................	2	1	1	1	0	0	0	2	0	1	2	229,325
Tempe................................	1	1	0	0	0	0	0	1	0	0	1	169,812
Tucson................................	4	2	3	0	0	0	0	1	4	3	1	527,328
Yuma..................................	4	6	1	3	0	0	0	5	7	2	0	92,075
Universities and Colleges												
Northern Arizona University	2	1	7	0	0	0	0	8	0	1	1	26,594
Metropolitan Counties	3	3	1	1	0	0	0					
Maricopa	3	0	1	0	0	0	0	1	0	2	1	
Pinal..................................	0	1	0	0	0	0	0	0	1	0	0	
Yavapai	1	0	0	0	0	0	0	0		1	0	
Yuma..................................	1	1	0	0	1	0	0	1	1	1	0	
ARKANSAS.......................................												
Total	5	1	1	1	0	0	0					
Cities	3	1	1	0	0	0	0					
Fort Smith...........................	3	0	1	0	0	0	0	1	1	2	0	87,989
Rogers	0	1	0	0	0	0	0	0	1	0	0	61,105
Universities and Colleges	1	0	0	0	0	0	0					
University of Arkansas, Fayetteville	1	0	0	0	0	0	0	0	0	1	0	25,341
Metropolitan Counties	1	0	0	0	0	0	0					
Pulaski...............................	1	0	0	0	0	0	0	0	0	1	0	
Nonmetropolitan Counties..............	0	0	0	1	0	0	0					
Baxter................................	0	0	0	1	0	0	0	0	0	1	0	
CALIFORNIA....................................												
Total	305	128	187	111	4	2	22					
Cities	291	117	166	87	1	0	6					
Adelanto.............................	1	0	0	1	0	0	0	0	1	0	1	31,213
Alameda	3	0	1	0	0	0	0	2	2	0	0	77,048
Alhambra............................	1	0	0	0	0	0	0	0	0	1	0	84,931
Antioch..............................	1	0	1	1	0	0	2	0	2	2	1	108,223

(Number.)

State/agency	Number of incidents per bias motivation							Number of incidents per quarter				Population[1]
	Race	Religion	Sexual orientation	Ethnicity	Disability	Gender	Gender identity	1st quarter	2nd quarter	3rd quarter	4th quarter	
Apple Valley	2	0	0	0	0	0	0	1	1	0	0	71,329
Arcata	1	0	0	0	0	0	0	0	0	0	1	17,748
Arvin	0	0	1	0	0	0	0	0	1	0	0	20,541
Azusa	0	1	0	0	0	0	0	0	0	1	0	48,224
Bakersfield	4	0	1	1	0	0	0	1	0	2	3	367,406
Barstow	1	0	0	0	0	0	0	1	0	0	0	23,349
Berkeley	0	2	0	1	0	0	0	2	0	1	0	117,753
Beverly Hills[2]	0	1	0	0	0	0	0	0	0	1	0	34,788
Brea	1	0	0	0	0	0	0	0	0	1	0	41,359
Brentwood	2	0	0	0	0	0	0	1	0	1	0	55,826
Buellton	0	1	0	0	0	0	0	0	0	1	0	4,997
Buena Park	0	0	1	1	0	0	0	0	2	0	0	83,414
Burbank	0	1	0	0	0	0	0	0	1	0	0	105,041
Camarillo	2	0	1	0	0	0	0	1	2	0	0	66,272
Carson	0	1	0	1	0	0	0	0	0	2	0	92,838
Central Marin	0	0	0	1	0	0	0	0	1	0	0	34,450
Cerritos	0	0	1	0	0	0	0	1	0	0	0	49,867
Chico	2	1	0	0	0	0	0	1	0	2	0	88,562
Chino	1	0	0	2	0	0	0	1	0	1	1	81,600
Chino Hills	1	0	0	0	0	0	0	0	1	0	0	76,972
Chula Vista	2	0	1	0	0	0	0	3	0	0	0	259,894
City of Angels	0	1	0	0	0	0	0	0	1	0	0	3,716
Claremont	0	4	0	1	0	0	0	1	0	2	2	36,042
Clearlake	1	0	0	0	0	0	0	0	1	0	0	14,914
Coalinga	1	0	0	0	0	0	0	0	0	1	0	16,445
Colusa	0	0	0	1	0	0	0	0	0	1	0	5,942
Compton	3	0	0	0	0	0	0	0	2	1	0	98,224
Cupertino	0	1	0	0	0	0	0	1	0	0	0	60,564
Daly City[2]	1	0	0	1	0	0	0	0	0	1	1	105,628
Dana Point	2	1	0	0	0	0	0	1	0	2	0	34,244
Davis	1	1	0	0	0	0	0	0	0	2	0	66,360
Dublin	2	0	0	0	0	0	0	0	0	2	0	53,795
El Cerrito	1	0	0	7	0	0	0	5	1	2	0	24,485
El Monte	4	1	0	0	0	0	0	2	0	1	2	116,220
Escondido	3	1	0	0	0	0	0	0	2	2	0	149,839
Eureka	1	0	0	0	0	0	0	1	0	0	0	26,843
Fairfield	0	0	0	1	0	0	0	0	0	0	1	110,300
Fontana	1	0	0	2	0	0	0	1	0	0	2	204,532
Fort Bragg	0	1	0	0	0	0	0	0	1	0	0	7,245
Fremont	0	1	0	0	0	0	0	1	0	0	0	227,575
Fresno	6	1	3	2	0	0	0	4	2	2	4	513,187
Fullerton	0	0	1	0	0	0	0	0	1	0	0	139,895
Galt	1	1	0	0	0	0	0	1	1	0	0	24,671
Gardena	1	0	0	0	0	0	0	0	0	1	0	60,233
Garden Grove	0	0	2	0	0	0	0	0	1	0	1	176,106
Gilroy	0	0	2	0	0	0	0	1	0	1	0	52,415
Glendale	0	2	0	0	0	0	0	1	0	1	0	197,079
Goleta	0	1	0	1	0	0	0	0	1	1	0	30,669
Grass Valley	0	0	0	1	0	0	0	0	0	1	0	12,777
Grover Beach	1	0	0	0	0	0	0	0	0	1	0	13,497
Hawaiian Gardens	1	0	0	0	0	0	0	0	1	0	0	14,490
Hayward	2	0	1	0	0	0	0	0	1	0	2	153,319
Healdsburg	0	1	0	0	0	0	0	0	0	1	0	11,569
Hemet	1	0	0	0	0	0	0	0	0	1	0	82,412
Hercules	1	0	0	0	0	0	0	0	0	1	0	25,026
Hesperia	1	0	0	0	0	0	0	0	0	1	0	92,592
Highland	2	0	1	0	0	0	0	0	1	1	1	54,559
Huntington Beach	1	1	0	1	0	0	0	1	0	2	0	199,152
Imperial Beach	0	1	0	0	0	0	0	1	0	0	0	27,234
Inglewood	0	0	1	0	0	0	0	0	0	0	1	111,997
Ione	1	0	0	0	0	0	0	1	0	0	0	6,773
Irvine	3	1	0	0	0	0	0	0	1	2	1	242,971
Laguna Niguel	0	1	0	0	0	0	0	0	0	1	0	65,033
Lake Forest	1	0	0	0	0	0	1	1	0	0	1	79,748
Lancaster	1	1	1	1	1	0	0	1	4	0	0	160,190
La Puente	1	0	0	0	0	0	0	0	0	1	0	40,583
La Quinta	1	0	0	1	0	0	0	0	1	1	0	39,753
Livermore	0	0	1	2	0	0	0	3	0	0	0	86,147
Lomita	0	1	0	0	0	0	0	0	0	0	1	20,677
Long Beach	4	2	4	0	0	0	0	2	4	2	2	471,123
Los Angeles	44	41	41	14	2	0	10	26	35	47	44	3,906,772

(Number.)

State/agency	Number of incidents per bias motivation							Number of incidents per quarter				Population[1]
	Race	Religion	Sexual orientation	Ethnicity	Disability	Gender	Gender identity	1st quarter	2nd quarter	3rd quarter	4th quarter	
Los Gatos	2	0	0	1	0	1	0	0	1	2	1	30,614
Lynwood	1	1	0	0	0	0	1	1	1	1	0	71,812
Malibu	1	0	0	0	0	0	0	0	0	0	1	12,912
Mammoth Lakes	1	0	0	1	0	0	0	0	2	0	0	8,033
Manteca	0	1	0	0	0	0	0	1	0	0	0	73,055
Marina	1	0	0	1	0	0	0	2	0	0	0	20,530
Menifee	1	0	0	0	0	0	0	0	1	0	0	84,843
Merced	0	0	1	0	0	0	0	0	1	0	0	81,603
Modesto	2	0	1	1	0	0	0	1	1	1	1	205,820
Monrovia	1	0	0	0	0	0	0	0	1	0	0	37,225
Montclair	3	0	0	0	0	0	0	1	1	1	0	38,347
Monterey	1	0	1	0	0	0	0	0	0	2	0	28,512
Monterey Park	1	0	0	0	0	0	0	0	0	1	0	61,284
Moorpark	1	0	0	0	0	0	0	1	0	0	0	35,299
Moreno Valley	4	0	0	0	0	0	0	0	0	0	4	202,911
Murrieta	0	0	1	0	0	0	0	0	0	0	1	108,376
National City	0	0	1	0	0	0	0	1	0	0	0	60,130
Newark	2	0	0	0	0	0	0	0	2	0	0	44,467
Newport Beach	0	1	1	0	0	0	0	1	0	1	0	87,759
Norco	0	0	0	1	0	0	0	0	1	0	0	26,933
Norwalk	11	0	0	0	0	0	0	1	6	2	2	106,838
Oakland	6	2	5	1	0	0	0	2	4	4	4	409,994
Oceanside	2	0	0	2	0	0	0	2	1	0	1	174,102
Orange	1	2	0	0	0	0	0	1	1	0	1	140,767
Oxnard	2	1	0	1	0	0	0	1	2	0	1	204,159
Palmdale	2	0	0	1	0	0	0	0	2	0	1	158,210
Palm Springs	0	2	1	0	0	0	0	1	2	0	0	46,665
Palo Alto	2	1	0	0	0	0	0	0	2	1	0	67,169
Paramount	0	0	2	0	0	0	0	0	2	0	0	55,194
Pasadena	3	0	1	0	0	0	0	0	0	0	4	140,373
Paso Robles	2	0	0	0	0	0	0	1	0	1	0	31,117
Pico Rivera	0	0	0	1	0	0	0	0	1	0	0	63,970
Piedmont	0	1	0	0	0	0	0	0	0	1	0	11,170
Pittsburg	0	1	0	0	0	0	0	1	0	0	0	67,509
Placentia	1	0	0	1	0	0	0	0	0	1	1	52,513
Pomona	1	0	1	0	0	0	0	0	2	0	0	151,899
Poway	0	1	0	0	0	0	0	0	0	0	1	49,786
Rancho Cucamonga	2	0	0	0	0	0	0	0	0	0	2	172,694
Red Bluff	2	0	1	0	0	0	0	1	0	1	1	14,103
Redding	1	1	2	0	0	0	0	0	2	1	1	91,426
Redlands	0	0	2	1	0	0	0	1	0	1	1	70,295
Redondo Beach	3	0	1	0	0	0	0	1	3	0	0	68,075
Ripon[2]	1	0	1	0	0	0	0	1	1	0	0	14,859
Riverside	8	0	2	3	0	0	0	4	4	2	3	319,453
Roseville	1	1	1	0	0	0	0	1	1	0	1	128,997
Sacramento	1	0	5	1	0	0	0	1	2	2	2	482,767
Salinas	0	0	1	0	0	0	0	0	1	0	0	156,908
San Bernardino	1	0	0	0	0	0	0	1	0	0	0	214,588
San Clemente	0	1	0	1	0	0	0	0	0	2	0	65,397
San Diego	8	5	13	8	0	0	3	7	13	11	6	1,368,690
San Dimas	1	0	0	0	0	0	0	0	0	0	1	33,953
San Francisco	2	4	11	3	0	0	2	7	5	5	5	850,294
San Jose	5	1	1	4	0	0	0	2	1	6	2	1,009,679
San Leandro	0	0	1	0	0	0	1	0	2	0	0	88,690
San Luis Obispo	1	0	0	0	0	0	0	0	0	1	0	46,672
San Marcos	0	0	1	0	0	0	0	0	0	1	0	90,799
San Mateo	2	0	0	0	0	0	0	1	1	0	0	102,082
San Rafael	0	0	1	1	0	0	0	1	0	1	0	59,292
San Ramon	0	0	1	0	0	0	0	0	1	0	0	75,049
Santa Ana	4	1	1	1	0	0	0	1	2	2	2	336,462
Santa Clarita	2	1	1	4	0	0	0	1	5	1	1	206,930
Santa Cruz	4	1	2	0	1	0	0	4	4	0	0	63,440
Santa Monica	0	1	0	0	0	0	0	0	0	1	0	93,151
Santee	0	0	0	1	0	0	0	0	0	1	0	56,737
Sierra Madre	1	0	0	0	0	0	0	0	1	0	0	11,090
Simi Valley	3	1	0	0	0	0	0	1	1	1	1	126,604
Sonora	1	1	0	0	0	0	0	1	0	1	0	4,786
South Gate	0	0	1	0	0	0	0	0	0	1	0	95,981
Stockton	1	1	0	1	0	0	0	1	1	1	0	299,519
Sunnyvale	0	1	0	0	0	0	0	1	0	0	0	149,384

Table 13. Hate Crime Incidents Per Bias Motivation and Quarter, by Selected State and Agency, 2014—*Continued*

(Number.)

State/agency	Number of incidents per bias motivation							Number of incidents per quarter				Population[1]
	Race	Religion	Sexual orientation	Ethnicity	Disability	Gender	Gender identity	1st quarter	2nd quarter	3rd quarter	4th quarter	
Taft	0	1	0	0	0	0	0	0	0	1	0	8,895
Tehachapi	1	0	0	0	0	0	0	0	0	1	0	12,997
Temple City	1	0	1	0	0	0	0	1	1	0	0	36,272
Torrance	0	0	1	0	0	0	0	0	0	1	0	147,971
Tracy	1	0	0	1	0	0	0	0	1	1	0	85,078
Turlock	0	0	1	0	0	0	0	0	0	1	0	70,786
Twentynine Palms	0	0	0	0	0	0	1	0	1	0	0	25,936
Ukiah	1	0	0	0	0	0	0	0	0	0	1	15,836
Union City	3	0	0	0	0	0	0	2	1	0	0	73,268
Vacaville	1	0	0	0	0	0	0	0	0	0	1	94,701
Ventura	1	0	0	0	0	0	0	0	0	0	1	109,246
Victorville	1	1	1	0	0	0	0	0	0	1	2	122,316
Visalia	1	0	1	0	0	0	0	1	1	0	0	128,488
Vista	2	1	0	0	0	0	0	1	1	0	1	97,651
Walnut Creek	1	1	0	0	0	0	0	0	0	0	2	67,555
Waterford	0	0	0	1	0	0	0	0	1	0	0	8,646
West Covina	1	0	0	1	0	0	0	1	0	0	1	108,136
West Hollywood	1	1	4	1	0	0	0	1	3	1	2	35,507
Windsor	0	0	1	0	0	0	0	0	0	0	1	27,350
Yorba Linda	0	1	0	0	0	0	0	1	0	0	0	67,702
Yuba City	0	0	0	1	0	0	0	0	0	1	0	65,525
Yucaipa	0	0	1	0	0	0	0	0	1	0	0	52,794
Yucca Valley	1	0	0	0	0	0	0	0	0	1	0	21,228
Universities and Colleges	8	2	6	2	0	0	0					
California State Polytechnic University, San Luis Obispo	0	0	0	1	0	0	0	0	0	0	1	19,703
California State University												
East Bay	0	0	1	0	0	0	0	0	0	1	0	14,526
San Jose	2	0	0	0	0	0	0	0	0	2	0	31,278
Riverside Community College	1	0	0	0	0	0	0	1	0	0	0	36,233
University of California												
Berkeley	2	2	4	0	0	0	0	2	4	2	0	36,198
Davis	2	0	1	0	0	0	0	0	2	1	0	33,307
San Diego	1	0	0	1	0	0	0	0	0	2	0	29,517
Metropolitan Counties	30	9	25	12	0	1	1					
Fresno	0	0	0	1	0	0	0	1	0	0	0	
Imperial	0	0	1	0	0	0	0	0	1	0	0	
Los Angeles	7	3	3	5	0	0	0	5	7	5	1	
Marin	0	1	0	0	0	0	0	0	1	0	0	
Merced	0	0	1	0	0	0	0	0	1	0	0	
Orange	1	0	1	0	0	0	0	1	1	0	0	
Riverside	2	0	1	0	0	0	0	0	1	2	0	
Sacramento	1	0	3	0	0	1	1	2	2	2	0	
San Bernardino	2	0	2	0	0	0	0	1	0	2	1	
San Diego	10	1	4	2	0	0	0	3	6	5	3	
San Mateo	1	0	0	0	0	0	0	1	0	0	0	
Santa Barbara	1	1	0	0	0	0	0	0	1	1	0	
Santa Clara	1	0	3	0	0	0	0	0	1	1	2	
Santa Cruz	0	1	2	4	0	0	0	0	4	2	1	
Shasta	1	0	0	0	0	0	0	1	0	0	0	
Sonoma	0	0	1	0	0	0	0	0	1	0	0	
Stanislaus	0	0	1	0	0	0	0	0	0	1	0	
Ventura	0	2	1	0	0	0	0	1	1	1	0	
Yolo	0	0	1	0	0	0	0	1	0	0	0	
Yuba[2]	3	0	0	0	0	0	0	2	0	0	1	
Nonmetropolitan Counties												
Amador	0	0	1	0	0	0	0	1	0	0	0	
Calaveras	2	0	0	0	0	0	0	1	0	0	1	
Glenn	1	0	0	0	0	0	0	1	0	0	0	
Humboldt	0	0	1	0	0	0	0	0	1	0	0	
Tuolumne	2	0	0	0	0	0	0	0	0	1	1	
State Police Agencies	1	0	0	0	0	0	0					
Highway Patrol, San Diego County	1	0	0	0	0	0	0	0	0	1	0	
Other Agencies	14	1	11	6	0	0	0					

Table 13. Hate Crime Incidents Per Bias Motivation and Quarter, by Selected State and Agency, 2014—*Continued*

(Number.)

State/agency	Number of incidents per bias motivation							Number of incidents per quarter				Population[1]
	Race	Religion	Sexual orientation	Ethnicity	Disability	Gender	Gender identity	1st quarter	2nd quarter	3rd quarter	4th quarter	
Department of Parks and Recreation, San Diego Coast	1	0	0	0	0	0	0	0	1	0	0	
Los Angeles County Metropolitan Transportation Authority	1	0	0	0	0	0	0	0	0	0	1	
Los Angeles Transportation Services Bureau	6	0	5	4	0	0	0	1	3	6	5	
Port of San Diego Harbor	1	0	1	1	0	0	0	2	0	0	1	
San Francisco Bay Area Rapid Transit												
Alameda County	2	0	4	0	0	0	0	0	4	1	1	
Contra Costa County	1	1	1	1	0	0	0	1	2	1	0	
San Francisco County	2	0	0	0	0	0	0	1	1	0	0	
COLORADO												
Total	38	11	26	16	5	0	0					
Cities	38	14	32	12	1	0	0					
Arvada	1	0	0	0	0	0	0	0	1	0	0	113,008
Aurora	1	1	2	0	0	0	0	1	1	2	0	350,948
Brighton	0	0	1	0	0	0	0	0	0	0	1	36,185
Canon City	1	0	0	0	0	0	0	1	0	0	0	16,291
Castle Rock	0	1	0	1	0	0	0	0	0	1	1	54,253
Centennial	1	2	0	0	0	0	0	0	0	2	1	107,485
Colorado Springs	5	0	1	1	0	0	0	1	3	3	0	444,949
Commerce City	0	0	0	1	0	0	0	0	1	0	0	50,754
Denver	6	0	7	3	0	0	0	1	4	7	4	665,353
Durango	0	1	2	0	0	0	0	0	3	0	0	17,710
Fort Collins	3	0	0	0	0	0	0	0	1	2	0	154,015
Fort Morgan	1	0	0	1	0	0	0	2	0	0	0	11,422
Glendale	0	0	1	0	0	0	0	1	0	0	0	4,558
Glenwood Springs	2	0	0	0	0	0	0	0	1	1	0	9,909
Golden	1	0	0	0	0	0	0	0	0	0	1	19,556
Grand Junction	0	1	2	0	0	0	0	0	0	1	2	59,972
Greenwood Village	1	1	0	0	1	0	0	1	1	0	1	14,824
Gunnison	0	0	0	1	0	0	0	1	0	0	0	5,865
Idaho Springs	1	0	0	0	0	0	0	0	1	0	0	1,677
Lakewood	0	0	0	1	0	0	0	0	1	0	0	148,236
Lone Tree	0	1	0	0	0	0	0	0	0	1	0	13,824
Longmont	2	0	0	1	0	0	0	0	2	1	0	90,813
Loveland	0	1	0	0	0	0	0	1	0	0	0	72,465
New Castle	1	0	0	0	0	0	0	0	0	1	0	4,595
Parachute	1	0	0	0	0	0	0	1	0	0	0	1,100
Pueblo	0	0	1	1	1	0	0	1	1	1	0	108,591
Steamboat Springs	0	0	0	3	0	0	0	1	0	0	2	12,114
Sterling	2	0	0	0	0	0	0	1	1	0	0	14,584
Universities and Colleges	1	0	1	0	0	0	0					
University of Colorado												
Boulder	1	0	0	0	0	0	0	0	1	0	0	32,017
Colorado Springs	0	0	1	0	0	0	0	1	0	0	0	11,321
Metropolitan Counties	6	1	6	1	3	0	0					
Douglas	1	0	0	0	0	0	0	1	0	0	0	
El Paso	1	0	3	0	0	0	0	1	0	0	3	
Gilpin	1	0	0	0	0	0	0	1	0	0	0	
Jefferson	1	0	0	0	0	0	0	1	0	0	0	
Larimer	0	1	3	1	3	0	0	0	3	4	1	
Mesa	1	0	0	0	0	0	0	1	0	0	0	
Teller	1	0	0	0	0	0	0	0	0	1	0	
Nonmetropolitan Counties	1	1	2	1	0	0	0					
La Plata	0	1	2	0	0	0	0	0	3	0	0	
Montezuma	1	0	0	0	0	0	0	0	0	1	0	
Summit	0	0	0	1	0	0	0	0	0	0	1	
CONNECTICUT												
Total	57	31	23	11	1	0	0					
Cities	56	26	22	10	1	0	0					
Bloomfield	3	0	3	1	0	0	0	1	1	4	1	20,718
Bridgeport	3	0	1	1	0	0	0	0	3	2	0	147,822

(Number.)

State/agency	Number of incidents per bias motivation							Number of incidents per quarter				Population[1]
	Race	Religion	Sexual orientation	Ethnicity	Disability	Gender	Gender identity	1st quarter	2nd quarter	3rd quarter	4th quarter	
Bristol	1	1	1	0	0	0	0	2	0	1	0	60,590
Brookfield	0	1	0	0	0	0	0	0	1	0	0	16,957
Canton	0	1	0	0	0	0	0	0	0	1	0	10,372
Cheshire	1	0	0	0	0	0	0	0	1	0	0	29,120
Coventry	0	1	0	0	0	0	0	0	0	0	1	12,403
Danbury	1	0	1	0	0	0	0	1	1	0	0	84,281
Derby	0	1	0	0	0	0	0	0	0	0	1	12,776
East Hartford	1	0	0	0	0	0	0	0	1	0	0	51,185
Easton	0	1	0	0	0	0	0	0	0	0	1	7,645
Enfield	0	1	0	0	0	0	0				1	44,769
Fairfield	0	0	1	0	0	0	0	1	0	0	0	61,146
Farmington	0	0	0	1	0	0	0	0	0	1	0	25,678
Glastonbury	1	0	0	0	0	0	0	0	0	0	1	34,850
Greenwich	0	0	1	0	0	0	0	1	0	0	0	62,676
Groton Town	1	1	1	0	0	0	0	1	1	0	1	30,339
Hamden	1	0	0	0	0	0	0	0	0	0	1	61,599
Manchester[2]	5	1	0	0	1	0	0	2	2	1	2	58,204
Meriden	1	0	0	0	0	0	0	0	0	1	0	60,352
Middlebury	1	0	0	0	0	0	0	0	0	0	1	7,569
Middletown	5	0	1	0	0	0	0	3	1	0	2	47,256
Milford	2	0	0	1	0	0	0	0	1	1	1	53,222
New Britain	0	0	1	0	0	0	0	0	0	0	1	72,864
New Haven	4	0	3	1	0	0	0	2	4	0	2	130,882
Newington	0	1	0	0	0	0	0	1	0	0	0	30,803
New Milford	0	2	0	0	0	0	0	0	2	0	0	27,681
Newtown	2	1	0	0	0	0	0	1	1	1	0	28,243
North Haven	0	1	0	0	0	0	0	0	0	1	0	23,901
Norwalk	1	1	0	0	0	0	0	0	0	2	0	88,232
Norwich	1	0	0	0	0	0	0	1	0	0	0	40,296
Old Saybrook	4	0	0	0	0	0	0	0	3	1	0	10,249
Plainfield	1	0	0	0	0	0	0	0	0	1	0	15,186
Plymouth	0	1	0	0	0	0	0	1	0	0	0	12,002
Redding	0	1	0	1	0	0	0	0	1	0	1	9,348
Seymour	1	1	0	0	0	0	0	0	1	1	0	16,579
Shelton	1	0	0	0	0	0	0	0	0	0	1	41,353
Southington	0	0	0	2	0	0	0	0	1	0	1	43,786
Stamford	1	3	4	1	0	0	0	0	0	3	6	127,385
Stratford	1	1	2	0	0	0	0	1	1	2	0	52,279
Torrington	2	0	0	0	0	0	0	1	0	1	0	35,432
Vernon	2	0	2	0	0	0	0	0	1	2	1	29,158
Wallingford	0	0	0	1	0	0	0	0	0	0	1	45,137
Waterbury	3	1	0	0	0	0	0	0	3	1	0	109,495
Watertown	1	0	0	0	0	0	0	0	1	0	0	22,161
West Hartford	1	0	0	0	0	0	0	0	0	0	1	63,360
West Haven	1	0	0	0	0	0	0	0	1	0	0	54,917
Wilton	0	1	0	0	0	0	0	0	0	1	0	18,807
Winchester	0	2	0	0	0	0	0	0	0	0	2	10,960
Windsor	1	0	0	0	0	0	0	0	1	0	0	29,154
Woodbridge	1	0	0	0	0	0	0	0	0	0	1	8,945
Universities and Colleges												
Southern Connecticut State University	0	0	1	0	0	0	0	1	0	0	0	10,804
University of Connecticut, Storrs, Avery Point and Hartford[3]	0	2	0	0	0	0	0	0	0	0	2	
State Police Agencies												
Connecticut State Police	1	3	0	1	0	0	0	2	0	3	0	
DELAWARE												
Total	7	2	3	1	0	0	0					
Cities												
Camden	1	0	0	0	0	0	0	0	0	1	0	3,518
Newark	1	0	0	0	0	0	0	0	0	0	1	32,813
Rehoboth Beach	0	0	0	1	0	0	0	0	0	1	0	1,416
Wilmington	1	0	1	0	0	0	0	0	1	1	0	71,713
Metropolitan Counties	2	0	1	0	0	0	0					
New Castle County Police Department	2	0	1	0	0	0	0	0	0	2	1	

(Number.)

State/agency	Number of incidents per bias motivation							Number of incidents per quarter				Population[1]
	Race	Religion	Sexual orientation	Ethnicity	Disability	Gender	Gender identity	1st quarter	2nd quarter	3rd quarter	4th quarter	
State Police Agencies	1	2	1	0	0	0	0					
Kent County	0	0	1	0	0	0	0	1	0	0	0	
New Castle County	0	2	0	0	0	0	0	0	1	1	0	
Sussex County	1	0	0	0	0	0	0	0	0	1	0	
Other Agencies	1	0	0	0	0	0	0					
State Fire Marshal	1	0	0	0	0	0	0	0	0	0	1	
DISTRICT OF COLUMBIA												
Total	13	8	29	4	1	0	15					
Cities	12	8	28	4	1	0	15					
Washington[2]	12	8	28	4	1	0	15	15	17	25	11	658,893
Other Agencies	1	0	1	0	0	0	0					
Metro Transit Police	1	0	1	0	0	0	0	0	0	1	1	
FLORIDA												
Total	34	12	12	6	1	0	0					
Cities	16	10	8	4	1	0	0					
Cape Coral	1	0	0	0	0	0	0	0	1	0	0	168,712
Clewiston	1	0	0	0	0	0	0	0	0	1	0	7,141
Coral Gables	0	1	0	0	0	0	0	0	0	0	1	50,316
Delray Beach	0	0	0	1	0	0	0	0	0	1	0	64,917
Gainesville	0	0	0	0	1	0	0	0	1	0	0	128,185
Jupiter	0	0	1	0	0	0	0	0	0	0	1	59,039
Kissimmee	0	0	1	1	0	0	0	0	1	0	1	66,623
Largo	0	0	0	1	0	0	0	0	0	0	1	78,502
Margate	0	1	0	0	0	0	0	0	0	1	0	55,982
Miami Beach	1	4	1	0	0	0	0	2	0	4	0	91,771
Miramar	1	0	0	0	0	0	0	0	1	0	0	132,352
North Miami	0	0	1	0	0	0	0	0	0	0	1	61,501
North Miami Beach	0	2	0	0	0	0	0	0	1	1	0	43,657
Ocoee	0	0	1	0	0	0	0	0	0	0	1	40,029
Orlando	3	0	2	0	0	0	0	0	2	3	0	259,675
Oviedo	1	0	0	0	0	0	0	1	0	0	0	37,467
Palm Bay	1	0	0	0	0	0	0	0	0	1	0	105,287
Pensacola	0	1	0	0	0	0	0	0	0	0	1	52,873
Port St. Lucie	0	0	1	0	0	0	0	0	0	0	1	172,453
Temple Terrace	1	0	0	0	0	0	0	0	1	0	0	25,335
Titusville	1	0	0	0	0	0	0	0	1	0	0	44,310
Weston	1	0	0	0	0	0	0	0	0	0	1	69,129
West Palm Beach	4	1	0	0	0	0	0	1	0	3	1	103,028
Winter Garden	0	0	0	1	0	0	0	0	1	0	0	38,454
Metropolitan Counties	18	2	4	2	0	0	0					
Alachua	1	0	0	0	0	0	0	0	0	0	1	
Charlotte	0	0	1	0	0	0	0	0	1	0	0	
Clay	1	0	1	0	0	0	0	0	0	1	1	
Highlands	1	0	0	0	0	0	0	0	0	1	0	
Lee	1	2	0	0	0	0	0	2	0	0	1	
Manatee	4	0	0	0	0	0	0	0	0	2	2	
Orange	0	0	2	1	0	0	0	1	1	1	0	
Pasco	1	0	0	0	0	0	0	0	0	0	1	
Seminole	0	0	0	1	0	0	0	0	0	1	0	
Sumter	3	0	0	0	0	0	0	0	0	0	3	
Volusia	3	0	0	0	0	0	0	2	0	1	0	
Wakulla	2	0	0	0	0	0	0	0	0	0	2	
Walton	1	0	0	0	0	0	0	1	0	0	0	
GEORGIA												
Total	21	3	12	3	2	0	0					
Cities	2	1	9	0	1	0	0					
Atlanta	2	1	9	0	1	0	0	5	3	5	0	454,363
Metropolitan Counties	19	2	3	3	1	0	0					
Cobb County Police Department	16	2	2	3	1	0	0	5	5	10	4	
Gwinnett County Police Department	2	0	0	0	0	0	0	1	1	0	0	

(Number.)

State/agency	Number of incidents per bias motivation							Number of incidents per quarter				Population[1]
	Race	Religion	Sexual orientation	Ethnicity	Disability	Gender	Gender identity	1st quarter	2nd quarter	3rd quarter	4th quarter	
Henry County Police Department	1	0	1	0	0	0	0	0	1	0	1	
IDAHO												
Total	13	2	3	7	0	0	0					
Cities	13	1	3	4	0	0	0					
Boise	6	0	2	4	0	0	0	2	3	5	2	216,260
Coeur d'Alene	1	0	0	0	0	0	0	0	0	1	0	46,952
Jerome	1	0	0	0	0	0	0	0	0	1	0	11,064
Lewiston	1	0	0	0	0	0	0	1	0	0	0	32,521
Nampa	3	0	1	0	0	0	0	0	0	2	2	87,735
Payette	1	0	0	0	0	0	0	0	0	1	0	7,417
Pocatello	0	1	0	0	0	0	0	0	0	1	0	54,360
Metropolitan Counties	0	0	0	1	0	0	0					
Ada	0	0	0	1	0	0	0	0	0	0	1	
Nonmetropolitan Counties	0	1	0	2	0	0	0					
Cassia	0	0	0	2	0	0	0	0	1	1	0	
Teton	0	1	0	0	0	0	0	0	0	1	0	
ILLINOIS												
Total	57	14	26	12	0	0	0					
Cities	52	12	24	11	0	0	0					
Addison	0	0	0	1	0	0	0	0	0	1	0	37,480
Arlington Heights	0	1	0	0	0	0	0	0	0	0	1	76,200
Aurora	2	0	1	1	0	0	0	0	0	3	1	200,419
Bartlett	1	0	0	0	0	0	0	1	0	0	0	41,784
Batavia	0	0	0	1	0	0	0	1	0	0	0	26,445
Beardstown	0	1	0	0	0	0	0	0	1	0	0	5,919
Bloomington	1	0	2	0	0	0	0	0	1	1	1	79,451
Cairo	1	0	0	0	0	0	0	0	0	0	1	2,580
Centralia	1	0	0	0	0	0	0	0	0	0	1	12,727
Chicago	22	6	17	5	0	0	0	11	17	13	9	2,724,121
Crest Hill	1	0	0	0	0	0	0	0	0	0	1	20,763
Crystal Lake	1	0	0	0	0	0	0	1	0	0	0	40,294
De Kalb	2	0	0	0	0	0	0	1	1	0	0	43,791
Eureka	1	0	0	0	0	0	0	0	1	0	0	5,397
Galesburg	1	0	0	0	0	0	0	1	0	0	0	31,538
Glenview	0	0	0	1	0	0	0	0	1	0	0	45,588
Grayslake	0	1	0	0	0	0	0	0	1	0	0	21,132
Hillsboro	1	0	0	0	0	0	0	0	1	0	0	6,123
Hoffman Estates	1	0	0	0	0	0	0	0	0	1	0	52,512
Homewood	1	0	0	0	0	0	0	0	0	0	1	19,470
Joliet	1	0	0	0	0	0	0	0	0	0	1	147,838
La Grange	1	0	0	0	0	0	0	0	0	0	1	15,774
La Salle	0	0	1	0	0	0	0	1	0	0	0	9,368
Lombard	0	1	0	0	0	0	0	0	0	0	1	44,026
Lyons	0	0	1	0	0	0	0	0	0	1	0	10,793
Normal	1	1	0	0	0	0	0	0	1	1	0	55,185
Oak Lawn	1	0	0	0	0	0	0	0	0	1	0	57,159
O'Fallon	1	0	0	0	0	0	0	0	1	0	0	29,255
Palestine	1	0	0	0	0	0	0	0	1	0	0	1,331
Peoria	0	1	1	0	0	0	0	2	0	0	0	116,923
Plano	0	0	1	0	0	0	0	0	0	0	1	11,147
Rantoul	1	0	0	0	0	0	0	1	0	0	0	13,060
Rockford	0	0	0	1	0	0	0	0	0	1	0	149,586
Schaumburg	1	0	0	0	0	0	0	1	0	0	0	75,060
Shiloh	1	0	0	0	0	0	0	0	0	1	0	12,991
Springfield	2	0	0	0	0	0	0	0	0	2	0	117,134
Streamwood	0	0	0	1	0	0	0	0	1	0	0	40,456
Urbana	1	0	0	0	0	0	0	0	1	0	0	41,805
Wamac	1	0	0	0	0	0	0	0	1			1,144
West Chicago	1	0	0	0	0	0	0	0	0	0	1	27,636
Wood River	1	0	0	0	0	0	0	0	0	1	0	10,370
Universities and Colleges	1	1	0	0	0	0	0					
Northwestern University, Chicago	1	0	0	0	0	0	0	0	0	1	0	430
University of Illinois, Urbana	0	1	0	0	0	0	0	0	0	1	0	44,942

Table 13. Hate Crime Incidents Per Bias Motivation and Quarter, by Selected State and Agency, 2014—*Continued*

(Number.)

State/agency	Number of incidents per bias motivation							Number of incidents per quarter				Population[1]
	Race	Religion	Sexual orientation	Ethnicity	Disability	Gender	Gender identity	1st quarter	2nd quarter	3rd quarter	4th quarter	
Metropolitan Counties	3	1	1	1	0	0	0					
Champaign	0	0	1	0	0	0	0	0	0	0	1	
Lake	1	0	0	0	0	0	0	0	0	0	1	
Peoria	2	0	0	1	0	0	0	0	1	1	1	
Winnebago	0	1	0	0	0	0	0	0	1	0	0	
Nonmetropolitan Counties	1	0	1	0	0	0	0					
Fulton	1	0	1	0	0	0	0	2	0	0	0	
INDIANA												
Total	25	9	6	8	0	2	0					
Cities	21	9	5	6	0	0	0					
Anderson	1	0	0	0	0	0	0	0	0	0	1	55,545
Bloomington	7	1	1	1	0	0	0	1	2	2	5	83,075
Columbus	0	4	0	0	0	0	0	0	1	3	0	46,196
Fishers	0	1	0	0	0	0	0	0	0	1	0	85,597
Fort Wayne	2	0	0	0	0	0	0	0	1	1	0	257,172
Indianapolis	7	3	4	5	0	0	0	3	4	7	5	858,238
Shelbyville	4	0	0	0	0	0	0	0	0	2	2	19,278
Universities and Colleges	1	0	0	0	0	0	0					
Purdue University	1	0	0	0	0	0	0	0	0	1	0	39,794
Nonmetropolitan Counties	1	0	0	0	0	0	0					
Montgomery	1	0	0	0	0	0	0	0	0	0	1	
State Police Agencies	2	0	1	2	0	2	0					
Decatur County	0	0	0	1	0	0	0	1	0	0	0	
Marion County	0	0	0	1	0	1	0	1	0	0	1	
Putnam County	1	0	0	0	0	0	0	0	1	0	0	
Scott County	0	0	0	0	0	1	0	1	0	0	0	
Vanderburgh County	0	0	1	0	0	0	0	0	1	0	0	
Wayne County	1	0	0	0	0	0	0	1	0	0	0	
IOWA												
Total	8	0	0	2	1	0	0					
Cities	6	0	0	2	0	0	0					
Ames	1	0	0	0	0	0	0	0	1	0	0	62,514
Atlantic	1	0	0	0	0	0	0	0	0	1	0	6,898
Bettendorf	1	0	0	1	0	0	0	0	0	1	1	35,045
Cedar Rapids	1	0	0	0	0	0	0	1	0	0	0	128,901
Council Bluffs	0	0	0	1	0	0	0	1	0	0	0	61,864
Des Moines	1	0	0	0	0	0	0	0	0	1	0	208,250
Fort Dodge	1	0	0	0	0	0	0	0	1	0	0	24,524
Universities and Colleges	1	0	0	0	1	0	0					
Iowa State University	1	0	0	0	0	0	0	1	0	0	0	32,955
University of Iowa	0	0	0	0	1	0	0	1	0	0	0	29,748
Nonmetropolitan Counties	1	0	0	0	0	0	0					
Hardin	1	0	0	0	0	0	0	0	1	0	0	
KANSAS												
Total	43	8	10	11	1	0	0					
Cities	33	6	9	9	1	0	0					
Abilene	0	1	0	0	0	0	0	0	1	0	0	6,617
Burlington	1	0	0	0	0	0	0	0	0	0	1	2,620
Dodge City	1	0	0	0	0	0	0	0	0	1	0	28,325
Edwardsville	0	1	0	0	0	0	0	0	1	0	0	4,357
Elwood	1	0	0	0	0	0	0	0	1	0	0	1,190
Goddard	1	0	0	0	0	0	0	0	0	1	0	4,624
Hays	0	0	0	1	0	0	0	0	0	1	0	21,167
Haysville	1	0	0	0	0	0	0	0	1	0	0	11,046
Hiawatha	0	0	1	0	0	0	0	0	1	0	0	3,180
Hutchinson	2	0	0	2	0	0	0	1	2	1	0	41,807
Junction City	1	0	0	0	0	0	0	0	0	1	0	25,786

(Number.)

State/agency	Number of incidents per bias motivation							Number of incidents per quarter				Population[1]
	Race	Religion	Sexual orientation	Ethnicity	Disability	Gender	Gender identity	1st quarter	2nd quarter	3rd quarter	4th quarter	
Kansas City	1	0	0	0	0	0	0		0	1	0	149,103
Lawrence	6	0	3	3	1	0	0	4	7	2	0	91,524
Leavenworth	4	0	0	0	0	0	0	0	3	0	1	36,018
Leawood	0	1	0	0	0	0	0	0	1	0	0	33,266
McPherson	0	0	1	0	0	0	0	0	1	0	0	13,369
Mulvane	2	0	0	0	0	0	0	0	0	0	2	6,322
Osawatomie	1	0	0	0	0	0	0	1	0	0	0	4,369
Ottawa	0	0	0	1	0	0	0	1	0	0	0	12,439
Overland Park	1	0	0	0	0	0	0			0	1	183,108
Paola	1	0	0	0	0	0	0	0	0	1	0	5,634
Pittsburg	0	1	0	0	0	0	0	0	1	0	0	20,431
Salina	1	1	0	0	0	0	0	0	2	0	0	47,850
Wellington	1	0	0	0	0	0	0	0	0	1	0	7,919
Wichita	7	1	4	2	0	0	0	3	1	7	3	387,493
Metropolitan Counties	2	0	1	0	0	0	0					
Jackson	1	0	0	0	0	0	0	0	1	0	0	
Jefferson	0	0	1	0	0	0	0	0	0	1	0	
Riley County Police Department	1	0	0	0	0	0	0	0	1	0	0	
Nonmetropolitan Counties	7	1	0	2	0	0	0					
Ellis	2	0	0	0	0	0	0	1	0	0	1	
Ford	0	1	0	0	0	0	0	0	0	1	0	
Greenwood	1	0	0	0	0	0	0	1	0	0	0	
Kearny	1	0	0	0	0	0	0	1	0	0	0	
Lyon	0	0	0	1	0	0	0	0	0	1	0	
Saline	3	0	0	0	0	0	0	0	1	2	0	
Wichita	0	0	0	1	0	0	0	0	1	0	0	
Other Agencies	1	1	0	0	0	0	0					
Johnson County Park	0	1	0	0	0	0	0	0	1	0	0	
Unified School District, Goddard	1	0	0	0	0	0	0	0	0	1	0	
KENTUCKY												
Total	115	13	19	11	4	0	1					
Cities	78	6	17	8	4	0	1					
Ashland	1	0	0	0	0	0	0	1	0	0	0	21,321
Augusta	1	0	0	0	0	0	0	1	0	0	0	1,177
Bowling Green	5	0	0	0	0	0	0	2	1	1	1	62,117
Cadiz	1	0	0	0	0	0	0	0	1	0	0	2,665
Campbellsville	1	0	0	0	0	0	0	0	0	1	0	10,840
Carrollton	2	0	0	0	0	0	0	1	0	0	1	4,009
Cold Spring	2	0	0	0	0	0	0	1	0	1	0	6,191
Covington	3	0	1	2	0	0	0	1	1	3	1	41,072
Cynthiana	0	0	0	0	1	0	0	1	0	0	0	6,334
Dayton	0	0	1	0	0	0	0	0	0	1	0	5,377
Elizabethtown	0	0	1	0	0	0	0	0	1	0	0	30,208
Elkton	1	0	0	0	0	0	0	0	0	0	1	2,179
Florence	2	0	0	0	0	0	0	1	0	1	0	31,769
Franklin	1	0	0	0	0	0	0	0	1	0	0	8,745
Georgetown	2	0	0	0	0	0	0	1	0	0	1	31,280
Glasgow	0	0	1	0	0	0	0	0	1	0	0	14,315
Harrodsburg	1	0	0	0	0	0	0	1	0	0	0	8,380
Hazard	1	0	0	0	0	0	0	1	0	0	0	5,415
Henderson	1	0	0	1	0	0	0	0	1	0	1	28,843
Hopkinsville	3	0	0	0	0	0	0	0	0	2	1	32,697
Jamestown	1	0	0	0	0	0	0	0	0	0	1	1,823
Jeffersontown	1	0	0	1	0	0	0	0	1	0	1	27,124
Lebanon	1	0	0	0	0	0	0	1	0	0	0	5,653
Lexington[2]	14	2	7	3	1	0	0	3	6	11	7	311,848
London	1	0	0	0	0	0	0	0	0	1	0	8,115
Louisville Metro	3	2	2	0	1	0	1	3	0	2	4	677,710
Ludlow	1	0	0	0	0	0	0	0	0	1	0	4,552
Mayfield	1	0	0	0	0	0	0	0	0	0	1	10,130
Maysville	2	0	0	0	0	0	0	0	0	2	0	8,895
Morgantown	0	0	1	0	0	0	0	1	0	0	0	2,462
Murray	1	0	0	0	0	0	0	1	0	0	0	18,188
Newport	2	0	0	1	0	0	0	2	0	0	1	15,357
Nicholasville	1	0	0	0	0	0	0	0	0	0	1	28,889

State/agency	Number of incidents per bias motivation							Number of incidents per quarter				Population[1]
	Race	Religion	Sexual orientation	Ethnicity	Disability	Gender	Gender identity	1st quarter	2nd quarter	3rd quarter	4th quarter	
Owensboro	4	0	0	0	0	0	0	2	0	1	1	58,659
Owingsville	1	0	0	0	0	0	0	1	0	0	0	1,573
Paducah	4	0	0	0	0	0	0	0	2	2	0	25,017
Paris	1	0	0	0	0	0	0	0	1	0	0	9,754
Raceland	0	0	1	0	0	0	0	0	0	0	1	2,376
Richmond	3	0	0	0	0	0	0	1	1	1	0	32,828
Russell Springs	1	0	0	0	0	0	0	0	0	1	0	2,509
Russellville	1	0	0	0	0	0	0	0	1	0	0	7,053
Shepherdsville	1	0	0	0	0	0	0	0	0	1	0	11,788
Shively	1	0	1	0	0	0	0	1	0	0	1	15,669
Somerset	1	0	0	0	0	0	0	1	0	0	0	11,503
Stanford	1	0	0	0	0	0	0	1	0	0	0	3,654
St. Matthews	0	1	0	0	0	0	0	0	0	0	1	17,945
Versailles	1	0	0	0	0	0	0	0	0	0	1	8,973
Vine Grove	1	0	0	0	0	0	0	0	1	0	0	5,479
Williamstown	0	1	0	0	0	0	0	1	0	0	0	3,958
Winchester	0	0	1	0	1	0	0	1	1	0	0	18,387
Universities and Colleges	3	0	0	0	0	0	0					
Eastern Kentucky University	1	0	0	0	0	0	0	0	0	0	1	16,111
Morehead State University	1	0	0	0	0	0	0	1	0	0	0	11,358
University of Kentucky	1	0	0	0	0	0	0	0	0	0	1	28,435
Metropolitan Counties	13	2	1	3	0	0	0					
Boone	4	1	0	0	0	0	0	0	1	3	1	
Bullitt	1	0	0	0	0	0	0	0	1	0	0	
Campbell County Police Department	1	0	0	0	0	0	0	0	0	1	0	
Christian	2	0	0	0	0	0	0	0	1	0	1	
Gallatin	1	0	0	0	0	0	0	1	0	0	0	
Kenton	2	0	0	2	0	0	0	0	1	1	2	
Oldham County Police Department	0	0	0	1	0	0	0	0	1	0	0	
Pendleton[2]	1	0	0	0	0	0	0	0	0	1	0	
Shelby	1	0	0	0	0	0	0	1	0	0	0	
Warren	0	1	1	0	0	0	0	1	0	1	0	
Nonmetropolitan Counties	8	2	1	0	0	0	0					
Adair	1	0	0	0	0	0	0	1	0	0	0	
Breckinridge	1	0	0	0	0	0	0	0	0	0	1	
Hopkins	0	1	0	0	0	0	0	0	0	0	1	
Laurel	1	0	0	0	0	0	0	0	0	0	1	
Lewis	0	0	1	0	0	0	0	0	1	0	0	
Marion	1	0	0	0	0	0	0	0	0	1	0	
Marshall	0	1	0	0	0	0	0	1	0	0	0	
McCracken	1	0	0	0	0	0	0	1	0	0	0	
Nelson	1	0	0	0	0	0	0	1	0	0	0	
Ohio	2	0	0	0	0	0	0	1	0	1	0	
State Police Agencies	9	2	0	0	0	0	0					
State Police:												
Cannabis Suppression Section	3	1	0	0	0	0	0	0	1	3	0	
Frankfort	1	0	0	0	0	0	0	0	0	0	1	
Hazard	1	1	0	0	0	0	0	0	1	0	1	
Henderson	1	0	0	0	0	0	0	0	0	0	1	
Madisonville	1	0	0	0	0	0	0	0	1	0	0	
Mayfield	1	0	0	0	0	0	0	0	0	1	0	
Pikeville	1	0	0	0	0	0	0	1	0	0	0	
Other Agencies	4	1	0	0	0	0	0					
Fayette County Schools	1	0	0	0	0	0	0	0	1	0	0	
Greater Hardin County Narcotics Task Force	1	1	0	0	0	0	0	2	0	0	0	
Park Security	1	0	0	0	0	0	0	0	0	0	1	
Pennyrile Narcotics Task Force	1	0	0	0	0	0	0	0	0	1	0	
LOUISIANA												
Total	3	0	5	0	1	0	0					
Cities	2	0	2	0	1	0	0					
Bernice	1	0	0	0	0	0	0	0	0	1	0	1,637
Harahan	1	0	0	0	0	0	0		1			9,319

(Number.)

State/agency	Number of incidents per bias motivation							Number of incidents per quarter				Population[1]
	Race	Religion	Sexual orientation	Ethnicity	Disability	Gender	Gender identity	1st quarter	2nd quarter	3rd quarter	4th quarter	
New Orleans............................	0	0	2	0	1	0	0	1	1		1	387,113
Universities and Colleges	0	0	1	0	0	0	0					
University of New Orleans....................	0	0	1	0	0	0	0		0	0	1	9,323
Metropolitan Counties	1	0	2	0	0	0	0					
Calcasieu................................	1	0	1	0	0	0	0	0	1	0	1	
Lafayette................................	0	0	1	0	0	0	0	0	1			
MAINE................................												
Total	11	8	8	1	0	0	0					
Cities	11	7	7	1	0	0	0					
Augusta................................	1	1	0	1	0	0	0	1	1	0	1	18,717
Bath................................	1	0	0	0	0	0	0	0	0	1	0	8,325
Gouldsboro................................	0	0	1	0	0	0	0	0	0	1	0	1,746
Hampden................................	0	1	0	0	0	0	0	1	0	0	0	7,303
Old Orchard Beach........................	2	0	1	0	0	0	0	0	1	2	0	8,705
Portland................................	0	3	1	0	0	0	0	2	0	0	2	66,380
Rumford................................	1	0	0	0	0	0	0	1	0	0	0	5,705
Saco................................	2	1	2	0	0	0	0	0	1	3	1	18,974
Searsport................................	1	0	0	0	0	0	0	1	0	0	0	2,627
South Portland........................	1	0	1	0	0	0	0	0	1	1	0	25,327
Waterville................................	0	0	1	0	0	0	0	0	1	0	0	16,022
Westbrook................................	1	0	0	0	0	0	0	0	0	0	1	17,809
Wiscasset................................	1	1	0	0	0	0	0	0	0	0	2	3,645
Metropolitan Counties	0	1	0	0	0	0	0					
Sagadahoc................................	0	1	0	0	0	0	0	0	0	0	1	
Nonmetropolitan Counties..............	0	0	1	0	0	0	0					
Kennebec	0	0	1	0	0	0	0	0	1	0	0	
MARYLAND................................												
Total	9	2	2	3	0	0	0					
Cities	4	0	0	2	0	0	0					
Baltimore................................	1	0	0	1	0	0	0	0	1	0	1	623,513
Cambridge................................	1	0	0	0	0	0	0	0	1	0	0	12,669
Salisbury................................	2	0	0	0	0	0	0	2	0	0	0	31,779
Thurmont	0	0	0	1	0	0	0	0	0	1	0	6,463
Universities and Colleges	0	0	1	0	0	0	0					
St. Mary's College	0	0	1	0	0	0	0	1	0	0	0	1,858
Metropolitan Counties	4	2	1	0	0	0	0					
Montgomery County Police Department................	3	2	1	0	0	0	0	1	1	4	0	
Prince George's County Police Department................	1	0	0	0	0	0	0	0	0	0	1	
State Police Agencies........................	1	0	0	1	0	0	0					
Carroll County	0	0	0	1	0	0	0	0	0	1	0	
Worcester County	1	0	0	0	0	0	0	0	1	0	0	
MASSACHUSETTS........................												
Total	128	57	80	33	10	18	49					
Cities	108	45	78	29	10	15	49					
Acton................................	0	3	0	0	0	0	0	0	0	2	1	23,193
Agawam................................	1	0	1	0	0	0	0	0	0	0	2	28,769
Amherst................................	2	0	0	0	0	0	0	1	0	0	1	38,977
Arlington................................	0	0	2	0	1	0	2	0	1	2	2	44,439
Attleboro................................	1	0	0	0	0	0	1	0	0	1	1	44,084
Barnstable................................	2	1	0	0	0	0	0	2	0	1	0	44,642
Belmont................................	0	0	0	0	0	0	1	0	0	0	1	25,550
Beverly................................	0	0	1	0	0	0	0	1	0	0	0	41,023
Billerica................................	0	1	0	0	0	0	0	0	0	1	0	42,393
Boston................................	46	6	39	4	0	0	0	16	32	27	20	654,413
Braintree................................	1	1	0	0	0	0	0	1	0	0	1	37,067

(Number.)

State/agency	Number of incidents per bias motivation							Number of incidents per quarter				Population[1]
	Race	Religion	Sexual orientation	Ethnicity	Disability	Gender	Gender identity	1st quarter	2nd quarter	3rd quarter	4th quarter	
Brockton	0	1	0	0	0	0	0	0	1	0	0	94,427
Brookline	1	0	0	0	0	0	0	1	0	0	0	59,413
Burlington	0	1	0	0	0	0	0	0	1	0	0	25,765
Cambridge	3	2	5	2	1	0	0	3	3	3	4	108,201
Chicopee	1	0	0	0	0	0	0	0	0	0	1	55,831
Cohasset	0	0	0	1	0	0	0	0	0	1	0	8,493
Danvers	0	0	0	0	1	2	0	0	1	1	1	27,809
Deerfield	0	0	1	0	0	0	0	0	1	0	0	5,080
Dracut	0	1	0	0	0	0	0	0	1	0	0	31,067
Easthampton	0	0	1	0	0	0	0	0	0	1	0	15,954
East Longmeadow	0	0	0	0	1	0	0	0	1	0	0	16,092
Edgartown	0	0	1	1	0	0	0	0	1	1	0	4,331
Everett	0	0	0	1	1	0	0	1	0	1	0	43,368
Fall River	3	0	0	0	0	0	0	2	0	1	0	88,915
Gloucester	0	0	0	0	0	2	0	0	1	1	0	29,383
Grafton	0	0	0	0	0	1	0	0	1	0	0	18,301
Great Barrington	1	0	0	0	0	0	0	0	0	1	0	6,971
Harvard	0	1	0	0	0	0	0	1	0	0	0	6,597
Haverhill[2]	1	1	2	2	0	1	5	2	3	2	5	62,552
Hingham	0	1	0	0	0	0	0	0	0	1	0	22,940
Hudson	0	0	1	0	0	0	0	0	0	1	0	19,765
Leominster	0	1	0	0	0	0	0	0	1	0	0	41,179
Lunenburg	0	1	0	0	0	0	0	0	0	1	0	11,238
Lynn	4	2	4	2	2	3	4	1	13	5	2	92,131
Malden[2]	4	0	1	0	1	0	1	0	1	3	3	60,925
Marblehead	0	1	0	0	0	0	0	1	0	0	0	20,332
Marlborough	1	0	0	0	0	0	0	0	1	0	0	39,748
Mattapoisett	1	0	0	0	0	0	0	1	0	0	0	6,219
Medford	3	1	0	1	0	1	3	1	5	3	0	57,551
Melrose	0	0	2	0	0	0	0	0	0	1	1	27,940
Merrimac	1	0	0	0	0	0	0	0	0	1	0	6,697
Middleboro	0	1	0	0	0	0	0	0	0	0	1	23,784
Monson	0	1	0	0	0	0	0	0	0	1	0	8,762
Needham	1	0	0	0	0	0	0	0	0	0	1	29,990
New Bedford	2	0	1	2	0	0	0	2	1	1	1	95,366
Newton	2	3	0	0	0	0	4	0	2	3	4	88,881
Norfolk	0	0	1	0	0	0	0	0	1	0	0	11,835
Northampton	1	0	0	0	0	0	0	1	0	0	0	28,465
North Andover	0	0	0	1	0	0	0	0	1	0	0	29,502
North Reading	0	0	0	0	1	0	0	0	0	0	1	15,537
Norton	1	0	0	0	0	0	9	0	5	4	1	19,477
Oxford	0	0	1	0	0	0	0	0	1	0	0	13,869
Pittsfield	0	0	0	1	0	0	0	1	0	0	0	43,895
Plymouth	3	2	0	1	0	0	0	2	2	2	0	58,292
Quincy	7	3	3	1	1	0	6	2	6	8	5	94,035
Raynham	1	0	0	0	0	0	0	0	0	0	1	13,635
Revere	0	0	1	2	0	0	0	2	1	0	0	54,402
Salem	0	2	2	0	0	0	0	1	1	1	1	42,847
Sharon	0	1	0	0	0	0	0	0	0	1	0	18,177
Somerville[2]	1	4	1	1	0	2	2	2	3	3	3	79,798
South Hadley	1	0	0	0	0	0	0	0	1	0	0	17,747
Springfield	1	0	0	0	0	0	0	1	0	0	0	153,766
Swampscott	0	0	0	2	0	0	1	1	1	0	1	14,028
Taunton	3	0	1	0	0	1	7	1	5	4	2	56,277
Upton	0	1	0	0	0	0	0	1	0	0	0	7,719
Wakefield	0	0	1	0	0	0	0	0	0	0	1	26,394
Waltham	1	0	1	2	0	1	3	0	2	2	4	62,756
Ware	1	0	0	0	0	0	0	1	0	0	0	9,838
Webster	0	0	0	0	0	0	0	0	0	0	1	16,869
Westport	0	0	1	0	0	0	0	0	0	0	1	15,785
West Tisbury	0	0	0	0	0	1	0	0	0	1	0	2,908
Whitman	1	0	0	0	0	0	0	0	1	0	0	14,786
Williamstown	0	0	0	1	0	0	0	0	0	0	1	7,561
Winthrop	1	0	0	0	0	0	0	0	1	0	0	18,314
Woburn	0	0	0	1	0	0	0	1	0	0	0	39,401
Worcester	3	1	2	0	0	0	0	1	1	3	1	183,248
Universities and Colleges	17	11	2	3	0	3	0					
Assumption College	0	1	0	0	0	0	0	1	0	0	0	2,756
Boston University	1	0	0	2	0	0	0	0	0	2	1	32,411

(Number.)

State/agency	Number of incidents per bias motivation							Number of incidents per quarter				Population[1]
	Race	Religion	Sexual orientation	Ethnicity	Disability	Gender	Gender identity	1st quarter	2nd quarter	3rd quarter	4th quarter	
Clark University	1	0	0	0	0	0	0	0	0	1	0	3,551
Emerson College	0	1	0	0	0	0	0	1	0	0	0	4,561
Massachusetts College of Liberal Arts	0	1	0	0	0	0	0	0	0	0	1	1,716
Massachusetts Institute of Technology	2	0	0	0	0	2	0	0	2	0	2	11,301
Massasoit Community College	0	1	0	0	0	0	0	0	0	0	1	8,272
Mount Holyoke College	1	0	0	0	0	0	0	1	0	0	0	2,251
Northeastern University	0	1	1	0	0	0	0		1	1		20,053
Springfield Technical Community College	1	0	0	0	0	0	0	0	0	0	1	6,792
Tufts University, Medford	0	4	0	0	0	0	0	0	1	0	3	10,872
University of Massachusetts, Amherst	11	2	1	1	0	1	0	2	2	1	11	28,518
Other Agencies	3	1	0	1	0	0	0					
Massachusetts General Hospital	3	1	0	1	0	0	0	3		1	1	
MICHIGAN												
Total	195	32	42	31	9	2	0					
Cities	136	25	28	24	7	1	0					
Ann Arbor	1	2	3	1	0	0	0	2	3	1	1	117,768
Auburn Hills	3	0	0	0	0	0	0	0	1	1	1	21,859
Battle Creek	1	0	0	0	0	0	0	0	0	1	0	61,225
Bay City	3	0	0	0	0	0	0	0	1	2	0	34,307
Benton Harbor	1	0	0	0	1	0	0	0	0	1	1	10,014
Beverly Hills	2	0	0	0	0	0	0	0	0	1	1	10,493
Blackman Township	0	1	0	2	0	0	0	1	0	0	2	38,025
Buena Vista Township	1	0	0	0	0	0	0	0	1	0	0	8,348
Burton	2	0	0	0	0	0	0	0	0	1	1	28,996
Cadillac	1	0	0	0	0	0	0	0	0	1	0	10,261
Canton Township	2	0	0	0	0	0	0	0	1	1	0	89,073
Chikaming Township	0	0	0	1	0	0	0	1	0	0	0	3,074
Clay Township	1	0	0	0	0	0	0	0	1	0	0	8,895
Clinton Township	1	0	0	0	1	0	0	0	0	1	1	98,897
Clio	1	0	0	0	0	0	0	1	0	0	0	2,555
Coldwater	1	0	0	0	0	0	0	0	1	0	0	10,826
Dearborn	3	1	0	1	0	0	0	2	1	1	1	95,396
Dearborn Heights	1	1	0	1	0	0	0	2	0	0	1	56,366
Detroit	11	0	4	1	0	0	0	5	5	3	3	684,694
East Lansing	3	0	1	0	0	0	0	0	1	3	0	48,555
Eastpointe	0	0	1	0	0	0	0	0	1	0	0	32,674
Essexville	1	0	0	0	0	0	0	0	1	0	0	3,439
Farmington Hills	0	2	0	0	0	0	0	1	0	1	0	81,682
Ferndale	1	0	1	0	0	0	0	0	0	2	0	20,346
Flat Rock	2	0	0	0	0	0	0	1	1	0	0	9,819
Flint	9	0	1	1	1	0	0	1	1	4	6	99,166
Fraser	1	0	0	0	0	0	0	1	0	0	0	14,632
Galesburg	6	0	0	0	0	0	0	1	4	1	0	2,033
Genesee Township	0	0	0	1	0	0	0	0	0	1	0	20,665
Grand Rapids	2	1	1	0	0	0	0	1	1	2	0	193,385
Greenville	2	0	0	0	0	0	0	0	0	2	0	8,449
Grosse Pointe Farms	2	0	0	0	0	0	0	0	0	1	1	9,273
Grosse Pointe Park	1	0	0	0	0	0	0	0	0	1	0	11,281
Grosse Pointe Shores	1	0	0	0	0	0	0	0	0	1	0	2,946
Harper Woods	0	0	1	0	0	0	0	0	0	0	1	13,897
Holland	0	0	1	0	0	0	0	0	0	1	0	33,588
Holly	0	0	1	0	0	0	0	0	0	0	1	6,218
Houghton	1	0	0	0	0	0	0	1	0	0	0	7,632
Huntington Woods	1	1	0	0	0	0	0	0	0	2	0	6,385
Inkster	3	0	0	0	0	0	0	0	2	1	0	24,745
Jackson	4	0	0	0	0	0	0	2	0	2	0	33,404
Kalamazoo	0	0	0	1	2	0	0	0	1	0	2	75,857
Lansing	3	2	1	0	0	0	0	1	1	3	1	113,901
Lapeer	1	0	0	0	0	0	0	1	0	0	0	8,799
Lincoln Park	2	0	0	0	0	0	0	1	0	1	0	37,129
Livonia	1	0	0	1	0	0	0	0	1	1	0	94,833
Madison Township	0	1	0	0	0	0	0	1	0	0	0	8,558
Manistee	1	0	0	0	0	0	0	0	0	1	0	6,093
Marshall	2	0	0	0	0	0	0	0	0	2	0	7,028
Melvindale	0	0	1	0	0	0	0	0	0	1	0	10,428
Menominee	0	0	1	0	0	0	0	0	0	0	1	8,473

Table 13. Hate Crime Incidents Per Bias Motivation and Quarter, by Selected State and Agency, 2014—*Continued*

(Number.)

State/agency	Number of incidents per bias motivation							Number of incidents per quarter				Population[1]
	Race	Religion	Sexual orientation	Ethnicity	Disability	Gender	Gender identity	1st quarter	2nd quarter	3rd quarter	4th quarter	
Meridian Township	2	1	0	0	0	0	0	0	0	3	0	41,133
Monroe	1	0	0	0	0	0	0	1	0	0	0	20,327
Montrose Township	1	0	0	0	0	0	0	0	1	0	0	7,638
Mount Morris	0	0	0	1	0	0	0	0	0	0	1	2,993
Mount Pleasant	0	1	1	0	0	0	0	1	0	1	0	26,227
Mundy Township	1	0	0	0	0	0	0	0	1	0	0	14,723
Muskegon	0	0	0	2	0	0	0	0	0	2	0	36,964
Newaygo	1	0	0	0	0	0	0	1	0	0	0	1,965
Northville Township	0	2	1	1	0	0	0	1	1	1	1	28,801
Ontwa Township-Edwardsburg	2	0	0	0	0	0	0	1	0	1	0	6,519
Pittsfield Township	1	1	1	1	0	0	0	1	0	2	1	36,722
Prairieville Township	0	0	1	0	0	0	0	1	0	0	0	3,403
Richland Township, Saginaw County	1	0	0	0	0	0	0	0	0	1	0	4,040
Richmond	0	0	0	1	0	0	0	1	0	0	0	5,828
River Rouge	1	0	0	0	0	0	0	0	0	1	0	7,625
Riverview	3	0	0	0	0	0	0	0	2	1	0	12,205
Romeo	0	0	1	0	0	0	0	0	0	0	1	3,580
Romulus	1	0	0	0	0	0	0	0	0	1	0	23,415
Roseville	2	0	0	0	0	0	0	0	1	1	0	47,618
Royal Oak	1	0	0	0	0	0	0	0	0	1	0	59,377
Saginaw	2	0	3	0	0	1	0	1	2	2	1	50,030
Saline	1	0	0	0	0	0	0	0	1	0	0	9,146
Sault Ste. Marie	1	0	0	0	0	0	0	1	0	0	0	14,084
Shelby Township	1	2	0	0	0	0	0	0	0	1	2	76,556
Southfield	4	1	0	2	0	0	0	0	4	3	0	73,321
South Haven	0	0	1	0	0	0	0	0	0	0	1	4,375
St. Clair	1	0	0	1	0	0	0	0	0	0	2	5,401
St. Clair Shores	1	0	0	0	0	0	0	0	0	1	1	60,157
St. Joseph	0	0	0	0	1	0	0	0	0	0	1	8,247
Three Rivers	1	0	0	0	0	0	0	1	0	0	0	7,743
Traverse City	1	0	0	0	0	0	0	1	0	0	0	15,105
Trenton	1	0	0	0	0	0	0	1	0	0	0	18,404
Troy	0	1	0	1	0	0	0	0	0	2	0	83,279
Van Buren Township	1	0	0	0	0	0	0	0	0	1	0	28,269
Walled Lake	1	0	0	0	0	0	0	0	0	1	0	7,158
Warren	8	3	1	1	1	0	0	2	4	5	3	135,080
Wayland	1	0	0	0	0	0	0	0	0	0	1	4,077
West Bloomfield Township	2	1	0	0	0	0	0	0	0	1	2	66,222
Westland	1	0	0	0	0	0	0	0	1	0	0	82,246
Wyandotte	1	0	0	0	0	0	0	1	0	0	0	25,082
Wyoming	2	0	0	1	0	0	0	1	1	1	0	74,603
Ypsilanti	1	0	0	1	0	0	0	1	1	0	0	19,901
Universities and Colleges	**28**	**2**	**6**	**1**	**1**	**0**	**0**					
Central Michigan University	0	0	1	0	1	0	0	0	0	2	0	26,841
Eastern Michigan University	1	0	1	0	0	0	0	0	1	0	1	23,447
Ferris State University	0	0	1	0	0	0	0	0	0	0	1	14,707
Grand Rapids Community College	2	0	0	0	0	0	0	0	0	1	1	16,590
Lansing Community College	1	0	0	0	0	0	0	0	0	0	1	17,562
Michigan State University	24	0	1	0	0	0	0	23	0	2	0	49,317
Oakland University	0	0	1	0	0	0	0	0	0	0	1	20,169
Schoolcraft College	0	0	1	0	0	0	0			1	0	12,385
University of Michigan, Ann Arbor	0	2	0	1	0	0	0	1	1	1	0	43,710
Metropolitan Counties	**25**	**5**	**5**	**5**	**1**	**1**	**0**					
Genesee	1	2	1	0	0	0	0	2	1	0	1	
Jackson	2	0	0	1	0	0	0	1	0	1	1	
Kent	1	0	1	1	0	1	0	1	1	1	1	
Macomb	3	0	0	0	0	0	0	0	1	2	0	
Midland	0	0	0	1	0	0	0	0	1	0	0	
Monroe	1	0	0	0	0	0	0	0	1	0	0	
Oakland	7	1	1	1	1	0	0	2	1	6	2	
Ottawa	4	2	0	0	0	0	0	1	3	1	1	
Van Buren	2	0	0	1	0	0	0	1	0	1	1	
Washtenaw	4	0	2	0	0	0	0	2	2	2	0	
Nonmetropolitan Counties	**5**	**0**	**3**	**1**	**0**	**0**	**0**					
Allegan	0	0	0	1	0	0	0	0	0	0	1	
Gratiot	0	0	1	0	0	0	0	0	0	1	0	
Isabella	1	0	0	0	0	0	0	0	1	0	0	

(Number.)

State/agency	Number of incidents per bias motivation							Number of incidents per quarter				Population[1]
	Race	Religion	Sexual orientation	Ethnicity	Disability	Gender	Gender identity	1st quarter	2nd quarter	3rd quarter	4th quarter	
Newaygo	2	0	2	0	0	0	0	0	0	2	2	
Tuscola	1	0	0	0	0	0	0	0	0	0	1	
Wexford	1	0	0	0	0	0	0	0	0	1	0	
State Police Agencies	1	0	0	0	0	0	0					
State Police, Gratiot County	1	0	0	0	0	0	0	0	0	0	1	
MINNESOTA												
Total	55	15	16	10	2	0	0					
Cities	54	15	15	9	2	0	0					
Alexandria	0	0	1	0	0	0	0	0	0	1	0	11,713
Apple Valley	0	0	0	0	1	0	0	0	0	1	0	50,472
Blaine	3	0	1	1	0	0	0	1	1	1	2	61,187
Brooklyn Park	0	0	1	0	0	0	0	1	0	0	0	78,986
Crystal	1	0	0	0	0	0	0	0	0	0	1	22,692
Duluth	1	0	0	0	0	0	0	0	0	0	1	86,106
Eagan	4	1	0	0	0	0	0	0	0	5	0	65,754
Eveleth	1	0	0	0	0	0	0	1	0	0	0	3,693
Fridley	2	0	0	0	0	0	0	1	0	1	0	27,778
Inver Grove Heights	2	0	1	2	0	0	0	2	1	2	0	34,454
Jordan	0	0	0	1	0	0	0	0	0	0	1	5,977
Mankato	2	0	0	0	0	0	0	1	1	0	0	40,959
Maplewood	0	0	0	1	0	0	0	0	0	1	0	40,295
Marshall	1	0	0	0	0	0	0	1	0	0	0	13,433
Mendota Heights	1	0	1	0	0	0	0	0	2	0	0	11,196
Minneapolis	11	10	7	3	1	0	0	8	10	7	7	404,461
Minnetonka	0	1	0	0	0	0	0	0	0	1	0	51,769
Moorhead	1	0	0	0	0	0	0	0	1	0	0	39,707
Plymouth	4	0	1	1	0	0	0	2	2	2	0	74,833
Robbinsdale	1	0	0	0	0	0	0	1	0	0	0	14,387
Roseville	1	0	0	0	0	0	0	0	1	0	0	35,332
St. Cloud	4	1	0	0	0	0	0		3	1	1	66,366
St. Louis Park	0	1	1	0	0	0	0	0	0	2	0	47,957
St. Paul	14	1	1	0	0	0	0	5	4	4	3	297,984
Metropolitan Counties	1	0	1	1	0	0	0					
Anoka	1	0	0	0	0	0	0	0	0	1	0	
Carlton	0	0	1	0	0	0	0	0	1	0	0	
Wright	0	0	0	1	0	0	0	0	0	1	0	
MISSISSIPPI												
Total	0	0	1	0	0	0	0					
Nonmetropolitan Counties	0	0	1	0	0	0	0					
Adams	0	0	1	0	0	0	0	0	0	0	1	
MISSOURI												
Total	47	10	13	3	1	0	2					
Cities	39	9	10	2	1	0	2					
Bolivar	1	0	0	0	0	0	0	0	1	0	0	10,523
Columbia	1	0	0	0	0	0	0	0	0	1	0	116,847
Creve Coeur	0	0	1	0	0	0	0	0	1	0	0	17,874
Grain Valley	0	1	0	0	0	0	0	0	1	0	0	13,188
Grandview	0	0	0	1	0	0	0	0	1	0	0	25,512
Hazelwood	1	0	0	0	0	0	0	0	0	0	1	25,662
Independence	2	1	0	0	0	0	0	1	0	0	2	117,321
Jennings	5	0	0	0	0	0	0	0	0	0	5	14,762
Kansas City	17	5	7	1	0	0	1	6	9	11	5	468,417
Lee's Summit	2	0	0	0	0	0	0	0	0	2	0	93,594
Rich Hill	1	0	0	0	0	0	0	0	1	0	0	1,334
Rolla	1	0	1	0	0	0	0	0	0	2	0	19,876
Springfield	3	1	0	0	0	0	1	1	0	0	4	165,280
St. Charles	0	0	0	0	1	0	0	1	0	0	0	67,970
St. Louis	4	1	1	0	0	0	0	0	2	2	2	318,574
St. Peters	1	0	0	0	0	0	0	1	0	0	0	55,362
Universities and Colleges	2	0	2	0	0	0	0					
Northwest Missouri State University	0	0	1	0	0	0	0	0	0	1	0	6,485

Table 13. Hate Crime Incidents Per Bias Motivation and Quarter, by Selected State and Agency, 2014—*Continued*

(Number.)

State/agency	Number of incidents per bias motivation							Number of incidents per quarter				Population[1]
	Race	Religion	Sexual orientation	Ethnicity	Disability	Gender	Gender identity	1st quarter	2nd quarter	3rd quarter	4th quarter	
University of Missouri........................												
Columbia	1	0	0	0	0	0	0				1	34,616
Kansas City	0	0	1	0	0	0	0	0	0	0	1	15,718
St. Louis	1	0	0	0	0	0	0	0	0	0	1	16,809
Metropolitan Counties	4	1	0	1	0	0	0					
St. Charles	1	0	0	0	0	0	0	0	0	1	0	
St. Louis County Police Department	3	1	0	1	0	0	0	1	2	1	1	
Nonmetropolitan Counties..............	2	0	1	0	0	0	0					
Henry....................................	0	0	1	0	0	0	0	0	1	0	0	
Ozark...................................	1	0	0	0	0	0	0	0	0	1	0	
Stone....................................	1	0	0	0	0	0	0	0	1	0	0	
MONTANA												
Total	18	3	3	3	2	0	1					
Cities	7	2	3	2	0	0	1					
Billings..................................	1	2	2	0	0	0	1	2	1	1	2	110,245
Columbia Falls	1	0	0	0	0	0	0	0	1	0	0	4,824
Deer Lodge	2	0	0	0	0	0	0	0	0	1	1	3,084
Helena..................................	1	0	0	1	0	0	0	1	0	1	0	29,928
Kalispell................................	1	0	1	0	0	0	0	1	0	0	1	21,238
Missoula................................	1	0	0	1	0	0	0	1	1	0	0	69,674
Metropolitan Counties	5	1	0	0	0	0	0					
Missoula................................	5	1	0	0	0	0	0	5	0	1	0	
Nonmetropolitan Counties..............	6	0	0	1	2	0	0					
Flathead................................	1	0	0	0	0	0	0	0	1	0	0	
Lake.....................................	1	0	0	0	0	0	0	0	0	1	0	
Lewis and Clark	2	0	0	1	2	0	0	0	0	2	3	
Park.....................................	1	0	0	0	0	0	0	1	0	0	0	
Powell..................................	1	0	0	0	0	0	0	0	1	0	0	
NEBRASKA												
Total	30	1	10	6	0	0	0					
Cities	30	1	10	6	0	0	0					
Blair.....................................	0	0	1	0	0	0	0	1	0	0	0	7,986
Chadron................................	1	0	0	0	0	0	0	0	1	0	0	5,773
Crete....................................	0	0	1	0	0	0	0		0	1	0	7,171
Lincoln..................................	19	0	3	6	0	0	0	5	15	4	4	271,208
Nebraska City	1	0	0	0	0	0	0	0	0	0	1	7,243
Norfolk.................................	1	0	1	0	0	0	0	0	0	0	2	24,588
Omaha[2]	8	1	4	0	0	0	0	2	5	2	4	438,465
NEVADA												
Total	10	1	9	4	0	0	0					
Cities	10	1	9	4	0	0	0					
Henderson.............................	1	0	0	1	0	0	0	0	0	2	0	274,121
Las Vegas Metropolitan Police Department..................................	7	0	9	1	0	0	0	2	0	6	9	1,530,899
North Las Vegas......................	0	0	0	1	0	0	0	0		0	1	229,436
Reno.....................................	2	1	0	1	0	0	0	0	1	1	2	235,055
NEW HAMPSHIRE												
Total	9	1	4	0	0	0	0					
Cities	9	1	4	0	0	0	0					
Belmont................................	1	0	0	0	0	0	0	0	0	1	0	7,257
Concord................................	0	0	1	0	0	0	0	0	0	1	0	42,358
Dover....................................	1	1	0	0	0	0	0	0	0	2	0	30,633
Farmington............................	2	0	0	0	0	0	0	1	0	1	0	6,800
Laconia.................................	1	0	0	0	0	0	0	0	0	1	0	16,043
Lancaster..............................	1	0	0	0	0	0	0	0	1	0	0	3,421
Lebanon................................	1	0	0	0	0	0	0	1	0	0	0	13,716
New London..........................	0	0	1	0	0	0	0	1	0	0	0	4,620
Pelham..................................	1	0	0	0	0	0	0	1	0	0	0	13,133

(Number.)

State/agency	Number of incidents per bias motivation							Number of incidents per quarter				Population[1]
	Race	Religion	Sexual orientation	Ethnicity	Disability	Gender	Gender identity	1st quarter	2nd quarter	3rd quarter	4th quarter	
Pembroke	0	0	1	0	0	0	0	0	0	0	1	7,125
Plymouth	1	0	1	0	0	0	0	0	1	0	1	6,989
NEW JERSEY												
Total	160	115	32	29	0	0	0					
Cities	157	112	31	28	0	0	0					
Aberdeen Township	1	0	0	1	0	0	0	0	0	0	2	18,215
Asbury Park	0	0	0	1	0	0	0	0	0	1	0	15,789
Atlantic Highlands	1	0	1	0	0	0	0	1	0	1	0	4,346
Berkeley Township	0	1	0	0	0	0	0	0	1	0	0	41,957
Bordentown Township	0	1	0	0	0	0	0	0	0	0	1	11,438
Bradley Beach	1	0	0	0	0	0	0	0	1	0	0	4,270
Brick Township	1	0	0	0	0	0	0	0	1	0	0	75,995
Byram Township	1	1	0	0	0	0	0	1	0	1	0	8,117
Carteret	0	1	0	0	0	0	0	0	1	0	0	24,264
Clark Township	1	0	0	0	0	0	0	0	1	0	0	15,308
Collingswood	1	0	0	0	0	0	0	0	0	1	0	13,855
Colts Neck Township	0	3	0	0	0	0	0	0	1	2	0	10,084
Cranbury Township	1	1	0	1	0	0	0	2	0	1	0	3,929
Denville Township	0	1	0	0	0	0	0	1	0	0	0	16,917
Dunellen	1	0	1	0	0	0	0	1	1	0	0	7,388
East Brunswick Township	3	5	1	0	0	0	0	3	2	0	4	48,391
East Hanover Township	0	3	0	0	0	0	0	0	1	0	2	11,338
Egg Harbor Township	1	0	0	0	0	0	0	0	0	0	1	43,992
Elk Township	1	0	0	0	0	0	0	0	1	0	0	4,262
Englewood	0	1	0	0	0	0	0	1	0	0	0	27,665
Evesham Township	8	1	2	1	0	0	0	1	3	1	7	45,623
Ewing Township	0	2	0	1	0	0	0	2	1	0	0	36,787
Fair Lawn	1	1	0	0	0	0	0	2	0	0	0	33,174
Fort Lee	1	3	0	1	0	0	0	1	2	2	0	36,226
Freehold	0	0	1	0	0	0	0	0	0	1	0	12,042
Freehold Township	1	2	0	0	0	0	0	0	1	1	1	36,033
Galloway Township	2	0	0	0	0	0	0	0	0	2	0	37,716
Glassboro	2	0	0	0	0	0	0	1	1	0	0	19,082
Glen Ridge	1	0	0	0	0	0	0	0	1	0	0	7,658
Hackettstown	1	0	0	0	0	0	0	1	0	0	0	9,576
Hamilton Township, Atlantic County	2	0	0	0	0	0	0	0	0	2	0	26,802
Hamilton Township, Mercer County	0	0	0	1	0	0	0	1	0			89,138
Harrison Township	2	0	0	0	0	0	0	1	1	0	0	12,812
Highland Park	3	1	0	0	0	0	0	1	1	1	1	14,478
Hightstown	1	0	0	1	0	0	0	0	1	0	1	5,592
Hillsborough Township	0	3	1	0	0	0	0	0	2	2	0	39,522
Hoboken	5	0	1	2	0	0	0	3	2	1	2	53,303
Holmdel Township	1	0	0	0	0	0	0	0	1	0	0	16,699
Hopewell Township	1	0	0	0	0	0	0	0	0	1	0	18,416
Howell Township	2	3	1	1	0	0	0	1	4	1	1	51,884
Jackson Township	1	0	0	0	0	0	0	0	0	0	1	56,347
Jersey City	0	1	2	1	0	0	0	2	1	1	0	260,005
Keansburg	3	0	0	1	0	0	0	1	1	1	1	9,991
Kearny	1	2	0	0	0	0	0	0	1	0	2	41,964
Lacey Township	1	0	1	0	0	0	0	2	0	0	0	28,100
Lakewood Township	7	8	0	0	0	0	0	1	5	7	2	93,749
Lawrence Township, Mercer County	0	2	0	0	0	0	0	0	0	2	0	33,133
Little Egg Harbor Township	3	1	1	0	0	0	0	3	1	1	0	20,401
Little Falls Township	3	0	1	0	0	0	0	0	0	0	4	14,564
Livingston Township	0	1	0	0	0	0	0	0	0	1	0	29,694
Lodi	1	0	0	0	0	0	0	0	1	0	0	24,648
Lopatcong Township	0	1	0	0	0	0	0	1	0	0	0	8,056
Madison	1	0	0	0	0	0	0	0	1	0	0	16,380
Manalapan Township	0	2	1	1	0	0	0	1	2	1	0	40,063
Manasquan	1	0	0	0	0	0	0	0	0	0	1	5,721
Manchester Township	0	1	0	0	0	0	0	0	1	0	0	43,394
Mansfield Township, Burlington County	0	2	0	0	0	0	0	0	0	0	2	8,568
Mansfield Township, Warren County	0	1	0	0	0	0	0	0	0	1	0	7,550
Mantua Township	0	0	1	0	0	0	0	0	0	1	0	15,105
Maple Shade Township	1	0	0	0	0	0	0	0	1	0	0	19,024
Marlboro Township	0	2	1	0	0	0	0	0	0	1	2	40,351
Medford Township	3	3	0	1	0	0	0	3		0	4	23,343

State/agency	Number of incidents per bias motivation							Number of incidents per quarter				Population[1]
	Race	Religion	Sexual orientation	Ethnicity	Disability	Gender	Gender identity	1st quarter	2nd quarter	3rd quarter	4th quarter	
Mendham	1	0	0	0	0	0	0	0	1	0	0	5,029
Metuchen	1	0	0	0	0	0	0	0	1	0	0	13,823
Middlesex	1	0	0	0	0	0	0	0	0	0	1	13,876
Middle Township	0	1	0	0	0	0	0	1	0	0	0	18,883
Middletown Township	1	2	0	0	0	0	0	1	2	0	0	66,223
Monroe Township, Gloucester County	2	0	0	0	0	0	0	0	0	1	1	36,933
Monroe Township, Middlesex County .	8	2	0	1	0	0	0	3	4	3	1	42,333
Moorestown Township	1	0	0	0	0	0	0	1	0	0	0	20,651
Morris Township	0	1	0	0	0	0	0	0	0	0	1	22,614
Mount Laurel Township	1	0	0	0	0	0	0	0	1	0	0	41,698
Mount Olive Township	1	1	0	0	0	0	0	1	0	0	1	28,891
Neptune City	1	0	0	0	0	0	0	0	1	0	0	4,831
Neptune Township	7	2	3	0	0	0	0	2	1	7	2	27,812
Newark	5	0	0	0	0	0	0	0	0	0	5	279,110
New Brunswick	3	1	2	0	0	0	0	2	0	1	3	56,193
New Providence	1	1	0	0	0	0	0	1	0	1	0	12,387
Newton	1	0	0	0	0	0	0	0	0	0	1	7,897
North Bergen Township	0	0	2	1	0	0	0	1	2	0	0	62,817
North Brunswick Township	0	0	1	1	0	0	0	0	0	1	1	42,526
Nutley Township	1	1	0	0	0	0	0	1	1	0	0	28,625
Ocean City	0	2	0	0	0	0	0	0	0	2	0	11,392
Oradell	0	2	0	0	0	0	0	0	0	0	2	8,175
Palmyra	1	0	0	0	0	0	0	0	0	1	0	7,353
Paramus	1	1	0	0	0	0	0	0	0	1	1	26,791
Parsippany-Troy Hills Township	0	1	0	0	0	0	0	0	1	0	0	54,025
Passaic	0	2	0	1	0	0	0	2	0	1	0	71,228
Pemberton Township	2	0	0	0	0	0	0	0	1	0	1	27,916
Pine Hill	0	0	1	0	0	0	0	0	1	0	0	10,583
Piscataway Township	0	2	0	0	0	0	0	1	1	0	0	59,089
Pitman	5	1	1	0	0	0	0	0	4	1	2	8,941
Point Pleasant	1	0	0	0	0	0	0	0	1	0	0	18,547
Randolph Township	3	3	0	2	0	0	0	2	5	1	0	26,055
Readington Township	1	0	0	0	0	0	0	0	1	0	0	16,081
Ridgefield Park	0	1	0	0	0	0	0	0	1	0	0	12,990
Ridgewood	0	1	0	1	0	0	0	0	1	0	1	25,482
Riverdale	0	1	0	0	0	0	0	1	0	0	0	4,162
Riverton	1	0	0	0	0	0	0	1	0	0	0	2,771
Robbinsville Township	1	1	1	0	0	0	0	0	3	0	0	14,176
Roxbury Township	0	1	0	0	0	0	0	0	0	0	1	23,640
Rumson	0	2	0	0	0	0	0	0	0	0	2	6,980
South Brunswick Township	0	2	1	4	0	0	0	1	2	3	1	45,096
South Plainfield	1	0	0	0	0	0	0	0	1	0	0	23,911
Springfield	1	0	0	0	0	0	0	0	0	0	1	17,104
Spring Lake	0	1	0	0	0	0	0	0	1	0	0	3,003
Stratford	1	1	0	0	0	0	0	2	0	0	0	6,943
Trenton	1	0	0	0	0	0	0	0	0	1	0	84,324
Union Beach	0	0	1	0	0	0	0	1	0	0	0	5,701
Union City	1	3	0	1	0	0	0	3	0	0	2	68,787
Union Township	1	0	0	0	0	0	0	0	0	0	1	57,830
Verona	0	2	0	0	0	0	0	2	0	0	0	13,771
Vineland	0	0	0	1	0	0	0	1	0	0	0	61,115
Voorhees Township	0	1	0	0	0	0	0	0	0	1	0	29,240
Weehawken Township	0	1	0	0	0	0	0	0	0	0	1	13,579
Westampton Township	0	1	0	0	0	0	0	0	0	1	0	8,772
West Deptford Township	2	0	0	0	0	0	0	1	0	0	1	21,490
West Long Branch	2	0	0	0	0	0	0	1	1	0	0	8,615
West Milford Township	3	1	0	0	0	0	0	0	0	2	2	26,623
Winslow Township	1	0	0	0	0	0	0	0	0	1	0	39,139
Woodbridge Township	3	4	0	0	0	0	0	2	3	1	1	100,969
Woodbury	13	1	1	0	0	0	0	5	4	1	5	10,071
Woodstown	1	0	0	0	0	0	0	0	0	0	1	3,478
Metropolitan Counties	2	0	1	1	0	0	0					
Camden County Police Department	2	0	1	1	0	0	0	2	1	0	1	
State Police Agencies	1	3	0	0	0	0	0					
Monmouth County	0	3	0	0	0	0	0	0	0	3	0	
Sussex County	1	0	0	0	0	0	0	1	0	0	0	

Table 13. Hate Crime Incidents Per Bias Motivation and Quarter, by Selected State and Agency, 2014—*Continued*

(Number.)

State/agency	Number of incidents per bias motivation							Number of incidents per quarter				Population[1]
	Race	Religion	Sexual orientation	Ethnicity	Disability	Gender	Gender identity	1st quarter	2nd quarter	3rd quarter	4th quarter	
NEW MEXICO												
Total	6	4	1	2	0	0	0					
Cities	4	4	1	1	0	0	0					
Albuquerque	4	4	1	1	0	0	0		6		4	558,874
Universities and Colleges	1	0	0	0	0	0	0					
University of New Mexico	1	0	0	0	0	0	0			1		28,592
Metropolitan Counties	1	0	0	1	0	0	0					
Bernalillo	1	0	0	1	0	0	0		1		1	
NEW YORK												
Total	108	287	110	35	1	0	4					
Cities	64	187	92	30	0	0	4					
Albany	1	1	1	0	0	0	0	1	2	0	0	98,595
Buffalo	10	0	4	1	0	0	0	2	5	4	4	258,419
Carthage Village	0	0	0	1	0	0	0	0	0	1	0	3,710
Cheektowaga Town	4	0	0	0	0	0	0	0	1	3	0	78,209
Clarkstown Town	0	1	0	0	0	0	0	0	0	0	1	81,435
Cortland	0	2	0	0	0	0	0	0	2	0	0	19,032
Crawford Town	1	1	0	0	0	0	0	2	0	0	0	9,240
Dobbs Ferry Village	1	0	0	0	0	0	0	0	0	1	0	11,102
Fishkill Town	0	1	0	0	0	0	0	0	0	1	0	21,502
Freeport Village	0	0	1	0	0	0	0	0	0	0	1	43,234
Geddes Town	1	0	0	0	0	0	0	0	0	1	0	10,436
Geneseo Village	0	0	0	0	0	0	1	0	0	1	0	7,914
Greenburgh Town	0	0	0	1	0	0	0	1	0	0	0	45,133
Lake Placid Village	1	0	0	0	0	0	0	0	0	1	0	2,460
Manlius Town	0	0	1	0	0	0	0	0	0	0	1	24,577
Middletown	0	2	0	0	0	0	0	2	0	0	0	27,700
Monroe Village	1	1	0	0	0	0	0	0	0	2	0	8,627
Mount Vernon	1	0	0	0	0	0	0	1	0	0	0	68,442
New Rochelle	1	2	1	2	0	0	0	1	3	2	0	80,030
New York	37	168	78	22	0	0	2	60	68	107	72	8,473,938
Niagara Falls	0	0	0	1	0	0	0	0	1	0	0	49,300
Oneonta City	0	1	0	0	0	0	0	0	0	0	1	13,961
Orangetown Town	1	4	0	1	0	0	0	0	0	5	1	37,677
Poughkeepsie	1	0	0	0	0	0	0	0	1	0	0	30,554
Poughkeepsie Town	1	0	0	0	0	0	0	0	0	0	1	43,599
Rochester	1	0	2	0	0	0	0	1	2	0	0	210,347
Southold Town	0	0	1	0	0	0	0	0	0	1	0	19,991
Spring Valley Village	0	1	0	0	0	0	1	0	0	0	2	32,586
Yonkers	1	1	3	1	0	0	0	0	4	1	1	200,624
Yorktown Town	0	1	0	0	0	0	0	0	0	0	1	36,989
Universities and Colleges	2	10	3	1	0	0	0					
Cornell University	0	0	1	0	0	0	0	0	1	0	0	21,593
State University of New York												
Binghamton	0	1	0	0	0	0	0	1	0	0	0	16,077
Stony Brook	1	1	0	0	0	0	0	1	0	1	0	24,143
State University of New York Agricultural and Technical College												
Cobleskill	0	0	0	1	0	0	0	0	0	0	1	2,453
Morrisville	0	3	0	0	0	0	0	3	0	0	0	3,028
State University of New York College ..												
Buffalo	0	1	1	0	0	0	0	1	1	0	0	11,091
New Paltz	0	1	0	0	0	0	0	0	0	1	0	7,578
Oneonta	0	1	0	0	0	0	0	0	0	0	1	6,034
Oswego	0	1	0	0	0	0	0	1	0	0	0	8,117
Potsdam	1	1	1	0	0	0	0	1	1	0	1	4,042
Metropolitan Counties	31	75	14	3	1	0	0					
Erie	0	0	1	0	0	0	0	0	0	1	0	
Nassau	17	21	2	1	0	0	0	7	16	13	5	
Niagara	0	0	0	0	1	0	0	0	1	0	0	
Ontario	0	1	0	0	0	0	0	0	0	1	0	
Suffolk County Police Department	14	53	9	2	0	0	0	15	20	19	24	
Washington	0	0	1	0	0	0	0	0	0	0	1	
Westchester Public Safety	0	0	1	0	0	0	0	1	0	0	0	

State/agency	Number of incidents per bias motivation							Number of incidents per quarter				Population[1]
	Race	Religion	Sexual orientation	Ethnicity	Disability	Gender	Gender identity	1st quarter	2nd quarter	3rd quarter	4th quarter	
State Police Agencies	5	3	1	1	0	0	0					
Chenango County	1	0	0	0	0	0	0	0	1	0	0	
Columbia County	0	0	1	0	0	0	0	0	1	0	0	
Essex County	1	1	0	0	0	0	0	0	0	2	0	
Herkimer County	0	0	0	1	0	0	0	0	1	0	0	
Orange County	0	1	0	0	0	0	0	0	1	0	0	
Otsego County	1	0	0	0	0	0	0	1	0	0	0	
Suffolk County	1	0	0	0	0	0	0	0	1	0	0	
Tompkins County	1	0	0	0	0	0	0	0	0	1	0	
Washington County	0	1	0	0	0	0	0	0	1	0	0	
Other Agencies	6	12	0	0	0	0	0					
New York City Metropolitan Transportation Authority	5	5	0	0	0	0	0	1	4	0	5	
State Park:												
Long Island Region	0	7	0	0	0	0	0	0	4	1	2	
New York City Region	1	0	0	0	0	0	0	0	0	0	1	
NORTH CAROLINA												
Total	85	19	23	11	2	0	0					
Cities	67	11	17	9	2	0	0					
Asheville	2	0	2	0	0	0	0	2	0	0	2	88,184
Burlington	0	0	1	0	0	0	0	0	1	0	0	51,627
Chapel Hill	2	0	0	0	0	0	0	1	0	1	0	60,190
Charlotte-Mecklenburg	11	5	5	3	1	0	0	6	10	5	4	856,916
Fayetteville	7	0	1	0	0	0	0	0	6	1	1	205,306
Greensboro	5	0	1	0	0	0	0	0	3	0	3	282,203
Greenville	3	1	0	0	0	0	0	1	0	2	1	90,198
High Point	1	0	0	1	0	0	0	0	2	0	0	108,540
Hillsborough	2	0	0	0	0	0	0	0	1	1	0	6,451
Hope Mills	2	1	0	1	0	0	0	1	3	0	0	16,399
Jacksonville	1	0	0	0	0	0	0	0	1	0	0	68,651
Lenoir	1	0	0	0	0	0	0	0	1	0	0	17,994
Mount Airy	1	0	0	0	0	0	0	0	0	0	1	10,420
Oxford	3	0	0	0	0	0	0	2	0	1	0	8,748
Raleigh	14	2	4	4	1	0	0	1	5	10	9	438,363
Roanoke Rapids	3	0	0	0	0	0	0	2	1	0	0	15,602
Salisbury	1	0	0	0	0	0	0	1	0	0	0	33,627
Stallings	0	0	1	0	0	0	0	1	0	0	0	14,848
Waynesville	1	0	0	0	0	0	0	0	0	1	0	9,712
Williamston	1	0	0	0	0	0	0	0	0	1	0	5,345
Wilmington	2	2	2	0	0	0	0	3	2	0	1	113,418
Wilson	4	0	0	0	0	0	0	2	1	0	1	49,731
Universities and Colleges	2	6	1	0	0	0	0					
East Carolina University	0	4	0	0	0	0	0	0	1	1	2	26,887
Fayetteville State University	1	0	0	0	0	0	0	0	0	1	0	6,179
North Carolina School of the Arts	1	0	0	0	0	0	0	1	0	0	0	912
University of North Carolina:												
Asheville	0	1	0	0	0	0	0	1	0	0	0	3,784
Wilmington	0	0	1	0	0	0	0	1	0	0	0	13,937
Western Carolina University	0	1	0	0	0	0	0	0	0	1	0	10,107
Metropolitan Counties	13	2	4	1	0	0	0					
Buncombe	2	0	1	0	0	0	0	0	1	1	1	
Cumberland	1	0	0	0	0	0	0	0	0	0	1	
Currituck	2	0	0	0	0	0	0	1	0	1	0	
Forsyth	3	2	0	0	0	0	0	0	2	2	1	
Gaston County Police Department	2	0	0	0	0	0	0	0	2	0	0	
Guilford	1	0	2	1	0	0	0	0	3	1	0	
Iredell	1	0	0	0	0	0	0	0	0	1	0	
New Hanover	0	0	1	0	0	0	0	0	0	1	0	
Rockingham	1	0	0	0	0	0	0	0	0	0	1	
Nonmetropolitan Counties	3	0	1	1	0	0	0					
Pasquotank	3	0	0	0	0	0	0	1	0	0	2	
Surry	0	0	0	1	0	0	0	0	0	0	1	
Wilkes	0	0	1	0	0	0	0	0	1	0	0	

Table 13. Hate Crime Incidents Per Bias Motivation and Quarter, by Selected State and Agency, 2014—*Continued*

(Number.)

State/agency	Number of incidents per bias motivation							Number of incidents per quarter				Population[1]
	Race	Religion	Sexual orientation	Ethnicity	Disability	Gender	Gender identity	1st quarter	2nd quarter	3rd quarter	4th quarter	
NORTH DAKOTA.............................												
Total	25	3	4	8	0	0	0					
Cities	19	3	4	5	0	0	0					
Bismarck...	5	1	0	2	0	0	0	0	4	3	1	68,492
Devils Lake...	1	0	0	0	0	0	0	0	1	0	0	7,286
Fargo...	5	1	2	1	0	0	0	1	5	0	3	115,686
Grand Forks.......................................	1	0	0	1	0	0	0	0	1	1	0	55,438
Mandan..	1	0	0	0	0	0	0	0	1	0	0	20,253
Minot...	1	1	0	0	0	0	0	1	1	0	0	47,682
Rolla..	0	0	1	0	0	0	0	0	1	0	0	1,350
Tioga...	0	0	0	1	0	0	0	0	0	0	1	1,661
West Fargo...	5	0	1	0	0	0	0	0	2	2	2	30,970
Metropolitan Counties	4	0	0	0	0	0	0					
Cass..	2	0	0	0	0	0	0	1	0	0	1	
Morton...	2	0	0	0	0	0	0	0	1	0	1	
Nonmetropolitan Counties.............	2	0	0	3	0	0	0					
Bottineau...	0	0	0	1	0	0	0	1	0	0	0	
Dunn...	1	0	0	0	0	0	0	0	0	1	0	
McLean..	0	0	0	1	0	0	0	0	0	1	0	
Rolette...	0	0	0	1	0	0	0	1	0	0	0	
Ward...	1	0	0	0	0	0	0	0	1	0	0	
OHIO												
Total	244	26	69	56	8	0	0					
Cities	220	23	61	54	7	0	0					
Akron...	2	1	1	0	0	0	0	1	0	3	0	197,891
Athens..	0	0	1	0	0	0	0	0	0	1	0	24,083
Austintown...	1	0	0	0	0	0	0	0	0	0	1	35,997
Barberton	2	0	0	0	0	0	0	0	1	1	0	26,286
Bath Township, Summit County	1	0	0	0	0	0	0	1	0	0	0	9,805
Bellbrook..	1	0	0	0	0	0	0	1	0	0	0	7,044
Bellefontaine......................................	1	0	0	0	0	0	0	0	0	0	1	13,156
Brunswick Hills Township	0	0	1	0	0	0	0	0	1	0	0	10,202
Butler Township	0	0	0	0	1	0	0	0	0	0	1	7,864
Canton...	1	0	0	0	0	0	0	0	1	0	0	72,391
Carroll Township................................	0	0	0	0	1	0	0	0	0	1	0	2,121
Celina..	2	0	1	0	0	0	0	0	2	1	0	10,370
Cincinnati...	35	3	5	11	0	0	0	8	22	13	11	297,671
Circleville...	0	0	1	0	0	0	0	1	0	0	0	13,469
Cleveland...	3	0	2	0	0	0	0	0	3	0	2	388,655
Columbus[2].......................................	89	8	17	34	1	0	0	30	42	44	33	830,811
Dayton...	6	1	2	1	0	0	0	1	1	3	5	143,217
East Palestine.....................................	1	0	0	0	0	0	0	1	0	0	0	4,601
Forest Park...	1	0	0	0	0	0	0	0	0	0	1	18,724
Garfield Heights.................................	3	1	2	0	3	0	0	3	3	2	1	28,273
Grove City	4	1	0	0	0	0	0	3	2	0	0	37,945
Groveport...	0	0	0	1	0	0	0	0	1	0	0	5,700
Hamilton Township, Warren County....	1	0	0	0	0	0	0	1	0	0	0	21,920
Heath	0	0	1	0	0	0	0	0	1	0	0	10,485
Hubbard...	1	0	0	0	0	0	0	1	0	0	0	7,724
Huber Heights.....................................	1	1	0	0	0	0	0	0	1	0	1	38,137
Hudson...	0	0	1	0	0	0	0	0	0	1	0	22,526
Independence.....................................	1	0	0	0	0	0	0	0	1	0	0	7,147
Jackson Township, Stark County	0	0	0	0	1	0	0	0	0	0	1	40,645
Lakewood...	3	0	0	0	0	0	0	0	0	1	2	50,923
Lancaster	4	0	0	0	0	0	0	1	2	0	1	39,453
Leipsic...	0	1	0	0	0	0	0	1	0			2,035
Lima..	0	0	1	0	0	0	0			1	0	38,265
Lockland..	3	0	0	0	0	0	0	0	1	0	2	3,434
Lorain..	2	0	4	2	0	0	0	1	1	3	3	63,619
Louisville..	1	0	0	0	0	0	0	0	0	1	0	9,150
Mansfield..	1	0	0	1	0	0	0	0	0	2	0	46,145
Marysville...	1	0	0	0	0	0	0	0	1	0	0	22,460
Mason..	1	0	0	0	0	0	0	0	0	0	1	31,416
Maumee...	0	1	0	0	0	0	0	0	0	0	1	14,062

Table 13. Hate Crime Incidents Per Bias Motivation and Quarter, by Selected State and Agency, 2014—*Continued*

(Number.)

State/agency	Number of incidents per bias motivation							Number of incidents per quarter				Population[1]
	Race	Religion	Sexual orientation	Ethnicity	Disability	Gender	Gender identity	1st quarter	2nd quarter	3rd quarter	4th quarter	
Medina	0	1	0	1	0	0	0	1	0	0	1	26,551
Miamisburg	0	1	0	1	0	0	0	0	2	0	0	20,109
Milton Township	1	0	0	0	0	0	0	0	1	0	0	2,488
Minster	0	0	1	0	0	0	0	1	0	0	0	2,835
Monroe	0	0	1	0	0	0	0	1				15,498
Montgomery	1	0	0	0	0	0	0	0	0	0	1	10,395
Montpelier	1	0	0	0	0	0	0	0	0	1	0	4,048
Moraine	2	0	0	0	0	0	0	1	0	0	1	6,331
Mount Healthy	1	0	0	0	0	0	0	1	0	0	0	6,051
Napoleon	0	0	2	0	0	0	0	0	1	1	0	8,687
New Albany	0	1	0	0	0	0	0	0	0	0	1	9,111
Newton Falls	0	0	1	0	0	0	0	0	0	0	1	4,701
Niles	1	0	0	0	0	0	0	0	0	1	0	18,848
Northwood	0	1	0	0	0	0	0	0	0	1	0	5,364
Norwood	3	0	0	0	0	0	0	1	0	1	1	19,027
Oregon	0	0	0	1	0	0	0	0	0	1	0	20,207
Parma	3	0	0	0	0	0	0	0	1	0	2	80,168
Pomeroy	1	0	0	0	0	0	0	1	0	0	0	1,842
Powell	1	0	0	0	0	0	0	0	1	0	0	12,410
Powhatan Point	1	0	0	0	0	0	0	0	0	1	0	1,577
Springfield	1	0	0	0	0	0	0	0	0	0	1	58,891
Springfield Township, Hamilton County	1	0	0	0	0	0	0	0	0	1	0	36,479
St. Clair Township	1	0	0	0	0	0	0	0	0	1	0	7,793
Streetsboro	1	0	0	0	0	0	0	1	0	0	0	16,152
Tipp City	1	0	0	0	0	0	0	0	1	0	0	9,839
Toledo	12	0	8	0	0	0	0	2	8	8	2	281,150
Trotwood	1	0	0	0	0	0	0	0	1	0	0	24,193
Urbana	0	0	2	0	0	0	0	1	0	1	0	11,584
Van Wert	0	0	1	0	0	0	0	1	0	0	0	10,763
Walbridge	1	0	0	0	0	0	0	1	0	0	0	3,068
Warren	1	0	0	0	0	0	0	0	1	0	0	40,592
Warren Township	1	0	0	0	0	0	0	0	1	0	0	5,395
Washington Court House	0	0	1	0	0	0	0	0	1	0	0	14,072
Wauseon	1	0	0	0	0	0	0	0	1	0	0	7,292
Weathersfield	1	0	0	0	0	0	0	1	0	0	0	8,145
West Chester Township	0	1	0	0	0	0	0	0	0	0	1	59,629
Westerville	2	0	0	0	0	0	0	1	1	0	0	37,836
Wilmington	2	0	2	0	0	0	0	0	2	0	2	12,455
Worthington	1	0	1	0	0	0	0	0	1	1	0	13,903
Xenia	2	0	1	1	0	0	0	1	1	1	1	25,932
Zanesville	1	0	0	0	0	0	0	1	0	0	0	25,415
Universities and Colleges	2	1	1	0	0	0	0					
Capital University	0	1	1	0	0	0	0	0	0	0	2	3,628
Ohio State University, Columbus	2	0	0	0	0	0	0	1	0	1	0	57,466
Metropolitan Counties	17	0	2	0	1	0	0					
Butler	1	0	0	0	0	0	0	0	1	0	0	
Clark	1	0	0	0	0	0	0	1	0	0	0	
Fairfield	0	0	0	0	1	0	0	1	0	0	0	
Greene	7	0	0	0	0	0	0	0	3	1	3	
Madison	1	0	0	0	0	0	0	0	1	0	0	
Montgomery	2	0	0	0	0	0	0	2	0	0	0	
Perry	1	0	0	0	0	0	0	0	0	1	0	
Portage	1	0	0	0	0	0	0	1				
Richland	0	0	2	0	0	0	0	1	1	0	0	
Summit	2	0	0	0	0	0	0	0	0	0	2	
Warren	1	0	0	0	0	0	0	0	1	0	0	
Nonmetropolitan Counties	5	2	5	2	0	0	0					
Ashland	0	1	0	0	0	0	0	0	0	1	0	
Auglaize	0	0	1	0	0	0	0	0	1	0	0	
Coshocton	0	0	1	0	0	0	0	0	0	0	1	
Fayette	0	0	0	1	0	0	0	0	0	0	1	
Knox	1	0	0	0	0	0	0	0	1	0	0	
Morgan	1	0	0	0	0	0	0	1	0	0	0	
Muskingum	1	0	0	0	0	0	0	0	1	0	0	
Paulding	1	0	1	0	0	0	0	0	0	2	0	
Preble	0	1	0	0	0	0	0	1	0	0	0	

Table 13. Hate Crime Incidents Per Bias Motivation and Quarter, by Selected State and Agency, 2014—*Continued*

(Number.)

State/agency	Number of incidents per bias motivation							Number of incidents per quarter				Population[1]
	Race	Religion	Sexual orientation	Ethnicity	Disability	Gender	Gender identity	1st quarter	2nd quarter	3rd quarter	4th quarter	
Ross..........................	1	0	1	1	0	0	0	0	0	0	3	
Shelby.........................	0	0	1	0	0	0	0	0	0	0	1	
OKLAHOMA..................................												
Total	13	4	10	5	1	0	0					
Cities	9	3	7	4	1	0	0					
Bethany...................................	1	0	0	0	0	0	0	1	0	0	0	19,683
Catoosa..................................	0	0	0	1	0	0	0	1	0	0	0	7,161
Edmond...................................	1	1	0	0	0	0	0	0	0	0	2	88,383
Fort Gibson............................	0	0	0	1	0	0	0	0	0	1	0	4,115
Hobart....................................	1	0	0	0	0	0	0	0	1	0	0	3,694
Mooreland...............................	1	0	0	0	0	0	0	0	0	1	0	1,285
Muskogee................................	2	0	0	0	1	0	0	0	2	1	0	38,759
Norman...................................	1	0	0	0	0	0	0	0	1	0	0	119,956
Oklahoma City........................	2	2	4	1	0	0	0	2	3	4	0	617,975
Sapulpa..................................	0	0	1	1	0	0	0	1	0	1	0	20,896
The Village..............................	0	0	1	0	0	0	0	0	1	0	0	9,336
Woodward	0	0	1	0	0	0	0	0	0	0	1	12,980
Universities and Colleges	1	0	1	0	0	0	0					
University of Central Oklahoma..........	1	0	1	0	0	0	0	0	1	1	0	17,220
Nonmetropolitan Counties..............	3	1	2	1	0	0	0					
Delaware	0	1	0	0	0	0	0	1	0	0	0	
Marshall..................................	0	0	1	0	0	0	0	0	0	1	0	
Payne......................................	2	0	1	0	0	0	0	0	3	0	0	
Tillman	1	0	0	0	0	0	0	0	0	1	0	
Woodward	0	0	0	1	0	0	0	0	1	0	0	
OREGON..												
Total	9	3	6	8	0	0	0					
Cities	6	1	5	7	0	0	0					
Grants Pass.............................	1	0	0	0	0	0	0	0	1	0	0	35,192
Independence..........................	0	0	0	1	0	0	0	1	0	0	0	8,672
Madras....................................	1	0	0	0	0	0	0	1	0	0		6,376
Medford..................................	0	0	1	0	0	0	0	0	0	1	0	78,356
Pendleton................................	1	0	0	0	0	0	0	0	0	0	1	17,006
Redmond.................................	0	0	1	0	0	0	0	0	1	0	0	27,733
Reedsport...............................	0	0	1	0	0	0	0	0	0	1	0	4,075
Salem......................................	1	0	1	2	0	0	0	2	0	2	0	162,028
Springfield...............................	2	0	1	3	0	0	0	1	2	1	2	60,377
Sutherlin.................................	0	1	0	1	0	0	0	0	2	0	0	7,729
Metropolitan Counties	1	0	0	1	0	0	0					
Deschutes................................	1	0	0	0	0	0	0	1	0	0	0	
Yamhill....................................	0	0	0	1	0	0	0	1	0	0	0	
Nonmetropolitan Counties..............	2	2	1	0	0	0	0					
Douglas	1	0	1	0	0	0	0	0	0	1	1	
Hood River...............................	0	2	0	0	0	0	0	0	0	2	0	
Wasco......................................	1	0	0	0	0	0	0		0	1	0	
PENNSYLVANIA................................												
Total	34	8	1	7	0	0	0					
Cities	27	6	0	7	0	0	0					
Abington Township, Montgomery County	0	1	0	1	0	0	0	0	0	0	2	55,628
Allentown................................	1	0	0	0	0	0	0	0	1	0	0	118,710
Economy..................................	5	0	0	0	0	0	0	1	1	3	0	9,323
Ferguson Township	0	1	0	0	0	0	0	0	0	0	1	18,198
Hazleton..................................	0	0	0	1	0	0	0	0	0	0	1	25,023
Horsham Township[2]	0	1	0	0	0	0	0	0	1	0	0	26,481
Lehighton................................	1	0	0	0	0	0	0	0	0	0	1	5,395
Mercersburg.............................	1	0	0	0	0	0	0	0	0	0	1	1,557
Philadelphia.............................	8	1	0	2	0	0	0	1	6	3	1	1,559,062
Pittsburgh................................	6	2	0	1	0	0	0	1	1	3	4	307,613
Portage...................................	1	0	0	0	0	0	0	1	0	0	0	2,550

Table 13. Hate Crime Incidents Per Bias Motivation and Quarter, by Selected State and Agency, 2014—*Continued*

(Number.)

State/agency	Race	Religion	Sexual orientation	Ethnicity	Disability	Gender	Gender identity	1st quarter	2nd quarter	3rd quarter	4th quarter	Population[1]
Reading	2	0	0	0	0	0	0	0	1	1	0	87,848
Scranton	1	0	0	0	0	0	0	0	0	1	0	75,749
Southwest Mercer County Regional	1	0	0	0	0	0	0	0	0	0	1	10,160
State College	0	0	0	1	0	0	0	0	0	0	1	56,551
Washington Township, Franklin County	0	0	0	1	0	0	0	0	0	0	1	14,468
Universities and Colleges	4	1	1	0	0	0	0					
Lock Haven University	1	0	0	0	0	0	0	1	0	0	0	5,260
Pennsylvania State University:												
Altoona	1	0	0	0	0	0	0	1	0	0	0	3,861
University Park	2	1	1	0	0	0	0	2	2	0	0	46,615
State Police Agencies	3	1	0	0	0	0	0					
Huntingdon County	1	0	0	0	0	0	0	0	1	0	0	
Skippack	1	1	0	0	0	0	0	0	0	1	1	
Perry County	1	0	0	0	0	0	0	0	0	1		
RHODE ISLAND												
Total	1	1	1	1	0	0	0					
Cities	1	1	1	1	0	0	0					
Charlestown	0	0	1	0	0	0	0	1	0	0	0	7,798
Pawtucket	1	0	0	0	0	0	0	0	0	1	0	71,443
Providence	0	0	0	1	0	0	0	0	0	0	1	178,640
West Warwick	0	1	0	0	0	0	0	1	0	0	0	28,934
SOUTH CAROLINA												
Total	23	7	10	4	5	0	0					
Cities	15	2	4	2	1	0	0					
Abbeville	0	0	1	0	0	0	0	0	0	1	0	5,163
Bluffton	0	0	0	1	0	0	0	0	0	1	0	13,755
Cayce	1	0	0	0	0	0	0	0	1	0	0	12,939
Charleston	2	0	0	0	0	0	0	1	0	0	1	129,867
Chester	1	0	0	0	0	0	0	0	0	1	0	5,529
Columbia	1	0	1	0	0	0	0	0	1	0	1	134,124
Darlington	0	0	0	0	1	0	0	1	0	0	0	6,223
Landrum	2	0	0	0	0	0	0	0	0	2		2,458
Lexington	0	0	0	1	0	0	0	0	0	1	0	19,998
Mauldin	1	0	0	0	0	0	0	0	0	1	0	24,869
Moncks Corner	1	0	0	0	0	0	0	1	0	0	0	9,471
Myrtle Beach	1	0	0	0	0	0	0	0	1	0	0	29,686
Pacolet	0	0	1	0	0	0	0	1	0	0	0	2,297
Simpsonville	1	0	0	0	0	0	0	0	1	0	0	19,918
St. George	2	0	0	0	0	0	0	1	0	1		2,157
Ware Shoals	1	0	1	0	0	0	0	1	1	0	0	2,171
Winnsboro	1	2	0	0	0	0	0	0	3	0	0	3,395
Universities and Colleges	0	0	1	0	0	0	0					
University of South Carolina, Upstate	0	0	1	0	0	0	0	0	1	0	0	5,445
Metropolitan Counties	6	1	2	2	0	0	0					
Anderson	1	0	0	0	0	0	0	0	1	0	0	
Greenville	1	0	0	0	0	0	0	1	0	0	0	
Lancaster	1	0	1	0	0	0	0	0	1	1	0	
Pickens	1	0	0	1	0	0	0	0	1	1	0	
Richland	1	0	0	0	0	0	0	0	0	0	1	
Spartanburg	0	1	0	0	0	0	0	0	0	0	1	
Sumter	0	0	1	1	0	0	0	0	0	1	1	
York	1	0	0	0	0	0	0	1	0	0	0	
Nonmetropolitan Counties	1	4	3	0	4	0	0					
Abbeville	0	2	0	0	0	0	0	1	0	0	1	
Cherokee	0	0	1	0	4	0	0	1	0	4		
Greenwood	0	0	1	0	0	0	0	0	1	0	0	
Orangeburg	0	2	0	0	0	0	0	0	0	0	2	
Williamsburg	1	0	1	0	0	0	0	1	1	0	0	

Table 13. Hate Crime Incidents Per Bias Motivation and Quarter, by Selected State and Agency, 2014—*Continued*

(Number.)

State/agency	Number of incidents per bias motivation							Number of incidents per quarter				Population[1]
	Race	Religion	Sexual orientation	Ethnicity	Disability	Gender	Gender identity	1st quarter	2nd quarter	3rd quarter	4th quarter	
SOUTH DAKOTA												
Total	9	2	3	2	1	0	1					
Cities	6	2	3	2	0	0	1					
Aberdeen	0	0	0	0	0	0	1			1		27,629
Canton	1	0	0	0	0	0	0	0	0	1	0	3,321
Rapid City	0	0	2	1	0	0	0	2	0	1	0	71,481
Sioux Falls	0	1	1	0	0	0	0	0	0	0	2	167,339
Spearfish	3	0	0	0	0	0	0	0	0	2	1	11,246
Sturgis	1	0	0	0	0	0	0	1	0	0	0	6,950
Vermillion	0	1	0	0	0	0	0	1	0	0	0	10,723
Watertown	1	0	0	1	0	0	0	0	1	1	0	22,118
Metropolitan Counties	2	0	0	0	0	0	0					
Minnehaha	1	0	0	0	0	0	0	0	0	0	1	
Pennington	1	0	0	0	0	0	0	0	1	0	0	
Nonmetropolitan Counties	1	0	0	0	1	0	0					
Charles Mix	1	0	0	0	0	0	0	0	1	0	0	
Hamlin	0	0	0	0	1	0	0	0	1	0	0	
TENNESSEE												
Total	82	14	20	73	5	0	0					
Cities	58	9	15	62	4	0	0					
Atoka	0	0	0	7	0	0	0	0	3	2	2	8,926
Baxter	1	0	0	0	0	0	0	0	1	0	0	1,397
Benton	1	0	0	0	0	0	0	0	1	0	0	1,316
Bristol	2	2	0	3	1	0	0	2	0	5	1	26,603
Camden	1	0	0	0	0	0	0	0	0	0	1	3,630
Chattanooga	9	1	1	0	0	0	0	2	4	2	3	174,449
Clarksville	7	1	4	1	0	0	0	3	4	2	4	144,639
Columbia	3	0	0	0	0	0	0	0	3	0	0	35,760
Covington	0	0	0	7	0	0	0	0	0	0	7	9,060
Crossville	1	0	0	0	0	0	0	0	1	0	0	11,339
Decaturville	0	1	0	0	0	0	0	0	0	1	0	869
Dyersburg	1	0	0	0	0	0	0	0	0	1	0	16,970
Elizabethton	2	0	1	0	0	0	0	1	1	0	1	14,375
Gallatin	0	1	0	0	0	0	0	1	0	0	0	32,756
Greeneville	2	1	0	26	0	0	0	4	7	4	14	15,011
Jackson	1	0	0	0	0	0	0	0	0	0	1	67,869
Jefferson City	3	0	0	0	0	0	0	0	0	3	0	8,211
Kingston	1	0	0	0	0	0	0	1	0	0	0	5,843
Knoxville	7	1	0	1	0	0	0	0	3	3	3	184,362
Lebanon	0	0	1	0	0	0	0	0	0	1	0	28,963
Mason	1	0	0	0	0	0	0	0	0	1	0	1,608
Memphis	4	0	3	3	3	0	0	1	7	3	2	654,922
Millington	1	0	1	1	0	0	0	0	2	1	0	11,095
Monteagle	0	0	1	0	0	0	0	0	0	0	1	1,177
Morristown	0	0	0	1	0	0	0	0	0	0	1	29,401
Munford	0	0	0	9	0	0	0	2	4	2	1	6,046
Nashville	7	0	3	1	0	0	0	3	5	1	2	647,689
Parsons	1	0	0	0	0	0	0	1	0	0	0	2,345
Ridgely	0	0	0	1	0	0	0	1	0	0	0	1,759
Savannah	1	0	0	0	0	0	0	0	0	1	0	7,134
Sharon	0	0	0	1	0	0	0	0	0	0	1	920
Spring Hill	0	1	0	0	0	0	0	0	0	1	0	33,472
Tullahoma	1	0	0	0	0	0	0	0	0	0	1	18,887
Universities and Colleges	1	3	1	0	0	0	0					
Middle Tennessee State University	1	3	0	0	0	0	0	0	2	1	1	23,881
Vanderbilt University	0	0	1	0	0	0	0	1	0	0	0	12,757
Metropolitan Counties	19	2	3	8	1	0	0					
Cheatham	1	0	0	0	0	0	0	0	0	0	1	
Hamilton	1	0	1	0	0	0	0	0	0	1	1	
Jefferson	0	0	0	1	0	0	0	0	1	0	0	
Knox	3	0	0	0	0	0	0	0	0	2	1	
Marion	0	0	0	3	0	0	0	0	0	3	0	

Table 13. Hate Crime Incidents Per Bias Motivation and Quarter, by Selected State and Agency, 2014—*Continued*

(Number.)

State/agency	Race	Religion	Sexual orientation	Ethnicity	Disability	Gender	Gender identity	1st quarter	2nd quarter	3rd quarter	4th quarter	Population[1]
Montgomery	0	1	0	0	0	0	0	0	0	0	1	
Robertson	1	0	0	0	0	0	0	1	0	0	0	
Rutherford	0	0	1	0	0	0	0	1	0	0	0	
Shelby	12	0	1	4	0	0	0	4	3	3	7	
Sullivan	0	0	0	0	1	0	0	1	0	0	0	
Washington	1	1	0	0	0	0	0	0	0	2	0	
Nonmetropolitan Counties	3	0	1	3	0	0	0					
Claiborne	1	0	0	0	0	0	0	0	0	1	0	
Lauderdale	1	0	0	0	0	0	0	0	0	0	1	
Lewis	0	0	1	0	0	0	0	0	0	1	0	
Monroe	0	0	0	1	0	0	0	0	0	1	0	
Overton	1	0	0	0	0	0	0	0	0	0	1	
Van Buren	0	0	0	2	0	0	0	0	0	2	0	
Other Agencies	1	0	0	0	0	0	0					
Nashville International Airport	1	0	0	0	0	0	0	0	1	0	0	
TEXAS												
Total	68	19	40	15	0	1	2					
Cities	59	16	38	15	0	1	1					
Austin	0	1	2	1	0	0	0	0	2	0	2	903,924
Baytown	0	0	1	0	0	0	0	0	0		1	76,253
Beaumont	3	0	1	0	0	0	0	2	1	1	0	117,898
Brownwood	0	0	1	0	0	0	0	1	0	0	0	18,890
Cedar Park	0	1	0	0	0	0	0	0	0	1	0	63,681
Center	1	0	0	0	0	0	0	0	0	1	0	5,302
College Station	0	0	1	0	0	0	0	0	0	1	0	101,483
Conroe	1	0	0	0	0	0	0	0	1	0	0	64,446
Corpus Christi	5	1	0	0	0	0	0	1	1	3	1	319,211
Dallas	4	1	10	0	0	0	0	1	11	2	1	1,272,396
Denison	1	1	0	1	0	0	0	1	1	0	1	22,838
El Paso	1	0	0	0	0	0	0	0	0	0	1	680,273
Fort Worth	1	0	0	2	0	0	0	0	0	0	3	804,907
Freer	0	0	1	0	0	0	0	0	0	1	0	2,778
Galveston	1	0	1	0	0	0	0	0	1	1	0	48,961
Garland	0	0	1	0	0	0	0	1	0	0	0	236,414
Georgetown	1	0	0	0	0	0	0	0	1	0	0	56,782
Gilmer	2	0	0	0	0	0	0	0	0	2	0	5,168
Harlingen	1	0	0	0	0	0	0	1	0	0	0	65,808
Hempstead	2	0	0	0	0	0	0	0	2	0	0	6,482
Houston	4	5	6	1	0	0	0	3	4	3	6	2,219,933
Iowa Park	1	0	0	0	0	0	0	0	1	0	0	6,404
Keller	1	0	0	0	0	0	0	0	0	0	1	43,711
Kilgore	0	0	1	0	0	0	0	1	0	0	0	14,789
Killeen	1	0	0	0	0	0	0	0	1	0	0	139,211
Lampasas	1	0	0	1	0	0	0	0	1	0	1	6,957
Lancaster	1	0	0	0	0	0	0	1	0	0	0	38,402
League City	0	1	0	0	0	0	0	0	1	0	0	92,790
Longview	3	0	0	3	0	0	0	3	2	1	0	81,659
Lubbock	1	0	0	0	0	0	0	0	1	0	0	241,826
McKinney	3	3	1	1	0	0	0	2	1	4	1	152,806
Mercedes	0	0	0	1	0	0	0	0	0	0	1	16,488
New Braunfels	0	0	0	1	0	0	1	0	0	1	1	64,622
Odessa	1	0	0	1	0	1	0	0	1	2	0	113,619
Pearland	2	0	2	0	0	0	0	2	0	1	1	102,516
Richardson	1	1	0	0	0	0	0	0	0	2	0	105,744
Rockwall	0	0	0	1	0	0	0	1	0	0	0	41,688
San Antonio	7	1	5	1	0	0	0	6	4	3	1	1,428,465
Sherman	1	0	0	0	0	0	0	1	0	0	0	39,522
South Padre Island	1	0	0	0	0	0	0	1	0	0	0	2,916
Spur	2	0	0	0	0	0	0	0	2	0	0	1,226
Sugar Land	1	0	0	0	0	0	0	0	0	0	1	85,055
Tomball	1	0	2	0	0	0	0	3	0	0	0	11,214
Vernon	0	0	1	0	0	0	0	0	0	1	0	10,589
Victoria	1	0	0	0	0	0	0	0	0	1	0	65,726
Wichita Falls	1	0	1	0	0	0	0	0	1	1	0	104,949
Universities and Colleges	3	3	1	0	0	0	1					
Paris Junior College	2	0	0	0	0	0	0	1		1	0	5,301

Table 13. Hate Crime Incidents Per Bias Motivation and Quarter, by Selected State and Agency, 2014—Continued

(Number.)

State/agency	Number of incidents per bias motivation							Number of incidents per quarter				Population[1]
	Race	Religion	Sexual orientation	Ethnicity	Disability	Gender	Gender identity	1st quarter	2nd quarter	3rd quarter	4th quarter	
Sul Ross State University....................	0	0	0	0	0	0	1	0	0	1	0	2,842
Tarleton State University.....................	0	0	1	0	0	0	0	0	0	0	1	13,307
Texas A&M University, Corpus Christi ..	0	1	0	0	0	0	0	1	0	0	0	10,913
Texas Christian University	1	1	0	0	0	0	0	0	1	1	0	9,925
Texas State University, San Marcos.......	0	1	0	0	0	0	0	0	1	0	0	35,546
Metropolitan Counties	5	0	1	0	0	0	0					
Harris..	1	0	0	0	0	0	0	0	0	1	0	
Kaufman..	2	0	0	0	0	0	0	0	1	1	0	
Travis	1	0	0	0	0	0	0	0	0	1	0	
Williamson...	1	0	1	0	0	0	0	0	2	0	0	
Other Agencies................................	1	0	0	0	0	0	0					
Independent School District, Pfluger-ville...	1	0	0	0	0	0	0	0	1	0	0	
UTAH												
Total	26	17	3	4	0	0	0					
Cities	15	9	2	3	0	0	0					
Bountiful...	1	1	0	0	0	0	0	0	1	1	0	43,115
Brigham City......................................	2	0	2	0	0	0	0	1	1	1	1	18,579
Centerville	0	1	0	0	0	0	0	0	1	0	0	16,953
Clinton	1	0	0	0	0	0	0	0	1	0	0	21,029
Farmington..	1	0	0	0	0	0	0	0	1	0	0	22,471
Murray...	1	0	0	0	0	0	0	0	0	0	1	49,083
North Salt Lake	1	0	0	1	0	0	0	0	2	0	0	17,170
Ogden	0	1	0	0	0	0	0	0	0	1	0	84,557
Roosevelt...	3	0	0	1	0	0	0	0	0	2	2	6,935
Salt Lake City.....................................	0	1	0	0	0	0	0	0	0	0	1	192,368
Tooele...	0	1	0	0	0	0	0	0	0	0	1	32,502
Tremonton	2	0	0	0	0	0	0	2	0	0	0	7,965
West Bountiful...................................	1	0	0	0	0	0	0	0	1	0	0	5,398
West Jordan.......................................	1	0	0	0	0	0	0	0	1	0	0	111,618
West Valley..	1	4	0	1	0	0	0	2	1	1	2	134,590
Universities and Colleges	1	1	0	0	0	0	0					
University of Utah	1	1	0	0	0	0	0	1	0	1	0	32,077
Metropolitan Counties	4	3	0	1	0	0	0					
Davis...	0	0	0	1	0	0	0	0	0	0	1	
Salt Lake County Unified Police Department	1	3	0	0	0	0	0	1	3	0	0	
Tooele...	3	0	0	0	0	0	0	0	1	1	1	
Nonmetropolitan Counties.............	1	1	0	0	0	0	0					
Carbon..	1	0	0	0	0	0	0	1	0	0	0	
Duchesne...	0	1	0	0	0	0	0	0	0	0	1	
State Police Agencies......................	2	2	1	0	0	0	0					
Utah Highway Patrol..........................	2	2	1	0	0	0	0	1	3	0	1	
Other Agencies................................	3	1	0	0	0	0	0					
Utah Transit Authority.......................	3	1	0	0	0	0	0	1	0	2	1	
VERMONT												
Total	7	3	1	0	4	0	0					
Cities	5	3	1	0	4	0	0					
Bellows Falls......................................	1	0	0	0	0	0	0	0	1	0	0	3,058
Burlington..	2	0	0	0	0	0	0	2	0	0	0	42,252
Essex...	0	2	0	0	0	0	0	0	0	1	1	20,755
Manchester..	1	0	0	0	0	0	0	1	0	0	0	4,335
Middlebury	0	0	1	0	1	0	0	0	1	1		8,504
Randolph...	0	1	0	0	0	0	0	0	0	0	1	4,752
South Burlington................................	0	0	0	0	3	0	0	1	2	0	0	18,779
Winooski	1	0	0	0	0	0	0	0	0	0	1	7,232
Universities and Colleges	1	0	0	0	0	0	0					
University of Vermont	1	0	0	0	0	0	0	1	0	0	0	12,723

(Number.)

State/agency	Number of incidents per bias motivation							Number of incidents per quarter				Population[1]
	Race	Religion	Sexual orientation	Ethnicity	Disability	Gender	Gender identity	1st quarter	2nd quarter	3rd quarter	4th quarter	
Nonmetropolitan Counties.............	1	0	0	0	0	0	0					
Lamoille...	1	0	0	0	0	0	0	1	0	0	0	
VIRGINIA												
Total	67	16	22	12	1	0	0					
Cities	30	8	15	6	1	0	0					
Alexandria	1	0	0	0	0	0	0	0	0	1	0	151,065
Bristol..	1	0	0	0	0	0	0	0	1	0	0	17,225
Charlottesville.................................	1	1	0	0	0	0	0	0	0	2	0	44,574
Chesapeake......................................	5	1	0	0	0	0	0	4	1	1	0	232,489
Falls Church	1	0	0	0	0	0	0	0	1	0	0	13,794
Fredericksburg	2	0	0	0	0	0	0	0	1	0	1	29,158
Front Royal	1	0	0	0	0	0	0	0	0	1	0	15,009
Hampton..	1	0	0	1	0	0	0	0	1	0	1	136,590
Harrisonburg....................................	0	1	0	1	0	0	0	0	1	1	0	52,026
Leesburg..	0	0	1	0	0	0	0	0	1	0	0	48,913
Lynchburg..	1	0	0	0	0	0	0	0	0	1	0	78,639
Manassas..	2	0	0	0	0	0	0	0	2	0	0	42,641
Newport News..................................	0	0	4	0	0	0	0	2	0	2	0	182,374
Norfolk..	2	0	7	3	0	0	0	1	2	5	4	247,078
Portsmouth......................................	3	1	0	0	0	0	0	0	0	3	1	96,435
Purcellville......................................	1	0	0	0	0	0	0	0	1	0	0	8,821
Rich Creek	0	1	0	0	0	0	0	1	0	0	0	760
Richmond...	0	1	1	1	0	0	0	1	0	2	0	216,747
Staunton..	0	0	1	0	0	0	0	0	0	0	1	24,499
Suffolk...	1	0	0	0	0	0	0	0	1	0	0	85,987
Vienna..	0	0	0	0	1	0	0	0	1	0	0	16,527
Virginia Beach..................................	5	2	1	0	0	0	0	3	2	1	2	451,102
West Point.......................................	2	0	0	0	0	0	0	2	0	0	0	3,345
Universities and Colleges	2	0	3	0	0	0	0					
George Mason University...................	2	0	1	0	0	0	0	0	2	0	1	33,917
Northern Virginia Community College	0	0	1	0	0	0	0	1	0	0	0	51,803
Radford University............................	0	0	1	0	0	0	0	0	0	0	1	9,928
Metropolitan Counties	31	8	4	6	0	0	0					
Albemarle County Police Department..	2	0	1	0	0	0	0	1	0	1	1	
Amherst..	1	0	0	0	0	0	0	0	0	1	0	
Arlington County Police Department...	3	0	0	0	0	0	0	0	0	1	2	
Bedford..	1	0	0	0	0	0	0	0	1	0	0	
Chesterfield County Police Department	2	1	0	0	0	0	0	1	0	1	1	
Clarke..	1	0	0	0	0	0	0	0	0	1	0	
Dinwiddie...	1	0	0	0	0	0	0	0	1	0		
Fairfax County Police Department	4	6	1	3	0	0	0	1	5	5	3	
Fluvanna...	1	0	0	0	0	0	0	1	0	0	0	
Goochland..	1	0	0	0	0	0	0	0	0	0	1	
Greene	2	0	0	0	0	0	0	0	0	1	1	
Henrico County Police Department	1	0	1	0	0	0	0	1	0	1	0	
Loudoun...	0	0	0	1	0	0	0	0	0	1	0	
New Kent..	1	0	0	0	0	0	0	0	0	1	0	
Powhatan...	0	0	0	1	0	0	0	0	1	0	0	
Prince George County Police Depart-ment.	1	0	0	0	0	0	0	0	0	1	0	
Roanoke County Police Department....	4	0	0	0	0	0	0	0	0	3	1	
Spotsylvania.....................................	1	0	0	0	0	0	0	0	0	0	1	
Stafford..	3	1	1	0	0	0	0	0	3	2	0	
Warren...	1	0	0	0	0	0	0	1	0	0	0	
York...	0	0	0	1	0	0	0	0	1	0	0	
Nonmetropolitan Counties.............	4	0	0	0	0	0	0					
Accomack...	1	0	0	0	0	0	0	1	0	0	0	
Pittsylvania.......................................	2	0	0	0	0	0	0	0	0	0	2	
Tazewell...	1	0	0	0	0	0	0	0	1	0	0	
WASHINGTON												
Total	176	50	43	27	3	8	1					
Cities	152	40	34	21	2	5	0					
Aberdeen..	1	0	0	0	0	0	0	0	1	0	0	16,243

State/agency	Number of incidents per bias motivation							Number of incidents per quarter				Population[1]
	Race	Religion	Sexual orientation	Ethnicity	Disability	Gender	Gender identity	1st quarter	2nd quarter	3rd quarter	4th quarter	
Auburn	1	0	1	0	0	0	0	1	0	0	1	76,020
Bainbridge Island	0	2	0	0	0	0	0	0	0	2	0	23,228
Bellingham	2	0	0	2	0	0	0	1	1	2	0	83,048
Bonney Lake	0	1	0	0	0	0	0	1	0	0	0	18,519
Bothell	1	3	0	0	0	0	0	4	0	0	0	36,087
Bremerton	2	1	0	0	0	0	0	1	1	1	0	39,359
Burien	3	0	0	0	0	0	0	1	2	0	0	50,284
Centralia	2	0	0	0	0	0	0	2	0	0	0	16,677
Colfax	0	0	0	1	0	0	0	0	0	1	0	2,856
East Wenatchee	1	0	0	0	0	0	0	1	0	0	0	13,539
Eatonville	1	0	0	0	0	0	0	0	1	0	0	2,824
Everett	3	0	0	0	0	0	0			2	1	105,911
Federal Way	0	4	0	0	0	0	0	1	2	0	1	93,551
Fife	3	0	0	2	0	0	0	1	0	2	2	9,479
Fircrest	1	0	0	0	0	0	0	0	0	1	0	6,644
Kent	10	1	5	0	0	0	0	3	4	6	3	125,837
Kirkland	0	1	1	1	0	0	0	2	0	0	1	85,352
Lacey	1	1	0	0	0	0	0	0	1	0	1	45,525
Lakewood	4	0	1	0	0	0	0	1	2	0	2	59,313
Longview	1	0	0	0	0	0	0	1	0	0	0	36,459
Monroe	0	0	0	0	0	2	0	0	1	1	0	17,826
Moses Lake	0	1	0	0	0	0	0	0	0	0	1	21,580
Mountlake Terrace	1	0	0	0	0	0	0	1	0	0	0	20,871
Mount Vernon	1	0	0	0	0	0	0	0	0	1	0	32,805
Normandy Park	3	0	0	0	0	0	0	1	1	0	1	6,610
Ocean Shores	0	0	1	0	0	0	0	0	0	1	0	5,622
Olympia	1	0	0	1	0	0	0	0	0	0	2	48,763
Port Angeles	0	0	0	0	1	0	0	1	0	0	0	19,220
Port Townsend	1	0	0	0	0	0	0	0	0	1	0	9,231
Pullman	2	0	0	0	0	0	0	1	0	0	1	31,810
Puyallup	3	0	0	0	0	0	0	1	0	1	1	39,016
Quincy	0	0	0	1	0	0	0	0	1	0	0	7,355
Renton	12	4	0	1	0	0	0	4	5	4	4	98,240
Ridgefield	1	0	0	0	0	0	0	0	0	0	1	5,856
Ritzville	0	0	0	1	0	0	0	0	0	1	0	1,681
Sammamish	0	1	0	0	0	0	0	1	0	0	0	51,016
Seattle	64	10	21	9	0	3	0	21	27	29	30	663,410
Sequim	1	1	0	0	0	0	0	1	0	0	1	6,682
Shelton	0	2	0	0	0	0	0	0	0	2	0	9,724
Spokane[2]	7	3	1	0	0	0	0	1	4	1	5	211,025
Spokane Valley	3	1	0	0	0	0	0	1	1	2	0	91,382
Tacoma	3	0	2	0	0	0	0	4	1	0	0	204,722
Vancouver	6	0	0	0	0	0	0	0	4	1	1	168,688
Walla Walla	4	1	1	1	1	0	0	0	2	3	3	31,833
Woodinville	1	0	0	1	0	0	0	2	0	0	0	11,408
Yakima	1	2	0	0	0	0	0	0	2	1	0	93,667
Universities and Colleges	3	1	2	0	0	2	1					
University of Washington	2	1	1	0	0	2	1	0	2	0	5	43,762
Washington State University, Pullman	0	0	1	0	0	0	0	0	1	0	0	27,642
Western Washington University	1	0	0	0	0	0	0	0	0	0	1	14,950
Metropolitan Counties	18	6	7	4	1	1	0					
Clark	1	0	1	0	0	0	0	1	1	0	0	
King	3	3	4	2	0	0	0	2	2	4	4	
Kitsap	2	0	0	0	0	0	0	1	0	0	1	
Pend Oreille	1	0	0	0	0	0	0	0	0	1	0	
Pierce	2	0	0	0	0	0	0	1	0	0	1	
Skagit	1	0	0	0	0	0	0	1	0	0	0	
Snohomish	2	0	0	0	0	0	0	1	1	0	0	
Spokane	1	0	1	0	0	0	0	0	0	1	0	
Stevens[2]	1	1	0	0	0	0	0	0	1	0	1	
Thurston	0	0	1	1	0	0	0	0	1	1	0	
Walla Walla	0	0	0	1	0	0	0	0	0	0	1	
Whatcom	4	2	0	0	1	1	0	0	2	3	3	
Nonmetropolitan Counties	2	2	0	0	0	0	0					
Garfield	1	0	0	0	0	0	0	0	0	0	1	
Grays Harbor	1	0	0	0	0	0	0	1	0	0	0	
San Juan	0	1	0	0	0	0	0	1	0	0	0	

Table 13. Hate Crime Incidents Per Bias Motivation and Quarter, by Selected State and Agency, 2014—*Continued*

(Number.)

State/agency	Race	Religion	Sexual orientation	Ethnicity	Disability	Gender	Gender identity	1st quarter	2nd quarter	3rd quarter	4th quarter	Population[1]
								Number of incidents per bias motivation				
Whitman	0	1	0	0	0	0	0	0	0	1	0	
Other Agencies	1	1	0	2	0	0	0					
Port of Seattle	1	1	0	2	0	0	0	0	2	0	2	
WEST VIRGINIA												
Total	17	2	4	1	2	0	0					
Cities	11	0	1	1	1	0	0					
Charleston	3	0	1	1	0	0	0	0	1	2	2	50,693
Chester	1	0	0	0	0	0	0	0	0	1	0	2,542
Fairmont	1	0	0	0	1	0	0	1	0	0	1	18,835
Hinton	1	0	0	0	0	0	0	0	1	0		2,566
Moundsville	1	0	0	0	0	0	0	0	1	0	0	8,846
Weirton	1	0	0	0	0	0	0	0	0	1	0	19,476
Winfield	3	0	0	0	0	0	0	2	1	0	0	2,331
Universities and Colleges	2	1	0	0	0	0	0					
West Virginia State University	1	1	0	0	0	0	0	0	1	1	0	2,677
West Virginia University	1	0	0	0	0	0	0	1	0	0	0	29,466
Metropolitan Counties	4	1	3	0	1	0	0					
Brooke	1	0	0	0	0	0	0	0	0	0	1	
Fayette	0	0	1	0	0	0	0	0	0	1	0	
Hancock	1	0	0	0	0	0	0	0	0	0	1	
Kanawha	1	0	1	0	1	0	0	0	0	0	3	
Marshall	0	0	1	0	0	0	0	0	1	0	0	
Ohio	1	0	0	0	0	0	0	0	0	1	0	
Raleigh	0	1	0	0	0	0	0	0	1	0	0	
WISCONSIN												
Total	28	6	9	5	3	0	0					
Cities	18	4	9	4	0	0	0					
Appleton	1	0	2	0	0	0	0	0	1	1	1	73,841
Fond du Lac	1	0	0	0	0	0	0	0	1	0	0	42,953
Janesville	2	0	0	0	0	0	0	0	0	0	2	63,885
La Crosse	3	0	0	0	0	0	0	1	1	0	1	51,564
Madison	3	1	4	2	0	0	0	1	2	3	4	245,788
Milwaukee	5	2	2	2	0	0	0	2	4	1	4	600,374
Oak Creek	1	0	0	0	0	0	0	0	0	1	0	35,138
River Falls	0	0	1	0	0	0	0	0	0	1	0	15,250
Stevens Point	1	0	0	0	0	0	0	0	0	1	0	26,665
Waupun	1	1	0	0	0	0	0	1	0	1	0	11,326
Universities and Colleges	4	0	0	0	0	0	0					
University of Wisconsin												
Eau Claire	2	0	0	0	0	0	0	0	0	0	2	10,923
Milwaukee	1	0	0	0	0	0	0	0	0	0	1	27,416
Stout	1	0	0	0	0	0	0	0	0	0	1	9,313
Metropolitan Counties	3	0	0	1	1	0	0					
Columbia	0	0	0	0	1	0	0	0	0	0	1	
Fond du Lac	2	0	0	0	0	0	0	0	0	1	1	
Iowa	0	0	0	1	0	0	0	0	0	1	0	
Washington	1	0	0	0	0	0	0	0	1	0	0	
Nonmetropolitan Counties	3	2	0	0	2	0	0					
Burnett	1	1	0	0	0	0	0	0	1	1	0	
Juneau	0	0	0	0	1	0	0	0	0	1	0	
Sauk	0	0	0	0	1	0	0	0	1	0	0	
Sawyer	2	0	0	0	0	0	0	0	0	1	1	
Vilas	0	1	0	0	0	0	0	0	1	0	0	

[1] Population figures are published only for the cities. The figures listed for the universities and colleges are student enrollment and were provided by the United States Department of Education for the 2013 school year, the most recent available. The enrollment figures include full-time and part-time students.
[2] Includes one incident reported with more than one bias motivation.
[3] Student enrollment figures were not available.

METHODOLOGY

The Federal Bureau of Investigation (FBI) began the procedures for implementing, collecting, and managing hate crime data after Congress passed the Hate Crime Statistics Act in 1990. This act required the collection of data "about crimes that manifest evidence of prejudice based on race, religion, sexual orientation, or ethnicity." Beginning in 2013, law enforcement agencies could submit hate crime data in accordance with a number of program modifications. In 1994, the Hate Crime Statistics Act was amended to include bias against persons with disabilities. The Church Arson Prevention Act, which was signed into law in July 1996, removed the sunset clause from the original statute and mandated that the collection of hate crime data become a permanent part of the UCR program. In 2009, Congress further amended the Hate Crime Statistics Act by passing the Matthew Shepard and James Byrd, Jr., Hate Crime Prevention Act. The amendment includes the collection of data for crimes motivated by bias against a particular gender and gender identity, as well as for crimes committed by, and crimes directed against, juveniles. In response to the Shepard/Byrd Act, the FBI modified its data collection so that reporting agencies could indicate whether hate crimes were committed by, or directed against, juveniles.

Definitions

Hate crimes include any crime motivated by bias against race, religion, sexual orientation, ethnicity/national origin, and/or disability. Because motivation is subjective, it is sometimes difficult to know with certainty whether a crime resulted from the offender's bias. Moreover, the presence of bias alone does not necessarily mean that a crime can be considered a hate crime. Only when law enforcement investigation reveals sufficient evidence to lead a reasonable and prudent person to conclude that the offender's actions were motivated, in whole or in part, by his or her bias should an incident be reported as a hate crime.

Data Collection

The UCR (Uniform Crime Reporting) program collects data about both single-bias and multiple-bias hate crimes. A single-bias incident is defined as an incident in which one or more offense types are motivated by the same bias. A multiple-bias incident is defined as an incident in which more than one offense type occurs and at least two offense types are motivated by different biases.

A table enumerating selected places in the United States that did not report hate crimes in 2014 is available at https://www.fbi.gov/about-us/cjis/ucr/hate-crime/2014/tables/table-14/table_14_hate_crime_zero_data_submitted_per_quarter_by_state_and_agency_2014.xls/view.

Crimes Against Persons, Property, or Society

The UCR program's data collection guidelines stipulate that a hate crime may involve multiple offenses, victims, and offenders within one incident; therefore, the Hate Crime Statistics program is incident-based. According to UCR counting guidelines:

- One offense is counted for each victim in *crimes against persons*
- One offense is counted for each offense type in *crimes against property*
- One offense is counted for each offense type in *crimes against society*

Victims

In the UCR program, the victim of a hate crime may be an individual, a business, an institution, or society as a whole.

Offenders

According to the UCR program, the term *known offender* does not imply that the suspect's identity is known; rather, the term indicates that some aspect of the suspect was identified, thus distinguishing the suspect from an unknown offender. Law enforcement agencies specify the number of offenders, and when possible, the race of the offender or offenders as a group.

Race/Ethnicity

The UCR program uses the following racial designations in its Hate Crime Statistics program: White; Black; American Indian or Alaskan Native; Asian; Native Hawaiian or Other Pacific Islander; and Multiple Races, Group. In addition, the UCR program uses the ethnic designations of Hispanic or Latino and Not Hispanic or Latino.

The law enforcement agencies that voluntarily participate in the Hate Crime Statistics program collect details about an offender's bias motivation associated with 11 offense types already being reported to the UCR program: murder and nonnegligent manslaughter, rape, aggravated assault, simple assault, and intimidation (crimes against persons); and robbery, burglary, larceny-theft, motor vehicle theft, arson, and destruction/damage/vandalism (crimes against property). The law enforcement agencies that participate in the UCR program via the National Incident-Based Reporting System (NIBRS) collect data about additional offenses for *crimes against persons* and *crimes against property*. These data appear in the category of other. These agencies also collect hate crime data for the category called *crimes against society*, which includes drug or narcotic offenses, gambling offenses, prostitution offenses, and weapon law violations.

Changes to the Data Collection

Beginning in 2013, law enforcement agencies could submit hate crime data in accordance with a number of program modifications. Descriptions of those modifications, which are again included in the published data, follow.

Addition of Gender and Gender Identity Bias Categories

In response to the Matthew Shepard and James Byrd Jr. Hate Crimes Prevention Act of 2009 (Shepard/Byrd Act), the FBI began accepting data on crimes motivated by gender (male and female) bias and gender identity (transgender and gender nonconforming) bias from contributors.

Involvement of Juveniles

Also in response to the Shepard/Byrd Act, the FBI modified its data collection so that reporting agencies could indicate whether hate crimes were committed by, or directed against, juveniles. Therefore, in addition to reporting the number of individual victims, in 2013, law enforcement began reporting the number of victims who are 18 years of age or older and the number of victims under the age of 18.

Revision of Sexual-Orientation Bias Types

Following the passage of the Shepard/Byrd Act, the FBI updated select sexual-orientation bias types at the recommendation of the Criminal Justice Information Services (CJIS) Advisory Policy Board (APB) and with input from the Hate Crime Coalition. The sexual-orientation bias types were revised from anti-male homosexual, anti-female homosexual, anti-homosexual, anti-heterosexual, and anti-bisexual to anti-gay (male); anti-lesbian; anti-lesbian, gay, bisexual, and transgender (mixed group); anti-heterosexual; and anti-bisexual.

Additional Bias Types per Offense

At the recommendation of the CJIS APB and with the approval of the FBI Director, the UCR Program began permitting law enforcement agencies to report four additional bias types per offense instead of one.

Revision of Race and Ethnicity Categories

To comply with a directive from the U.S. Government's Office of Management and Budget (OMB), the UCR Program expanded its race categories and changed its ethnicity categories. The race categories were expanded from four (White, Black, American Indian or Alaskan Native, and Asian or Other Pacific Islander) to five (White, Black or African American, American Indian or Alaska Native, Asian, and Native Hawaiian or Other Pacific Islander). The ethnicity categories changed from "Hispanic" and "Other Ethnicity/National Origin" to "Hispanic or Latino" and "Not Hispanic or Latino."

Revision to the Definition of Rape

At the recommendation of the CJIS APB and with the approval of the FBI Director, the UCR Program initiated the collection of rape data under a revised definition and removed the term "forcible" from the offense name in 2013. The changes bring uniformity to the offense in both the Summary Reporting System (SRS) and the National Incident-Based Reporting System (NIBRS) by capturing data (1) without regard to gender, (2) including penetration of any bodily orifice by any object or body part, and (3) including offenses where physical force is not involved. Beginning in 2013, the UCR Program defined rape as follows:

Rape (revised definition): Penetration, no matter how slight, of the vagina or anus with any body part or object, or oral penetration by a sex organ of another person, without the consent of the victim. (This includes the offenses of rape, sodomy, and sexual assault with an object as converted from data submitted via the NIBRS.)

Rape (legacy definition): The carnal knowledge of a female forcibly and against her will.

From the NIBRS

For all law enforcement agencies that submitted their hate crime data via the NIBRS in 2014, the UCR Program combined the agencies' totals for the offenses of rape (which includes both male and female victims), sodomy, and sexual assault with an object to derive rape figures in accordance with the broader revised definition. In addition, the UCR Program published any offenses of fondling, incest, and statutory rape submitted via the NIBRS in the crimes against persons category of *other*.

From the SRS

The UCR Program's revised definition of rape is the same definition adopted specifically for the SRS and includes the offenses of rape, sodomy, and sexual assault with an object (without any breakdowns for individual offenses). Likewise, the UCR Program's legacy definition of rape is the same definition formerly used in the SRS as forcible rape. Although some SRS agencies were able to apply the revised definition to their data collection procedures, not all agencies were able to do so. Therefore, the UCR Program published the rape data of law enforcement agencies that submitted their hate crime data via the SRS electronic record layout, or the Microsoft Excel Workbook Tool in accordance with the rape definition (revised or legacy) the agency applied in 2014.

PART 6

Jail Inmates at Midyear, 2014

HIGHLIGHTS

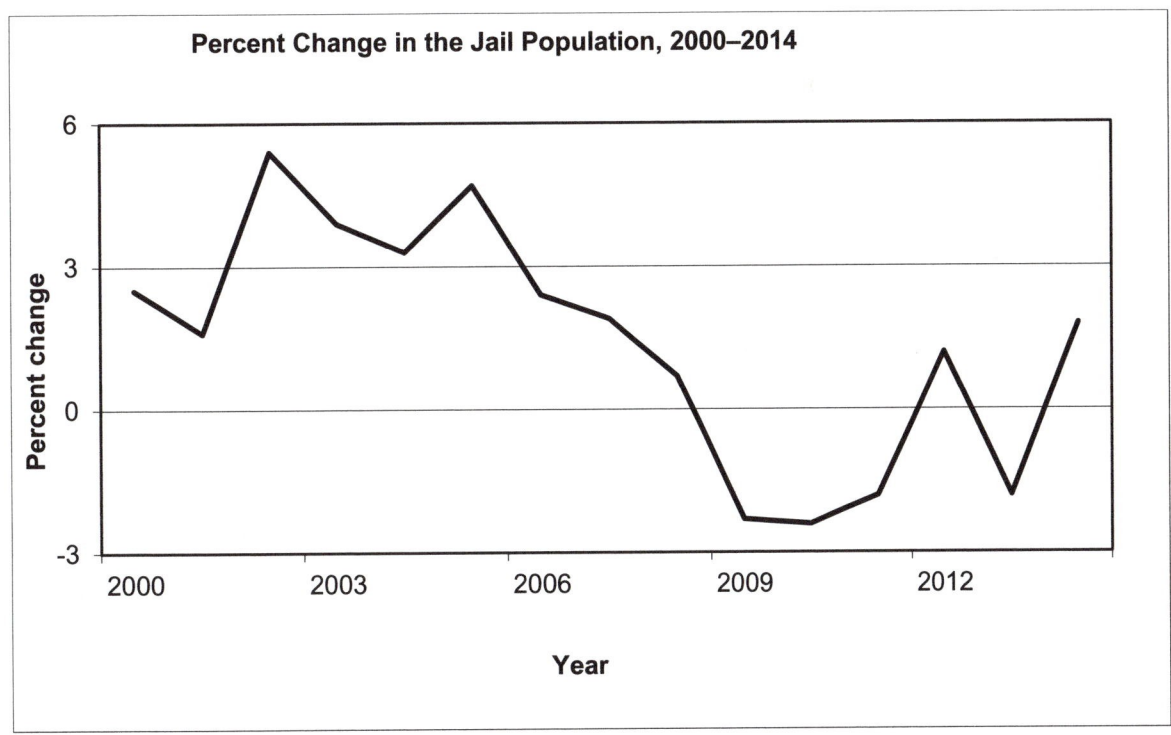

Percent Change in the Jail Population, 2000–2014

- The number of inmates confined in county and city jails was an estimated 744,600 at midyear 2014, which was significantly lower than the peak of 785,500 inmates at midyear 2008.

- At midyear 2014, the jail incarceration rate decreased from a peak of 259 per 100,000 population in 2007 to 234 per 100,000 population.

- An 18.1 percent between midyear 2010 and 2014 was noted for the female jail population, while the male population declined 3.2 percent.

- White inmates accounted for 47 percent of the total jail population, Black inmates represented 35 percent of the population, and inmates of Hispanic or Latino ethnicity represented 15 percent of the population.

- About 4,200 juveniles age 17 years or younger were held in local jails at midyear 2014. They accounted for 0.6 percent of the confined population, down from 1.2 percent at midyear 2000.

Table 1. Inmates Confined in Local Jails at Midyear, Average Daily Population, and Incarceration Rates, 2000–2014

(Number; percent.)

Year	Inmates confined at midyear[1]			Average daily population[2]			Jail incarceration rate[3]	
	Total	Year-to-year change		Total	Year-to-year change		Adults and juveniles[4]	Adults only
		Number	Percent		Number	Percent		
2000...............................	621,149	15,206	2.5	618,319	10,341	1.7	220	292
2001...............................	631,240	10,091	1.6	625,966	7,647	1.2	222	294
2002...............................	665,475	34,235	5.4	652,082	26,116	4.2	231	307
2003...............................	691,301	25,826	3.9	680,760	28,678	4.4	238	315
2004...............................	713,990	22,689	3.3	706,242	25,482	3.7	243	322
2005...............................	747,529	33,539	4.7	733,442	27,200	3.9	252	334
2006...............................	765,819	18,290	2.4	755,320	21,878	3	256	338
2007...............................	780,174	14,355	1.9	773,138	17,818	2.4	259	340
2008...............................	785,533	5,359	0.7	776,573	3,435	0.4	258	338
2009...............................	767,434	-18,099	-2.3	768,135	-8,438	-1.1	250	327
2010...............................	748,728	-18,706	-2.4	748,553	-19,582	-2.5	242	315
2011...............................	735,601	-13,127	-1.8	735,565	-12,988	-1.7	236	307
2012...............................	744,524	8,923	1.2	737,369	1,804	0.2	237	308
2013...............................	731,208	-13,316	-1.8	731,352	-6,017	-0.8	231	299
2014*.............................	744,592	13,384	1.8	738,975	7,623	1	234	302
Average annual change.........................								
2000–2013...............................			1.3			1.3		
2013–2014...............................			1.8			1		

Note: Detail may not sum to total because of rounding.
* = Comparison year on confined inmates and average daily population.
[1] Number of inmates held on the last weekday in June.
[2] Sum of all inmates in jail each day for a year, divided by the number of days in the year.
[3] Number of inmates confined at midyear per 100,000 U.S. residents.
[4] Juveniles are persons age 17 or younger at midyear.

Table 2. Number of Inmates in Local Jails, by Characteristics, Midyear 2000 and 2005–2014

(Number.)

Characteristic	2000	2005	2006	2007	2008	2009	2010	2011[1]	2012[1]	2013[1]	2014*,[1]
Total[2]	621,149	747,529	765,819	780,174	785,533	767,434	748,728	735,601	744,524	731,208	744,592
Sex											
Male	550,162	652,958	666,819	679,654	685,862	673,728	656,360	642,300	645,900	628,900	635,500
Female	70,987	94,571	99,000	100,520	99,670	93,706	92,368	93,300	98,600	102,400	109,100
Adult	613,534	740,770	759,717	773,341	777,829	760,216	741,168	729,700	739,100	726,600	740,400
Male	543,120	646,807	661,164	673,346	678,657	667,039	649,284	636,900	640,900	624,700	631,600
Female	70,414	93,963	98,552	99,995	99,172	93,176	91,884	92,800	98,100	101,900	108,800
Juvenile[3]	7,615	6,759	6,102	6,833	7,703	7,218	7,560	5,900	5,400	4,600	4,200
Held as adult[4]	6,126	5,750	4,835	5,649	6,410	5,846	5,647	4,600	4,600	3,500	3,700
Held as juvenile	1,489	1,009	1,268	1,184	1,294	1,373	1,912	1,400	900	1,100	500
Race/Hispanic origin[5]											
White[6]	260,500	331,000	336,500	338,200	333,300	326,400	331,600	329,400	341,100	344,900	352,800
Black/African American[6]	256,300	290,500	295,900	301,700	308,000	300,500	283,200	276,400	274,600	261,500	263,800
Hispanic/Latino	94,100	111,900	119,200	125,500	128,500	124,000	118,100	113,900	112,700	107,900	110,600
American Indian/Alaska Native[6,7]	5,500	7,600	8,400	8,600	9,000	9,400	9,900	9,400	9,300	10,200	10,400
Asian/Native Hawaiian/Other Pacific Islander[6,7]	4,700	5,400	5,100	5,300	5,500	5,400	5,100	5,300	5,400	5,100	6,000
Two or more races[6]	NC	1,000	700	800	1,300	1,800	800	1,200	1,500	1,600	1,000
Conviction status[5,8]											
Convicted	271,300	284,400	290,000	296,700	291,200	290,100	291,300	289,600	293,100	278,000	277,100
Unconvicted	349,800	463,200	475,800	483,500	494,200	477,300	457,400	446,000	451,400	453,200	467,500

Note: Detail may not sum to total because of rounding.
NC = Not collected.
* = Comparison year for each characteristic.
[1] Data for 2011–2014 are adjusted for nonresponse and rounded to the nearest 100.
[2] Midyear count is the number of inmates held on the last weekday in June.
[3] Persons age 17 or younger at midyear.
[4] Includes juveniles who were tried or awaiting trial as adults.
[5] Data adjusted for nonresponse and rounded to the nearest 100.
[6] Excludes persons of Hispanic or Latino origin.
[7] Previous reports combined American Indians and Alaska Natives and Asians, Native Hawaiians, and other Pacific Islanders into an Other race category.
[8] Includes juveniles who were tried or awaiting trial as adults.

Table 3. Percent of Inmates in Local Jails, by Characteristics, Midyear 2000 and 2005–2014

(Percent.)

Characteristic	2000	2005	2006	2007	2008	2009	2010	2011	2012	2013	2014
Sex											
Male	88.6	87.3	87.1	87.1	87.3	87.8	87.7	87.3	86.8	86.0	85.3
Female	11.4	12.7	12.9	12.9	12.7	12.2	12.3	12.7	13.2	14.0	14.7
Adult	98.8	99.1	99.2	99.1	99.0	99.1	99.0	99.2	99.3	99.4	99.4
Male	87.4	86.5	86.3	86.3	86.4	86.9	86.7	86.6	86.1	85.4	84.8
Female	11.3	12.6	12.9	12.8	12.6	12.1	12.3	12.6	13.2	13.9	14.6
Juvenile[1]	1.2	0.9	0.8	0.9	1.0	0.9	1.0	0.8	0.7	0.6	0.6
Held as adult[2]	1.0	0.8	0.6	0.7	0.8	0.8	0.8	0.6	0.6	0.5	0.5
Held as juvenile	0.2	0.1	0.2	0.2	0.2	0.2	0.3	0.2	0.1	0.1	0.1
Race/Hispanic origin[3]											
White[3]	41.9	44.3	43.9	43.3	42.5	42.5	44.3	44.8	45.8	47.2	47.4
Black/African American[3]	41.3	38.9	38.6	38.7	39.2	39.2	37.8	37.6	36.9	35.8	35.4
Hispanic/Latino	15.2	15.0	15.6	16.1	16.4	16.2	15.8	15.5	15.1	14.8	14.9
American Indian/Alaska Native[4,5]	0.9	1.0	1.1	1.1	1.1	1.2	1.3	1.3	1.2	1.4	1.4
Asian/Native Hawaiian/Other Pacific Islander[4,5]	0.8	0.7	0.7	0.7	0.7	0.7	0.7	0.7	0.7	0.7	0.8
Two or more races[4]	NC	0.1	0.1	0.1	0.2	0.2	0.1	0.2	0.2	0.2	0.1
Conviction status[5]											
Convicted	44.0	38.0	37.9	38.0	37.1	37.8	38.9	39.4	39.4	38.0	37.2
Unconvicted	56.0	62.0	62.1	62.0	62.9	62.2	61.1	60.6	60.6	62.0	62.8

Note: Percentages are based on the total number of inmates held on the last weekday in June. Detail may not sum to total because of rounding.
NC = Not collected.
[1] Persons age 17 or younger at midyear.
[2] Includes juveniles who were tried or awaiting trial as adults.
[3] Data adjusted for nonresponse.
[4] Excludes persons of Hispanic or Latino origin.
[5] Previous reports combined American Indians and Alaska Natives and Asians, Native Hawaiians, and other Pacific Islanders into an Other race category.

Table 4. Inmates Confined in Local Jails at Midyear, by Size of Jurisdiction, 2013–2014

(Number; percent.)

Jurisdiction size[1]	Inmates confined at midyear[2]		Difference	Percent change	Percent of all inmates	
	2013	2014			2013	2014
Total	731,208	744,592	13,384	1.8	100.0	100.0
49 or fewer	23,545	25,058	1,513	6.4	3.2	3.4
50 to 99	38,970	42,172	3,202	8.2	5.3	5.7
100 to 249	95,031	96,443	1,412	1.5	13.0	13.0
250 to 499	102,362	101,609	-753	-0.7	14.0	13.6
500 to 999	123,155	128,070	4,915	4.0	16.8	17.2
1,000 and over	348,145	351,239	3,094	0.9	47.6	47.2

Note: Detail may not sum to total because of rounding. All comparisons by jurisdiction size are not significant at the 95%-confidence level.
[1] Standardized on the average daily population (ADP) for the 12-month period ending June 30, 2006, the first year in the current Annual Survey of Jails sample. ADP is the sum of all inmates in jail each day for a year, divided by the number of days in the year.
[2] Number of inmates held on the last weekday in June.

Table 5. Rated Capacity of Local Jails and Percent of Capacity Occupied, 2000 and 2005–2014

(Number; percent.)

| Year | Rated capacity[1] | Year-to-year change in rated capacity[2] | | Percent of capacity occupied[3] | |
		Number	Percent	Midyear[4]	Average daily population[5]
2000..	677,787	25,466	3.9	92.0	91.2
2005..	786,954	33,398	4.1	95.0	93.2
2006..	794,984	8,638	1.0	96.3	95.0
2007..	810,543	15,863	2.0	96.3	95.4
2008..	828,714	18,171	2.2	94.8	93.7
2009..	849,895	21,181	2.6	90.3	90.4
2010..	857,918	8,023	0.9	87.3	87.3
2011..	870,422	12,504	1.5	84.5	84.5
2012..	877,396	6,974	0.8	84.9	84.0
2013..	872,943	-4,453	-0.5	83.8	83.8
2014*..	890,486	17,543	2.0	83.6	83.0
Average annual change..........................					
2000–2013......................................	2.0	17,199			
2013–2014......................................	2.0	17,543			

* Comparison year on rated capacity and percent of capacity occupied.
[1] Maximum number of beds or inmates assigned by a rating official to a facility, excluding separate temporary holding areas.
[2] Increase or reduction in the number of beds during the 12 months ending midyear of each year. Number and percentage change for 2000 are calculated using the rated capacity of 652,321 for 1999.
[3] Based on the confined inmate population divided by the rated capacity and multiplied by 100.
[4] Number of inmates held on the last weekday in June.
[5] Sum of all inmates in jail each day for a year, divided by the number of days in the year.

Table 6. Percent of Jail Capacity Occupied at Midyear, by Size of Jurisdiction, 2013–2014

(Percent.)

Jurisdiction size	2013	2014
Total	83.8	83.6
49 or fewer...	64.4	67
50–99...	69.4	74.2
100–249...	77.9	78.7
250–499...	87.3	86.7
500–999...	84.9	85
1,000 or more..	87.9	86.5

Note: Number of inmates held on the last weekday in June divided by the rated capacity multiplied by 100. Jurisdiction size is standardized on the average daily population for the 12-month period ending June 30, 2006, the first year in the current Annual Survey of Jails sample.
*Comparison year on percent of capacity occupied at midyear.

Table 7. Average Daily Jail Population, Admissions, and Turnover Rate, by Size of Jurisdiction, Week Ending June 30, 2013 and 2014

(Number; rate.[1])

| Jurisdiction size[2] | Average daily population[3] | | | Estimated number of admissions during last week of June | | Weekly turnover rate[1] | |
	2013	2014	Difference	2013	2014*	2013	2014*
Total	731,352	738,975	7,623	224,536	218,924	60.2	58.1
49 or fewer..............................	23,301	23,490	189	15,296	12,610	121.1	104.2
50–99......................................	38,721	40,554	1,833	16,315	18,763	83.6	87.2
100–249..................................	93,653	96,200	2,547	32,470	32,087	67.9	65.5
250–499..................................	102,045	99,889	-2,156	35,003	33,527	66.3	65.0
500–999..................................	123,220	125,954	2,734	46,806	35,430	75.5	56.1
1,000 or more	350,412	352,888	2,476	78,645	86,507	44.3	48.5

Note: Detail may not sum to total because of rounding. See Methodology for more detail on estimation procedures. All comparisons by average daily population are not significant at the 95%-confidence level.
* Comparison year on admissions and weekly turnover rate.
[1] Calculated by adding weekly admissions and releases, dividing by the average daily population (ADP), and multiplying by 100.
[2] Standardized on the ADP for the 12-month period ending June 30, 2006, the first year in the current Annual Survey of Jails sample.
[3] Sum of all inmates in jail each day for a year.

Table 8. Inmate Population in Jail Jurisdictions Reporting on Confined Persons Being Held for U.S. Immigration and Customs Enforcement (ICE), Midyear 2002–2014

(Number; percent.)

Year	Jurisdictions reporting on holdings for ICE[1]	Inmates confined at midyear[2]	Confined persons held at ICE at midyear	
			Number	Percent of all inmates
2002	2,961	626,870	12,501	2.0
2003	2,940	637,631	13,337	2.1
2004	2,962	673,807	14,120	2.1
2005	2,824	703,084	11,919	1.7
2006	2,784	698,108	13,598	1.9
2007	2,713	683,640	15,063	2.2
2008	2,699	704,278	20,785	3.0
2009	2,643	685,500	24,278	3.5
2010	2,531	622,954	21,607	3.5
2011	2,758	672,643	22,049	3.3
2012	2,716	690,337	22,870	3.3
2013	2,685	673,707	17,241	2.6
2014	2,634	654,730	16,384	2.5

Note: Data are based on the reported data and were not estimated for survey item nonresponse. Comparisons were not tested due to changing coverage each year.

[1] Not all jurisdictions reported on holdings for ICE.

[2] Number of inmates held on the last weekday in June in jails reporting complete data or the number of inmates held for ICE.

Table 9. Persons Under Jail Supervision, by Confinement Status and Type of Program, Midyear 2000 and 2006–2014

(Number.)

Confinement status and type of program	2000	2006	2007	2008	2009	2010	2011	2012	2013	2014*
Total	687,033	826,041	848,419	858,385	837,647	809,360	798,417	808,622	790,649	808,070
Held in jail[1]	621,149	765,819	780,174	785,533	767,434	748,728	735,601	744,524	731,208	744,592
Supervised outside of a jail facility[2]	65,884	60,222	68,245	72,852	70,213	60,632	62,816	64,098	59,441	63,478
Weekend programs[3]	14,523	11,421	10,473	12,325	11,212	9,871	11,369	10,351	10,950	9,698
Electronic monitoring	10,782	10,999	13,121	13,539	11,834	12,319	11,950	13,779	12,023	14,223
Home detention[4]	332	807	512	498	738	736	809	2,129	1,337	646
Day reporting	3,969	4,841	6,163	5,758	6,492	5,552	5,200	3,890	3,683	4,413
Community service	13,592	14,667	15,327	18,475	17,738	14,646	11,680	14,761	13,877	14,331
Other pretrial supervision	6,279	6,409	11,148	12,452	12,439	9,375	10,464	7,738	7,542	8,634
Other work programs[5]	8,011	8,319	7,369	5,808	5,912	4,351	7,165	7,137	5,341	7,003
Treatment programs[6]	5,714	1,486	2,276	2,259	2,082	1,799	2,449	2,164	2,002	2,100
Other	2,682	1,273	1,857	1,739	1,766	1,983	1,731	2,149	2,687	2,430

* Comparison year by status and program.
[1] Number of inmates held on the last weekday in June.
[2] Number of persons under jail supervision but not confined on the last weekday in June. Excludes persons supervised by a probation or parole agency.
[3] Offenders serve their sentences of confinement on weekends only (i.e., Friday to Sunday).
[4] Includes only persons without electronic monitoring.
[5] Includes persons in work release programs, work gangs, and other alternative work programs.
[6] Includes persons in drug, alcohol, mental health, and other medical treatment.

Table 10. Number of Inmates in Local Jails, by Characteristics, Midyear 2000 and 2005–2014

(Number.)

Characteristic	2000	2005	2006	2007	2008	2009	2010	2011	2012	2013	2014*
Male	547,624	652,958	666,819	679,654	685,862	673,728	650,341	633,171	636,708	602,193	617,842
Female	70,659	94,571	99,000	100,520	99,670	93,706	91,521	91,923	97,190	98,015	106,081
Adult	610,703	740,770	759,717	773,341	777,829	760,216	734,372	719,253	728,547	695,817	719,857
Male	540,614	646,807	661,164	673,346	678,657	667,039	643,331	627,777	631,802	598,228	614,102
Female	70,089	93,963	98,552	99,995	99,172	93,176	91,042	91,476	96,745	97,589	105,754
Juvenile	7,580	6,759	6,102	6,833	7,703	7,218	7,490	5,840	5,351	4,391	4,067
Held as adult	6,126	5,750	4,835	5,649	6,410	5,846	5,596	4,490	4,489	3,366	3,581
Held as juvenile	1,454	1,009	1,268	1,184	1,294	1,373	1,895	1,350	862	1,025	485
Race/Hispanic origin											
White	236,969	315,598	323,474	327,864	320,111	289,606	274,907	298,663	304,762	297,745	314,846
Black/African American	233,078	276,959	284,412	292,457	295,747	266,638	234,738	250,577	245,376	225,751	235,436
Hispanic/Latino	85,612	106,707	114,564	121,660	123,376	109,998	97,869	103,274	100,682	93,133	98,714
American Indian/Alaska Native	4,974	7,270	8,052	8,347	8,638	8,328	8,223	8,527	8,292	8,793	9,285
Asian/Native Hawaiian/Other Pacific Islander	4,304	5,130	4,940	5,181	5,267	4,785	4,225	4,776	4,826	4,386	5,388
Two or more races	NC	975	633	754	1,237	1,563	689	1,070	1,320	1,419	906
Conviction status											
Convicted	245,698	270,712	280,914	289,098	272,291	250,920	234,566	250,464	248,800	234,134	240,944
Unconvicted	316,728	440,873	460,837	470,960	462,052	412,914	368,411	385,631	383,152	381,588	406,565

NC = Not collected.

METHODOLOGY

About the Report

This report presents estimates of the number of jail inmates at midyear 2014 by sex, race, Hispanic origin, and conviction status. It provides estimates of year-to-year changes from midyear 2000 to midyear 2014 in the number of inmates held, average daily population, rated capacity of local jails, and percent of capacity occupied. It also includes statistics, by jurisdiction size, on changes in the number of inmates, number of admissions, and weekly turnover rate between 2013 and 2014. Estimates and standard errors are based on data collected from the *Annual Survey of Jails*.

For more information, please see http://www.bjs.gov/index.cfm?ty=pbdetail&iid=5299.

Terms and Definitions

Admissions: Persons who are officially booked and housed in jails by formal legal document and the authority of the courts or some other official agency. Jail admissions include persons sentenced to weekend programs and those who are booked into the facility for the first time. Excluded from jail admissions are inmates re-entering the facility after an escape, work release, medical appointment or treatment facility appointment, and bail and court appearances. BJS collects jail admissions for the last 7 days in June.

Average daily population (ADP): The average is derived by the sum of inmates in jail each day for a year, divided by the number of days in the year (i.e., between July 1, 2013, and June 30, 2014).

Average annual change: The mean average change across a 12-month time period.

Calculating annual admissions: BJS collects the number of jail admissions during the last 7 days in June. Annual jail admissions are calculated by multiplying weekly admissions by the sum of 365 days divided by 7 days.

Calculating weekly jail turnover rate: This rate is calculated by adding admissions and releases and dividing by the average daily population.

Inmates confined at midyear: The number of inmates held in custody on the last weekday in June.

Jail incarceration rate: The number of inmates held in the custody of local jails, per 100,000 U.S. residents.

Percent of capacity occupied: This percentage is calculated by taking the number of inmates (midyear or average daily population), dividing by the rated capacity, and multiplying by 100.

Rated capacity: The number of beds or inmates assigned by a rating official to a facility, excluding separate temporary holding areas.

Releases: Persons released after a period of confinement (e.g., sentence completion, bail or bond releases, other pretrial releases, transfers to other jurisdictions, and deaths). Releases include those persons who have completed their weekend program and who are leaving the facility for the last time. Excluded from jail releases are temporary discharges including work release, medical appointment or treatment center, court appearance, furlough, day reporting, and transfers to other facilities within the jail's jurisdiction.

Standard errors and tests of significance: As with any survey, the ASJ estimates are subject to error arising from sampling rather than using a complete enumeration of the jail population. A common way to express this sampling variability is to construct a 95 percent confidence interval around each survey estimate. Typically, multiplying the standard error by 1.96 and then adding or subtracting the result from the estimate produces the confidence interval. This interval expresses the range of values that could result among 95 percent of the different samples that could be drawn.

Under jail supervision but not confined: This classification includes all persons in community-based programs operated by a jail facility. These programs include electronic monitoring, house arrest, community service, day reporting, and work programs. The classification excludes persons on pretrial release and who are not in a community-based program run by the jail, as well as persons under supervision of probation, parole, or other agencies; inmates on weekend programs; and inmates who participate in work release programs and return to the jail at night.

Weekend programs: Offenders in these programs are allowed to serve their sentences of confinement only on weekends (i.e., Friday to Sunday).

About the Data

Annual Survey of Jails

In years between the complete census of local jails, the Bureau of Justice Statistics (BJS) conducts the Annual Survey of Jails (ASJ). ASJ uses a stratified probability sample of jail jurisdictions to estimate the number and characteristics of local inmates nationwide. The 2014 ASJ sample consisted of 891 jail jurisdictions, represented by 942 jail facilities (referred to as reporting units). This sample represents about 2,750 jail jurisdictions nationwide.

Local jail jurisdictions include counties (parishes in Louisiana) or municipal governments that administer one or more local jails. In the sampling design, the jail jurisdictions nationwide were grouped into 10 strata. The 10 strata were defined by the interaction of two variables: the jail jurisdiction average daily population (ADP) in 2005, and whether in 2005 the jurisdiction held at least one juvenile. For 8 of the 10 strata, a random sample of jail jurisdictions was selected. For the remaining two strata, all jurisdictions were included in the sample. One stratum consisted of all jails (70) that were operated jointly by two or more jurisdictions (referred to as multi-jurisdictional jails). The other stratum (referred to as certainty stratum) consisted of all jail jurisdictions (267) that held juvenile inmates at the time of the 2005 Census of Jail Inmates and had an ADP of 500 or more inmates during the 12 months ending June 30, 2005; held only adult inmates and had an ADP of 750 or more.

The sampling design used for the 2014 ASJ is the same as the design used for the 2013 ASJ. The 2013 ASJ differed from the 2006–2012 ASJs in that it included in the sample, with a probability of one, all California jail jurisdictions in response to the two enacted laws—AB 109 and AB 117 by the California State Legislature and governor—to reduce the number of inmates housed in state prisons starting October 1, 2011. The inclusion of all California jail jurisdictions resulted in an additional 21 jail jurisdictions (for a total sample size of 891 jurisdictions). Since the enactment of the two laws in recent years, the California jail population has experienced changes in size that cannot be compared to the changes of any other state in the U.S. For this reason, the California jail jurisdictions were put in separate strata so that they could represent only California jurisdictions. The same sampling design was adopted for the California jurisdictions. BJS obtained data from sampled jail jurisdictions by mailed and web-based survey questionnaires. After follow-up phone calls and facsimiles, the item response rate for jails that responded to the survey was nearly 100 percent for critical items, such as the number of inmates confined, ADP, and rated capacity. (See appendix tables 1 to 7 for standard errors associated with reported estimates from the 2014 ASJ.) Response rate, nonresponse adjustment, and out-of-scope jail facilities.

The 2014 ASJ sample initially comprised 942 reporting units. However, 12 units were out-of-scope for the 2014 data collection because they had closed either permanently or temporarily, which resulted in a sample of 930 active respondents. Ninety-three percent (or 878) of the 930 active individual reporting units responded to the 2014 data collection, and 52 active individual reporting units did not respond to the survey. BJS implemented nonresponse weight adjustment procedures to account for unit nonresponse, as it did in 2011 to 2013.

PART 7

Law Enforcement Officers Killed and Assaulted, 2014

HIGHLIGHTS

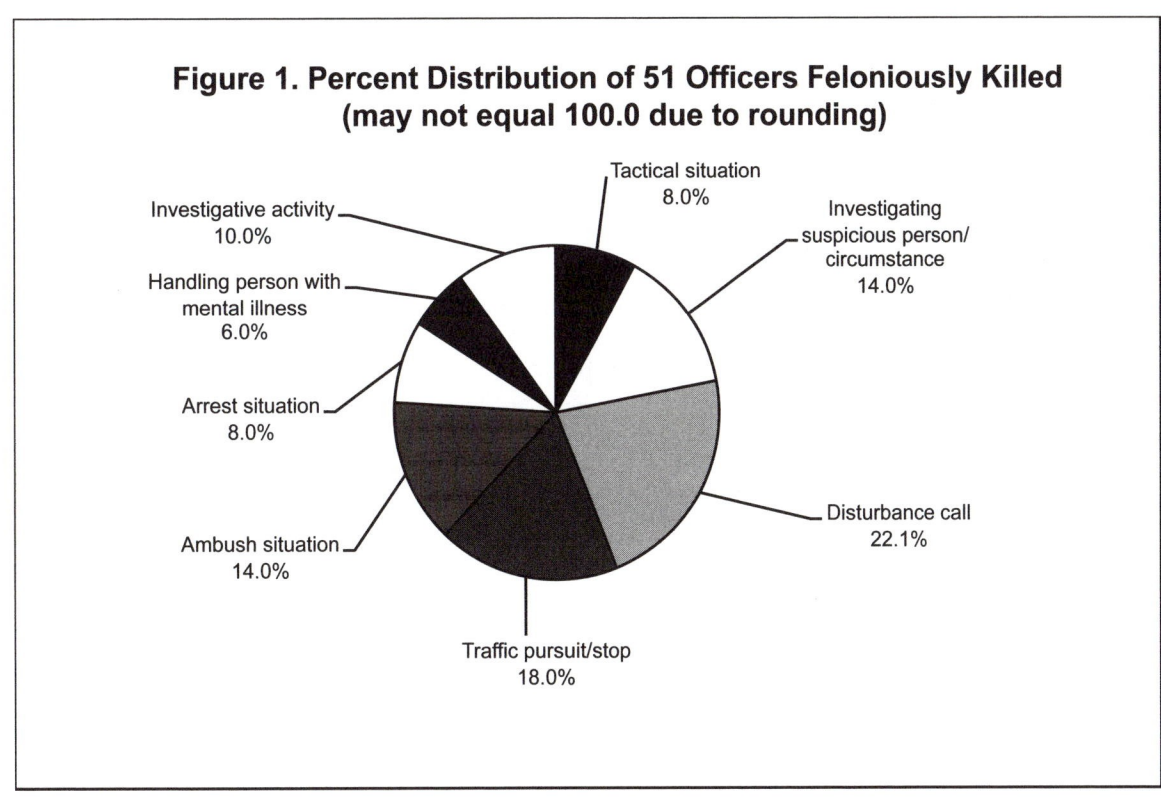

Figure 1. Percent Distribution of 51 Officers Feloniously Killed (may not equal 100.0 due to rounding)

- Tactical situation 8.0%
- Investigating suspicious person/circumstance 14.0%
- Investigative activity 10.0%
- Handling person with mental illness 6.0%
- Arrest situation 8.0%
- Ambush situation 14.0%
- Traffic pursuit/stop 18.0%
- Disturbance call 22.1%

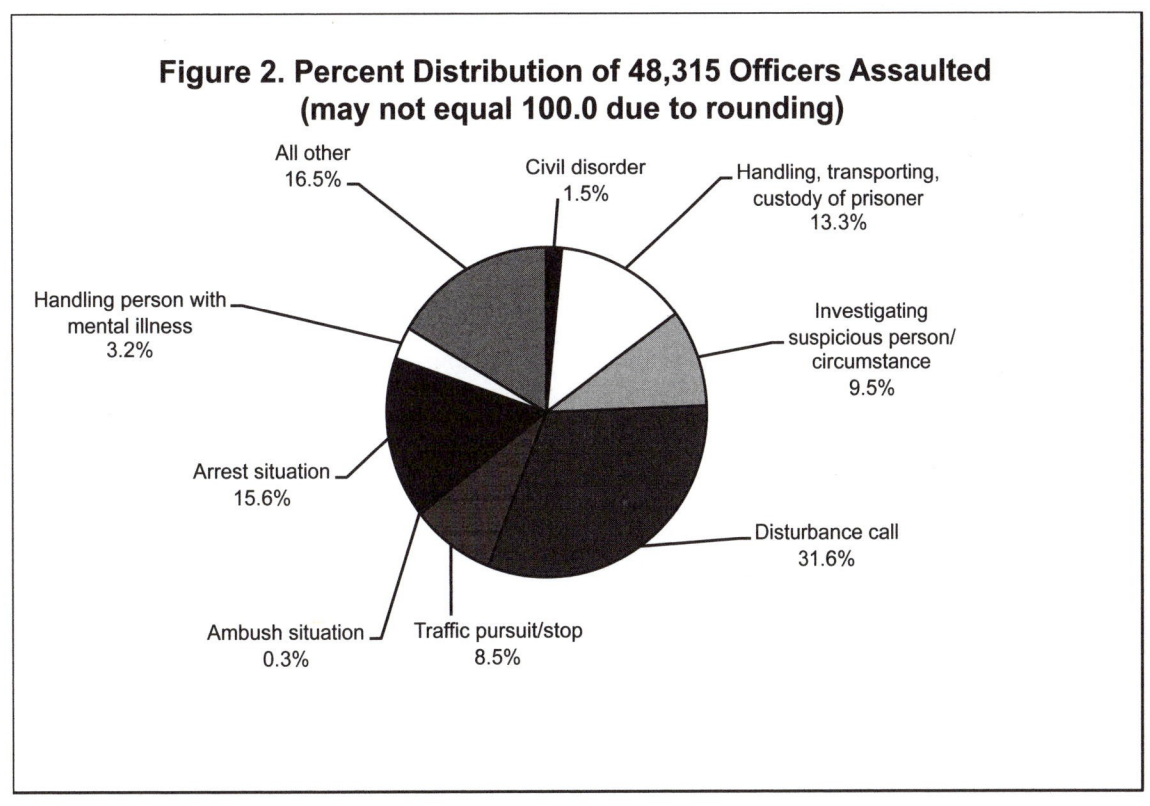

Figure 2. Percent Distribution of 48,315 Officers Assaulted (may not equal 100.0 due to rounding)

- All other 16.5%
- Civil disorder 1.5%
- Handling, transporting, custody of prisoner 13.3%
- Handling person with mental illness 3.2%
- Investigating suspicious person/circumstance 9.5%
- Arrest situation 15.6%
- Ambush situation 0.3%
- Traffic pursuit/stop 8.5%
- Disturbance call 31.6%

- In 2014, 51 law enforcement officers died from injuries incurred in the line of duty during felonious incidents. Of the officers feloniously killed, 27 were employed by city police departments, including 8 who were members of law enforcement agencies in cities with 250,000 or more inhabitants. Line-of-duty deaths occurred in 24 states and Puerto Rico.

- The average age of the officers who died in 2014 was 39 years old. The slain officers' average length of law enforcement service was 13 years. These data were unchanged from 2013.

- In 2014, 45 law enforcement officers died as the result of accidents that occurred in the line of duty. Accidental line-of-duty deaths of law enforcement officers occurred in 22 states and in Puerto Rico.

- Law enforcement agencies (11,151 participated, representing 76.4 percent of the nation's population) reported that 48,315 officers were assaulted while performing their duties in 2014.

- The U.S. Department of Homeland Security employed 4 of the federal officers killed between 2010 and 2014; the other 5 fatalities were employed with the U.S. Department of Justice (3) and the U.S. Department of the Interior (2).

Table 1. Law Enforcement Officers Feloniously Killed, by Region, Geographic Division, and State/Territory, 2005–2014

(Number.)

Area	Total	2005	2006	2007	2008	2009	2010	2011	2012	2013	2014
Number of Victim Officers	505	55	48	58	41	48	56	72	49	27	51
Northeast	58	5	7	7	3	7	3	10	6	2	8
New England	9	1	1	2	0	0	1	0	2	1	1
Connecticut	0	0	0	0	0	0	0	0	0	0	0
Maine	0	0	0	0	0	0	0	0	0	0	0
Massachusetts	4	0	0	1	0	0	1	0	1	1	0
New Hampshire	4	0	1	1	0	0	0	0	1	0	1
Rhode Island	1	1	0	0	0	0	0	0	0	0	0
Vermont	0	0	0	0	0	0	0	0	0	0	0
Middle Atlantic	49	4	6	5	3	7	2	10	4	1	7
New Jersey	7	0	1	2	0	1	0	2	0	0	1
New York	19	2	3	2	0	0	0	4	2	1	5
Pennsylvania	23	2	2	1	3	6	2	4	2	0	1
Midwest	88	10	6	9	9	5	10	21	6	4	8
East North Central	54	3	5	8	6	2	8	12	2	3	5
Illinois	14	0	2	1	3	2	4	1	0	1	0
Indiana	10	0	1	3	0	0	0	2	0	1	3
Michigan	13	1	1	1	1	0	3	4	1	1	0
Ohio	14	2	1	2	2	0	1	4	1	0	1
Wisconsin	3	0	0	1	0	0	0	1	0	0	1
West North Central	34	7	1	1	3	3	2	9	4	1	3
Iowa	2	0	0	0	0	0	0	1	0	1	0
Kansas	8	2	1	0	0	1	0	1	2	0	1
Minnesota	8	2	0	0	0	1	2	1	1	0	1
Missouri	12	3	0	1	3	0	0	3	1	0	1
Nebraska	0	0	0	0	0	0	0	0	0	0	0
North Dakota	1	0	0	0	0	0	0	1	0	0	0
South Dakota	3	0	0	0	0	1	0	2	0	0	0
South	228	28	22	32	20	21	22	29	22	15	17
South Atlantic	112	13	11	14	13	7	11	18	10	5	10
Delaware	2	0	0	0	0	1	0	1	0	0	0
District of Columbia	1	0	1	0	0	0	0	0	0	0	0
Florida	35	2	3	6	3	3	4	6	2	2	4
Georgia	20	5	2	0	2	0	5	3	1	0	2
Maryland	6	1	0	2	1	0	1	0	0	1	0
North Carolina	17	1	0	3	2	3	1	2	3	0	2
South Carolina	10	1	0	3	2	0	0	2	1	0	1
Virginia	15	3	4	0	3	0	0	3	0	1	1
West Virginia	6	0	1	0	0	0	0	1	3	1	0
East South Central	41	9	4	3	2	5	4	6	5	3	0
Alabama	12	1	2	1	0	4	1	1	2	0	0
Kentucky	6	2	0	1	1	0	0	0	1	1	0
Mississippi	14	6	1	0	0	0	3	1	1	2	0
Tennessee	9	0	1	1	1	1	0	4	1	0	0
West South Central	75	6	7	15	5	9	7	5	7	7	7
Arkansas	7	0	1	1	0	1	2	1	0	0	1
Louisiana	18	2	2	5	2	0	3	0	2	1	1
Oklahoma	4	1	1	0	0	2	0	0	0	0	0
Texas	46	3	3	9	3	6	2	4	5	6	5
West	109	10	11	9	9	13	18	10	9	6	14
Mountain	45	4	4	4	2	2	11	5	5	1	7
Arizona	19	1	0	3	2	0	5	3	2	0	3
Colorado	8	1	2	0	0	1	1	2	1	0	0
Idaho	1	0	0	1	0	0	0	0	0	0	0
Montana	3	0	0	0	0	0	2	0	0	0	1
Nevada	5	0	1	0	0	0	1	0	1	0	2
New Mexico	4	2	1	0	0	1	0	0	0	0	0
Utah	5	0	0	0	0	0	2	0	1	1	1
Wyoming	0	0	0	0	0	0	0	0	0	0	0
Pacific	64	6	7	5	7	11	7	5	4	5	7
Alaska	4	0	0	0	0	0	2	0	0	0	2
California	44	6	6	4	3	5	5	3	2	5	5
Hawaii	1	0	0	1	0	0	0	0	0	0	0
Oregon	4	0	0	0	2	0	0	2	0	0	0
Washington	11	0	1	0	2	6	0	0	2	0	0
Puerto Rico and other outlying areas	22	2	2	1	0	2	3	2	6	0	4
American Samoa	0	0	0	0	0	0	0	0	0	0	0
Guam	0	0	0	0	0	0	0	0	0	0	0
Mariana Islands	0	0	0	0	0	0	0	0	0	0	0
Puerto Rico	21	2	2	1	0	2	3	2	5	0	4
U.S. Virgin Islands	1	0	0	0	0	0	0	0	1	0	0

Table 2. Law Enforcement Officers Feloniously Killed, by Population Group/Agency Type, 2005–2014

(Number.)

Area	Total	2005	2006	2007	2008	2009	2010	2011	2012	2013	2014
Number of Victim Officers	505	55	48	58	41	48	56	72	49	27	51
Group I (cities 250,000 and over)	103	12	8	12	12	15	13	13	6	4	8
Group II (cities 100,000–249,999)	47	6	4	9	1	3	3	9	4	2	6
Group III (cities 50,000–99,999)	34	4	2	5	1	4	3	9	2	2	2
Group IV (25,000–49,999)	30	2	3	2	5	1	6	4	2	3	2
Group V (cities 10,000–24,999)	30	2	3	3	3	3	2	5	3	2	4
Group VI (cities under 10,000)	51	10	3	5	0	6	5	10	4	3	5
Metropolitan counties	100	6	15	11	9	8	9	14	11	6	11
Nonmetropolitan counties	41	4	3	4	4	4	6	4	5	3	4
State agencies	35	5	4	6	3	1	5	0	5	2	4
Federal agencies	12	2	1	0	3	1	1	2	1	0	1
Puerto Rico and other outlying areas	22	2	2	1	0	2	3	2	6	0	4

Table 3. Law Enforcement Officers Feloniously Killed, by Time of Incident, 2005–2014

(Number.)

Time of day	Total	2005	2006	2007	2008	2009	2010	2011	2012	2013	2014
Number of Victim Officers	505	55	48	58	41	48	56	72	49	27	51
Total A.M. hours	223	21	17	24	24	21	23	36	24	13	20
12:01 a.m.–2 a.m.	60	4	5	13	9	3	7	7	5	3	4
2:01 a.m.–4 a.m.	42	4	4	4	4	1	4	9	3	3	6
4:01 a.m.–6 a.m.	22	1	3	0	2	2	3	2	3	3	3
6:01 a.m.–8 a.m.	22	2	2	2	0	5	2	5	3	0	1
8:01 a.m.–10 a.m.	27	5	0	1	4	8	1	3	4	1	0
10:01 a.m.–noon	50	5	3	4	5	2	6	10	6	3	6
Total P.M. hours	279	34	30	34	17	27	33	36	23	14	31
12:01 p.m.–2 p.m.	36	1	5	6	0	5	2	5	2	3	7
2:01 p.m.–4 p.m.	49	7	4	6	4	3	4	6	3	3	9
4:01 p.m.–6 p.m.	38	4	5	2	2	3	4	8	3	1	6
6:01 p.m.–8 p.m.	42	6	4	7	4	3	4	5	6	2	1
8:01 p.m.–10 p.m.	57	6	5	9	2	10	10	3	6	2	4
10:01 p.m.–midnight	57	10	7	4	5	3	9	9	3	3	4
Not reported	3	0	1	0	0	0	0	0	2	0	0

Table 4. Law Enforcement Officers Feloniously Killed, by Day of Incident, 2005–2014

(Number.)

Day of the week	Total	2005	2006	2007	2008	2009	2010	2011	2012	2013	2014
Number of Victim Officers	505	55	48	58	41	48	56	72	49	27	51
Sunday	66	9	2	4	6	9	5	13	7	2	9
Monday	62	8	11	4	1	5	6	12	5	3	7
Tuesday	72	7	3	7	7	6	11	11	10	5	5
Wednesday	66	5	11	8	6	4	12	8	5	3	4
Thursday	87	10	11	10	7	7	11	9	9	6	7
Friday	73	9	5	12	8	4	6	11	5	5	8
Saturday	79	7	5	13	6	13	5	8	8	3	11

Table 5. Law Enforcement Officers Feloniously Killed, by Month of Incident, 2005–2014

(Number.)

Month	Total	2005	2006	2007	2008	2009	2010	2011	2012	2013	2014
Number of Victim Officers..............................	505	55	48	58	41	48	56	72	49	27	51
January...	45	6	1	6	8	1	4	9	6	2	2
February..	36	3	6	5	4	1	4	3	4	5	1
March...	49	6	5	8	0	6	5	9	1	1	8
April..	37	6	2	2	1	8	1	9	4	3	1
May...	44	6	6	7	2	0	7	3	3	1	9
June...	43	3	4	4	6	6	4	6	4	2	4
July...	43	4	0	6	4	7	7	8	2	1	4
August..	51	7	7	5	4	4	4	7	8	2	3
September..	42	3	5	7	6	4	1	1	5	4	6
October...	31	2	6	4	1	2	5	5	1	1	4
November...	30	7	1	0	1	4	6	2	4	0	5
December...	54	2	5	4	4	5	8	10	7	5	4

Table 6. Law Enforcement Officers Feloniously Killed, by Age Group of Victim Officer, 2005–2014

(Number.)

Age group	Total	2005	2006	2007	2008	2009	2010	2011	2012	2013	2014
Number of Victim Officers...........................	505	55	48	58	41	48	56	72	49	27	51
Under 25 years	25	2	1	7	2	1	3	2	2	0	5
25–30 years	83	9	9	7	7	9	12	17	8	2	3
31–35 years	113	15	10	17	7	8	13	11	12	9	11
36–40 years	99	9	17	8	11	11	9	12	8	7	7
41–45 years	76	12	3	4	3	13	7	10	8	4	12
46–50 years	58	7	3	7	4	3	5	13	6	1	9
51–55 years	30	1	4	5	5	0	1	4	5	2	3
56–60 years	14	0	0	1	2	3	4	3	0	1	0
Over 60 years	7	0	1	2	0	0	2	0	0	1	1
Average age (years).................................	38	37	38	38	39	38	38	38	38	39	39

Table 7. Law Enforcement Officers Feloniously Killed, by Years of Service of Victim Officer, 2005–2014

(Number.)

Years of service	Total	2005	2006	2007	2008	2009	2010	2011	2012	2013	2014
Number of Victim Officers...........................	505	55	48	58	41	48	56	72	49	27	51
Less than 1	9	2	0	2	0	0	1	0	2	0	2
1–5...	147	20	16	17	15	13	22	17	12	4	11
6–10..	131	10	13	17	11	12	13	24	13	10	8
11–15...	76	7	9	7	6	9	6	8	5	8	11
16–20...	69	9	4	7	2	6	9	8	10	1	13
21–25...	41	5	4	5	4	3	1	12	1	1	5
26–30...	21	2	1	3	3	4	1	1	4	2	0
More than 30	9	0	1	0	0	0	3	2	1	1	1
Not reported..	2	0	0	0	0	1	0	0	1	0	0
Average years of service...........................	11	10	11	10	10	12	10	12	12	13	13

Table 8. Law Enforcement Officers Feloniously Killed, by Profile of Victim Officer, Averages, 1995–2014

(Number.)

Characteristic	2014	5-year averages		10-year averages	
		2005–2009	2010–2014	1995–2004	2005–2014
Age	39	38	38	37	38
Years of service	13	11	12	10	11
Height	5'10"	5'11"	5'11"	5'11"	5'11"
Weight	204	200	204	198	202

Note: The deaths of the 72 law enforcement officers that resulted from the events of September 11, 2001, are not included in this table.

Table 9. Law Enforcement Officers Feloniously Killed, by Race and Sex of Victim Officer, 2005–2014

(Number.)

Characteristic	Total	2005	2006	2007	2008	2009	2010	2011	2012	2013	2014
Number of Victim Officers	505	55	48	58	41	48	56	72	49	27	51
Race											
White	439	47	41	48	30	42	48	68	43	25	47
Black	55	8	5	9	10	3	7	3	6	2	2
Asian/Pacific Islander	6	0	1	1	0	1	1	0	0	0	2
American Indian/Alaska Native	5	0	1	0	1	2	0	1	0	0	0
Sex											
Male	484	54	45	58	37	47	54	69	44	25	51
Female	21	1	3	0	4	1	2	3	5	2	0

Table 10. Law Enforcement Officers Feloniously Killed, by Victim Officer's Use of Weapon During Incident, 2005–2014

(Number.)

Characteristic	Total	2005	2006	2007	2008	2009	2010	2011	2012	2013	2014
Number of Victim Officers	505	55	48	58	41	48	56	72	49	27	51
Fired own weapon	112	15	11	11	11	12	17	18	6	6	5
Attempted to use own weapon	72	6	7	17	4	9	7	10	2	3	7
Did not attempt to use own weapon	257	24	22	25	14	18	20	43	38	18	35
Use of weapon not required	64	10	8	5	12	9	12	1	3	0	4

Table 11. Law Enforcement Officers Feloniously Killed, by Victim Officer's Weapon Stolen[1] by Offender, 2005–2014

(Number.)

Characteristic	Total	2005	2006	2007	2008	2009	2010	2011	2012	2013	2014
Number of Victim Officers	505	55	48	58	41	48	56	72	49	27	51
Total, weapon stolen	52	9	4	4	5	7	7	5	3	2	6
Killed with own weapon	14	5	0	2	1	1	4	1	0	0	0
Killed with weapon other than own	37	4	4	2	4	5	3	4	3	2	6
Killed with weapon, information not reported	1	0	0	0	0	1	0	0	0	0	0
Total, weapon not stolen	450	46	43	53	36	41	48	67	46	25	45
Killed with own weapon	13	1	1	0	3	1	2	2	1	1	1
Killed with weapon other than own	437	45	42	53	33	40	46	65	45	24	44
Killed with weapon, information not reported	0	0	0	0	0	0	0	0	0	0	0
Total, weapon stolen, information not reported	3	0	1	1	0	0	1	0	0	0	0
Killed with own weapon	0	0	0	0	0	0	0	0	0	0	0
Killed with weapon other than own	2	0	0	1	0	0	1	0	0	0	0
Killed with weapon, information not reported	1	0	1	0	0	0	0	0	0	0	0

Note: Weapon is inclusive of all weapon types that may be issued to a law enforcement officer.
[1] The term "stolen" indicates the weapon was taken from the scene of the incident.

Table 12. Law Enforcement Officers Feloniously Killed with Own Weapons, by Victim Officer's Type of Weapon, 2005–2014

(Number.)

Type of weapon	Total	2005	2006	2007	2008	2009	2010	2011	2012	2013	2014
Number of Victim Officers Killed with Own Weapon	27	6	1	2	4	2	6	3	1	1	1
Total, handgun	26	6	1	2	4	2	5	3	1	1	1
.38 caliber	2	0	0	0	1	0	0	1	0	0	0
.40 caliber	15	5	1	1	3	1	1	2	0	0	1
.45 caliber	2	1	0	0	0	0	1	0	0	0	0
9 millimeter	6	0	0	1	0	1	3	0	0	1	0
Not reported	1	0	0	0	0	0	0	0	1	0	0
Rifle, total	0	0	0	0	0	0	0	0	0	0	0
Shotgun, total	1	0	0	0	0	0	1	0	0	0	0
12 gauge	1	0	0	0	0	0	1	0	0	0	0

Table 13. Law Enforcement Officers Feloniously Killed, by Population Group/Agency Type, by Type of Assignment, 2014

(Number.)

Area	Total	2-officer vehicle	1-officer vehicle		Foot patrol		Other[1]		Off duty
			Alone	Assisted	Alone	Assisted	Alone	Assisted	
Number of Victim Officers.................................	51	7	12	12	0	0	4	11	5
Group I (cities 250,000 and over)	8	4	0	3	0	0	0	1	0
Group II (cities 100,000–249,999)	6	1	1	1	0	0	0	2	1
Group III (cities 50,000–99,999)	2	0	2	0	0	0	0	0	0
Group IV (25,000–49,999)	2	0	0	2	0	0	0	0	0
Group V (cities 10,000–24,999)	4	0	2	1	0	0	0	0	1
Group VI (cities under 10,000)	5	0	3	0	0	0	2	0	0
Metropolitan counties	11	0	2	4	0	0	0	3	2
Nonmetropolitan counties	4	0	1	1	0	0	1	1	0
State agencies	4	2	1	0	0	0	1	0	0
Federal agencies	1	0	0	0	0	0	0	1	0
Puerto Rico and other outlying areas	4	0	0	0	0	0	0	3	1

[1] Includes detectives, officers on special assignments, undercover officers, and officers on other types of assignments not listed.

Table 14. Law Enforcement Officers Feloniously Killed, by Circumstance at Scene of Incident, 2005–2014

(Number.)

Circumstance	Total	2005	2006	2007	2008	2009	2010	2011	2012	2013	2014
Number of Victim Officers	505	55	48	58	41	48	56	72	49	27	51
Disturbance call	62	7	8	5	1	6	6	10	4	4	11
Disturbance (bar fight, person with firearm, etc.)	39	2	6	3	1	4	2	5	3	3	10
Domestic disturbance (family quarrel, etc.)	23	5	2	2	0	2	4	5	1	1	1
Arrest situation	95	8	12	17	9	8	14	10	7	6	4
Burglary in progress/pursuing burglary suspect	9	1	0	1	2	1	3	0	1	0	0
Robbery in progress/pursuing robbery suspect	39	4	6	7	1	3	6	6	3	3	0
Drug-related matter	8	0	2	1	1	0	1	0	2	0	1
Attempting other arrest	39	3	4	8	5	4	4	4	1	3	3
Civil disorder (mass disobedience, riot, etc.)	0	0	0	0	0	0	0	0	0	0	0
Handling, transporting, custody of prisoner	11	1	1	1	1	2	1	1	3	0	0
Investigating suspicious person/circumstance	68	7	6	4	7	4	8	12	8	5	7
Ambush situation	36	4	1	9	1	6	2	2	3	1	7
Unprovoked attack	57	4	9	7	5	9	11	6	1	4	1
Investigative activity (surveillance, search, interview, etc.)	25	4	0	1	2	0	2	4	6	1	5
Handling person with mental illness	9	2	1	0	0	0	0	0	3	0	3
Traffic pursuit/stop	93	15	8	11	8	8	9	14	9	2	9
Felony vehicle stop	33	5	0	5	5	2	3	7	5	0	1
Traffic violation stop	60	10	8	6	3	6	6	7	4	2	8
Tactical situation (barricaded offender, hostage taking, high-risk entry, etc.)	49	3	2	3	7	5	3	13	5	4	4

Table 15. Law Enforcement Officers Feloniously Killed, by Circumstance at Scene of Incident, by Region, 2014

(Number.)

Circumstance	Total	Northeast	Midwest	South	West	Puerto Rico and other outlying areas
Number of Victim Officers..	51	8	8	17	14	4
Disturbance call	11	1	2	6	2	0
Disturbance (bar fight, person with firearm, etc.)...............................	10	1	2	6	1	0
Domestic disturbance (family quarrel, etc.)	1	0	0	0	1	0
Arrest situation	4	0	0	0	2	2
Burglary in progress/pursuing burglary suspect	0	0	0	0	0	0
Robbery in progress/pursuing robbery suspect	0	0	0	0	0	0
Drug-related matter	1	0	0	0	0	1
Attempting other arrest..	3	0	0	0	2	1
Civil disorder (mass disobedience, riot, etc.)	0	0	0	0	0	0
Handling, transporting, custody of prisoner......................................	0	0	0	0	0	0
Investigating suspicious person/circumstance	7	0	1	3	3	0
Ambush situation..	7	4	0	1	2	0
Unprovoked attack	1	1	0	0	0	0
Investigative activity (surveillance, search, interview, etc.)...................	5	0	2	0	1	2
Handling person with mental illness	3	1	0	2	0	0
Traffic pursuit/stop	9	1	3	2	3	0
Felony vehicle stop	1	0	0	1	0	0
Traffic violation stop	8	1	3	1	3	0
Tactical situation (barricaded offender, hostage taking, high-risk entry, etc.)	4	0	0	3	1	0

Table 16. Law Enforcement Officers Feloniously Killed, by Circumstance at Scene of Incident, by Region, 2005–2014

(Number.)

Circumstance	Total	Northeast	Midwest	South	West	Puerto Rico and other outlying areas
Number of Victim Officers..........................	505	58	88	228	109	22
Disturbance call	62	6	12	32	10	2
Disturbance (bar fight, person with firearm, etc.)....................	39	4	9	19	5	2
Domestic disturbance (family quarrel, etc.)	23	2	3	13	5	0
Arrest situation	95	15	16	37	18	9
Burglary in progress/pursuing burglary suspect	9	1	2	4	1	1
Robbery in progress/pursuing robbery suspect	39	11	8	11	5	4
Drug-related matter	8	0	0	4	1	3
Attempting other arrest...	39	3	6	18	11	1
Civil disorder (mass disobedience, riot, etc.)	0	0	0	0	0	0
Handling, transporting, custody of prisoner..........................	11	1	0	8	0	2
Investigating suspicious person/circumstance	68	5	14	31	17	1
Ambush situation..	36	9	6	14	5	2
Unprovoked attack	57	6	12	24	15	0
Investigative activity (surveillance, search, interview, etc.)..............	25	1	5	8	6	5
Handling person with mental illness	9	1	2	3	3	0
Traffic pursuit/stop	93	9	12	47	24	1
Felony vehicle stop	33	3	4	21	5	0
Traffic violation stop	60	6	8	26	19	1
Tactical situation (barricaded offender, hostage taking, high-risk entry, etc.)	49	5	9	24	11	0

Table 17. Law Enforcement Officers Feloniously Killed, by Type of Weapon, 2005–2014

(Number.)

Type of weapon	Total	2005	2006	2007	2008	2009	2010	2011	2012	2013	2014
Number of Victim Officers	505	55	48	58	41	48	56	72	49	27	51
Total firearms	466	50	46	56	35	45	55	63	44	26	46
Handgun	343	42	36	39	25	28	38	50	34	18	33
Rifle	84	3	8	8	6	15	15	7	7	5	10
Shotgun	38	5	2	8	4	2	2	6	3	3	3
Type of firearm not reported	1	0	0	1	0	0	0	0	0	0	0
Knife or other cutting instrument	2	0	0	0	0	0	0	1	1	0	0
Bomb	2	0	0	0	2	0	0	0	0	0	0
Blunt instrument	0	0	0	0	0	0	0	0	0	0	0
Personal weapons	5	0	0	0	0	0	0	2	2	0	1
Vehicle	30	5	2	2	4	3	1	6	2	1	4
Other	0	0	0	0	0	0	0	0	0	0	0

Table 18. Law Enforcement Officers Feloniously Killed, by Number of Victim Officers Wearing Uniform, Body Armor, or Holster, 2005–2014

(Number.)

Characteristic	Total	2005	2006	2007	2008	2009	2010	2011	2012	2013	2014
Number of Victim Officers	505	55	48	58	41	48	56	72	49	27	51
Wearing uniform	398	43	32	41	31	40	47	61	40	20	43
Wearing body armor	338	34	27	36	32	36	38	51	26	19	39
In uniform	308	32	22	33	26	32	35	46	25	18	39
Not in uniform	29	2	4	3	6	4	3	5	1	1	0
Wearing uniform not reported	1	0	1	0	0	0	0	0	0	0	0
Wearing holster	464	49	43	52	37	45	53	67	43	27	48
In uniform	392	43	32	40	30	39	46	59	40	20	43
Not in uniform	71	6	10	12	7	6	7	8	3	7	5
Wearing uniform not reported	1	0	1	0	0	0	0	0	0	0	0

Table 19. Law Enforcement Officers Feloniously Killed, Age Group of Known Offender, 2005–2014

(Number.)

Age group	Total	2005	2006	2007	2008	2009	2010	2011	2012	2013	2014
Number of Known Offenders	563	56	59	66	42	45	80	76	52	28	59
Under 18	28	2	4	7	3	2	1	5	1	0	3
18–24	174	19	26	26	8	14	24	20	15	9	13
25–30	130	15	9	10	10	6	23	19	14	7	17
31–35	77	8	7	6	4	9	12	9	6	6	10
36–40	48	2	2	4	5	5	8	7	4	2	9
41–45	39	2	6	3	7	5	6	3	6	0	1
46–50	26	6	1	2	3	1	0	5	2	3	3
51–55	18	0	2	3	1	2	3	4	1	1	1
56–60	12	0	1	2	1	0	2	4	0	0	2
Over 60	5	2	0	0	0	1	1	0	1	0	0
Not reported	6	0	1	3	0	0	0	0	2	0	0
Average age	30	30	28	28	32	31	31	32	31	31	31

Table 20. Law Enforcement Officers Feloniously Killed, by Profile of Known Offender, Averages, 1995–2014

(Number.)

Characteristic	2014	5-year averages		10-year averages	
		2005–2009	2010–2014	1995–2004	2005–2014
Age	31	30	31	29	30
Height	5'10"	5'9"	5'10"	5'10"	5'10"
Weight	180	177	181	174	179

Note: The 14 known offenders involved in the events of September 11, 2001, are not included in this table.

Table 21. Law Enforcement Officers Feloniously Killed, by Race and Sex of Known Offender, 2005–2014

(Number.)

Characteristic	Total	2005	2006	2007	2008	2009	2010	2011	2012	2013	2014
Number of Known Offenders	563	56	59	66	42	45	80	76	52	28	59
Race											
White..	309	36	25	35	20	28	32	44	32	15	42
Black...	224	20	31	26	21	17	39	28	17	12	13
Asian/Pacific Islander	10	0	0	4	1	0	2	1	1	0	1
American Indian/Alaska Native	9	0	0	0	0	0	4	2	1	0	2
Not reported	11	0	3	1	0	0	3	1	1	1	1
Sex											
Male..	545	56	58	65	40	43	78	74	50	27	54
Female..	18	0	1	1	2	2	2	2	2	1	5

Table 22. Law Enforcement Officers Feloniously Killed, by Status of Known Offender at Time of Incident, 2005–2014

(Number.)

Characteristic	Total	2005	2006	2007	2008	2009	2010	2011	2012	2013	2014
Number of Known Offenders	563	56	59	66	42	45	80	76	52	28	59
Under judicial supervision...											
Total..	147	25	15	19	12	13	19	17	10	6	11
Probation...	65	11	5	10	4	7	9	7	5	2	5
Parole..	52	10	5	7	5	3	8	4	3	2	5
Halfway house	2	1	0	0	0	0	0	1	0	0	0
Escapee from penal institution.................	6	2	3	0	0	0	1	0	0	0	0
Conditional release, pending criminal prosecution	22	1	2	2	3	3	1	5	2	2	1
Known to agency as:											
User of controlled substance	106	18	9	9	11	10	19	13	6	3	8
Dealer of controlled substance	80	13	11	9	5	5	7	9	6	4	11
Possessor of controlled substance	80	12	7	12	9	2	12	9	5	2	10
Use of controlled substance											
Under influence...	68	9	5	8	3	1	11	8	11	1	11
Not under influence	92	10	8	14	11	9	10	15	5	5	5
Unknown to victim officer's agency	367	37	40	41	28	29	54	48	28	21	41
Not reported	36	0	6	3	0	6	5	5	8	1	2
Use of alcohol..											
Intoxicated/under influence.....................	51	6	4	11	2	2	7	7	7	3	2
Not intoxicated/under influence..............	119	15	10	11	13	11	16	16	9	4	14
Unknown to victim officer's agency	356	35	39	41	27	26	52	48	27	20	41
Not reported	37	0	6	3	0	6	5	5	9	1	2
Known to agency as having prior mental disorders........	30	3	4	4	2	3	2	7	2	2	1
Relationship between victim officer and offender											
Through law enforcement	59	11	5	6	5	3	8	11	4	3	3
Through non-law enforcement	5	0	1	1	0	0	1	0	0	2	0
No known relationship	462	45	46	56	37	33	66	60	41	23	55
Unknown to victim officer's agency	1	0	1	0	0	0	0	0	0	0	0
Not reported	36	0	6	3	0	9	5	5	7	0	1

Table 23. Law Enforcement Officers Feloniously Killed, by Criminal History of Known Offender, 2005–2014

(Number.)

Characteristic	Total	2005	2006	2007	2008	2009	2010	2011	2012	2013	2014
Number of Known Offenders	563	56	59	66	42	45	80	76	52	28	59
Prior criminal arrest...	470	53	43	60	36	35	71	64	38	20	50
Convicted on prior criminal charge................................	357	41	31	46	24	28	55	52	30	13	37
Received juvenile conviction on prior criminal charge	93	8	9	14	6	8	10	19	7	2	10
Received parole/probation on prior criminal charge	281	34	22	39	18	26	41	44	19	9	29
Prior arrest for:..											
Crime of violence	254	25	26	32	17	23	44	37	17	12	21
Murder..	20	1	3	2	1	2	7	1	2	0	1
Drug law violation......................................	248	26	27	38	19	13	39	27	17	8	34
Assaulting an officer/resisting arrest........	128	12	11	20	6	9	20	23	9	4	14
Weapons violation.....................................	229	21	25	29	14	18	40	33	17	7	25

Table 24. Law Enforcement Officers Feloniously Killed, by Disposition of Known Offender, 2003–2012

(Number.)

Disposition	2003–2007	2008–2012	2003–2012
Number of Known Offenders	300	295	595
Fugitive	0	4	4
Arrested and charged	214	185	399
Guilty of murder	152	97	249
Received death sentence	50	16	66
Received life imprisonment	77	58	135
Received prison term (ranging from 5 years to 999 years)	25	23	48
Guilty of lesser offense related to murder	25	15	40
Guilty of crime other than murder	11	9	20
Acquitted/dismissed/nolle prosequi	16	17	33
Indeterminate charge and sentence	0	1	1
Committed to psychiatric institution	5	4	9
Case pending/disposition unknown	4	40	44
Died in custody prior to sentencing	1	2	3
Not arrested	86	106	192
Justifiably killed	55	65	120
Justifiably killed by victim officer	18	21	39
Justifiably killed by person(s) other than victim officer	37	44	81
Committed suicide	25	36	61
Murdered while at large	0	0	0
Died under other circumstance	4	4	8
Other	2	1	3

Table 25. Law Enforcement Officers Accidentally Killed, by Region, Geographic Division, and State/Territory, 2005–2014

(Number.)

Area	Total	2005	2006	2007	2008	2009	2010	2011	2012	2013	2014
Number of Victim Officers................................	599	67	66	83	68	48	72	53	48	49	45
Northeast...	73	7	5	6	11	6	8	8	9	5	8
New England	18	2	1	2	1	2	3	2	4	0	1
Connecticut.................................	4	0	1	0	1	0	2	0	0	0	0
Maine......................................	1	0	0	0	0	0	0	1	0	0	0
Massachusetts.............................	12	2	0	2	0	2	1	1	3	0	1
New Hampshire............................	0	0	0	0	0	0	0	0	0	0	0
Rhode Island...............................	1	0	0	0	0	0	0	0	1	0	0
Vermont...................................	0	0	0	0	0	0	0	0	0	0	0
Middle Atlantic................................	55	5	4	4	10	4	5	6	5	5	7
New Jersey.................................	16	3	1	2	2	0	4	1	1	0	2
New York...................................	25	1	2	2	3	3	1	5	2	3	3
Pennsylvania..............................	14	1	1	0	5	1	0	0	2	2	2
Midwest	84	13	14	11	5	9	14	7	3	4	4
East North Central	59	9	14	5	5	6	7	3	3	4	3
Illinois....................................	17	3	6	1	0	0	3	0	1	2	1
Indiana....................................	14	3	2	2	2	2	2	0	0	0	1
Michigan..................................	10	3	2	0	0	2	0	1	0	1	1
Ohio.......................................	13	0	3	2	2	1	1	2	1	1	0
Wisconsin.................................	5	0	1	0	1	1	1	0	1	0	0
West North Central	25	4	0	6	0	3	7	4	0	0	1
Iowa.......................................	2	0	0	1	0	0	0	1	0	0	0
Kansas....................................	3	0	0	1	0	0	2	0	0	0	0
Minnesota.................................	1	0	0	1	0	0	0	0	0	0	0
Missouri	17	4	0	3	0	2	4	3	0	0	1
Nebraska..................................	1	0	0	0	0	1	0	0	0	0	0
North Dakota	0	0	0	0	0	0	0	0	0	0	0
South Dakota..............................	1	0	0	0	0	0	1	0	0	0	0
South...	299	30	26	46	32	21	39	27	28	31	19
South Atlantic................................	130	12	11	22	14	12	16	16	14	9	4
Delaware..................................	0	0	0	0	0	0	0	0	0	0	0
District of Columbia........................	2	0	0	1	0	0	1	0	0	0	0
Florida....................................	27	3	2	8	4	1	4	1	2	1	1
Georgia...................................	30	3	3	3	3	2	3	6	4	2	1
Maryland..................................	13	0	0	2	3	0	3	2	3	0	0
North Carolina.............................	18	1	0	4	2	3	0	4	2	1	1
South Carolina.............................	13	3	1	1	1	2	2	1	0	2	0
Virginia...................................	25	2	5	2	1	3	3	2	3	3	1
West Virginia..............................	2	0	0	1	0	1	0	0	0	0	0
East South Central	50	4	6	6	4	4	6	3	3	7	7
Alabama..................................	17	2	1	3	2	1	0	2	1	3	2
Kentucky..................................	5	0	2	1	0	0	1	0	1	0	0
Mississippi................................	14	0	1	2	1	2	2	0	0	4	2
Tennessee.................................	14	2	2	0	1	1	3	1	1	0	3
West South Central	119	14	9	18	14	5	17	8	11	15	8
Arkansas..................................	10	2	1	0	2	1	0	0	0	4	0
Louisiana..................................	21	2	2	4	0	1	3	3	2	3	1
Oklahoma.................................	15	3	1	0	3	1	1	0	2	2	2
Texas.....................................	73	7	5	14	9	2	13	5	7	6	5
West..	133	14	20	19	17	12	11	10	8	9	13
Mountain	58	3	9	10	6	8	4	4	6	4	4
Arizona...................................	19	2	4	2	2	1	1	2	1	2	2
Colorado..................................	8	1	0	2	0	0	0	0	4	0	1
Idaho......................................	2	0	0	0	0	2	0	0	0	0	0
Montana..................................	6	0	2	1	1	1	0	1	0	0	0
Nevada...................................	5	0	0	1	1	2	0	0	0	1	0
New Mexico...............................	11	0	1	4	1	2	1	0	0	1	1
Utah......................................	5	0	1	0	1	0	2	0	1	0	0
Wyoming..................................	2	0	1	0	0	0	0	1	0	0	0
Pacific......................................	75	11	11	9	11	4	7	6	2	5	9
Alaska....................................	1	0	0	0	0	0	0	0	0	1	0
California..................................	63	10	9	7	11	3	6	5	0	3	9
Hawaii....................................	4	0	1	0	0	0	0	1	2	0	0
Oregon....................................	1	0	0	1	0	0	0	0	0	0	0
Washington...............................	6	1	1	1	0	1	1	0	0	1	0
Puerto Rico and other outlying areas.................	10	3	1	1	3	0	0	1	0	0	1
American Samoa	0	0	0	0	0	0	0	0	0	0	0
Guam...	1	0	0	1	0	0	0	0	0	0	0
Mariana Islands..............................	0	0	0	0	0	0	0	0	0	0	0
Puerto Rico..................................	8	3	1	0	2	0	0	1	0	0	1
U.S. Virgin Islands...........................	1	0	0	0	1	0	0	0	0	0	0

Table 26. Law Enforcement Officers Accidentally Killed, by Population Group/Agency Type, 2005–2014

(Number.)

Area	Total	2005	2006	2007	2008	2009	2010	2011	2012	2013	2014
Number of Victim Officers..................................	599	67	66	83	68	48	72	53	48	49	45
Group I (cities 250,000 and over).........................	63	4	7	4	10	4	9	5	9	5	6
Group II (cities 100,000–249,999).......................	39	4	6	7	5	3	3	3	3	4	1
Group III (cities 50,000–99,999).........................	33	2	3	6	4	3	2	5	1	5	2
Group IV (25,000–49,999).................................	35	7	2	5	2	1	6	3	6	1	2
Group V (cities 10,000–24,999)...........................	22	4	2	4	3	1	2	0	1	3	2
Group VI (cities under 10,000)............................	59	8	5	8	8	4	4	7	2	6	7
Metropolitan counties.......................................	133	15	19	19	14	10	13	11	12	10	10
Nonmetropolitan counties.................................	60	6	4	6	5	11	9	3	4	5	7
State agencies...	114	12	15	14	13	10	19	12	6	8	5
Federal agencies	31	2	2	9	1	1	5	3	4	2	2
Puerto Rico and other outlying areas..................	10	3	1	1	3	0	0	1	0	0	1

Table 27. Law Enforcement Officers Accidentally Killed, by Time of Incident, 2005–2014

(Number.)

Time of day	Total	2005	2006	2007	2008	2009	2010	2011	2012	2013	2014
Number of Victim Officers............................	599	67	66	83	68	48	72	53	48	49	45
Total A.M. hours	277	32	26	37	32	23	39	22	25	16	25
12:01 a.m.–2 a.m.	70	9	5	8	10	8	10	5	6	3	6
2:01 a.m.–4 a.m.	61	7	5	9	7	2	8	9	5	5	4
4:01 a.m.–6 a.m.	38	9	4	3	5	4	4	3	4	1	1
6:01 a.m.–8 a.m.	36	0	5	2	3	3	5	3	5	3	7
8:01 a.m.–10 a.m.	33	4	2	8	3	2	4	1	4	2	3
10:01 a.m.–noon..	39	3	5	7	4	4	8	1	1	2	4
Total P.M. hours	316	34	40	46	36	25	32	31	23	30	19
12:01 p.m.–2 p.m..	55	6	9	10	6	4	4	6	3	3	4
2:01 p.m.–4 p.m..	46	4	3	7	5	3	5	6	5	4	4
4:01 p.m.–6 p.m..	47	5	10	6	4	3	3	7	2	4	3
6:01 p.m.–8 p.m..	37	9	3	3	3	3	5	4	2	3	2
8:01 p.m.–10 p.m..	64	5	6	12	7	8	6	3	5	10	2
10:01 p.m.–midnight..	67	5	9	8	11	4	9	5	6	6	4
Not reported..	6	1	0	0	0	0	1	0	0	3	1

Table 28. Law Enforcement Officers Accidentally Killed, by Day and Time of Incident, 2005–2014

(Number.)

Time of day	Total	Sunday	Monday	Tuesday	Wednesday	Thursday	Friday	Saturday
Number of Victim Officers.......................	45	9	5	9	4	5	8	5
Total A.M. hours	25	5	2	3	3	5	6	1
12:01 a.m.–2 a.m.	6	0	0	2	0	2	2	0
2:01 a.m.–4 a.m.	4	2	0	1	1	0	0	0
4:01 a.m.–6 a.m.	1	1	0	0	0	0	0	0
6:01 a.m.–8 a.m.	7	1	2	0	2	0	2	0
8:01 a.m.–10 a.m.	3	0	0	0	0	1	1	1
10:01 a.m.–noon....................................	4	1	0	0	0	2	1	0
Total P.M. hours	19	4	2	6	1	0	2	4
12:01 p.m.–2 p.m.	4	1	0	2	0	0	1	0
2:01 p.m.–4 p.m.	4	1	1	1	0	0	0	1
4:01 p.m.–6 p.m.	3	0	1	1	0	0	0	1
6:01 p.m.–8 p.m.	2	1	0	0	0	0	0	1
8:01 p.m.–10 p.m.	2	0	0	0	1	0	0	1
10:01 p.m.–midnight.............................	4	1	0	2	0	0	1	0
Not reported..	1	0	1	0	0	0	0	0

Table 29. Law Enforcement Officers Accidentally Killed, by Day of Incident, 2005–2014

(Number.)

Day of the week	Total	2005	2006	2007	2008	2009	2010	2011	2012	2013	2014
Number of Victim Officers....................	599	67	66	83	68	48	72	53	48	49	45
Sunday	84	7	12	11	10	5	11	7	6	6	9
Monday...	66	3	4	6	12	8	8	7	7	6	5
Tuesday	80	6	12	11	8	5	7	10	5	7	9
Wednesday...	78	18	7	17	7	7	8	2	2	6	4
Thursday...	86	7	11	11	11	9	10	10	8	4	5
Friday..	113	13	14	16	11	7	17	7	8	12	8
Saturday	92	13	6	11	9	7	11	10	12	8	5

Table 30. Law Enforcement Officers Accidentally Killed, by Month of Incident, 2005–2014

(Number.)

Month	Total	2005	2006	2007	2008	2009	2010	2011	2012	2013	2014
Number of Victim Officers.........................	599	67	66	83	68	48	72	53	48	49	45
January..	49	2	6	2	7	9	8	4	4	1	6
February	41	3	6	6	6	4	9	4	1	0	2
March..	43	6	5	6	3	2	3	8	3	5	2
April..	47	2	6	14	0	5	6	1	3	5	5
May...	60	4	4	9	6	6	4	8	4	9	6
June...	50	5	3	8	4	3	15	5	4	2	1
July..	45	8	4	4	3	3	3	5	8	6	1
August...	44	5	8	6	8	4	4	3	2	3	1
September...	53	10	5	3	9	2	6	4	6	3	5
October	71	10	7	14	9	4	10	2	4	5	6
November..	47	5	8	7	9	2	1	3	5	3	4
December..	49	7	4	4	4	4	3	6	4	7	6

Table 31. Law Enforcement Officers Accidentally Killed, by Age Group of Victim Officer, 2005–2014

(Number.)

Age group	Total	2005	2006	2007	2008	2009	2010	2011	2012	2013	2014
Number of Victim Officers	599	67	66	83	68	48	72	53	48	49	45
Under 25	36	4	1	10	2	7	2	2	2	2	4
25–30	120	14	21	11	17	13	15	10	6	6	7
31–35	114	20	15	20	11	8	15	3	9	4	9
36–40	107	13	10	15	14	7	13	11	6	10	8
41–45	77	5	9	9	10	4	5	8	13	9	5
46–50	62	4	2	10	6	7	8	9	8	5	3
51–55	41	2	4	2	4	2	6	5	3	8	5
56–60	26	4	2	5	3	0	5	2	1	2	2
Over 60	12	1	2	1	1	0	2	3	0	0	2
Not reported	4	0	0	0	0	0	1	0	0	3	0
Average age (years)	38	37	36	37	38	35	39	41	40	41	39

Table 32. Law Enforcement Officers Accidentally Killed, by Years of Service of Victim Officer, 2005–2014

(Number.)

Years of service	Total	2005	2006	2007	2008	2009	2010	2011	2012	2013	2014
Number of Victim Officers	599	67	66	83	68	48	72	53	48	49	45
Less than 1	30	3	3	4	3	2	4	2	2	2	5
1–5	191	26	24	32	19	20	24	13	9	9	15
6–10	158	15	20	24	18	12	18	13	14	12	12
11–15	66	6	5	7	9	4	8	7	9	8	3
16–20	70	8	9	8	9	4	8	6	8	7	3
21–25	30	5	1	4	3	2	2	5	3	5	0
26–30	28	1	1	1	3	4	4	3	3	3	5
More than 30	23	3	3	2	3	0	4	4	0	2	2
Not reported	3	0	0	1	1	0	0	0	0	1	0
Average years of service	11	10	10	9	11	9	11	13	12	13	10

Table 33. Law Enforcement Officers Accidentally Killed, by Profile of Victim Officer, Averages, 1995–2014

(Number.)

Characteristic	2014	5-year averages		10-year averages	
		2005–2009	2010–2014	1995–2004	2005–2014
Age	39	37	40	37	38
Years of service	10	10	12	10	11
Height	5'11"	5'11"	5'11"	5'11"	5'11"
Weight[1]	204	200	210	195	204

Table 34. Law Enforcement Officers Accidentally Killed, by Race and Sex of Victim Officer, 2005–2014

(Number.)

Characteristic	Total	2005	2006	2007	2008	2009	2010	2011	2012	2013	2014
Number of Victim Officers...	599	67	66	83	68	48	72	53	48	49	45
Race											
White..	516	59	59	70	59	44	60	45	36	41	43
Black...	61	7	4	8	7	4	8	7	10	6	0
Asian/Pacific Islander	12	1	3	1	1	0	1	1	2	0	2
American Indian/Alaska Native	2	0	0	0	0	0	2	0	0	0	0
Not reported	8	0	0	4	1	0	1	0	0	2	0
Sex											
Male	570	64	64	79	61	48	67	50	46	49	42
Female	29	3	2	4	7	0	5	3	2	0	3

Table 35. Law Enforcement Officers Accidentally Killed, by Circumstance at Scene of Incident, 2005–2014

(Number.)

Circumstance	Total	2005	2006	2007	2008	2009	2010	2011	2012	2013	2014
Number of Victim Officers...	599	67	66	83	68	48	72	53	48	49	45
Automobile accident..	348	39	38	49	39	34	45	30	23	23	28
Motorcycle accident...	54	4	8	6	6	3	7	4	6	4	6
Aircraft accident	18	2	3	3	2	1	2	1	3	1	0
Struck by vehicle..	97	11	13	12	13	7	11	5	10	9	6
Traffic stop, roadblock, etc.	31	5	4	7	1	3	4	3	2	1	1
Directing traffic, assisting motorist, etc.	66	6	9	5	12	4	7	2	8	8	5
Accidental shooting	29	4	4	4	2	2	3	4	2	2	2
Crossfire, mistaken for subject, firearm mishap............................	22	2	3	4	2	2	1	3	2	2	1
Training session	3	1	0	0	0	0	1	0	0	0	1
Self-inflicted, cleaning mishap (not apparent or confirmed suicide).................	4	1	1	0	0	0	1	1	0	0	0
Drowning	11	2	0	2	1	0	0	3	0	2	1
Fall...	14	3	0	1	0	0	1	2	3	4	0
Other accidental	28	2	0	6	5	1	3	4	1	4	2

Table 36. Law Enforcement Officers Accidentally Killed, by Circumstance at Scene of Incident, by Type of Assignment, 2014

(Number.)

Circumstance	Total	2-officer vehicle	1-officer vehicle		Foot patrol		Other[1]		Off duty
			Alone	Assisted	Alone	Assisted	Alone	Assisted	
Number of Victim Officers	45	5	27	5	0	1	0	6	1
	28	4	18	2	0	0	0	3	1
Automobile accident									
Wearing seatbelt	15	2	11	1	0	0	0	0	1
Not wearing seatbelt	10	2	5	1	0	0	0	2	0
Seatbelt usage not reported	3	0	2	0	0	0	0	1	0
Motorcycle accident	6	0	5	1	0	0	0	0	0
Aircraft accident	0	0	0	0	0	0	0	0	0
Struck by vehicle	6	0	3	2	0	1	0	0	0
Traffic stop, roadblock, etc.	1	0	0	1	0	0	0	0	0
Directing traffic, assisting motorist, etc.	5	0	3	1	0	1	0	0	0
Accidental shooting	2	0	0	0	0	0	0	2	0
Crossfire, mistaken for subject, firearm mishap	1	0	0	0	0	0	0	1	0
Training session	1	0	0	0	0	0	0	1	0
Self-inflicted, cleaning mishap (not apparent or confirmed suicide)	0	0	0	0	0	0	0	0	0
Drowning	1	0	1	0	0	0	0	0	0
Fall	0	0	0	0	0	0	0	0	0
Other accidental	2	1	0	0	0	0	0	1	0

[1] Includes detectives, officers on special assignments, undercover officers, and officers on other types of assignments not listed.

Table 37. Law Enforcement Officers Assaulted, by Region and Geographic Division, 2014

(Number; rate.)

Characteristic	Total[1]	Rate per 100 officers	Assaults with injury	Rate per 100 officers	Number of reporting agencies	Population covered	Number of officers employed
Number of Victim Officers	48,315	9.0	13,654	2.5	11,151	243,753,902	536,119
Northeast	5,831	4.6	2,061	1.6	2,596	46,342,595	126,496
New England	1,623	6.3	556	2.2	749	11,905,908	25,797
Middle Atlantic	4,208	4.2	1,505	1.5	1,847	34,436,687	100,699
Midwest	6,595	9.2	2,028	2.8	2,654	36,893,333	71,933
East North Central	2,739	7.7	912	2.6	1,085	18,973,909	35,548
West North Central	3,856	10.6	1,116	3.1	1,569	17,919,424	36,385
South	20,222	9.7	5,015	2.4	4,148	91,621,346	209,384
South Atlantic	12,693	10.4	2,674	2.2	1,799	50,948,722	122,108
East South Central	2,628	8.9	844	2.9	931	12,763,344	29,571
West Soiuth Central	4,901	8.5	1,497	2.6	1,418	27,909,280	57,705
West	15,667	12.2	4,550	3.5	1,753	68,896,628	128,306
Mountain	4,428	12.2	1,152	3.2	665	18,684,501	36,359
Pacific	11,239	12.2	3,398	3.7	1,088	50,212,127	91,947

[1] Regional and divisional totals do not include data for West Virginia which were not available for inclusion in this table.

Table 38. Law Enforcement Officers Assaulted, by Population Group, 2014

(Number; rate.)

Characteristic	Total	Rate per 100 officers	Assaults with injury	Rate per 100 officers	Number of reporting agencies	Population covered	Number of officers employed
Number of Victim Officers...............	48,315	9.0	13,654	2.5	11,151	243,753,902	536,119
Group I (cities 250,000 and over).....................	13,414	10.3	3,195	2.5	68	50,720,361	129,738
Group II (cities 100,000–249,999)...................	5,820	13.4	1,872	4.3	184	27,356,968	43,341
Group III (cities 50,000–99,999)....................	5,253	13.4	1,729	4.4	397	27,442,401	39,314
Group IV (cities 25,000–49,999)....................	3,628	10.0	1,076	3.0	653	22,428,079	36,327
Group V (cities 10,000–24,999)....................	3,347	8.4	984	2.5	1,395	22,228,944	40,074
Group VI (cities under 10,000)1	3,481	5.4	1,155	1.8	5,748	18,291,193	64,930
Metropolitan counties1.............................	11,443	8.0	3,083	2.2	1,102	56,086,868	143,060
Nonmetropolitan counties1	1,929	4.9	560	1.4	1,604	19,199,088	39,335

[1] Includes universities and colleges, state police agencies, and/or other agencies to which no population is attributed.

Table 39. Law Enforcement Officers Assaulted, by Time of Incident, Number of Assaults, and Percent Distribution, 2005–2014

(Number; percent.)

Characteristic	Total	Percent distribution	2005 Total	2005 Percent distribution	2006 Total	2006 Percent distribution	2007 Total	2007 Percent distribution	2008 Total	2008 Percent distribution
Total Number of Victim Officers	563,030	100.0	57,820	100.0	59,396	100.0	61,257	100.0	61,087	100.0
Total A.M. hours	227,093	40.3	23,070	39.9	23,964	40.3	24,488	40.0	24,637	40.3
12:01 a.m.–2 a.m..................................	85,524	15.2	8,325	14.4	8,823	14.9	9,318	15.2	9,585	15.7
2:01 a.m.–4 a.m....................................	52,874	9.4	5,438	9.4	5,505	9.3	5,862	9.6	5,879	9.6
4:01 a.m.–6 a.m....................................	20,084	3.6	2,048	3.5	2,169	3.7	2,157	3.5	2,114	3.5
6:01 a.m.–8 a.m....................................	14,262	2.5	1,549	2.7	1,548	2.6	1,476	2.4	1,480	2.4
8:01 a.m.–10 a.m..................................	23,665	4.2	2,518	4.4	2,621	4.4	2,489	4.1	2,376	3.9
10:01 a.m.–noon	30,684	5.4	3,192	5.5	3,298	5.6	3,186	5.2	3,203	5.2
Total P.M. hours	335,937	59.7	34,750	60.1	35,432	59.7	36,769	60.0	36,450	59.7
12:01 p.m.–2 p.m.	34,337	6.1	3,532	6.1	3,599	6.1	3,659	6.0	3,558	5.8
2:01 p.m.–4 p.m.	42,138	7.5	4,268	7.4	4,508	7.6	4,464	7.3	4,286	7.0
4:01 p.m.–6 p.m.	50,861	9.0	5,366	9.3	5,307	8.9	5,573	9.1	5,274	8.6
6:01 p.m.–8 p.m.	59,845	10.6	6,160	10.7	6,309	10.6	6,372	10.4	6,611	10.8
8:01 p.m.–10 p.m.	70,667	12.6	7,276	12.6	7,487	12.6	7,825	12.8	7,853	12.9
10:01 p.m.–midnight	78,089	13.9	8,148	14.1	8,222	13.8	8,876	14.5	8,868	14.5

Table 39. Law Enforcement Officers Assaulted, by Time of Incident, Number of Assaults, and Percent Distribution, 2005–2014—*Continued*

(Number; percent.)

Characteristic	2009 Total	2009 Percent distribution	2010 Total	2010 Percent distribution	2011 Total	2011 Percent distribution	2012 Total	2012 Percent distribution	2013 Total	2013 Percent distribution	2014 Total	2014 Percent distribution
Total Number of Victim Officers	58,364	100.0	56,491	100.0	55,631	100.0	53,867	100.0	50,802	100.0	48,315	100.0
Total A.M. hours	23,586	40.4	22,807	40.4	22,703	40.8	22,056	40.9	20,662	40.7	19,120	39.6
12:01 a.m.–2 a.m.	9,323	16.0	8,829	15.6	8,555	15.4	8,188	15.2	7,679	15.1	6,899	14.3
2:01 a.m.–4 a.m.	5,653	9.7	5,390	9.5	5,293	9.5	5,212	9.7	4,623	9.1	4,019	8.3
4:01 a.m.–6 a.m.	2,082	3.6	1,987	3.5	2,126	3.8	1,973	3.7	1,817	3.6	1,611	3.3
6:01 a.m.–8 a.m.	1,389	2.4	1,428	2.5	1,438	2.6	1,367	2.5	1,258	2.5	1,329	2.8
8:01 a.m.–10 a.m.	2,192	3.8	2,291	4.1	2,213	4.0	2,272	4.2	2,336	4.6	2,357	4.9
10:01 a.m.–noon	2,947	5.0	2,882	5.1	3,078	5.5	3,044	5.7	2,949	5.8	2,905	6.0
Total P.M. hours	34,778	59.6	33,684	59.6	32,928	59.2	31,811	59.1	30,140	59.3	29,195	60.4
12:01 p.m.–2 p.m.	3,414	5.8	3,307	5.9	3,297	5.9	3,395	6.3	3,303	6.5	3,273	6.8
2:01 p.m.–4 p.m.	4,232	7.3	4,361	7.7	4,145	7.5	4,083	7.6	3,828	7.5	3,963	8.2
4:01 p.m.–6 p.m.	5,315	9.1	5,045	8.9	4,826	8.7	4,839	9.0	4,654	9.2	4,662	9.6
6:01 p.m.–8 p.m.	6,269	10.7	6,088	10.8	6,032	10.8	5,603	10.4	5,434	10.7	4,967	10.3
8:01 p.m.–10 p.m.	7,337	12.6	7,195	12.7	6,808	12.2	6,684	12.4	6,177	12.2	6,025	12.5
10:01 p.m.–midnight	8,211	14.1	7,688	13.6	7,820	14.1	7,207	13.4	6,744	13.3	6,305	13.0

Note: Assault figures published in prior years' editions of Law Enforcement Officers Killed and Assaulted have been updated for inclusion in this table. Because of rounding, percentages may not add to 100.0.

Table 40. Law Enforcement Officers Assaulted, by Type of Weapon and Percent Injured, 2005–2014

(Number; percent.)

Characteristic	Total	Percent injured	Firearm		Knife or other cutting instrument		Other dangerous weapon		Personal weapons		Number of reporting agencies	Population covered	Number of officers employed
			Total	Percent injured	Total	Percent injured	Total	Percent injured	Total	Percent injured			
Total Number of Victim Officers	563,030	27.0	21,652	9.3	9,668	12.7	78,663	23.7	453,047	28.7			
2005..	57,820	27.4	2,157	8.7	1,059	11.5	8,379	24.6	46,225	29.1	10,119	222,873,755	489,393
2006..	59,396	26.7	2,290	9.5	1,055	12.7	8,611	23.6	47,440	28.4	10,596	227,360,586	504,147
2007..	61,257	25.9	2,216	8.7	1,028	10.5	8,692	22.2	49,321	27.6	10,973	234,734,286	523,944
2008..	61,087	26.0	2,292	8.3	958	13.0	8,466	22.8	49,371	27.7	10,835	238,730,830	541,906
2009..	58,364	26.0	2,007	8.1	886	12.4	7,966	23.5	47,505	27.4	11,691	245,925,716	560,387
2010..	56,491	26.5	1,925	11.1	918	12.1	7,413	23.8	46,235	27.8	11,826	248,726,641	557,884
2011..	55,631	26.6	2,240	9.0	1,003	15.0	7,856	22.4	44,532	28.5	12,031	254,534,862	539,282
2012..	53,867	27.7	2,276	9.9	909	13.1	7,435	24.2	43,247	29.6	11,794	250,150,500	525,217
2013..	50,802	29.1	2,299	10.7	901	14.0	7,042	27.0	40,560	30.8	11,958	256,689,224	551,893
2014..	48,315	28.3	1,950	9.4	951	13.2	6,803	23.4	38,611	30.4	11,151	243,753,902	536,119

Note: Assault figures published in prior years' editions of Law Enforcement Officers Killed and Assaulted have been updated for inclusion in this table.

Table 41. Law Enforcement Officers Assaulted, by Region, Geographic Division, and State, by Type of Weapon, 2014

(Number.)

Characteristic	Total	Firearm	Knife or other cutting instrument	Other dangerous weapon	Personal weapons	Number of reporting agencies	Population covered	Number of officers employed
Total Number of Victim Officers	48,315	1,950	951	6,803	38,611	11,151	243,753,902	536,119
Northeast...	5,831	118	68	492	5,153	2,596	46,342,595	126,496
New England..	1,623	14	8	161	1,440	749	11,905,908	25,797
Connecticut..	682	2	3	66	611	102	3,596,677	8,584
Maine..	156	3	0	9	144	131	1,329,570	1,962
Massachusetts.......................................	141	1	0	17	123	235	4,150,245	9,357
New Hampshire.....................................	249	3	2	31	213	146	1,153,071	2,207
Rhode Island..	324	3	3	31	287	48	1,055,173	2,493
Vermont..	71	2	0	7	62	87	621,172	1,194
Middle Atlantic..	4,208	104	60	331	3,713	1,847	34,436,687	100,699
New Jersey...	1,569	19	15	128	1,407	516	8,373,056	25,435
New York...	717	8	12	48	649	380	16,751,520	55,382
Pennsylvania..	1,922	77	33	155	1,657	951	9,312,111	19,882
Midwest...	6,595	322	123	908	5,242	2,654	36,893,333	71,933
East North Central....................................	2,739	129	47	329	2,234	1,085	18,973,909	35,548
Illinois[1]	87	3	0	10	74	1	149,586	280
Indiana...	876	25	9	54	788	81	2,870,608	4,587
Michigan...	988	81	29	169	709	591	9,714,636	16,745
Ohio..	166	0	1	10	155	43	913,189	1,875
Wisconsin..	622	20	8	86	508	369	5,325,890	12,061
West North Central...................................	3,856	193	76	579	3,008	1,569	17,919,424	36,385
Iowa..	577	15	14	104	444	218	2,942,244	4,421
Kansas..	230	14	4	34	178	64	485,067	2,273
Minnesota...	381	19	5	89	268	328	5,456,172	8,854
Missouri..	2,223	137	42	289	1,755	535	5,822,620	14,411
Nebraska...	98	0	1	19	78	202	1,702,176	3,336
North Dakota..	155	0	0	7	148	108	738,176	1,541
South Dakota..	192	8	10	37	137	114	772,969	1,549
South..	20,222	870	383	3,024	15,945	4,148	91,621,346	209,384
South Atlantic...	12,693	419	203	1,626	10,445	1,799	50,948,722	122,108
Delaware...	376	24	2	83	267	55	934,360	2,180
District of Columbia[2]................................	741	9	17	132	583	1	658,893	3,935
Florida..	5,232	165	74	775	4,218	296	15,805,943	35,842
Georgia...	1,035	47	41	111	836	390	8,064,133	20,591
Maryland...	1,875	21	24	181	1,649	139	4,251,772	12,551
North Carolina......................................	1,870	72	24	144	1,630	353	9,063,195	21,307
South Carolina......................................	325	30	7	60	228	287	3,847,745	8,830
Virginia...	1,239	51	14	140	1,034	278	8,322,681	16,872
West Virginia[3]								
East South Central....................................	2,628	248	82	540	1,758	931	12,763,344	29,571
Alabama..	38	1	0	6	31	123	1,800,559	4,295
Kentucky...	851	59	6	164	622	310	3,678,379	6,613
Mississippi...	125	8	0	17	100	46	769,700	1,951
Tennessee..	1,614	180	76	353	1,005	452	6,514,706	16,712
West South Central...................................	4,901	203	98	858	3,742	1,418	27,909,280	57,705
Arkansas...	158	6	7	30	115	267	2,660,276	5,344
Louisiana...	1,126	19	3	419	685	75	2,055,185	6,706
Oklahoma..	716	39	17	123	537	313	3,712,410	6,489
Texas..	2,901	139	71	286	2,405	763	19,481,409	39,166
West..	15,667	640	377	2,379	12,271	1,753	68,896,628	128,306
Mountain..	4,428	252	153	667	3,356	665	18,684,501	36,359
Arizona...	1,660	104	47	202	1,307	74	5,149,240	9,461
Colorado...	985	64	32	183	706	212	5,132,949	11,334
Idaho...	275	12	9	40	214	108	1,632,930	2,690
Montana..	290	3	6	36	245	62	696,297	1,085
Nevada...	365	33	20	76	236	35	2,834,483	5,391
New Mexico..	595	32	37	112	414	58	1,399,507	3,149
Utah..	216	3	2	17	194	63	1,306,340	1,966
Wyoming...	42	1	0	1	40	53	532,755	1,283
Pacific..	11,239	388	224	1,712	8,915	1,088	50,212,127	91,947
Alaska..	477	19	14	53	391	32	732,371	1,251
California...	9,000	326	168	1,396	7,110	682	38,795,537	76,309
Hawaii[4]..	44	0	0	9	35	1	162,229	358
Oregon...	578	9	10	60	499	143	3,490,222	5,058
Washington..	1,140	34	32	194	880	230	7,031,768	8,971

[1] Data represents the number of assaults on officers reported by the Rockford Police Department.
[2] Data represents the number of assaults on officers reported by the Metropolitan Police Department.
[3] Data for West Virginia were not available for inclusion in this table.
[4] Data represents the number of assaults on officers reported by the Maui Police Department.

Table 42. Law Enforcement Officers Assaulted, by Circumstance at Scene of Incident, by Type of Weapon and Percent Distribution, 2014

(Number; percent.)

Circumstance	Total	Percent distribution	Firearm		Knife or other cutting instrument		Other dangerous weapon		Personal weapons	
			Total	Percent distribution	Total	Percent distribution	Total	Percent distribution	Total	Percent distribution
Total Number of Victim Officers	48,315	100.0	1,950	4.0	951	2.0	6,803	14.1	38,611	79.9
Disturbance call	14,901	100.0	574	3.9	404	2.7	1,444	9.7	12,479	83.7
Burglary in progress/pursuing burglary suspect......	697	100.0	40	5.7	22	3.2	117	16.8	518	74.3
Robbery in progress/pursuing robbery suspect.......	419	100.0	78	18.6	30	7.2	73	17.4	238	56.8
Attempting other arrest	7,343	100.0	228	3.1	106	1.4	773	10.5	6,236	84.9
Civil disorder (mass disobedience, riot, etc.)	713	100.0	25	3.5	9	1.3	190	26.6	489	68.6
Handling, transporting, custody of prisoner...........	6,303	100.0	20	0.3	31	0.5	673	10.7	5,579	88.5
Investigating suspicious person/circumstance	4,486	100.0	270	6.0	92	2.1	627	14.0	3,497	78.0
Ambush situation...	167	100.0	44	26.3	4	2.4	21	12.6	98	58.7
Handling person with mental illness.....................	1,499	100.0	92	6.1	85	5.7	172	11.5	1,150	76.7
Traffic pursuit/stop..	4,022	100.0	270	6.7	34	0.8	1,333	33.1	2,385	59.3
All other	7,765	100.0	309	4.0	134	1.7	1,380	17.8	5,942	76.5

Note: Because of rounding, percentages may not add to 100.0.

Table 43. Federal Officers Killed and Assaulted, by Department and Agency, by Number of Victim Officers and Known Offenders, 2013 and 2014

(Number; percent.)

Department/agency	Victim officers		Known offenders	
	2013	2014	2013	2014
Total Number of Victim Officers/Known Offenders..	1,774	1,410	1,177	892
U.S. Capitol Police..	13	3	9	2
U.S. Department of Homeland Security..	590	535	70	111
U.S. Customs and Border Protection (CBP)...	555	500	48	80
CBP, Office of Air and Marine[1]	27	11		1
CBP, Office of Border Patrol[2]	468	373		
CBP, Office of Field Operations...	60	116	48	79
U.S. Immigration and Customs Enforcement[3]		8		5
U.S. Secret Service..	35	27	22	26
U.S. Department of the Interior...	875	607	842	594
Bureau of Indian Affairs...	806	550	776	544
Bureau of Land Management...	5	5	5	5
National Park Service..	59	47	57	43
U.S. Fish and Wildlife Service (FWS)...	5	5	4	2
FWS, National Wildlife Refuge System..	5	5	4	2
FWS, Office of Law Enforcement	0	0	0	0
U.S. Department of Justice..	293	257	253	178
Bureau of Alcohol, Tobacco, Firearms and Explosives	14	10	14	11
Federal Bureau of Investigation...	31	11	19	6
U.S. Drug Enforcement Administration	7	6	13	10
U.S. Marshals Service..	241	230	207	151
U.S. Department of the Treasury	0	1	0	2
Internal Revenue Service...	0	1	0	2
Treasury Inspector General for Tax Administration..	0	0	0	0
U.S. Postal Inspection Service	3	7	3	5

[1] For 2013, known offender data were not reported by the CBP, Office of Air and Marine.
[2] For 2013 and 2014, known offender data were not reported by the CBP, Office of Border Patrol.
[3] For 2013, data were not reported by the U.S. Immigration and Customs Enforcement.

Table 44. Federal Officers Killed and Assaulted, by Department and Agency, by Extent of Injury to Victim Officer, 2010–2014

(Number; percent.)

Department/agency	2010			2011			2012			2013			2014		
	Killed	Injured	Not injured	Killed	Injured	Not injured	Killed	Injured	Not injured	Killed	Injured	Not injured	Killed	Injured	Not injured
Total Number of Victim Officers/Known Offenders...............	1	351	1,534	3	254	1,432	1	206	1,096	4	292	1,478	0	170	867
U.S. Capitol Police...	0	1	9	0	8	13	0	1	3	0	6	7	0	0	3
U.S. Department of Homeland Security.........................	1	144	858	1	90	745	0	20	83	2	122	466	0	39	123
U.S. Customs and Border Protection (CBP).................	1	141	846	0	82	720	0	12	40	2	121	432	0	18	109
CBP, Office of Air and Marine.........................	0	0	27	0	0	25	0	0	9	0	0	27	0	0	11
CBP, Office of Border Patrol[1,2,3].....................	1	133	754	0	71	628				2	98	368			
CBP, Office of Field Operations......................	0	8	65	0	11	67	0	12	31	0	23	37	0	18	98
U.S. Immigration and Customs Enforcement[4,5]..........	0	2	1	1	4	0	0	6	6				0	7	1
U.S. Secret Service.......................................	0	1	11	0	4	25	0	2	37	0	1	34	0	14	13
U.S. Department of the Interior..............................	0	130	520	0	113	423	1	151	709	1	106	768	0	84	523
Bureau of Indian Affairs[6]................................	0	114	430	0	88	337	0	112	604	1	94	711	0	69	481
Bureau of Land Management...........................	0	0	4	0	0	7	0	0	5	0	0	5	0	1	4
National Park Service....................................	0	14	84	0	25	76	1	37	99	0	12	47	0	13	34
U.S. Fish and Wildlife Service (FWS)..................	0	2	2	0	0	3	0	2	1	0	0	5	0	1	4
FWS, National Wildlife Refuge System...........	0	2	0	0	0	3	0	1	1	0	0	5	0	1	4
FWS, Office of Law Enforcement	0	0	2	0	0	0	0	1	0	0	0	0	0	0	0
U.S. Department of Justice...................................	0	73	135	2	41	246	0	32	297	1	58	234	0	46	211
Bureau of Alcohol, Tobacco, Firearms and Explosives	0	3	21	0	2	22	0	0	20	0	2	12	0	5	5
Federal Bureau of Investigation.........................	0	7	7	0	7	22	0	2	22	0	11	20	0	3	8
U.S. Drug Enforcement Administration[7]...............	0	4	1	0	0	0	0	0	0	1	0	6	0	0	6
U.S. Marshals Service...................................	0	59	106	2	32	202	0	30	255	0	45	196	0	38	192
U.S. Department of the Treasury	0	1	8	0	0	0	0	2	0	0	0	0	0	0	1
Internal Revenue Service...............................	0	0	8	0	0	0	0	2	0	0	0	0	0	0	1
Treasury Inspector General for Tax Administration..................	0	1	0	0	0	0	0	0	0	0	0	0	0	0	0
U.S. Postal Inspection Service	0	2	4	0	2	5	0	0	4	0	0	3	0	1	6

[1] For 2012, extent of injury data for 555 victim officers were not reported by the CBP, Office of Border Patrol.
[2] For 2013, detailed incident data were not reported by the CBP, Office of Border Patrol, for the 2 killed victim officers; therefore, the deaths were not represented in the feloniously killed section of this publication.
[3] For 2014, extent of injury data for 373 victim officers were not reported by the CBP, Office of Border Patrol.
[4] For 2011, detailed incident data were not reported by the U.S. Immigration and Customs Enforcement for the killed victim officer; therefore, the death was not represented in the feloniously killed section of this publication.
[5] For 2013, data were not reported by the U.S. Immigration and Customs Enforcement.
[6] For 2013, detailed incident data were not reported by the Bureau of Indian Affairs for the killed victim officer; therefore, the death was not represented in the feloniously killed section of this publication.
[7] For 2013, detailed incident data were not reported by the U.S. Drug Enforcement Administration for the killed victim officer; therefore, the death was not represented in the feloniously killed section of this publication.

METHODOLOGY

When an officer is killed in the line of duty, the FBI gathers data about circumstances pertaining to the death. The data come from various sources:

- City, university and college, county, state, tribal, and federal law enforcement agencies participating in the Uniform Crime Reporting Program may report line-of-duty deaths that occur in their jurisdictions.

- FBI field offices report line-of-duty deaths of law enforcement officers that occur in the United States and its outlying areas.

- Several nonprofit organizations, such as the Concerns of Police Survivors and the National Law Enforcement Officers Memorial Fund, which provide various services to the families of fallen officers, also furnish information about line-of-duty deaths.

When the FBI receives notification of a line-of-duty death, the Law Enforcement Officers Killed and Assaulted (LEOKA) Program's staff works with FBI field offices to contact the fallen officer's employing agency and request additional details about the fatal incident. The LEOKA staff also obtains criminal history data from the FBI's Interstate Identification Index about individuals who are identified in connection with line-of-duty felonious deaths.

The data in *Law Enforcement Officers Killed and Assaulted* pertain to felonious deaths, accidental deaths, and assaults of duly sworn city, university and college, county, state, tribal, and federal law enforcement officers who, at the time of the incident, met the following criteria:

- They were working in an official capacity, whether on or off duty.

- They had full arrest powers.

- They ordinarily wore/carried a badge and a firearm.

- They were paid from governmental funds set aside specifically for payment of sworn law enforcement representatives.

Officers who died are included if their deaths are directly related to injuries received during the incidents.

The FBI publishes *Law Enforcement Officers Killed and Assaulted* each year to provide information about officers who were killed, feloniously or accidentally, and officers who were assaulted while performing their duties. The FBI collects these data through the Uniform Crime Reporting (UCR) Program.

Data Considerations

When reviewing the tables, charts, and summaries presented in this publication, readers should be aware of certain features of the Law Enforcement Officers Killed and Assaulted (LEOKA) data collection process that could affect their interpretation of the information.

- The data in the tables and charts reflect the number of victim officers, not the number of incidents or weapons used.

- The UCR Program considers any parts of the body that can be used as weapons (such as hands, fists, or feet) to be personal weapons and designates them as such in its data.

- Law enforcement agencies use a different methodology for collecting and reporting data about officers who were killed than the methodology used for those who were assaulted. As a result, information about officers killed and information about officers assaulted reside in two separate databases, and the data are not comparable.

- Because the information in the tables of this publication is updated each year, the FBI cautions readers against making comparisons between the data in this publication and those in prior editions.

History

Beginning in 1937, the FBI's UCR Program collected and published statistics on law enforcement officers killed in the line of duty in its annual publication, *Crime in the United States*. Statistics regarding assaults on officers were added in 1960. In June 1971, executives from the law enforcement conference, "Prevention of Police Killings," called for an increase in the FBI's involvement in preventing and investigating officers' deaths. In response to this directive, the UCR Program expanded its collection of data to include more details about the incidents in which law enforcement officers were killed and assaulted.

Using this comprehensive set of data, the FBI began in 1972 to produce two reports annually, the *Law Enforcement Officers Killed Summary* and the *Analysis of Assaults on Federal Officers*. These two reports were combined in 1982 to create the annual publication, *Law Enforcement Officers Killed and Assaulted*.

PART 8

Probation and Parole, 2014

HIGHLIGHTS

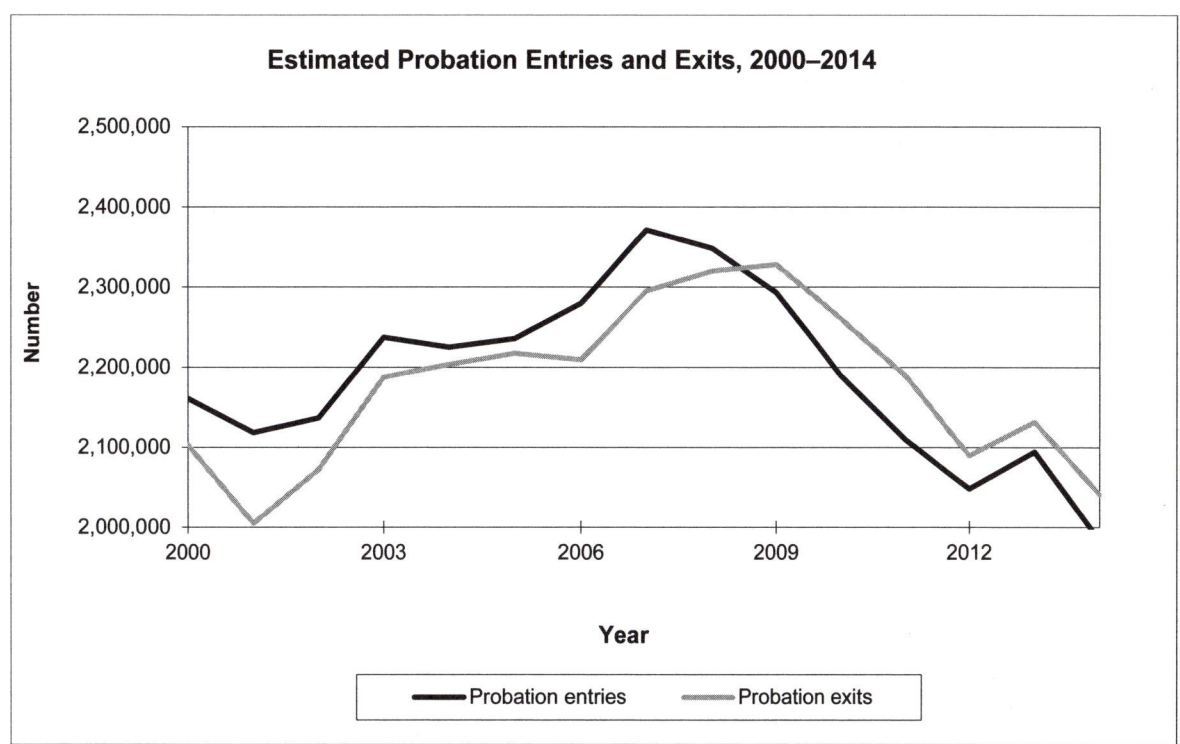

Estimated Probation Entries and Exits, 2000–2014

- At yearend 2014, an estimated 4,708,100 adults were under community supervision, down by about 45,300 offenders from yearend 2013.

- Approximately 1 in 52 adults in the United States was under community supervision at yearend 2014.

- Between yearend 2013 and 2014, the adult probation population declined by 1.2 percent, about 46,500 offenders, falling to an estimated 3,864,100 offenders at yearend 2014.

- The adult parole population increased by about 1,600 offenders between yearend 2013 and 2014 to an estimated 856,900 offenders at yearend 2014; this represented a 0.2 percent increase from yearend 2013.

- Parole entries and exits each declined 1.5 percent from yearend 2013 to yearend 2014.

- The reincarceration rate among parolees at risk of violating their conditions of supervision remained stable at about 9 percent from 2013 to 2014.

Table 1. U.S. Adult Residents on Community Supervision, Probation, and Parole, 2000–2014

(Number; percent.)

Year	Community supervision population	Probation	Parole
2000	4,564,900	3,839,400	725,500
2001	4,665,700	3,934,500	731,100
2002	4,748,100	3,995,000	753,100
2003	4,847,300	4,073,800	773,500
2004	4,916,300	4,140,400	775,900
2005	4,946,600	4,162,300	784,400
2006	5,035,000	4,236,800	798,200
2007	5,119,000	4,293,000	826,100
2008	5,094,400	4,270,100	828,200
2009	5,015,900	4,196,200	824,100
2010	4,886,000	4,053,600	840,700
2011	4,813,000	3,969,400	854,600
2012	4,785,900	3,940,800	857,800
2013	4,753,400	3,910,600	855,200
2014	4,708,100	3,864,100	856,900
Percent change, 2007–2011	-8.0	-10.0	3.7
Percent change, 2013–2014	-1.0	-1.2	0.2

Note: Counts rounded to the nearest 100. Detail may not sum to total due to rounding. Counts based on most recent data and may differ from previously published statistics. Reporting methods for some probation agencies changed over time.

Table 2. U.S. Adult Residents on Community Supervision, Probation, and Parole, 2000, 2005–2014

(Number; rate.)

Year	Number per 100,000 U.S. adult residents			U.S. adult residents on		
	Community supervision[1]	Probation	Parole	Community supervision[2]	Probation	Parole
2000	2,162	1,818	344	1 in 46	1 in 55	1 in 291
2005	2,215	1,864	351	1 in 45	1 in 54	1 in 285
2006	2,228	1,875	353	1 in 45	1 in 53	1 in 283
2007	2,239	1,878	361	1 in 45	1 in 53	1 in 277
2008 [3]	2,202	1,846	358	1 in 45	1 in 54	1 in 279
2009	2,146	1,795	353	1 in 47	1 in 56	1 in 284
2010	2,066	1,714	355	1 in 48	1 in 58	1 in 281
2011	2,014	1,661	358	1 in 50	1 in 60	1 in 280
2012	1,982	1,632	355	1 in 50	1 in 61	1 in 284
2013	1,947	1,602	350	1 in 51	1 in 62	1 in 286
2014	1,910	1,568	348	1 in 52	1 in 64	1 in 288

Note: Detail may not sum to total due to rounding. Rates based on most recent data and may differ from previously published statistics. Rates based on the community supervision, probation, and parole population counts as of December 31 of the reporting year and the estimated U.S. adult resident population on January 1 of each subsequent year.
[1] Includes adults on probation and adults on parole. For 2008 to 2014, detail may not sum to total because the community supervision rate was adjusted to exclude parolees who were also on probation.
[2] Includes adults on probation and parole.
[3] See Methodology for estimating change in population counts.

Table 3. Rate of Probation Exits, by Type of Exit, 2008–2014

(Rate per 100 probationers; months.)

Type of exit	2008	2009	2010	2011	2012	2013	2014
Total exit rate[1]	55	55	55	55	53	54	55
Completion	35	36	36	36	36	36	35
Incarceration[2]	9	9	9	9	8	8	8
Absconder	2	2	1	1	1	1	1
Discharged to custody, detainer, or warrant	--	--	--	--	--	--	1
Other unsatisfactory[3]	6	6	6	5	5	6	7
Transferred to another probation agency	--	--	--	--	--	--	--
Death	--	--	--	--	--	--	--
Other[4]	2	2	2	2	2	2	2
Estimated mean time served on probation (months)[5]	21.8	21.6	21.7	22.0	22.8	22.1	21.9

Note: Detail may not sum to total due to rounding. Rates based on most recent data and may differ from previously published statistics.
-- = Less than 0.5 per 100 probationers.
[1] The ratio of the number of probationers exiting supervision during the year to the average daily probation population (i.e., average of the January 1 and December 31 populations within the reporting year).
[2] Includes probationers who were incarcerated for a new offense and those who had their current probation sentence revoked (e.g., violating a condition of supervision).
[3] Includes probationers discharged from supervision who failed to meet all conditions of supervision, including some with only financial conditions remaining, some who had their probation sentence revoked but were not incarcerated because their sentence was immediately reinstated, and other types of unsatisfactory exits. Includes some early terminations and expirations of sentence.
[4] Includes, but not limited to, probationers who were discharged from supervision through a legislative mandate because they were deported or transferred to the jurisdiction of Immigration and Customs Enforcement; were transferred to another state through an interstate compact agreement; had their sentence dismissed or overturned by the court through an appeal; had their sentence administratively closed, deferred, or terminated by the court; were awaiting a hearing; and were released on bond.
[5] Calculated as the inverse of the exit rate times 12 months.

Table 4. Rate of Parole Exits, by Type of Exit, 2008–2014

(Rate per 100 parolees; months.)

Type of exit	2008	2009	2010	2011	2012	2013[1]	2014[1]
Total exit rate[2]	69	70	67	63	58	54	53
Completion	34	35	35	33	33	33	33
Returned to incarceration	24	24	22	20	15	14	14
With new sentence	6	6	6	5	5	4	4
With revocation	17	17	16	13	8	9	8
Other/unknown	1	1	1	2	1	2	1
Absconder	7	6	6	6	6	4	3
Other unsatisfactory[3]	1	1	1	1	1	1	1
Transferred to another state	1	1	1	1	1	0	0
Death	1	1	1	1	1	1	1
Other[4]	1	2	1	2	1	1	1
Estimated mean time served on parole (months)[5]	17.4	17.1	17.9	19.1	20.7	22.1	22.7

Note: Rate per 100 parolees. Detail may not sum to total due to rounding. Rates based on most recent data and may differ from previously published statistics. Except as noted, rates based on parolees with known type of exit.
[1] Type of exit includes imputed data for California, based on information provided for 2012.
[2] The ratio of the number of parolees exiting supervision during the year to the average daily parole population (i.e., average of the January 1 and December 31 populations within the reporting year).
[3] Includes parolees discharged from supervision who failed to meet all conditions of supervision, including some who had their parole sentence revoked but were not incarcerated because their sentence was immediately reinstated, and other types of unsatisfactory exits. Includes some early terminations and expirations of sentence reported as unsatisfactory exits.
[4] Includes, but not limited to, parolees discharged from supervision because they were deported or transferred to the jurisdiction of Immigration and Customs Enforcement, had their sentence terminated by the court through an appeal, or were transferred to another state through an interstate compact agreement and discharged to probation supervision.
[5] Calculated as the inverse of the exit rate times 12 months.

Table 5. Parolees on Probation Excluded from the January 1 and December 31 Community Supervision Populations, 2008–2014

(Number.)

Year	January 1st[1]	December 31st
2008	3,562	3,905
2009	3,905	4,959
2010	8,259	8,259
2011	8,259	10,958
2012	10,958	12,672
2013	12,672	12,511
2014	12,511	12,919

Note: Counts based on most recent data and may differ from previously published statistics.
[1] For 2008–2009 and 2011–2014, data were based on the count as of December 31 of the prior reporting year. For 2010, the count as of December 31, 2010, was used as a proxy because additional states reported these data in 2010.

Table 6. Change in the Number of Adults on Probation, Based on Reporting Changes, 2000–2014

(Number.)

Year	December 31st probation population	Change[1]
2000	3,839,374	-13,323
2001	3,934,537	-2,982
2002	3,994,979	28,902
2003	4,073,792	18,856
2004	4,140,436	3,154
2005	4,162,286	4,262
2006	4,236,827	-21,675
2007	4,292,950	-59,275
2008	4,270,105	-33,666
2009	4,198,155	-73,122
2010	4,053,605	-2,399
2011	3,971,319	9,771
2012	3,940,820	4,975
2013	3,910,647	19,163
2014	3,864,114	NA

Note: Counts based on most recent data and may differ from previously published statistics.
NA = Not available.
[1] Calculated as the difference between the January 1 probation population in the year of the reporting change and the December 31 probation population in the year prior to the reporting change.

Table 7. Change in the Number of Adults on Parole, Based on Reporting Changes, 2000–2014

(Number.)

Year	December 31st probation population	Change[1]
2000	725,527	-1,629
2001	731,147	1,186
2002	753,141	-2,207
2003	773,498	23,614
2004	775,875	-4,023
2005	784,354	-3,738
2006	798,202	1,656
2007	826,097	-4,920
2008	828,169	1,391
2009	824,115	13,703
2010	840,676	-78
2011	854,581	-2,190
2012	857,796	-18,245
2013	855,232	-15,681
2014	856,872	NA

Note: Counts based on most recent data and may differ from previously published statistics.
NA = Not available.
[1] Calculated as the difference between the January 1 parole population in the year of the reporting change and the December 31 parole population in the year prior to the reporting change.

Table 8. Adults Under Community Supervision, 2014

(Number; percent.)

Jurisdiction	Community supervision population, 1/1/14[1]	Entries		Exits		Community supervision population, 12/31/14[1]	Change, 2014		Number under community supervision per 100,000 adult residents, 12/31/14[3]
		Reported	Imputed[2]	Reported	Imputed[2]		Number	Percent	
U.S. Total....................................	4,766,700	2,408,500	2,527,300	2,452,900	2,582,600	4,708,100	-58,600	-1.2	1,910
Federal[4]	128,500	54,200	54,200	55,200	55,200	128,400	-100	-0.1	52
State..	4,638,200	2,354,300	2,473,100	2,397,700	2,527,400	4,579,700	-58,500	-1.3	1,858
Alabama[4,5]	58,600	23,500	24,600	20,400	21,400	61,400	2,900	4.9	1,637
Alaska...............................	9,500	6,400	6,400	6,600	6,600	9,300	-200	-1.9	1,689
Arizona[4]	78,500	38,300	38,300	36,000	36,000	80,700	2,300	2.9	1,568
Arkansas.........................	49,900	19,100	19,100	19,600	19,600	49,300	-600	-1.2	2,174
California[5]....................	383,600	190,300	219,000	186,900	220,500	382,600	-1,000	-0.3	1,283
Colorado[4,5]....................	89,700	61,700	62,200	62,100	62,800	89,100	-600	-0.7	2,150
Connecticut	47,700	24,700	24,700	24,600	24,600	45,600	-2,000	-4.3	1,613
Delaware...........................	16,700	12,700	12,700	13,100	13,100	16,300	-400	-2.1	2,223
District of Columbia	12,200	6,000	6,000	6,900	6,900	11,400	-900	-7.1	2,075
Florida[4,5]...........................	237,700	161,300	166,500	168,600	174,100	231,600	-6,100	-2.6	1,450
Georgia[4,6].......................	539,500	295,700	295,700	341,600	341,600	491,800	-47,700	-8.8	6,433
Hawaii...............................	23,200	5,500	5,500	6,200	6,200	22,500	-800	-3.2	2,015
Idaho	36,900	15,500	15,500	14,800	14,800	37,700	800	2	3,109
Illinois..............................	153,400	83,700	83,700	85,400	85,400	151,800	-1,600	-1.1	1,532
Indiana.............................	133,600	86,600	86,600	92,100	92,100	128,100	-5,500	-4.2	2,545
Iowa..................................	34,700	19,900	19,900	19,100	19,100	35,500	800	2.2	1,485
Kansas..............................	20,500	24,700	24,700	24,800	24,800	20,400	-100	-0.6	931
Kentucky...........................	67,300	35,900	35,900	32,500	32,500	70,800	3,500	5.3	2,077
Louisiana..........................	69,300	30,400	30,400	29,200	29,200	70,600	1,300	1.8	1,990
Maine	6,700	3,200	3,200	3,300	3,300	6,600	-100	-2.1	614
Maryland[4]	93,800	45,600	45,600	48,300	48,300	91,100	-2,700	-2.9	1,962
Massachusetts...........................	69,900	80,300	80,300	79,900	79,900	70,200	300	0.5	1,305
Michigan[4,5]........................	198,000	108,600	120,700	106,600	118,100	199,000	1,000	0.5	2,582
Minnesota........................	104,300	54,200	54,200	54,200	54,200	104,300	0	--	2,488
Mississippi.......................	38,600	16,500	16,500	10,100	10,100	44,300	5,700	14.8	1,953
Missouri	70,600	39,200	39,200	44,000	44,000	65,800	-4,800	-6.8	1,404
Montana[4,5]........................	9,400	4,800	4,900	4,400	4,500	9,700	300	3.5	1,211
Nebraska..........................	14,800	10,600	10,600	11,500	11,500	14,000	-800	-5.2	986
Nevada.............................	17,600	9,400	9,400	9,100	9,100	18,000	300	1.9	818
New Hampshire........................	6,300	4,200	4,200	4,200	4,200	6,300	0	0.7	592
New Jersey.......................	127,500	47,500	47,500	44,200	44,200	130,800	3,300	2.6	1,881
New Mexico[5]....................	18,800	7,800	9,900	7,800	10,400	18,100	-700	-3.9	1,141
New York	152,800	49,000	49,000	52,700	52,700	149,100	-3,600	-2.4	958
North Carolina	100,600	65,100	65,100	64,700	64,700	99,300	-1,300	-1.3	1,290
North Dakota	5,500	5,100	5,100	4,400	4,400	6,200	700	12.3	1,068
Ohio[4,5]..............................	260,000	127,500	147,500	129,600	152,700	256,200	-3,800	-1.5	2,853
Oklahoma	29,800	12,400	12,400	11,000	11,000	31,100	1,400	4.6	1,059
Oregon	60,000	24,000	24,000	22,200	22,200	61,900	1,800	3.1	1,977
Pennsylvania...........................	275,800	165,500	165,500	159,900	159,900	281,400	5,600	2	2,783
Rhode Island[5]	23,400	300	4,700	200	4,100	24,100	600	2.7	2,848
South Carolina	40,300	16,000	16,000	16,500	16,500	40,000	-400	-1	1,060
South Dakota.......................	8,800	5,300	5,300	4,700	4,700	9,400	600	6.5	1,458
Tennessee.........................	79,500	28,700	28,700	31,600	31,600	76,400	-3,000	-3.8	1,505
Texas.................................	507,000	186,500	186,500	196,900	196,900	496,900	-10,100	-2	2,481
Utah..................................	14,500	8,100	8,100	7,200	7,200	15,300	800	5.8	744
Vermont............................	6,900	3,900	3,900	4,000	4,000	6,800	-100	-1.7	1,339
Virginia	55,800	28,900	28,900	29,200	29,200	56,700	900	1.6	875
Washington[4,5]...........................	98,700	49,400	63,600	39,400	57,600	104,000	5,300	5.4	1,893
West Virginia[4]	9,700	2,000	2,900	2,700	2,700	9,900	200	2	675
Wisconsin[4,5]...........................	64,500	**	29,400	**	29,300	64,500	0	--	1,444
Wyoming	5,700	3,100	3,100	3,000	3,000	5,900	200	3	1,325

Note: All calculations are based on unrounded numbers. Counts were rounded to the nearest 100. Detail may not sum to total due to rounding. Counts based on most recent data and may differ from previously published statistics. See Methodology. Due to nonresponse or incomplete data, the community supervision population for some jurisdictions on December 31, 2014, does not equal the population on January 1, 2014, plus entries, minus exits.
-- = Less than 0.05%.
** = Not known.
[1] The January 1 population excludes 12,511 offenders and the December 31 population excludes 12,919 offenders under community supervision who were on both probation and parole.
[2] Reflects reported data, excluding jurisdictions for which data were unavailable.
[3] Computed using the estimated U.S. adult resident population in each jurisdiction on January 1, 2015.
[4] See <http://www.bjs.gov/content/pub/pdf/ppus14.pdf> for more detail.
[5] Data for entries and exits were estimated for nonreporting agencies.
[6] Counts include private agency cases and may overstate the number of persons under supervision.

Table 9. Adults on Probation, 2014

(Number; percent.)

Jurisdiction	Probation population, 1/1/14[1]	Entries		Exits		Probation population, 12/31/14[1]	Change, 2014		Number under Probation per 100,000 adult residents, 12/31/14[3]
		Reported	Imputed[2]	Reported	Imputed[2]		Number	Percent	
U.S. Total.....................................	3,929,810	1,983,385	2,067,100	2,041,230	2,130,700	3,864,114	-65,696	-1.7	1,568
Federal[4]	19,118	9,197	9,197	10,090	10,090	19,121	3	--	8
State..	3,910,692	1,974,188	2,057,900	2,031,140	2,120,600	3,844,993	-65,699	-1.7	1,560
Alabama[3,4]	50,698	20,998	22,100	18,147	19,200	53,640	2,942	5.8	1,429
Alaska.................................	7,167	5,342	5,342	5,432	5,432	7,077	-90	-1.3	1,287
Arizona[4]	70,827	26,493	26,493	24,088	24,088	73,232	2,405	3.4	1,422
Arkansas..................................	29,107	9,623	9,623	10,726	10,726	28,192	-915	-3.1	1,244
California	294,057	169,167	169,167	168,310	168,310	295,475	1,418	0.5	991
Colorado[3,4]	78,843	53,393	53,900	53,026	53,800	78,988	145	0.2	1,907
Connecticut	45,039	22,568	22,568	22,376	22,376	43,070	-1,969	-4.4	1,522
Delaware.................................	16,039	12,227	12,227	12,601	12,601	15,665	-374	-2.3	2,131
District of Columbia	7,042	4,666	4,666	5,224	5,224	6,484	-558	-7.9	1,185
Florida[3,4]	233,017	155,099	160,400	162,272	167,700	227,087	-5,930	-2.5	1,422
Georgia[4,5]	518,507	283,648	283,648	329,168	329,168	471,067	-47,440	-9.1	6,161
Hawaii.....................................	21,576	4,658	4,658	5,303	5,303	20,931	-645	-3	1,877
Idaho	33,062	13,212	13,212	12,848	12,848	33,450	388	1.2	2,761
Illinois.....................................	123,862	56,639	56,639	58,317	58,317	122,184	-1,678	-1.4	1,233
Indiana....................................	123,261	78,020	78,020	82,707	82,707	118,574	-4,687	-3.8	2,356
Iowa..	29,301	16,335	16,335	15,707	15,707	29,929	628	2.1	1,252
Kansas.....................................	16,446	21,050	21,050	21,168	21,168	16,328	-118	-0.7	746
Kentucky..................................	53,350	26,728	26,728	25,971	25,971	54,107	757	1.4	1,587
Louisiana.................................	41,761	13,658	13,658	14,440	14,440	40,979	-782	-1.9	1,155
Maine	6,710	3,195	3,195	3,335	3,335	6,570	-140	-2.1	612
Maryland[4]	81,304	40,585	40,585	42,350	42,350	79,539	-1,765	-2.2	1,713
Massachusetts...........................	67,784	77,736	77,736	77,246	77,246	68,274	490	0.7	1,269
Michigan[3,4]	179,567	98,486	110,600	96,451	108,000	180,583	1,016	0.6	2,343
Minnesota................................	98,267	48,033	48,033	48,639	48,639	97,661	-606	-0.6	2,330
Mississippi...............................	31,675	9,959	9,959	6,583	6,583	34,398	2,723	8.6	1,517
Missouri	51,197	25,376	25,376	29,270	29,270	47,303	-3,894	-7.6	1,009
Montana[3,4]	8,362	4,171	4,300	3,889	4,000	8,621	259	3.1	1,075
Nebraska..................................	13,545	9,108	9,108	9,812	9,812	12,940	-605	-4.5	911
Nevada....................................	12,102	5,201	5,201	5,276	5,276	12,027	-75	-0.6	548
New Hampshire.........................	3,994	2,736	2,736	2,820	2,820	3,910	-84	-2.1	368
New Jersey................................	112,598	41,600	41,600	38,300	38,300	115,898	3,300	2.9	1,667
New Mexico[3]	16,690	6,773	8,900	6,829	9,500	16,060	-630	-3.8	1,013
New York..................................	107,730	27,984	27,984	31,460	31,460	104,254	-3,476	-3.2	670
North Carolina	94,437	54,086	54,086	56,718	56,718	90,918	-3,519	-3.7	1,181
North Dakota	4,947	3,944	3,944	3,306	3,306	5,585	638	12.9	967
Ohio[3,4]	243,282	119,293	139,300	121,913	145,000	238,915	-4,367	-1.8	2,660
Oklahoma	27,208	11,605	11,605	10,245	10,245	28,568	1,360	5	972
Oregon	36,957	14,454	14,454	13,488	13,488	37,923	966	2.6	1,212
Pennsylvania.............................	171,970	100,272	100,272	95,505	95,505	176,737	4,767	2.8	1,748
Rhode Island[3]	22,988	**	4,500	**	3,900	23,595	607	2.6	2,793
South Carolina	35,300	13,652	13,652	13,856	13,856	35,096	-204	-0.6	931
South Dakota	6,262	3,674	3,674	3,133	3,133	6,803	541	8.6	1,054
Tennessee	65,751	24,133	24,133	26,802	26,802	62,950	-2,801	-4.3	1,239
Texas.......................................	398,607	150,244	150,244	160,750	160,750	388,101	-10,506	-2.6	1,938
Utah..	11,188	6,090	6,090	5,295	5,295	11,983	795	7.1	583
Vermont...................................	5,791	3,306	3,306	3,435	3,435	5,662	-129	-2.2	1,120
Virginia....................................	54,020	28,465	28,465	28,648	28,648	54,966	946	1.8	848
Washington[3,4]...........................	89,199	43,876	58,100	34,658	52,800	94,112	4,913	5.5	1,713
West Virginia[3,4].........................	7,174	**	900	882	882	7,174	/	:	488
Wisconsin[3,4]..............................	46,140	**	22,900	**	22,800	46,212	72	0.2	1,034
Wyoming..................................	4,984	2,627	2,627	2,415	2,415	5,196	212	4.3	1,165

Note: Counts based on most recent data and may differ from previously published statistics. Counts may not be actual as reporting agencies may provide estimates on some or all detailed data. Due to nonresponse or incomplete data, the probation population for some jurisdictions on December 31, 2014, does not equal the population on January 1, 2014, plus entries, minus exits. Reporting methods for some probation agencies changed over time and probation coverage was expanded in 1998 and 1999.
-- = Less than 0.05%.
** = Not known.
: = Not calculated.
/ = Not reported.
[1] Detail may not sum to total due to rounding. Reflects reported data, excluding jurisdictions for which data were unavailable.
[2] Computed using the estimated U.S. adult resident population in each jurisdiction on January 1, 2015.
[3] Data for entries and exits were estimated for nonreporting agencies.
[4] See <http://www.bjs.gov/content/pub/pdf/ppus14.pdf> for more detail.
[5] Includes private agency cases and may overstate the number of persons under supervision.

Table 10. Characteristics of Adults on Probation, 2000, 2013, and 2014

(Percent.)

Characteristic	2000	2013	2014
Total	100.0	100.0	100.0
Sex			
Male	78.0	75.0	75.0
Female	22.0	25.0	25.0
Race/Hispanic origin			
White[1]	54.0	54.0	54.0
Black/African American[1]	31.0	30.0	30.0
Hispanic/Latino	13.0	14.0	13.0
American Indian/Alaska Native[1]	1.0	1.0	1.0
Asian/Native Hawaiian/Other Pacific Islander[1]	1.0	1.0	1.0
Two or more races[1]	NA	--	--
Status of supervision			
Active	76.0	69.0	73.0
Residential/other treatment program	NA	1.0	1.0
Financial conditions remaining	NA	1.0	1.0
Inactive	9.0	6.0	5.0
Absconder	9.0	9.0	7.0
Supervised out of jurisdiction	3.0	2.0	2.0
Warrant status	NA	9.0	6.0
Other	3.0	3.0	4.0
Type of offense			
Felony	52.0	55.0	56.0
Misdemeanor	46.0	43.0	42.0
Other infractions	2.0	2.0	2.0
Most serious offense			
Violent	NA	19.0	19.0
Domestic violence	NA	4.0	4.0
Sex offense	NA	3.0	3.0
Other violent offense	NA	12.0	12.0
Property	NA	29.0	28.0
Drug	24.0	25.0	25.0
Public order	24.0	17.0	16.0
DWI/DUI	18.0	14.0	14.0
Other traffic offense	6.0	2.0	2.0
Other[2]	52.0	10.0	11.0

Note: Detail may not sum to total due to rounding. Counts based on most recent data and may differ from previously published statistics. See Methodology. Characteristics based on probationers with known type of status.
-- = Less than 0.5%.
NA = Not available.
[1] Excludes persons of Hispanic or Latino origin.
[2] Includes violent and property offenses in 2000 because those data were not collected separately.

Table 11. Adults on Parole, 2014

(Number; percent.)

Jurisdiction	Parole population, 1/1/14	Entries		Exits		Parole population, 12/31/14[1]	Change, 2014		Number on parole per 100,000 adult residents, 12/31/14[2]
		Reported	Imputed[1]	Reported	Imputed[1]		Number	Percent	
U.S. Total.................	849,359	425,134	460,200	411,694	451,900	856,872	7513	0.9	348
Federal[3]	109,356	45,000	45,000	45,118	45,118	109,265	-91	-0.1	44
State................	740,003	380,134	415,200	366,576	406,800	747,607	7604	1.0	303
Alabama[3]	7,884	2,475	2,475	2,262	2,262	8,097	213	2.7	216
Alaska................	2,303	1,072	1,072	1,165	1,165	2,210	-93	-4.0	402
Arizona................	7,636	11,779	11,779	11,913	11,913	7,502	-134	-1.8	146
Arkansas................	21,589	9,459	9,459	8,910	8,910	21,743	154	0.7	959
California[3,4,5]	89,527	21,157	49,800	18,546	52,200	87,104	-2423	-2.7	292
Colorado................	10,846	8,296	8,296	9,075	9,075	10,067	-779	-7.2	243
Connecticut	2,640	2,137	2,137	2,213	2,213	2,564	-76	-2.9	91
Delaware................	657	507	507	488	488	676	19	2.9	92
District of Columbia	5,601	1,336	1,336	1,657	1,657	5,280	-321	-5.7	965
Florida................	4,683	6,166	6,166	6,330	6,330	4,519	-164	-3.5	28
Georgia................	25,931	12,002	12,002	12,386	12,386	25,547	-384	-1.5	334
Hawaii................	1,647	827	827	934	934	1,540	-107	-6.5	138
Idaho	3,851	2,318	2,318	1,952	1,952	4,217	366	9.5	348
Illinois................	29,586	27,094	27,094	27,036	27,036	29,644	58	0.2	299
Indiana................	10,340	8,554	8,554	9,413	9,413	9,481	-859	-8.3	188
Iowa................	5,595	3,574	3,574	3,400	3,400	5,769	174	3.1	241
Kansas................	4,065	3,628	3,628	3,642	3,642	4,051	-14	-0.3	185
Kentucky[3]................	14,019	9,207	9,207	6,497	6,497	16,729	2710	19.3	491
Louisiana................	27,615	16,716	16,716	14,712	14,712	29,619	2004	7.3	835
Maine	22	0	0	1	1	21	-1	-4.5	2
Maryland[3]................	12,464	5,051	5,051	5,978	5,978	11,537	-927	-7.4	248
Massachusetts................	2,106	2,514	2,514	2,671	2,671	1,949	-157	-7.5	36
Michigan................	18,439	10,114	10,114	10,140	10,140	18,413	-26	-0.1	239
Minnesota................	5,997	6,193	6,193	5,548	5,548	6,642	645	10.8	158
Mississippi................	6,901	6,529	6,529	3,547	3,547	9,883	2982	43.2	436
Missouri	19,402	13,842	13,842	14,749	14,749	18,495	-907	-4.7	395
Montana................	1,020	601	601	527	527	1,094	74	7.3	136
Nebraska................	1,235	1,500	1,500	1,668	1,668	1,067	-168	-13.6	75
Nevada................	5,522	4,194	4,194	3,789	3,789	5,927	405	7.3	270
New Hampshire................	2,256	1,489	1,489	1,360	1,360	2,385	129	5.7	224
New Jersey................	14,918	5,871	5,871	5,900	5,900	14,889	-29	-0.2	214
New Mexico................	2,132	1,062	1,062	939	939	2,255	123	5.8	142
New York................	45,039	21,063	21,063	21,213	21,213	44,889	-150	-0.3	288
North Carolina	7,171	10,975	10,975	8,014	8,014	10,025	2854	39.8	130
North Dakota	548	1,114	1,114	1,078	1,078	584	36	6.6	101
Ohio................	16,797	8,210	8,210	7,686	7,686	17,321	524	3.1	193
Oklahoma	2,554	784	784	778	778	2,560	6	0.2	87
Oregon	23,088	9,559	9,559	8,683	8,683	23,964	876	3.8	766
Pennsylvania................	103,802	65,246	65,246	64,419	64,419	104,629	827	0.8	1,035
Rhode Island	435	254	254	221	221	468	33	7.6	55
South Carolina	5,477	2,361	2,361	2,613	2,613	5,225	-252	-4.6	139
South Dakota................	2,577	1,579	1,579	1,545	1,545	2,611	34	1.3	404
Tennessee................	13,732	4,539	4,539	4,773	4,773	13,498	-234	-1.7	266
Texas................	111,302	36,213	36,213	36,103	36,103	111,412	110	0.1	556
Utah................	3,265	1,964	1,964	1,917	1,917	3,312	47	1.4	161
Vermont................	1,098	558	558	549	549	1,107	9	0.8	219
Virginia................	1,800	446	446	515	515	1,732	-68	-3.8	27
Washington[3]................	9,500	5,515	5,515	4,789	4,789	9,880	380	4.0	180
West Virginia................	2,553	1,977	1,977	1,781	1,781	2,749	196	7.7	187
Wisconsin[3,4]................	20,083	**	6,500	**	6,500	20,010	-73	-0.4	448
Wyoming................	753	513	513	551	551	715	-38	-5.0	160

Note: Counts based on most recent data and may differ from previously published statistics. See Methodology. Counts may not be actual as reporting agencies may provide estimates on some or all detailed data. Due to nonresponse or incomplete data, the parole population for some jurisdictions on December 31, 2014, does not equal the population on January 1, 2014, plus entries, minus exits.
** = Not known.
[1] Detail may not sum to total due to rounding. Reflects reported data, excluding jurisdictions for which data were unavailable.
[2] Computed using the estimated U.S. adult resident population in each jurisdiction on January 1, 2015.
[3] See <http://www.bjs.gov/content/pub/pdf/ppus14.pdf> for more detail.
[4] Data for entries and exits were estimated for nonreporting agencies.
[5] Includes post-release community supervision and mandatory supervision parolees: 41,947 on January 1, 2014; and 21,157 entries, 18,546 exits, and 46,575 on December 31, 2014.

Table 12. Adults Entering Parole, by Type of Entry, 2014

(Number.)

Jurisdiction	Total reported	Discretionary[1]	Mandatory[2]	Reinstatement[3]	Term of supervised release[4]	Other[5]	Not reported
U.S. Total..	425,134	193,556	108,898	12,811	80,195	4,828	24,846
Federal..	45,000	177	163	0	44,660	0	0
State...	380,134	193,379	108,735	12,811	35,535	4,828	24,856
Alabama	2,475	**	**	**	**	**	2,475
Alaska	1,072	95	778	193	0	6	0
Arizona	11,779	34	11	142	10,664	928	0
Arkansas[6]..	9,459	8,175	1,284	0	0	0	0
California	21157	**	**	**	**	**	21,157
Colorado..	8,296	2,770	2,924	2,401	0	201	0
Connecticut	2,137	1,084	**	**	1,053	0	0
Delaware..	507	**	**	**	**	**	507
District of Columbia	1,336	188	0	0	1,148	0	0
Florida	6,166	36	5,544	0	580	6	0
Georgia[6]...	12,002	12,002	0	**	0	0	0
Hawaii..	827	746	69	12	NA	NA	0
Idaho[6]...	2,318	1,784	0	534	0	0	0
Illinois[6]..	27,094	7	25,510	322	**	859	396
Indiana	8,554	0	8,554	0	0	0	0
Iowa...	3,574	3,574	0	0	0	0	0
Kansas	3,628	0	1	112	3,477	37	1
Kentucky	9,207	6,115	3,092	0	0	0	0
Louisiana	16,716	848	15,669	177	13	9	0
Maine	0	0	0	0	0	0	0
Maryland..	5,051	2,535	2,516	**	**	NA	0
Massachusetts[6]................................	2,514	2,266	0	199	49	0	0
Michigan	10,114	8,860	621	633	NA	0	0
Minnesota	6,193	0	6,193	0	0	0	0
Mississippi	6,529	5,280	**	1,147	**	**	102
Missouri	13,842	10,759	782	1,171	0	1,130	0
Montana	601	601	0	0	0	0	0
Nebraska	1,500	1,463	0	37	0	0	0
Nevada...	4,194	2,820	1,228	146	NA	0	0
New Hampshire.................................	1,489	751	0	593	**	134	11
New Jersey	5,871	3,737	2,134	0	0	0	0
New Mexico	1,062	0	1,041	21	0	0	0
New York	21,063	5,451	6,818	0	7,975	819	0
North Carolina	10,975	35	396	0	10,544	NA	0
North Dakota	1,114	1,114	0	0	0	0	0
Ohio...	8,210	51	7,885	274	0	0	0
Oklahoma	784	784	**	**	**	**	0
Oregon	9,559	2,212	7,287	6	13	**	41
Pennsylvania[6]..................................	65,246	61,400	0	3,846	0	0	0
Rhode Island	254	254	NA	NA	NA	MA	0
South Carolina	2,361	861	1,500	0	0	0	0
South Dakota....................................	1,579	612	806	**	19	142	0
Tennessee	4,539	4,397	1	128	0	13	0
Texas...	36,213	34,646	502	475	**	434	156
Utah..	1,964	1,809	0	45	0	110	0
Vermont[6]	558	416	NA	142	NA	NA	0
Virginia	446	152	294	0	0	0	0
Washington......................................	5,515	220	5,295	**	**	**	0
West Virginia....................................	1,977	1,977	0	0	0	0	0
Wisconsin	**	**	**	**	**	**	**
Wyoming	513	458	0	55	0	0	0

Note: Detail may not sum to total due to rounding. Counts based on most recent data and may differ from previously published statistics.
NA = Not applicable.
** = Not known.
[1] Includes persons entering due to a parole board decision.
[2] Includes persons whose release from prison was not decided by a parole board, persons entering due to determinate sentencing, good-time provisions, or emergency releases.
[3] Includes persons returned to parole after serving time in a prison due to a parole violation. Depending on the reporting jurisdiction, reinstatement entries may include only parolees who were originally released from prison through a discretionary release, only those originally released through a mandatory release, or a combination of both types. May also include those originally released through a term of supervised release.
[4] Includes persons sentenced by a judge to a fixed period of incarceration based on a determinate statute immediately followed by a period of supervised release in the community.
[5] Includes parolees who were transferred from another state, reinstated to parole following a board hold, placed on supervised release from jail, released to a drug or alcohol transition program, or released from prison through a conditional medical release to parole. Also includes juvenile offenders with a determinant sentence that transferred from the juvenile justice system to adult parole upon reaching the maximum age of the juvenile systemís authority, offenders released to parole supervision on parole/discretionary mandatory supervision or mandatory supervision in the custody of a criminal justice agency other than a prison or jail, and others.
[6] Some or all detailed data were estimated for type of sentence.

Table 13. Characteristics of Adults on Parole, 2000, 2013, and 2014

(Percent.)

Characteristic	2000	2013	2014
Total	100.0	100.0	100.0
Sex			
Male	88.0	88.0	88.0
Female	12.0	12.0	12.0
Race/Hispanic origin			
White[1]	38.0	43.0	43.0
Black/African American[1]	40.0	38.0	39.0
Hispanic/Latino	21.0	17.0	16.0
American Indian/Alaska Native[1]	1.0	1.0	1.0
Asian/Native Hawaiian/Other Pacific Islander[1]	--	1.0	1.0
Two or more races[1]	NA	--	--
Status of supervision			
Active	83.0	84.0	84.0
Inactive	4.0	5.0	5.0
Absconder	7.0	6.0	6.0
Supervised out of state	5.0	4.0	4.0
Financial conditions remaining	NA	--	0.0
Other	1.0	1.0	2.0
Maximum sentence to incarceration			
Less than 1 year	3.0	5.0	6.0
1 year or more	97.0	95.0	94.0
Most serious offense			
Violent	NA	29.0	31.0
Sex offense	NA	10.0	7.0
Other violent offense	NA	20.0	24.0
Property	NA	22.0	22.0
Drug	NA	32.0	31.0
Weapon	NA	4.0	4.0
Other[2]	NA	13.0	12.0

Note: Detail may not sum to total due to rounding. Counts based on most recent data and may differ from previously published statistics. See Methodology. Characteristics based on parolees with known type of status.
-- = Less than 0.5%.
NA = Not available.
[1] Excludes persons of Hispanic or Latino origin, unless specified.
[2] Includes public order offenses.

Table 14. Adults Exiting Parole, by Type of Exit, 2014

(Number.)

Jurisdiction	Total reported	Completion	Returned to incarceration		To receive treatment	Other/ unknown	Absconder	Other unsatisfactory[1]	Death	Other[2]	Unknown or not reported
			With new sentence	With revocation							
U.S. Total..................................	411,694	242,344	31,867	64,472	2,638	9,197	7,919	6,901	5,558	9,198	31,600
Federal..	45,118	27,770	1,390	7,887	**	**	1,066	277	637	0	6,091
State..	366,576	214,574	30,477	56,585	2,638	9,197	6,853	6,624	4,921	9,198	25,509
Alabama	2,262	1,369	403	130	**	**	**	**	95	265	0
Alaska	1,165	450	59	656	**	X	X	X	X	0	0
Arizona	11,913	6,683	2	2,272	0	0	0	2,845	42	69	0
Arkansas[3].....................	8,910	3,466	908	4,358	0	0	0	0	178	0	0
California[3].....................	18,546	**	**	**	**	**	**	**	**	**	18,546
Colorado[3].....................	9,075	4,070	850	3,951	0	0	58	0	71	75	0
Connecticut	2,213	1,203	**	**	**	882	128	0	**	0	0
Delaware......................	488	290	11	32	**	**	**	47	6	102	0
District of Columbia	1,657	729	0	0	0	423	0	239	39	227	0
Florida..........................	6,330	4,097	387	814	**	**	**	**	60	682	290
Georgia[3]......................	12,386	9,364	344	747	**	1,324	221	0	96	290	0
Hawaii...........................	934	427	2	312	0	2	107	0	16	68	0
Idaho[3]..........................	1,952	724	0	722	0	479	0	0	23	4	0
Illinois[3]........................	27,036	15,516	1,785	7,050	**	**	879	**	121	1,030	655
Indiana.........................	9,413	4,774	618	1,684	0	0	1,644	0	97	596	0
Iowa.............................	3,400	1,911	551	801	0	2	0	108	27	0	0
Kansas	3,642	3,033	150	0	0	49	282	0	19	109	0
Kentucky......................	6,497	3,313	1,567	345	0	1,169	0	0	102	1	0
Louisiana......................	14,712	7,195	1,264	853	X	1,276	~	753	188	3,183	0
Maine	1	0	0	1	0	0	0	0	0	0	0
Maryland.......................	5,978	3,405	814	831	**	X	**	827	91	10	0
Massachusetts[3]..............	2,671	2,057	96	475	0	21	0	0	22	0	0
Michigan........................	10,140	7,019	1,268	1,684	X	X	X	X	169	X	0
Minnesota.....................	5,548	2,752	122	2,649	0	0	0	0	25	0	0
Mississippi....................	3,547	2,058	**	**	**	938	22	444	32	7	46
Missouri	14,749	5,926	1,083	3,739	747	1,673	1,388	**	172	0	21
Montana	527	297	5	212	0	0	0	0	13	0	0
Nebraska.......................	1,668	1,151	72	423	**	2	**	**	5	0	15
Nevada[3].......................	3,789	2,741	358	196	X	414	40	0	40	0	0
New Hampshire...............	1,360	557	**	803	X	X	**	X	**	**	0
New Jersey	5,900	4,284	118	1,339	0	0	0	0	102	57	0
New Mexico	939	603	**	**	**	**	85	166	37	48	0
New York	21,213	11,100	1,400	6,610	1,888	0	0	X	215	X	0
North Carolina	8,014	6,048	524	401	X	0	862	106	73	0	0
North Dakota	1,078	756	42	245	**	**	28	**	5	0	2
Ohio..............................	7,686	5,157	1,431	97	0	0	165	0	176	660	0
Oklahoma	778	677	26	39	**	**	**	**	36	**	0
Oregon	8,683	4,944	813	1,891	3	3	**	724	131	50	124
Pennsylvania[3]	64,419	43,575	6,119	5,608	0	0	806	188	767	1,549	5,807
Rhode Island	221	166	12	37	**	0	0	0	6	0	0
South Carolina	2,613	2,197	91	253	0	0	0	0	34	38	0
South Dakota	1,545	956	82	457	X	25	0	X	24	1	0
Tennessee.....................	4,773	2,696	1,090	834	0	0	0	0	153	0	0
Texas............................	36,103	27,577	5,479	1,299	X	500	X	0	1,248	0	0
Utah..............................	1,917	340	246	1,088	0	0	0	162	26	55	0
Vermont[3]......................	549	364	76	89	X	15	0	X	5	0	0
Virginia	515	222	150	86	**	**	12	**	22	22	1
Washington....................	4,789	4,711	**	**	**	**	**	**	78	**	0
West Virginia..................	1,781	1,267	25	333	0	0	125	0	31	0	0
Wisconsin	**	**	**	**	**	**	**	**	**	**	**
Wyoming	551	357	34	139	**	**	1	15	3	0	2

Note: Detail may not sum to total due to rounding. Counts based on most recent data and may differ from previously published statistics.
X = Not applicable.
** = Not known.
[1] Includes persons discharged because of release to special sentence, violations, deportations, incarceration, and revocations. Includes some early terminations and expirations of sentence.
[2] Includes 2,160 parolees who were transferred to another state and 7,038 parolees who exited for other reasons. Other reasons include, but are not limited to, parolees who had a pending revocation warrant; were discharged to probation, detainer, or another criminal justice status; were deported or transferred to the jurisdiction of Immigration and Customs Enforcement; were transferred to another state through an interstate compact agreement; were pardoned; or had their sentence terminated by the court through an appeal.
[3] Some or all data were estimated for type of exit.

METHODOLOGY

About the Data

The Bureau of Justice Statistics' (BJS) Annual Probation Survey and Annual Parole Survey began in 1980 and collects data from probation and parole agencies in the United States that supervise adults. In these data, adults are persons subject to the jurisdiction of an adult court or correctional agency. Juveniles prosecuted as adults in a criminal court are considered adults. Juveniles under the jurisdiction of a juvenile court or correctional agency are excluded from these data.

The National Criminal Justice Information and Statistics Service of the Law Enforcement Assistance Administration, BJS's predecessor agency, began a statistical series on parole in 1976 and on probation in 1979. The two surveys collect data on the total number of adults supervised in the community on January 1 and December 31 each year, the number of entries and exits to supervision during the reporting year, and characteristics of the population at yearend.

Both surveys cover all 50 states, the District of Columbia, and the federal system. BJS depends on the voluntary participation of state central reporters and separate state, county, and court agencies for these data. During 2013, Westat (Rockville, MD) served as BJS's collection agent for the 50 states and the District of Columbia. Data for the federal system were provided directly to BJS from the Office of Probation and Pretrial Services, Administrative Office of the United States Courts through the Federal Justice Statistics Program.

Probation

The 2014 Annual Probation Survey was sent to 467 respondents: 35 central state reporters; 426 separate state, county, or court agencies, including the state probation agency in Pennsylvania, which also provided data for 65 counties in Pennsylvania; the District of Columbia; and the federal system. States with multiple reporters were Alabama (3), Colorado (8), Florida (41), Georgia (2), Idaho (2), Kentucky (3), Michigan (131), Missouri (2), Montana (4), New Mexico (2), Ohio (186), Oklahoma (3), Pennsylvania (2), Tennessee (3), and Washington (32). Of the 461 agencies on the agency frame, 1 locality in Alabama, 1 in Colorado, 6 in Florida, 14 in Michigan, 1 in Montana, 17 in Ohio, and 5 in Washington did not provide data for the 2014 collection. For these localities, the agency's most recent December 31 population was used to estimate the populations on January 1 and December 31, 2014.

Parole

The 2014 Annual Parole Survey was sent to 53 respondents: 50 central state reporters, including the state parole agency in Pennsylvania, which also provided one separate summary record for the state's 65 counties; the District of Columbia; and the federal system. Data for the federal system were provided directly to the BJS Federal Justice Statistics Program, which obtained data from the Office of Probation and Pretrial Services, Administrative Office of the United States Courts. In this report, federal parole includes a term of supervised release from prison, mandatory release, parole, military parole, and special parole. A term of supervised release is ordered at the time of sentencing by a federal judge, and it is served after release from a federal prison sentence.

In each collection year, respondents are asked to provide both the January 1 and December 31 population counts. At times, the January 1 count may differ from the December 31 count of the prior year. The difference reported may have resulted from administrative changes, such as implementing new information systems, leading to data review and cleanup; reconciling probationer records; reclassifying offenders, including those on probation to parole and offenders on dual community supervision statuses; and including certain probation populations not previously reported (e.g., supervised for an offense of driving while intoxicated or under the influence, some probationers who had absconded, and some on an inactive status). The discrepancy between the yearend 2013 and the beginning year 2014 probation counts resulted in an increase of 19,163 probationers. The discrepancy between the yearend and beginning year parole population count resulted in a decrease of 15,681 parolees from December 31, 2013, to January 1, 2014.

The number of probation agencies included in the survey expanded in 1998 and continued to expand through 1999 to include misdemeanor probation agencies in a few states that fell within the scope of this survey. For a discussion of this expansion, see *Probation and Parole in the United States, 2010* (NCJ 236019, BJS web, November 2011).

Technically, the change in the probation and parole populations from the beginning of the year to the end of the year should equal the difference between entries and exits during the year. However, those numbers may not be equal. Some probation and parole information systems track the number of cases that enter and exit community supervision, not the number of offenders. This means that entries and exits may include case counts as opposed to counts of offenders, while the beginning and yearend population counts represent individuals. Additionally, all of the data on entries and exits may not have been logged into the information systems, or the information systems may not have fully processed all of the data before the data were submitted to BJS. At the national level, 7,851 probationers were the difference between the change in the probation population measured by the difference between January 1 and December 31, 2014, populations and the difference between probation entries and exits during 2014. For parole, 5,927 parolees were the difference between the change in the parole population measured by the difference between January 1 and December 31, 2014, populations and the difference between parole entries and exits during 2014.

PART 9

Human Trafficking, 2014

HIGHLIGHTS

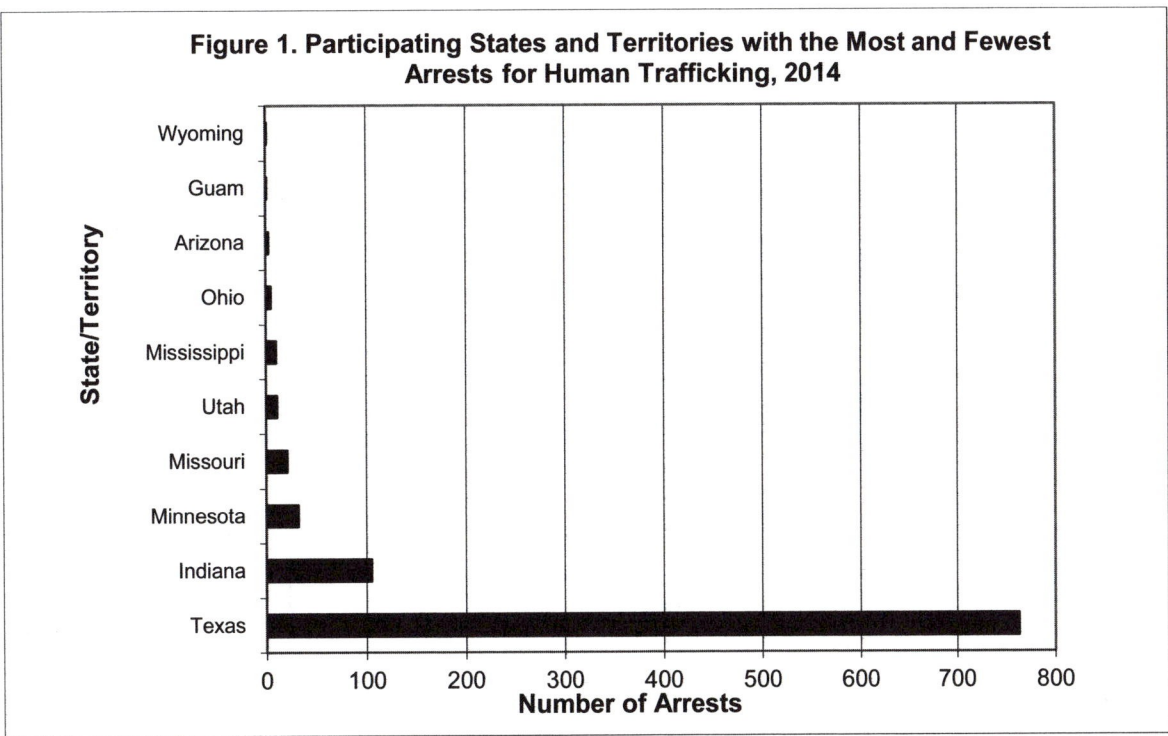

Figure 1. Participating States and Territories with the Most and Fewest Arrests for Human Trafficking, 2014

- Of the participating states, Texas had the highest number of participating agencies in the contribution of human trafficking data (1,074), followed by Illinois (716) and Florida (698).

- Adult males represented the highest number of arrestees for human trafficking crimes.

- Texas and Indiana had the highest incidences of arrests of persons of non—Hispanic or Latino ethnicity for human trafficking crimes (485 and 77, respectively).

Table 1. Human Trafficking, by Participating State/Territory, 2014

(Number.)

State	Number of participating agencies
Alaska	20
Arizona	6
California[1]	2
Colorado	249
Delaware	60
Florida	698
Guam	1
Hawaii	2
Idaho[1]	2
Illinois	716
Indiana	78
Kansas	5
Massachusetts	7
Michigan	657
Minnesota	9
Missouri	636
Mississippi	68
Montana	117
Nevada	35
Ohio	78
Oklahoma	65
Oregon	111
South Dakota	137
Tennessee	467
Texas	1,074
Utah	142
U.S. Virgin Islands	1
Washington	247
Wyoming	61

[1] Data submitted through the Bureau of Indian Affairs.

Table 2. Human Trafficking, Offenses and Clearances by Participating State/Territory, 2014

(Number.)

State	Commercial sex acts			Involuntary servitude			Total		
	Offenses	Total cleared	Clearances under 18	Offenses	Total cleared	Clearances under 18	Offenses	Total cleared	Clearances under 18
Alaska	11	3	0	0	0	0	11	3	0
Arizona	15	8	0	0	0	0	15	8	0
California	0	0	0	0	0	0	0	0	0
Colorado	11	0	0	2	0	0	13	0	0
Delaware	0	0	0	0	0	0	0	0	0
Florida	57	44	0	3	3	0	60	47	0
Guam	0	0	0	0	0	0	0	0	0
Hawaii	0	0	0	0	0	0	0	0	0
Idaho	0	0	0	0	0	0	0	0	0
Illinois	50	0	0	17	0	0	67	0	0
Indiana	0	0	0	0	0	0	0	0	0
Kansas	1	1	0	0	0	0	1	1	0
Massachusetts	6	4	0	1	0	0	7	4	0
Michigan	2	2	0	1	0	0	3	2	0
Minnesota	22	5	0	1	1	0	23	6	0
Missouri	5	2	1	1	0	0	6	2	1
Mississippi	0	0	0	0	0	0	2	1	0
Montana	1	0	0	0	0	0	1	0	0
Nevada	0	0	0	0	0	0	0	0	0
Ohio	0	0	0	0	0	0	0	0	0
Oklahoma	10	7	0	0	0	0	10	7	0
Oregon	0	0	0	0	0	0	0	0	0
South Dakota	0	0	0	0	0	0	0	0	0
Tennessee	29	0	0	1	0	0	30	0	0
Texas	78	22	5	113	17	3	191	39	8
Utah	0	0	0	0	0	0	0	0	0
U. S. Virgin Islands	0	0	0	0	0	0	0	0	0
Washington	2	0	0	0	0	0	2	0	0
Wyoming	0	0	0	1	0	0	1	0	0

Table 3. Human Trafficking Arrests, by Age, State, and Participating State/Territory, 2014

(Number.)

State and offense	Juvenile		Adult	
	Juvenile male	Juvenile female	Adult male	Adult female
Arizona				
Commercial sex acts	0	0	0	0
Involuntary servitude	0	0	3	0
Guam				
Commercial sex acts	0	0	0	0
Involuntary servitude	1	0	0	0
Indiana				
Commercial sex acts	6	2	47	27
Involuntary servitude	8	11	2	2
Minnesota				
Commercial sex acts	1	1	25	5
Involuntary servitude	0	0	0	0
Missouri				
Commercial sex acts	3	0	8	1
Involuntary servitude	0	0	4	5
Mississippi				
Commercial sex acts	3	0	1	0
Involuntary servitude	2	4	0	0
Ohio				
Commercial sex acts	0	0	4	1
Involuntary servitude	0	0	0	0
Texas				
Commercial sex acts	5	30	513	153
Involuntary servitude	13	24	18	7
Utah				
Commercial sex acts	0	0	0	0
Involuntary servitude	0	0	10	1
Wyoming				
Commercial sex acts	0	1	0	0
Involuntary servitude	0	0	0	0

Table 4. Human Trafficking Arrests, by Race, Age, and Participating State/Territory, 2014

(Number.)

Area and offense	Juvenile						Adult					
	White	Black or African American	American Indian or Alaska Native	Asian	Native Hawaiian or Other Pacific Islander	Total	White	Black or African American	American Indian or Alaska Native	Asian	Native Hawaiian or Other Pacific Islander	Total
Arizona												
Commercial sex acts	0	0	0	0	0	0	0	0	0	0	0	0
Involuntary servitude	0	0	0	0	0	0	2	1	0	0	0	3
Guam												
Commercial sex acts	0	0	0	0	0	0	0	0	0	0	0	0
Involuntary servitude	0	0	0	0	1	1	0	0	0	0	0	0
Indiana												
Commercial sex acts	6	2	0	1	0	9	60	11	0	0	1	72
Involuntary servitude	17	2	0	0	0	19	1	0	0	3	0	4
Minnesota												
Commercial sex acts	0	2	0	0	0	2	11	18	0	1	0	30
Involuntary servitude	0	0	0	0	0	0	0	0	0	0	0	0
Missouri												
Commercial sex acts	3	0	0	0	0	3	7	1	0	1	0	8
Involuntary servitude	0	0	0	0	0	0	6	3	0	0	0	9
Mississippi												
Commercial sex acts	0	0	0	0	0	0	1	0	0	0	0	1
Involuntary servitude	0	3	0	0	0	3	0	0	0	0	0	0
Ohio												
Commercial sex acts	0	0	0	0	0	0	6	0	0	0	0	6
Involuntary servitude	0	0	0	0	0	0	0	0	0	0	0	0
Texas												
Commercial sex acts	19	16	0	0	0	35	567	98	0	1	0	666
Involuntary servitude	34	3	0	0	0	37	20	5	0	0	0	25
Utah												
Commercial sex acts	0	0	0	0	0	0	0	0	0	0	0	0
Involuntary servitude	0	0	0	0	0	0	11	0	0	0	0	11
Wyoming												
Commercial sex acts	1	0	0	0	0	1	0	0	0	0	0	0
Involuntary servitude	0	0	0	0	0	0	2	0	0	0	0	2

Table 5. Human Trafficking Arrests, by Ethnicity, Age, and Participating State/Territory, 2014

(Number.)

Area and offense	Juvenile			Adult		
	Hispanic or Latino	Not Hispanic or Latino	Total	Hispanic or Latino	Not Hispanic or Latino	Total
Arizona..						
Commercial sex acts	0	0	0	0	0	0
Involuntary servitude..............................	0	0	0	0	3	3
Guam..						
Commercial sex acts	0	0	0	0	0	0
Involuntary servitude..............................	0	1	1	0	0	0
Indiana...						
Commercial sex acts	0	6	6	0	71	71
Involuntary servitude..............................	0	13	13	0	3	3
Minnesota..						
Commercial sex acts	0	2	2	0	30	30
Involuntary servitude..............................	0	0	0	0	0	0
Missouri...						
Commercial sex acts	0	0	0	0	0	0
Involuntary servitude..............................	0	0	0	0	0	0
Mississippi...						
Commercial sex acts	0	0	0	0	2	2
Involuntary servitude..............................	0	0	0	0	0	0
Ohio..						
Commercial sex acts	0	0	0	0	0	0
Involuntary servitude..............................	0	0	0	0	0	0
Texas...						
Commercial sex acts	15	20	35	201	465	666
Involuntary servitude..............................	25	12	37	14	11	25
Utah..						
Commercial sex acts	0	0	0	0	0	0
Involuntary servitude..............................	0	0	0	0	11	11
Wyoming...						
Commercial sex acts	0	1	1	0	0	0
Involuntary servitude..............................	0	0	0	0	0	0

Note: The ethnicity totals are representative of those agencies that provided ethnicity breakdowns. Not all agencies provide ethnicity data; therefore, the race and ethnicity totals will not equal.

METHODOLOGY

In January 2013, the national UCR Program began collecting offense and arrest data regarding human trafficking as authorized by the *William Wilberforce Trafficking Victims Protection Reauthorization Act of 2008*. The act requires the FBI to collect human trafficking offense data and to make distinctions between prostitution, assisting or promoting prostitution, and purchasing prostitution.

To comply with the Wilberforce Act, the national UCR Program created two additional offenses in the Summary Reporting System and the National Incident-Based Reporting System for which the UCR Program collects both offense and arrest data. The definitions for these offenses are:

Human Trafficking/Commercial Sex Acts: inducing a person by force, fraud, or coercion to participate in commercial sex acts, or in which the person induced to perform such act(s) has not attained 18 years of age.

Human Trafficking/Involuntary Servitude: the obtaining of a person(s) through recruitment, harboring, transportation, or provision, and subjecting such persons by force, fraud, or coercion into involuntary servitude, peonage, debt bondage, or slavery (not to include commercial sex acts).

The data in the tables included in this report reflect the offenses and arrests recorded by state and local law enforcement agencies (LEAs) that currently have the ability to report the data to the national UCR Program. As such, they should not be interpreted as a definitive statement of the level or characteristics of human trafficking as a whole.

In addition to the data reported to the UCR Program, it is important to note that this is only one view of a complex issue— the law enforcement perspective. The investigation of human trafficking by local, state, tribal, and federal LEAs is one facet of this crime. However, due to the nature of human trafficking, many of these crimes are never reported to law enforcement. In addition to the law enforcement facet in fighting these crimes, there are victim service organizations whose mission it is to serve the needs of the victims of human trafficking. In order to have the complete picture of human trafficking, it would be necessary to gather information from all of these sources.

Table 1

The FBI collects these data through the Uniform Crime Reporting (UCR) Program's Summary Reporting System and National Incident-Based Reporting System. This table includes the states that have added human trafficking offenses to their data collection and the number of agencies per state participating in the UCR Program. Even though a state program included human trafficking, the individual agencies in that state may or may not have added it to their collections.

Indiana, Mississippi, and portions of Ohio have no UCR state program to manage the collection of UCR data within the state. Each law enforcement agency is responsible for reporting its crime data directly to the FBI.

Table 2

The FBI collects these data through the Uniform Crime Reporting (UCR) Program's Summary Reporting System and National Incident—Based Reporting System. This table provides the volume of human trafficking offenses as reported by state. For UCR purposes, juveniles are individuals under the age of 18 years. Adults are 18 years of age and older.

The data used in creating this table were from all law enforcement agencies submitting one or more human trafficking incidents for at least 1 month of the calendar year. The published data, therefore, do not necessarily represent reports from each participating agency for all 12 months of the calendar year. When the FBI determines that an agency's data collection methodology does not comply with national UCR guidelines, the figure(s) for that agency's offense(s) will not be included in the table, and the discrepancy will be explained in a footnote.

Table 3

The FBI collects these data through the Uniform Crime Reporting (UCR) Program's Summary Reporting System and National Incident- Based Reporting System.

This table provides the number of juvenile and adult male and female persons arrested for human trafficking offenses by state in 2014. These data represent the number of persons arrested; however, some persons may be arrested more than once during a year. Therefore, the statistics in this table could, in some cases, represent multiple arrests of the same person. For UCR purposes, juveniles are under the age of 18 years. Adults are 18 years of age and older. The data used in creating this table were from all law enforcement agencies submitting one or more human trafficking arrests for at least 1 month of the calendar year. The published data, therefore, do not necessarily represent reports from each participating agency for all 12 months of the calendar year.

Table 4

The FBI collects these data through the Uniform Crime Reporting (UCR) Program's Summary Reporting System and National Incident- Based Reporting System.

This table provides the number of persons arrested for human trafficking offenses by state in 2014 broken down by race of the arrestee. These data represent the number of persons arrested; however, some persons may be arrested more than once during a year. Therefore, the statistics in this table could, in some cases, represent multiple arrests of the same person. For UCR purposes, juveniles are individuals under the age of 18 years. Adults are 18 years of age and older. The data used in creating this table were from all law enforcement agencies submitting one or more human trafficking arrests for at least 1 month of

the calendar year. The published data, therefore, do not necessarily represent reports from each participating agency for all 12 months of the calendar year.

Table 5

This table provides the number of persons arrested for human trafficking offenses by state in 2014 broken down by ethnicity of the arrestee. These data represent the number of persons arrested; however, some persons may be arrested more than once during a year. Therefore, the statistics in this table could, in some cases, represent multiple arrests of the same person. For UCR purposes, juveniles are individuals under the age of 18 years. Adults are 18 years of age and older. The data used in creating this table were from all law enforcement agencies submitting one or more human trafficking arrests for at least 1 month of the calendar year. The published data, therefore, do not necessarily represent reports from each participating agency for all 12 months of the calendar year.

APPENDIX: SOURCES FOR TABLES

Part 1. Criminal Victimization, 2014

1 Bureau of Justice Statistics, National Crime Victimization Survey, 2005, 2013, and 2014.
2 Bureau of Justice Statistics, National Crime Victimization Survey, 2005–2014.
3 Bureau of Justice Statistics, National Crime Victimization Survey, 2005, 2013, and 2014.
4 Bureau of Justice Statistics, National Crime Victimization Survey, 2005, 2013, and 2014.
5 Bureau of Justice Statistics, National Crime Victimization Survey, 2005, 2013, and 2014.
6 Bureau of Justice Statistics, National Crime Victimization Survey, 2005, 2013, and 2014.
7 Bureau of Justice Statistics, National Crime Victimization Survey, 2005, 2013, and 2014.
8 Bureau of Justice Statistics, National Crime Victimization Survey, 2005, 2013, and 2014.
9 Bureau of Justice Statistics, National Crime Victimization Survey, 2005, 2013, and 2014.
10 Bureau of Justice Statistics, National Crime Victimization Survey, 2005, 2013, and 2014.
11 Bureau of Justice Statistics, National Crime Victimization Survey, 2013–2014; and FBI, Preliminary Semiannual Uniform Crime Report, January–June 2014, http://www.fbi.gov/about-us/cjis/ucr/crime-in-the-u.s/2014/preliminary-semiannual-uniform-crime-report-january-june-2014/tables/table-3.
12 Bureau of Justice Statistics, National Crime Victimization Survey, 2005–2014.

Part 2. Correctional Populations in the United States, 2014

1 Bureau of Justice Statistics, Annual Probation Survey, Annual Parole Survey, Annual Survey of Jails, Census of Jail Inmates, and National Prisoner Statistics program, 2000, 2005–2010, and 2013–2014.
2 Bureau of Justice Statistics, Annual Probation Survey, Annual Parole Survey, Annual Survey of Jails, Census of Jail Inmates, and National Prisoner Statistics program, 2000, 2005–2014; and U.S. Census Bureau, postcensal estimated resident population for January 1 of the following year, 2001, and 2006–2015.
3 Bureau of Justice Statistics, Annual Probation Survey, Annual Parole Survey, Annual Survey of Jails, and National Prisoner Statistics program, 2007 and 2014.
4 Bureau of Justice Statistics, Annual Probation Survey, Annual Parole Survey, Annual Survey of Jails, and National Prisoner Statistics program, 2000–2014.
5 Bureau of Justice Statistics, Annual Probation Survey, Annual Parole Survey, Deaths in Custody Reporting Program, and National Prisoner Statistics program, 2014; and U.S. Census Bureau, unpublished U.S. resident population estimates within jurisdiction on January 1, 2015.
6 Bureau of Justice Statistics, Annual Probation Survey, Annual Parole Survey, and National Prisoner Statistics program, 2000–2014.
7 Bureau of Justice Statistics, Annual Probation Survey, Annual Parole Survey, Deaths in Custody Reporting Program, and National Prisoner Statistics program, 2014; and U.S. Census Bureau, unpublished U.S. resident population estimates within jurisdiction on January 1, 2015.
8 Bureau of Justice Statistics, Annual Survey of Jails, and National Prisoner Statistics program, 2000 and 2013–2014; and U.S. Census Bureau, postcensal estimated resident populations for January 1 of the following year, 2001, 2014, and 2015.
9 Bureau of Justice Statistics, National Prisoner Statistics program and Survey of Jails in Indian Country, 2000, 2005, and 2013–2014.
10 Bureau of Justice Statistics, National Prisoner Statistics program, Census of Jail Inmates, and Annual Survey of Jails, 2004–2014; and U.S. Census Bureau, postcensal estimated resident population for January 1 of the following year, 2005–2015.

Part 3. Crime in the United States, 2014

1   United States Department of Justice, Federal Bureau of Investigation, Uniform Crime Reports, 2014.
2   United States Department of Justice, Federal Bureau of Investigation, Uniform Crime Reports, 2014.
3   United States Department of Justice, Federal Bureau of Investigation, Uniform Crime Reports, 2014.
4   United States Department of Justice, Federal Bureau of Investigation, Uniform Crime Reports, 2014.
5   United States Department of Justice, Federal Bureau of Investigation, Uniform Crime Reports, 2014.
6   United States Department of Justice, Federal Bureau of Investigation, Uniform Crime Reports, 2014.
7   United States Department of Justice, Federal Bureau of Investigation, Uniform Crime Reports, 2014.
8   United States Department of Justice, Federal Bureau of Investigation, Uniform Crime Reports, 2014.
9   United States Department of Justice, Federal Bureau of Investigation, Uniform Crime Reports, 2014.
10 United States Department of Justice, Federal Bureau of Investigation, Uniform Crime Reports, 2014.
11 United States Department of Justice, Federal Bureau of Investigation, Uniform Crime Reports, 2014.
12 United States Department of Justice, Federal Bureau of Investigation, Uniform Crime Reports, 2014.
13 United States Department of Justice, Federal Bureau of Investigation, Uniform Crime Reports, 2014.
14 United States Department of Justice, Federal Bureau of Investigation, Uniform Crime Reports, 2014.
15 United States Department of Justice, Federal Bureau of Investigation, Uniform Crime Reports, 2014.
16 United States Department of Justice, Federal Bureau of Investigation, Uniform Crime Reports, 2014.
17 United States Department of Justice, Federal Bureau of Investigation, Uniform Crime Reports, 2014.
18 United States Department of Justice, Federal Bureau of Investigation, Uniform Crime Reports, 2014.
19 United States Department of Justice, Federal Bureau of Investigation, Uniform Crime Reports, 2014.
20 United States Department of Justice, Federal Bureau of Investigation, Uniform Crime Reports, 2014.
21 United States Department of Justice, Federal Bureau of Investigation, Uniform Crime Reports, 2014.
22 United States Department of Justice, Federal Bureau of Investigation, Uniform Crime Reports, 2014.
23 United States Department of Justice, Federal Bureau of Investigation, Uniform Crime Reports, 2014.
24 United States Department of Justice, Federal Bureau of Investigation, Uniform Crime Reports, 2014.
25 United States Department of Justice, Federal Bureau of Investigation, Uniform Crime Reports, 2014.
26 United States Department of Justice, Federal Bureau of Investigation, Uniform Crime Reports, 2014.
27 United States Department of Justice, Federal Bureau of Investigation, Uniform Crime Reports, 2014.
28 United States Department of Justice, Federal Bureau of Investigation, Uniform Crime Reports, 2014.
29 United States Department of Justice, Federal Bureau of Investigation, Uniform Crime Reports, 2014.
30 United States Department of Justice, Federal Bureau of Investigation, Uniform Crime Reports, 2014.
31 United States Department of Justice, Federal Bureau of Investigation, Uniform Crime Reports, 2014.
32 United States Department of Justice, Federal Bureau of Investigation, Uniform Crime Reports, 2014.
33 United States Department of Justice, Federal Bureau of Investigation, Uniform Crime Reports, 2014.
34 United States Department of Justice, Federal Bureau of Investigation, Uniform Crime Reports, 2014.
35 United States Department of Justice, Federal Bureau of Investigation, Uniform Crime Reports, 2014.
36 United States Department of Justice, Federal Bureau of Investigation, Uniform Crime Reports, 2014.
37 United States Department of Justice, Federal Bureau of Investigation, Uniform Crime Reports, 2014.
38 United States Department of Justice, Federal Bureau of Investigation, Uniform Crime Reports, 2014.
39 United States Department of Justice, Federal Bureau of Investigation, Uniform Crime Reports, 2014.
40 United States Department of Justice, Federal Bureau of Investigation, Uniform Crime Reports, 2014.
41 United States Department of Justice, Federal Bureau of Investigation, Uniform Crime Reports, 2014.
42 United States Department of Justice, Federal Bureau of Investigation, Uniform Crime Reports, 2014.
43 United States Department of Justice, Federal Bureau of Investigation, Uniform Crime Reports, 2014.
44 United States Department of Justice, Federal Bureau of Investigation, Uniform Crime Reports, 2014.
45 United States Department of Justice, Federal Bureau of Investigation, Uniform Crime Reports, 2014.

Part 4. Capital Punishment, 2013

1	Bureau of Justice Statistics, National Prisoner Statistics Program (NPS-8), 2013.
1A	Bureau of Justice Statistics, National Prisoner Statistics Program (NPS-8), 2013.
2	Bureau of Justice Statistics, National Prisoner Statistics Program (NPS-8), 2013
3	Bureau of Justice Statistics, National Prisoner Statistics Program (NPS-8), 2013
4	Bureau of Justice Statistics, National Prisoner Statistics Program (NPS-8), 2013.
5	Bureau of Justice Statistics, National Prisoner Statistics Program (NPS-8), 2013.
6	Bureau of Justice Statistics, National Prisoner Statistics Program (NPS-8), 2013.
7	Bureau of Justice Statistics, National Prisoner Statistics Program (NPS-8), 2013.
8	Bureau of Justice Statistics, National Prisoner Statistics Program (NPS-8), 2013.
9	Bureau of Justice Statistics, National Prisoner Statistics Program (NPS-8), 2013.
10	Bureau of Justice Statistics, National Prisoner Statistics Program (NPS-8), 2013.
11	Bureau of Justice Statistics, National Prisoner Statistics Program (NPS-8), 2013.
12	Bureau of Justice Statistics, National Prisoner Statistics Program (NPS-8), 2013.
13	Bureau of Justice Statistics, National Prisoner Statistics Program (NPS-8), 2013.
14	Bureau of Justice Statistics, National Prisoner Statistics Program (NPS-8), 2013.
15	Bureau of Justice Statistics, National Prisoner Statistics Program (NPS-8), 2013.
16	Bureau of Justice Statistics, National Prisoner Statistics Program (NPS-8), 2013.
17	Bureau of Justice Statistics, National Prisoner Statistics Program (NPS-8), 2013.

Part 5. Hate Crime Statistics, 2014

1	Federal Bureau of Investigation, Hate Crime Statistics, 2014.
2	Federal Bureau of Investigation, Hate Crime Statistics, 2014.
3	Federal Bureau of Investigation, Hate Crime Statistics, 2014.
4	Federal Bureau of Investigation, Hate Crime Statistics, 2014.
5	Federal Bureau of Investigation, Hate Crime Statistics, 2014.
6	Federal Bureau of Investigation, Hate Crime Statistics, 2014.
7	Federal Bureau of Investigation, Hate Crime Statistics, 2014.
8	Federal Bureau of Investigation, Hate Crime Statistics, 2014.
9	Federal Bureau of Investigation, Hate Crime Statistics, 2014.
10	Federal Bureau of Investigation, Hate Crime Statistics, 2014.
11	Federal Bureau of Investigation, Hate Crime Statistics, 2014.
12	Federal Bureau of Investigation, Hate Crime Statistics, 2014.
13	Federal Bureau of Investigation, Hate Crime Statistics, 2014.

Part 6. Jail Inmates at Midyear, 2014

1	Bureau of Justice Statistics, Annual Survey of Jails, midyear 2000–2004 and midyear 2006–2014; and Census of Jail Inmates, midyear 2005.
2	Bureau of Justice Statistics, Annual Survey of Jails, midyear 2000 and midyear 2006–2014; and Census of Jail Inmates, midyear 2005.
3	Bureau of Justice Statistics, Annual Survey of Jails, midyear 2000 and midyear 2006–2014; and Census of Jail Inmates, midyear 2005.
4	Bureau of Justice Statistics, Annual Survey of Jails, midyear 2013–2014.
5	Bureau of Justice Statistics, Annual Survey of Jails, midyear 2000 and midyear 2006–2014; and Census of Jail Inmates, midyear 2005.
6	Bureau of Justice Statistics, Annual Survey of Jails, midyear 2013–2014.
7	Bureau of Justice Statistics, Annual Survey of Jails, midyear 2013–2014.
8	Bureau of Justice Statistics, Annual Survey of Jails, midyear 2002–2004 and midyear 2006–2014; and Census of Jail Inmates, midyear 2005.
9	Bureau of Justice Statistics, Annual Survey of Jails, midyear 2000 and midyear 2006–2014.
10	Bureau of Justice Statistics, Annual Survey of Jails, midyear 2000 and midyear 2006–2014; and Census of Jail Inmates, midyear 2005.

Part 7. Law Enforcement Officers Killed and Assaulted, 2014

1   United States Department of Justice, Federal Bureau of Investigation, Uniform Crime Reports, 2014.
2   United States Department of Justice, Federal Bureau of Investigation, Uniform Crime Reports, 2014.
3   United States Department of Justice, Federal Bureau of Investigation, Uniform Crime Reports, 2014.
4   United States Department of Justice, Federal Bureau of Investigation, Uniform Crime Reports, 2014.
5   United States Department of Justice, Federal Bureau of Investigation, Uniform Crime Reports, 2014.
6   United States Department of Justice, Federal Bureau of Investigation, Uniform Crime Reports, 2014.
7   United States Department of Justice, Federal Bureau of Investigation, Uniform Crime Reports, 2014.
8   United States Department of Justice, Federal Bureau of Investigation, Uniform Crime Reports, 2014.
9   United States Department of Justice, Federal Bureau of Investigation, Uniform Crime Reports, 2014.
10   United States Department of Justice, Federal Bureau of Investigation, Uniform Crime Reports, 2014.
11   United States Department of Justice, Federal Bureau of Investigation, Uniform Crime Reports, 2014.
12   United States Department of Justice, Federal Bureau of Investigation, Uniform Crime Reports, 2014.
13   United States Department of Justice, Federal Bureau of Investigation, Uniform Crime Reports, 2014.
14   United States Department of Justice, Federal Bureau of Investigation, Uniform Crime Reports, 2014.
15   United States Department of Justice, Federal Bureau of Investigation, Uniform Crime Reports, 2014.
16   United States Department of Justice, Federal Bureau of Investigation, Uniform Crime Reports, 2014.
17   United States Department of Justice, Federal Bureau of Investigation, Uniform Crime Reports, 2014.
18   United States Department of Justice, Federal Bureau of Investigation, Uniform Crime Reports, 2014.
19   United States Department of Justice, Federal Bureau of Investigation, Uniform Crime Reports, 2014.
20   United States Department of Justice, Federal Bureau of Investigation, Uniform Crime Reports, 2014.
21   United States Department of Justice, Federal Bureau of Investigation, Uniform Crime Reports, 2014.
22   United States Department of Justice, Federal Bureau of Investigation, Uniform Crime Reports, 2014.
23   United States Department of Justice, Federal Bureau of Investigation, Uniform Crime Reports, 2014.
24   United States Department of Justice, Federal Bureau of Investigation, Uniform Crime Reports, 2014.
25   United States Department of Justice, Federal Bureau of Investigation, Uniform Crime Reports, 2014.
26   United States Department of Justice, Federal Bureau of Investigation, Uniform Crime Reports, 2014.
27   United States Department of Justice, Federal Bureau of Investigation, Uniform Crime Reports, 2014.
28   United States Department of Justice, Federal Bureau of Investigation, Uniform Crime Reports, 2014.
29   United States Department of Justice, Federal Bureau of Investigation, Uniform Crime Reports, 2014.
30   United States Department of Justice, Federal Bureau of Investigation, Uniform Crime Reports, 2014.
31   United States Department of Justice, Federal Bureau of Investigation, Uniform Crime Reports, 2014.
32   United States Department of Justice, Federal Bureau of Investigation, Uniform Crime Reports, 2014.
33   United States Department of Justice, Federal Bureau of Investigation, Uniform Crime Reports, 2014.
34   United States Department of Justice, Federal Bureau of Investigation, Uniform Crime Reports, 2014.
35   United States Department of Justice, Federal Bureau of Investigation, Uniform Crime Reports, 2014.
36   United States Department of Justice, Federal Bureau of Investigation, Uniform Crime Reports, 2014.
37   United States Department of Justice, Federal Bureau of Investigation, Uniform Crime Reports, 2014.
38   United States Department of Justice, Federal Bureau of Investigation, Uniform Crime Reports, 2014.
39   United States Department of Justice, Federal Bureau of Investigation, Uniform Crime Reports, 2014.
40   United States Department of Justice, Federal Bureau of Investigation, Uniform Crime Reports, 2014.
41   United States Department of Justice, Federal Bureau of Investigation, Uniform Crime Reports, 2014.
42   United States Department of Justice, Federal Bureau of Investigation, Uniform Crime Reports, 2014.
43   United States Department of Justice, Federal Bureau of Investigation, Uniform Crime Reports, 2014.
44   United States Department of Justice, Federal Bureau of Investigation, Uniform Crime Reports, 2014.

Part 8. Probation and Parole, 2014

1   Bureau of Justice Statistics, Annual Probation Survey and Annual Parole Survey, 2000–2014.

2   Bureau of Justice Statistics, Annual Probation Survey and Annual Parole Survey, 2000, 2005–2014; and U.S. Census Bureau, National Intercensal Estimates, 2001, 2005–2010, and Population Estimates, January 1, 2011–2015.

3   Bureau of Justice Statistics, Annual Probation Survey and Annual Parole Survey, 2008–2014.

4   Bureau of Justice Statistics, Annual Parole Survey, 2008–2014.

5   Bureau of Justice Statistics, Annual Probation Survey and Annual Parole Survey, 2008–2014.

6   Bureau of Justice Statistics, Annual Parole Survey, 2000–2014.

7   Bureau of Justice Statistics, Annual Parole Survey, 2000–2014.

8   Bureau of Justice Statistics, Annual Probation Survey and Annual Parole Survey, 2014.

9   Bureau of Justice Statistics, Annual Probation Survey and Annual Parole Survey, 2014.

10   Bureau of Justice Statistics, Annual Probation Survey, 2000, 2013, and 2014.

11   Bureau of Justice Statistics, Annual Parole Survey, 2014.

12   Bureau of Justice Statistics, Annual Parole Survey, 2014.

13   Bureau of Justice Statistics, Annual Parole Survey, 2000, 2013, and 2014.

14   Bureau of Justice Statistics, Annual Parole Survey, 2014.

Part 9. Human Trafficking, 2014

1   United States Department of Justice, Federal Bureau of Investigation, Uniform Crime Reports, 2014.

2   United States Department of Justice, Federal Bureau of Investigation, Uniform Crime Reports, 2014.

3   United States Department of Justice, Federal Bureau of Investigation, Uniform Crime Reports, 2014.

4   United States Department of Justice, Federal Bureau of Investigation, Uniform Crime Reports, 2014.

5   United States Department of Justice, Federal Bureau of Investigation, Uniform Crime Reports, 2014.

INDEX

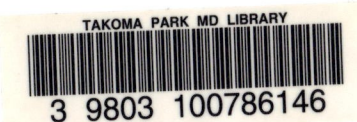

arrests by race, 271
offenses and clearances, 269
participating territories, 268
Law enforcement officers killed and assaulted, 221, 226, 234

TERRORISM
Federal capital offenses, 137
THEFT
see **CRIME IN THE UNITED STATES**
TORTURE
Federal capital offenses, 137
TRAIN WRECKING
Federal capital offenses, 137
TREASON
Federal capital offenses, 137

U
UNIFORMS
Law enforcement officers killed and assaulted
number of victim officers wearing, 230
UNIVERSITIES
Hate crimes, 170

V
VICTIMIZATION
see **CRIMINAL VICTIMIZATION**
VICTIM SERVICE AGENCIES

Victims receiving assistance from, 8
VIOLENT CRIME
see **CRIME IN THE UNITED STATES**

W
WEAPONS
Aggravated assault, types of weapons used, 122
Criminal victimizations, 4
Justifiable homicide by weapon, law enforcement, 121
Justifiable homicide by weapon, private citizen, 121
Law enforcement officers killed and assaulted
officers assaulted, by type of weapon, 242, 244
type of weapon, 230
victim officer's type of weapon, 225
victim officer's use of weapon, 224
victim officer's weapon stolen, 225
Murder, types of weapons used, percent distribution by region, 113
Murder circumstances, by weapon, 118
Murder victims, by weapons, 114
Robbery, types of weapons used, 122
WEAPONS OF MASS DESTRUCTION
Federal capital offenses, 137
WEEKEND PROGRAMS
Types of programs of jail supervision, 213
WHITE RACE
see **RACE**